STUDIES IN THE SEMANTIC STRUCTURE OF HINDI

Studies in the Semantic Structure of Hindi

(Synonymous Nouns and Adjectives with *karanā*)

KALI CHARAN BAHL

The University of Chicago

VOLUME I

MOTILAL BANARSIDASS

Delhi :: Varanasi :: Patna

First Edition 1974

ISBN 0—8426—0682—3

Head Office : BUNGALOW ROAD, JAWAHARNAGAR, DELHI-7
Branches: 1. CHOWK, VARANASI-1 (U.P.)
2. ASHOK RAJPATH, PATNA-4 (BIHAR)

Printed in India

BY SHANTILAL JAIN, AT SHRI JAINENDRA PRESS, BUNGALOW ROAD, JAWAHARNAGAR, DELHI-7, AND PUBLISHED BY SUNDARLAL JAIN FOR MOTILAL BANARSIDASS, BUNGALOW ROAD, JAWAHARNAGAR, DELHI-7

TO

Vimla

whose contribution to this work cannot be told in words and without whose help it could not have become what it is.

CONTENTS

PREFACE

The author's interest in modern standard Hindi dates back to 1960-61 when he became associated with a research project for the preparation of *A Reference Grammar of Hindi* at The University of Chicago. While working on this project generally but more so upon the completion of this grammar in 1967, it became apparent to him that for the purpose of preparing a systematic and deeper interpretation of the syntactico-semantic structure of the language, substantially more data was needed on almost every aspect of the language than was available then. It is, therefore, only appropriate to say that the *Studies in the Semantic Structure of Hindi* aims at fulfilling that need in the form of a dictionary of conjunct verbs.

The study of modern standard Hindi, in spite of all the attention it has received in the past from an international community of scholars, cannot boast of showing any marked trend towards the development of a sufficiently sophisticated understanding of its semantic structure. The reasons for such a state of affairs are only too well-known to discuss here. We only wish to say that the *Studies in the Semantic Structure of Hindi* lays a foundation which, we hope, will ultimately aid in the development of such an understanding by making a modest beginning in this direction.

Though the need for a study such as this one became apparent to the author very early yet the actual systematic work was undertaken only in June, 1966, under the "Project for the Preparation of a Medium Sized Dictionary of Hindi Verbs". This project was funded by The Office of Education, U.S. Department of Health, Education and Welfare under contract No. HEW OEC 3-6-061386 which officially terminated in August, 1970.

The procedures we followed in this research project were twofold, namely, (i) the ones concerning the gathering of the data, and (ii) the ones concerning the processing of the data. The procedures involved in the processing of the data have been explained in detail in the "Introduction" (sections 3 and 4). We shall, therefore, confine ourselves to an outline of the procedures followed by us in gathering the data for the present as well as the subsequent volumes of the *Studies in the Semantic Structure of Hindi*. These procedures essentially consisted of reading of all the texts reported in Appendix I and marking on them sentences or contexts of verbs as well as conjunct verbs to be taken down on slips. These slips consisted of 'zip out' blanks which could produce up to four copies at a time. Entries for all the verbs in the language were developed from these slips. Within each verb, further categories and sub-categories were established on the basis of the classification of sentences illustrated by the verb लेना (*lenā*) "to take" in sub-section 3.6.3 of the "Introduction", including several sub-categories depending on the non-finite occurrence of these verbs etc.

The total number of works selected for this purpose is about 450, each with an average length of 200 pages. About 70 per cent of these texts were read completely and excerpts selected from them. The rest were read only in parts to select instances of the occurrence of verbs as were not available but known to occur in the language. Utmost care was taken to repeat instances of a given phenomenon in a single work of an author as well as several works of the same author. This procedure was also extended to all the texts of all the authors as have been used. We started with the assumption that there may be some regional variations in the writings of modern standard Hindi writers depending upon their linguistic background and so forth. So we selected such authors from all over India as we could find, some well-known, others not as known. Such an assumption, however, proved to be superfluous because we found the language to be remarkably well standardized in every respect.

However, we wish to point out that the language of the modern standard Hindi newspapers and plays presented several kinds of problems. Most modern standard Hindi newspapers (including some periodicals) do not seem to conform to the natural idiom of the language, especially in their reporting of daily news items. Due to this difficulty we did not find it particularly useful to gather data from newspapers except in a few selected instances. Modern Hindi plays, on the other hand, exhibit too many instances of the occurrence of elliptical sentences in their dialogue. Such elliptical sentences, though perfectly good modern standard Hindi sentences, cannot be suitable as examples for the illustration of the occurrence of conjunct verbs in view of the principles explained in sub-section 4.7 of the "Introduction". For this reason, we have made a very limited use of modern Hindi plays for the gathering of our data.

Not all the instances of the occurrence of a given conjunct verb on our files are reported in sections three onwards of the articles in the *Studies*. The examples reported were selected on the basis of the principles discussed in the "Introduction". Since the gathering of the data as well as processing them had to be carried out simultaneously to some extent, it is likely that some instances of the occurrence of a given conjunct verb in a particular text may have been left out, though they may fare better than the ones reported in the articles. In some cases references to the texts have also been accidentally omitted but in no case were any sentences coined for the purpose of illustrating the occurrence of a given conjunct verb.

The task of collecting these data was a mammoth one and required considerable care and control. We, therefore, take this opportunity to thank everybody who participated in this work from time to time.

The processing of the data involved simultaneously controlling modern standard Hindi as well as English. A number of Hindi-knowing speakers of English helped us in this process. Notable among them is Richard A. Williams who tested every generic as well as specific definition of every noun and adjective against the translation given for the occurrence of these nouns and adjectives in conjunct verbs. However, the ultimate responsibility for this task is the author's alone.

Richard A. Williams, William F. Henderson III and Anjani K. Sinha read the "Introduction" and suggested many improvements. Arden Rappaport and Mrs. Nirmala Shrivastava also helped us in many ways.

Long periods of time usually intervene between the preparation and publication of a study such as this one, especially when it is a first work of its kind. Continued endurance, and sustaining the burden of the pressure of the work involved in it, would have become an insurmountable problem if we had not received encouragement and help from Edward C. Dimock Jr., A. K. Ramanujana and J. A. B. van Buitenen during these long years of work.

We are also grateful to the Committee on Southern Asian Studies at The University of Chicago whose generous assistance made the publication of this work possible.

We are also thankful to Shri N. P. Jain of Motilal Banarsidass who took a personal interest in the publication of this work and whose men have done a commendable job of putting this difficult work together.

Chicago
March, 1974

Kali Charan Bahl

INTRODUCTION

1. Scope of this study

1.1. ***Studies in the Semantic Structure of Hindi*** (Synonymous Nouns and Adjectives with the verb *karanā*, volume I), is the first in a series of works, the major aim of which is the study of the semantic structure of modern standard Hindi (hereafter abbreviated MSH). More specifically, this volume forms a part of a three-volume study concerned with the presentation of a semantic description of synonymous nouns and adjectives known to occur in MSH "conjunct verbs", that is, formed with the verb करना (*karanā*) "to do".

The category of conjunct verbs (sometimes labelled "nominal compound verbs") is a phenomenon well-known in MSH grammars, where the chief concern of grammarians has been to recognize conjunct verbs in the language and to offer an interpretation of sentences containing them. The major contribution in such an approach lies in its view that there are in the language, besides what is usually known as verbs, a special category of noun or adjective plus verb sequences which are viewed semantically (or conceptually) as units functioning as verbs.

1.2. As early as Gilchrist (A.D. 1796) there began a series of works written by various traditional grammarians whose main concern was the recognition of this category rather than a presentation of the grammatical structure of sentences containing such conjunct verbs. These traditional grammarians, in addition to Gilchrist, are represented by Kellogg (1875), Platts (1878), Bailey (1956), Guru (1922), Sharma (1958) and Dimshits (1966). In addition to these traditional grammarians there exist schools of scholars who either offer formal or structural justification for the recognition and extent of the category of conjunct verbs [Burton-Page (1957)], or whose primary aim is the application of a particular theory of language description to the study of MSH as a whole, and secondarily offer an interpretation of the grammatical structure of sentences containing conjunct verbs. The latter technique is manifestly the aim of Kachru (1966), along with whom may be included Verma (1971), which has important bearing on the views expressed in the former. Lastly there are two scholars who remain in separate categories by themselves. One is Bahri (1959), dealing with a comparative philological exploration of the semantics of MSH. The other is Hacker (1961), a work of considerable importance, as it for the first time seriously and very cogently questions the validity of the application of any formal or structuralist approach to the study of MSH without recourse to "meaning", and thus forms a link between Burton-Page (1957) and Kachru (1966), on the one hand, and the work of the present author [more particularly Bahl (1967)], on the other.

In section 2 we shall briefly discuss the contribution of these scholars to the area of conjunct verbs in MSH. But we would like to point out that the scholarly works we have chosen to examine are by no means the only works dealing with our specific problem, or with MSH grammar in general. As far as our discussion is concerned, we believe these works more than adequately represent the various noticeable trends concerning the category of conjunct verbs in MSH. And thus we have chosen to deal with the various trends which are manifest in these works, rather than describe the development of grammatical thought concerning the category of conjunct verbs in a chronological fashion.

1.3. In section 3 of the "Introduction" we shall present our views regarding the category of conjunct verbs essentially in programmatic terms rather than offer a definitive theoretical interpretation of the phenomenon. We have adopted this approach because we believe (and, have repeatedly demonstrated in section 2), that a definitive theoretical interpretation is an endeavor which, if it is not to become a mere exposition of a particular theory of language description, as most of the theoretical works on MSH grammar tend to be, should be undertaken after more than superficial knowledge of the phenomenon is gained through an adequate and thorough investigation.[1]

1. As we have said in sub-section 5.5, the goal of the *Studies in the Semantic Structure of Hindi* is a modest one, that is, it aims at making the area of conjunct verbs in the language more accessible to the scholarly world than it has been so far. Such a goal could be achieved in two different ways. A linguist could illustrate the existence of the linguistic universals implied in conjunct verbs by preparing suitable description of the syntactico-semantic structure of this segment of MSH, or he could develop an account of such universals and use MSH data to justify such a development. We have indicated at length in section 2 that the grammarians, who have tried the former approach, have failed to produce any satisfactory description of the phenomena. We, therefore, strongly feel the need for concentrating on the later approach. We also feel that the development of linguistic universals as may be involved in conjunct verbs also requires a more substantial understanding of the phenomenon gained through a familiarity with an adequate amount of data before such a step can be taken. It is apparent from our discussion in section 2 of the "Introduction" that the grammarians of MSH tend to take an overly simplistic view of the language primarily due to their inability to generate enough data on conjunct verbs. Therefore, it is desirable that the *Studies in the Semantic Structure of Hindi* should first aim at satisfying the dictionary aspect of the problem, and to this extent it should also remain relatively free from any preoccupation with a particular theory of language description. To the extent that these data cannot be generated in a vacuum, the *Studies in the Semantic Structure of Hindi* should engage in its main pursuit with a view as would be consistent with the need for developing linguistic universals as are implied in conjunct verbs. Therefore, it is appropriate to say that the *Studies in the Semantic Structure of Hindi* does two things at the same time

In section 4 we shall deal more specifically with the semantic complexity of nouns and adjectives occurring in करना (*karanā*) "to do" conjunct verbs, as well as with the verb करना (*karanā*) itself in its function as a formative element in conjunct verbs.

1.4. Since the format of this work is that of a dictionary in the sense that our representation of the semantic complexity of nouns and adjectives occurring in करना (*karanā*) "to do" conjunct verbs is expressed by means of a system of paraphrases in English designed to read like dictionary definitions, we will of necessity comment upon the present state of MSH lexicography (with special reference to the problem at hand) in section 5.

It may not be entirely out of place to mention here that the present state of MSH lexicography is quite chaotic. It will, therefore, be well within the scope of this "Introduction" to comment in section 5 upon the misgivings about the various strata of the lexicon of the language persisting in scholarly works on MSH.

1.5. Before we set about the main task of this "Introduction", it is necessary to explain the general format of our presentation in the *Studies in the Semantic Structure of Hindi*, Synonymous Nouns and Adjectives with the verb *karanā*, volume I (hereafter abbreviated SSSH). The present volume of the SSSH contains 120 independent articles on an equal number of groups of synonymous nouns and adjectives occurring in करना (*karanā*) "to do" conjunct verbs in MSH. Each article contains several sections : section one of each article gives a definition of the generic meaning of the group, followed by definitions of the specific meanings of all the individual members in the group; section two takes note of the grammatical information pertinent to the group; and sections three onwards contain illustrations of the occurrence of these nouns and adjectives in करना (*karanā*)

that is, it generates data on conjunct verbs by dealing with one formative verb at a time and by providing a step-by-step description of the conjunct verbs formed with that verb (and is, for this reason, a dictionary of conjunct verbs) but it does so in a manner which, we believe, is theoretically more interesting (see sections 3 and 4 of the "Introduction" for a discussion of some of the theoretical problems involved in conjunct verbs in MSH).

It may not, therefore, be out of place here to say that we have engaged in speculation about the category of conjunct verbs within the limits just stated and only to the extent that it does not take precedence over our primary goal. Such a speculation is based on two different sources, that is (i) modern theories of the generative semanticists, and (ii) Indo-Aryan philosophies of language. The influence of the former is quite explicit in the "Introduction". However, the ideological contribution of the Indo-Aryan philosophies of language to our discussion concerning the category of conjunct verbs (particularly to our notions of "concept" and its related "behavioral manifestations)" as well as to the general problem of development of linguistic universals as implied in the area of conjunct verbs, is deliberately left implicit for the reasons discussed in sub-section 5.5 of this "Introduction".

"to do" conjunct verbs in a wide variety of contexts as is deemed necessary to exemplify the co-occurrence restrictions on these nouns and adjectives, or required by the necessity of the variety of translation equivalents of a given conjunct verb in English. In section four of the "Introduction" we shall discuss the theoretical justification for the procedures followed in the articles, namely, the formulation of the definitions of generic and specific meanings of nouns and adjectives in section one, our conceptualization of the grammatical information as well as the extent to which it is considered pertinent to an adequate description of a given group of synonyms as provided in section two of the articles, and the translation equivalents of the individual conjunct verbs as given in English in sections three onwards.

1.6. The English paraphrases containing semantic definitions of nouns and adjectives as given in section one of the articles, and the rendering of the individual occurrences of the conjunct verbs in various contexts by means of translation equivalents in English could as well be formulated in MSH. But in the latter case, we believe such a work, while being inherently useful and significant, would not then be as readily within the grasp of a speaker of English who wants to understand MSH sentences like a native speaker of the language. Keeping this in mind, we have formulated the paraphrases containing the definitions of generic as well as specific meanings of nouns and adjectives and suggested translation equivalents of the conjunct verbs in English. In doing so we have strictly based ourselves on *Webster's Third New International Dictionary of the English Language.*[1] If there is any difficulty in the interpretation of our definitions or translation equivalents, we recommend that this dictionary be consulted.

1.7. The data reported in these articles has been selected from more than 450 different MSH prose texts in varied fields ranging from literature to the physical sciences. They have been carefully chosen to reflect co-occurrence restrictions, as well as the necessity of illustrating translation equivalents (in English) of the conjunct verbs in as many context types as we have been able to establish.[2] Each example illustrating a context type is followed by a coded reference to the text from which it is taken and the page number on which it occurs. The list containing the coded references to the texts used by us as well as complete bibliographic information is contained in Appendix I entitled "List of the Sources of the Data".

2. Existing grammatical treatment of conjunct verbs

2.1. The traditional grammarians of MSH, as we have remarked earlier, are more interested in the recognition of the phenomenon of conjunct

1. G. & C. Merriam Company (Springfield, Massachusetts, 1967)
2. These context types are established on the basis of principles discussed in sections 3 and 4 of the "Introduction".

verbs in the language than in offering any linguistic interpretation of the sentences containing them. This recognition ultimately led to the establishment of the grammatical category of conjunct verbs. But before we begin our evaluation of the individual contributions of traditional grammarians towards the recognition and establishment of this category, it would be interesting to take note of the twofold process by which this was accomplished.

In their examination of the language MSH grammarians noted that (i) some noun or adjective plus verb sequences have a unitary status as opposed to others [such as the expression को दान देना (*ko dāna denā*) "to give (someone something) in alms" versus the expression को पुस्तक देना (*ko pustaka denā*) "to give (someone) a book"], and (ii) the noun or adjective plus verb sequences which have such a unitary status [such as दान देना (*dāna denā*)] function like ordinary verbs. This traditional grammarians' conception of the unitary status of some noun or adjective plus verb sequences is based on the fact that such sequences have translation equivalents in English which are single verbs.[1] The translation equivalence of one word lexical items like verbs in English with verb plus verb, or noun or adjective plus verb sequences in MSH (on the basis of which the identity of the overall category of compound verbs was established), later became a theoretical assumption. It was assumed, that generally speaking, modern Indo-Aryan languages have lexical items consisting of one word each, just as in the case of English, but occasionally one may find that there are significant exceptions in the area of verbs. In other words, lexically speaking it is necessary to recognize (i) verbs which consist of one word each, (ii) verbs, which are single lexical items consisting of one word each, but which may occasionally occur with other verbs, and (iii) verbs which are single lexical items but consist of more than one word each, that is nouns or adjectives plus verbs. The notion of compound verbs as it has been propounded by various grammarians of modern Indo-Aryan languages is thus based on the traditional assumption (accepted in linguistics until very recently) that lexical items consist of single words, and anything to the contrary is either a grammatically specifiable phrase or a lexical unit consisting of more than one word, that is to say a compound.

The term "compound verb", as it is applied in MSH grammars (and in the grammars of other modern Indo-Aryan languages as well), has the peculiarity that it refers to these grammarians' conception of single lexical items consisting of more than one word each. Therefore, it was thought to be the task of the grammarians to recognize and establish in grammar the status of verb plus verb as well as noun or adjective plus verb sequences by distinguishing amongst them those sequences which can be given a unitary interpretation and those which can-

1. Some grammarians, notably Guru (1922) and Sharma (1958) (discussed in sub-section 2.1.6), do not assume any notion of semantic unity between various constituents of conjunct verbs on the basis of their translational equivalence in English.

not. In other words, the establishment of the grammatical category of compound verbs (both in its broad as well as narrow senses) and the grammatical category of conjunct verbs are a manifestation of this trend. As far as the problem of the grammatical category of conjunct verbs is concerned, traditional grammarians isolated such noun or adjective plus verb sequences in the language which, on the basis of their translation equivalence in English or otherwise, have a unitary status in the lexicon of MSH, while, at the same time, the structuralists provided one or the other kind of theoretical justification for the category. One can, of course, surmise a converse of this situation by saying that, if the grammar of English had been described in terms of the grammar of MSH, the grammarian then would have come up with one-word lexical items (that is, verbs) in English which are syntactically (or semantically) complex, that is, correspond to noun or adjective plus sequences in MSH.

What has resulted in this discussion of one-word lexical items versus more-than-one-word lexical items is that the grammatical characterization of the categories of compound and conjunct verbs in modern Indo-Aryan languages including MSH has tended to evolve around a controversy as to the unitary lexical status of these verbs rather than a systematic grammatical description of them. That is, the grammarians of MSH, due to their sole preoccupation with this mode of enquiry, have completely ignored the need for a systematic investigation of the syntactico-semantic phenomena pertaining to the category of conjunct verbs in the underlying structure of the language.

With these preliminary remarks concerning the nature of the existing grammatical literature on the category of conjunct verbs in MSH, we will now proceed to an assessment of the contributions made by individual grammarians who are all in agreement with the interpretation of conjunct verbs as lexical items consisting of more than one word each. For convenience of reference we shall label grammarians following this trend as "lexical interpretationists". This will be followed by a discussion of the contribution of those grammarians who do not subscribe to the views of the lexical interpretationists and whose works suggest alternative modes of enquiry stemming from a variety of considerations including the study of the semantic structure of MSH. We shall refer to the grammarians of this group as "semanticists".[1]

2.1.1. An account of the trend represented by the lexical interpretationists must begin with Gilchrist (1796), who, in Chapter V, Section IV

1. By the use of labels "lexical interpretationists" and "semanticists" we merely intend to refer to the practices of the grammarians of MSH concerning the category of conjunct verbs rather than identify them with the two schools of thought among the transformational-generative grammarians (though at times such an implication may be unavoidable due to the inherent nature of the phenomenon of conjunct verbs).

(entitled "Of the General Formation and Arrangement of Verbs, as Neuter, Active, Causal, etc. with Practical Remarks on the Compound, Frequentative, Inceptive, and other Verbs, in the Hindoostanee Language"), introduces the general subject of compound verbs (page 154). Here he presents his classification of them in terms of Class I containing various verb plus verb compounds, and Classes II and III referring to two kinds of conjunct verbs. The two classes of conjunct verbs are described in the following terms.[1]

> Class II is appropriated to the compounds from a substantive, and one or other of the subservient verbs enumerated in the note below..., which in this complex state so very frequently supersede the more elegant verbs, (many of which are now becoming obsolete) or supply the want of those that do not occur uncompounded in this language;...
>
> Class III. In this are exhibited the verbs formed by adjectives with करना (*karanā*), and other subservient transitives, besides होना (*honā*), हो जाना (*ho jānā*), आना (*ānā*) etc. the first of which in general form active, while the latter produce a numerous tribe of neuter, intransitive and inceptive verbs.

A few examples of each of these two classes are reproduced below from among many given by Gilchrist.

दर्द (*darda*)—करना (*karanā*), होना (*honā*), आना (*ānā*), (v. n.) and—लाना (*lānā*) (v. a.) "to pain, to feel".

खबर (*khabara*)—देना (*denā*), करना (*karanā*), पहुँचाना (*pahũcānā*), लाना (*lānā*), etc. "to inform", etc.

गर्म (*garma*)—करना (*karanā*), "to heat",—होना (*honā*), "to be hot",—हो जाना (*ho jānā*) or आना (*ānā*), "to grow or become hot".

His term "subservient verbs", which is applicable to the second members in compound (that is, verb plus verb) as well as conjunct (that is, noun or adjective plus verb) verbs, is probably meant to underline Gilchrist's assumption of some similarity in the function of these "subservient verbs" in both types of verbal constructions. He also states in a footnote (page 157) that "Many of the following (that is, the subservient verbs) have already appeared under Class I (that is, verb plus verb compounds)".

1. All MSH data cited in this "Introduction" or reproduced from other works will be given in Devanagari script with Roman transliteration in parentheses irrespective of the fact as to how they are quoted in the original works. The glosses or translations of MSH examples in English are approximate, and have no purpose other than increasing the usefulness of these data as examples illustrating grammatical phenomena in MSH.

Gilchrist's assumption of the functional similarity of subservient verbs in compound as well as conjunct verbs persisted in the grammars of MSH until it was proven otherwise in Burton-Page (1957) (to be discussed in sub-section 2.2).

Gilchrist also tried to present a kind of systematization of "the various significations" of these subservient verbs when they occur with nouns. According to him, for example, the verb करना (*karanā*) "to do" has the following significations in this environment:

> to do, act, make, try, perform, execute, commit, excite, use, consider,...

2.1.2. Kellogg (1875) exhibits considerable improvement on Gilchrist (1796). He labels these conjunct verbs as "nominal compound verbs" and describes them (in section 448, page 271) in the following terms.

> 448. Sometimes a substantive or adjective is so combined with a verb as to form, conjointly with it, but one conception. Such combinations as these have been called *Nominal Compounds.* Of these, the largest part are formed with the verbs, करना (*karanā*) "to do", or "to make", and होना (*honā*) "to be"; but several other verbs are also employed in the same way. These may often be rendered into English by a single word: as e.g., खड़ा होना (*kharā honā*) "to stand (intr.)"; खड़ा करना (*kharā karanā*) "to stand (trans.)"; प्राप्त करना (*prāpta karanā*) "to obtain", समाप्त होना (*samāpta honā*) "to be completed"; मोल लेना (*mola lenā*) "to buy", etc. etc.

Kellogg also refers to the semantic difference between his *Nominal Compound* verbs and ordinary verbs in the language in the following terms:

> Very commonly, when it is intended to express special respect, or when, as in poetry, an elevated diction is desired, a Nominal verb, formed by the combination of a Sanskrit noun or participle with होना (*honā*) "to be" करना (*karanā*) "to do", or some other Hindi verb, is preferred to the corresponding simple verb. In such cases, the slight modification of the meaning may often be well expressed by the use in English of different words. Examples are दर्शन करना (*darśana karanā*) "to behold", for देखना (*dekhanā*) "to see"; भोजन करना (*bhojana karanā*) for खाना (*khānā*) "to eat"; गमन or गमन करना (*gamana* or *gamana karanā*) "to go", for जाना (*jānā*); प्रस्थान करना (*prasthāna karanā*) or प्रस्थित होना (*prasthita honā*) "to depart", for the more colloquial चला जाना (*calā jānā*) "to go away"; etc. etc. This matter is deserving of special attention by the student of Hindi conversation and composition.

In sections 450-460 (pages 272-276) Kellogg gives a list of various combinations of nouns with करना (*karanā*) "to do" illustrating the postpositions or cases governed by these nominal compounds. He also observes that "...not infrequently the compound takes a different meaning, according as it is used in regimen with one or another case". Besides the variety of combinations with करना (*karanā*) "to do", Kellogg lists examples with the verbs खाना (*khānā*) "to eat", देना (*denā*) "to give", मारना (*māranā*) "to hit" and "a number of additional combinations of frequent occurrence".

Kellogg (1875) is probably the only work which seeks to list conjunct verbs, and, therefore, has had considerable influence on later grammarians who almost unanimously believe conjunct verbs to be formed in MSH with the verb करना (*karanā*) "to do" alone. One does come across an occasional mention of conjunct verbs formed with verbs other than करना (*karanā*) "to do" in the works of these grammarians, but that fact never figures significantly in their discussion.

It may also be mentioned here that no grammarian after Kellogg (1875) has discussed the distinction between "nominal compound verbs" like दर्शन करना (*darśana karanā*) "to behold" and their corresponding simple verbs like देखना (*dekhanā*) "to see". Some grammarians [especially Verma (1971)], however, do mention this fact, only to dismiss rather than explore the distinction pointed out by Kellogg. Semantic significance of the occurrence of nouns (forming conjunct verbs) with more than one postposition as suggested by Kellogg is generally ignored in the later works excepting Bahl (1967).

2.1.3. Platts (1878), otherwise a work of little importance, is worth noting here since it figures in the characterization of the category of conjunct verbs in Bailey (1956) and Burton-Page (1957). Platts labels these conjunct verbs as "nominal compound verbs" also, but adds that "but not a few of these are, strictly speaking, not compound verbs,..." This characterization of Platts' was probably instrumental in providing clues for the resolution of the confusion created by the use of the terms "compound verbs" (both in the narrow as well as broad senses of the term), on the one hand, and "conjunct verbs", on the other [especially in Bailey (1956) and Burton-Page (1957)]. In addition, Platts takes note of a "few compounds formed by prefixing a Persian preposition or adverb to a Hindi verb".

2.1.4. Bailey (1956) is another work which figures prominently in Burton-Page (1957), containing rudimentaries of the structuralist interpretation of the category of conjunct verbs. The author introduced the term "conjunct verb" to refer to what has been called "nominal compound verbs" by earlier grammarians. His definition of the category of conjunct verbs is essentially based on Platts (1878), or if we may say so, a mere restatement of Platts. However, the original contribution of this work lies in its recognition of three different constructions of conjunct verbs with the verb करना (*karanā*) "to do". Why Bailey, who was familiar with Kellogg's work, chose to deal with just the three constructions with the verb करना (*karanā*) alone, ignoring everything else, is not made explicit. We reproduce below his section on these three constructions :

(i) First Construction : the two are joined so closely as to become one word, and the gender of the noun does not matter. Thus with feminine nouns :—

याद करना
(*yāda karanā*)
"learn by heart, remember"
उसने अपना सबक याद किया
(*usane apanā sabaka yāda kiyā*)
"he learnt his lesson"

(ii) Second Construction : noun with का (*kā*), की (*kī*) according to gender.

(a) Feminine Nouns :—

तारीफ करना
(*tārīfa karanā*)
"to praise"
मैंने उसकी तारीफ की
(*maine usakī tārīfa kī*)
"I praised him"

(b) Similar are masculine nouns, as :—

का बन्दोबस्त करना
(*kā bandobasta karanā*)
"arrange for"
का इन्तेजाम करना
(*kā intezāma karanā*)
"arrange for"
का फैसला करना
(*kā faisalā karanā*)
"decide"

(iii) Third Construction: this like (i), but with this important difference, that the gender of the noun affects the verb. This is seen in the past tenses of the verb, when the noun is feminine. There are not so many in this class as in (i).

उसे मलामत की
(*use malāmata kī*)
"rebuked him"
उसने उसे ताकीद की
(*usane use tākīda kī*)
"he urged him"

Bailey also recognizes two kinds of constructions with the verb देना (*denā*) "to give". His first देना (*denā*) construction [e.g., को धोखा देना (*ko dhokhā denā*) "to deceive"] is an instance of his third करना (*karanā*) "to do" construction, and his second देना (*denā*) construction [e.g., करार देना (*karāra denā*) "to fix, decide"] is an instance of his first करना (*karanā*) "to do" construction.

2.1.5. Before passing on to a consideration of the views of the other grammarians concerning the category of conjunct verbs in MSH, it would be worthwhile to summarize the contribution of Kellogg (1875) and Bailey (1956), as both these works figure very prominently in later discussion, though for different reasons.

It can be said that both Kellogg and Bailey consider it necessary to recognize some noun or adjective plus verb combinations in Hindi/Urdu as having special status in grammar, since such combinations, if looked at from the point of view of English, form single "concepts" (for Kellogg) and verbs (for Bailey). However, Bailey is not certain as to "whether such verbs are real verbs or are two distinct ideas". Both approach the problem of "nominal compound" or "conjunct" verbs giving the similar impression that the phenomenon of compounding of verbs in modern Indo-Aryan is an important discovery, and their description of them an important methodological advance. Their interpretation of conjunct verbs as lexical items consisting of more than one word each, which was quite in accordance with the then prevailing views in linguistics, later became the sole aim of the linguists of the so-called structuralist school, and has persisted in the grammars of modern Indo-Aryan languages, including MSH, ever since.

Both Kellogg and Bailey clearly give the impression that these conjunct verbs are almost exclusively formed with the verb करना (*karanā*) "to do" in vastly larger numbers than with any other verb [with the possible exception of होना (*honā*) "to be" etc.], a belief so prevalent that later grammarians almost exclusively rely upon these two works as their only sources of data.

There is, however, an important difference between Kellogg (1875) and Bailey (1956). Kellogg is describing, what we may call standard literary Hindi, whereas Bailey is describing colloquial (or spoken dialect) Urdu. Such a problem, though not directly pertinent to the category of conjunct verbs as far as we are concerned, will nevertheless, be discussed from the point of view of the lexicographical difficulties it presents in MSH in section 5 of this "Introduction".

2.1.6. Both Guru (1922) and Sharma (1958), unlike Gilchrist (1796), Kellogg (1875), Platts (1878) and Bailey (1956), do not start with the assumption of some sort of conceptual or semantic unity between nouns or adjectives and verbs in conjunct verbs. They are in favor of restricting the category of conjunct verbs only to those noun or adjective plus verb sequences which are morpho-syntactically unanalyzable into any of the known categories, and, are thus residual in nature. In order to further explicate the views of these two grammarians, we would like to reproduce below section 268 (b) and (c) from Sharma (1958), which incorporates the views of Guru (1922).

> 268. (b) It is important to remember that nouns or adjectives, when combined with a verb, forgo their independent existence and become a part of the verb. They have, consequently, no grammatical relation with any other word in the sentence. Thus in a sentence like मैं राम को क्षमा करता हूँ (*mãĩ Rāma ko kṣamā karatā hū̃*) "I forgive Rāma" the noun क्षमा (*kṣamā*) "forgiveness" is a component of the verb, and is not related to मैं (*mãĩ*) "I" or राम (*Rāma*) "a proper name", nor is it the object of the verb करना (*karanā*) "to do"; राम (*Rāma*), obviously, is the object of the verb क्षमा करना (*kṣamā karanā*) "to forgive". Further we cannot regard क्षमा (*kṣamā*) "forgiveness" either as the primary object of the verb करना (*karanā*) "to do" [because करना (*karanā*) does not take two objects], or as a predicative word referring to the object [because क्षमा (*kṣamā*) and राम (*Rāma*) do not refer to the same thing,...].
>
> (c) In contrast with the above, in a sentence like मैं भोजन करता हूँ (*mãĩ bhojana karatā hū̃*) "I take meals", भोजन करना (*bhojana karanā*) is not a compound, since here भोजन (*bhojana*) "meals" is obviously the object of (*karanā*) "to do" and has its own existence. In the same way काम करना (*kāma karanā*) "to do work" is not a compound, since काम (*kāma*) "work" does have an independent existence in such sentences as मैंने आपका काम किया (*mãĩne āpakā kāma kiyā*) "I did your work" [where काम (*kāma*) "work" is related to आप (*āpa*) and is not a component of the verb].

By the application of the criterion of independent morpho-syntactic status advanced by both Guru and Sharma, one could say that these two grammarians would include in the category of conjunct verbs (i) almost all adjective plus verb sequences, except when the adjectives are interpreted as predicative complements, but not (ii) all noun plus verb sequences.

On the other hand, Gilchrist, Kellogg, Platts and Bailey do not seem to advance any such restriction. In view of this difference in opinion, it seems necessary to clarify the position of both Guru and Sharma vis-a-vis Gilchrist, Kellogg, Platts and Bailey. We will now try to explain this situation by means of a few examples. For instance, in the following two sentences

(1) पाठ का आरम्भ करो
(pāṭha kā ārambha karo)
"Start reading !"

(2) पाठ आरम्भ करो
(pāṭha ārambha karo)
"Begin the lesson"

containing the noun plus verb sequence आरम्भ करना *(ārambha karanā)*, the noun आरम्भ *(ārambha)* does have "an independent existence" of its own (from the verb) in sentence (1) where it is grammatically related to the noun पाठ *(pāṭha)* by means of the postposition का *(kā)* "of", whereas no such relationship exists between आरम्भ *(ārambha)* "beginning" and पाठ *(pāṭha)* "lesson" in sentence (2). According to the view adopted by Gilchrist, Kellogg, Platts and Bailey the expression आरम्भ करना *(ārambha karanā)* "to begin, to start" is a conjunct verb in both sentences, whereas, according to both Guru and Sharma, it can be interpreted as a conjunct verb only in the second.

The difference in these two positions can be explained when we take both Guru and Sharma not to be in favor of interpreting the occurrence of a given noun plus verb sequence as a lexical item consisting of more than one word unless it fails to satisfy the criterion of independent morpho-syntactic status. By the application of this criterion as it has been applied by both Guru and Sharma, one can group all the nouns occurring with the verb करना *(karanā)* "to do" into three classes, that is, (i) nouns like प्रशंसा *(praśaṁsā)* "praise" as in की प्रशंसा करना *(kī praśaṁsā karanā)* "to praise someone" which always have independent morpho-syntactic status, (ii) nouns like आरम्भ *(ārambha)* "beginning" which may or may not have independent morpho-syntactic status (as illustrated above), and finally (iii) nouns like स्वीकार *(svīkāra)* "acceptance" and क्षमा *(kṣamā)* "forgiveness" which never have independent morpho-syntactic status in MSH sentences in the manner discussed by both Guru and Sharma. Without going into the details of this three-way classification of nouns in conjunct verbs at this stage (a problem which will be discussed in sub-section 3.6.6 of this "Introduction"), we would like to state that the term conjunct verb is applicable to the instances of nouns in all the three classes when they occur with the verb करना *(karanā)* "to do". The value of this restricted definition of the term conjunct verb advanced by both Guru and Sharma, neither of whom start with any conceptual or semantic unity on the basis of their translation into English, lies chiefly in the fact that these grammarians have pointed out an important distinction which has gone completely unnoticed in any subsequent treatment of conjunct verbs.

2.1.7. Dimshits (1966) is another work which, though it makes no original contribution to the discussion concerning the category of conjunct verbs, is worth mentioning here by reason of its representing an extreme position among the lexical interpretationists. In its characterization of the category of conjunct verbs, Dimshits (1966) essentially follows the position taken by both Guru and Sharma, but, following the biases of the Soviet lexicologists, it discusses the category of conjunct verbs in the chapter on word derivations in MSH. So according to Dimshits (1966), the category of conjunct verbs is a subclass of *nāmika kriyā* "denominalized verbs". The term *jaṭila nāmika kriyā* "complex denominalized verbs" is used to refer to those noun plus verb sequences which have a unitary status as conjunct verbs, without, however, going into any discussion. The rest of the treatment of conjunct verbs in this work is a summary of the statements made by other grammarians which merely serves to exhibit the author's familiarity with the discussion that has already taken place concerning this category in MSH.

2.2. Burton-Page (1957) and Kachru (1966) are two lexical interpretationists whose major aim is to provide a theoretical basis for the specification and structuralist delimitation of the broad category of conjunct verbs in MSH. Both authors, by distinguishing such noun or adjective plus verb sequences which are conjunct verbs in the underlying structure of MSH (that is, are lexical items consisting of more than one word each) from those which are not, endeavor to establish the category of conjunct verb in the sentence structure of the language. It should be noted here that both scholars are interested in analyzing as many noun or adjective plus verb sequence types as possible in terms of sentential phrases, and, therefore, exhibit some important differences between them as to which particular noun or adjective plus verb sequence types can be interpreted as belonging to the structurally specified category of conjunct verbs. The result attained through this method, no matter how accomplished it may seem from the point of view of the lexical interpretationistic approach, is nevertheless devoid of any theoretical interest.[1]

With these preliminary remarks concerning Burton-Page (1957) and Kachru (1966), we will now proceed to discuss them individually. Since Kachru (1966), which is supposedly an improvement over Burton-Page (1957), does not discuss its significant differences from the latter, we will include in this section a brief discussion of Verma (1971), a work

1. Our reasons for such a statement are discussed at some length in sections 3 and 4 of the "Introduction".

which provides some basis for an understanding of the motivation behind the interpretation of the phenomenon of conjunct verbs in Kachru (1966).

2.2.1. Burton-Page (1957) embodies two proposals regarding the category of conjunct verbs—(i) concerning the morpho-syntactic specification of conjunct verbs, and (ii) as to the delimitation of the category of conjunct verbs by suggesting alternative interpretation of the underlying structure of sentences containing noun plus verb sequences included by Bailey in his second and third constructions.

By means of contrasting the range of occurrence of formative verbs with that of explicators (or operators, as Burton-Page prefers to call them), this paper clarifies the confusion persisting since Gilchrist (1796) regarding the function of "subservient verbs" in the overall category of compound verbs. Following this line of argument, Burton-Page proposes the following reasons for separating compound and conjunct verbs.

> The final verbal element in *NV* (i.e., conjunct verbs) is thus clearly to be separated from the final verbal element in VO (i.e., verb plus verb compounds) on the basis of their different paradigmatic potentialities. This, with the difference in syntactical implication of *NV* and VO which has already been referred to, is sufficient justification for separating 'compound' and 'conjunct' verbs.[1]

Burton-Page takes exception with Bailey regarding his second and third constructions. His argument in respect to the second construction is reproduced below.

> But if प्रशंसा करना (*praśaṁsā karanā*) is...regarded as *NV*, how is उसकी (*usakī*) to be regarded? To consider the group उसकी प्रशंसा करना (*usakī praśaṁsā karanā*) as *NV* would involve the proliferation of such 'verbs' to the point of absurdity—although an impersonal किसी की प्रशंसा करना (*kisī kī praśaṁsā karanā*) "to extol something" would not be inappropriate as a suitable dictionary entry. If, on the other hand, उसकी (*usakī*) were regarded as constituting N_2 by itself, this would imply that the relationship between उसकी (*usakī*) and प्रशंसा (*praśaṁsā*) were different from that between उसकी (*usakī*) and कहानी (*kahānī*). This cannot be justified. It is therefore suggested that the type be analyzed as
>
> | N_1 | N_2 | V_1 |
> |---|---|---|
> | (*maine* | *usakī praśaṁsā* | *kī*) |
>
> "I extolled him (did his praise)."
>
> and that the question of प्रशंसा करना (*praśaṁsā karanā*) being considered as *NV* does not arise.

1. Burton-Page's original symbolization of the category of conjunct verbs is modified by *NV* for typographical reasons.

Similarly by showing that को शिक्षा देना (*ko śikṣā denā*) "to instruct someone" is parallel to को किताब देना (*ko kitāba denā*) "to give someone a book", Burton-Page decides in favor of excluding noun plus verb sequences like शिक्षा देना (*śikṣā denā*) "to instruct", which form part of Bailey's third construction, from the category of conjunct verbs.

Therefore, according to Burton-Page, conjunct verbs in MSH are limited to the type of noun or adjective plus verb sequences constituting Bailey's first construction only. This, incidentally, is the precise conclusion of Guru (1922) and Sharma (1958). Since we propose to discuss the nature of Burton-Page's arguments in our treatment of Hacker (1961) in sub-section 2.3.2, further examination of the validity of his specification and delimitation of the category of conjunct verbs is not necessary. However, it should be pointed out that Burton-Page gives no reason as to why he chose to deal with Bailey's classification of conjunct verbs and disregard completely a somewhat more detailed presentation of "nominal compound verbs" as discussed by Kellogg (1875). The variety of करना (*karanā*) "to do" conjunct verbs discussed by Kellogg, if brought into the picture, would immediately point out the triviality of Burton-Page's argument, which accounts for no more than a tiny fraction of the data. The only contribution of Burton-Page (1957) is thus historical, representing the then prevailing tendencies of the London School.

2.2.2. Kachru (1966) is a work concerned with a basic description of some syntactic structures of MSH, and, therefore, is not concerned with a detailed analysis of the sentences involving conjunct verbs. It offers three-way syntactical interpretation of four kinds of sentences, all traditionally believed (though not by all grammarians) to be formed with conjunct verbs. Kachru's examples illustrating these four kinds of sentences are reproduced below.

(1) राम ने गुरु को प्रणाम किया
(*rāma ne guru ko praṇāma kiyā*)
"Ram did obeisance to his teacher"

(2) मैं उसको पसन्द करता हूं
(*mãĩ usako pasanda karatā hū̃*)
"I like him"

(3) सिपाही ने चोर का पीछा किया
(*sipāhī ne cora kā pīchā kiyā*)
"The constable followed the thief"

(4) उसने दरवाजा बन्द किया
(*usane darvāzā banda kiyā*)
"He closed the door"

According to Kachru the noun and verb sequences as they occur in sentences (1) and (2), that is, प्रणाम करना (*praṇāma karanā*) "to do obeisance", and पसन्द करना (*pasanda karanā*) "to like" are conjunct verbs in the underlying structure of MSH, whereas noun plus verb sequences like पीछा करना (*pīchā karanā*) "to follow", as it occurs in sentence (3), and adjective plus verb sequences like बन्द करना (*banda karanā*) "to close", as it occurs in sentence (4), are not. In sentence (3) चोर का पीछा (*cora kā pīchā*) is the direct object of the verb करना (*karanā*) "to do", and in sentence (4) दरवाजा बन्द (*darvāzā banda*) is a surface manifestation of an embedded sentence labelled as Verbal Complementation.

A comparison of Kachru (1966) with Burton-Page (1957) reveals some interesting differences between the two. Kachru's sentence (1) as reproduced above corresponds to Bailey's third construction, sentence (2) to Bailey's first construction, and sentence (3) to Bailey's second construction. Kachru's sentence (4) would probably also belong to Bailey's first construction, though Bailey does not explicitly discuss adjective plus verb sequences in the context of his three constructions. According to Burton-Page (1957) noun or adjective plus verb sequences, as exemplified by Kachru's sentences (2) and (4), are conjunct verbs in the underlying structure of MSH. Since Kachru (1966) does not give any reason for the interpretation of प्रणाम करना (*praṇāma karanā*) "to do obeisance" [as it occurs in sentence (1)] as a conjunct verb, and Burton-Page (1957) does not explicitly discuss this type of sequence, we must now turn to Verma (1971) in order to further understand the nature of the structuralist basis of delimitation of the surface phenomenon of Conjunct verbs in MSH.

2.2.3. Verma (1971), a review of Kachru (1966), speaks of the latter's attempt "to solve the nagging problem of 'conjunct verbs' " in the following terms.

> There is no doubt that lots of verbal phrases are cavalierly treated as conjunct verbs when there are more satisfying alternative analyses possible as shown by Kachru. The question is further vitiated because of the grammatical characterization of the noun (+postposition) preceding the so-called conjunct verbs which, for some reason everyone would like to see analyzed only as the object (or subject, if intransitive) of these conjunct verbs.

The above passage contains, as far as this "Introduction" is concerned, a statement of the current trend in the study of the phenomenon of conjunct verbs in MSH. It not only states the goals of the lexical interpretationists, but also reveals the limitations of their approach.

The "nagging problem of 'conjunct verbs' " facing these structuralists stems from their desire to seek a basis for the establishment of the immediate constituents in sentences containing the surface phenomenon of conjunct verbs so that (i) the analysis does not end up at the level of the lexicon with lexical units consisting of more than one word each, and (ii) the phrase structure of these noun or adjective plus verb sequences is specified in terms of the sentence structure of the language. By specification of the phrase structure of these noun or adjective plus verb sequences, these grammarians imply the positing of some sort of higher syntactic units, that is, subject plus predicate or object plus verb or the like, or transformationally derived structures, an analysis which would yield more-than-one-word lexical items within the thus limited area of conjunct verbs only at the level of the lexicon. This search for a basis for the establishment of the immediate constituents is further motivated by the grammarians' desire to free themselves of the prejudices of the traditional grammarians who, as we have seen, posited the category of conjunct verbs in MSH on the basis of their translational equivalence in English. Following this line of approach, Kachru (1966) is probably willing to have "conjunct verbs" either as a residual category in the sense of Guru (1927) and Sharma (1958) (though with some exceptions) [Kachru's sentence (2)] or as a structurally specifiable noun plus verb sequence in the sense of Burton-Page (1957) [Kachru's sentence (1)].

Verma (1971), therefore, seeks to provide a further basis for a structuralist treatment of "conjunct verbs" in the above noted two categories as posited in Kachru (1966). This is a logical consequence of the approach followed by both Kachru (1966) and Verma (1971), and probably the only theoretically interesting thing to do. Verma's observation in this regard is as follows :

> Maybe, they all have the same deep structure with surface variations in which the selection of the postposition is determined by the verbal complex, if not also by different case relations. After all, even unitary verbs are known to have their postpositional preferences: पूछना (*pūchanā*) "to ask" takes से (*se*) "from" [cf. प्रश्न करना (*praśna karanā*)], धमकाना (*dhamakānā*) "to threaten" takes को (*ko*) "to" [cf. धमकी देना (*dhamakī dena*)].

There are two other questions raised by Verma (1971) which, we believe, need some comment here. Firstly, question is raised in Verma's remark as to "Why is it that all these 'conjunct verbs' typically have करना (*karanā*) 'to do' as their verb?" We may posit two reasons for this, i.e., (i) no grammarian or lexicographer of MSH has ever reported anything like an adequate datum on conjunct verbs, and (ii) the lexical interpretationists' overwhelming predilection for करना (*karanā*) "to do" conjunct verbs alone lies in the fact that these grammarians also make a distinction between conjunct verbs and idioms. Any noun or adjective plus verb sequence intuitively felt to be an idiom is, therefore, automatically excluded from consideration.

The second question raised by Verma (1971) is its argument of similarity of postpositional preferences between verbs and conjunct verbs which the reviewer would probably like to be used as a basis for analyzing the noun plus verb sequences posited by Kachru (1966) as conjunct verbs. It is not clear from the review as to how Verma would actually apply this argument, but it raises another important question concerning the nature of the differences between the semantic complexity of verbs and their related conjunct verbs. Kellogg (1875), as pointed out in sub-section 2.1.2, raised this point very explicitly, even if in somewhat different terms, but no grammarian of MSH has ever considered this matter worthy of investigation. We will discuss this problem in section 4 of this "Introduction".

2.3. The three works constituting the semanticist approach, that is, Bahri (1959), Hacker (1961) and Bahl (1967), serve to bring into focus a variety of phenomena completely ignored by the lexical interpretationists in their discussion of the category of conjunct verbs in MSH. They either by implication [only Bahri (1959)] or expressly set out to explore the semantic structure of the language, completely abandoning the lexical interpretationists' goal of specifying and delimiting the noun or adjective plus verb sequences as conjunct verbs. Bahri (1959), which essentially involves the traditional grammarians' approach, seeks to present within the overall category of verbs a systematization of idiomatic verbal phrases, almost all of which are conjunct verbs of the types discussed neither by the traditional grammarians nor by the structuralists. Hacker (1961), by bringing in fresh evidence from the language, points out that the application of mechanical techniques (such as those practised by structuralists) are inadequate if "the task is set of determining the syntactico-semantic or meaning qualifying" functions. This is probably another way of saying that a linguist's conceptualization of the grammatical structure of a language in terms of a particular theory is not an end in itself, if one takes that conceptualization as equivalent to the underlying structure of that language. Thus Hacker, by asserting that "the value of theories must be measured by the results of their application and not by their systematic appearance", and by pointing out that "purely formal analysis is not only insufficient for a description of syntactic conditions but is sometimes positively misleading", opens the way for a fresh investigation of the phenomenon of conjunct verbs in MSH. This was the aim of Bahl (1967) out of which grew the present volume (as well as others mentioned by us in sub-section 1.1 of this "Introduction"). With these initial remarks concerning the semanticist approach towards the study of conjunct verbs in MSH, we, in the remainder of this section, pass on to a discussion of the individual contribution of these works.

2.3.1. Bahri (1959), as the author states, aims "to sketch a provisional plan in a domain which has not yet been exploited, and demands the combined labor of several generations of philologists". The most important feature of this work is its effort "to explain the genius of Hindi". The work presents a kind of overview of the "semantic genius" of MSH which at times is superficial and sketchy, but generally suggestive. The category of conjunct verbs, or more precisely, information concerning the category of conjunct verbs is scattered throughout the book, especially in sections on "Close and Loose Compounds","Verbal Idioms" and "Idiomatic Verbs". We shall, therefore, try to summarize the contents of these sections to the extent that they pertain to the problem of exploring the semantic structure of MSH with particular reference to the category of conjunct verbs.

In section (IX, ii), the author introduces the category of conjunct verbs in the following terms:

> Hindi also has special devices of forming verbs by adding the same formative verbs, as enumerated above, to nouns, participles and adjectives and gerunds. Such nominal verbs may be considered along with idiomatic usages for which see VII.4. and also p. 259.

He also comments that करना (*karanā*) "to do" and होना (*honā*) "to be" are profusely used for such formations. Doing and being, he notes, "make up the spirit of a verb". His observation regarding the identity of "formative verbs in nominal verbs" with "auxiliary verbs in compound verbs" has been discussed earlier, and needs no comment here.

In his section on idioms, Bahri discusses two types of noun plus verb combinations. The first are "verbal idioms" in which "the verb alone implies a metaphorical meaning without affecting the substantive". His examples are दिन काटना (*dina kāṭanā*) "to pass the day", कैद काटना (*kaida kāṭanā*) "to complete imprisonment" and so on. The second type of idioms are labelled "substantival idioms" in which "the substantive is transferred in meaning, without a change in the meaning of verb". His examples are अन्धेरा (*andherā*) "darkness" referring to grief as in अन्धेरा छाना (*andherā chānā*), गिनती (*ginatī*) "counting" referring to importance as in गिनती में होना (*ginatī mẽ honā*), and so forth. It may be pointed out that both classes of idiomatic noun plus verb combinations listed by Bahri are in fact semantically complex expressions which are idioms, not because they are semantically unanalyzable but only because (as Bahri uses the term idiom) they are in some ways peculiar. We would, therefore, like to assert that most of such idiomatic noun plus verb combinations are conjunct verbs of one kind or the other which will be discussed in somewhat more detail in section 3 of this "Introduction".

In the section of the book dealing with the "Basis of Idioms", Bahri presents six different classes of "idioms" on the basis of their formation. We reproduce these six classes with Bahri's labels and a few examples in each class.

(i) The human body

आंख चढ़ाना
"(*ā̃kha caṛhānā*)
"(lit. to raise the eye) to be angry"

दिल लगाना
(*dila lagānā*)
"(lit. to stick one's heart to) to become attached to, to fall in love"

नाक काटना
(*nāka kāṭanā*)
"(lit. to cut someone's nose) to cause someone to loose respect"

हाथ खोलना
(*hātha kholanā*)
"(lit. to open hands) to spend money"

(ii) Immediate surroundings

चोला बदलना
(*colā badalanā*)
"(lit. to change the shirt) to transmigrate"

नमक मिर्च मिलाना
(*namaka mirca milānā*)
"(lit. to mix salt and pepper) to exaggerate"

(iii) Organic life

दुम हिलाना
(*duma hilānā*)
"(lit. to move the tail) to flatter"

उड़ती चिड़िया पकड़ना
(*uṛatī ciṛiyā pakaṛanā*)
"(lit. to catch the flying bird) to rely on uncertainty"

(iv) Inorganic life

हवा हो जाना
(*havā ho jānā*)
"(lit. to become wind) to run fast, to disappear"

हवा लगना
(*havā laganā*)
"(lit. to be touched by air or climate) to be affected"

(v) Habits, customs and superstitions

लाल पीला होना
(*lāla pīlā honā*)
"(lit. to be red and pale) to be angry"

छाती ठोकना
(*chātī ṭhokanā*)
"(lit. to pat the chest) to show courage"

(vi) History, myth and tradition
बीड़ा उठाना
(*bīṛā uṭhānā*)
"(lit. to take up a betel leaf) to take up a challenge"

Bahri (1959) also presents a semantic categorization of idioms in terms of three broad categories labelled as (i) general, which involves restriction (referring to specialization of meaning), generalization, pejoration and amelioration, synecdoche (referring to those phrases which are specific in form and general meaning), and metonymy, (ii) concretion (involving comparison of "abstract life to the concrete life") and (iii) idiomatic verbs (a sub-category which includes single verbs as well as noun plus verb sequences of various sorts).

Towards the end of this section Bahri makes an interesting observation which we reproduce here in its entirety since we feel it has bearing on the further study of the semantic complexity of conjunct verbs in MSH.

> Why a particular verb should have been used with a particular noun for a particular meaning is a subject for further study, to which help will be found in previous chapters. But it will be seen that the concrete literal meaning is in the centre of all the various idiomatic by-meanings.

2.3.2. Hacker (1961), as the title of the paper suggests, primarily concentrates "On the problem of a method for treating the compound and conjunct verbs in Hindi", and is probably the only work which deals more than superficially with this problem. It, therefore, has important bearing upon the discussion that has taken place about the category of conjunct verbs in MSH. Most of the paper is, in fact, a discussion of the implications of the following three questions posed by Hacker:

(1) Does the structuralist way of treatment actually or potentially add anything new to our knowledge of the syntax of Hindi ?

(2) Is there any prospect of an actual or potential structuralist syntax providing a workable basis for, affording substantial aid to, a description more accurate and more comprehensive than those given by previous grammars, of the meaning of the compound verbs or the syntactico-semantic function of the 'operators' (hitherto called auxiliary verbs) in Hindi ?

(3) What is the proper method for ascertaining that meaning or syntactico-semantic function ?

Hacker uses the term "compound verb" in two different senses: (i) in the narrow sense referring to compound verbs (that is verb plus verb sequences) as opposed to conjunct verbs (that is, noun or adjective plus verb sequences), and (ii) in the broad sense to refer to the phenomenon of compounding of conjunct verbs as well as of ordinary verbs (in the narrow sense) by means of explicators. It is on the basis of the application of the term compound verb in its broad sense that Hacker rejects Burton-Page's specification and delimitation of the category of conjunct verbs by pointing out a certain parallelism between dependent occurrences of explicators with verbs as well as conjunct verbs. He states that "Whenever a noun of a conjunct included in a compound verb is assignable to a meaning group, it is a group of verbs, not of object". Illustration of this point is given by several examples, a few of which we reproduce below.

> A group of verbs frequently compounded with बैठना (*baiṭhanā*) has the common feature that all of them denote some sort of aggression. In some instances, the verb is simple one (e.g., मारना (*māranā*), चुराना (*curānā*), डांटना (*ḍā̃ṭanā*), in other cases it is a conjunct [आघात करना (*āghāta karanā*), चोरी करना (*corī karanā*) निन्दा करना (*nindā karanā*)]. When conjuncts are employed, the use of the 'operator' is, of course, not determined by the meaning of the simple verb करना (*karanā*) that is a component of the conjunct; for there is no affinity of the meaning of करना (*karanā*) to the function of बैठना (*baiṭhanā*). Since the notion of aggression, which is determinant of the use of बैठना (*baiṭhanā*) is expressed by a noun [e.g., आघात (*āghāta*)], it is this noun (which, at a lower level is analyzable as the "object" N_2) or, more exactly, this noun in conjunction with the verb, that causes the use of the 'operator'.

In other words, use of the criterion of occurrence of conjunct verbs as well as verbs with explicators, a criterion employed by Burton-Page to isolate conjunct from compound verbs (in the narrow sense of the term), is an important argument in proving that the lexical interpretationists' formal or structural specification and delimitation of the category of conjunct verbs involves faulty assumptions. We will present more information in this context in section 3 of the "Introduction".

In view of this situation, Hacker (1961) proposes a new definition of conjunct verbs in the following terms:

> Therefore, the definition of the conjunct verb should include formal and semantic criteria. A conjunct verb is a combination of a substantive or an adjective (which may be a Sanskrit past participle) with a verb. The verb has very little of special content in it but denotes only the general concept of action [करना (*karanā*), देना (*denā*), etc.] or process or state [होना (*honā*)], the special content of the action or process or state being expressed by the noun [e.g., सर्वनाश करना (*sarvanāśa+karanā*), कैदी बनाना (*qaidī+banānā*), विकल होना (*vikala+honā*)].

Before we pass on to an evaluation of the contribution of Bahl (1967), it is necessary to clarify some misgivings in Hacker (1961) as to the nature of the dependent occurrence of explicators with verbs in compound verb formations in general. Hacker (1961), though he correctly points out the existence of the dependent occurrence of explicators with verbs in compound verbs (in the narrow sense of the term), as well as with conjunct verbs, fails to specify certain properties of verbs (that is, both formative verbs which form conjunct verbs, as well as other verbs) in regard to their ability to constrain the dependent occurrence of explicators with them in compound verbs (in the broad sense of the term). By "ability of the verbs to constrain the dependent occurrence of explicators with them" we mean the existence of a compatible versus incompatible relation between formative and other verbs, on the one hand, and explicators, on the other. In other words, we wish to point out that no blanket rules can be formulated concerning the selection of explicators by conjunct verbs, in the manner explained by Hacker, without at first specifying which explicators are compatible with a given formative verb. In addition, the class of such explicators compatible with a given formative verb is established independently of any consideration as to whether a given verb may or may not be a formative verb, or if a formative verb, whether or not it occurs with a particular noun or adjective. Hacker's argument concerning the existence of dependent occurrence of explicators with verbs in compound verbs (as we have tried to paraphrase his discussion on the subject) should, therefore, be amended to be "the existence of dependent occurrence of compatible explicators..." It is, therefore, correct to say that the formative verbs do play a part in the selection of explicators in (compound) conjunct verbs, a fact which is not taken into account by Hacker and grossly misconceived by both Burton-Page and Kachru. This fact, however, does not controvert Hacker's argument in any way.

There is another implication of the dependent occurrence of explicators in compound verbs (in the broad sense of the term) not stated by Hacker. It concerns the notion of maximum dependence between verbs or conjunct verbs, on the one hand, and the explicators, on the other, as explained in Bahl (1967). We shall now discuss the notion of maximum independence in order to bring out the significance of the relevance of the notion of maximum dependence to a specification of the category of conjunct verbs in MSH.

Almost all the grammarians of MSH (and other Indo-Aryan languages as well) operate under the assumption that subsidiary verbs (or explicators) modify or add to the meaning of main verbs in compound verb formations. This assumption led them to establish the category of compound verbs as comprising two components, that is, the primary verbs and their explicators, which were interpreted as being independent of each other. This interpretation involved the grammarians' belief that simple verbs in all the possible environments of their occurrence in MSH sentences can be compounded by means of explicators. This relation of maximum independence between the main (or primary verbs) and their explicators underlies the phrase structure rule (introducing the category of explicators in structuralist grammars) expressed in the form Verb Phrase→Verb (+Explicator). Having thus established the category of compound verbs, that is, formally introducing in the grammar verbs which may consist of more than one word each, the only task left for the grammarians is to list all the possible combinations of verbs (or conjunct verbs) plus explicators as possible lexical items in the language. An example of this type of situation is the "List of V's and Operators" as given in Kachru (1966) on pages 52-57. This list of "V's and Operators", as we have commented earlier, is not a list of "operators" which actually occur in sentences, but of explicators which are compatible with the verbs with which they are listed. In order to demonstrate the futility of such lists as a means of specifying the dependent occurrence of compatible explicators with verbs, one needs only to cite some instances of sentences which contain compound verbs and their non-sentence counterparts. In such instances each non-sentence is ungrammatical due to the occurrence of an explicator listed as compatible with the verb, whereas in each case, dropping the particular explicator will yield a grammatically well-formed sentence. A few such sentence pairs are given below. The intended senses in which the unstarred sentences are grammatical and starred sentences are ungrammatical are given below each.

(1) राम पढ़ाई में उससे आगे निकल गया है
(*rāma paṛhāī mẽ usa se āge nikala gayā hai*)
"Ram has gone ahead of him in studies."

(1a) *राम पढ़ाई में उससे पीछे निकल गया है
(**rāma paṛhāī mẽ usa se pīche nikala gayā*)
"Ram turned out to be behind him in studies."

(2) उसके मुंह से बात तक नहीं निकल रही
(*usa ke mũha se bāta taka nahī̃ nikala rahī*)
"He is unable to say a word even."

(2a) *उसके मुंह से कभी भी बात तक नहीं निकल रही
(**usa ke mũha se kabhī bhī bāta taka nahī̃ nikala rahī*)
"He never said a word."

In view of the possibilities of the occurrence or non-occurrence of compatible explicators, as illustrated in the above noted sentences as well as by Hacker (1961), we made the following proposal in Bahl (1967).

> The other possibility of analysis as suggested...is to limit ourselves to the interpretation of the grammatical relationship between a verb and the explicator, disregarding the problem of contrast between simple and compound verbs. The grammatical relationship between a verb and its explicators, we believe, can be satisfactorily understood on the basis of positing maximum dependence between the two. This means that the rule Verb Phrase→Verb (+Explicator) is no longer a valid interpretation. It is replaced by the rule Verb Phrase→Verb+Explicator.

We would now like to amend our original proposal by saying that the grammatico-semantic functions of the explicators can only be understood by regarding them (that is, the compatible explicators) as having a relation of maximum dependent occurrence with their (primary) verbs or conjunct verbs.

Hacker's definition of a conjunct verb, as reproduced earlier, is not clear as to how the immediate constituents of compound conjunct verbs are to be interpreted in view of this newly proposed relationship of maximum dependence between verbs or conjunct verbs and the explicators which actually occur with them in MSH sentences. We think it is necessary to clarify this matter in order that a further investigation of the phenomenon of conjunct verbs can be carried out on the lines envisaged by Hacker in his proposed conceptualization of the category of conjunct verbs.

As far as conjunct verbs are concerned there are only two possible ways of interpreting their immediate constituents, that is, (i) noun or adjective+formative verb/explicator, or (ii) noun or adjective/formative verb+explicator. We propose that the second possibility is the only one worth entertaining here because (i) a compatibility versus incompatibility relation exists only between formative verbs and their explicators, and (ii) (in view of Hacker's demonstration of the dependent occurrence of explicators with conjunct verbs) maximum dependence exists between the two constituents of compound conjunct verbs, that is, the nouns or adjectives, on the one hand, and their formative verbs (whether simple or compound) on the other.

Before we proceed to a discussion of the contribution of Bahl (1967), we would like to point out that our application of the terms "compound verbs" and "conjunct verbs", in view of the proposed relation of maximum dependence between their constituents, should not be confused with their traditional or structuralist usages. Our "Introduction" will continue to employ these two terms in the sense we have delimited above.

2.3.3. Bahl (1967) is essentially an exploratory study. Its section on "Action Noun Phrases" (pages 120-173) deals with the phenomenon of conjunct verbs in MSH, aiming primarily towards investigation of the problem by bringing in fresh evidence from the language. It begins with the conceptualization of the category of conjunct verbs in MSH as given in Hacker (1961) and states that the term "conjunct verb" as used by the grammarians of the languages includes several grammatically divergent phenomena, illustrated by the sentences given below.

(1) मैंने उसको शिक्षा दी
(*mãĩ ne usa ko śikṣā dī*)
"I instructed him."

(2) मैंने उसकी प्रशंसा की
(*mãĩ ne usa kī praśaṁsā kī*)
"I praised him."

(3) मैंने उसको किताब दान दी
(*mãĩ ne usa ko kitāba dāna dī*)
"I gave him a book in alms."

(4) मुझे यह किताब इनाम मिली
(*mujhe yaha kitāba ināma milī*)
"I got this book as a prize."

(5) उसने मुझे काबू कर लिया
(*usa ne mujhe kābū kara liyā*)
"He subjugated me."

(6) उसने गीत याद कर लिया
(*usa ne gīta yāda kara liyā*)
"He memorized the song."

(7) वह बहुत विकल हो रहा है
(*vaha bahuta vikala ho rahā hai*)
"He is getting disturbed very much."

While commenting upon the above noted examples, Bahl (1967) introduces the notion of "Action Noun Phrase". These comments are reproduced below.

In the above noted sentences, the sequences उसको शिक्षा (*usa ko śikṣā*) and उसकी प्रशंसा (*usa kī praśaṁsā*) are action noun phrases, the nouns दान (*dāna*) and इनाम (*ināma*)[with the ellipsis of the postposition में (*mẽ*) after both] are adverbs, and the nouns काबू (*kābū*) [with the ellipsis of the postposition में (*mẽ*)], याद (*yāda*) as well as the adjective विकल (*vikala*) are complements.

We would like to amend the application of the notion of Action Noun Phrase (hereafter abbreviated as ANP) in the manner it occurs in Bahl (1967) by saying that all the underlined noun or adjective plus verb sequences in the above noted examples are instances of conjunct verbs in MSH, and the term ANP should include all the nominal as well as adjectival phrases occurring with the various verbs in the above noted sentences. Such a statement is necessary since the restricted application of the term ANP to उसको शिक्षा (*usa ko śikṣā*) in (1) and उसकी प्रशंसा (*usa kī praśaṁsā*) in (2), and consequently the exclusion of the noun or adjective plus verb sequences as they occur in the rest of the sentences from the category of conjunct verbs, is an error. Our reasons for this amendment of the proposed notion of ANP as it exists in Bahl (1967) are discussed below.

It is obvious that Bahl (1967), by introducing the notion of ANP, proposes to investigate the phenomenon of conjunct verbs by concentrating on their nominal and verbal constituents separately, rather than attempting to establish the unitary status of these noun or adjective plus verb sequences in the lexicon of the language, as has been done by other grammarians of the language. At the same time, Bahl (1967) tacitly assumes that only those nominal or adjectival constituents, which occur as ANP's with verbs [as in sentences (1) and (2) above], should be included in the category of conjunct verbs. Evidence from the sentence structure of MSH may be employed to contradict this tacit assumption in Bahl (1967). The traditional grammarians of MSH would without question interpret the noun or adjective plus verb sequences दान देना (*dāna denā*) "to give something in alms", इनाम मिलना (*ināma milanā*) "to get something as a prize", काबू करना (*kābū karanā*) "to bring someone under one's control", याद कर लेना (*yāda kara lenā*) "to memorize" and विकल होना (*vikala honā*) "to be restless" as instances of conjunct verbs as they occur in sentences (3-7) noted above. But at the same time, they failed to notice that the sentences containing such noun or adjective plus verb sequences have other related sentences which should also be accounted for. For instance, sentence (3) is related to (3a) and (3b).

(3a) मैंने उसको गाय का दान दिया
(mãĩ ne usa ko gāya kā dāna diyā)
"I made him the gift of a cow."

(3b) मैंने उसको गाय दान में दी
(mãĩ ne usa ko gāya dāna mẽ dī)
"I gave him the cow in gift."

Similarly sentences (4) and (5) are respectively related to sentences (4a) and (4b), and (5a) and (5b).

(4a) मुझे इस किताब का इनाम मिला
(mujhe isa kitāba kā ināma milā)
"I got the prize of this book."

(4b) मुझे यह किताब इनाम में मिली
(mujhe yaha kitāba ināma mẽ milī)
"I got this book as a prize."

(5a) उसने मुझ पर काबू कर लिया
(usa ne mujha para kābū kara liyā)
"He subjugated me."

(5b) उसने मुझे काबू में कर लिया
(usa ne mujhe kābū mẽ kara liyā)
"He subjugated me."

Sentence (6) matches sentences (6a) and (6b).

(6a) उसने मोहन को बहुत याद किया
(usa ne mohana ko bahuta yāda kiyā)
"He remembered Mohan very much."

(6b) उसने मोहन की बहुत याद की
(usa ne mohana kī bahuta yāda kī)
"He remembered Mohan very much."

Sentence (7) involves the ellipsis of the constituent N के लिए (*N ke liye*) before the adjective विकल (*vikala*) "disturbed", and corresponds to sentence (7a).

(7a) वह इस बात के लिये बहुत विकल हो रहा है
(vaha isa bāta ke liye bahuta vikala ho rahā hai)
"He is getting very much disturbed about this matter."

Bahl (1967), because of its failure to perceive the apparent relationship between two sets of sentences, as noted above, quite arbitrarily determined to exclude the noun or adjective plus verb sequences of the types illustrated in sentences (3-7) from the category of conjunct verbs. As we will discuss in sub-section 3.6.6 the noun plus verb sequences occurring in sentences (3-6) are respectively related to noun postposition noun plus verb sequences as they occur in sentences (3a), (4a), (5a) and (6b), and sentences (3a), (4a), (5a) and (6a) are sentences with conjunct verbs also. We will also discuss the nature of adjective plus verb sequences in sub-section 4.2.1, where we will try to spell out the distinction between such adjective plus verb sequences as are regarded as conjunct verbs (or more precisely, as are conjunct verbs in the language) by the traditional grammarians, but interpreted otherwise by some structuralists.

The introduction of the notion of ANP in Bahl (1967) to cover a variety of noun postposition noun sequences is a significant step towards an investigation of the category of conjunct verbs in MSH. This notion, in its amended form (as suggested above), covers a wide variety of noun postposition noun or adjective sequences. That, and other related structures, as discussed above, will form the basis of the discussion of the phenomenon of conjunct verbs in section 3 of this "Introduction". We will also use the term ANP in the sense proposed here throughout this "Introduction", with the exception that in section two of the articles in SSSH, the application of this term will be restricted to noun postposition noun sequences only. The term "verbalizer verbs" as it occurs in Bahl (1967), referring to the verbs occurring with ANP's to form conjunct verbs, will be replaced by "formative verbs" in this "Introduction".

Since we propose to discuss the two constituents of conjunct verbs, that is, the ANP's and their formative verbs, in somewhat more detail in the next section [which will incorporate as well as amend the contents of Bahl (1967)], we feel it is not necessary to go into other contributions of Bahl (1967) in this sub-section.

3. Conjunct verbs in MSH.

3.1. As has been demonstrated in section 2, the grammarians of MSH have generally included among conjunct verbs such noun or adjective plus verb sequences as are either translatable in English by single verbs or come very close to being conceived of as grammatical units. In addition, we have noted that these grammarians also speak of the occurrence of such nouns or adjectives with a few verbs like करना (*karanā*) "to do", होना (*honā*) "to be", आना (*ānā*) "to come", देना (*denā*) "to give", खाना (*khānā*) "to eat" and so forth. They all, however, give the impression that the expressions treated as conjunct verbs are peculiar to modern Indo-Aryan languages including MSH, constituting grammatical exceptions which, even though having a marginal status in the languages, nevertheless deserve attention. As one looks at these works in a chronological fashion, one cannot fail to observe that fewer and fewer instances of expressions forming the basis of grammatical discussion concerning the category of conjunct verbs occur in these grammars culminating in the belief that conjunct verbs typically have करना (*karanā*) "to do" as their formative verb.

Due to the prevalence of this trend of thought, we feel that an investigation of the phenomena of conjunct verbs must start afresh. Such an investigation, if it is to contribute significantly to the study of the semantic structure of MSH, should base itself on new evidence collected primarily for this purpose concerning the category of conjunct verbs. Therefore, in the sub-sections that follow, we try to present as much fresh evidence about conjunct verbs as possible within the limitations of this "Introduction", followed by a discussion, and not an interpretation, of this evidence.

3.2. In this sub-section we propose to deal with ANP's, that is, phrases referring to the nominal or adjectival constituents of conjunct verbs denoting the special content of the action or process or state. These ANP's consist of N_2(oun) post(position) N_1(oun) or Adj(ective) sequences and a variety of related structures which occur with V(erbs) to form conjunct verbs.[1] The grammarians of MSH have concentrated on[N_1 or Adj+V] sequences disregarding the occurrence of [N_2 post] with [N_1 or Adj]. These grammarians have also disregarded the fact that these same [N_2 post N_1 or Adj] sequences occur in MSH sentences in environments other than that of verbs. For this reason we argued in sub-section 2.3.2 in favor of positing [N_2 post N_1 or Adj] and [V] (that is, verbs with or without explicators) as the two constituents in conjunct verbs. The grammarians of MSH, as we have tried to show in section 2, have insisted on studying conjunct verbs by positing [N_2 post] and [N_1 or Adj+V] as two constituents. Thus the treatment of conjunct verbs in MSH grammars is erroneous on two counts, that is, (i) it involves a complete lack of any attempt to take into account the occurrence of those [N_2 post N_1 or Adj] sequences (which occur with verbs to form conjunct verbs) in environments other than that of [V]'s and (ii) as a result of this one-sided emphasis they do not study these nominal and verbal constituents of conjunct verbs either independently of each other, or when they have a "unitary status" as conjunct verbs.

To illustrate our view, we give below some instances of the occurrence of का प्रयोग (*kā prayoga*) with the verb करना (*karanā*) "to do" as well as in

1. The symbols like N_2 post N_1 etc. are throughout this "Introduction" enclosed in square brackets to avoid any confusion.

environments where it is not followed by any verbs, referring to the act of using something.

(1) स्वास्थ्य तथा सफाई के प्रदत्त बजट का प्रयोग करने के लिये ग्रामीण जनों को प्रोत्साहित करना
(*svāsthya tathā saphāī ke pradatta bajaṭa kā prayoga karane ke liye grāmīṇa janõ ko protsāhita karanā . . .*)
"To encourage village people to make use of the budget allocated for sanitation and health."

(2) देश के समस्त लोग नई नई विधियों को सीखने तथा उनका प्रयोग करने में तत्पर हैं।
(*deśa ke samasta loga naī naī vidhiyõ ko sīkhane tathā unakā prayoga karane mẽ tatpara hãĩ*)
"All the people of the country are engaged in learning newer methods as well as making use of them."

(3) १ अक्तूबर १९६२ से लम्बाई नापने के लिये मीटरका प्रयोग जरूरी हो जायगा।
(1 *aktūbara* 1962 *se lambāī nāpane ke liye mīṭara kā prayoga zarūrī ho jāyagā*)
"The use of meter will become mandatory for measuring length from October 1, 1962."

(4) पशु-शक्ति के प्रयोग के साथ ही नये और अधिक कुशल औजारों का आविष्कार और विकास होता गया।
(*paśu-śakti ke prayoga ke sātha hī naye aura adhika kuśala auzārõ kā āviṣkāra aura vikāsa hotā gayā*)
"The invention and development of newer and better implements took place along with the use of animal power."

The above examples are sufficient to illustrate the fact that these [N_2 post N_1] sequences are verbal in nature, that is, represent or refer to actions (or more precisely, to concepts of actions) of one sort or another, independently of the [V]'s with which they form conjunct verbs.

This situation can be contrasted with the occurrence of nouns or adjectives which may or may not be verbal, depending upon the environment in which they occur. We may illustrate this with the occurrence of the noun भोजन (*bhojana*) "eating ; that which is eaten (i.e., food)" and adjective ठीक (*ṭhika*) "fixed ; appropriate, right".

(5) मोहन भोजन कर रहा है।
(*mohana bhojana kara rahā hai*)
"Mohan is eating."

(6) मोहन भोजन बना रहा है ।
(*mohana bhojana banā rahā hai*)
"Mohan is preparing the food."

(7) यह मशीन अब बिल्कुल ठीक हो गई है ।
(*yaha maśīna aba bilkula ṭhīka ho gayī hai*)
"This machine is now completely fixed."

(8) यह मशीन आपके लिये बिल्कुल ठीक है ।
(*yaha maśīna āpake liye bilkula ṭhīka hai*)
"This machine is just right for you."

In sentence (5) the noun भोजन (*bhojana*) (where it means "eating") is verbal, whereas in sentence (6) (where it refers to "food") it is not. These two occurrences of the noun भोजन (*bhojana*) with the verbs करना (*karanā*) "to do" and बनाना (*banānā*) "to make" can be contrasted with its occurrence in environments other than that of verbs. We illustrate this below :

(9) फलों के भोजन से स्वास्थ्य अच्छा रहता है ।
(*phalõ ke bhojana se svāsthya acchā rahatā hai*)
"By eating fruit (one's) health remains in good condition".

(10) भोजन में विटामिन, प्रोटीन आदि पदार्थों का होना स्वास्थ्य के लिये आवश्यक है ।
(*bhojana mẽ viṭāmina proṭīna ādi padārthõ kā honā svāsthya ke liye āvaśyaka hai*)
"It is necessary for good health that there should be substances like vitamins, proteins etc. in the food."

In sentence (9) the phrase फलों का भोजन (*phalõ kā bhojana*) can be substituted by फलों का भोजन करने (*phalõ kā bhojana karane*) "by eating fruit", whereas no such substitution is possible in sentence (10). Therefore, the noun भोजन (*bhojana*) "eating; food" is verbal only in sentence (9); similarly in sentence (7) the [Adj+V] sequence ठीक हो गई है (*ṭhīka ho gayī hai*) "is fixed" is a conjunct verb, whereas the sequence ठीक है (*ṭhīka hai*) "is right or appropriate", as it occurs in sentence (8), is not.

Without going into the details of the grammatico-semantic interpretation of the above noted sentences at this stage of our investigation, we would like to point out the necessity of distinguishing the verbal occurrence of nouns and adjectives in MSH sentences from their non-verbal occurrences. As may be seen, it is necessary to make this distinction independently of whether or not the nouns or adjectives, which refer to various concepts of actions, occur with verbs to form conjunct verbs. It is, therefore, appropriate to say that by ANP we mean only the [N_2 post N_1 or

Adj] sequences which, by virtue of their [N_1]'s, or [Adj]'s are realized in the sentence structure of MSH in their manifestations as verbal occurrences. We believe it is necessary to start with this assumption for a proper investigation of the phenomenon of conjunct verbs.

With these preliminary remarks concerning the [N_1]'s and [Adj]'s occurring in ANP's, we will first proceed to a discussion of the working of these [N_2 post N_1 or Adj] sequences in the environment of [V]'s, and then to a discussion of these [V]'s in the environment of their co-occurring [N_2 post N_1 or Adj] sequences. What is postulated here is designed to be a first step towards a somewhat more systematic account of करना (*karanā*) "to do" conjunct verbs presented in section 4 of this "Introduction"; although we attempt to shed as much light as possible on the general phenomenon of conjunct verbs in MSH.

We also feel, that, at this stage of our investigation of conjunct verbs in MSH, it is possible to make general statements about [N_1] nouns without restricting them to their occurrence with ANP's which form conjunct verbs with any particular verb. On the other hand, it is not possible to discuss [Adj]'s in the same manner, that is, without bringing in a discussion of a wide variety of formative verbs. Due to limitations of space, we, therefore, propose to discuss the occurrence of [Adj]'s only in करना (*karanā*) "to do" conjunct verbs, which appears in sub-section 4.2.1.

3.3. Broadly speaking the nouns occurring as [N_1] nouns in ANP's are lexically either abstract nouns such as ध्यान (*dhyāna*)"attention", or common nouns referring to concrete objects, such as हाथ (*hātha*) "hand", which serve as instruments of various activities. The occurrence of abstract nouns in conjunct verbs is well-known in MSH grammars. But no grammar of the language has ever proposed the inclusion of [N_2 post N_1+V] sequences with common nouns occurring as [N_1] nouns in the category of conjunct verbs, partly because such sequences were set aside as idioms [as explained in sub-section 2.3.1 while discussing Bahri (1959)], and partly because the grammarians' hold to a one-sided preoccupation with the notion of the unitary status of [N_1+V]'s. It so happens that [N_2 post N_1+V] sequences, in which [N_1]'s are common nouns, are not felt as idioms (though there are some exceptions) when their co-occurring [N_2 post]'s are either not taken into consideration or dropped. For example, the expression हाथ (*hātha*) "hand" plus करना (*karanā*) "to do" can occur in sentences like हाथ नीचे करो (*hātha nīce karo* !) "Put your hands down!" and is not considered to be an idiom in such sentences. Also these [N_2 post N_1] sequences with common nouns occurring as [N_1]'s generally assume verbal occurrences in the environment of [V]'s only, that is, in conjunct verbs.

Below we give a few examples of the [N_2 post N_1+V] conjunct verbs illustrating the occurrence of the noun हाथ (*hātha*) "hand" as an [N_1].

(1) N की ओर हाथ उठाना
(*N kī ora hātha uṭhānā*)
"to raise one's hand in the direction of someone (or something) (in order to point at him or it) i.e., to point at or towards the N"

(2) N पर हाथ बैठाना
(*N para hātha baiṭhānā*)
"to try to get one's hands accustomed to manipulating something (by repeatedly working on it) i.e., to practise with the N."

(3) N पर हाथ उठाना
(*N para hātha uṭhānā*)
"to position one's hand above someone (with the intention of hitting him) i.e., to try to hit someone."

(4) N में हाथ डालना
(*N mẽ hātha ḍālanā*)
"to put one's hands into something (by engaging them in the manipulation of it) i.e., to start doing the N."

(5) N को हाथ लगाना
(*N ko hātha lagānā*)
"to deliberately let one's hand come into contact with something (with a variety of intentions) i.e., to touch the N, to pollute the N, to feel the N, and so forth."

(6) N से दो हाथ करना
(*N se do hātha karanā*)
"to stand in a posture with one's hands raised in the direction of someone (who is also in a similar posture) i.e., (to be ready) to have a duel with N."

The exclusion by traditional grammarians of expressions like the above containing common nouns from the category of conjunct verbs, and as a result, their relegation to the category of idioms, does not mean that such expressions are felt to be unanalyzable. On the contrary, they are regarded as analyzable, as, for instance, Bahri (1959), but in a manner or on the basis of principles which are felt to be inconsistent with grammar. We propose that the grammarians of MSH have in the past regarded such expressions as idioms because they posited the occurrence of nouns like हाथ (*hātha*) "hand", in idiomatic as well as non-idiomatic expressions, as being one and the same thing, that is, referring to "hands" as parts of the human body. We, on the contrary, stipulate that the noun हाथ (*hātha*) "hand", when it occurs in idiomatic expressions of the type we have listed above and which we would like to include in the category of conjunct verbs, does not refer to the part of the human body called "hand". It, rather, refers only to the MSH "concept of hand", which according to the cultural practices (and probably folk-beliefs as well) is an instrument of various activities. For example, the expressions with the noun हाथ (*hātha*) listed above respectively presuppose इशारा करने के लिये (*iśārā karane ke liye*) "in order to point at" (1), आदत डालने के लिये (*ādata ḍālane ke liye*) "to become accustomed to" (2), मारने के लिये (*mārane ke liye*) "in order to hit" (3), and so on. It is presuppositions like those we have just listed, and which refer to various activities, that define the occurrence of common nouns as instruments of those activities. The common noun हाथ (*hātha*) "hand" occurs in the above noted conjunct verbs, not as referring to a certain part (or parts) of the human body, but as a symbolic concept and functions like abstract nouns, which by their occurrence in ANP's denote special content of action, process or state. The conjunct verbs containing common nouns serve as references to actions presupposed by their modalities or instrumentations, and the $[N_1]$ common nouns occurring in them are symbolic concepts referring to such modalities or instrumentations. Expressions like those with the noun हाथ (*hātha*) "hand" which we have given above, as well as those quoted from Bahri (1959) in sub-section 2.3.1, abound in MSH. Fairly comprehensive lists of such expressions exist in Tiwari (1964)

3.3.1. Within the two broad classes of $[N_1]$ nouns noted above, it is necessary to recognize two varieties of $[N_1]$ phrases—(i) in which an $[N_1]$ noun is preceded by a specificant consisting of a noun and a postposition, and (ii) in which an $[N_1]$ noun is followed by a determinant consisting of a postposition and a noun. The following sentences illustrate this situation.

(1) मैं आपको इस मेहरबानी के लिये धन्यवाद देता हूं।
(*mãĩ āpako isa meharabānī ke liye dhanyavāda detā hū̃*)
"I thank you for this kindness."

(2) मैं आपको आपकी सफलता के उपलक्ष्य में बधाई देता हूं।
(*mãĩ āpa ko āpa kī saphalatā ke upalakṣya mẽ badhāī detā hū̃*)
"I congratulate you for your success."

(3) स्त्रियाँ भी मुस्करा कर उन पर नयनों की कटार चला रही थीं।
(*striyā̃ bhī muskarākara una para nayanõ kī kaṭāra calā rahī thī̃*)
"The women, by their smiles, were brandishing their dagger- (like) eyes at them."

(4) क्षणभर में उनके मन में भावों का तूफान उठ आया।
(*kṣaṇa-bhara mẽ unake mana mẽ bhāvõ kā tūphana uṭha āyā*)
"In a moment his mind was stormed with emotions."

In sentences (1) and (2) इस मेहरबानी के लिये (*isa meharabānī ke liye*) "for this kindness" and आपकी सफलता के उपलक्ष्य में (*āpa kī saphalatā ke upalakṣya mẽ*) "for your success" are respectively specificants of the N_1 nouns धन्यवाद (*dhanyavāda*) "expression of thanks" and बधाई (*badhāī*) "congratulations". On the other hand, in sentences (3) and (4), the phrases नयनों की कटार (*nayanõ kī kaṭāra*) and भावों का तूफान (*bhāvõ kā tūphāna*) have the nouns कटार (*kaṭāra*) "dagger" and तूफान (*tūphāna*) "storm" as determinants of the modalities of the activities denoted respectively by the nouns नयनों (*nayanõ*) "eyes" and भावों (*bhāvõ*) "emotions".

There is a considerable variety of these specificants and determinants of activities denoted by [N_1] nouns in the language. A systematization of them is, however, outside the scope of this "Introduction", and, therefore, will not be discussed here.

3.3.2. Common nouns like हाथ (*hātha*) "hand" may occur as [N_1] nouns in [N_2 post N_1], or they may, as specificants or determinants of the activities denoted by their [N_1] nouns, replace these [N_1] nouns in sentences. This kind of substitution of [N_1] nouns by means of their specificants and determinants will be labelled as substitution of [N_1], that is, an activity by its instrumentations or modalities. The phenomena is illustrated by the examples given below.

(1) मोहन ने राम से जूतों की मार खाई।
(*mohana ne rāma se jūtõ kī māra khāī*)
"Mohan took a beating from Ram with shoes."

(1a) मोहन ने राम से जूते खाये।
(*mohana ne rāma se jūte khāye*)
"Mohan took (a beating) from Ram (with) shoes."

(2) क्षणभर में उनके मन में भावों का तूफान उठ आया।
(*kṣaṇa bhara mẽ una ke mana mẽ bhāvõ kā tūphāna uṭha āyā*)
"In a moment, there arose a storm of feelings in his mind."

(2a) क्षणभर में उनके मन में एक तूफान-सा उठ आया।
(*kṣaṇa bhara mẽ una ke mana mẽ eka tūphāna sā uṭha āyā*)
"In a moment, there arose a storm (of feelings) in his mind."

Here it is noteworthy that quite a few of the so-called idiomatic verbal expressions of traditional grammarians involve substitution of an activity denoted by an [N_1] noun by nouns denoting instrumentations of that activity.

The kind of substitution of an activity by its instrumentation or modality, as we have illustrated above, should be distinguished from the occurrence of the modalities of an activity since the nouns denoting various modalities of such an activity are in themselves independent nouns.

This situation can be illustrated by the occurrence of the nouns क्रोध (*krodha*) "anger", गुस्सा (*gussā*) "displeasure", तैश (*taiśa*) "furiousness", ताव (*tāva*) "heat", (*garmī*) "heat", and रोष (*roṣa*) "anger" etc. in the sentence frame,

(3) N को भी——आ गया/गई
(*N ko bhī——ā gayā/gayī.*)
"The N too became angry etc."

all referring to a person's (that is, the one referred to by the N) getting or becoming angry. All these nouns are modalities of "ANGER" (**क्रोध**) in the sense that they all serve to characterize the manifestations of the emotional state of "ANGER" (**क्रोध**) in the variety of ways as can be specified in MSH.[1] The phenomenon will be discussed further in sub-section 4.4. dealing with the synonymy of nouns and adjectives occurring in conjunct verbs formed with the verb करना (*karanā*) "to do".

3.3.3. Nouns denoting various activities undergo various modifications in their meanings depending upon their linking postposition (that is, the [post] in [N_2 post N_1]), on the one hand, and the formative verbs of their ANP's, on the other. Below we give examples of the occurrences of the ANP's N का ध्यान (*N kā dhyāna*) and N पर ध्यान (*N para dhyāna*) with a variety of verbs illustrating the various nuances of the meaning of noun ध्यान (*dhyāna*).

(1) किसी को किसी बात का ध्यान होना
(*kisī ko kisī bāta kā dhyāna honā*)
"for someone to be aware of something ; awareness"

उसे इसका तनिक भी ध्यान न था कि बात इतनी बढ़ जायगी।
(*use isakā tanika bhī dhyāna na thā ki bāta itanī baṛha jāyagī*)
"He wasn't even the slightest bit aware that the matter would grow to such proportions."

(2) किसी को किसी का ध्यान आना
(*kisī ko kisī kā dhyāna ānā*)
"for someone to think of someone ; thought"

पर जब-जब मुझे उसका ध्यान आता है मन चंचल हो उठता है।
(*para jaba jaba mujhe usakā dhyāna ātā hai mana cañcala ho uṭhatā hai*).
"But whenever I think of her my mind becomes troubled."

1. The abstract [N_1]'s, [Adj]'s or [V]'s will be written in capitals in Roman or indicated by bold types in Devanagari. Also the abstract verb TAKE, for example, is not a synonym of the lexical item "to take" etc. For more discussion about this convention and some other related problems see Bahl and Sinha (1972).

(3) किसी का ध्यान टूटना
(kisī kā dhyāna ṭūṭanā)
"for someone's reverie to break ; reverie"

दादा ने नाम लिया तो निन्नी का ध्यान टूटा ।
(dādā ne nāma liyā to ninnī kā dhyāna ṭūṭā)
"When her older brother called her name then Ninni's reverie was broken."

(4) किसी बात का ध्यान करना
(kisī bāta kā dhyāna karanā)
"to muse over ; reflection"

कदाचित् प्रतापी जयित्र चन्द्र के अपार धैर्य और साहस का ध्यान कर रही थी ।
(...kadācit pratāpī jayitra candra ke apāra dhairya aura sāhasa kā dhyāna kara rahī thī).
"Perhaps she was musing over the limitless fortitude and courage of the splendid Jayitra Candra."

(5) किसी वस्तु का ध्यान करना
(kisī vastu kā dhyāna karanā)
"to focus one's mind upon something ; the act of focusing."

मैं अवश्य तपस्या बढ़ाऊंगी और केवल गुरु चरणों का ही ध्यान किया करूंगी ।
(mãĩ avaśya tapasyā baṛhāū̃gī auru kevala guru caraṇõ kā hī dhyāna kiyā karū̃gī)
"I will certainly expand my practice of asceticism and will only focus my mind upon the sacred feet of the Guru"

(6) किसी का ध्यान लगाना
(kisī kā dhyāna lagānā)
"to meditate ; meditation"

आजकल सुमन्त पुरी जी बहुत ध्यान लगाते हैं, एकान्त में रहते हैं ।
(ājakala sumantapurī jī bahuta dhyāna lagāte hãĩ, ekānta mẽ rahate hãĩ)
"These days Sumantapuri ji meditates over prolonged periods of time, and stays alone."

(7) किसी का ध्यान रखना
(kisī kā dhyāna rakhanā)
"to look after someone ; looking after"

नागरत्ना को अपने लौट आने तक मनिमेखला का ध्यान रखने...का आदेश दे वह दूत के साथ रथ पर चली।
(*nāgaratnā ko apane lauṭa āne taka manimekhalā kā dhyāna rakhane ...kā ādeśa de vaha dūta ke sātha ratha para calī*)
"She instructed Nagaratna to look after Manimekhala until she comes back and then accompanied the messenger on the chariot."

(8) किसी बात पर ध्यान देना
(*kisī bāta para dhyāna denā*)
"to pay heed to, heed"

उन्होंने कभी उस बात पर ध्यान ही नहीं दिया।
(*unhõ ne kabhī usa bāta para dhyāna hī nahī̃ diyā*)
"He never paid any heed to that matter."

(9) किसी का किसी बात पर ध्यान होना
(*kisī kā kisī bāta para dhyāna honā*)
"to have one's mind on ; mind"

मन्सूर का ध्यान अब उस प्लेन पर नहीं था जिसे बनाने वह निकले थे।
(*mansūra kā dhyāna aba usa plena para nahī̃ thā jise banāne vaha nikale the*)
"Mansur's mind was then not on the plan which he had set out to prepare."

(10) किसी का किसी चीज पर ध्यान खिंच आना
(*kisī kā kisī cīja para dhyāna khĩca ānā*)
"for someone's attention to be attracted towards something ; attention"

मीता का ध्यान चाकलेट पर खिंच आया।
(*mītā kā dhyāna cākaleṭa para khĩca āyā*)
"Mita's attention was (suddenly) attracted towards the chocolate."

Several examples of the occurrence of the noun आवाज (*āvāza*) "sound", as given below, also illustrate the variety of ways this noun serves to characterize the modalities of the activities it refers to.[1]

(11) के विरुद्ध आवाज उठाना
(*ke viruddha āvāza uṭhānā*)
"to object ; objection"

1. The noun आवाज़ (*āvāza*) "sound" in all these examples means "noises made by human speech organs", and, therefore, refers to the activity as well as the product of the human speech organs.

(12) पर आवाज़ उठाना
(*para āvāza uṭhānā*)
"to express concern over; concern"

(13) पर आवाज़ कसना
(*para āvāza kasanā*)
"to taunt someone; remark, taunt"

(14) के कान में आवाज़ पड़ना
(*ke kāna mẽ āvāza paṛanā*)
"to overhear; the act of overhearing"

(15) के कान में आवाज़ डालना
(*ke kāna mẽ āvāza ḍālanā*)
"to suggest; suggestion"

(16) को आवाज़ देना
(*ko āvāza denā*)
"to call; call"

(17) को आवाज़ लगाना
(*ko āvāza lagānā*)
"to summon; summon"

(18) की आवाज़ बैठना
(*kī āvāza baiṭhanā*)
"to have a hoarse voice; hoarse voice"

(19) की आवाज़ खुल जाना
(*kī āvāza khula jānā*)
"to have a clear voice; clear voice"

(20) की आवाज़ मर जाना
(*kī āvāza mara jānā*)
"to have a low voice; low voice"

(21) की आवाज़ उखड़ना
(*kī āvāza ukhaṛanā*)
"to falter (while singing or talking); faltering voice"

3.4. It is extremely difficult at this stage of our investigation of the language to discuss the variety of [N_2 post N_1] sequences which occur in the language, as well as the number of formative verbs with which they occur as conjunct verbs, short of listing them in a suitable manner. Such an enterprise, we believe, would not only be cumbersome and consume too much space, but would also serve no useful purpose other than that of convincing the reader of the immensity of the phenomena. Therefore, we would like to adopt an alternative approach involving an examination of the occurrence of some selected ANP's with a variety of verbs in order to learn more about their semantic complexity. Such an examination can proceed along two lines—(i) an examination of the occurrence of individual ANP's with a variety of formative verbs, and (ii) an examination of a variety of ANP's occurring with a formative verb. In the next two sub-sections we shall present data along these two lines and discuss some of the conclusions which emerge from them.

Before we proceed, however, we would like to say that our presentation of this data is only a poor substitute for a description to be prepared of all the ANP's occurring with all the formative verbs along the lines of the करना (*karanā*) "to do" conjunct verbs we have initiated in this volume of the SSSH. Preparation of such a description is a necessary first step towards a systematic enquiry into the phenomenon of conjunct verbs in MSH. Our presentation of the data along the lines suggested above is, therefore, aimed at an exploration of the regularities of the occurrence of ANP's with verbs other than करना (*karanā*) "to do", as well as the regularities of the occurrence of different verbs with an ANP.

3.4.1. We would like to begin an examination of the occurrence of individual ANP's with a variety of formative verbs with the ANP N पर नज़र (*N para nazara*). The various conjunct verbs formed with this ANP are listed below.

(1) N पर नज़र जाना
(*N para nazara jānā*)
"for one's vision to turn towards"

(2) N पर नज़र पड़ना
(*N para nazara paṛanā*)
"to happen to look at something"

(3) N पर नज़र डालना
(*N para nazara ḍālanā*)
"to take a look at"

(4) N पर नज़र रखना
(*N para nazara rakhanā*)
"to keep looking at"

(5) N पर नज़र रहना
(*N para nazara rahanā*)
"to have one's vision set on something"

(6) N पर नजर दौड़ाना
(N para nazara dauṛānā)
"to take quick look at"

(7) N पर नजर जमाना
(N para nazara jamānā)
"to fix one's vision on something"

(8) N पर नजर मारना
(N para nazara māranā)
"to go through something"

(9) N पर नजर ठहरना
(N para nazara ṭhaharanā)
"to be able to fixedly look at something"

(10) N पर नजर टिकना
(N para nazara ṭikanā)
"to be able to concentrate one's vision on something"

(11) N पर नजर होना
(N para nazara honā)
"to have one's eyes on something"

In Bahl (1967) (pages 138-139), we commented as follows regarding the occurrence of the various verbs with the ANP N पर नजर (*N para nazara*).

> All the verbs जा- (*jā-*) "to go", पड़- (*paṛa-*) "to fall", डाल- (*ḍāla-*) "to throw", रख- (*rakha-*) "to keep", रह- (*raha-*) "to remain", दौड़ा- (*dauṛā-*) "to cause to run", जमा- (*jamā-*) "to fix", मार- (*māra-*) "hit", ठहर- (*ṭhahara-*) "to stay", टिक- (*ṭika-*) "to become stabilized", and हो- (*ho-*) "to be" by virtue of their occurrence with the action noun phrase N पर नज़र (*N para nazara*) besides acting as its verbalizers, cluster around a single verbal concept which in the above examples is N पर नज़र जाना (*N para nazara jānā*) "for one's vision to turn towards". In other words, the action denoted by the verb जा- (*jā-*) "to go", that is, "movement away from a point" is implied by the action noun phrase N पर नज़र (*N para nazara*). Only the verb जा (*jā*) "to go" can be considered as an empty verb (or a true verbalizer verb) with this action noun phrase. The rest of the verbs do add their semantic content to the action noun phrase. Traditional statements about conjunct verbs, if they have any meaning at all, apply only to N पर नज़र जाना (*N para nazara jānā*) "for one's vision

to turn towards" but don't say anything about the rest of the verbal concepts mentioned above.

In other words, all the conjunct verbs with N पर नज़र (*N para nazara*), with the exception of N पर नज़र जाना (*N para nazara jānā*) "for one's vision to turn towards" imply N पर नज़र जाना (*N para nazara jānā*) in their underlying structure and are analyzable as N पर नज़र जाना (*N para nazara jānā*) plus x, where x represents the semantic content of the verbs other than जाना (*jānā*) "to go". Traditional grammarians, who concentrated on conjunct verbs (that is, [N_1 + V]'s) as lexical items consisting of more than one word each, that is, noun plus verb sequences having unitary conceptual (or semantic) status, interpreted only sequences like N पर नज़र जाना (*N para nazara jānā*) "for one's vision to turn towards" as a conjunct verb and relegated the rest of the conjunct verbs to the category of idioms [or more specifically, to the category of "verbal idioms" "in which the verb alone implies a metaphorical meaning without affecting the substantive" as discussed by Bahri (1959) and referred to by us in sub-section 2.3.1]. A great majority of conjunct verbs in MSH are of this type.

Since we have discussed above an ANP in which the postposition happens to be पर (*para*) "on, at" etc., we would like to pursue the matter of the occurrence of this postposition in a variety of other ANP's in order to see what kinds of problems it presents.

We give below several instances of the ANP's of the type [N_2 पर N_1] ([*N_2 para N_1*]) occurring with a variety of verbs with their approximate equivalents in English.

(12) N पर आरोप लगाना
(*N para āropa lagānā*)
"to accuse"

(13) N पर बल देना
(*N para bala denā*)
"to emphasize"

(14) N पर प्रहार करना
(*N para prahāra karanā*)
"to hit"

(15) N पर सन्देह करना
(*N para sandeha karanā*)
"to suspect"

(16) N पर तरस खाना
(*N para tarasa khānā*)
"to pity"

(17) N पर जोर डालना
(*N para jora ḍālanā*)
"to pressurize"

(18) N पर गुस्सा निकालना
(*N para gussā nikālanā*)
"to take it out on"

(19) N पर आतंक जमाना
(*N para ātaṁka jamānā*)
"to terrorize"

(20) N पर पर्दा डालना
(*N para pardā ḍālanā*)
"to (try to) conceal"

All the above noted examples suggest that the English verbs "accuse", "emphasize", "hit" and so on, are semantically complex lexical items. Also the MSH counterparts of these verbs suggest some possible ways of handling them in the prelexical syntax of English, that is, by interpreting "accuse", "emphasize" and "hit" etc., as respectively consisting of "put the blame on", "put the emphasis on" and "direct one's blows at" etc. The other implication of these examples is that whereas English combines semantic materials to generate lexical items like "accuse" etc., MSH does not do so.[1] Therefore, the grammarians of MSH should abandon the approach of trying to describe conjunct verbs as any form of units.

Above we have discussed a few instances of the ANP's involving [N_2 पर N_1] ([N_2 *para* N_1]), and have tried to demonstrate that lexical materials which manifest themselves in the surface structure of MSH also combine themselves into semantically complex lexical items in English. We now proceed to discuss some other peculiarities of these [N_2 पर N_1] ([N_2 *para* N_1]) ANP's, confining ourselves to the various आना (*ānā*) "to come" conjunct verbs in MSH. There are three categories of such ANP's in the language, examples of each of which are given below.

(i) N_3 *ko* [N_2 *para* N_1] *ānā*

(21) किसी को किसी की अकल पर अफसोस आना
(*kisī ko kisī kī akala para aphasosa ānā*)
"(for someone) to feel sorry for someone's (lack) of wisdom"

1. For further implications of this approach see James D. McCawley, "Prelexical Syntax" in Richard J. O'Brien, S.J. (editor) *Monograph Series on Languages and Linguistics*, Georgetown University, School of Languages and Linguistics, Number 24, 1971.

(22) किसी को किसी की बात पर यकीन आना
(kisī ko kisī kī bāta para yakīna ānā)
"(for someone) to feel certain about something"

(23) किसी को किसी पर रहम आना
(kisī ko kisī para rahama ānā)
"(for someone) to feel pitiful towards someone"

(24) किसी को किसी पर क्रोध आना
(kisī ko kisī para krodha ānā)
"(for someone) to be angry or upset about (something done by) someone"

(ii) [N_2 *para* N_1] *ānā*

(25) किसी पर आफत आना
(kisī para āphata ānā)
"(for) some mishap to happen to someone"

(26) किसी पर बदनामी आना
(kisī para badanāmī ānā)
"(for someone) to be victimized by some infamy"

(27) किसी पर संकट आना
(kisī para saṁkaṭa ānā)
"(for someone) to be in a state of crisis"

(28) किसी पर मुसीबत आना
(kisī para musībata ānā)
"(for someone) to be in a state of misfortune"

(iii) [N_3 *ke* N_2 *para* N_1] *ānā*
N_2

(29) किसी के चेहरे पर खुशी आना
(kisī ke cehare para khuśī ānā)
"(for someone) to look happy or cheerful"

(30) किसी के चेहरे पर रौनक आना
(kisī ke cehare para raunaka ānā)
"(for someone) to appear gay and happy (as a normal disposition)"

(31) किसी के मुख पर कठोरता आ जाना
(kisī ke mukha para kaṭhoratā ā jānā)
"(for someone) to put on a relentless disposition"

(32) पेड़ों पर जवानी आना
(perõ para javānī ānā)
"(for trees) to become youthful"

(33) किसी पर बुढ़ापा आना
(kisī para buṛhāpā ānā)
"(for someone) (suddenly) to look older than one really is"

(34) किसी के चेहरे पर निखार आना
(kisī ke cehare para nikhāra ānā)
"(for someone) to put on an appearance of elegance"

The $[N_1]$ nouns in category (i) refer to various psychological or mental states resulting from a disturbed homeostasis and characterize $[N_3]$'s (that is, someone's) response to a stimulus denoted by $[N_2]$ at whom (or which) such responses are directed. The $[N_1]$ nouns in category (ii) refer to various environmental conditions which come upon an individual denoted by $[N_2]$. And finally, the $[N_1]$ nouns in category (iii) refer to certain psycho-physical states characteristic of someone's mental make-up.

The ANP's in category (i) also occur with the verb करना (*karanā*) "to do".

(35) राम को मोहन पर बड़ा क्रोध आया।
(rāma ko mohana para baṛā krodha āyā)
"Ram was very angry with Mohan"

(36) राम ने मोहन पर बड़ा क्रोध किया।
(rāma ne mohana para baṛā krodha kiyā)
Ram let his anger out on Mohan"

Another feature of sentences with conjunct verbs in category (i) is that, for example, [N_3 *ko* N_2 *para krodha*] *ānā* match क्रोध में आना (*krodha mẽ ānā*) with suitable adjustment of the constituents [N_3 *ko*] and [N_2 *para*], as illustrated in the following sentence.

(37) राम ने क्रोध में आकर मोहन को बड़ा मारा
(rāma ne krodha mẽ ākara mohana ko baṛā mārā)
"Ram got angry and beat Mohan soundly"

The sentence (37) is in fact a paraphrase of the sentence (36). In other words, $[N_1]$ nouns in category (i) of the ANP's with आना (*ānā*) "to come" are a class of nouns denoting various psychological states characterizing an individual's response (referring to what one does) to a variety of factors, in the environment.

All the ANP's with आना (*ānā*) "to come" with $[N_1]$ nouns in the category (ii) also form conjunct verbs with पड़ना (*paṛanā*) "to fall" with the exception of बदनामी (*badanāmī*) [sentence (26)] as illustrated below.

(38) किसी पर आफत पड़ना
(*kisī para āphata paṛanā*)
"to meet with a mishap"

(39) किसी पर संकट पड़ना
(*kisī para saṁkaṭa paṛanā*)
"to meet with a crisis"

(40) किसी पर मुसीबत पड़ना
(*kisī para musībata paṛanā*)
"to meet with misfortune"

All the above noted instances of [N_1+*paṛanā*] can also have matching sentences with [N_1 *meṁ paṛanā*), such as आफत में पड़ना (*āphata meṁ paṛanā*) "to be overcome by mishap". Therefore, all the $[N_1]$ nouns in category (ii) represent conditions referring to predicaments of someone who is viewed as an involuntary victim of those predicaments. However, the occurrence of the noun बदनामी (*badanāmī*) as $[N_1]$ noun in ANP with आना (*ānā*) "to come", by virtue of the occurrence of this noun with the verbs होना (*honā*) "to be" and करना (*karanā*) "to do" as illustrated below, represents an instance of nouns which refer to predicaments of someone by his own doing.

(41) इस से राम की बहुत बदनामी होती है।
(*isa se rāma kī bahuta badanāmī hotī hai*)
"Ram is much maligned because of this."

(42) वह राम की बहुत बदनामी करता है।
(*vaha rāma kī bahuta badanāmī karatā hai*)
"He slanders Ram a great deal."

The आना (*ānā*) "to come" ANP's with $[N_1]$ nouns in category (iii) also occur with verbs झलकना (*jhalakanā*) "to reflect (intr.)" and छाना (*chānā*) "to spread, to reflect" etc. as illustrated by the sentence given below.

(43) अचानक उसके चेहरे पर खुशी झलक आई।
(*acānaka usake cehare para khuśī jhalaka āī*)
"Suddenly there was happiness reflected on his face".

The psycho-physical states denoted by these [N_1] nouns fall in the category of *Ensuants* [or अनुभाव (*anubhāva*)] as they are known in the tradition of Indian poetic theory.[1]

3.4.2. So far we have discussed ANP's consisting of [N_2 post N_1] sequences only. There are in MSH a variety of [N_2 post N_1] sequences which drop their [N_2 post]'s under a variety of syntactic conditions. There are still others which do not occur with [N_2 post]. We would like to illustrate this situation with a few examples of conjunct verbs with लेना (*lenā*) "to take".

(1) N का निर्णय लेना
(*N kā nirṇaya lenā*)
"to informally decide to do something"

(2) N की अनुमति लेना
(*N kī anumati lenā*)
"to have the permission of someone"

(3) N का चुम्बन लेना
(*N kā cumbana lenā*)
"to kiss someone"

(4) N में दिलचस्पी लेना
(*N mẽ dilacaspī lenā*)
"to take an interest in something (i.e., by cultivating such an interest or as a pastime)"

(5) N में रुचि लेना
(*N mẽ ruci lenā*)
"to take interest in something (as a natural or inborn trait)"

There are some [N_1] nouns [like करवट (*karavaṭa*) "the act of lying on one's side (while sleeping)" and सांस (*sā̃sa*) "breath"] which normally do not occur with [N_2 post] as ANP's with लेना (*lenā*) "to take" as illustrated below.

(6) उसने सारी रात करवटें लेते हुए बिताई।
(*usa ne sārī rāta karavaṭẽ lete hue bitāī*)
"She spent all night shifting from side to side."

1. These ensuants are described in Viśvanātha Kavirāja, *Sāhitya Darpaṇa* (The Mirror of Composition), English translation by Pramadadasa Mitra (Calcutta, 1875), section 163, page 95. These ensuants generally refer to various "bodily effects" which are regarded as the natural consequences of various emotional or mental states.

(7) वह बड़े जोर-जोर से सांस ले रहा है।
(vaha baṛe zora zora se sā̃sa le rahā hai)
"He is breathing very heavily."

The $[N_1]$ nouns like the ones illustrated in sentences (6) and (7) above may sometimes occur with $[N_2$ post$]$ also. A few examples are given below to illustrate this situation.

(8) N की करवट लेना
(N kī karavaṭa lenā)
"to take a turn for N (i.e., a temporary change in someone's disposition)"

. . .हरियाली ने लिली के मन को एक राहत दी, थके हुए मन ने उल्लास की एक करवट ली।
(...hariyālī ne lilī ke mana ko eka rāhata dī, thake hue mana ne ullāsa kī eka karavaṭa lī)
"The green grass made Lili's mind feel at ease (once again), and her disposition reversed to its jovial state".

(9) N की सांस लेना
(N *kī sā̃sa lenā*)
"to breathe a sigh of relief"

विपत्ति बड़ी मुश्किल से टली और तब कहीं उसने सुख की सांस ली।
(vipatti baṛī muśkila se ṭalī aura taba kahī̃ usane sukha kī sā̃sa lī)
"The trouble was finally over and then he breathed a sigh of relief."

As the above noted two sentences illustrate, the normal (involuntary) activities of "changing sides (while sleeping)" and "breathing" respectively referred to by करवट लेना (*karavaṭa lenā*) "to change sides" and सांस लेना (*sā̃sa lenā*) "to breathe" take on a new dimension of meaning when preceded by $[N_2$ post$]$. In other words, by the occurrence of $[N_2$ post$]$ with them such $[N_1]$ nouns become specific in relation to the $[N_2]$ nouns which precede them. This sort of occurrence and non-occurrence of $[N_2$ post$]$ with $[N_1]$'s will be respectively referred to by specifying the occurrence of an $[N_1]$ noun as being [+relative] and [—relative].

The distinction between [+relative] and [—relative] occurrence of $[N_1]$ nouns in ANP's is an important distinction in MSH because प्यार करना (*pyāra karanā*) "to love" and घृणा करना (*ghṛṇā karanā*) "to hate" etc. are not the same thing as are किसी को प्यार करना (*kisī ko pyāra karanā*) "to love someone" and किसी से घृणा करना (*kisī se ghṛṇā karanā*) "to hate someone" etc. Some of the implications of this distinction are discussed in the next sub-section.

3.4.3. It is a well-known fact that most of the [N_1] nouns are generally handled in MSH dictionaries (both monolingual as well as bilingual) as polysemous lexical items. It is the purpose of this sub-section to demonstrate the correlation between semantic definitions of some of these nouns as given in dictionaries and their occurrence in different ANP's, and then raise some important questions about the notion of polysemy as it is applicable to these nouns.

Below we list some ANP's in order to show the contrast between the two occurrences of a given [N_1] noun with at least two different [N_2 post] constituents involving पर (*para*) "on, at" versus का/की (*kā/kī*) "of", के बारे में (*ke bāre mẽ*) "about" versus का/की (*kā/kī*) "of", से (*se*) "with" versus का/की (*kā/kī*) "of", में (*mẽ*) "in" versus से (*se*) "with", पर (*para*) "on, at" versus को (*ko*) "to", and को (*ko*) "to" versus का/की (*kā/kī*) "of". The formative verbs in each case will be kept constant. The meanings appearing on the right hand side of these conjuncts refer only to the [N_1] nouns.

(1)	N पर विचार करना (*N para vicāra karanā*)	"topic of discussion"
(1a)	N का विचार करना (*N kā vicāra karanā*)	"thought"
(2)	N पर खोज चलना (*N para khoja calanā*)	"research"
(2a)	N की खोज चलना (*N kī khoja calanā*)	"search"
(3)	N पर अधिकार रखना (*N para adhikāra rakhanā*)	"hold"
(3a)	N का अधिकार रखना (*N kā adhikāra rakhanā*)	"right"
(4)	N पर भरोसा रखना (*N para bharosā rakhanā*)	"reliance"
(4a)	N का भरोसा रखना (*N kā bharosā rakhanā*)	"dependence"
(5)	N पर विश्वास करना (*N para viśvāsa karanī*)	"faith"
(5a)	N का विश्वास करना (*N kā viśvāsa karanā*)	"trust"

(6) N के बारे में चिन्ता करना "concern"
(*N ke bāre mẽ cintā karanā*)

(6a) N की चिन्ता करना "worry"
(*N kī cintā karanā*)

(7) N के बारे में अनुमान लगाना "surmise"
(*N ke bāre mẽ anumāna lagānā*)

(7a) N का अनुमान लगाना "guess"
(*N kā anumāna lagānā*)

(8) N के बारे में कोशिश करना "endeavor"
(*N ke bāre mẽ kośiśa karanā*)

(8a) N की कोशिश रखना "try"
(*N kī kośiśa karanā*)

(9) N से पहचान रखना "acquintance"
(*N se pahacāna rakhanā*)

(9a) N की पहचान करना "familiarity"
(*N kī pahacāna rakhanā*)

(10) N से राय लेना "consultation"
(*N se rāya lenā*)

(10a) N की राय लेना "opinion"
(*N kī rāya lenā*)

(11) N से बदला उतारना "vengeance"
(*N se badalā utāranā*)

(11a) N का बदला उतारना "recompense"
(*N kā badalā utāranā*)

(12) N में अनुराग रखना "passion"
(*N mẽ anurāga rakhanā*)

(12a) N से अनुराग रखना "attachment"
(*N se anurāga rakhanā*)

(13) N पर जोर देना "emphasis"
(*N para jora denā*)

(13a) N को जोर देना "pressure"
(*N ko jora denā*)

(14) N को साथ देना "company"
(*N ko sātha denā*)

(14a) N का साथ देना "association"
(*N kā sātha denā*)

The problem we wish to pose is : should the two or more occurrences of a noun like भरोसा (*bharosā*) "reliance, dependence" [examples (4) and (4a)], be regarded as two occurrences of the same noun or of two different nouns. In other words, it is quite valid to ask if this noun is in fact a polysemous noun or not in the semantic structure of MSH.

The situation we have just illustrated is further complicated if we observe the [−relative] occurrence of [N_1] nouns in some ANP's, where it may not always be possible to tell which one of the several [N_2 post] is intended to be implied by the speaker, or where (as we would like to argue) no [N_2 post] may be involved. For example, in a sentence like अरे तुम, जरा भरोसा तो रखो (*are tuma, zarā bharosā to rakho* !) "Hey you, keep patience !", it may not always be possible to tell whether the speaker means N पर भरोसा (*N para bharosā*) or N का भरोसा (*N kā bharosā*), or neither of them. If we choose the third possibility, we would be required to add a third meaning to the list of meanings of this noun different from both "reliance" and "dependence". In such a situation, the usual method would be treat the sentence अरे तुम, जरा भरोसा तो रखो (*are tuma, zarā bharosā to rakho* !) "Hey you, keep patience !" as an ambiguous sentence and interpret the ANP in it as consisting of N पर भरोसा (*N para bharosā*), N का भरोसा (*N kā bharosā*) and भरोसा (*bharosā*).

We feel that the occurrence of the noun भरोसा (*bharosā*) "reliance, dependence" in the above sentence without [N_2 post] does not involve the ellipsis of [N_2 post] with it, and, therefore, the usual method of resolution of ambiguity, as suggested above, is not applicable in this instance. While we do not want to altogether rule out the existence of some form of ambiguity resulting from the ellipsis of [N_2 post]'s in conjunct verbs which can be resolved by the usual methods, we do postulate the [−relative] occurrence of [N_1] nouns in conjuncts as distinct from elliptical conjunct verbs. It is also to be noted that, according to the view we have taken, N पर भरोसा (*N para bharosā*), N का भरोसा (*N kā bharosā*) and भरोसा (*bharosā*) are to be interpreted as instances of three different ANP's. However, the occurrence of an [N_1] noun in more than one ANP, as we have just illustrated, is not a sufficient condition for positing such a noun as a polysemous lexical item in the semantic structure of the language. Therefore, the conclusion arrived at by the method of resolution of ambiguity, that is to treat the [N_1] noun भरोसा (*bharosā*) as a polysemous noun, is not a proper solution of the problem, for it leads to a ridiculous proliferation of the polysemous lexical items in the language. We believe, such a solution is also contrary to the overwhelming tendency of MSH.

It is clear from our discussion that we do not regard a semantic characterization of [N_1]'s and [Adj]'s based on the notion of polysemy as being sufficiently deep and significant as far as the phenomenon of conjunct verbs is concerned in MSH. We, therefore, propose that in all the three occurrences of the ANP's with the [N_1] noun भरोसा (*bharosā*), we have the same [N_1] noun भरोसा (*bharosā*), two instances of which are [+relative] and one [—relative]. Consequently, the variety of surface meanings of this noun based on the notion of polysemy are all derivable from an underlying common meaning. It is, therefore, necessary to devise methods which would enable us to arrive at deeper semantic characterization of [N_1] nouns in the language. We would like to say that [N_1] nouns occurring in ANP's are concepts, a fact to which we alluded to in sub-section 3.3, and will discuss further in section 4.

3.5. In view of the avowed goal of the SSSH of preparing a step-by-step description of the semantic complexity of conjunct verbs, taking the ANP's occurring with a formative verb at a time, it is necessary to explain its divergence from the practices of MSH dictionaries and grammars on two points. They are : (i) imposition of certain limitations on the inclusion of synonyms in the groups of nouns and adjectives treated in the SSSH, and (ii) the view we hold concerning the category of gender in nouns in the language. A proper understanding of these matters is a prerequisite towards a fruitful inquiry into the various aspects of the semantic complexity of [N_1]'s and [Adj]'s in the language.

3.5.1. A detailed discussion of the notion of synonym and the way we have employed this notion in setting forth our system of semantic representations of [N_1]'s and [Adj]'s occurring in करना (*karanā*) "to do" conjunct verbs appears in sub-section 4.4. In this sub-section, we shall, therefore, explain the limitations we have imposed on the inclusion of nouns and adjectives among the groups we have treated in the present volume and propose to deal with in the volumes yet to appear.

It is a matter of common practice among the lexicographers and grammarians of MSH that they do not explicitly take note of the considerable divergence that exists in their sharing of common syntactic environments by the nouns and adjectives usually treated as synonyms of each other. Such a practice has led them to treat some nouns indiscriminately as semantic equivalents of each other, and ignore certain aspects of the semantic complexity of others. For instance, there are nouns like जल (*jala*) and पानी (*pānī*) listed in MSH dictionaries as equivalents of each other meaning "water". Both the nouns, though they are synonyms of each other, do not share all the environments of occurrence with each other. जल (*jala*) occurs in conjunct verbs like N पर जल चढ़ाना (*N para jala caṛhānā*) referring to the ritual practice of offering water to an image, and cannot be replaced in this conjunct verb by its synonym पानी (*pānī*). On the other hand, पानी (*pānī*) occurs in conjunct verb N को पानी देना (*N ko pānī denā*) meaning "to water (a plant etc.)", and cannot be replaced in this conjunct verb by its synonym जल (*jala*).

The other situation can be illustrated by means of the nouns पीड़ा (*pīṛā*) "pain", दुख (*dukha*) "grief", कष्ट (*kaṣṭa*) "trouble", तकलीफ (*takalīpha*) "trouble, inconvenience", व्यथा (*vyathā*) "distress", शोक (*śoka*) "mourning", वेदना (*vedanā*) "agony", संताप (*santāpa*) "torment", all referring to the actively felt state or condition of physical and/or mental distress caused by a variety of agents. They all occur in this general meaning in ANP's which form conjunct verbs with the verb होना (*honā*) "to be". However, only पीड़ा (*pīṛā*) "pain", दुख (*dukha*) "grief", कष्ट (*kaṣṭa*) "trouble" and तकलीफ (*takalīpha*) "trouble, inconvenience" occur in conjunct verbs formed with the verbs देना (*denā*) "to give" and पहुंचाना (*pahũcānā*) "to cause to reach". On the basis of their occurrence with देना (*denā*) "to give" and पहुंचाना (*pahũcānā*) "to cause to reach", the nouns पीड़ा (*pīṛā*) "pain", दुख (*dukha*) "grief", कष्ट (*kaṣṭa*) "trouble" and तकलीफ (*takalīpha*) "trouble, inconvenience" can be interpreted as representing modalities of "physical and/or mental distress" suffered by one through a variety of acts one performs on being compelled by someone.

It is, therefore, only expedient in a step-by-step description such as the one we are envisaging in the SSSH, that only the synonymous [N_1]'s and [Adj]'s which occur in ANP's forming conjuncts with a given verb should be so treated in the context of that verb, irrespective of the fact that these nouns and adjectives may have other synonyms in the language which do not occur in ANP's forming conjuncts with that particular verb as a formative. Such a limitation is necessary for a systematic and proper handling of the data at any given state of the investigation of the language. The procedure as suggested would automatically account for other synonyms of any given [N_1] (or [N_1]'s) or [Adj] (or [Adj]'s) without at any time barring any aspect of its (or their) semantic complexity from vision at any given stage. It is, therefore, unnecessary to say that our grouping of synonyms, as presented in this volume as well as in volumes yet to appear, does presuppose this limitation.

3.5.2. The role of the grammatical category of gender in MSH nouns, in spite of all the discussion that has taken place concerning the category, is still very much a mystery. It goes without saying that it is absolutely necessary to properly understand the ways in which the category of gender affects the semantic complexity of nouns in the language, and any description of the semantic complexity of these nouns would be incomplete without systematically accounting for this aspect. We have discussed the problem of gender of nouns from various points of view elsewhere,[1] and, here repeat, that we do not regard the gender of nouns in the language as fixed. That is to say, we do not regard any divergence in the gender usage of a noun, (such as the occurrence of a noun, commonly understood to be a masculine noun, in feminine gender or vice versa) as may be dictated by the requirements of the semantic structure of MSH in a particular context, as a sufficient condition to render the sentence containing that noun as an ungrammatical sentence. In other words, any deviations in the gender usage of nouns as just stipulated (if we may use the term deviation here) are not grammatical mistakes or dialectal variations etc., as lexicographers as well as grammarians of the language would have us believe. A few examples of such divergent usages of the gender of [N_1] nouns are given below.

(1) वह चुपचाप उनके कमरे से निकल आई थी, अपने कमरे में आकर उनके जगने का इन्तजार करती रही थी ।
(*vaha cupacāpa unake kamare se nikala āī thī. apane kamare mẽ ākara unake jagane kā intezāra karatī rahī thī*)
"She quitely slipped out of her room and came into her own room where she waited for her to wake up."

(2) उसका वह आम का पेड़, जिसके पकने की उसने बेसब्री से इन्तजार की थी...।
(*usakā vaha āma kā peṛa, jisake pakane kī usane besabrī se intezāra kī thī...*)
"That mango tree of hers, for the ripening of whose fruit she had waited impatiently..."

Since the problem of gender requires independent discussion, we shall throughout assume that the gender of nouns in MSH is determined (semantically as mentioned above) but not fixed.

3.6. We have already noted that the grammarians of MSH report the occurrence of very few formative verbs in conjuncts, a fact which leads one to suppose that most of these grammarians have not really confronted themselves with a sizable body of the data on conjunct verbs which actually occur in the language. We shall, therefore, devote the rest of this section to a discussion of the occurrence of formative verbs in conjuncts.

3.6.1. Some general regularities can be observed concerning the occurrence of verbs as formative verbs in conjuncts. It can be safely assumed

1. For a discussion concerning the category of gender in nouns, see Bahl (1967), pp. 77-78, Bahl (1969), section 3.4.1 (pp. 166-167), and Bahl (to appear), section 3.3.2. The traditional view regarding the category of gender has been to regard violations of gender as grammatical mistakes originating from a lack of standardization in the gender usage of nouns in modern Indo-Aryan languages. We have argued at length in the works just mentioned that such is not the case.

that (a) onomatopoetic and (b) denominalized verbs do not occur as formative verbs in conjuncts. There seems, however, to be no inherent restriction on the formation of conjunct verbs with any other kind of verbs in the language. Therefore, it seems only appropriate to say that conjunct verbs, in the sense we have used the term in sub-section 2.3.2, involve a wide variety of verbs other than the ones repeatedly noticed by the grammarians of the language. So instead of listing such formative verbs or the conjunct verbs formed with them, we can only say that we have data on more than 2,000 verbs in MSH, quite a few of which form a variety of conjunct verbs. However, at the moment we are in no position to offer an overall and inclusive account of conjunct verbs, and more particularly, of the functions of formative verbs. We will, therefore, in the following sub-sections be content with the presentation of a fragmentary picture.

3.6.2. The problem of isolating the meanings of formative verbs in conjuncts by means of the methods of abstraction followed by lexicographers of MSH is a fairly complicated matter. It is complicated even further if we bring it to bear upon several aspects of the complexity of conjunct verbs observed earlier in this "Introduction". If we adhere to the usual practices in this respect, followed by lexicographers of MSH, then Hacker's remark that formative verbs have very little special content in them must be regarded as an oversimplification, since his notion of the general concept of action [करना (*karanā*), देना (*denā*) etc.] or process or state [होना (*honā*)] does not lend itself to analysis in a satisfactory manner in terms of the traditional methods of lexicographers of MSH.

Before we go any further into this problem, we would like to point out that there is a fundamental difference between what happens to nouns semantically when they occur as [N_1] nouns in ANP's, and what happens to verbs when they occur as formative verbs in conjuncts. It is fairly easy to discern that [N_1] nouns, by their occurrence in a variety of ANP's which in turn form conjuncts with various formative verbs, seem to combine more and more semantic content from the contexts of their occurrence. The dictionaries of MSH handle this situation by treating these [N_1] nouns as polysemous lexical items. Our examples of the nouns ध्यान (*dhyāna*) "attention" and आवाज (*āvāza*) "sound" given in sub-section 3.3.3 illustrate this situation. Exactly the opposite of this happens to verbs, that is, they tend to lose their semantic content through their occurrence as formative verbs. This is an obvious consequence of the assumption of close relationship of nouns and adjectives with verbs in conjunct verbs made by the traditional grammarians. Hacker's remark about very little special content in formative verbs, as well as his notion of the general concept of action indicated by them, probably involves a realization of the close relationship between nouns (as well as adjectives) and verbs in conjunct verbs on his part. In the next sub-section, we shall, therefore, try to understand the implications of Hacker's observation by presenting almost all the known types of MSH sentences occurring with the verb लेना (*lenā*) "to take".

3.6.3. All sentences with the verb लेना (*lenā*) "to take" fall into three groups, briefly described as follows.

Within group I, there are several categories of लेना (*lenā*) "to take" sentences.

(a) This category of sentences has this verb as ले आना (*le ānā*), ले जाना (*le jānā*) and ले चलना (*le calanā*), and involves the speaker's description of one person's (that is, the subject noun's) causing another animate being that is, (the object noun) to move along with him (that is, the subject noun) to or from a place etc., whether expressed or implied. The verb in these contexts may occur with an adverbial noun followed by one of the postpositions में (*mẽ*) "in", के अन्दर (*ke andara*) "inside", के भीतर (*ke bhītara*) "within", की ओर (*kī ora*) "towards", की तरफ (*kī tarapha*) "in the general direction of", तक (*taka*) "upto", के बाहर (*ke bāhara*) "outside", के साथ (*ke sātha*) "along with", के पास (*ke pāsa*) "to (a person or place)", and से (*se*) "from" etc.

A few sentences are given below to illustrate the occurrence of this verb in group I (a).

(1) भगौती सूका को बरबस खींचता हुआ बाहर ले जाता है।
(*bhagautī sūkā ko barabasa khĩcatā huā bāhara le jātā hai*)
"Dragging her forcibly, Bhagauti takes Suka out(side)."

(2) भेड़ पालक सर्दियों में भेड़ों को निचले स्थानों में ले आते हैं।
(*bheṛapālaka sardiyõ mẽ bheṛõ ko nicale sthānõ mẽ le āte hãĩ*)
"Shepherds bring their sheep to places of lower altitude in winter."

(b) This category of sentences has this verb as ले लेना (*le lenā*) and लेना (*lenā*), and involves the speaker's description of a person's (that is, the subject noun's) act of causing another person (that is, the object noun) to move (literally or figuratively) or be with oneself. The verb in such sentences always occurs with an adverbial modifier consisting of a noun followed by one of the postpositions के नीचे (*ke nīce*) "under", के अन्दर (*ke andara*) "inside", में (*mẽ*) "in", के लिये (*ke liye*) "for", के निकट (*ke nikaṭa*) "near", and के साथ (*ke sātha*) "along with" etc. The sentences given below illustrate some of the occurrences of the verb लेना (*lenā*) "to take" in this category.

(3) जग्गु ने सन्ती को समझाया कि मोटर वाले जहां तक सम्भव हो किसी को नीचे नहीं लेते।
(*jaggu ne santī ko samajhāyā ki moṭaravāle jahā̃ taka sambhava ho kisī ko nīce nahī̃ lete*)

Jaggu tried to explain this to Santi that car drivers, as far as possible, do not run-over people [lit., take them under (the car)]."

(4) पहाड़ी ने राम शरण को कोठरी में लेकर किवाड़ मूंद लिये ।
(*pahāṛī ne rāma śaraṇa ko koṭharī mẽ lekara kivāṛa mũda liye...*)
"The Pahari took Rama Sarana inside the chamber (that is, let him inside the chamber) and shut the doors..."

Within the sentences in which the verb लेना (*lenā*) "to take" occurs with N में (*N mẽ*) "in N", there are a variety of sentences which all presuppose N के रूप में (*N ke rūpa mẽ*) "as N, in the form of N" as an additional adverbial constituent (which may be expressed or implied) and occur with a variety of meanings. A few such instances are given below.

(5) किसी को नौकरी में ले लेना
(*kisī ko naukarī mẽ le lenā*)
"to hire someone (as an N)"

(6) किसी को किसी संस्था में ले लेना
(*kisī ko kisī saṁsthā mẽ le lenā*)
"to enroll someone (as a member) in a society"

(7) किसी को गोद (में) ले लेना
[*kisī ko goda (mẽ) le lenā*]
"to adopt someone (as a son)"

(8) किसी को हिरासत में ले लेना
(*kisī ko hirāsata mẽ le lenā*)
"to arrest someone (as a prisoner)"

There are other sentences within this category such as किसी को गिनती में लेना (*kisī ko ginatī mẽ lenā*) "to consider someone an important person" and किसी को अपने विश्वास में लेना (*kisī ko apane viśvāsa mẽ lenā*) "to take someone into one's confidence", and so forth, which form another group of N में लेना (*N mẽ lenā*) sentences in which the nouns like गिनती (*ginatī*) "count" and विश्वास (*viśvāsa*) "trust, confidence" figuratively refer to some kind of a fold etc.

(c) This category of sentences has the verb लेना (*lenā*) "to take" as ले लेना (*le lenā*) only, and all refer to the speaker's description of a person's (that is, the subject noun's) act of taking or acquiring something, such as an object (taken for a specific purpose), food or drink, any medicine (to be taken internally only), any piece of real estate, money or any other valuable or material object etc.

A few instances of this type of sentence which also involves various adverbial modifications are given below.

(9) कोई चीज किसी के हाथ से ले लेना
(koī cīja kisī ke hātha se le lenā)
"to take something from someone's hand (that is, to accept something from someone)"

(10) कोई चीज किसी स्थान से ले लेना
(koī cīja kisī sthāna se le lenā)
"to take something from a place (that is, to remove something from a place)"

A few instances of sentences in this category involving adverbials plus the verb लेना (*lenā*) "to take" are wrongly regarded as conjunct verbs. We list below such instances with the adverbials underlined.

(11) कोई चीज मोल लेना
(koī cīja mola lenā)
"to acquire something (by paying for it) (that is, to buy something)"

(12) कोई परिस्थिति मोल लेना
(koī paristhiti mola lenā)
"to cause oneself to confront (some undesirable) situation by one's own doing (just as one buys something)"

(13) कोई चीज वापिस ले लेना
(koī cīja vāpisa le lenā)
"to take something back"

(14) कोई चीज मुफ्त लेना
(koī cīja mufta lenā)
"to acquire something for free"

(15) कोई काम अपने ऊपर ले लेना
(koī kāma apane ūpara le lenā)
"to undertake to do something"

(16) कोई चीज, बात या व्यक्ति विशेष (के कार्य) को (उदाहरण के रूप में) लेना
[*koī cīja, bāta yā vyakti viśeṣa (ke kārya) ko (udāharaṇa ke rūpa mẽ) lenā*]
"to cite or take something or someone's doing something as an example"

In group II there are sentences involving a wide variety of लेना (*lenā*) "to take" conjunct verbs, the ANP's of which have the structures [N_2 का

N_1] ([N_2 *kā* N_1]), [N_2 में N_1] ([N_2 *mẽ* N_1]), [N_2 से N_1] ([N_2 *se* N_1]) and [N_1]. A few sentences illustrating some of these conjunct verbs are given below.

(17) मैं भैरवपाद की अनुमति ले लेता हूं ।
(*maĩ bhairavapāda kī anumati le letā hū̃*)
"Let me obtain Bhairavapāda's permission."

(18) सूर्यगढ़ से साम्यवादी दल ने चन्द्रशेखर सिंह को खड़ा करने का निर्णय लिया है।
(*sūryagaṛha se sāmyavādī dala ne candraśekhara sĩha ko khaṛā karane kā nirṇaya liyā hai*)
"The communist party of Suryagarh has decided to nominate Chandrashekhara Singh."

Sentences with लेना (*lenā*) "to take" conjunct verbs, as those listed above, are different from sentences in group I because the verb लेना (*lenā*) "to take" in such sentences does not readily yield to abstraction of its lexical meaning, as we have tried earlier with sentences of group I. For example, in the following conjunct verbs

(19) किसी काम में रुचि लेना
(*kisī kāma mẽ ruci lenā*)
"to take interest in something"

(20) किसी काम में दिलचस्पी लेना
(*kisī kāma mẽ dilacaspī lenā*)
"to cultivate an interest in something"

(21) किसी काम के लिये किसी की अनुमति लेना
(*kisī kāma ke liye kisī kī anumati lenā*)
"to obtain someone's permission for doing something"

(22) किसी काम के बारे में किसी की राय लेना
(*kisī kāma ke bāre mẽ kisī kī rāya lenā*)
"to seek someone's opinion about something"

(23) सामाजिक न्याय के लिये हिंसा और घृणा का आश्रय लेना
sāmājika nyāya ke liye hiṁsā aura ghṛṇā kā āśraya lenā)
"to resort to violence and hatred for the sake of social justice"

(24) किसी काम में किसी की मदद लेना
(*kisī kāma mẽ kisī kī madada lenā*)
"to seek someone's help in something"

(25) किसी बात में किसी की आड़ लेना
(*kisī bāta mẽ kisī kī āṛa lenā*)
"to use someone as a pretext in some matter"

(26) किसी से बचने के लिये किसी चीज की ओट लेना
(*kisī se bacane ke liye kisī cīja kī oṭa lenā*)
"to take a shelter behind something in order to protect one-self from someone or something"

(27) किसी काम के द्वारा किसी की इज्जत लेना
(*kisī kāma ke dvārā kisī kī ijjata lenā*)
"to try to bring dishonor to someone by some act"

(28) किसी से काम लेना
(*kisī se kāma lenā*)
"to use someone as a help"

(29) किसी का धर्म लेना
(*kisī kā dharma lenā*)
"to cause someone to do something contrary to his religion"

(30) कुछ करने का निर्णय लेना
(*kucha karane kā nirṇaya lenā*)
"to decide to do something"

if we try to abstract the lexical meaning of the verb लेना (*lenā*) by examining their English glosses, we may come up with a common meaning which can be roughly rendered into English by the verb "TAKE". But this abstracted common meaning indicated by the verb "TAKE" is not to be taken as the translation equivalent of the MSH लेना (*lenā*) in English as far as its occurrence in the above noted conjunct verbs is concerned. If we momentarily disregard English and try to perform the same process using MSH as the metalanguage, we can say that in all the instances of the conjunct verbs listed above, the verb लेना (*LENĀ*) "to take" occurs as an abstract metalinguistic lexical item which is different from the phonologically similar lexical item लेना (*lenā*) occurring in sentences of group I. In other words, this is as far as we can go in a dictionary in terms of the lexical interpretationism practised by the structuralists as described in sub-section 2.2. The result of attempting to interpret the occurrence of, for example, अनुमति लेना (*anumati lenā*) as it occurs in instance (21) as a conjunct verb, that is, a lexical item consisting of more than one word, is an explicit recognition of the fact that the occurrence of लेना (*lenā*) in this conjunct verb as a lexical abstraction differs from the occurrences of this verb in sentences of group I. Thus what appears to be two words in the surface structure of MSH [that is, अनुमति लेना (*anumati lenā*)] becomes a lexical unit at par with the verb लेना (*lenā*) "to take" (as it occurs in sentences of group I) in the deep structure of the language. Such a conception of the notion of conjunct verbs in MSH is far from satisfactory as it is just another way of stating the traditional grammarians' assumption of semantic affinity between nouns or adjectives and verbs in conjunct verbs.

Of the लेना (*lenā*) "to take" sentences in group II, we may say that the meaning of this verb as a formative is semantically more abstract than its meaning in sentences in group I. Before we try to offer an interpretation of Hacker's characterization of formative verbs as concepts, we would like to complete our discussion of all the लेना (*lenā*) "to take" sentences.

In group III, we include sentences like the following.

(31) अब मुझे यह अवसर मिला है, इसे क्यों छोड़ूं ? जमींदारी की लालसा लिये हुए क्यों मरूं ?
(*aba mujhe yaha avasara milā hai, ise kyõ choṛũ? jamīndārī kī lalasā liye hue kyõ marũ?*)
"Now this opportunity has presented itself to me. Why should I let it pass? Why should I die with my ambition to be a landlord (i.e., still unfulfilled)?"

(32) यह मुहल्ला उजाड़खण्ड में सदा नई आस लेकर जीता है।
(*yaha muhallā ujāṛakhaṇḍa mẽ sadā naī āsa lekara jītā hai*)
"This neighbor hood lives on amidst desolation with an ever new expectation."

(33) और मैं यह आशा लिये हुए चला गया कि एक कल ऐसा आयेगा जब मैं तुमसे यह सब कह सकूंगा।
(*aura mãĩ yaha āśā liye hue calā gayā ki eka kala aisā āyegā jaba mãĩ tuma se yaha saba kaha sakũgā*)
"And I left with the hope that that tomorrow would come when I would be able to tell you all this."

These three sentences illustrate the non-finite occurrence of conjunct verbs N की लालसा लिये हुए (*N kī lalasā liye hue*), आस लेकर (*āsa lekara*), and आशा लिये हुए (*āśā liye hue*) which do not occur otherwise, that is as finite verbs in MSH sentences. Though the non-finite occurrence of the verb लेना (*lenā*) is peculiar in these sentences, and this fact has important bearing on its occurrence as a formative verb in these three conjuncts, we believe such a situation does not in any way affect the inclusion of these three sentences with those of group II for the purpose of understanding the semantic complexity of लेना (*lenā*) "to take" as a formative verb.

And finally, we would like to include a variety of sentences with the verb लेना (*lenā*) "to take" as illustrated below in group IV.

(43) इटालियन को शायद विश्वास नहीं हुआ, वह शायद निश्चय नहीं कर पा रहा था कि मैं किस सीमा तक पी चुका हूं...किस सीमा तक वह मुझे गम्भीरता से ले सकता है।

(*iṭāliyana ko śāyada viśvāsa nahī̃ huā, vaha śāyada niścaya nahī̃ kara pā rahā thā ki maĩ kisa sīmā taka pī cukā hū̃...kisa sīmā taka vaha mujhe gambhīratā se le sakatā hai*)

"The Italian perhaps did not believe me, perhaps he was unable to make up his mind about the quantity of liquor I had already consumed...to what extent he could take me seriously."

(44) इतनी बड़ी बात को कैसे चुपचाप ले लिया।

(*itanī baṛī bāta ko kaise cupacāpa le liyā*)

"(I don't know), how did he take such an important matter without saying anything."

A common feature of the above noted sentences is their representation of the speaker's observation about the subject noun's behavior rather than a description or indication of his doing something. The occurrence of the verb लेना (*lenā*) in such sentences resembles the occurrence of the verb "to take" in such English expressions as "Take it easy !" The difference between English and MSH on this point lies in the fact that the speaker in the former can tell another person to take it easy etc. He can also make an observation about the subject noun's behavior, for example, the sentence "He took it very lightly." In MSH only the latter type of usages of the लेना (*lenā*) exist.

3.6.4. With this preliminary and somewhat sketchy presentation of all the known sentence types which occur with the verb लेना (*lenā*) "to take" in MSH, which have a bearing on the problem at hand, we will now try to explain some of the implications of Hacker's observation regarding the formative verbs as concepts. Our primary interest in this discussion is the occurrence of लेना (*lenā*) "to take" as a formative verb only, and that is limited to sentences in groups II and III. Sentences in group I will also figure in our discussion for several reasons which will subsequently become clear. However, the sentences of the type in group IV have no direct bearing on the problem, and will be omitted from further discussion.

Below we reproduce the instances of लेना (*lenā*) conjunct verbs as given earlier with their approximate paraphrases in MSH.

(19) किसी काम में रुचि लेना
(*kisī kāma mẽ ruci lenā*)
"to take interest in something"

(19a) किसी काम को रुचिपूर्वक करना
(*kisī kāma ko rucipūrvaka karanā*)
"to do something in a manner characteristic of one's interest in it"

(20) किसी काम में दिलचस्पी लेना
(*kisī kāma mẽ dilacaspī lenā*)
"to cultivate an interest in something"

(20a) किसी काम को दिलचस्पी के साथ करने का प्रयत्न करना
(*kisī kāma ko dilacaspī ke sātha karane kā prayatna karanā*)
"to try to do something as if one has interest in it"

(21) किसी काम के लिये किसी की अनुमति लेना
(*kisī kāma ke liye kisī kī anumati lenā*)
"to obtain someone's permission for doing something"

(21a) किसी की अनुमति होने पर ही किसी काम को करने में प्रवृत्त होना
(*kisī kī anumati hone para hī kisī kāma ko karane mẽ pravṛtta honā*)
"to engage in the act of doing something with someone's permission"

(22) किसी काम के बारे में किसी की राय लेना
(*kisī kāma ke bāre mẽ kisī kī rāya lenā*)
"to seek someone's opinion about something"

(22a) किसी काम के बारे में किसी से उसकी राय जानने का प्रयत्न करना
(*kisī kāma ke bāre mẽ kisī se usakī rāya jānane kā prayatna karanā*)
"to try to find out someone's opinion about something"

(23) सामाजिक न्याय के लिये हिंसा और घृणा का आश्रय लेना
(*sāmājika nyāya ke liye hiṁsā aura ghṛṇā kā āśraya lenā*)
"to resort to violence and hatred for the sake of social justice"

(23a) हिंसा और घृणा के आश्रय से सामाजिक न्याय की प्रतिष्ठा करने का प्रयत्न करना
(*hiṁsā aura ghṛṇā ke āśraya se sāmājika nyāya kī pratiṣṭhā karane kā prayatna karanā*)
"to try to establish social justice through the means of violence and hatred"

(24) किसी काम में किसी की मदद लेना
(*kisī kāma mẽ kisī kī madada lenā*)
"to seek someone's help in something"

(24a) किसी की मदद से कोई काम करना
(*kisī kī madada se koī kāma karanā*)
"to do something with someone's help"

(25) किसी बात में किसी की आड़ लेना
(*kisī bāta mẽ kisī kī āṛa lenā*)
"to use someone as a pretext in some matter"

(25a) किसी की आड़ में कोई बात करना
(*kisī kī āṛa mẽ koī bāta karanā*)
"to do something under another person's pretext"

(26) किसी से बचने के लिये किसी चीज की ओट लेना
(*kisī se bacane ke liye kisī cīja kī oṭa lenā*)
"to try to protect oneself from someone by taking a cover of something"

(26a) किसी चीज की ओट से किसी से बचने का प्रयत्न करना
(*kisī cīja kī oṭa se kisī se bacane kā prayatna karanā*)
"to try to protect oneself from someone (by taking) a cover of something"

(27) किसी काम के द्वारा किसी की इज्जत लेना
(*kisī kāma ke dvārā kisī kī ijjata lenā*)
"to try to bring dishonor to someone by some act"

(27a) किसी की इज्जत का ख्याल न करके कोई काम करना
(*kisī kī ijjata kā khyāla na karake koī kāma karanā*)
"to do something with no regard for someone's honor"

(28) किसी से काम लेना
(*kisī se kāma lenā*)
"to use someone as a help"

(28a) किसी का किसी काम में प्रयोग करना
(*kisī kā kisī kāma mẽ prayoga karanā*)
"to use someone in some work"

(29) किसी का धर्म लेना
(*kisī kā dharma lenā*)
"to cause someone to do something contrary to his religion"

(29a) किसी को उसके धर्म के विरुद्ध कार्य करने में प्रवृत्त होने के लिये बाध्य करके उससे वह कार्य करवाना
(*kisī ko usake dharma ke viruddha kārya karane mẽ pravṛtta hone ke liye bādhya karake usase vaha kārya karavānā*)
"to cause someone to engage in doing something contrary to his religion"

(30) कुछ करने का निर्णय लेना
(*kucha karane kā nirṇaya lenā*)
"to decide to do something"

(30a) निर्णायक रूप में कुछ करने का विचार कर लेना
(*nirṇāyaka rūpa mẽ kucha karane kā vicāra kara lenā*)
"to intend definitely to do something"

A comparison of the abstracted लेना (*lenā*) "to take" conjunct verbs with their paraphrases reveals that the two are related to each other in linguistically significant ways. In order to explain the significance of the relation between a conjunct verb and its paraphrase, we give below two sentences illustrating the occurrence of the conjunct verb किसी काम में रुचि लेना (*kisī kāma mẽ ruci lenā*) and its paraphrase:

(1) मोहन पढ़ने-लिखने में बहुत रुचि लेता है।
(*mohana paṛhane-likhane mẽ bahuta ruci letā hai*)
"Mohan takes a great deal of interest in reading and writing."

(1a) मोहन अपना पढ़ने-लिखने का काम बहुत रुचिपूर्वक करता है।
(*mohana apanā paṛhane-likhane kā kāma bahuta rucipūrvaka karatā hai*)
"Mohan does his reading and writing with a characteristic display of interest in it."

In other words, sentence (1) embodies the speaker's generalization (that the person named Mohan takes an active interest in reading and writing) which is based on the fact [as indicated in sentence (1a) which is a paraphrase of sentence (1)] that that person does reading and writing in a manner characteristic of his interest in those acts. Similarly, it can be said that "to cultivate an interest in something" is "to try to do something as if one has interest in it", or "to resort to violence and hatred for the sake of social justice" is "to try to establish social justice by resorting to violence and hatred" and so forth. Without going into any further details, we propose that the paraphrases of the conjunct verbs as given above are respectively related to their conjunct verbs as the description of facts (behavior etc.) and as the speaker's generalization based on those facts. Also the statements of facts embodying these paraphrases are generally the sentences of the type included in group I, or if they contain other conjunct verbs, they can also be further paraphrased in terms of sentences of the type included in group I.

On the basis of the paraphrase of (1) in terms of (1a), we can say that the two constituents of the conjunct verb in (1), that is, लेना (*lenā*) "to take" and पढ़ने-लिखने के काम में रुचि (*paṛhane-likhane ke kāma mẽ ruci*) "interest in reading and writing" respectively correspond to the two constituents of the paraphrase in (1a), that is, पढ़ने-लिखने का काम N पूर्वक करना (*paṛhane-likhane kā kāma N pūrvaka karanā*) "to do reading and writing in a manner characteristic of...." and रुचि (*ruci*) "interest". In other words the meaning of लेना (*lenā*) "to take" as a formative verb, as it occurs in the conjunct verb किसी काम में रुचि लेना (*kisī kāma mẽ ruci lenā*) "to take interest in something" [example (19)] is represented by the expression कोई काम N पूर्वक करना (*koī kāma N pūrvaka karanā*) "to do something in a manner characteristic of...." It should also be noted that the expression कोई काम N पूर्वक करना (*koī kāma* N *pūrvaka karanā*) "to do something in a manner characteristic of....." as the suggested semantic representation of लेना (*lenā*) "to take" is an abstraction covering all the possible specific activities like पढ़ना-लिखना (*paṛhanā-likhanā*) "to read and write" etc. in which one could be interested.

Hacker's observation concerning the formative verbs as concepts, therefore, can be interpreted by saying that the semantic content of a formative verb can be represented in a variety of ways by means of paraphrases, in the manner attempted for the verb लेना (*lenā*) "to take". These paraphrases may involve sentences with other conjunct verbs, but ultimately all of them are linguistically reducible to sentences of the type included in group I, that is, sentences with non-conjunct verbs.

It should, therefore, be clear by now that MSH sentences with conjunct verbs, as we have tried to demonstrate above, are characteristically different from sentences with non-conjunct verbs (or single verbs) by virtue of the fact that the former can be systematically analyzed in terms of the latter. In addition, the paraphrases of the लेना (*lenā*) "to take" conjunct verbs, as given above, represent semantic materials of these conjunct verbs. These semantic materials systematically combine to generate sentences with conjunct verbs.

It would be safe to assume at this stage of our investigation (of the semantic structure of MSH) that the analysis of the semantic functions of all the formative verbs as concepts of action or process or state has to be carried out by describing conjunct verbs formed with each and every verb individually, prior to saying anything further about the phenomenon of conjunct verbs in the language. In addition, an analysis of conjunct verbs simultaneously involves two sorts of operations as discussed above in a somewhat simplified manner. That is, (i) determination and description of the semantic complexity of [N_1]'s and [Adj]'s occurring in ANP's, and (ii) determination and specification of the semantic functions of the formative verbs. We shall discuss this matter further in section 4.

3.6.5. In this sub-section, we would like to point out several kinds of disparities between transitive and intransitive verbs in their function as formative verbs in conjuncts.

There are some related transitive and intransitive verbs like लगाना (*lagānā*) "to attach" and लगना (*laganā*) "to be attached" which act like independent verbs in the role of formatives. For example, all the ANP's listed below with the verb लगना (*laganā*) "to be attached" do not occur with the transitive counterpart of this verb.

(1) किसी से शर्म लगना
(kisī se śarma laganā)
"to feel embarrassed of something"

(2) किसी से भय लगना
(kisī se bhaya laganā)
"to feel scared of something"

(3) किसी को हवा लग जाना
(kisī ko havā laga jānā)
"(for someone) to be under the weather"

(4) किसी को चोट लग जाना
(kisī ko coṭa laga jānā)
"(for someone) to get hurt"

Similarly there are some ANP's in the language which occur with the verb लगाना (*lagānā*) "to attach" but do not occur with its intransitive counterpart. A few examples are given below.

(5) किसी का ध्यान लगाना
(kisī kā dhyāna lagānā)
"to meditate"

(6) किसी काम में हाथ लगाना
(kisī kāma mẽ hātha lagānā)
"to begin doing something"

(7) किसी वस्तु को हाथ लगाना
(kisī vastu ko hātha lagānā)
"to touch something (as in a ritual)"

There are also verbs like देना (*denā*) "to give" and मिलना (*milanā*) "to get", which, though semantically discreet, come very close to being respectively transitive and intransitive counterparts of each other as formative verbs. A few examples are given below.

(8) किसी को आदर देना
(*kisī ko ādara denā*)
"to give someone honor"

(8a) किसी को आदर मिलना
(*kisī ko ādara milanā*)
"(for someone) to get honor"

(9) किसी को किसी वस्तु का दान देना
(*kisī ko kisī vastu kā dāna denā*)
"to give someone the gift of something"

(9a) किसी को किसी वस्तु का दान मिलना
(*kisī ko kisī vastu kā dāna milanā*)
"(for someone) to get the gift of something"

Quite a few ANP's exist which do not occur with transitive verbs, but are used only with the causal forms of transitive verbs.

(10) किसी को यकीन दिलाना
(*kisī ko yakīna dilānā*)
"to convince someone"

(11) किसी को किसी बात की याद दिलाना
(*kisī ko kisī bāta kī yāda dilānā*)
"to remind someone of something"

(12) किसी को विश्वास दिलाना
(*kisī ko viśvāsa dilānā*)
"to try to make someone believe one"

(13) किसी का हौसला बंधाना
(*kisī kā hausalā bandhānā*)
"to encourage someone"

There are quite a few transitive verbs in the language, which, when occurring with ANP's, form intransitive conjunct verbs. Several examples of such conjunct verbs are given below.

(14) दर्द करना as in उसका दांत दर्द कर रहा है।
(darda karanā) as in *(usakā dẫta darda kara rahā hai)*
"to hurt" as in "His tooth is hurting"

(15) आग पकड़ना
(āga pakaṛanā)
"to catch fire"

(16) शोभा देना
(śobhā denā)
"(for something) to be worthy of someone"

3.6.6. Finally, we would like to mention briefly some instances of the occurrence of some ANP's with several formative verbs where [N_2 post N_1]'s undergo structural changes like those discussed in sub-sections 2.1.6. and 2.3.3.

In the following sentence

(1) जिस दिन सवेरे कोई उसका मुंह देख लेता, उस दिन उसे इस बात की चिन्ता लग जाती कि. . .आज दिन कैसा बीतेगा।
(jisa dina savere koī usakā mũha dekha letā, usa dina use isa bāta kī cintā laga jātī ki....āja dina kaisā bītegā)
"Whenever someone happened to catch a glimpse of his face in the morning, he would become concerned about (the expectation of) having a rough time that day."

(2) क्या अब से वह केवल कुछ लोगों को प्रसन्न करने और अपने विषय भोग की चिन्ता में लगा रहने के सिवा और कोई ढंग का काम नहीं करेगा।
(kyā aba se vaha kevala kucha logõ ko prasanna karane aura apane viṣaya bhoga kī cintā mẽ lagā rahane ke sivā aura koī ḍhaṅga kā kāma nahī̃ karegā)
"From now on won't he do anything besides trying to please a few people and care about (the fulfilment) of his worldly desires?"

the N_2 को (N की) चिन्ता लग जाना [*N_2 ko(N kī) cintā laga jānā*] "for someone to become concerned about" [in sentence (1)] corresponds to the occurrence of N की चिन्ता में लगे रहना (*N kī cintā mẽ lage rahanā*) "to care about" in sentence (2). Similarly, the occurrence of सज्जन के मन की ईमानदारी जोश के साथ उबल कर बाहर आई (*sajjana ke mana kī īmānadārī jośa ke sātha ubala kara bāhara āī*) "Sajjan's sense of honesty passionately boiled over" in sentence (3) below

(3) कारुणिक परिस्थिति में उसकी मृत्यु हो जाने से सज्जन के मन की ईमानदारी जोश के साथ उबल कर बाहर आई।

(..*kāruṇika paristhiti mẽ usakī mṛtyu ho jāne se sajjana ke mana kī īmānadārī jośa ke sātha ubala kara bāhara āī*)
"Sajjan's sense of honesty passionately boiled over due to her death under pathetic circumstances."

corresponds to सज्जन के मन की ईमानदारी का जोश उबल कर बाहर आ गया (*sajjana ke mana kī īmānadārī kā jośa ubala kara bāhara ā gayā*) "Sajjan's passion for honesty boiled over" in sentence (4).

(4) ···कारुणिक परिस्थिति में उसकी मृत्यु हो जाने से सज्जन के मन की ईमानदारी का जोश उबल कर बाहर आ गया ।
(...*kāruṇika paristhiti mẽ usakī mṛtyu ho jāne se sajjana ke mana kī īmānadārī kā jośa ubala kara bāhara ā gayā*)
"Sajjan's passion for honesty boiled over due to her death under pathetic circumstances."

Similarly, सज्जन का क्रोध उबल पड़ा (*sajjana kā krodha ubala paṛā*) "Sajjana's anger boiled over" in sentence (5)

(5) यह बात सुनकर सज्जन का क्रोध उबल पड़ा ।
(*yaha bāta sunakara sajjan kā krodha ubala paṛā*)
"On hearing this Sajjan's anger boiled over."

corresponds to शिवा क्रोध से उबल पड़ा (*śivā krodha se ubala paṛā*) "Shiva was enraged" in sentence (6).

(6) यह देखते ही शिवा क्रोध से उबल पड़ा... ।
(*yaha dekhate hī śivā krodha se ubala paṛā*...)
"Shivā was enraged when he saw this..."

It is only appropriate to point out at this stage of the investigation of the phenomenon that the sentences (1), (3) and (5) are respectively related to sentences (2), (4) and (6), and a systematic treatment of conjunct verbs in MSH would not be complete without accounting for the variety of structures illustrated in sentences (2), (4) and (6).

4. The *karanā* conjunct verbs in MSH

4.1. In this section we shall discuss the करना (*karanā*) "to do" conjunct verbs. In doing so we shall (i) try to take up some of the problems which we did not carry to their full conclusion in section 3, and (ii) present an overall picture of the semantic complexity of (*karanā*) "to do" conjunct verbs themselves.

Our treatment of the करना (*karanā*) "to do" conjunct verbs as envisaged in the SSSH involves the following assumptions regarding the semantic complexity of their two constituents, that is, the [N_1]'s and [Adj]'s which occur in ANP's, on the one hand, and the formative verb करना (*karanā*) "to do", on the other.

(i) The [N_1]'s and [Adj]'s occurring in ANP's in MSH are generalized concepts, the term "concept" being taken to mean a fairly definite and independent mental formulation determined by consideration of instances.

(ii) Every occurrence of an [N_1] or [Adj] term in ANP's in MSH sentences constitutes an attempt on the part of the speaker of the language to instantiate the generalized concept represented by that term.

(iii) Every occurrence of a generalized concept (represented by a term denoting that concept) in a conjunct verb with the verb करना (*karanā*) "to do" in MSH sentences serves to instantiate that generalized concept by referring to a specific behavioral manifestation of it in a given context type.

(iv) Every actual (that is, existing in act) behavioral manifestation serving as an instantiation of a generalized concept represents a process. The term representing that generalized concept will be marked by the feature [+process].

(v) A reference to the factual (that is, restricted to, involving, or based on fact, especially as opposed to the imaginative or theoretical) behavioral manifestation of a generalized concept will be indicated by marking the term representing that concept by the feature [−process].

In the rest of this section we shall try to explicate by means of suitable examples the general nature of these assumptions.

4.2. In sub-section 3.3 we remarked that the common nouns, when they occur in ANP's, do not refer to concrete objects but occur as symbolic concepts which function like abstract nouns which by their occurrence in ANP's denote special content of action or process or state. In sub-section 3.4.3 we discussed the polysemy of [N_1] abstract nouns and came to the following conclusions.

> It is clear from our discussion that we do not regard a semantic characterization of [N_1]'s and [Adj]'s based on the notion of polysemy as being sufficiently deep and significant as far as the phenomenon of conjunct verbs is concerned in

MSH. We, therefore, propose that in all the three occurrences of the ANP's with the $[N_1]$ noun भरोसा (*bharosā*), we have the same $[N_1]$ noun भरोसा (*bharosā*), two instances of which are [+relative] and one [−relative]. Consequently, the variety of surface meanings of this noun based on the notion of polysemy are all derivable from an underlying common meaning. It is, therefore, necessary to devise methods which would enable us to arrive at deeper semantic characterization of $[N_1]$ nouns in the language. We would like to say that $[N_1]$ nouns occurring in ANP's are concepts, a fact to which we alluded to in sub-section 3.3, and will discuss further in section 4.

We would like to pursue these matters further in this sub-section, that is, to discuss the nature of $[N_1]$ abstract nouns as concepts, as we indicated in our first assumption. Such a discussion, we believe, will also dispense with the necessity of positing these abstract nouns as polysemous lexical items in the language.

Our first assumption clearly states that the $[N_1]$ abstract nouns are generalized concepts which are (i) fairly definite mental formulations, and (ii) are determined by consideration of instances. We shall now try to explicate these two characteristics of concepts by means of a few examples of the occurrence of the conjunct verb की धृष्टता करना (*kī dhṛṣṭatā karanā*).

(1) की धृष्टता करना
(*kī dhṛṣṭatā karanā*)
"to act presumptuously"

यह कहकर सम्राट बिम्बसार शिलाखण्ड पर बैठ गये। बोले क्षमा करना, वृद्ध हूं, इसलिये आपके सम्मुख बैठने की धृष्टता कर बैठा हूं।
(*yaha kahakara samrāṭa bimbasāra śilākhaṇḍa para baiṭha gaye. bole kṣamā karanā vṛddha hū̃, isa liye āpake sammukha baiṭhane kī dhṛṣṭatā kara baiṭhā hū̃*)
"After saying this the Emperor Bimbasāra sat down on a boulder and said, 'Forgive me, I'm an old man, that is why, (I feel), I have acted presumptuously in sitting before you.'"

(2) की धृष्टता करना
(*kī dhṛṣṭatā karanā*)
"to take the liberty of, to act presumptuously"

आप लखनऊ आयें यह सुझाने की धृष्टता तो नहीं कर सकता, मेरी अपात्रता के अलावा लखनऊ की घटनाओं का भी स्मरण कराया जाना आप नापसन्द करेंगी।

(*āpa lakhanaū āyẽ yaha sujhāne kī dhṛṣṭatā to nahī̃ kara sakatā, merī apātratā ke alāvā lakhanaū kī ghaṭanāõ kā bhī smaraṇa karāyā jānā āpa nāpasanda karẽgī*)

"I cannot take the liberty of suggesting to you that you come to Lucknow. In addition to my unworthiness, you might dislike being reminded of the events of Lucknow."

Both the examples given above involve a reference to the speaker's admission that he is being insolent in taking a seat in the presence of someone [in sentence (1)], and suggesting that the addressee visit Lucknow [in sentence(2)]. But it is also noteworthy that both the instances of the speaker's conduct in fact have nothing to do with his characterization of them as instances of the behavior of an insolent person, unless, of course, he knows beforehand what constitutes an instance of conduct markedly divergent from the norms of propriety in a given circumstance and at a given time. In other words, taking a seat in the presence of someone superior to oneself with the knowledge that one should not do so [in sentence (1)], and suggesting something to another person knowing that it is likely to hurt that person's feelings [in sentence (2)] are two factors contributing to the speaker's characterization of his act of taking a seat, and his suggesting to the addressee that she visit Lucknow, as instances of a behavior markedly divergent from the norms of propriety. Therefore, one could say that the speaker's characterization of his behavior as being insolent involves his notion of "insolence", on the one hand, as well as his specific behavior (in a given time and place) which exhibits this "insolence", on the other.

In other words, all the occurrences of the [N_1] abstract noun धृष्टता (*dhṛṣṭatā*) "insolence" in conjunct verbs presuppose the speaker's explicit recognition of his behavior as being markedly divergent from the norms of propriety, that is, a form of behavior which violates a code of conduct or oversteps certain norms. These norms of behavior are of the form "one should not take a seat in the presence of a superior", "one should not suggest something to another person knowing that it is likely to hurt that person's feelings" and so forth. The MSH notion of धृष्टता (*dhṛṣṭatā*) "insolence" constitutes a violation of such norms of behavior by someone who is expected to know these norms and behave accordingly. It is in this sense MSH notion of धृष्टता (*dhṛṣṭatā*) "insolence" is a fairly definite mental formulation, that is, a concept. Likewise all the [N_1] nouns described in the SSSH are also concepts.

Our definition of [N_1] abstract nouns as concepts stipulates that they are concepts which are not only definite, but also independent mental formulations. We would now like to comment on this aspect of our definition. One could perhaps say that there is no natural or inherent relationship, as in the above noted examples, between a person's notion of "insolence" and his behavior which exhibits it since any or all the instances of a person's conduct can be characterized as being markedly divergent from the norms of propriety [and can be referred to by the speaker by the [N_1] abstract noun धृष्टता (*dhṛṣṭatā*)], if appropriate presuppositions of the form mentioned above concerning the notion of "insolence" are fulfilled. It is by virtue of these presuppositions alone that a person's conduct is viewed to be insolent, and not otherwise. We would now like to illustrate this situation by means of a different variety of examples.

(3) हीरा ने यह कह कर कि वह अपने घमण्ड में भूला हुआ है और आरजू विनती न सुनेगा उसके प्रति चिन्ता व्यक्त की ।

(*hīrā ne yaha kahakara ki vaha apane ghamaṇḍa mẽ bhūlā huā hai aura ārajū vinatī na sunegā usake prati cintā vyakta kī*)

"Hira, by saying that he was lost in his haughtiness and would not listen to their requests and entreaties, expressed his concern about him."

(3a) हीरा ने चिन्तित स्वर में कहा, "वह अपने घमण्ड में भूला हुआ है, आरजू विनती न सुनेगा ।"

(*hīra ne cintita svara mẽ kahā, "vaha apane ghamaṇḍa mẽ bhūlā huā hai, ārajū vinatī na sunegā*)

"Hira said in a worried tone, "He is lost in his haughtiness and won't listen to our requests and entreaties." "

(4) एक बालक ने कहा, "ऐसे बैल किसी के पास न होंगे।" दूसरे ने उसका समर्थन किया, 'इतनी दूर से दोनों अकेले चले आये।"

(*eka bālaka ne kahā, "aise baila kisī ke pāsa na hõge." dūsare ne usakā samarthana kiyā, "itanī dūra se donõ akele cale āye."*)

"One boy said, "Nobody has such bulls." The other supported him (by saying that) they (that is, the bulls) came back from such a distance all by themselves." "

(4a) एक बालक ने कहा, "ऐसे बैल किसी के पास न होंगे।" दूसरे ने उसके समर्थन में कहा, "इतनी दूर से दोनों अकेले चले आये।"

(*eka bālaka ne kahā, "aise baila kisī ke pāsa na hõge. dūsare ne usake samarthana mẽ kahā, "itanī dūra se donõ akele cale āye."*)

"One boy said, "Nobody has such bulls." The other supporting him said, "They came back from such a distance all by themselves." "

In the above noted examples, the underlined expressions in (3a) and (4a) are paraphrases of the underlined expressions in (3) and (4) respectively, that is, "to say something in a worried tone" is "to express one's concern", and "to say something supporting someone" is to support someone". In both the instances of someone's behavior as described in (3a) and (4a) there is a reference to his act of saying something, but this same act of saying something is interpreted as व्यक्त करना (*vyakta karanā*) "to express" in the environment of चिन्तित स्वर में (*cintita svara mẽ*) "in a worried tone", as in (3), and का समर्थन करना (*kā samarthana karanā*) "to support" in the environment of समर्थन में (*samarthana mẽ*) "in support", as in (4). It is obvious from these examples that it is not by virtue of the fact that someone said something that "saying something" is interpreted as "expressing something" in (3) and "supporting someone" in (4). In other words, the same act of saying something underlies two different conjunct verbs as illustrated in sentences (3) and (4), and it is so interpreted by means of these conjunct verbs because "saying something" presupposes "a particular tone (in which something is said)" in the former sentence, and "supporting someone" in the latter. Therefore, one could say that the concepts of "expressing" and "supporting", while they necessarily involve acts like "saying" etc. as their behavioral manifestations, are independent mental formulations, and every instance of the occurrence of [N_1]'s referring to these concepts involves determination of such concepts by means of their characteristic presuppositions manifested behaviorally as explained above.

It could perhaps be said that presuppositions like "one should not take a seat in the presence of someone superior", and so on, are not universal among the speakers who form the speech community of MSH, but the fact remains that presuppositions like the one just mentioned do exist as universals.

4.2.1. The [Adj]'s occurring in करना (*karanā*) "to do" conjunct verbs are also concepts, that is definite and independent mental formulations of various states or conditions presupposed to be induced or brought into being by a variety of causes. In order to illustrate the nature of [Adj]'s as concepts we reproduce below two sentences containing the occurrence of the conjunct verbs बाध्य करना (*bādhya karanā*) "to compel" and तंग करना (*taṅga karanā*) "to bother."

(1) को बाध्य करना
(*ko bādhya karanā*).
"to prevail upon"

इन सब कारणों के अलावा देश-काल की विशेष परिस्थितियां भी राज्यों को सामाजिक विधान बनाने को बाध्य करती हैं।
(*ina sabu kāraṇõ ke alāvā deśa-kāla kī viśeṣa paristhitiyā̃ bhī rājyõ ko sāmājika vidhāna banāne ko bādhya karatī hãĩ*)
"Besides all these reasons, the conditions pertaining to space and time also prevail upon the states to have (some sort of) social order."

(2) को तंग करना
(*ko taṅga karanā*)
"to annoy"

बच्चे ताई को बहुत तंग करते हैं, वह पूजा करने या जप करने बैठती हैं तो...।
(*bacce tāī ko bahuta taṅga karate hãĩ, vaha pūjā karane yā japa karane baiṭhatī hãĩ to....*)
"Children annoy tāi very much. (Whenever) she sits down to worship or recite..."

These sentences can be paraphrased as follows.

(1a) इन सब कारणों के अलावा देश-काल की विशेष परिस्थितियों से बाध्य हो कर भी राज्य सामाजिक विधान बनाते हैं।
(*ina saba kāraṇõ ke alāvā deśa-kāla kī viśeṣa paristhitiyõ se bādhya hokara bhī rājya sāmājika vidhāna banāte hãĩ*)
"Besides these reasons, states resort to the (act of) creating some sort of social order (when) compelled by the conditions of time and place."

(2a) बच्चों से ताई बहुत तंग आ जाती हैं, वह पूजा करने या जप करने बैठती हैं तो....।
(*baccõ se tāī bahuta taṅga ā jātī hãĩ, vaha pūjā karane yā japa karane baiṭhatī hãĩ to...*)
"Tāi (usually feels) very much annoyed by the children. (Whenever) she sits down to worship or recite..."

The important difference between sentences (1) and (1a), and (2) and (2a) is that what appears as the subject in (1) and (2) is represented adverbially as the cause in their respective paraphrases in (1a) and (2a). In addition, a comparison between (1) and(2) and their respective paraphrases reveals that [Adj]'s forming conjunct verbs with the verb करना (*karanā*) "to do", such as बाध्य (*bādhya*) "compelled" and तंग (*taṅga*) "constrained", which appear as lexically single items in करना (*karanā*) "to do" conjunct verbs are, in fact, semantically complex lexical items consisting of बाध्य होना (*bādhya honā*) "to be compelled" and तंग आ जाना (*taṅga ā jānā*) "to be constrained " etc.

The analyzability of single lexical items like these [Adj]'s as semantically complex items, however, does not eliminate them from the category of adjectives occurring in करना (*karanā*) "to do" conjunct verbs.[1] This fact only serves to point out that [Adj]'s occurring in करना (*karanā*) "to do" conjunct verbs are also semantically complex just as are the [N_1]'s, but in-

1. This view may be compared with the analysis of sentence (4) उसने दरवाजा बन्द किया (*usane darvāzā banda kiyā*) in Kachru (1966) as discussed in sub-section 2.2.2

volve different steps of analysis due to the differences in their semantic complexity.

Before proceeding we would like to summarize the difference between [Adj]'s and [N_1]'s as concepts by stipulating that [Adj]'s are a variety of states or conditions presupposed to be induced by causes of various sorts.

We have also chosen the [Adj]'s बाध्य (*bādhya*) "compelled" and तंग (*taṅga*) "constrained" to illustrate another aspect of the semantic complexity of these adjectives. It has already been demonstrated that [Adj+V] sequences like बाध्य करना (*bādhya karanā*) "to compell" and तंग करना (*taṅga karanā*) "to constrain" can be analyzed as बाध्य होना + करना (*bādhya honā + karanā*) and तंग आ जाना + करना (*taṅga ājānā + karanā*) respectively. We now propose that the sentence (1a) can be further paraphrased as follows.

(1b) इन सब कारणों के अलावा देश-काल की विशेष परिस्थितियों से बंध जाने की अवस्था आ जाने पर भी राज्य सामाजिक विधान बनाते हैं।
(*ina saba kāraṇõ ke alāvā deśa-kāla kī viśeṣa paristhitiyõ se b̃adha jāne kī avasthā ā jāne para bhī rājya sāmājika vidhāna banāte hãĩ*)
"Besides all these reasons, states also resort to the act of creating some sort of social order on getting tied down to a state of the (internally emerged) conditions pertaining to time and space."

In this context बाध्य (*bādhya*) "compelled" is analyzable into बंध जाने की अवस्था (*b̃adha jāne kī avasthā*) "state of getting tied down." However, no such analysis can be proposed for तंग आ जाना (*taṅga ā jānā*) "to become constrained".

4.2.2. In this sub-section, we demonstrate that our definitions of the generic meanings of [N_1]'s and [Adj]'s in section one of the articles in SSSH are statements of presuppositions and presupposed causes respectively which semantically represent these [N_1]'s and [Adj]'s. The purpose behind this demonstration is twofold, that is, (i) to establish the linguistic adequacy of our definitions, and (ii) to dispense with the necessity of positing these [N_1]'s and [Adj]'s as polysemous lexical items.

We have already discussed the nature of the relationship between [N_1 or Adj+V] sequences and their paraphrases in sub-section 3.6.4 as well as in sub-sections 4.2. and 4.2.1. In sub-section 3.6.1 we stated that all [N_1 or Adj+V] sequences can be paraphrased by means of a variety of [Adv(erb)+V] sequences [that is, by means of the sentences of the type included in group I with the verb लेना (*lenā*) "to take"]. In addition, we remarked that these [Adv+V] sequences represent the semantic materials which combine to yield lexical items in conjunct verbs such as [N_1]'s and [Adj]'s, on the one hand, and [V]'s, on the other. In subsection 4.2 and 4.2.1 we established that these [N_1]'s and [Adj]'s are concepts which are semantically characterized by their respective presuppositions and presupposed causes. Thus we now propose that our statements in section one of the articles in SSSH containing definitions of the generic meanings of [N_1]'s and [Adj]'s are in fact semantic representations embodying such presuppositions and presupposed causes. In order to demonstrate that such, in fact, is the case, we will discuss [N_1]'s first and then do the same thing for [Adj]'s. The procedure to be followed consists essentially of determination of the "fairly definite and independent mental formulations", "by consideration of instances" as stated in our first assumption in sub-section 4.1.

We give below a few sentences illustrating the occurrence of the [N_1] noun क्रोध (*krodha*) "anger".

(1) राम ने उसके अशिष्ट व्यवहार के कारण मोहन पर बड़ा क्रोध किया ।
(*rāma ne usake aśiṣṭa vyavahāra ke kāraṇa mohana para baṛā krodha kiyā*)
"Due to his inedcent behavior Ram let his anger out on Mohan".

(1a) राम ने उसके अशिष्ट व्यवहार के कारण क्रोध में आकर मोहन को बहुत गालियां दीं ।
(*rāma ne usake aśiṣṭa vyavahāra ke kāraṇa krodha mẽ ākara mohana ko bahuta gāliyā̃ dī̃*)
"Ram, having been angered at the indecent behavior of Mohan, abused him very much."

(1b) राम को मोहन पर उसके अशिष्ट व्यवहार के कारण बड़ा क्रोध आया ।
(*rāma ko mohana para usake aśiṣṭa vyavahāra ke kāraṇa baṛā krodha āyā*)
"Ram was very angry at Mohan because of his indecent behavior".

(1c) मोहन ने राम से अशिष्ट व्यवहार किया जिसके कारण उसको मोहन पर बड़ा क्रोध आया ।
(*mohana ne rāma se aśiṣṭa vyavahāra kiyā jisa ke kāraṇa usa ko mohana para baṛā krodha āyā*)
"Mohan treated Ram indecently (and) because of that Ram was very angry at him."

Each of the above noted sentences is successively a paraphrase of the former. पर क्रोध करना (*para krodha karanā*) in (1) is represented by क्रोध में आकर गालियां देना (*krodha mẽ ākara gāliyā̃ denā*) in (1a), क्रोध में आना (*krodha mẽ ānā*) in (1b) is further related to को क्रोध आना (*ko krodha ānā*) in (1b) and (1c). In other words, as we have already tried to explain, the [N_1] क्रोध (*krodha*) "anger" appears as a single lexical item in (1) but in fact it is a surface manifestation of the semantically complex sequence consisting of क्रोध (*krodha*) "anger" plus the verb आना (*ānā*) "to come". It is at this level that our definition of the generic meaning of (*krodha*) "anger" is applicable to the concept of क्रोध (*KRODHA*) "anger". We reproduce below section one of article 5 from SSSH, volume I for comparison.

1. Both क्रोध (*krodha*) and गुस्सा (*gussā*) refer to one's behavior (verbal or otherwise) expressing emotional excitement aroused or induced by intense displeasure. क्रोध (*krodha*) names the emotional state of anger as well as its outward manifestation, implying a grievance and a desire or intent to revenge or punish. गुस्सा (*gussā*) refers to the emotional reaction of an angry individual.

As our definition of the generic meaning of the noun क्रोध (*krodha*) "anger" implies, it is applicable to this noun in all the known possible environments of its occurrence. In view of the distinction between verbal and non-verbal nouns, as explained in sub-section 3.2, this noun in all its possible environments of occurrence, where it is verbal, always implies the verb आना (*ānā*) "to come", though this verb may not appear with it in some of its surface manifestations. For example, the occurrence of क्रोध से (*krodha se*) "with anger (that is, angrily)" in the following sentence

(2) वह बड़े क्रोध से बोला
(*vaha baṛe krodha se bolā*)
"He spoke very angrily"

is analyzable as (2a)

(2a) वह इस तरह से बोला जैसे वह बड़े क्रोध में हो ।
(*vaha isa taraha se bolā jaise vaha baṛe krodha mẽ ho*)
"He spoke in a manner which indicated that he was angry."

and (2a) as (2b),

(2b) वह इस तरह से बोला जैसे वह बड़े क्रोध में आया हुआ हो ।
(*vaha isa taraha se bolā jaise vaha baṛe krodha mẽ āyā huā ho*)
"He spoke in a manner as if he was overcome by the state of anger."

and (2b) as (2c).

(2c) वह इस तरह से बोला जैसे उसे बड़ा क्रोध आ गया हो ।
(*vaha isa taraha se bolā jaise use baṛā krodha ā gayā ho*)
"He spoke in a manner as if he had become very angry."

Another kind of situation can be illustrated by the [N_1] noun प्रशंसा (*praśaṁsā*) "praise" as it occurs in the following sentence.

(3) राम ने मोहन की विद्वत्ता की बहुत प्रशंसा की ।
(*rāma ne mohana kī vidvattā kī bahuta praśaṁsā kī*)
"Ram highly praised the scholarship of Mohan."

(3a) राम ने (मोहन की विद्वत्ता की प्रशंसा में) कहा, "मोहन बड़ा विद्वान है ।"
[*rāma ne* (*mohana kī vidvattā kī praśaṁsā meṁ*) *kahā*, "*mohana baṛā vidvāna hai.*"]
"Ram (praising the scholarship of Mohan) said, "Mohan is a great scholar." "

A comparison of sentence (3) with its paraphrase as contained in (3a) reveals that the noun प्रशंसा (*praśaṁsā*) "praise" (probably) does not imply any other verb as does the noun क्रोध (*krodha*) "anger". Our definition of the generic meaning of this noun in SSSH, volume I does take this fact into account. We reproduce below section one of article 2 in this volume to facilitate comparison.

1. प्रशंसा (*praśaṁsā*), सराहना (*sarāhanā*), तारीफ (*tārīpha*) all refer to the expression of one's feeling of admiration in a variety of ways. प्रशंसा (*praśaṁsā*) implies a recognition of superiority, and is often motivated. सराहना (*sarāhanā*) is applied to anything from a warmly expressed commendation to the expression of one's appreciation based on some sort of understanding. तारीफ (*tārīpha*) refers to expression of one's feeling about what is pleasing or what one regards with favor.

We have already given examples of the occurrence of the [Adj] (*bādhya*) "compelled" in sub-section 4.2.1. Therefore, we reproduce below section one of article 128, SSSH, volume II to facilitate comparison.[1]

1. All these terms suggest a recourse to action on the part of the object of the sentence, the outcome of which may or may not be favorable to him, but which is prompted and limited by the pressures of some inner compulsion or overriding or influential outside force. The terms, however, differ in reference to the specification of the manner or mode in which the object noun is described as being affected by the source of influence.

1. The other adjectives described in this article, besides बाध्य (*bādhya*) "compelled", are लाचार (*lācāra*) "helpless", विवश (*vivaśa*) "obligated" and मजबूर (*majabūra*) "forced".

4.3. Our second assumption concerning the instantiation of a generalized concept by the speaker has threefold implications. Firstly it is meant to underline the fact that all करना (*karanā*) "to do" conjunct verbs can be generated in a grammar of MSH by systematically combining their semantic materials contained in their paraphrases in terms of sentences with [Adv+V] sequences. We have discussed this matter in sufficient detail in the previous sub-section, as well as in sub-section 3.6.3 and 3.6.4. While doing so, we have not gone through all the necessary steps that are required to analytically establish the relationship between sentences with conjunct verbs and their paraphrases in terms of sentences with [Adv+V] sequences because such an endeavor is outside the scope of this "Introduction". There are, however, other bearings of the distinction between these two types of sentences in the semantic structure of MSH, bearings which are involved in the other implications of our second assumption.

We can state the second implication by saying that sentences with करना (*karanā*) "to do" conjunct verbs have grammatico-semantic functions different from their related sentences containing their paraphrases in terms of [Adv+V] sequences. These two sorts of sentences, as far as the native speakers of MSH are concerned, involve two different speech acts.[1]

The phenomenon of speech acts as involved in these two kinds of sentences has not yet been investigated, but we believe that a description of the semantic structure of sentences with करना (*karanā*) "to do" conjunct verbs in terms of their semantic materials as represented by their paraphrases would be incomplete without positing them as two different speech acts. We alluded to this sort of distinction in sub-section 2.2.3 while discussing the problem of "similarity of postpositional preferences bet-

1. The notion of speech act is described in John R. Searle, *Speech Acts*, An Essay in the Philosophy of Language, Cambridge University Press (Cambridge, 1970). There is, however, another way of characterising the relationship between sentences with conjunct verbs and their paraphrases in terms of (Adv+V)'s according to the inherent relationship between concepts (contained in sentences with conjunct verbs) and their behavioral manifestations (described by the paraphrases of conceptual sentences in terms of (Adv+V)'s) posited by the *Advaita Vedānta* and *Sāṁkhya* theories of causation. According to the *satkāryavāda* ("effect pre-exists in cause") principle of these two schools of Indian philosophy, the behavioral manifestions of a concept (which underlies them) constitute an effect which pre-exists in the cause (that is, in the concept to which it is related). On this basis, one could say that the sentences with conjunct verbs are conceptual sentences representing causes of the descriptive sentences (involving paraphrases of conceptual sentences) referring to the effects of those causes as perceived by the senses (including the mind). We will not go into these matters in any detail in this "Introduction" for the reasons mentioned in sub-section 5.5. For further information concerning the principle of *satkāryavāda*, see Eliot Deutch, *Advaita Vedānta*, East-West Centre Press (Honolulu, 1969), page 35, footnote.

ween verbs and conjunct verbs" raised by Verma (1971). For instance, sentence (1) as given below with the conjunct verb से प्रश्न करना (*se praśna karanā*)

(1) बादशाह ने उस यात्रीदल के सम्बन्ध में और भी कई प्रश्न किये। अयाज ने सब बातों का उत्तर दे दिया।

(bādaśāha ne usa yātrī-dala ke sambandha mẽ aura bhī kaī praśna kiye. Ayāza ne saba bātõ kā uttara de diyā)

"The king asked (him) many other questions concerning the party of travellers. Ayaz satisfied him with his replies on all the matters."

and its related paraphrase as illustrated by (1a) below,

(1a) बादशाह ने अयाज से उस यात्रीदल के सम्बन्ध में और भी कई बातें पूछीं। अयाज ने सब बातों का उत्तर दे दिया।

(bādaśāha ne ayāza se usa yātrī-dala ke sambandha mẽ aura bhī kaī bātẽ pūchī̃. ayāz ne saba bātõ kā uttara de diyā)

"The king asked Ayaz about many other matters concerning the party of travellers. Ayaz satisfied him with his replies on all these matters."

apart from being related to each other in the manner discussed above, constitute instances of two different speech acts based on the fact that the native speaker of MSH has a freedom to choose between them. Our second assumption concerning the instantiation of a generalized concept by the speaker, therefore, is expressly designed to underline the necessity of taking into account the speaker's freedom of choice as illustrated above. However, by "the speaker's freedom of choice" we do not mean to imply that sentences (1) and (1a) as given above are free-variants of each other in the sense that their meaning differences are explainable only in terms of factors not contained within the semantic structure of MSH. We will discuss this matter further in section 5. Therefore, we would like to repeat that sentences (1) and (1a), as far as we are concerned, are synonymous sentences constituting, however, two different speech acts.

The third implication of our second assumption is that there is no restriction on what can or cannot form the basis of the speaker's instantiation of a generalized concept, except that which is indicated by the presuppositions involved in a particular instance. We have already discussed this matter in sub-section 4.2 while explaining the relationship between sentences (3) and (4), on the one hand, and (3a) and (4a), on the other. We will, however, explain this matter once more in terms of the third implication just stated.

For example the following sentence

(2) मोहन ने श्याम से टेलीफोन पर कहा, "राम आज सात बजे से पहले ही घर चला गया है।"
(*mohana ne śyāma se ṭelīphona para kahā, "rāma āja sāta baje se pahale hī ghara calā gayā hai"*)
"Mohan said to Shyam over the telephone, "Ram left for home today before seven.""

can form the basis of a variety of concepts which the speaker might generalize from it. This is illustrated by the following sentences.

(2a) मोहन ने श्याम को टेलीफोन पर राम के आज सात बजे से पहले ही घर चले जाने की खबर कर दी।
(*mohana ne śyāma ko ṭelīphona para rāma ke āja sāta baje se pahale hī ghara cale jāne kī khabara kara dī*)
"Mohan informed Shyam over the telephone about Ram's leaving for home today before seven."

(2b) मोहन ने श्याम से टेलीफोन पर राम के आज सात बजे से पहले ही घर चले जाने के बारे में शिकायत कर दी।
(*mohana ne śyāma se ṭelīphona para rāma ke āja sāta baje se pahale hī ghara cale jāne ke bāre mẽ śikāyata kara dī*)
"Mohan complained to Shyam over the telephone about Ram's leaving for home today before seven."

The speaker's two different interpretations of sentence (2) by means of (2a) and (2b) are based on the fact that his presuppositions underlying (2a) and (2b) are different, that is, (2a) presupposes (2) in the form of (2c)

(2c) मोहन ने श्याम से उसे खबर करने के लिये टेलीफोन पर कहा, "..."
(*mohana ne śyāma se use khabara karane ke liye ṭelīphona para kahā, "...."*)
"Mohan said to Shyam over the telephone in order to inform him, "...""

and (2b) presupposes (2) to be in the form of (2d).

(2d) मोहन ने श्याम से टेलीफोन पर शिकायत भरे स्वर में कहा, "..."
(*mohana ne śyāma se ṭelīphona para śikāyata bhare svara mẽ kahā, "..."*)
"Mohan said to Shyam over the telephone in a complaining tone, "...""

It, therefore, becomes necessary to say that what does or does not constitute a basis for the instantiation of a generalized concept by the speaker is determined by the presuppositions involved in a particular instance.[1]

4.4. The explication of the mutual semantic relationship between $[N_1]$'s and [Adj]'s as discussed in the SSSH necessarily involves a discussion of the notion of synonymy as we have employed it. The notion of synonymy, as the term is generally understood to refer to some sort of semantic similarity between lexical items, is a vague notion. Therefore, we propose to deal with this notion by discussing the manner in which we have usefully employed it in formulating our definitions of the generic and specific meanings of synonymous $[N_1]$'s and [Adj]'s which occur in ANP's forming conjunct verbs with the verb करना (*karanā*) "to do" in MSH.

Two or more $[N_1]$'s and [Adj]'s which share the same presuppositions, as stated in the form of generic definitions contained in section one of the articles, are synonyms with each other. On this basis, nouns like प्रशंसा (*praśaṁsā*) "praise", सराहना (*sarāhanā*) "appreciation" and तारीफ (*tārīpha*) "liking", which occur in ANP's forming conjunct verbs with करना (*karanā*) "to do" and share the same presuppositions, are synonymous with each other. On the other hand, nouns like आज्ञा (*ājñā*) "instruction" and अनुमति (*anumati*) "consent", which may ultimately be analyzed as sharing the same presuppositions, are not treated as synonyms with each other since अनुमति (*anumati*) "consent" does not occur in ANP's which form conjunct verbs with करना (*karanā*) "to do".

The sharing of presuppositions by two or more $[N_1]$'s and [Adj]'s should be distinguished from a sharing of any similarity in behavioral manifestations as contained in the paraphrases of sentences with conjunct verbs. Although the noun खबर (*khabara*) "information" and शिकायत (*śikāyata*) "complaint" share the same behavioral manifestations, that is, the activity of "saying something", they are not synonyms with each other because they involve different presuppositions.

Synonymy, a relation which obtains between generalized concepts by virtue of their sharing common presuppositions by means of the nouns and adjectives denoting them, involves two kinds of relationships between nouns and adjectives which are synonymous with each other. Below we discuss these relationships within the limitations just imposed.

4.4.1. Synonymy, we propose, is a relation between nouns which are related to each other along a scale of specificity versus genericity. We will illustrate this kind of synonymy by discussing the four nouns प्रयोग (*prayoga*), उपयोग (*upayoga*), व्यवहार (*vyavahāra*) and इस्तेमाल (*istemāla*) dealt

1. The speaker who instantiates a generalized concept (that is, the speaker of a sentence with करना (*karanā*) "to do" conjunct verb), as our discussion implies throughout, should be distinguished from the speaker of sentence (2) represented here in the person of a man named Mohan.

with in article 1, SSSH, volume I. Section one of this article is reproduced below.

1. प्रयोग (*prayoga*), उपयोग (*upayoga*), व्यवहार (*vyavahāra*), इस्तेमाल (*istemāla*) are synonymous nouns meaning use of a thing (or a person) as a means to an end. प्रयोग (*prayoga*) implies suitability, उपयोग (*upayoga*) refers to the use of an object for a purpose other than that for which it is primarily meant, व्यवहार (*vyavahāra*) stresses customary, habitual use, and इस्तेमाल (*istemāla*) indicates nothing more than the idea of use. In careful writings इस्तेमाल (*istemāla*) occurs in contexts where the distinctions indicated by प्रयोग (*prayoga*), उपयोग (*upayoga*) and व्यवहार (*vyavahāra*) are to be definitely avoided.

In the way we have set up the definitions of these nouns, प्रयोग (*prayoga*) can be substituted by उपयोग (*upayoga*), उपयोग (*upayoga*) by व्यवहार (*vyavahāra*) and व्यवहार (*vyavahāra*) by इस्तेमाल (*istemāla*) in the contexts of occurrence of each ; and all three nouns can be substituted by the noun इस्तेमाल (*istemāla*) as well, with some modification in the sentences. Below we give one sentence illustrating the occurrence of the conjunct verb का प्रयोग करना (*kā prayoga karanā*) with three additional sentences in which this conjunct verb is substituted by its synonymous conjunct verbs. In the three sentences where the substitution of का प्रयोग करना (*kā prayoga karanā*) is illustrated by its synonymous conjuncts, the synonymous expression and our modifications of the original sentence are underlined.

(1) श्रीमती आनन्द प्राय: सभी भाषाओं के एकाध अश्लील-कहावत, अश्लील-शब्द, और अश्लील-आशय के वाक्य जानती है और <u>अवसर देखकर उनका प्रयोग भी करती है</u>।

(*śrīmatī ānanda prāyaḥ sabhī bhāṣāõ ke ekādha aślīla-kahāvata, aślīla-śabda, aura aślīla-āśaya ke vākya jānatī hai, aura, <u>avasara dekhakara unakā prayoga bhī karatī hai</u>*)

"Shrimati Anand knows some obscene expressions, obscene words and sentences having obscene connotations of almost all the languages. And <u>she uses them on appropriate occasions.</u>"

(2) श्रीमती आनन्द प्राय: सभी भाषाओं के एकाध अश्लील-कहावत, अश्लील-शब्द और अश्लील-आशय के वाक्य जानती है। और, कभी-कभी उनका इस ढंग <u>से उपयोग करती है कि सुननेवाला हंसे बिना नहीं रहता</u>।

(*śrīmatī ānanda prāyaḥ sabhī bhāṣāõ ke ekādha aślīla-kahāvata, aślīla-śabda, aura aślīla-āśaya ke vākya jānatī hai, aura, <u>kabhī-kabhī unakā isa prakāra se upayoga karatī hai ki sunanevālā hãse binā nahī̃ rahatā</u>*)

"Shrimati Anand knows some obscene expressions, obscene words and sentences having obscene connotations of almost all the languages. And, sometimes employs them in such a way that the listener cannot help laughing."

(3) श्रीमती आनन्द प्रायः सभी भाषाओं के एकाध अश्लील-कहावत, अश्लील-शब्द, और अश्लील-आशय के वाक्य जानती है। और, बात-बात में उनका व्यवहार करती है।

(*śrīmatī ānanda prāyaḥ sabhī bhāṣāõ ke ekādha aślīla-kahāvata, aślīla-śabda, aura aślīla-āśaya ke vākya jānatī hai, aura, bāta-bāta mẽ unakā vyavahāra karatī hai*)

"Shrimati Anand knows some obscene expressions, obscene words and sentences having obscene connotations of almost all the languages. And (she) uses them in conversation now and then

(4) श्रीमती आनन्द प्रायः सभी भाषाओं के एकाध अश्लील-कहावत, अश्लील-शब्द, और अश्लील-आशय के वाक्य जानती है। और, जाने-अनजाने उनका इस्तेमाल कर देती है।

(*śrīmatī ānanda prāyaḥ sabhī bhāṣāõ ke ekādha aślīla-kahāvata, aślīla-śabda, aura aślīla-āśaya ke vākya jānatī hai. aura, jāne-anajāne unakā istemāla kara detī hai*)

"Shrimati Anand knows some obscene expressions, obscene words, and sentences having obscene connotations of almost all the languages. And, (she) uses them indiscriminately (in the sense that whether it is appropriate to use such expressions or not)."

As we have tried to illustrate by means of the four examples given above, the noun प्रयोग (*prayoga*) is the most marked noun in the group, and इस्तेमाल (*istemāla*) is the least marked. On the basis of the semantic relationship of markedness versus unmarkedness, the following set of rules can be formulated for these nouns using the term USE as a label for the semantic field represented by them.

(i) USE → ± suitability
(ii) —suitability → ± secondariness
(iii) —secondariness → ± convention

These rules can be expressed by means of a tree-diagram as follows:—

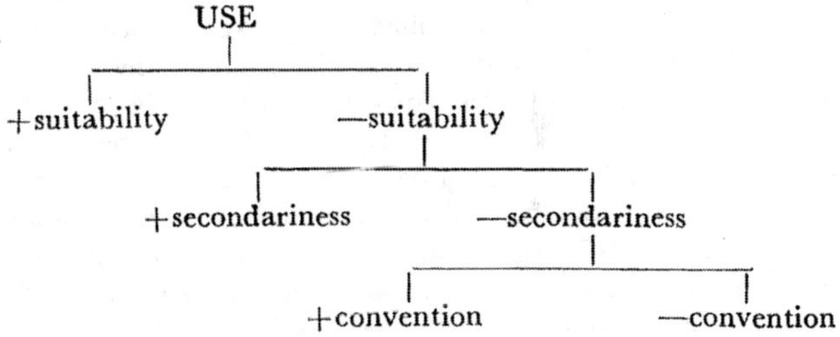

Nouns like the ones discussed above, which are synonyms with each other by virtue of the fact that their mutual semantic relationship can be expressed in terms of a scale of markedness versus unmarkedness, are related to each other along the dimension of specific versus generic. For instance, the noun प्रयोग (*prayoga*) (which is the most marked member in the group) is a specific noun in relation to its generic counterpart इस्तेमाल (*istemāla*) (which is the least marked member in the group). The other two nouns form intermediate categories on this scale of specificity versus genericity.

It follows, therefore, that the specific meanings of such nouns are derivable from their common presuppositions by systematically combining semantic materials pertaining to the linguistic modes of specificity as may be involved in a group. These linguistic modes of specificity which distinguish nouns from each other also consist of presuppositions involved in the specific behavioral manifestations indicated by the paraphrases. Sentences (1-4) given above illustrate this point. Our formulations of the definitions of the specific meanings of nouns in section one of the articles are, therefore, related to the definitions of their generic meanings and to each other in the manner explained above.

The definitions of the specific meanings of adjectives in section one of the articles are also related to the definitions of their generic meanings and to each other in the manner of nouns like प्रयोग (*prayoga*), व्यवहार (*vyavahāra*) etc.

4.4.2. There are, however, nouns in MSH which are not related to each other in the manner of nouns discussed in sub-section 4.4.1 above. We illustrate this situation by discussing the nouns described in article 67 in SSSH, volume I. Section one of this article is reproduced below.

1. All these nouns refer to the modalities of expression of praise. आत्मसंकीर्तन (*ātmasaṅkīrtana*) is self-glorification through the use of such sentences as involve the occurrence of one's own name

repeatedly (with reference to statements of one's own accomplishments). आत्मश्लाघा (*ātmaślāghā*) is applied to an exaggerated reference to one's own or someone else's quality or qualities. गुणगान (*guṇagāna*) is talking about the praiseworthy qualities of someone (generally with a motive) or of oneself (as if one were singing a song). बखान (*bakhāna*) is relating repetitiously the pleasing qualities or characteristics of someone. The term may be used as a dignified reference to someone's profuse abuse of another in public. स्तुति (*stuti*) is singing religious praises in order to perform worship, and वाहवाह (*vāhavāha*) [which is lit. using the interjectional particle वाह (*vāha*) more than once] is public approbation implying a degree of pleasure and satisfaction. The term usually contains a somewhat slighting reference to the one expressing approbation, because it carries a strong implication of being impulsive.

These nouns are grouped together not because they are synonyms with each other in the manner of nouns like प्रयोग (*prayoga*) etc., but because they represent various specific modalities of the activity denoted by the generic noun प्रशंसा (*praśaṁsā*) "praise". We give below the conjunct verbs formed with these nouns along with their paraphrases to illustrate the relationship between the generic activity denoted by the noun प्रशंसा (*praśaṁsā*) "praise" and its specific modalities described in article 67, SSSH, volume I.

(1) आत्मसंकीर्तन करना
(*ātmasaṁkīrtana karanā*)
"to indulge in self-glorification"

(1a) अपने मुंह से बढ़ा-चढ़ाकर दूसरों को प्रभावित करने के लिये अपनी प्रशंसा करना
(*apane mũha se baṛhā-caṛhākara dūsarõ ko prabhāvita karane ke liye apanī praśaṁsā karanā*)
"to praise oneself in exaggerated terms in order to impress others"

(2) आत्मश्लाघा करना
(*ātmaślāghā karanā*)
"to boast about oneself"

(2a) अपने मुंह से अपने गुणों का कथन करके अपनी प्रशंसा करना
(*apane mũha se apane guṇõ kā kathana karake apanī praśaṁsā karanā*)
"to extol one's own virtues"

(3) का गुणगान करना
(kā guṇagāna karanā)
"to sing someone's praises"

(3a) किसी के गुणों का गीत गाने के समान वर्णन करके उसकी प्रशंसा करना
(kisī ke guṇõ kā gīta gāne ke samāna varṇana karake usakī praśaṁsā karanā)
"to praise someone by describing his virtues in the manner of singing a song"

(4) का बखान करना
(kā bakhāna karanā)
"to speak repeatedly of someone"

(4a) किसी के गुणों का प्रसन्नतापूर्वक बार-बार कथन करके उसकी प्रशंसा करना
(kisī ke guṇõ kā prasannatāpūrvaka bāra-bāra kathana karake usakī praśaṁsā karanā)
"to praise someone by repeatedly talking about his virtues"

(5) किसी की स्तुति करना
(kisī kī stuti karanā)
"to extol someone"

(5a) किसी की पूज्य-भाव से प्रशंसा करना
(kisī kī pūjya-bhāva se praśaṁsā karanā)
"to praise someone in venerable terms"

(6) किसी की वाह्-वाह् करना
(kisī kī vāha-vāha karanā)
"to applaud someone"

(6a) वाह्-वाह् शब्द कहकर किसी की प्रशंसा करना
(vāhavāha śabda kahakara kisī kī praśaṁsā karanā)
"to express one's admiration for someone by saying the words *vāhavāha*"

As the above noted paraphrases imply, the relationship between the generic activity denoted by the noun प्रशंसा (*praśaṁsā*) "praise" and its specific modalities can be expressed by means of the following diagram.

प्रशंसा
(*praśaṁsā*)

आत्मसंकीर्तन	आत्मश्लाघा	गुणगान	बखान	स्तुति	वाह्-वाह्
(*ātmasaṅkīrtana*)	(*ātmaślāghā*)	(*guṇagāna*)	(*bakhāna*)	(*stuti*)	(*vāhavāha*)

4.5. Now we would like to discuss the verb करना (*karanā*) "to do" in its function as a formative verb in conjuncts, that is, as a general concept of action, as mentioned in sub-section 2.3.2 and discussed at some length earlier in this section. In the following sub-sections we present more data to this end (while trying to avoid repetition as far as possible), and concentrate more specifically on the kinds of behavioral manifestations of concepts this verb represents as well as some other related matters.

4.5.1. To illustrate the function of करना (*karanā*) "to do" as a general concept of action with ANP's involving $[N_1]$ nouns, we give below a few sentences containing the occurrence of पर/से घृणा करना (*para/se ghṛṇā karanā*) "to despise someone; to hate".

(1) अब धर्म नहीं रहा...गुरुदीन ने नाक सिकोड़ कर जैसे किसी पर घृणा करते हुए कहा।
(*aba dharma nahī̃ rahā...gurudīna ne nāka sikoṛakara jaise kisī para ghṛṇā karate hue kahā*)
"Nowadays moral standards have declined", said Gurudin, wrinkling his nose as if he were despising someone."

(2) अपने अर्धचेतन मन में शिवप्रसाद उनसे इतनी घृणा करते थे कि आज तक उनका नाम तक जानने की इच्छा उन्होंने न प्रकट की थी।
(*apane ardhacetana mana mẽ śivaprasāda unase itanī ghṛṇā karate the ki āja taka unakā nāma taka jānane kī icchā unhõne na prakaṭa kī thī*).
"Shivaprasad hated him so much in his subconscious mind that he never manifested a desire to know his (that is, another person's) name."

In the first sentence there is a reference by the speaker to the subject-noun's gestural behavior, that is, his act of wrinkling his nose etc. by means of the expression नाक सिकोड़कर (*nāka sikoṛakara*) and verbal behavior, that is, his saying the sentence अब धर्म नहीं रहा (*aba dharma nahī̃ rahā*) "nowadays moral standards have declined". For the purpose of clarifying the relationship between the conjunct verb पर घृणा करना (*para ghṛṇā karanā*) "to despise" and its behavioral manifestations as expressed in this sentence, it can be paraphrased as follows in English.

> (I am saying that) Gurudin hates/despises him (that is, some other person not named in the context) (because he, that is, Gurudin) said (about him) while wrinkling his nose (which I, the speaker take as a gestural indication of Gurudin's feeling of hatred for that person) that moral standards have declined these days (an expression which I, the speaker take as a valid reason for Gurudin's despising that person).

In the second sentence there is a reference by the speaker to the subject-noun's not expressing any desire to know another person's name, which is also an instance of a specific behavioral manifestation of घृणा (*ghṛṇā*) "hatred", though a negative one. As far as the speaker is concerned, the subject-noun's behavior described in the above noted two examples, that is, wrinkling his nose and commenting upon the decline of moral standards [in (1)], and never manifesting any desire to know another person's name [in (2)] are behavioral manifestations of his (that is, the subject noun's) feeling of hatred for the persons referred to in these examples. Sentence (1) illustrates both gestural as well as verbal manifestation of "hatred", whereas example (2) implies only its gestural manifestation. It can thus be said that the verb करना (*karanā*) "to do" as a formative verb occurs in conjunct verbs as a general concept of action and refers to a variety of gestural and non-gestural (including verbal) modes of behavior. These modes of behavior are systematically interpreted by the native speakers of MSH as manifesting the concepts denoted by [N_1] nouns. As we shall try to explain in sub-section 4.7, these modes of behavior as involved in particular contexts of the occurrence of conjunct verbs form the basis of our renderings of these conjunct verbs into English in sections three onwards in the articles.

4.5.2. We have already discussed in sub-section 4.2.1 that all [Adj]'s occurring in करना (*karanā*) "to do" conjunct verbs refer to various states or conditions presupposed to be induced or brought into being by a variety of causes. The verb करना (*karanā*) "to do" in its function as a formative verb is a general concept of action [in Adj + करना (*karanā*) "to do" conjuncts] referring to the causal presuppositions of the concepts of states or conditions denoted by the [Adj]'s. A few sentences with the [Adj] प्रमाणित (*pramāṇita*) referring to the "inducement of factual or authoritative evidence in order to make something acceptable beyond a reasonable doubt" are reproduced below from article 59 of SSSH, volume I to prove this point.

(1) यह बात विज्ञान ने विशेष करके विद्युतशक्ति, चुम्बकशक्ति और आणविक रचना से प्रमाणित कर दी है।

(*yaha bāta vijñāna ne viśeṣa karake vidyuta śakti, cumbaka śakti aura āṇavika racanā se pramāṇita kara dī hai*)

"Science has conclusively proved this matter especially by means of electricity, magnetic power and atomic structure."

(2) बीरू बाबू ने रिक्शा खरीदने की रसीद दिखा कर रिक्शा पर अपना अधिकार प्रमाणित कर दिया।

(*bīrū bābū ne rikṣā kharīdane kī rasīda dikhākara rikṣā para apanā adhikāra pramāṇita kara diyā*)

"Biru Babu conclusively proved his claim to the rickshaw by showing the receipt for its purchase."

In both the examples, the verb करना)*karanā*) "to do" [occurring as कर देना (*kara denā*)] refers to whatever arguments, evidence or the like that are"adduced by way of proof or disproof of the genuineness, validity or truth" of बात (*bāta*) "matter under consideration" [in (1)] and अधिकार (*adhikāra*) "right of ownership" [in (2)] as may be implied in these contexts.

4.5.3. Having clarified the notion of the general concept of action denoted by the verb करना (*karanā*)) "to do" in conjunct verbs, we should state that our intention behind positing no limit as to what does or does not constitute the specific behavioral manifestation of a concept, was that (i) the conjunct verbs in MSH are "stable collocations" which tend to preserve their semantic content,[1] whereas (ii) their behavioral manifestations may undergo changes in the speech community. This can be easily seen from the major literary trends in MSH poetry and fiction which may be viewed as quests by poets and writers of fiction for re-alignment of changed stereotypes of the modes of behavior with the semantic content of linguistic concepts.[2] It is due to this property of the concepts denoted by [N_1]'s and [Adj]'s that we have called them "generalized concepts" [assumption (i), sub-section 4.1.]

As noted above, the verb करना (*karanā*) "to do" as a general concept of action represents the specific behavioral manifestations of concepts denoted by [N_1]'s and [Adj]'s which occur in ANP's forming conjuncts with it, and there is no limitation as to what does or does not constitute the behavioral manifestations of a concept. The fact remains, however, that [N_1]'s and [Adj]'s can be grouped together on the basis of the similarity in their behavioral manifestations represented by the verb करना (*karanā*) "to do". The following examples illustrate this point.

(1) किसी की प्रशंसा करना
(*kisī kī praśaṁsā karanā*)
"to praise someone"

(1a) कि .ी की प्रशंसा में कुछ कहना
(*kisī kī praśaṁsā meṁ kucha kzhanā*)
"to say something in praise of someone"

1. We owe this notion to Uriel Weinreich, "Problems in the Analysis of Idioms' in Jaan Puhvel (editor), *Substance and Structure of Language*, University of California Press (Berkeley and Los Angeles, 1969).

2. See for instance, Richard A. Williams' translation of Mohan Rakesh's short story *Gunāhe Belazzata* "Savorless Sins" to appear in *Mahfil*. In his introductory note to the translation, the translator tries to explain that Rakesh's technique essentially consists of presenting a conflict between जीवन (*jīvana*) "the life one would like to live" and जिन्दगी (*zindagī*) "the life one actually lives" in the life of the main character of the story.

(2) किसी की शिकायत करना
(kisī kī śikāyata karanā)
"to complain about someone"

(2a) शिकायत के स्वर में किसी के बारे में कुछ कहना
(śikāyata ke svara mẽ kisī ke bāre mẽ kucha kahanā)
"to say something about someone in a complaining tone"

(3) किसी बात पर आपत्ति करना
(kisī bāta para āpatti karanā)
"to object to something"

(3a) आपत्ति के स्वर में किसी बात के बारे में कुछ कहना
(āpatti ke svara mẽ kisī bāta ke bāre mẽ kucha kahanā)
"to say something about some matter in an objecting tone"

(4) किसी से प्रश्न करना
(kisī se praśna karanā)
"to ask someone a question"

(4a) किसी से प्रश्न के रूप में कुछ कहना
(kisī se praśna ke rūpa mẽ kucha kahanā)
"to say something to someone in the form of a question"

(5) किसी से आग्रह करना
(kisī se āgraha karanā)
"to urge someone"

(5a) किसी से आग्रह के स्वर में कुछ कहना
(kisī se āgraha ke svara mẽ kucha kahanā)
"to say something to someone in an urging tone"

(6) किसी का समर्थन करना
(kisī kā samarthana karanā)
"to support someone"

(6a) किसी के समर्थन में कुछ कहना
(kisī ke samarthana mẽ kucha kahanā)
"to say something in support of someone"

All the conjunct verbs listed above [that is, examples (1-6)] involve the manifest behavior of "saying something", as indicated by their respective paraphrases in examples (1a-6a). A categorization of [N_1]'s and [Adj]'s on the basis of similarity and difference in their behavioral manifestations needs to be worked out and, therefore, will not be discussed here.

4.6. Our fourth and fifth assumptions, referring to the [±process] occurrence of $[N_1]$'s involve certain aspects of the semantic complexity of these concepts as implied in the variety of sentences discussed by us in sub-section 3.6.6.

As our fourth assumption states, every [+process] occurrence of a term involves a reference to the speaker's application of a generalized concept denoted by an $[N_1]$ noun to the actual specific behavioral manifestation of it. The [-process] occurrence of an $[N_1]$ or [Adj] means that the speaker is not applying the term denoted by a generalized concept to its actual specific behavioral manifestation. All [-process] occurrences of $[N_1]$'s with करना (*karanā*) "to do", therefore, signify instantiation of those concepts by reference to their factual behavioral manifestations which the speaker knows for a fact to be a stereotype of one sort or an other. All the occurrences of [Adj]'s with the verb करना (*karanā*) "to do" are inherently [-process] because these adjectives refer to specific behavioral manifestations by signifying their resultant states or conditions. It, therefore, follows that while all [Adj]'s are [-process], the $[N_1]$'s, according to the feature specification of their occurrence as [+process], or [-process], can be grouped into three categories, that is, (i) $[N_1]$'s which are always [+process], (ii) $[N_1]$'s which are always [-process], and (iii) $[N_1]$'s which can be both [+process] and [-process].

We would now like to clarify the distinction between actual and factual behavioral manifestations as it is involved in the [+process] or [-process] feature specification of $[N_1]$ nouns. The sentence (1) below illustrates the [+process] occurrence of the $[N_1]$ noun अनुभव (*anubhava*) "experience, feeling", and the sentence (2) its [-process] occurrence.

(1) हम कभी-कभी अपने क्षुद्र स्वार्थों पर बड़े-बड़े आदर्शों का बलिदान करते समय गर्व का अनुभव करते हैं ।
(*hama kabhī-kabhī apane kṣudra svārthõ para baṛe-baṛe ādarśõ kā balidāna karate samaya garva kā anubhava karate hãĩ*)
"We sometimes take pride in sacrificing great ideals for petty self-interests."

(2) हम यह कहने में हमेशा गर्व अनुभव करते हैं कि हमारा अमरीका सिर्फ शक्तिशाली ही नहीं है, सिर्फ स्वतन्त्र ही नहीं है बल्कि सुन्दर भी है ।
(*hama yaha kahane mẽ hameśā garva anubhava karate hãĩ ki hamārā amarīkā sirpha śaktiśālī hī nahĩ hai, sirpha svatantra hī nahĩ hai balki sundara bhī hai*)
"We are always proud to say that our America is not only a powerful country, it is not only a free country, but it is also a beautiful country."

Sentence (1) can be paraphrased as follows :—

(1a) हम गर्व का अनुभव करते हुए कभी-कभी अपने क्षुद्र स्वार्थों पर बड़े-बड़े आदर्शों का बलिदान कर देते हैं।
(hama garva kā anubhava karate hue kabhī-kabhī apane kṣudra svārthõ para baṛe-baṛe ādarśõ kā balidāna kara dete hãĩ)
"We sometimes sacrifice great ideals for our petty self-interests, taking pride (in our acts)."

However, if the compound conjunct verb का बलिदान कर देना (*kā balidāna kara denā*) "to make a sacrifice" is substituted in (1a) by its simple counterpart का बलिदान करना (*kā balidāna karanā*), the sentence is rendered ungrammatical [as (1b) below] in the sense of (1a).

(1b) *हम गर्व का अनुभव करते हुए कभी-कभी अपने क्षुद्र स्वार्थों पर बड़े-बड़े आदर्शों का बलिदान करते हैं।
(**hama garva kā anubhava karate hue kabhī-kabhī apane kṣudra svārthõ para baṛe-baṛe ādarśõ kā balidāna karate hãĩ*)

Sentence (2) can similarly be paraphrased as follows :—

(2a) हम हमेशा गर्व अनुभव करते हुए यह कहते हैं कि. . . ।
(hama hameśā garva anubhava karate hue yaha kahate hãĩ ki...)
"We always say with a feeling of pride that..."

but the substitution of कहते हैं (*kahate hãĩ*) in (2a) by its compound counterpart कह देते हैं (*kaha dete hãĩ*), as indicated in (2b) below, renders the paraphrase ungrammatical.

(2b) *हम हमेशा गर्व अनुभव करते हुए यह कह देते हैं कि. . .।
(**hama hameśā garva anubhava karate hue yaha kaha dete hãĩ ki...*)

However, if गर्व अनुभव करते हुए (*garva anubhava karate hue*) "with a feeling of pride" is substituted by गर्व का अनुभव करते हुए (*garva kā anubhava karate hue*) "taking pride" in (2b), then the occurrence of कह देते हैं (*kaha dete hãĩ*) yields a grammatically well-formed sentence such as (2c).[1]

(2c) हम हमेशा गर्व का अनुभव करते हुए यह कह देते हैं कि. . . ।
(hama hameśā garva kā anubhava karate hue yaha kaha dete hãĩ ki...)
"We take pride in asserting that. . ."

We have tried to demonstrate above that there is a dependence between grammatically well-formed paraphrases of sentences (1) and (2)

1. The substitution of the compound verb by its simple counterpart in sentence (2c) also involves a change in its meaning. This fact is indicated in the English translation given under the sentence (2c).

and the occurrence of compound and simple verbs in the sentences containing these paraphrases and that this is true in the sense that the[+process] occurrence of अनुभव (*anubhava*) "experience, feeling" requires the occurrence of a compound verb in the paraphrases [as in sentence (1a)], and the [—process] occurrence of this noun requires the occurrence of a simple verb in the paraphrase [as in sentence (2a)]. Paraphrase (1a) of sentence (1) illustrates the speaker's reference to the actual behavioral manifestations of the [+process] occurrence of the noun अनुभव (*anubhava*) "experience, feeling" indicated by the compound conjunct verb का बलिदान कर देना (*kā balidāna kara denā*) "to make a sacrifice of". On the other hand, paraphrase (2a) of sentence (2) illustrates the speaker's reference to the factual behavioral manifestations of the [-process] occurrence of this noun indicated by the simple verb कहना (*kahanā*) "to say".

The occurrence or non-occurrence of compound verbs in the paraphrases is just one of the semantic distinctions involved in the [±process] specification of [N_1]'s. Another sort of distinction is discussed below by means of the illustration of the [±process] occurrence of the noun व्यवहार (*vyavahāra*) "customary use". Sentences (3) and (4) below illustrate the [+process] and [-process] occurrences respectively of this noun.

(3) बहुत से लोग झूठे बांटों का व्यवहार करके लोगों को ठगते हैं।
(*bahuta se loga jhūṭhe bā̃ṭõ kā vyavahāra karake logõ ko ṭhagate hãĩ*)
"Many people cheat others by using counterfeit weights (as a customary mode of cheating)."

(4) बहुत से लोग झूठे बांट व्यवहार करके लोगों को ठगते हैं।
(*bahuta se loga jhūṭhe bā̃ṭa vyavahāra karake logõ ko ṭhagate hãĩ*)
"(I know that) many people cheat others by using counterfeit weights."

Sentence (3) is related to sentence (3a).

(3a) बहुत से लोग लोगों को ठगने के लिये झूठे बांटों का व्यवहार करते हैं।
(*bahuta se loga logõ ko ṭhagane ke liye jhūṭhe bā̃ṭõ kā vyavahāra karate hãĩ*)
"Many people customarily make use of counterfeit weights (that is, actually use them as a means) for cheating others."

Similarly sentence (4) is related to sentences (4a) and (4b).

(4a) बहुत से लोग लोगों को ठगने के लिये झूठे बांट व्यवहार करते हैं।
(*bahuta se loga logõ ko ṭhagane ke liye jhūṭhe bā̃ṭa vyavahāra karate hãĩ*)
"Many people use counterfeit weights for the purpose of cheating others."

(4b) बहुत से लोग लोगों को ठगने में झूठे बांट व्यवहार करते हैं।
(bahuta se loga logõ ko ṭhagane mẽ jhūṭhe bā̃ṭa vyavahāra karate hãĩ)
"Many people employ counterfeit weights in cheating others."

whereas sentence (3) has no counterpart like (4b) of (4).

(3b) *बहुत से लोग लोगों को ठगने में झूठे बांटों का व्यवहार करते हैं।
*(*bahuta se loga logõ ko ṭhagane mẽ jhūṭhe bā̃ṭõ kā vyavahāra karate hãĩ)*

In other words, sentence (4) is an ambiguous sentence, that is, it can be either interpreted to mean that "some people achieve their end of cheating others by (the means of) making use of counterfeit weights" (4a), or that "making use of counterfeit weights is just one of the modes (employed by many people) in cheating others" (4b). On the other hand, "the act of cheating others" involved in their "(actual) customary use of counterfeit weights by many people", as indicated by sentences (3) and (3a), is an actual behavioral manifestation of the concept of "customary mode of behavior in the act of using something for some purpose".

It is also a property of the [-process] [N_1]'s which occur with the verb करना (*karanā*) "to do" that they resemble nouns which act as determinants in conjunct verbs, as discussed in sub-section 3.3.1. However, there is a subtle difference in the semantic characteristics of determinants discussed by us in sub-section 3.3.1 and the determinant-like functions of [N_1] nouns in their [-process] occurrence with the verb करना (*karanā*) "to do" in conjuncts. We give below a few sentences to illustrate this situation.

(5) उसके हृदय में भावों का तूफान उठ आया।
(usake hṛdaya mẽ bhāvõ kā tūphāna uṭha āyā)
"A storm of feelings arose in his mind."

(6) ईश्वर-प्रेमी जब लौकिक दुखों से पीड़ित होता है तब वह अपनी अवस्था में पूर्ण शान्ति का अनुभव करता है।
(īśvara premī jaba laukika dukhõ se pīṛita hotā hai taba vaha apanī avasthā mẽ pūrṇa śānti kā anubhava karatā hai)
"A godly person, even though he may be going through this-worldly pains, experiences a completely calm state of mind in that condition of his."

(7) एक विचित्र-सी शान्ति वह अनुभव कर रहे थे अपने अन्दर।
(eka vicitra-sī śānti vaha anubhava kara rahe the apane andara)
"He felt within himself a strange sort of quietude (at that time)."

(8) अलहना मां के आदेश का पालन करना जानता है, पर कठिनाई यह है कि विधाता इस काम में उसके विरुद्ध है ।
(*alahanā mā̃ ke ādeśa kā pālanā karanā jānatā hai, para kaṭhināī yaha hai ki vidhātā isa kāma mẽ usake viruddha hai*)
"Alahana knows how to carry out the order (that is, observe or live up to the directive) of his mother, but the difficulty is that the Almighty is against him in this matter."

(9) हमें भगवती त्रिपुर सुन्दरी का आदेश पालन करना चाहिये ।
(*hamẽ bhagavatī tripura sundarī kā ādeśa pālana karanā cāhiye*)
"It is expected (of us) that we should follow the directive of Bhagavati Tripura Sundari."

In sentence (5) the noun तूफान (*tūphāna*) "storm" occurs as a determinant of the intensity of भाव (*bhāva*) "emotional feelings". Thus the sentence can be paraphrased as (5a) below.

(5a) उसके हृदय में भाव तूफान की तरह उठ आये ।
(*usa ke hṛdaya mẽ bhāva tūphāna kī taraha uṭha āye*)
"Feelings arose in his mind like a storm."

On the other hand, the nouns अनुभव (*anubhava*) "experience, feeling" and पालन (*pālana*) "observance" as [-process] [N_1]'s in sentences (7) and (9) (in contrast to their respective [+process] occurrences in (6) and (8)] occur as the determinants of "the consciousness of the subjective state of quietude" on the part of the subject-noun, as opposed to "someone's mentally responding to a state of vicissitude calmly" [sentence (6)], and as "someone's doing something mechanically or reflexively" as a valid instance of "doing something", as opposed to "someone's doing something consciously or non-reflexively" [sentence (8)]. In other words, a person's "composed appearance" implied in sentence (7) is a determinant of the fact of his being "mentally in a state of quietude". Similarly "mechanically or reflexively doing something" as implied in sentence (9) is construed to be a determinant of the concept of "observance of something."

Though we are not in a position to discuss any further the implications of the [±process] occurrence of [N_1]'s as well as of the necessity of our saying that all [Adj]'s are inherently [-process] at this state of our investigation of the language, we would like to say that the phenomena have been variously illustrated in the articles, especially in section three onwards.

4.7. We have already stated in sub-section 1.5 that instances of the occurrences of all the करना (*karanā*) "to do" conjunct verbs reported in section three onwards in the articles have also been rendered into English. It is, therefore, necessary to explain the distinction between the definitions of $[N_1]$'s and [Adj]'s in section one of the articles and the renderings of the conjunct verbs in English in section three onwards.

Our renderings of the individual occurrences of conjunct verbs in section 3 onwards of the articles are based on assumptions 1-5, as stated in sub-section 4.1 and discussed in this section. While our definitions of the generic as well as specific meanings of $[N_1]$'s and [Adj]'s are so formulated that they are independent of the occurrence of their ANP's in करना (*karanā*) "to do" conjunct verbs, our rendering of the individual conjunct verbs in English are not. We may also point out that the latter (that is, the English renderings of conjunct verbs) are derivable from the former (that is, from the generic as well as specific meanings), but the reverse does not hold true. For the purpose of explaining this process of deriving the meaning of the individual occurrence of a conjunct verb from the generic as well as specific meanings of its $[N_1]$ or [Adj], we reproduce below a few sentences illustrating the occurrence of the conjunct verb का ध्यान करना (*kā dhyāna karanā*) from article 65 of SSSII, volume I. Each sentence is followed by an approximate paraphrase of the conjunct in MSH which is also translated in English.

(1) का ध्यान करना
(*kā dhyāna karanā*)
"to concentrate on"

सज्जन मौसम से ज्यादा शास्त्री जी की बातों का ध्यान कर रहा है। शास्त्री जी की बातों से आज उसके मन की अनेक शंकाएं दूर हुई हैं।
(*sajjana mausama se jyādā śāstrī jī kī bātõ kā dhyāna kara rahā hai. śāstrī jī kī bātõ se āja usake mana kī aneka śaṅkāẽ dūra huī haĩ*)
"Sajjan is concentrating more on Shastri ji's talks than on the weather. Today, by means of Shastri ji's words, several of his mental doubts have been removed."

(1a) ध्यानपूर्वक सुनना
(*dhyānapūrvaka sunanā*)
"to concentrate on, to listen to someone attentively"

(2) का ध्यान करना
(*kā dhyāna karanā*)
"to be musing over"

. . . कदाचित् प्रतापी जयित्र चन्द्र के अपार धैर्य और साहस का ध्यान कर रही थीं।
(*. . .kadācit pratāpī jayitra candra ke apāra dhairya aura sāhasa kā dhyāna kara rahī thī*)
". . .perhaps (she) was musing over the limitless fortitude and courage of the splendid Jayitra Chandra."

(2a) किसी के अपार धैर्य और साहस की घटनाओं के ध्यान में खो जाना
(kisī ke apāra dhairya aura sāhasa kī ghaṭanāõ ke dhyāna mẽ kho jānā)
"to be musing over, to loose oneself while thinking about someone"

(3) का ध्यान करना
(kā dhyāna karanā)
"to observe, to follow carefully"

इसका परिणाम यह होता है कि वह निवास की अनिश्चितता के कारण स्वास्थ्य सम्बन्धी नियमों का ध्यान नहीं कर पाती ।
(isakā pariṇāma yaha hotā hai ki vaha nivāsa kī aniścitatā ke kāraṇa svāsthya sambandhī niyamõ kā dhyāna nahī̃ kara pātī)
"The result is that because of the uncertainty of the home, (the people) are not able to carefully follow the rules regarding good health."

(3a) स्वास्थ्य सम्बन्धी नियमों पर ध्यान पूर्वक चल पाना
(svāsthya sambandhī niyamõ para dhyānapūrvaka cala pānā)
"to follow carefully the rules of health"

All the above noted paraphrases of the conjunct verb का ध्यान करना (*kā dhyāna karanā*) represent some of the behavioral manifestations which can serve to instantiate the generalized concept of ध्यान (*dhyāna*), the definition of the specific meaning of which is reproduced below.

> ध्यान (*dhyāna*) refers to the state of intellectualization or the exercise of intellect (i.e., the power or faculty of knowing as distinguished from the power to feel and to will), and is, therefore, esoterically applied to indicate a mental state in which one takes into the mind or dwells upon any object of thought in order to give it an intellectual or rational form or content, or intellectually absorb its significance. In its popular usage it refers to the act of pursuing one's thoughts with complete absorption (often as in a reverie).

A comparison of the MSH paraphrases of the various occurrences of the conjunct verb का ध्यान करना (*kā dhyāna karanā*) as well as of the English translation of these paraphrases with the English renderings of the individual occurrences of this conjunct verb reveals a remarkaable similarity between them. Each paraphrase represents in a summary fashion a statement of the behavioral manifestations of the concept as implied by the verb करना (*karanā*) "to do" in the individual contexts of the occurrence of the noun ध्यान (*dhyāna*), and our renderings of the individual occurrences of the conjunct verb in English are in fact our approximations of the MSH paraphrases as given above in terms of [Adv+V] sentences, as we implied in the sentences just illustrated.

However, there is another kind of difference between the definitions of the generic as well as specific meanings of [N_1]'s and [Adj]'s in section one of the articles and the English renderings of their conjunct verbs in section three onwards. While formulating our definitions in section one of the articles we employ English as a sort of metalanguage, whereas no such intention is implied in the English renderings of the individual occurrences of the conjunct verbs in section three onwards of the articles.

5. Present state of MSH lexicography

5.1. In this section we will confine our comments to an assessment of the present state of MSH lexicography and some related problems without going into the history of its development. In doing so we will particularly concentrate on taking note of the manner in which nouns and adjectives occurring in conjunct verbs are handled in some of the well-known monolingual encyclopedic dictionaries including some studies dealing with synonyms in the language.

5.2. For the purpose of discussing the technique by which nouns and adjectives have been handled in MSH dictionaries, we reproduce in several sub-sections the entries for the nouns प्रशंसा (*praśaṁsā*) "praise", सराहना (*sarāhanā*) "appreciation" and तारीफ (*tārīpha*) "liking", as given in *Mānaka Hindī Koṣa* (hereafter abbreviated MHK), and deal with them individually.

5.2.1. MHK gives the following two definitions of the noun प्रशंसा (*praśaṁsā*) "praise".

1. प्रसन्नतापूर्वक किसी के अच्छे गुणों या कार्यों का किया जाने वाला उल्लेख जिससे समाज में उसका आदर तथा प्रतिष्ठा बढ़ती हो।
(*prasannatāpūrvaka kisī ke acche guṇõ yā kāryõ kā kiyā jānevālā ullekha jisase samāja mẽ usakā ādara tathā pratiṣṭhā baṛhatī ho*)
"Favorable mention of someone's good qualities or deeds which lends him more respect and eminence in the society"

2. प्रसन्न होकर यह कहना कि चीज बहुत अच्छी है, तथा गुण सम्पन्न है।
(*prasanna hokara yaha kahanā ki cīja bahuta acchī hai, tathā guṇa-sampanna hai*)
"Expressing one's pleasure about something by saying that it is good and possesses good qualities"

MHK has no examples of the occurrence of this noun in specific contexts. We, therefore, reproduce below two MSH contexts of the occurrence of this noun from article 2, SSSH, volume I, the first in the sense of the first definition of MHK, and the second in the sense of the second definition.

(1) उन दिनों नैषधकार महाकवि हर्ष का बड़ा सम्मान था। वे थे भी सम्मान के योग्य। महाराज उनकी बड़ी प्रशंसा किया करते थे।
(*una dinõ naiṣadhakāra mahākavi harṣa kā baṛā sammāna thā. ve the bhī sammāna ke yogya. mahārāja unakī baṛī praśaṁsā kiyā karate the*)
"In those days the great poet Harsha, the author of Naishadha, was very much respected. He was worthy of that respect. The emperor used to admire him very much."

(2) इन गुणों से मुग्ध होकर अनेक कवियों ने उनकी मुक्त कंठ से प्रशंसा की।
(*ina guṇõ se mugdha hokara aneka kaviyõ ne unakī mukta kaṇṭha se praśaṁsā kī*)
"Entranced by these virtues many poets lauded him."

A qualification of the paraphrase of the meanings of the noun by the expressions प्रसन्नतापूर्वक (*prasannatāpūrvaka*) "favorably" and प्रसन्न होकर (*prasanna hokara*) "on being pleased" in the two definitions of MHK, while being adequate enough to cover the meaning of the noun as it occurs in the above noted two contexts, prevents at the same time the application of both definitions to a variety of contexts of its occurrence in sentences of the language. We give below two examples of the occurrence of this noun not covered by either of the definitions in MHK.

(3) . . . किसान बनिये के पैरों से लिपट कर बोला, लक्ष्मी नारायण जी, खूब खाइये, जी भरकर खाइये। हे धर्मावतार, जो कुछ है, आपका ही तो है, आप बड़े आदमी हैं। . . . बनिया अपनी प्रशंसा सुनकर कुप्पा हो गया।
(*. . .kisāna baniye ke pairõ se lipaṭakara bolā, lakṣmī nārāyaṇa jī, khūba khāiye, jī bharakara khāiye. he dharmāvatāra, jo kucha hai, āpakā hī to hai. āpa baṛe ādamī hãī. . . .baniyā apanī praśaṁsā sunakara kuppā ho gayā*)
"The farmer touching the feet of the Baniya said, "Oh you the lord of wealth, eat as much as you can to your fill. Oh you, the incarnation of Dharma, whatever I have is yours. You are a great man...On hearing his praises the Baniya swelled up like a balloon."

(4) और फिर स्वयं उनकी प्रशंसा न करके आप उनकी चीजों की प्रशंसा कीजिये, उनकी रुचि की सराहना कीजिये, और फिर भले ही कवियों की अतिशयोक्ति का भी उल्लंघन करते हुए कहिये . . . ।

(*aura phira svayaṁ unakī praśaṁsā na karake āpa unakī cīzẽ kī praśaṁsā kījiye, unakī ruci kī sarāhanā kījiye, aura phira bhale hī kavizõ kī atiśayokti kā bhī ullaṅghana karate hue kahiye...*)
"And then rather than praising him you should admire his possessions, express appreciation for his good taste and going beyond the exaggeration of the poets you may say..."

The above noted two instances of the occurrence of the noun प्रशंसा (*praśaṁsā*) make reference to motivation of the subject noun other than those contained in the two definitions of MHK, that is, lavishing praises upon someone in order to mislead him. Our definition of the meaning of this noun as contained in section one of article 2 in SSSH, volume I encompasses all the known context types of the occurrence of the noun.

5.2.2. Curiously enough the noun सराहना (*sarāhanā*) "appreciation" is quickly dismissed in MHK by giving its MSH equivalents तारीफ (*tārīpha*) "liking" and प्रशंसा (*praśaṁsā*) "praise". Therefore nothing can be said about the treatment of this noun in MHK.

5.2.3. The noun तारीफ (*tārīpha*) has received somewhat longer treatment in MHK. We reproduce below its five definitions as given in MHK.

1. लक्षणों आदि से युक्त परिभाषा
(*lakṣaṇõ ādi se yukta paribhāṣā*)
"a definition embodying the characteristics (of something)"

2. उक्त प्रकार की परिभाषा से युक्त वर्णन या विवरण
(*ukta prakāra kī paribhāṣā se yukta varṇana yā vivaraṇa*)
"a description involving such a definition"

3. प्रशंसा (*praśaṁsā*) "praise", श्लाघा, (*ślāghā*) "applause"

4. प्रशंसनीय काम या बात
(*praśaṁsanīya kāma yā bāta*)
"any commendable episode or deed"

5. विशिष्टता, जैसे : यही तो आप में तारीफ है।
(*viśiṣṭatā, jaise: yahī to āpa mẽ tārīpha hai*)
"peculiarity, uniqueness, such as in: such is the uniqueness in you."

Our search for the contexts of the occurrence of this noun in MSH texts in the sense of definitions (1) and (2) has so far met with no success. We are, on the other hand, aware of the fact that the noun is used in Urdu in the sense of definitions (1) and (2) as given in MHK. But since the meaning of the noun is not set forth in MHK by means of paraphrases, we must conclude that this work fails to characterize properly the meaning of this noun also.

The above noted discussion of the treatment of three nouns प्रशंसा (*praśaṁśā*) "praise", सराहना (*sarāhanā*) "appreciation" and तारीफ (*tāripha*) "liking" in MHK, which is probably the best of the available dictionaries of MSH, speaks for itself. It also reveals some of the prejudices under which MSH lexicography is belaboring. We will deal with them in the next sub-section.

5.3. In view of the present state of MSH lexicography, there exists no strong trend towards the study of synonyms in the language. Nevertheless, significant work has been done in this area by Varmma (1957), (1959) and (1968). Another group of works, that is, Pal (1964), Jain (1966), Shivnath (1968) and Aruna (1968), though not directly concerned with the study of synonyms in MSH, are useful in their own right and are worth noting here. All these studies, in addition to being contributions valuable in their respective areas of MSH lexicography, can be regarded as indicators of the directions that the lexicographic study of the language should take.

The task of determining similarities and differences in the meanings of synonyms in a language is not always an easy one, especially in the case of MSH where, as we have illustrated above, the lexicographic tradition is not yet sufficiently strong and mature. This problem is further compounded by the nature of the lexical stock of MSH. It is a well-known fact that the lexical stock of MSH belongs to three different strata on the basis of its origin, that is, (i) the *tatsama* stratum representing borrowings from Sanskrit, (ii) the *tadbhava* stratum representing the lexicon inherited from the various stages of pre-modern Indo-Aryan, and (iii) borrowings from various known sources. Another category of lexicon is labelled *deśaja* which includes words belonging to unidentifiable sources and words of native origin as well as onomatopoetic words. This problem is further complicated by the recent attempts by the various Institutions and Agencies of the Government of India to coin technical and scientific terminology in order to facilitate the translation and writing of technical works in the language. Because of this situation, we believe it would be unfair to critically evalute the above-mentioned works. We, therefore, propose to limit ourselves to mentioning a few important relevant tendencies present in these works, especially in three studies of the late Ramchandra Varmma.

Varmma (1957), (1959) and (1968), if read in a sequence, very clearly indicate the author's concern with the standardization in the semantic usages of words in MSH. With this end in mind the author not only describes the meanings of words currently in use, but also goes to a considerable length in suggesting what words or expressions can be used as equivalents of certain words and expressions in English. A quick look at Varmma's works reveals that he has two distinct notions of the standardization of semantic usages of MSH words, that is, (i) from the point of view of the semantic structure of MSH itself, and (ii) from the point of view of the translation equivalents of these words in English. The first notion clearly falls within the purview of the lexicographer, whereas the second strictly belongs to the language planner. By this statement we do not mean to imply that the lexicographical investigation of MSH as well as its modernization by means of making available in it words and expressions comparable to English cannot be carried on simultaneously. We only wish to state that lexicographical study of MSH, or more specifically the study of its semantic structure, should not be made subservient to the requirement of its modernization by a lexicographer as Varmma has done. Varmma's predilection for modernization of MSH, which often takes precedence over lexicographical matters, is an important shortcoming in his three works.

Another noticeable tendency in Varmma (1957), (1959) and (1968) is the author's almost complete neglect of words of Perso-Arabic origin. Throughout, the author refers to such words by saying that, for example, इस्तेमाल (*istemāla*) "use" and तारीफ (*tārīpha*) "liking" etc. are used in a sense very similar to प्रयोग (*prayoga*) "suitable use" and प्रशंसा (*praśaṁsā*) "praise" respectively. Such statements could mean that either Varmma favors a puritanical view biased towards words of the *tatsama* stratum or treats words of Perso-Arabic origin as free-variants of their counterparts borrowed from Sanskrit since they belong to different strata of the lexicon of MSH. There are adherents as well as opponents of both these views. The consequence of such a tendency is that an adherence to the second view also leads one into believing that the meaning difference among synonymous words belonging to different strata of the lexicon of the language, if any, must be sought extra-linguistically. It is interesting to note here that some scholars have attempted to study the "language problems" in India as they pertain to MSH believing that there are no linguistically characterizable differences in the meanings of MSH lexical items which belong to different strata of its lexicon. One such study is Gupta and Gumperz (1968). In the next sub-section, we briefly comment on the MSH data presented in this short essay.

5.4 At the outset we must say that we are not concerned with the theory propounded by Gupta and Gumperz (1968), nor have we any interest in their conclusions regarding the "language problems" and "communication and control" in India. This short essay represents a popular belief concerning MSH held by linguists, pedagogists, as well as social scientists. Our sole interest, therefore, lies in looking upon this essay as a representative example of the existing scientific folklore of MSH about which not much has appeared in print. We, therefore, should clarify some of the misunderstandings as to the nature of lexicon of the language, and thus clear the way for its study in depth.

> The authors state the aim of their essay in the following terms. This essay explores the problem by examining the linguistic policies and practices of twentieth-century language societies in the North Indian state of Uttar Pradesh. We shall attempt to demonstrate the close interdependence between communication and political process by showing how the policies and activities of these interest groups both affect internal communication channels and are in turn affected by them.

After discussing the identity of the various interest groups concerned with MSH as well as their tendencies, the authors conclude as follows.

> In this sense, the Hindi scholars have interpreted the task of language development as being synonymous with increasing classicalization. But classicalization implies that the literary language diverges sharply from the common speeches, thus causing an increasing separation between the media of elite communication and mass comprehension. Evidently, the Hindi scholars are less concerned with standardizing the language for popular use than for retaining its purity from the contamination of the outside influences. Hence the policy of elitist sanctity has been of greater salience to their conception of language planning than the policy of extension of mass communication.

In order to prove that such is the case, the authors present some data with their comments. We reproduce below that data.

> Here are some examples of the new literary style. Items 1 and 2 are taken from signboards intended for the public. Item 3 is from the text of the Indian Constitution as given in the Government of India, Ministry of Law, Manual of Election Law. In each case *a* gives the official text, *b* the English translation, and *c* an approximate equivalent in the colloquial educated style.

Item 1

a. धूम्रपान वर्जित है।
(*dhūmrapāna varjita hai*)

b. smoking prohibited

c. सिगरेट पीना मना है।
(*sigareṭa pīna manā hai*)

Item 2

a. बिना आज्ञा प्रवेश निषेध।
(*binā ājñā praveśa niṣedha*)

b. entrance prohibited without permission

c. बिना आज्ञा अन्दर जाना मना है।
(*binā ājñā andara jānā manā hai*)

Item 3

a. राष्ट्रपति का निर्वाचन एक ऐसे निर्वाचक गण के सदस्य करेंगे जिसमें
(*rāṣṭrapati kā nirvācana eka aise nirvācaka gaṇa ke sadasya karẽge jisamẽ*)

b. the president's election will be done by the electors chosen to include

c. राष्ट्रपति का चुनाव एक ऐसे चुने हुए सदस्य करेंगे जिसमें
(*rāṣṭrapati kā cunāva eka aise cune hue sadasya karẽge jisamẽ*)

a. (k) संसद के दोनों सदनों के निर्वाचित सदस्य तथा
(*saṁsada ke donõ sadanõ ke nirvācita sadasya tathā*)

b. (a) the elected members of both houses of parliament and

c. (k) संसद की दोनों सभाओं के चुने हुए सदस्य और
(*saṁsada kī donõ sabhāõ ke cune hue sadasya aura*)

a. (kh) राज्यों की विधान सभाओं के निर्वाचित सदस्य होंगे
(*rājyõ kī vidhāna sabhāõ ke nirvācita sadasya hõge*)

b. (b) the elected members of the lower houses of state legislatures will be

c. (kh) राज्यों की विधान सभाओं के चुने हुए सदस्य होंगे
(*rājyõ kī vidhāna sabhāõ ke cune hue sadasya hõge*)

We have discussed the meaning differences between the noun निषेध (*niṣedha*) and the adjectives वर्जित (*varjita*) and मना (*manā*) in article 98, SSSH, volume I. Therefore, we would like to suggest that the MSH sentences given under item (1) sentence (a) is correctly translated by the authors, sentence (c) simply means "No smoking", and item (2) sentence (a) means "Entrance without permission is forbidden" and sentence (c) "Do not enter without permission".

The item (3) in this essay is more interesting because it displays an almost complete lack of understanding of the meanings of the words treated by the authors in it as free-variants of each other. For instance, निर्वाचन (*nirvācana*) refers to the process of election (as defined in the Constitution) whereas its colloquial counterpart चुनाव (*cunāva*) as suggested by the authors can mean both "election" as well as "selection". Similarly, निर्वाचित (*nirvācita*) means "elected" and its suggested colloquial counterpart चुने हुए (*cune hue*) can mean "elected, selected, (hand) picked" etc. The choice of MSH terms in the Constitution is not made merely for "technical reasons" alone. It is also governed by the semantic distinctions involved in these words. The conjoining particles (*tathā*) in MSH is a close equivalent of "as well as" in English, and if replaced by और (*aura*) "and" in the context noted above as contended by the authors, would destroy the intention of the Constitution which by these clauses lays down the process by which the election of a president in India is supposed to take place.

The existence of differences in the meanings of the so-called free-variants of Gupta and Gumperz (1968) does not, however, invalidate the central issue, that is, the study of the semantic complexity of the specific terms of Sanskritic origin as opposed to their generic counterparts in the "colloquial style". Therefore, without going into several other of the theoretical as well as factual misconceptions of this essay, we would like to say that there are some additional aspects of the semantic complexity of nouns and adjectives belonging to the *tatsama* stratum as opposed to the *tadbhava* cum Perso-Arabic strata in the lexicon of MSH, on the basis of which the speakers of the language choose synonyms from these two categories. Since this problem involves all the lexicons including the nouns and adjectives occurring in conjunct verbs, it would be more appropriate to discuss it elsewhere. Therefore, we conclude this sub-section by saying that the "interdependence between communication and political process" as demonstrated by Gupta and Gumperz (1968) is not a creation of the "interest groups", but rather based on some inherent aspects of the semantic complexity of the various strata of the lexicons of MSH. While we do not want to condone the failure on the part of the MSH scholars to explain the semantic complexity of the two strata of the lexicon of the language, we cannot help observing that the separation (that is, free variation) between "the media of elite communication (based on the *tatsama* stratum) and mass communication (based on the *tadbhava* cum Perso-Arabic strata) as posited by the authors of this essay is, thus, a logical extension of the scientific folklore of MSH.

5.5. A discussion of the semantic complexity of conjunct verbs and other related matters from the point of view of Indo-Aryan theories of meaning would have been appropriate in this "Introduction". But we have avoided any discussion of these theories for several important reasons. It is true that such discussion has already taken place in several studies, but most of it merely aims at bringing out "in a systematic form the linguistically relevant views on the different aspects of meaning given by various schools of thought in ancient India".[1] We concur with Murray B. Emeneau who states that

> Certainly in one other slowly awakening department of linguistics, that concerned with meaning, the West still has something to learn from India. There grammarians, literary theoreticians, and philosophers were all concerned with problems of meaning, and much was thought and written on the subject. Of this the West is for all practical linguistic purposes innocent. The Hindu treatises are in a difficult style, and a few in the West will be qualified to deal with them, as Sanskritists, philosophers, and linguistic scholars. Yet the results are likely to be worth the effort.[2]

but we must observe that the research on Indo-Aryan theories of meaning has so far not gone beyond some very crude correlation of them with modern theories. In view of the existence of this situation, we believe this "Introduction" is not a proper forum for initiating the sort of investigation that is necessary; although, we must observe, our discussion of the semantic complexity of conjunct verbs would have substantially gained from such an investigation.

We conclude this "Introduction" by quoting a part of the Preface of Betty Heimann (1951) as her remarks concerning nouns in Sanskrit are equally valid in the study of the semantic complexity of nouns and adjectives in MSH. We also believe that these passages succinctly and vividly portray our difficulties in describing the semantic structure of the language.

> From the very concreteness of Sanskrit linguistic expressions there radiate widely divergent meanings, and more divergent meanings in fact than in any other Indo-European language. The more dynamic the character of a language, the greater the impetus for such radiation, i.e., for divergency of the mean-

1. This is essentially the view taken by K. Kunjunni Raja, *Indian Theories of Meaning*, The Adyar Library and Research Centre (Madras, 1963).
2. Murray B. Emeneau, "India and Linguistics", *Journal of the American Oriental Society*, Volume 75 (1955) page 151. Since then a number of studies concerning the The Indo-Aryan philosophies of language and meaning have already appeared. They are described in J.F. Staal, "Sanskrit Philosophy of Language' in Thomas A. Sebeok (editor), *Current Trends in Linguistics*, Volume 5, Linguistics in South Asia, Mouton (The Hague and Paris, 1969).

ings derived. In the search for an adequate rendering of Sanskrit philosophical texts these principles have all to be kept in mind: the fundamental concreteness, the basic dynamics, the resultant ambiguity, and on top of it the necessary congruence of the term in question with the specific contexts in which it is introduced. The complex factors, their different valuation, or neglect of one of them, account for the great divergency of translation, i.e., interpretations.

After having completed the following monograph in 1945 I was fortunate enough once more to spend some years of study and teaching in the East itself. It has taught me that also modern Eastern students have to be reminded of the creative nature of their languages and to revitalize their terminology. They, too, have consciously to revive their abstract and stagnant use of terms by retracing the meanings from the original productive and concrete roots.

The SSSH is a first attempt of its kind. Therefore, we may only hope that we have made some contribution towards making MSH more accessible to the scholarly world than it has been so far.

BIBLIOGRAPHY OF WORKS CITED IN THE "INTRODUCTION"

Aruna, Sarnam Singh Sharma, *Hindī kī Tadbhava Śabdāvalī*, College Book Depot (Jaipur, 1968).

Bahl, Kali Charan, *A Reference Grammar of Hindi*, (The University of Chicago, 1967). Mimeographed.

— "Panjabi" in Thomas A. Sebeok (editor), *Current Trends in Linguistics*, Volume 5, Linguistics in South Asia, Mouton (The Hague and Paris, 1969).

— "On the Present State of Modern Rajasthani Grammar", *Paramparā*, Journal of Rajasthani Research Institute, Chaupasani, District Jodhpur, Rajasthan, India Volume 33-34 (1972), pages 1-76.

— Kali Charan and Sinha, Anjani K., "Some Aspects of the Semantic Complexity of *karanā* Conjunct Verbs in Hindi" in Edgar J. Polome (editor), *Studies in honor of Professor Archibald A. Hill* (in press).

Bahri, Hardev, *Hindi Semantics*, The Bharati Press (Allahabad, 1959).

Bailey, T. Grahame, *Teach Yourself Urdu*, J.R. Firth and A.H. Harley (editors) (London, 1956).

Burton-Page, J., "Compound and Conjunct Verbs in Hindi", *Bulletin of the School of Oriental and African Studies*, The University of London Volume 19 (1957), pages 469-478.

Dimshits, Z.M., *Hindī Vyākaraṇa kī Rūparekhā*, Rajkamal Prakashan (Delhi, 1966).

Gilchrist, John Borthwick, *A Grammar of the Hindustani Language*, (Calcutta, 1796). Reprinted by The Scolar Press Limited (Menston, 1970).

Gupta, Jyotindra Das and Gumperz, John J., "Language, Communication and Control in North India" in Joshua A. Fishman, Charles A. Ferguson and Jyotindra Das Gupta (Editors), *Language Problems of Developing Nations*, John Wiley and Sons Inc. (New York, 1968).

Guru, Kamata Prasad, *Hindī Vyākaraṇa*, Kāśī Nāgarī Pracāriṇī Sabhā, (Kāśī, 1922).

Hacker, Paul, "On the Problem of a Method for Treating the Compound and Conjunct Verbs in Hindi", *Bulletin of the School of Oriental and African Studies*, The University of London, Volume 24 (1961), pages 484-516.

Heimann, Betty, *The Significance of Prefixes in Sanskrit Philosophical Terminology*, Royal Asiatic Society Monograph, Volume XXV, (London, 1951).

Jain, Bhaidyal, *Hindī Śabda-racanā*, Bharatiya Gyana Pitha, (Vārānasī, 1966).

Kachru, Yamuna, *An Introduction to Hindi Syntax*, (Department of Linguistics, University of Illinois, Urbana, 1966). Mimeographed.

Kellogg, Rev. S.H., *A Grammar of the Hindi Language*, Routledge and Kegan Paul Ltd. (London, 1875). Reprinted (1955).

Paul, Keshavram, *Hindi mẽ prayukta Śabdõ mẽ Arthaparivartana*, Praci Prakashan (Meerut, 1964).

Platts, John T., *A Grammar of the Hindustani or Urdu Language*, Oxford University Press (London, 1878). Reprinted by Munshiram Manoharlal (Delhi, 1967).

Sharma, Aryendra, *A Basic Grammar of modern Hindi*, Government of India, Ministry of Education and Scientific Research(Delhi, 1958).,

Shivanath, *Hindī Bhāṣā kā Arthatāttvika Vikāsa*, Hindi Sahitya Sammelana, (Prayāga, 1968).

Tiwari, Bholanath, *Hindī Muhavirā Kośa*, Kitaba Mahal, (Allahabad, 1964).

Varmma, Ramchandra, *Śubda-Sādhanā*, Sahitya Ratna Mala Karyalaya (Banares, 1957).

— (editor), *Mānaka Hindī Kośa*, Hindi Sahitya Sammelana (Prayāga, 1965).

— *Śabdārthaka Jñāna Kośa*, Sabda Loka Prakashana (Vārānasī, 1959).

— *Śabdārtha Darśana*, Racana Prakashana, (Allahabad, 1968).

Verma, Manindra K., (reviewer), Kachru, Yamuna, *An Introduction to Hindi Syntax*, (Department of **Linguistics**, University of Illinois, Urbana 1966). Mimeographed, in *Indian Linguistics*, Volume 32.2, pages 156-164.

1. प्रयोग, उपयोग, व्यवहार, इस्तेमाल

1. **प्रयोग, उपयोग, व्यवहार, इस्तेमाल** are synonymous nouns meaning use of a thing (or a person) as a means to an end. प्रयोग implies suitability, उपयोग refers to the use of an object for a purpose other than that for which it is primarily meant, व्यवहार stresses customary, habitual use, and इस्तेमाल indicates nothing more than the idea of use. In careful writings इस्तेमाल occurs in contexts where the distinctions indicated by प्रयोग, उपयोग and व्यवहार are to be definitely avoided.

2.1. All these nouns in .. में ले- / ला - / आ - are synonymous with काम which indicates the use of an object as a means to an end implying that the object serves the purpose though it may not be in the right or desirable form, shape, quality or quantity.

2.2. Adverbials followed by के लिए, में, and पर refer to the end which the object of use is a means, and those followed by के रूप में, के बतौर, की तरह etc. to the means (i.e., the object of use) itself. के लिए denotes the intended result, में either refers to the mode of use or singles out the object of use from among the many which collectively serve as a means. पर refers to an end which itself is a means to an end implied in the sentence context. Only के लिए and में permit infinitives (as embedded sentences) and the rest of the postpositions do not.

2.3. None of the nouns take the plural. These nouns are ±process, and form ANP with का.

3. **का के लिए प्रयोग कर—"to use"**

परन्तु शिकार करने अथवा मछली पकड़ने के लिए कुछ उपकरणों की आवश्यकता होती है। इन उपकरणों में धनुष-बाण तथा जाल बहुत प्रमुख हैं । अनेक जन-जातियां इस काम के लिए भाले का भी प्रयोग करती हैं। (मानव, 450)

का के लिए उपयोग कर—"to make use of"

शिकार करने के लिए आदि मानव भाले, तीर-धनुष, फन्दों आदि का उपयोग करते हैं। (मानव, 452)

का के लिए व्यवहार कर—"to use, to make use of customarily"

बहुत से लोग झूठे बांटों का व्यवहार करके लोगों को ठगते हैं। (भारत, 34)

In the above sentence —झूठे बांटों का व्यवहार करके "by using counterfeit weights" being itself a means to an end, i.e., cheating, the adverb with के लिए is dropped. The sentence can also occur in the following form:

बहुत से लोग लोगों को ठगने के लिये झूठे बांटों का व्यवहार करते हैं।

का के लिए इस्तेमाल कर—"to use"

इस मिट्टी को अच्छी तरह मिलाने के लिये यह अच्छा होता है कि एक पगमिल का इस्तेमाल किया जाये। (ईंट, 78)

इस तरह से बना हुआ विशेष गुणकारी तेल, हर रोज इस्तेमाल करके बाल गिरने की मुसीबत से आप छुटकारा पाइये। (धर्मयुग, 40)

का में प्रयोग कर—"to employ, to use"

इन स्थानीय योजनाओं को क्रियान्वित करने में स्थानीय साधनों का ही प्रयोग किया जाता है। (सामुदा, 17)

का में उपयोग कर—"to make use of"

स्वयं वेश्याओं ने जो धन एकत्र कर रक्खा है उसका भी उपयोग नई जीवन परिस्थिति के निर्माण में किया जा सकता है। (नदु, 40)

का में व्यवहार कर—"to make use of, to employ"

प्रकाश और अंधकार का समुचित व्यवहार संवेदन के संवर्धन में कैसे किया जा सकता है। (कोणार्क, 101)

का पर प्रयोग कर—"to use"

अतः इन रोगों के इलाज में पेनिसिलिन ही ड्रग आफ च्वायस माना गया है। अन्य एण्टीबायटीक्स तब इस्तेमाल किये जाते हैं, जब पेनिसिलिन का प्रयोग रोगी पर नहीं किया जा सकता। (गरिमा, 127)

का के ऊपर प्रयोग कर—"to use"

पर उसने मेरे ऊपर भी अपने अस्त्र का प्रयोग करना चाहा था। (चारु, 165)

का पर उपयोग कर—"to make use of, to employ"

गोबर की खाद, कम्पोस्ट, हरी खाद आदि जैसी कार्बनिक खादों का उपयोग बिना किसी हानि के फसल पर किया जा सकता है (खाद, 12)

का पर इस्तेमाल कर—"to use, to apply"

यों श्रद्धा भी शक्ति है पर वह शक्ति गलत जगह पर क्यों इस्तेमाल की जाती है? कन्या बोली—"बात तो ठीक है पर—" (बूंद, 515)

का के रूप में प्रयोग कर—"to use, to utilize"

पाखाने का खाद के रूप में प्रयोग करने के लिये विधियों से परिचित कराना चाहिये। (सामुदा, 36)

"(People) should be made acquainted with the methods for using/utilizing human waste as manure."

का के बतौर उपयोग कर—"to make use of"

आज दिन तक भी वह धूर्ततापूर्ण स्वेच्छाशासन जारी है जो देश को पराधीन बनाए रखने और उस पराधीनता को बढ़ाने के लिए देशी सिपाहियों का ही बतौर साधनों के उपयोग करता है। (मुंदर, 22)

(को) के लिए प्रयोग कर—"to make use of"

कहा जाता है कि प्रारम्भ में इस काम के लिये केवल उन जानवरों की खालों को ही प्रयोग किया जाता था जो कि सरलता से धूप में सूख जाती थीं। (मानव, 450)

(को) के लिए उपयोग कर—"to utilize"

सभी नाइट्रोजनीय उर्वरक खेत की औसत दशाओं में फसलों की उपज बढ़ाने के लिये उपयोग किये जाते हैं। (खाद, 67)

(को) के लिए व्यवहार कर—"to make use of"

कहा जाता है कि गुफा को या ऐसे ही किसी स्थान को रहने के लिये व्यवहार करने का विचार सर्वप्रथम स्त्रियों के दिमाग में ही आया था। (मानव, 449)

(को) के लिए इस्तेमाल कर—"to use"

इस बिजली को ईंट पकाने के लिये भी इस्तेमाल किया जा सकता है, खासतौर पर उन स्थानों पर, जहां कोयला नहीं पाया जाता और जहां इसको मंगाना बहुत मंहगा पड़ता है। (ईंट, 48)

(को) में प्रयोग कर—"to use"

अब से पचास साल पहले संसार के सभी देशों में दियासिलाइयों में सिर्फ लाल फास्फोरस प्रयोग किया जाने लगा। (आग, 34)

(को) में उपयोग कर—"to employ"

जब बहुत अधिक मात्रा में ईंटों को बनाना होता है तो मिट्टी को मशीनों की सहायता से मिलाया जाता है। इस काम में जो मशीनें उपयोग की जाती हैं, उनको पगमिल कहते हैं। (ईंट, 27)

(को) में इस्तेमाल कर—"to make use of"

मैं कभी नावेल लिखूंगा, तो उन खतों को उसमें जरूर इस्तेमाल करूंगा। (अवध, 49)

(को) पर प्रयोग कर—"to use, to apply"

कुछ फेंक कर मारने से जोर से आघात पहुंचता है, यह ज्ञान आदि मानव को इसी से हुआ। इसी सिद्धान्त को उसने पशुओं पर भी प्रयोग किया। (मानव, 450)

(को) के रूप में उपयोग कर—"to employ"

मुद्रा को विनिमय के माध्यम के रूप में तब ही प्रयोग किया जा सकता है जब कि वस्तुओं के मूल्य मुद्रा में आंक लिये जावें। (एमाई, 78)

(को) के रूप में उपयोग कर—"to utilize"

मुद्रा प्रणाली के विकास के कारण ही बचत के एक बड़े अंश को पूंजी के रूप में उपयोग करने की सम्भावना उत्पन्न हो गई है। (एमाई, 34)

(को) के रूप में इस्तेमाल कर—"to use, to utilize"

वहां पर छोटे किन्तु निरन्तर चलने वाले भट्टों पर भी खोज हो रही है जिसमें ईंधन के रूप में कोयला इस्तेमाल किया जा सकता है (ईंट, 83)

4. **Other usages of प्रयोग कर—.**

का प्रयोग कर—"to use"

अनेक जन जातियां लकड़ी व धातु की कील का भी प्रयोग करती हैं जिनसे कि चमड़े आदि को खम्भों के साथ अटका दिया जाता है ताकि वह हवा में उड़ न जायें। (मानव, 452-3)

उसी प्रकार अगर हमें भूतकाल के विषय में कोई बात कहनी है तो उसी के अनुसार शब्द का प्रयोग करना पड़ेगा और अगर वर्तमान काल के विषय में कुछ कहना है तो उसी प्रकार के शब्दों को जोड़ना पड़ेगा। (मानव, 517)

मुद्रा की सहायता से ही उत्पादक अपने साधनों का इस प्रकार प्रयोग करने लगा है कि उसे अधिकतम आय हो। (एमाई, 51)

In all the above sentences के लिये adverbial is dropped because the purpose of the use of an object is expressed by a sentence in each case.

का प्रयोग कर—"to use"

स्त्री पुरुष में पुरुषत्व देखती है, साथ ही वह धन और वैभव भी देखती है। आप में दोनों हैं। आप इनका प्रयोग करें। इसके बाद आप अपनी उंगलियों के इशारे पर एक से एक सुंदरी स्त्रियों को नचा सकेंगे। (तीन, 77)

In the above sentence the use of प्रयोग is almost idiomatic.

अपने अधिकार का प्रयोग कर—"to exercise one's right"

गत आम चुनाव में... मतदाताओं में से ··· मतदाताओं ने ही अपने मतदान अधिकार का प्रयोग किया। (आज, 4)

शब्द etc. का प्रयोग कर दे—"to use, to employ word(s) (intentionally)"

वे जब-तब अंग्रेजी शब्दों का प्रयोग इसीलिए कर देते थे ताकि लोग यह न समझ लें कि वे अंग्रेजी जानते ही नहीं। (घनु, 58)

The occurrence of the explicator दे-with प्रयोग कर-is limited only with nouns meaning "words" "sentences" etc. The explicator ले-in this environment implies either one's ability to use certain words appropriately or to their use in the circumstances, contexts, etc., contrary to one's expectation.

शब्द का प्रयोग कर—"to use word(s)"

श्रीमती आनन्द, प्रायः सभी भाषाओं के एकाध अश्लील-कहावत, अश्लील-शब्द और अश्लील-आशय के वाक्य जानती है। और, अवसर देखकर उसका प्रयोग भी करती है। (दीर्घ, 22)

का प्रयोग करने दे—"to permit the use of N (human)"

चिमटा—हम लोग यह सब करना जानते हैं और करते रहे हैं इन बालकों का ऐसा प्रयोग नहीं करने देना चाहते हैं। आपका मुंह नहीं चलने देंगे। (खिलौने, 90)

5. **Other usages of उपयोग कर—.**

का उपयोग कर—"to utilize"

इतना धन कोई भी सरकार खर्च नहीं कर सकती पर गांवों में उपलब्ध अतिरिक्त श्रम का उपयोग करके ईंटें बनाई जा सकती हैं। (ईंट, 92)

का उपयोग कर ले—"to make use of something (contrary to expectation)"

प्रत्येक मनुष्य अपना काम सिद्ध करने के लिए ओझों और गुनियों की मुट्ठी गरम करके देव या दैवी से मनचाहा कौल प्राप्त कर लेता। गांव के उच्च वर्णीय ब्राह्मण भी इस शस्त्र का उपयोग कर लेते इसीलिए जिवा लुहार के प्रचार का कोई प्रभाव न पड़ता। (लाख, 102-3)

का उपयोग कर ले—"to make use of N (human)"

विवाहित स्त्री का कोई भी पति जो उपयोग करता है, उसी काम के लिए उसने उस ग्वालन की लड़की को रखा है न? (लाख, 81)

का पूरा-पूरा उपयोग कर ले—"to make full use of"

हमने अपने नये और दुर्बल देश के प्रत्येक साधन का पूरा-पूरा उपयोग करके एक महान साम्राज्य को परास्त किया। (अमरीका, 34)

दुर्घटना का उपयोग कर—"to make use of, to exploit"

राजनीति को मेरे परिवार की एक दुर्घटना का उपयोग करने का बहाना मिल गया इसलिए उसका महत्व बहुत बढ़ गया। (बूंद, 393)

6. **Other usages of इस्तेमाल कर—.**

को इस्तेमाल कर—"to use N (human)"

मुझे भी वह अच्छी लगी। इसलिए मैंने भी उसे इस्तेमाल किया। पर उसके बाद वह शादी-वादी की बात करने लगी। यह बला कौन पाले? इन बेड़ियों में कौन फंसे। (धनु, 159)

(को) उपयोग में लाकर इस्तेमाल कर—"to consume something by putting it to use"

सुखाने के लिये इसमें सायाबान होता है जो भट्टों के निकट ही बनाया जाता है। इससे भट्टे की व्यर्थ गर्मी ड्रायर उपयोग में लाकर इस्तेमाल की जाती है। (ईंट, 34)

(को) के पक्ष में इस्तेमाल कर—"to use something to one's own end or to one's advantage"

··· इतिहास दिखलाता है कि प्रत्येक सामाजिक वर्ग को जब कि वह राजनैतिक शक्ति का स्वामी बन जाता है, उसको अपने विशेष हित के पक्ष में इस्तेमाल करना पड़ता है। (भारत, 25)

सादगी इस्तेमाल कर—"to exercise frankness or to employ simplicity (in one's expression)"

"सामान आपस में बांट लेते हैं," बड़ी बहन ने सादगी इस्तेमाल की ···। (आकाश, 59)

2. प्रशंसा, सराहना, तारीफ

1. प्रशंसा, सराहना, तारीफ all refer to the expression of one's feeling of admiration in a variety of ways. प्रशंसा implies a recognition of superiority, and is often motivated. सराहना is applied to anything from a warmly expressed commendation to the expression of one's appreciation based on some sort of understanding. तारीफ refers to the expression of one's feelings about what is pleasing or what one regards with favour.

2. 1. प्रशंसा is a generic activity, the specific instances of which are स्तुति, गुणगान, यशोगान, वाहवाही, बड़ाई and a few others. All these specific nouns refer to the modalities of प्रशंसा. For example in the following contexts, the प्रशंसा given to a Brahmana by a farmer is characterized by the author as स्तुति, and that given to a Vaishya as प्रशंसा.

चना-चोरों का परिचय पाकर चतुर किसान आगे बढ़ा और पण्डित के चरण छूकर बोला—महाराज, आज हमारे पुरखों के पुण्य से आप जैसे देवता हमारी धरती पर पधारे हैं, हमारा तो सर्वस्व आप जैसे साधु-सन्तों के लिये है। देव...।

ब्राह्मण अपनी स्तुति सुनकर गद्गद् हो गया...। (लोक कथा, 8-9)

···किसान बनिये के पैरों से लिपटकर बोला—लक्ष्मीनारायण जी, खूब खाइए, जी भर कर खाइए। हे धर्मावतार, जो कुछ है आपका ही तो है। आप बड़े आदमी हैं...।

बनिया भी अपनी प्रशंसा सुनकर कुप्पा हो गया...। (लोक कथा, 9-10)

2. 2. All the nouns are + process. Both प्रशंसा and सराहना are not pluralized. They all form ANP with की.

3. An example of the variety of expressions characterized as सराहना is given below:

मुझे वृद्ध धीर शर्मा की समझदारी पर आश्चर्य हुआ। उन्होंने रानी को देखते ही कहा था, बेटा। अस्सी वर्ष के जीवन में प्रथम बार सौभाग्यवती पद्मिनी नारी को देख रहा हूं। अनुष्ठान के समय भी उन्होंने मेरी पीठ पर हाथ फेरते हुए कहा था, बेटा, तुम्हारे ग्रह-गण प्रसन्न हैं, तुम्हें साक्षात् पद्मिनी नारी प्राप्त करने का सौभाग्य प्राप्त हुआ है, और इसके बाद झमाझम पांच-सात श्लोक बोल गए...।

अन्तिम बार जब उन्होंने मेरे सौभाग्य की सराहना की और...(चारु, 29-30)

Parts of a context illustrating the noun तारीफ are also reproduced below :—

मंजे हुए, साफ-सुथरे पीतल के गिलास से दूध का घूंट भरते ही सत्यव्रत की आत्मा तृप्त होती चली गई। वास्तव में इतने अच्छे दूध की उसने आशा नहीं की थी। गूंगे की ईमानदारी पर उसे आन्तरिक खुशी हुई और इसीलिए पैसे देते वक्त उसने दूध के गिलास की ओर इशारा करते हुए निर्विकार भाव से उसकी शुद्धता की तारीफ की। (सवाल, 39)

4. की प्रशंसा कर—"to admire, to express one's admiration for someone"

उन दिनों नैषधकार महाकवि हर्ष का बड़ा सम्मान था। वे थे भी सम्मान के योग्य महाराज उनकी बड़ी प्रशंसा किया करते थे···। (चारु, 44)

की प्रशंसा कर—"to praise, to compliment"

अब मैं आपकी प्रशंसा ऐसे शब्दों में करूंगी जो आज तक किसी ने नहीं कहे होंगे। (बाल, 22)

की मुक्त कण्ठ से प्रशंसा कर—"to laud"

इन गुणों से मुग्ध होकर ही अनेक कवियों ने उनकी मुक्त कण्ठ से प्रशंसा की है। (ज्योति, 12)

5. **की सराहना कर—"to express one's appreciation for"**

और फिर स्वयं उनकी प्रशंसा न करके आप उनकी चीज़ों की प्रशंसा कीजिए, उनकी रुचियों की सराहना कीजिए और फिर भले ही कवियों की अतिशयोक्ति का भी उल्लंघन करते हुए कहिए... । (कहा, 77)

The above sentence may be compared with the following :—

मैं मन ही मन उसकी सुरुचि की प्रशंसा कर रहा था। (राकेश, 38)

"I was quietly admiring his good taste."

की सराहना कर—"to appreciate"

यह सही है कि पाई हुई इस अनमोल वस्तु की सराहना केवल दार्शनिक या कलाकार ही कर पाते हैं। (बूंद, 285)

6. **की तारीफ कर—"to praise"**

बीच-बीच में रामायण के सम्पुट पाठ की तरह वह प्रसंग और अवसर निकाल कर मेरी रचनाओं की, मेरे स्वभाव और मीठे व्यवहार की भी लगे हाथों तारीफ करते चलते थे। (सच, 28)

की तारीफ करता न अघा—"to laud"

घर-बाहर पास-पड़ोस का जो भी उनसे मिलता है, उनकी सूक्ष्म बुद्धि की तारीफ करता नहीं अघाता। (कहा, 11)

की तारीफ कर—"to praise, to express one's liking for"

नीलिमा : (उदास हंसी के साथ) तुम जो भी पहनोगी, सब उसी की तारीफ करेंगे। (भंवर, 68)

Contrast the above sentence with the following containing **की प्रशंसा कर—"to express admiration for"**

पीटर पुस्तक का वह पृष्ठ पढ़ने लगा, जिस पर से वह चिट्ठी नकल की जा रही थी। जान स्टोव के पास जा खड़ा हुआ और अनिता के शाल की प्रशंसा करने लगा। (जानवर, 155)

की निकम्मी तारीफ कर—"to praise someone in many different ways"

...अपनी खुदगर्जी के लिए मर्द औरत की जवानी का भिखारी बनकर उससे दान पाने के लिए निकम्मी तारीफें किया करता है। (बूंद, 355)

3. प्रतीक्षा, इन्तजार

1. Both प्रतीक्षा and इन्तजार refer to the activity of waiting. प्रतीक्षा stresses either one's attitude of expectancy, or one's concern or anxiety (generally expressed adverbially) about an outcome which is expected but inordinately delayed. इन्तजार is simply waiting in a state of readiness.

2. Both the nouns are+process, and do not take plural. They admit infinitives before की/का. A few sentences below illustrate the distinction between प्रतीक्षा and इन्तजार.

माधुरी ने सिर उठाकर देखा और कहा—आइए, हम लोग बड़ी देर से आपकी प्रतीक्षा कर रहे हैं। मां का दर्द आज बेहद बढ़ गया है। (तितली, 31)

"अरे हां, मैं तो भूल ही गया था, अच्छी याद दिलाई। लोग मेरा इंतजार कर रहे होंगे।"—यह कहते हुए अविनाश उठा। (तीन, 86)

ऐसा विचार करके उसने पंडित जी का सिर काटकर दूर एक कोने में छिपा दिया और स्वयं बैठकर उनके जगने की प्रतीक्षा करने लगा। (कथा, 65)

वह चुपचाप उनके कमरे से निकल आयी थी। अपने कमरे में आकर उनके जागने का इन्तजार करती रही थी। (मांस, 9)

गंगराज तथा हेमाद्री दोनों राजमाता के उद्देश्य की सिद्धि के अनुकूल अवसर की प्रतीक्षा कर रहे थे। (शांतला, 49)

मछुए और नाविक और सैलानी लोग हमेशा ज्वारों के इस बदलने वाले समय का इन्तजार किया करते हैं। (समुद्र, 36)

3.1. Adverbials occurring with it express concern or anxiety, e.g., आतुरता से "restlessly", अधीरता से "impatiently", स्थिरभाव से "in a composed manner", उत्सुकता से "anxiously", व्याकुलता से "restlessly", धैर्य से "patiently". Sometimes one's concern may be expressed by using a suitable adjective e.g., उत्कट प्रतीक्षा "intense waiting".

3.2. Time adverbials with से and तक also occur freely with both प्रतीक्षा and इन्तजार. It is common to express the state of the subject-noun (who is waiting) by means of participles, i.e.,.. बाहर टैरेस पर खड़े होकर अपने पति की प्रतीक्षा...,वह कमरे में बैठे हुए तुम्हारी प्रतीक्षा...,आप बैठी इन्तजार...,शेरनी की तरह बिफरती इन्तजार..., गजल गुनगुनाता हुआ इन्तजार...

3.3. Only इन्तजार admits adverbials with के लिए meaning "in order to".

अनेक बन्दरगाहों में तो बड़े जहाजों को प्रवेश करने और बाहर निकलने—दोनों कामों के लिए ऊंचे ज्वार का इन्तजार करना पड़ता है। (समुद्र, 40)

3.4. इन्तजार occurs as का इन्तजार more frequently but sometimes one may expect to find की इन्तजार also. This kind of divergence in the gender is systematic, and adds to the noun, though only partly, the features of प्रतीक्षा.

उसका वह आम का पेड़, जिसके पकने की उसने बेसब्री से इन्तजार की थी . . . ।
(जानवर, 117)

The usage of the noun इन्तजार is quite appropriate in a context such as above where the occurrence of प्रतीक्षा is ruled out.

3.5. की/का is often dropped before प्रतीक्षा and इन्तजार, more so with इन्तजार than with प्रतीक्षा as in the following examples.

मैंने कहा, नहीं गीरा, कुछ नहीं सुनाऊंगा, सुनाने को है ही क्या, चुपचाप सिर झुका लूंगा और प्रतीक्षा करूंगा कि तुम्हारे क्षमा-भरे करुणा भरे हाथ मेरे माथे को छू दें. . . ।
(नदी, 275)

"सीडी, कल रात तुम नहीं आये ? सब इन्तजार करते रहे।" मैंने कहा। (परिन्दे, 96)

Both the above sentences imply restriction on the occurrence of infinitives as embedded sentences. The problem requires further investigation.

3.6. इन्तजार also occurs with N के लिए, and in that case the infinitive cannot be embedded before the postposition. के लिये in the contexts such as illustrated below singles out some individual (s) who is/are considered worth waiting for.

शानदार पोर्टिको में श्रीमती कल्याणी महिपाल शुक्ल के लिए गाड़ी इतजार कर रही थी। (बूंद, 495)

. . . आप दोनों में से कोई भी इस काबिल नहीं कि जिसके लिए इन्तजार किया जाय।
(बूंद, 28)

4. Both प्रतीक्षा कर-and इन्तजार कर-occur as non-finite imperfectives in sentences with expressions denoting the passage of time, or with ऊब जा-थक जा-, तंग आ जा- etc., denoting various mental and/or physical states of the subject noun.

भाई चुप हो रहा। मैं इन्तजार करते-करते ऊब गया। कानपुर वाला बहाना अब नहीं चल सकता था। (तुला, 8)

और लाजवंती सोचती—काश, कहीं वर्षा हो जाये ! पर वर्षा थी, कि होने का नाम ही न लेती थी। इस तरह प्रतीक्षा करते-करते एक महीना बीत गया। (दुग्गल, 22)

5. प्रतीक्षा कर-"to expect" also permits the thing expected to occur as its subject and in that case the person who is waiting in expectation is expressed as the N, as in N की प्रतीक्षा.

की प्रतीक्षा कर—"to await"

मल्लिका:—कुछ समय पहले एक राजपुरुष से उनका साक्षात्कार हो चुका है।

निक्षेप:—उस कटुता को केवल तुम्हीं दूर कर सकती हो मल्लिका। अवसर किसी की प्रतीक्षा नहीं करता (आषाढ़, 33)

फिर हंसकर इस श्लेष का अर्थ समझाते हुए बोले, "सीढ़ी से भेंट नहीं होगी, परन्तु सिद्धि तुम्हारी प्रतीक्षा कर रही है। उठो, देर न करो। एक क्षण के विलम्ब से सारा काम नष्ट हो जाएगा।" (चारु, 14)

4. अतिक्रमण, उल्लंघन

1. Both अतिक्रमण and उल्लंघन refer to acting in a manner such that the action either implies or involves going beyond a prescribed limit. अतिक्रमण literally means stepping across, and therefore denotes any act that goes beyond the prescribed limit in the sense that it exceeds the limit with or without any implication of disregard. उल्लंघन literally means overstepping, and denotes an apparent violation or a deliberate disregard of the prescribed limit.

2. अतिक्रमण is$_{+}$ process and उल्लंघन$\pm$ process. Both nouns are not pluralized and do not permit infinitives before का.

3. **का अतिक्रमण कर—"to transcend"**

जिस तरह पार्थिव वायुमंडल व गुरुत्वाकर्षण की सीमा को पार कर वह आकाश के

नक्षत्रों की ओर बढ़ रहा है, वैसे ही सूक्ष्म रूप से वह अपनी पार्थिवता का अतिक्रमण कर देवत्व की ओर बढ़ रहा है। (अणु, 45)

साम्प्रदायिक अनुशासन जहां भी प्रगति चेतना में आड़े आये हैं, उनका उसने साहसपूर्वक अतिक्रमण किया है। (मूल्य, 134)

... जयदेव का अधूरा श्लोक स्वतः कृष्ण आकर पूरा कर देते हैं... प्रबलतम अन्तः-प्रेरणा जो अधिकतर मनुष्य की सचेतन मानसिक शक्तियों या वातावरण का अतिक्रमण कर जाती है... । (मूल्य, 157)

का अतिक्रमण कर—"to exceed"

चिन्तन-धाराओं की गति के अतिरिक्त पिछले १०० वर्षों में वास्तविक राजनीतिक इतिहास की गति ने कई बार मार्क्सीय पद्धति की अनिवार्यता का अतिक्रमण किया, (लेनिन द्वारा आयोजित रूसी क्रान्ति और माओ द्वारा आयोजित चीनी क्रांति ही स्वतः इसके सबसे बड़े प्रमाण हैं...)। (मूल्य, 110)

का अतिक्रमण कर—"to surpass"

इस बार गिलिन्स्की का क्रोध मर्यादा का अतिक्रमण कर गया। (काल, 52)

का अतिक्रमण कर—"to transcend, to transgress, to violate"

यह आत्मोपलब्धि रहस्यवादियों की उस साधना से भी पृथक् है जिसमें वे ये मानते हैं कि सामान्य मनुष्य की नियति से उसे क्या लेना देना, वे तो उसका अतिक्रमण कर सीधे किसी विराट ब्रह्म से साक्षात्कार कर उसी में पूर्णत्व की प्राप्ति कर लेंगे। (मूल्य, 35)

का अतिक्रमण कर—"to step across, to exceed, to violate"

अगर कहीं उनकी खींची हुई लक्ष्मण-रेखा (नहीं-नहीं, पत्नी-रेखा) का अतिक्रमण करके अपने पत्नीव्रत धर्म से मैं जरा भी डिगने लगता हूं... । (कहा, 13)

का अतिक्रमण कर—"to violate"

अब तो वह अपने दायरे के बाहर पैर रखती है—अपने कर्त्तव्य-क्षेत्र का अतिक्रमण करती है। (देश, 47)

जनता का जंगल ! सब मनुष्य जैसे समय और अवकाश का अतिक्रमण करके, बहुत शीघ्र अपना काम कर डालने में व्यस्त हैं ? (तितली, 219)

का अतिक्रमण कर जा—"to transcend, to surpass"

सूर्य के अध्ययन से और भी कई उपयोगी काम होते हैं परन्तु ज्योतिष ज्ञान ज्यों-ज्यों बढ़ता गया त्यों-त्यों ज्योतिषी की दृष्टि कोरी व्यावहारिक उपयोगिता की परिधि का अतिक्रमण करती गयी। (नक्षत्र, 33)

4. **का उल्लंघन कर—"to overstep, to violate"**

राज्य अपने नागरिकों पर बल प्रयोग द्वारा अपने नियम लादता है। परन्तु ऐसा करने में वह नैतिक नियमों का उल्लंघन नहीं कर सकता। (भारत, 29)

का उल्लंघन कर—"to violate"

राज्य आमतौर से समाज की प्रथाओं, रीति-रिवाजों और परम्पराओं का उल्लंघन नहीं करता।... साधारणतः राज्य इन सामाजिक संगठनों के अधिकारों की अवहेलना नहीं करता। (भारत, 29)

का उल्लंघन कर—"to encroach upon"

अपने देश में शान्ति बनाये रखने का तरीका यही है कि इस महान् नैतिक आदेश का पालन किया जाय कि किसी भी आदमी को दूसरों के उन अधिकारों का उल्लंघन नहीं करना चाहिए जो उसे संविधान ने प्रदान किये हैं। (अमरीका, 93)

का उल्लंघन कर—"to trespass"

खुली जगह लापता होती जा रही है और पुराने भू-चिन्हों का उल्लंघन करना आम बात हो गई है। (अमरीका, 41)

का उल्लंघन कर—"to infringe upon"

... कि उसे अपराधी ठहराने वाला कानून क्या वास्तव में ईश्वरीय कानून की सीमा का उल्लंघन नहीं करेगा। (सोमा, 78)

का उल्लंघन कर—"to act in contravention of"

बोधा प्रवान से उन्होंने कहा, प्रधान, मैंने तुम्हें सहायता का वचन दिया है, पर देवी इस युद्ध की अनुमति नहीं दे रही हैं। न तो मैं वचन-भंग कर सकता हूं, न देवी की आज्ञा का उल्लंघन कर सकता हूं। (चारु, 366)

का उल्लंघन कर—"to act in defiance of"

सद्भावना का प्रदर्शन करते हैं, किन्तु सामाजिक रीतियों का उल्लंघन करने से डरते हैं। (नदु, 37)

को उल्लंघन कर—"to exceed"

यदि वह (मानसिक रोग) उचित सीमा को उल्लंघन करते प्रतीत हों...। चमत्कार, 45)

उल्लंघन कर—"to disobey"

... अपने शिविर का नियम संयम इतना शुद्ध और पक्का है कि कोई आज्ञा उल्लंघन नहीं करता और न कोई करेगा। (कचनार, 234)

5. क्रोध, गुस्सा

1. Both क्रोध and गुस्सा refer to one's behaviour (verbal or otherwise) expressing emotional excitement aroused or induced by intense displeasure. क्रोध names the emotional state of anger as well as denotes its outward manifestation, implying a grievance and a desire or intent to revenge or punish. गुस्सा refers to the emotional reaction of an angry individual.

The sentences below illustrate the distinction between क्रोध and गुस्सा.

कोई-कोई संपादक तो यहां तक कहते हैं कि अपने ग्राहकों को प्रसन्न रखना हमारा कर्त्तव्य है। हम उनका खाते हैं तो उन्हीं का गावेंगे। सुभद्रा—तब तो ये लोग केवल पैसे के गुलाम हैं। इन पर क्रोध करने की जगह दया करनी चाहिये।

पद्मसिंह मेज पर से उठ आये। उत्तर लिखने का विचार छोड़ दिया। (सेवा,273-74)

वह बेहद थक गई थी, भूखी थी और उसे गुस्सा आ रहा था। वह एक जगह बैठकर अपने पर गुस्सा करने लगी। (आग, 19)

2. Both nouns are + process, and do not take plural. They form ANP with पर.

The N of N पर क्रोध is generally a person at whom the outward manifestation of anger is directed whereas the N of N पर गुस्सा may be a person (generally the subject himself represented by the pronominal अपना) or a thing which causes an individual to react in a state of anger.

छोटी छोटी बात पर गुस्सा करते थे। खाने में ज्यादा नुक्स निकालते थे। (जानवर, 102)

3. The N पर may be dropped before both क्रोध and गुस्सा. The variety of expressions which exist as a result of the dropping of N पर are illustrated below.

क्रोध कर—

—तीसरे मेरी आई अनायास ही भयानक क्रोध करने वाली थीं। (अपनी खबर, 36)

कहीं ऐसा न हो कि मन में छिपी हुई बात कह देने से मां और भी क्रोध कर बैठे...। (तितली, 122)

बात में सत्यांश था। वह क्रोध न करके अपनी सफाई देने की चेष्टा करने लगी। (तितली, 106)

मैं क्रोध न करूं तो कैसे बचूं ? लोग मुझको यों ही पागल कहते हैं । क्या मैं पागल हूं ? (बांस, 48)

गुस्सा कर—

...तुम नाराज हो जाओगे तो मुझे दो हजार रूबल दोगे और मैं गुस्सा करूंगा तो या तो तुम्हें दो हजार रूबल दूंगा या बीस वर्ष तक तुम्हारी गुलामी करता रहूंगा । (रूस, 2-3)

6. भूल, गल्ती

1. Both भूल and गल्ती (sp. var. गलती) denote a mistake made either through one's misunderstanding or misconception. भूल imputes the misunderstanding or misconception to the inadvertence or ignorance of one who makes a mistake whereas गल्ती has no such implication. Both the nouns are neutral as to culpability which may be implied or expressed in the context if intended, as illustrated in the context below.

नित्य-प्रति, सवेरे से शाम तक, और रात में भी, जाने कितनी चीजें हम देखते हैं और पहचानते हैं. . . , तो फिर यह कैसे स्वीकार किया जाय कि हम ठीक से नहीं देख पाते । वास्तव में हम पहचानने में भूल नहीं करते बल्कि दृष्टि-विलम्बना के कारण देखने की व्यवस्था में गल्ती करते हैं ।(प्रकाश, 30)

2. Both nouns are +process and admit plural. They form ANP with में or की which may take a noun or an infinitive. में refers to the source of the mistake, and की to its kind.

हिन्दू धर्म का आधार वेद है किन्तु बहुत ही थोड़े व्यक्ति उस आधार के शुद्ध रूप और मर्म से अवगत रहते हैं । अन्य धर्मग्रन्थ वेद-वृक्ष की शाखाओं की भांति हैं । प्रायः हम किसी एक शाखा के किसी एक भाग में बैठकर दो-एक सुस्वादु नश्वर फल चख कर ही सनातन धर्म के मूल्यों को आंकने लगते हैं । पर उस मूल का पता लगाने का किंचित् भी प्रयत्न नहीं करते, जिससे सनातन धर्म के वृक्ष की शाखाएं उत्पन्न होकर फैली हैं । इसलिए हम धर्म का व्यापक रूप समझने में प्रायः भूल कर जाते हैं । (धर्म, 9)

कर्नल....फिर आवाज को नीची सतह पर लाकर बोला—...देखिये महिपाल को समझने में आप गलती करती हैं । ये मैं मानता हूं कि महिपाल में बुराइयां हैं, पर ये भी आपको मानना पड़ेगा कि इनके जैसे भोला-भाला, दिल के साफ इन्सान आपको भी जमाना इक्के दुक्के देखने को मिलेंगे । (बूंद, 271)

कुछ क्षणों तक सामने रणचंडी के भयानक नृत्य पर उड़ती दृष्टि डालकर छत्रपति ने पहले की तरह गंभीर स्वर में कहा—तुमने स्त्री को कमजोर और तुच्छ समझने की भूल की है...। (बेटी, 65)

...और सैनिक में रचना भेजते समय साधु शब्दों के प्रयोग की गलती की जाय। (कहा, 95)

...भाषा में लिंग-सम्बन्धी भूलें सबसे बुरी समझी जाती हैं। किसी को इस प्रकार की भूलें करते देखकर लोग प्रायः कह बैठते हैं—उंह। उन्हें तो स्त्रीलिंग और पुल्लिग तक का ज्ञान नहीं है। (प्रयोग, 145)

भाषा न देखिये भाव देखिए इनका। भाषा की गलतियां बड़े बड़े साहित्यकार भी कर जाते हैं। (बूंद, 147)

3. The distinction implied by में and की is neutralized by the conjunctive participles as in

हमें विश्वास है कि बिलारी दरबार से संधि और युद्ध करने का अधिकार तुम्हें सौंपकर हमने भूल नहीं की है। (बेटी, 29)

प्रतिभा—मैंने पहली बार ही शादी करके गलती की। असल में मेरी प्रकृति शादी के अनुकूल ही नहीं। (भंवर, 61)

4. N में/की are often dropped before भूल and गल्ती, more so with भूल than गल्ती.

तुम भूल करती हो राजो। तितली को मधुबन के साथ परदेश जाना पड़े, यह भी मैं सह लूंगा... । (तितली, 102)

कर्नल के विरोध से सज्जन को महसूस होने लगा था कि उसने गलती की है, पर चूंकि वह गलती कर चुका था, इसलिये उस पर डटा रहना चाहता था।

5.1. Only गल्ती can occur with the conjunctive जानबूझ कर "deliberately".

5.2. The explicators which do not occur with भूल/गल्ती कर-are आ-, उठ-,पड़-,चल-,निकल-, and पा-. Among the ones which can occur, only रह-, चुक-,जा-,सक-,डाल-, and बैठ-are frequent.

7. कष्ट, तकलीफ

1. कष्ट and तकलीफ refer to the act of one's taking the trouble of doing something (for someone). कष्ट suggests a formal (sometimes figurative) acknowledgement of or reference to the trouble actually taken or not. तकलीफ imputes the trouble to the thing done, and therefore stresses a stronger implication of acknowledgement of or reference to

the trouble. कष्ट is a preferred term for use with negation in the contexts where the sense is to not bother to do something.

2. Both nouns are +process, and do not admit plural. They form ANP with का and की which almost exclusively are preceded by infinitives.

3. **का कष्ट कर—"to take the trouble of"**

आप यदि यहां आने का कष्ट करें तो जरा विस्तार से बातचीत हो। (धनु, 135)
आपने साथ आने का कष्ट किया, उस उपकार के लिए आभारी हूं। (जय, 99)

का कष्ट न कर—"to not bother to do something"

सफेद कार्क हेलमेट को उतारने का उन्होंने अभी तक कष्ट न किया था। (तीन, 28)

4. **की तकलीफ कर "to take the trouble of"**

सात महीने पूरे नहीं हो पाए थे कि एक दिन वीणा ने अपने पेट को पकड़कर, सारा संकोच और झिझक छोड़कर पति से कहा—मेरी तबीयत बहुत खराब है। क्या आप मुझे तुरन्त नर्सिंग होम में पहुंचा देने की तकलीफ करेंगे? (धनु, 145)

तकलीफ कर-, when used with negation, means "to not put oneself into any inconvenience", as illustrated below.

रास्ते में किसी चीज की तकलीफ न करना। (अंधा, 124)

This expression is almost formulaic.

5. N का/की with both कष्ट and तकलीफ may be substituted by N के लिए when one takes the trouble for someone else.

ब्यालू करते करते श्रीचन्द्र ने कहा—चन्दा, तुम मेरे लिए इतना कष्ट करती हो। (कंकाल, 154)

उसके ठहरने के लिए चन्द्र को कष्ट नहीं करना होगा, रियासत वालों का एक गेस्ट हाउस लखनऊ में है और वहीं उसे ठहरने की अनुमति मिल गयी है। (नदी, 47)

The expressions कष्ट कर-and तकलीफ कर are customarily employed in address form when one is confronted by the addressee, e.g., कहिये, आपने कैसे कष्ट किया, or कहिये, आपने कैसे तकलीफ की. The former is equivalent to the colloquial expression "What can I do for you?", and the latter to "How come you are here?" तकलीफ कर-indicates rudeness on the part of the speaker, as indicated by the sentence below.

कैसे तकलीफ की ? कन्या को यह रूखापन चुभा । उसे छिपाते हुए किंचित् मुस्करा कर उसने कहा...(बूंद, 371)

8. घृणा, नफरत

1. घृणा and नफरत denote expression of one's state of mind or feeling of antipathy, dislike and distaste, or refer to one's reaction to someone or something characteristic of such a state of mind.

Both the nouns denote the emotional state in abstract or to the actual experience of it. घृणा, however, is more often used as a designation for the emotion in abstract.

घृणा stresses aversion implying despite or disdain often with a cause, and नफरत, aversion accompanied by detestation and antagonism.

2. Both nouns are + process, and form ANP with से or को. घृणा occurs with पर also.

3. से घृणा कर—"to develop a dislike for"

इसलिए गांव के लोग जिवा से कुछ घृणा-सी करने लगे। (लाख, 4)

से घृणा कर—"to hate"

अपने अर्धचेतन मन में शिव प्रसाद उनसे इतनी घृणा करते थे कि आज तक उनका नाम तक जानने की इच्छा उन्होंने प्रकट न की थी। (धारा, 82)

उनके भाव और कर्म में विशुद्धता बसती है। इसलिए वे किसी से घृणा नहीं करते। (धर्म, 58)

पर घृणा कर—"to despise"

अब धर्म नहीं रहा—गुरुदीन ने नाक सिकोड़ कर जैसे किसी पर घृणा करते हुए कहा। (निरु, 49)

किसी पर घृणा करते हुए कहा, in the above context, can be rendered as "said···despitefully".

को घृणा कर—"to have an aversion to, to hate"

वैसे तुम कुछ भी कहो, मैं मनुष्य जीवन में, खुद अपने जीवन में, भी शृंगाररस का पूरा-पूरा महत्त्व स्वीकार करके भी तुम्हारे राधारमण और गोपीरमण—याने जिस रूप में तुम उसे देख रहे हो—उसे मैं अपने समूचे अंतःकरण से घृणा करती हूं (बूंद, 320)

In the above sentence...उसे मैं अपने समूचे अन्तःकरण से घृणा करती हूँ can be rendered in English by "...I hate that with all my heart."

4. **से नफरत कर—"to hate"**

न उससे नफरत की जा सकती है और न उसके बारे में आकर्षण लगता है। (धनु, 18)

बड़ी करुणाभरी दृष्टि से उन्होंने सज्जन की ओर देखा और बोली—गुनाह से भले ही नफरत करो सज्जन, लेकिन गुनाहगार को कलेजे से लगाए रक्खो। (बूंद, 235)

को नफरत कर—"to hate (oneself")

पत्नी के चले जाने के बाद महिपाल बड़ी देर तक क्षुब्ध-भाव से बैठा रहा। सदा की तरह इस समय भी अपनी विवशता अनुभव कर उसे अपने ऊपर खीज आ रही थी। एक जगह वह अपने आपसे बड़ी नफरत करता है। (बूंद, 109)

9. मूर्खता, बेवकूफी

1. Both मूर्खता and बेवकूफी refer to an act which does not commend itself in the judgement of others as judicious. मूर्खता stresses lack of wisdom, i.e., the lack of power of discerning properly as to what is right, and बेवकूफी implies the lack of knowledge, i.e., lack of acquaintance with facts. मूर्खता, therefore, is a stronger term which imputes the quality of foolishness to the individual rather than just the thing done. बेवकूफी may or may not have such an implication.

2. Both nouns are + process, and form ANP with की. They permit infinitives before की freely. N की may also be dropped before both of them.

3. लेकिन इन आवाजों के कोलाहल से हमें यह समझने की मूर्खता नहीं करनी चाहिए कि हम जिस राष्ट्र में रहते हैं वह अनेक खंडों में बंटा हुआ है। (अमरीका, 6)

4. पंडित जी को मूर्ख विद्वान् लिखने में कलम की कोई भूल नहीं, क्योंकि दुनिया में बहुत से प्राणी हैं जो अक्ल रखते हुए भी बेवकूफी करते हैं। (विचित्र, 64)

10. धृष्टता, गुस्ताखी

1. धृष्टता and गुस्ताखी both refer to one's conduct (in a given situation) markedly divergent from the norms of propriety. धृष्टता implies a sense of awareness of insolence on one's part and गुस्ताखी lacks this implication.

2. Both nouns are + process and form ANP with के साथ and की. Only गुस्ताखी admits plural when occurring with के साथ.

3. की धृष्टता कर—"to act presumptuously"

यह कह सम्राट् बिम्बसार शिलाखंड पर बैठ गए। बोले क्षमा करना, वृद्ध हूं इसलिए आपके सम्मुख बैठने की यह धृष्टता कर बैठा हूं। (दत्तकपुत्री, 115)

की धृष्टता कर—"to act presumptuously, to take the liberty of"

आप लखनऊ आवें यह सुझाने की धृष्टता तो नहीं कर सकता, मेरी अपात्रता के अलावा लखनऊ की घटनाओं का भी स्मरण कराया जाना आप नापसंद करेंगी। (नदी, 256)

की धृष्टता कर—"to take the liberty of"

चिरंतन मौन ही जिसका अभिशाप है उस पौरुष को मैंने वाणी देने की धृष्टता की है। (कोणार्क, 31)

4. के साथ गुस्ताखी कर—"to treat someone disrespectfully, to take liberty with"

अगर तुम लोगों ने देवियों के साथ जरा भी गुस्ताखी की, तुम्हारे हक में अच्छा न होगा। (सम, 78)

11. सफर, यात्रा

1. Both सफर and यात्रा refer to travelling from one place to another. सफर emphasizes the distance, and therefore implies the inconvenience, difficulty etc., as they affect the individual. यात्रा implies a destination, stresses a desire or a purpose, and thus the added implication of gaining experience through the fulfilment of one's desire or the accomplishment of one's purpose.

अभियान "expedition", प्रयाण "departure" प्रस्थान "departure" भ्रमण "tour", and दौरा 'tour" are related to यात्रा but cannot be considered as its synonyms.

2. Both सफर and यात्रा are + process, and form ANP with का and की. Only यात्रा can be pluralized.

3. का सफर कर—"to travel by"

टिकट भुवन ने वापस कर दिया, नया टिकट बारह के बाद मिलेगा—नयी तारीख हो जाने पर, क्योंकि रेखा इंटर का सफ़र करती थी, सेकेंड होता तो भी मिल जाता। (नदी, 121)

सफर कर—"to travel"

लोगों को जाने सफर में कैसे इतनी गहरी नींद आ जाती है? वह बोली, मुझे दो-दो रातें सफर करना हो तो भी मैं नहीं सो पाती। अपनी अपनी आदत होती है। क्यों? (कहानी, 115)

मैं बैठकर बहुत सोचने लगता हूं और मुझे कई बार लगने लगता है कि मेरी जिन्दगी का कोई मतलब नहीं है। मैं रात दिन बसों और गाड़ियों में सफर करता हूँ और होटलों का गंदा खाना खाता हूं . . . (राकेश, 60)

4. की यात्रा कर—"to take a trip to"

हम इस राजबाला के अमंगल दूर करने के निमित्त काशी की यात्रा कर रहे हैं, लेकिन अमंगल पग-पग पर हमारा बाधक सिद्ध हो रहा है। (चारु, 84)

की यात्रा कर—"to make a trip"

श्रीमती इंदिरा गांधी ने एशिया, यूरोप, अमेरिका और रूस की यात्राएं की हैं। (बाल, 1)

यात्रा कर—"to travel"

उस डिब्बे में बैठकर थोडी देर के लिए मैं अपने को यह मना सकी थी कि हम साथ ही साथ इस गाड़ी में यात्रा कर रहे हैं। पर अब—अब लगता है कि आप मुझे विदा कर चुके और उपचार बाकी है। (नदी, 123)

पहले सोचा था कि बम्बई से गोआ तक की यात्रा स्टीमर से करूंगा। (राकेश, 22)

कुछ सोचते हैं कि पृथ्वी को अपने साथ खींचता हुआ अन्तरिक्ष में यात्रा करता हुआ सूर्य कहीं सितारों की गर्द के विशाल बादलों में न पहुंच जाए। (समुद्र, 143)

की यात्रा करके लौट—"to return from one's trip to"

ये सीस्तान, कन्दहार, बुखारा और तुर्किस्तान का भ्रमण कर आए हैं, और हाल ही में नालन्दा, लक्ष्मणावती और कामरूप की यात्रा करके लौटे हैं। (चारु, 12)

12. दुराग्रह, हठ, ज़िद

1. दुराग्रह, हठ and ज़िद all refer to the act of repeating or pressing an utterance beyond a reasonable limit. They differ in their implication as to the characteristic display of temperament and the reaction they arouse in the mind of the other person (s), as well as in the nature of the utterances to which they are applied.

दुराग्रह is pressing a point through a variety of arguments or denying the truth of someone else's statement in an admittedly unreasonable and perverse manner to an extent that is characteristic of a pertinacious individual.

हठ is pressing something unreasonable, impractical or the like with a marked unyielding adherence and stolid determination by someone who is given to stubbornness either by nature or under the given circumstances.

ज़िद is repeated insistence with an intrinsic sense of affection by a friendly but obstinate individual, or a loved-one (generally a child) who has the prerogative of being unreasonable at times.

दुराग्रह, हठ, and ज़िद may be applied in their extended sense to refer to one's adverse attitude. In this extended sense दुराग्रह is applied to unworthy or ill-advised persistence, हठ to undesirable or unnecessary stubbornness, and ज़िद to the frivolity of one's obstinate nature.

2. All the nouns are +process, and form ANP with पर, से, के लिये and का (की for ज़िद). N post. may be dropped, and in that case only ज़िद can be pluralized. पर, से and का/की admit infinitives only, and के लिये both infinitives and nouns.

3. का दुराग्रह कर—"to press a point"

डा० सुमंत के तर्क के सामने प्रोफेसर ज्ञानशंकर निरुत्तर हो गए। उनके दोष-दर्शन के कारण उन्हें चोट तो लगी, मानसिक संताप भी हुआ पर स्वभाव से प्रांजल व्यक्ति होने के कारण अपनी गलती को अस्वीकार करने का दुराग्रह नहीं कर सके। (धनु, 18)

4. का हठ कर—"to insist on, to keep saying something insistently"

वर्षा उस समय जोर से होने लगी थी और नन्हा तुलसीराव अपनी मां की साड़ी का पल्लू पकड़े उसके साथ जाने का हठ कर रहा था, जबकि राशन अफसर श्री बालकृष्ण बिट्ठल राव कोलार्कर अपने बंगले में दाखिल हुए। (धारा, 57)

उन दिनों मेरी भांजी के विवाह की चिंता लगी हुई थी। मेरी पत्नी अपने जाति-समाज की परंपरा के अनुसार ही उसका विवाह करने का हठ कर रही थी। उसके हठ में समाज की नाड़ी बोल रही थी। (बूंद, 579)

(वह) ... दर्शन करने का हठ कर रही है। किसी बड़े दुःख में ग्रस्त जान पड़ती है। (कचनार, 178)

हठ कर—"to urge (someone) repeatedly, to insist on"

गुरुजी ने बहुत समझाया, लेकिन मेधावी बालक नहीं माना। उसने हठ करके भाष्याचार्य से जाने की स्वीकृति ले ही ली। (आदर्श, 20)

के लिये हठ कर—"to repeatedly ask for"

आप विश्वास न मानेंगे, एक बार उसने अपने साथी रामनेवाज़ के मामा की ऐसी सुंदर मूर्ति बनाई थी कि रामनेवाज़ उसे असली मामा मानकर घंटों उससे मिठाई के लिए हठ करता रहा और अंत में यही समझकर रूठ गया कि मामा नाराज़ हैं, इसीलिए चुप हैं। (कथा, 32)

के लिए हठ कर—"to be unyielding"

कन्या सज्जन को खड़ी देखती रही। जिस तरह सज्जन उत्तर न देने के लिए हठ कर रहा था उसी तरह कन्या का मन उत्तर पाने के लिए हठ पर जमा हुआ था। (बूंद, 374)

से हठ कर—"to be stubborn"

राजा : . . . तुम्हें मुझसे जरा भी मोह नहीं है क्या ?
रानी : और तुम्हें क्या मुझ से मोह है ?
राजा : है, यही तो बात है रानी, नहीं तो तुम मुझ से इस तरह का हठ नहीं करतीं। (नाटक, 31)

5. **पर ज़िद कर—"to insist upon"**

डरते थे कि कहीं वह इन रुपयों को अपनी लड़कियों के विवाह के लिए रख छोड़ने पर ज़िद न करने लगें। (सेवा, 164)

के लिए ज़िद कर—"to insist on"

न कभी नुमायश के लिए मचले, न सिनेमा देखने के लिए ज़िद करे। (सच, 52)

की ज़िद कर—"to insist on, to repeatedly ask for"

मनियां का बड़ा लड़का ऊपर जंगले के पास खड़ा होकर दादी का पल्ला खींचते हुये जलेबी खाने की ज़िद कर रहा था। (बूंद, 24)

की ज़िद कर—"to be repeatedly wanting to, insist on"

मितानसिंह चिता पर चढ़ जाने को ज़िद कर रहे थे और लोग उन्हें रोककर ढाढ़स दे रहे थे। (फूलो, 31)

ज़िद पर बैठ—"to start asking for again and again"

किन्तु मरदाने को तो सख्त प्यास लगी थी। बाबा नानक यह सुनकर चिंता में पड़ गये। इस जंगल में पानी तो दूर-दूर तक नहीं था और मरदाना ज़िद कर बैठता तो सबके लिये बड़ी मुश्किल हो जाती। (दुग्गल, 50)

13. अनुमान, अंदाजा, अंदाज

1. अनुमान, अन्दाजा, अन्दाज all refer to the act of forming an opinion or making a judgement, or to the opinion or judgement so formed or made, which by nature of the case may not be objective or definite. अनुमान implies knowledge or conviction (i.e., the state of being convinced as of the truth or rightness of one's belief) gained by intuition, अन्दाजा, direct knowledge by intuition, and अन्दाज, an opinion or judgement by conjecture.

अनुमान is synonymous with कल्पना when it refers to forming an idea or having in mind a notion of something. अनुमान stresses taking something for granted or as true or existent, especially as a basis for reasoning and कल्पना lacks this implication.

2. Both अनुमान and अन्दाज are ± process and अन्दाजा + process only. They form ANP with का and do not admit plural.

3. **का अनुमान कर—"to envision"**

आप अपनी आवश्यकताओं का ठीक अनुमान नहीं कर सकते। (कंकाल, 85)

का अनुमान कर—"to infer"

जिस प्रकार कर्म द्वारा फल का अनुमान किया जाता है उसी प्रकार फल द्वारा कर्म का भी अनुमान हो सकता है। (धर्म, 52)

का अनुमान कर—"to gather"

इससे यह अनुमान करता हूं कि मेरी बुद्धि मंद रही होगी और स्मरण शक्ति कच्ची। (गांधी, 5)

अनुमान कर—"to imagine"

खांडिक्य ने उसे दूर से आते देखकर अनुमान किया कि वह उसका वध करने आ रहा है। (भारक, 73)

अनुमान कर—"to estimate"

इससे इतनी बड़ी-बड़ी लहरें उठीं कि उनके बीच की दूरी ९० मील तक अनुमान की गई। (समुद्र, 33)

अनुमान कर—"to suppose"

एक समय अनुमान किया जाता था कि यह उस दशा में होता है जब कि कोई तारा आकाश में घूमता हुआ बिखरे हुए रजकणों से टकरा जाता है। (नक्षत्र, 15)

अनुमान कर—"to gather"

बोधा प्रधान ने अक्षोभ्य भैरव का जो रूप बताया था उस पर से मैंने अनुमान किया था कि अक्षोभ्य भैरव अक्खड़ और शुष्क तान्त्रिक होंगे, अभिचार के बल पर श्रद्धालु जनों पर आतंक जमाया करते होंगे...। (चारु, 401)

4. **का अंदाज़ा कर—"to estimate"**

...जैसे कसाई किसी पले हुए बकरे को देख-देख कर उसके गोश्त का अंदाजा करता है। (बाहों, 57)

5. **अंदाज़ कर—"to conjecture"**

वह तैरना नहीं जानता था इसलिए अंदाज किया जाता है कि उसकी मृत्यु होने में देर न लगी होगी। (धनु, 195)

का अंदाज़ कर—"to make a guess as to, to guess"

साधारण मनुष्य इस बात का कोई अंदाज़ नहीं कर सकता कि वह आज कहां है और कल कहां रहेगा। (नक्षत्र, 18)

का अंदाज़ कर—"to judge, to guess"

झाड़ियों की ओट खड़ा चन्द्रराव शत्रु के बदले हुए मोर्चे की दूरी का अंदाज़ कर रहा था। (ब्रेटी, 55)

अंदाज़ कर ले—"to guess"

उसने अंदाज़ कर लिया कि यही वीणा ज्ञानशंकर का प्रेमी है। (धनु, 163)

14. वरण, चयन, चुनाव

1. वरण, चयन and चुनाव refer to the exercise of one's judgement in order to fix upon one (or more) of a number of things as the one (or ones) to be taken, accepted, adopted, or the like. वरण is exercising one's preference implying a sense of discretion, चयन is making a selection (or selection-making in general) on a given basis, and चुनाव is an exercise in choice-making in general.

2. वरण is—process and चयन and चुनाव are+process only. They all form ANP with का and are not pluralized.

3. **का वरण को—"to take to, to conceive and develop a liking for"**

जब तक हम श्रेष्ठता का वरण नहीं कर लेते तब तक हमारा राष्ट्र महान नहीं हो सकता। (अमरीका, 38)

का वरण कर—"to take to something" (as a means of progression)

और गार्हस्थ्य लम्बी यात्रा है—वल्कि पथ-यात्रा नहीं, सागर-यात्रा, जिस में मोड़ पर नहीं, क्षण क्षण पर संकल्प-पूर्वक जोखम का वरण करना होता है और कोई लीकें आंकी हुई नहीं मिलतीं, नक्शे और कम्पास और अन्ततोगत्वा अपनी बुद्धि और अपने साहस के सहारे चलना होता है। (नदी, 74)

को वरण कर—"to take to (i. e. adapting oneself to)"

चुनाव स्पष्ट है, हम चाहें तो भय से वाणी को रुग्ण और जर्जर बना डालें—चाहें तो साहस को वरण कर अपनी वाणी को इस नयी मर्यादा की अपराजेय तेजस्विता से अभिषिक्त कर इतिहास को नया मोड़ दे दें। (मूल्य, 140)

को वरण कर—"to take on, to undertake; to take to"

इस बार मातृभूमि के उद्धार के लिये वह मृत्यु को वरण करने का संकल्प कर चुका है।

"This time he is decided upon (taking on) undertaking a deadly course for the emancipation of his mother-land."

4. का चयन कर—"to make a selection, to select"

दस्तकारी का चयन बालकों की पसन्द का ध्यान रख कर किया जाना चाहिए। (बुन, 28)

"It is desirable that a craft is selected keeping in mind the likes and dislikes of children."

का चयन कर—"to decide upon one's choice of, to pick"

योजना का चयन करते समय...। (सामुदा, 7)

5. का चुनाव कर—"to choose"

दस्तकारी का चुनाव करते समय बालकों की अवस्था को भी ध्यान में रखना चाहिये। (बुन, 28)

आज हमारे समाज में लड़कों को ही नहीं, बल्कि सुशिक्षित लड़कियों को भी, विशेषकर उच्च वर्ग की लड़कियों को, अपने जीवन साथी का चुनाव करने की स्वतंत्रता एक हद तक प्राप्त हो चुकी है। (भंवर, 29)

का चुनाव कर—"to pick"

...यह नहीं समझना चाहिए कि हम मन के विचारों और संस्कारों को अच्छी दिशा में नहीं ला सकते। जिन द्वारों और जिन साधनों द्वारा हम पर संस्कार अंकित होते हैं उन्हीं का चुनाव करके हम संस्कारों को बदल भी सकते हैं। (चमत्कार, 74)

नयी भेड़ें खरीदते समय भेड़ों का चुनाव सावधानी से करना चाहिए। (भेड़, 30)

का चुनाव कर—"to choose"

वह शर्त यह रहेगी कि पार्टनर्स का चुनाव ताशों पर न छोड़कर हम लोग स्वयं कर लें। (तीन, 61)

"The condition is this (i.e. I propose) that we choose partners ourselves..."

का चुनाव कर—"to make/take one's choice, to opt for, to choose"

यद्यपि तीनों का मिलन अंत में विवेक के संगम पर होता है, तथापि दृष्टि-भेद से एक का चुनाव प्रारंभिक अवस्था में करना पड़ता है। (धर्म, 113)

का चुनाव कर—"to make a selection, to select"

ऐसा वह तभी कर सकता है जब वह अपने क्षेत्र की जलवायु और चरागाह की परिस्थितियों के अनुकूल भेड़ों और मेढ़ों का ठीक तरह से चुनाव कर सकता है। इसलिए किसी विशेष नस्ल या किस्म का चुनाव करते हुए स्थानीय परिस्थितियों की ओर ध्यान रखना बहुत महत्त्वपूर्ण है। (भेड़, 28-29)

का चुनाव कर—"to pick"

बाद में इनसे अच्छी भेड़ों का चुनाव कर सकते हैं और कम आयु वाली नयी भेड़ें अधिक आयु वाली प्रौढ़ भेड़ों की अपेक्षा अपने आपको नयी परिस्थितियों के अनुकूल जल्दी बदल लेनी हैं। (भेड़, 30)

15. भेद, अन्तर

1. भेद and अन्तर refer to pointing out or marking the difference between things that are or seem to be very much and confusingly alike. भेद stresses the difference in kind, and is applied to the statement of such a difference between things which otherwise seem similar. अन्तर stresses the fact of relative difference between things which are confusingly alike. In sentences where both भेद and अन्तर imply disagreement, they respectively refer to the confusion aroused by discernment of difference between things otherwise considered similar and to the confusion due to differentiating between things which do not possess any distinguishing characteristics.

2. Both nouns are+process, and form ANP with के बीच and में. के बीच stresses or emphasizes the obvious and में lacks this implication. Both nouns do not admit plural.

3. के बीच भेद कर—"to differentiate between N and N, to make a distinction"

बच्ची ने जिस सहज भाव से गिरने और फिसल जाने के बीच भेद किया था, उससे मुझे बरबस हंसी आ गई और मैं हंसने लगा। (परिन्दे, 34)

में भेद कर—"to distinguish between N and N"

गांव के लोग हैरान थे कि तहसीलदार नूरी और जमालो में भेद क्यों करता है? दोनों लड़कियों की शक्ल सूरत इतनी मिलती थी कि स्वयं भूरेखां के पड़ोसी उन्हें पहचानने में भूल कर जाते थे। (डगर, 45)

4. के बीच अन्तर कर—"to differentiate between N and N, to recognize a difference between N and N"

अमेरिका को आक्रमणकारी और आक्रांत के बीच अंतर करना चाहिए।

के बीच अंतर कर—"to distinguish N from N"

इसलिए यह समझ में नहीं आता कि इन्हीं लेखकों के स्वतंत्र रूप से प्रकाशित होने वाले संग्रहों तथा एक सूत्र में पिरोये गये इन संग्रहों में किस आधार पर अन्तर किया जाए। (आकाश, भूमिका)

में अन्तर कर—"to distinguish between N and N"

भारत में समाज कल्याण के विभिन्न पहलुओं का विस्तृत अध्ययन करने से पहले यह समझना आवश्यक है कि यह समाज कल्याण क्या है? समाज कल्याण का अर्थ इसलिए भी जानना आवश्यक है क्योंकि बहुधा अनेक लेखक समाज कल्याण और कल्याणकारी राज्य द्वारा किये जाने वाले सर्वांगीण कल्याण में अन्तर नहीं करते। (भारत, 3)

16. उज्र, एतराज, आपत्ति

1. उज्र, एतराज and आपत्ति refer to the indication of one's dissent or opposition to somthing. उज्र is lack of concurrence indicated by one's manifestation of neither the will nor the desire to do something. एतराज is objecting to or disapproving something implying an unfavourable judgement. आपत्ति is objecting to something with words in a variety of ways.

2. All nouns are+process, and form ANP with में or पर. में is used when one has objection to doing something, and पर when one objects to something done by someone else, or has objection to someone's doing something.

3. **उज्र कर—"to show one's unwillingness"**

पर उसे रह-रह कर यही ख्याल आता था कि औरत भी एक अजीब किस्म की पहेली है। उस दिन तो उसने कोई उज्र नहीं किया था और आज एकदम फिरण्ट हो गई ? (धनु, 107-108)

4. **में एतराज कर—"to have an objection"**

और यह मानने में हमें एतराज नहीं करना चाहिए कि उनमें चोर भी होते हैं, और उनके अंग औज़ारों का काम करते हैं। (समुद्र, 69)

पर एतराज कर—"to object to, to disapprove"

अंग्रेज गवर्नर ने फिर जब्ती की आज्ञा उठा लिए जाने पर एतराज किया। (सुन्दर, झ)

5. **में आपत्ति कर—"to dislike, to be disinclined to"**

इतना सब होने पर भी ताई कन्या के हाथ का छुआ पानी पीने में अभी तक आपत्ति करती थीं। (बूंद, 558)

पर आपत्ति कर—"to object to"

शुक्ल :—मोती ने तुम्हारे यहाँ आने पर आपत्ति नहीं की थी। (सन्यासी, 37)

17. समता, बराबरी

1. समता and बराबरी are the expressions employed (generally in negative) when one person or a thing is referred to as having equality with another in some qualities. समता suggests comparability (i.e. having enough like qualities to make comparison appropriate), and बराबरी is likening to another in capabilities to perform and/or accomplish, implying competitiveness.

2. Both nouns are+process and form ANP with की. They do not admit plural.

3. **की समता कर—"to approach, to touch"**

खान-पान में, शुचि-रुचि में, देव-भक्ति में, कर्म-श्रद्धा में, शम-दमादि गुणों में, ज्ञान-मार्ग में प्रभु की समता कौन कर सकता है। (शांतला, 98)

4. **की बराबरी कर—"to touch"**

उस समय यूरोप का कोई देश सभ्यता के किसी अंग में भी भारत की बराबरी न कर सकता था। (सुन्दर, 112)

किन्तु कालिदास की बराबरी करने वाले अन्य कवि न होने के कारण दूसरी उंगली खाली रह गई। (ज्योति, 21)

18. विलम्ब, देर

1. Both विलम्ब and देर refer to the act of delaying or taking more time in doing something in a variety of ways. विलम्ब stresses more than required or necessary prolongation of time through hesitation or inadvertence but never deliberately, and देर is a neutral term lacking in the implications of विलम्ब. The sentences below illustrate this distinction.

में विलम्ब कर—"to linger"

इस चिन्ता में मैंने जरूर कुछ अनुचित विलम्ब किया होगा... (बाण, 49)

में देर कर—"to take (too much) time"

इसी झंझट में मैंने इतनी देर कर दी, पर आप जरूर-जरूर मेरी बात ठीक-ठीक समझेंगे और तब आपको यह देर भी अच्छी लगेगी। (नदी, 77)

2. Both nouns are +process and do not admit plural. They form ANP with the में which occurs with nouns as well as infinitives.

में विलम्ब न कर—"to hesitate"

···और बात से काम न चले तो शस्त्र उठाने में एक क्षण का भी विलम्ब न करना। (बेटी, 30)

में देर कर—"to put off (to a latter time)"

तुम भी मुझे भगवान के प्रसाद की तरह मिली हो कन्या। मैं तुम्हें ग्रहण करने में देर नहीं करना चाहता। (बूंद, 228)

3. विलम्ब may sometimes mean "intentionally delaying". Observe the contrast between विलम्ब and देर in the following sentences where the latter is qualified by जानबूझकर "deliberately".

विलम्ब कर—"to take some time"

किन्तु तुम थे थके हुए और तुम्हारी देह से पसीना निकल रहा था। उस दशा में ठंडा पानी देने से नुकसान होता। उसी से मैंने थोड़ा सा विलम्ब कर दिया। (रूस, 6)

देर कर—"to wait"

उसने बाजार में जानबूझकर देर कर दी और नौ बजे के बाद घर की तरफ चला। (डगर, 35)

4. देर occurs with N को also.

को देर कर—"to detain"

लेकिन—मैं आपको देर तो नहीं कर दे रही हूं? आपके मेज़बान—(नदी, 107)

5. By dropping N में both विलम्ब कर-and देर कर-occur as conjunctive participles in a variety of contexts.

तुम ठीक कहते हो नारायण, हम विलम्ब करके अपनी प्रजा की दृष्टि में अपराधी नहीं बनना चाहते। (बेटी, 35)

महिला ने विलम्ब न कर कन्धे पर उबहनी डालकर दोनों घड़े एक-एक कर उठा लिये। (निरु, 62)

मालती : बहुत से लड़के देर करके आते हैं और लेख नहीं लिखते। किसी को भी वे इस तरह नहीं निकाल बाहर करते। (सन्यासी, 24)

इनामदार सोचता शायद उसे उसकी करतूतों की सज़ा मिल रही थी। कितनी-कितनी देर करके वह रात को घर लौटता था। (दुग्गल, 131)

19. गणना, गिनती

1. Both गणना and गिनती refer to the act of ascertaining the total of units in a given collection by noting one after another or one group after another. The former implies determining the total by noting the known specifics of the objects or individuals in addition to the ascertainment of their total number. The latter has no such implication. The sentences below illustrate this distinction.

यदि भारत में अब तक खोले गये विकास खण्डों की गणना की जाय तो ग्रामीण क्षेत्रों में प्रशिक्षित महिलाओं की सेवाओं का ज्ञान होगा। (श्रम, 32)

छावनी के नायक चन्द्रराव ने मराठों के साज़-सामान और हरबा-हथियारों की गिनती करके उन्हें कब्जे में ले लिया। (बेटी, 22)

2. The difference in meaning between N की गणना/गिनती कर-on the one hand and गिन-"to count" on the other is illustrated in the sentence below.

फिर मीनू गेट के बाहर ईंटों के चबूतरे पर बैठकर सड़क पर आ जा रही मोटरों की गणना करने लगा। मीनू गिनता जा रहा था, गिनता जा रहा था ...। (दुग्गल, 158)

The verb गिन-simply refers to the process of counting (not ascertaining) by saying the numerals in succession.

3. Both गणना and गिनती are +process and form ANP with की which does not admit infinitives. Only गणना is pluralized. In the contexts where गणना can be pluralized, it means "calculation".

सभी गणनायें मुद्रा-प्राप्तियों (money yields) और मुद्रा-लागतों (money costs) के संदर्भ में की जाती हैं। (एमाई, 56)

4. Both गणना and गिनती, when they refer to the act of ascertaining the category or classifying an individual, a thing or an idea rather than the total in a given collection, require a noun phrase indicating the category or class followed by one of the postpositions में, अन्तर्गत, के साथ etc., as in भारत के मूर्धन्य विद्वानों और चिन्तकों में उनकी गणना...,जिनकी गणना...मुद्रा...के अन्तर्गत...,...दोनों ही नगरियों का अस्तित्व अतिप्राचीन था और उनकी गणना उस समय के अन्य कतिपय प्रमुख नगरों...के साथ...,... गांव वाले मेरी बेवकूफों में गिनती...

5. Only गणना permits the occurrence of nouns like विनिमय-अनुपात, etc., denoting something which can be mathematically or arithmetically determined.

20. मैत्री, मित्रता, दोस्ती

1. मैत्री, मित्रता and दोस्ती all refer to making friends with. मैत्री stresses the promotion of friendly disposition for one another, मित्रता implies a lack of hostile or antagonistic attitude, or refers to seeking the society of someone (often but not necessarily, in order to gain favours), and दोस्ती is intimate friendship marked by informal relationship.

2. All nouns are +process, and form ANP with के साथ or से.

3. **से मैत्री कर--"to befriend, to show a cordial regard for"**

मैंने छोटी-से-छोटी समझी जाने वाली जाति के लोगों से मैत्री की थी और अत्यन्त

पतित समझे जाने वालों में जाकर उनके निदारुण दुःख की ज्वाला का साक्षात् परिचय पाया था। (चारु, 147)

4. **से मित्रता कर—"to make friends with"**

मैं अब निश्चय कर चुका था कि अपनी लम्पटता की बदनामी को हमेशा के लिए धो दूंगा। आज मैं कुमार कृष्णवर्द्धन से मित्रता करूंगा और दस दिन के भीतर ही महा-धिराज का भी कृपापात्र बन जाऊंगा। (बाण, 6)

से मित्रता कर—"to maintain friendly relations with"

एक राष्ट्र अपने स्वार्थ के रक्षार्थ दूसरे राष्ट्र से मित्रता करता है। (वैदिक, 23)

5. **से दोस्ती कर—"to associate with, to keep company with"**

लोमड़ी ने अकड़कर, दुम फुलाकर कहा—दुश्मन को छल से मारो। पहले उससे दोस्ती करो, फिर उसे मार डालो। (बाल, 11, 19)

जमके दोस्ती कर—"to become a close friend (of)"

धावक ने हंसकर कहा—जब राजसभा से आ ही गये, तो हम लोगों को अस्पृश्य मानने से कैसे काम चलेगा। मैंने विनीत भाव से कहा—आर्य, मुझे अकारण लज्जा दे रहे हैं। परन्तु धावक मस्त आदमी था। उसने थोड़ी देर में ही जमके दोस्ती करली। देर तक वह इधर-उधर की बातें करता रहा। (बाण, 194-5)

21. संशय, संदेह, भ्रम, भरम, शक, आशंका, शंका

1. संशय, सन्देह, भ्रम, भरम, शक, आशंका and शंका are applied to expressions of one's feeling or a state of mind dominated by the feeling that one is not sure about someone or something. संशय refers to one's state of mind in which one is given to skepticism or mistrust or entertains a feeling of lack of certitude in something proposed for belief. सन्देह either refers to suspicion implying a conjecture or disinclination to accept the truth of something. भ्रम is misunderstanding implying one's inability to distinguish or discriminate (and thus confusing one thing for another). भरम is the suspicion of something unfavourable for oneself, in something done or said by someone else. The person concerned is presupposed to have such a nature or habitual disposition of mind toward such suspicions and on the occasion referred to chooses to give some indication of his anxiety. शक is indulgence in skepticism or contains reference to one's proneness to suspicion. आशंका refers to the expression of one's doubts or one's misgivings, because of uneasiness in a situation or mistrust of

a person, and शंका is applied to the expression of one's doubt implying uncertainty or misgivings about the truth, reality or validity of something.

2. All the nouns are +process, and do not admit plural except शंका. They form ANP with पर, के प्रति, में, का, के सम्बन्ध में, के विषय में and के बारे में. The N post is dropped when संशय etc. कर-is followed by a कि clause.

3. **पर संशय कर—"to mistrust"**

वे लोग संशय करेंगे कि हम अपने बाकी रुपये के लोभ में इसका उपचार कर रहे हैं। (कचनार, 122)

पर संशय कर लेना—"to be mistrustful, to be skeptical about"

अपने ज्ञान की सत्यता को कसौटी पर परखने के लिए भी संशय कर लेना चाहिए। (धर्म, 121)

4. **पर सन्देह कर—"to suspect"**

एक बार महर्षि गौतम ने अपनी स्त्री अहल्या के चरित्र पर सन्देह करके चिरकारी को उसका वध कर डालने को कहा। (भारक, 67-8)

जल्हन के सरल विश्वास पर सन्देह करने का मुझे क्या अधिकार है। (चारु, 391)

संदेह कर— "to suspect"

सबको यह विश्वास हो चला था कि अब सिकन्दर के प्राण नहीं बचेंगे, इसलिए हर-एक यह सोचता था कि यदि दवा देने के बाद सिकन्दर मर गया तो लोग सन्देह कर सकते हैं कि हकीम ने जानबूझकर उसकी हत्या की है। अपने ऊपर इस तरह का संकट मोल लेने को कौन तैयार होता। (आदर्श, 29-30)

के ऊपर संदेह कर—

मैं निर्दोष हूं, आप मेरे ऊपर किसी तरह का सन्देह न करें। (आदर्श, 32)

"Don't entertain any suspicions of me".

में संदेह कर —"to raise a doubt about, to be skeptical about"

ईश्वर के अस्तित्व में संदेह करना व्यर्थ है, क्योंकि ऐसा कोई भी मनुष्य नहीं है जो ईश्वर को किसी न किसी रूप में न मानता हो। (धर्म, 63)

का सन्देह कर—"to suspect"

सामान्य रूप में राजकीय नियंत्रण के अत्यधिक बढ़ जाने में उपरोक्त खतरों का सन्देह अवश्य किया जा सकता है। (भारत, 38)

वह भी इस बात को समझता था कि यदि उसकी दवा से सिकन्दर को लाभ न हुआ और वह मर ही गया तो लोग हत्या का सन्देह कर सकते हैं। (आदर्श, 30)

के प्रति संदेह कर—"to suspect one of, to suspect that one..."

पति के प्रति पर-स्त्रीगमन का सन्देह करते रहना, अथवा खुद पर-पुरुष की घात में रहना। (बूंद, 463)

पर के विषय में सन्देह कर—"to accuse someone"

जब से सुभद्रा ने सदन पर अपने कंगन के विषय में सन्देह किया था तब से पद्मसिंह उससे रुष्ट हो गये थे। (सेवा, 141)

5. का भ्रम कर—"to confuse one thing for another"

ऊन-उत्पादक भेड़ों के आस-पास के क्षेत्रों में इन रोयेंदार नस्ल की भेड़ों को छोटे पांव वाली सुगठित किस्म की भेड़ों का भ्रम करने लगते हैं और उन्हें नासमझी में विभिन्न किस्म की भेड़ें मानने लगते हैं। (भेड़, 13)

6. का भरम कर—"to entertain any suspicion about something (in one's mind)"

—फूलावन्ती, जिसे बोली-ठोली का अमल हो, बोल-कुबोल का परहेज न हो, उसके कहे का तू भरम करेगी? (मित्रो, 6)

धनवन्ती सयाने गले समझाकर बोली—बेटा, तुम्हारे बाप का जी राजी नहीं, इनके कहे का भरम न करना। (मित्रो, 8)

7. में शक कर—"to be skeptical about"

वह खुदा के इन्साफ में क्यों शक करे। (फूलो, 53)

जरा-जरा में शक कर—"to suspect (evil of every little thing)"

घर में तो मुन्ने की मां किसी स्त्री को देखकर सिर पर छत ले लेती है। ...पुरानी दकियानूस गंवार औरत है जरा-जरा में शक करने लगती है। (मनु, 55)

8. की आशंका कर—"to raise a doubt"

यहां एक बात और स्पष्ट कर देने की आवश्यकता प्रतीत होती है—कई लोग इस प्रकार की आशंका कर बैठते हैं कि मूलोद्योग पर इतना बल देने पर शिक्षालय कहीं उद्योग-शालाओं का रूप न ले लें और बालकों पर अत्यधिक श्रम का भार न डाल दें। (बुन, 27)

9. **के बारे में शंका कर—"to raise a doubt about (the validity of), to doubt"**

इसलिये मनुष्य कभी-कभी अपने सभी अनुभवों के बारे में शंका करते हुए पूछने लगता है—मैं जो देख रहा हूं वह वास्तव में है या नहीं। (पाश्चात्य, 2)

के सम्बन्ध में शंका कर—"to raise a doubt about, to be skeptical about"

आज का मनुष्य ईश्वर और आत्मा के सम्बन्ध में ही शंका नहीं करता ....। (पाश्चात्य, 2)

पर शंकाएं कर—"to express one's misgiving about"

अब यामिनी बाबू को नीली की मैत्री खटकने लगी, नीली के भविष्य पर अनेक प्रकार की शंकाएं उन्होंने कीं। निरू के प्रति जितने विरोधी भाव थे, एक साथ, तेज हवा में बादलों की तरह कट-छंट गये। (निरु, 18)

पर शंका कर—"to doubt, to suspect one of"

इतनी बाकायदा कार्रवाई के बाद किसी को महिला सेवा मंडल पर किसी प्रकार की शंका करने का अधिकार ही नहीं रह जाता। (बूंद, 501)

के प्रति शंका कर—"to doubt, to suspect"

राजा : नहीं रानी, तुमने मेरे प्रेम और विश्वास के प्रति शंका की थी, तभी मैं उसकी तुम्हारे लिये परीक्षा देना चाहता हूं। (नाटक, 67)

शंका कर—"to express one's doubt, to raise a doubt"

लेकिन, दादा, कपूर ने शंका की, एक बात अभी समझ में नहीं आई। जलना क्या है, समझ गया पर आप तो बताने जा रहे थे कि आग क्या है। (आग, 50)

22. अनुग्रह, कृपा, मेहरबानी

1. अनुग्रह, कृपा and मेहरबानी all refer to expression of one's feeling of gratitude by verbally acknowledging someone's act of kindness. अनुग्रह refers to an act of kindness done by a superior, and regarded as an obligation upon oneself by the one benefiting. कृपा is a reference to someone's kind disposition exhibited in the act, and मेहरबानी to a kindly act.

2. All the nouns are +process, and form ANP with के ऊपर or पर which may be optionally dropped.

3. **के ऊपर अनुग्रह कर—"to gratify, to confer a favor upon"**

भगवान ने उनके ऊपर अनुग्रह किया और प्रज्ञा के आलोक से उन्हें सत्यज्ञान की ओर उन्मुख किया। (चारु, 67)

अनुग्रह कर—"to do a great favor (for someone)"

भवन—डाक्टर, आपने बड़ा अनुग्रह किया। इस अवस्था में भी चले आए। (खिलौने, 34)

4. **के ऊपर कृपा कर—"to do a favor (for someone)"**

मुझे उन्होंने कई बार सहायता दी है। इसलिए आप भी मेरे ऊपर कृपा करें। भगवान आपका भला करें। (तुला, 57)

के ऊपर कृपा कर—"kindly, benignly"

मां, इसी शरीफ मुसलमान ने मेरे ऊपर कृपाकर यह वादा किया है कि यह चिट्ठी किसी न किसी तरह बच-बचाकर हावड़ा स्टेशन के डाकखाने में छोड़ आएगा। (ख़त, 73)

पर कृपा कर—"to do a favor (for someone), to render a service (to someone)"

दुष्यन्त ने कण्व के आश्रम की शकुन्तला से विवाह करके मनुष्य जाति पर कौन-सी कृपा की? (कहा, 96)

कृपा करके—"please!"

भइया गीदड़, मैं बड़ी प्यासी हूं। इतनी सब बात नहीं कह सकती, कृपा करके मुझे पहले थोड़ा-सा पानी पी लेने दो। (बाल, 11, 22)

रमाशंकर: हां, आप अखबारी दुनिया के लेखक—क्लास के लिए क्यों लिखें? कृपा कर क्लास से निकल जाइये। (सन्यासी, 21)

5. **मेहरबानी कर—"to do someone a favor, to be kind enough"**

आप एक मेहरबानी करेंगे? पुलिस वालों से कह दें, जल्द ही यहां से चले जायं। हम लोगों को फूट-फूट कर रोने के लिए भी अवकाश नहीं मिल रहा है। (बूंद, 56)

मेहरबानी करके—"kindly, would you be kind enough to..."

मेहरबानी करके आप मुझे अपने साथियों के साथ रहने से न रोकें। (परम, 5)

23. रहम, दया

1. रहम and दया both refer to an act of kindness motivated by compassion (i.e., deep feeling for and understanding of misery or suffering of others, and the concomitant desire to promote its alleviation). रहम stresses the benevolence of the agent or gratification in the one benefiting. दया lacks the overt signification of रहम, and thus also implies alleviation of misery or suffering through forbearance.

2. Both nouns are +process and form ANP with पर. They are not pluralized.

3. पर रहम कर—"to sympathize with"

मुझे और कुछ नहीं, चार रोटियां और चार गज़ कपड़े की ज़रूरत है। आपको भगवान ने चार पैसे दिए हैं। मेरी हालत पर रहम कीजिए। (ख़त, 99)

पर रहम कर—"to have mercy upon"

बतलाइये आप मुझे कैसे कन्विंस करेंगे कि स्विंग, ग़रीबों पर रहम करके उनका इलाज़ मुफ्त किया करो ? अगर ऐसा करूं तो दुनिया में ग़रीब इतने ज्यादा हैं कि मुझे अपने अमीर पेशेन्ट्स से फीस कमाने की फुरसत ही नहीं मिलेगी। (बूंद, 92)

4. पर दया कर—"to take pity on"

जुगनू—तो यह कहो, इनका कोई धरम-करम नहीं है। फिर भला ग़रीबों पर क्यों दया करने लगीं। (सम, 49)

पर दया कर—"to feel for, to have sympathy for"

सदन इस प्रकार सुमन से बचता था जैसे हम कुष्ट रोगी से बचते हैं, उस पर दया करते हुए भी उसके समीप जाने की हिम्मत नहीं रखते। (सेवा, 315-16)

दया कर—"to pity"

इन पर क्रोध करने की जगह दया करनी चाहिये। (सेवा, 274)

24. आलस्य, सुस्ती

1. आलस्य (Sp.var आलस) and सुस्ती both refer to slowing down or slackening in the performance of what one normally does or is expected to do. आलस्य implies evading or putting off the performance of one's obligation due to laziness, and सुस्ती is a reflection upon someone's habit of doing things slowly or taking more time than would be normally required under the given circumstances.

2. Both nouns are +process and form ANP with में. Only आलस्य forms ANP with से also. They are not pluralized.

3. में आलस्य कर—"to let up"

वह सत्य का पुजारी अपनी पूजा में कभी आलस्य और प्रमाद नहीं करता। (धर्म, 148)

आलस्य कर—"to laze around, to idle away"

कल से शायद काम करने लायक हो जाऊं, आज अभी और आलस करने का जी है। (नदी, 275)

से आलस्य कर—"to shirk from"

कहीं ऐसा न हो कि मणियां बीनने के कठिन काम से आलस्य करते हुए हम अपने घर के इस कूड़े-कचड़े की सड़ांध में घुटते बैठे रहे। (बूंद, 111)

4. **में सुस्ती कर—"to take it easy"**

चाय ले आने में चौबेजी और सुस्ती कर रहे थे। (तितली, 26)

25. इंगित, संकेत, इशारा

1. इंगित, संकेत, इशारा refer to the act of pointing something out to someone, either literally, with motion of hands or fingers, or figuratively; they refer also to anything communicated by such means. They may apply in situations in which one infers a fact or possibility, on more or less good grounds, from the characteristics of something.

इंगित is pointing in a direction by extending one's finger or hand, and implies nothing more than a visible indication by means of which something is made known or revealed. It also applies to the expression of one's belief that something points to or indicates another.

संकेत is pointing out or towards indirectly in order to call to someone's notice, or just signalling, hinting or suggesting something in order to convey an idea or the thought of something by indirect means. It applies to the expressions of one's inference that something suggests another, or when one chooses to allude to something rather than expressing oneself directly.

इशारा is a relatively colorless term referring to giving gestural indications in a variety of ways (often expressed in a sentence).

2. All the nouns are +process and form ANP with की ओर, को, का and से. Only इशारा can be pluralized.

3. **की ओर इंगित कर—"to point to"**

वस्तुतः प्रयोगवादी काव्य में लघु मानव की एक ऐसी धारणा को स्थान मिला है जो इतिहास की गति को एक अप्रत्याशित मोड़ दे सकने की क्षमता की ओर इंगित करती है। (निबंध, 672)

की ओर इंगित कर—"to point to"

उन्होंने मन्त्री की ओर इंगित करते हुए कहा, तातपाद को विश्राम की आवश्यकता है। (चारु, 233)

का इंगित कर— "to indicate"

उनकी व्याकुल आंखें केवल एक ही वस्तु की तलाश कर रही थीं—बत्तीस लक्षणों से सम्पन्न किशोरी, जिसके हाथ की रेखाएं उसे रानी से भी बड़ी बनाने का इंगित करती हैं। (चारु, 71)

इंगित कर—"to indicate"

उदासी एक चिह्न है, एक लक्षण है जो बहुधा इस बात को इंगित करती है कि एक नवीन शक्ति अभिव्यक्ति और प्रकाशन के लिए तड़प रही है। उसको टटोल कर कार्यान्वित करो। (चमत्कार, 42)

4. की ओर संकेत कर—"to point towards"

मैंने उस लम्बी सफेद इमारत की ओर संकेत किया, जिसकी खिड़कियों पर शाम की धूप गिर रही थी। (वे दिन, 118)

कलाकार वह कम्पास है जो तूफान में ठीक उत्तर की ओर संकेत करता है। (सन्यासी, 6)

आते-जाते लोग उसे देखते, जानने वाले उसकी ओर संकेत कर दूसरों को उसका नाम बतलाते, टिप्पणियां करते। (सुहाग, 231)

की ओर संकेत कर—"to point out"

...उन्होंने केवल हिंदू समाज के इन दोषों की ओर संकेत ही नहीं किया बल्कि अपनी ओर से जनता के कल्याण के बहुत से काम भी करने शुरू कर दिये। (भारत, 61)

बात यह है कि बिना इन बातों की ओर संकेत किये आधुनिक ज्योतिष की महत्ता की झलक नहीं मिलती। (नक्षत्र, 32)

की ओर संकेत कर—"to allude to"

भारतीय परम्पराओं में 'शिवेतरक्षतये' कहकर उसकी इस स्थिति की ओर संकेत किया गया...। (मूल्य, 151)

पर संकेत कर—"to hint at, to allude to"

मधूलिका अपनी दयनीय अवस्था पर संकेत करने देना नहीं चाहती थी। (अच्छी, 23)

संकेत कर--"to point out"

जैसा कि हम पहले संकेत कर चुके हैं कि . . . । (एमाई, 68)

वह सन्यासी के संकेत किये हुए कुटीर की ओर चली । (कंकाल, 55)

The-process occurrences of संकेत as in the above sentences are derivable from की ओर संकेत कर-by dropping की ओर.

को संकेत कर--"to signal someone to"

मराठा सेनापति ने सम्हल कर घुड़सवारों को दूसरी ओर हटने का संकेत किया किन्तु चन्द्रराव ने उसका संकेत समझ लिया था । (बेटी, 52)

को संकेत कर-may occur with infinitives followed by का (as in the above sentence) or by के लिये. का indicates a signal which may or may not be recognized by anyone other than the one it is meant for. के लिये implies a signal which is recognized by the one it is meant for as well as understood by a third party who is also concerned with the act denoted by the infinitive. The following sentence, therefore, means that "He motioned Choti and others (signifying that it is all right) to come."

शंकर ने आगे बढ़कर सज्जन से कहा---सज्जन जी, मेरी फेमिली के लोग आपसे मिलने के लिए उत्सुक हैं। कहकर उसने छोटी आदि को आने के लिए संकेत किया । सज्जन उसी बेलौस अदा से बाहिर निकल आया। सबसे परिचित होकर बड़ी खुशी हुई कहकर सज्जन फिर मुड़ा। (बूंद, 76)

The sentence below also indicates the suggestiveness of purpose implied by के लिये.

. . .बैठ जाओ (आसन पर अपने निकट बैठने के लिए संकेत करती है । मल्लिका नीचे बैठने लगती है । प्रियंगु संकेत से उसे रोक देती है ।) यहां पास बैठो । (आषाढ़, 71)

Both के लिये and का occur after infinitives but only का after nouns.

मिस खुरशेद ने इस तरह जुगनू की उपस्थिति का उसे संकेत किया कि जुगनू की नज़र पड़ जाय । (सम, 53)

से संकेत कर--"to hint, to suggest"

पर तुम्हें यह दुख देखना न पड़ता और उसके चले जाने पर भी एक बार मैंने तुमसे संकेत किया, पर तुम्हारी इच्छा न देख कर मैं कुछ न बोली । (कंकाल, 53)

और यह कहकर उन्होंने रानी मानकुमारी से उठने का संकेत किया । (सा सा, 207)

का संकेत कर—"to suggest"

हमने इस तरह कुछ दिशाओं का संकेत किया है, जिनमें शांति स्थापना के बीज निहित हैं। (अणु, 33)

का संकेत कर—"to suggest, to indicate"

शिवाजी की उंगलियां आपस में रगड़ खाकर उनके पश्चाताप का संकेत करने लगीं। (बेटी, 103)

का संकेत कर—"to point to"

इस अत्यन्त मर्मस्पर्शी क्षण का चित्रण करते हुए लेखक ने ··· मूल्यगत एकता का चतुर संकेत किया है। (मूल्य, 104-5)

5. को इशारा कर

इशारा seldom occurs in this environment without a qualifying phrase. Such qualifying phrases belong to the following categories:—

(i) noun denoting a body part से infinitive का, e.g., हाथ से उठने का with the restriction that either हाथ से or उठने का, or both may occur except when the infinitive का is represented by a कि clause.

(ii) conjunctive participial phrase, e.g., मुंह पर उंगली रख कर followed by infinitive का, as चुप रहने का.

(iii) noun denoting a body part का, e.g. हाथ का. The occurrences of इशारा in the first two categories do not require any explanation. In the third category, the nouns frequently employed are हाथ and आंख, the former signifies telling someone to wait or to stop, and the latter winking.

विरहेश ने अपनी जेब से एक पत्र निकालकर दिखलाया। बड़ी ने खिड़की से अपना पत्र हिलाया फिर हाथ का इशारा कर खिड़की से हट गई। (बूंद, 220)

गोली सिर्फ हंसा और मंदा को फिर आंख का इशारा कर चल दिया। (लाख, 28)

गोपाल के हाथ से आरा छूटकर गिर पड़ा। उस आदमी के भी छक्के छूट गये। गोपाल के धीरे से आंख का इशारा करते ही वह आदमी चुपचाप सटक गया। (लाख, 143)

इशारा may be used without any qualifying phrase where there is no possibility of ambiguity.

घोड़ों को इशारा कर—"to spur the horses"

और गंगादत्त ने मोहदत्त के रथ के बांके घोड़ों को इशारा किया। और क्षणभर बाद दोनों मित्र इन्द्रप्रस्थ की ओर सनकते नज़र आने लगे। (विचित्र, 51)

से इशारा कर—"to suggest to someone to"

शंकरलाल ने घड़ी की तरफ नज़र डालकर अपनी पत्नी से उठने का इशारा किया। (बूंद, 70)

की ओर इशारा कर—"to refer to (an event)"

...यह फोड़ा समस्त पूंजीवादी व्यवस्था के सीने में पल रहा था और जिस भयंकर विस्फोट की ओर वानगाघ ने इशारा किया था वह विस्फोट आया। (मूल्य, 45)

की ओर इशारा कर—"to point towards, to refer to"

गंगराज ने इस तरह मानों प्रभु के भाव को ताड़ लिया हो, शांतला और लक्ष्मी की ओर इशारा करते हुए कहा—यह है इनकी लावण्यमयी कन्या शांतला... (शांतला, 49)

इशारा कर—"to indicate"

दीवान ने गौरी को गहरी नज़रों से देखते हुए कहा था, "अब यहां भी यही बताना पड़ेगा... घर में वह जान खा गयी और यहां तुम... क्यों क्या बात है?" दीवान की आंखों का टेढ़ापन कुछ और इशारा कर रहा था। (मांस, 94)

6. **निर्लज्ज संकेत कर—"to make an indecent suggestion"**

फिर कुछ रुककर महंत ने एक निर्लज्ज संकेत किया। राजकुमारी उसे जहर के घूंट की तरह पी गई। उसने कहा—तो क्या चौबे यहीं हैं। (तितली, 180)

गंदे इशारे कर—"to make an obscene gesture"

तगड़े और बदसूरत मज़दूरों ने तब आंखें बचाकर गंदे इशारे किये थे। (मांस, 118)

26. प्रवर्तन, प्रारंभ, श्रीगणेश, सूत्रपात, समारंभ, आरंभ, शुरुआत, शुरू

1. प्रवर्तन, प्रारंभ, श्रीगणेश, सूत्रपात, समारम्भ, आरम्भ, शुरुआत and शुरू all refer to taking the first step or steps in a course, a process or an operation, or to set it going. प्रवर्तन is introducing a custom or a trend by bringing it into practice, प्रारम्भ is starting a process by performing or entering on the first stage of it, श्रीगणेश refers to making an auspicious beginning of something of personal concern, and सूत्रपात is either initiating a new trend, a course of development or refers to its inauguration through an event (occurring as the subject in the sentence). समारम्भ is the beginning or commence-

ment of what one undertakes to accomplish, or refers to the fact of one's taking upon oneself a big project (or a variety of projects) which is received with favor by others. आरम्भ is to begin or commence, i.e., to initiate formally by performing the first act, शुरुआत is to begin or make a beginning of a process by bringing about a start or establishing an origin of it, and शुरू is to begin an act by setting about it or start a process by getting into it or by performing or executing the first part of it.

2. प्रवर्तन, श्रीगणेश and शुरुआत are +process, प्रारम्भ, समारम्भ and आरम्भ are ±process, and शुरू-process only.

They form ANP with का (की for शुरुआत) which permits occurrence of infinitives freely. None of them is pluralized.

3. **का प्रवर्तन कर—"to introduce"**

कुशीनगर में जब भगवान् का वैशाखी पूर्णिमा को परिनिर्वाण हुआ तो जम्बूद्वीप के सभी भिक्षुओं ने समझा कि भगवान ने पृथ्वी का त्याग किया। परन्तु उनकी लीला अपरम्पार है। तुषित-लोक से वे फिर इस लोक में लौट आये और यहां उन्होंने चीनाचार की साधना का प्रवर्तन किया। (चारु, 67)

का प्रवर्तन कर—"to institute a constitutional reform"

पहाड़ी नेताओं की मांगों की पूर्ति के लिए केन्द्रीय सरकार ने एक नया महत्त्वपूर्ण संविधानिक प्रवर्तन किया।

4. **का प्रारंभ कर—"to start"**

...दस्तकारी बालक की इस क्रियात्मक तथा सृजनात्मक प्रवृत्ति को प्रोत्साहित करती है। अतः दस्तकारी द्वारा शिक्षा का प्रारम्भ किया जाना स्वाभाविक है। (बुन, 26)

का प्रारम्भ कर—"to inaugurate"

भारत में सामुदायिक विकास कार्यक्रम का प्रारम्भ राष्ट्रपिता महात्मा गांधी के जन्म दिवस 2 अक्तूबर 1952 को पं० जवाहरलाल नेहरू के द्वारा किया गया था। (सामुदा, 11)

को प्रारम्भ कर—"to start"

कम्पोस्ट खाद के निर्माण में प्रतिक्रिया को प्रारम्भ करने के लिये निम्न पदार्थ प्रारम्भक के रूप में काम आते हैं। (खाद, 36)

प्रारम्भ कर—"to start"

पर अब भी आप अपना जीवन नए सिरे से प्रारम्भ करें तो भी कुछ बिगड़ा नहीं। (धनु, 187)

एक बार यह भी सोचा था कि क्यों न राका को किसी-न-किसी बहाने कोई-न-कोई पत्र भेजना प्रारम्भ कर दूं। (सपना, 282)

5. **का श्रीगणेश कर—"to make an auspicious beginning of"**

जो भूतिकामी है वह किसी न किसी रूप में कार्यक्रम का श्रीगणेश आज ही कर सकते हैं। (चमत्कार, 23)

6. **का सूत्रपात कर—"to initiate"**

...प्रथम इतिहास प्रस्तुत करके परम्परा के ऐतिहासिक मूल्यांकन का जो सूत्रपात किया था उसको उनके परवर्ती समीक्षक आशा के अनुरूप नहीं बढ़ा पाये। (मूल्य, 149)

का सूत्रपात कर—"to inaugurate"

इस लड़ाई ने हमारे इतिहास में एक नये युग का सूत्रपात किया। (अमरीका, 19)

7. **का समारम्भ कर—"to undertake to do"**

और सचमुच आपने दुखी किसानों के लिए बहुत से उपकार करने का समारम्भ किया है। (तितली, 128)

8. **का आरम्भ कर—"to commence"**

अतः ग्रामवासी भाइयों को स्वास्थ्य के नियमों से अवगत कराने के उद्देश्य से इस पुस्तकमाला का आरम्भ किया गया है। (स्वस्थ, V)

आरम्भ कर—"to begin"

महेश्वर खाना आरम्भ करते हुए मेरी ओर देखकर बोले, आपको तो खाने का मज़ा क्या ही आयेगा...ऐसे बेवक्त खा रहे हैं। (कहानी, 60)

अश्क ने समाचार-पत्र के एक साधारण रिपोर्टर के रूप में जीवन आरम्भ करके...निम्न-मध्यवर्ग तथा उच्च-मध्यवर्ग के जीवन को बड़े निकट से देखा है और उसका जागरूक तथा सूक्ष्म अध्ययन किया है। (भंवर, 10)

मैं बिलकुल ठीक हूं, काम मैंने फिर आरम्भ कर दिया है। (नदी, 281)

"मेरे पेट से निकाल ले अपनी बासी रोटी!" बचन ने वाक्य आरम्भ किया था मीठी झिड़की के रूप में, पर समाप्त करते-करते उसकी आंखें गीली हो गईं। (जान, 34)

खुश्क ऊसर परिस्थितियों के कारण लोगों ने बढ़िया ऊन-उत्पादन के लिए भेड़ें पालना आरम्भ कर दिया है। (भेड़, 3)

9. **की शुरुआत कर—"to make a beginning, to begin"**

छोटे पैमाने पर शुरुआत करके हम फ्रैंकलिन रूज़वेल्ट द्वारा निर्धारित लक्ष्य...तक पहुंच पायेंगे। (अमरीका, 34)

10. **शुरू कर—"to begin by..."**

इस बीच में हेमाद्री ने बोलना शुरू किया, "मैं आशा करता हूं कि अक्क ने एक बात पर गौर किया ही होगा...।" (शांतला, 52)

शुरू कर—"to start"

दोनों जंगल में पहुंचे तो मालिक की स्त्री ने "कू-कू" बोलना शुरू कर दिया। (रूस, 4)

शुरू कर—"to begin by"

जगन : आप शुरू तो कीजिए किसी खेल में भाग लेना।

प्रतिभा : आप से परिचय हो गया है तो...(दोनों हाथ मस्तक तक ले जाती है) (भंवर, 82)

शुरू कर—"to start"

मिसेज़ सक्सेना ने इधर एक साल से कांग्रेस के कामों में भाग लेना शुरू कर दिया था और कांग्रेस-कमेटी ने उन्हें अपना मेम्बर चुन लिया था।। (सम, 64)

शुरू कर—"to begin"

जब मैंने ज़िरह शुरू की तो सब बगलें झांकने लगे। मैंने तीनों गवाहों को झूठा साबित कर दिया। उस समय जाने कैसे मुझे चोट सूझती गई। (सम, 5)

शुरू कर—"to start"

मैंने उनसे ज़िरह करनी शुरू की। मैंने भी इतने दिनों घास नहीं खोदी है। (सम, 5)

को शुरू कर—"to begin by"

लेकिन इस कहानी को अपने दुर्भाग्य के रोने से नहीं शुरू करूंगा। (बाण, 3)

शुरू कर—"to start"

जब दो वर्ष बाद हमने अपने दोस्तों के साथ संयुक्तरूप से मार्शल प्लान के अंतर्गत आर्थिक उन्नति का प्रयत्न शुरू किया तब हमें इस कथन की सचाई का पता चला। (अमरीका, 70)

और वह गम्भीर होकर बाल्कनी की तरफ देखने लगा। "काम शुरू किस दिन से कर रहे हो ?" मैंने पूछा। (जान, 59)

आगे उसे कई ईंटें मिलीं। उसने सबको बांधकर दौड़ना शुरू किया। (कथा, 22)

तोप खींचने वाले घोड़ों और सवारी की टट्टुओं ने भड़ककर बेतहाशा ढाल की ओर दौड़ना शुरू कर दिया। (बेटी, 22)

27. अहसान, उपकार, सलूक, हित, हितसाधन, भला, भलाई

1.1. अहसान, एहसान, उपकार, सलूक, हित, हितसाधन, भला and भलाई all refer to something or something done which is directly or indirectly beneficial to someone (i.e. the object). अहसान is an obligation (imposed on someone) with an expectation of return, उपकार is a favor done without an expectation of return or may refer to something which contributes to someone's welfare, and सलूक is a treatment meted out to someone with the thought that it is conducive to his welfare, but may or may not be so considered by the one benefiting. हित is the promotion of well-being motivated by favorable disposition, and हितसाधन is adoption of means of promotion of well-being by one who is capable of doing so either by virtue of authority or otherwise. भला refers to one's normal conduct or behavior leading to a desired result, and भलाई either to one's nature or to one's conduct beneficial to others without implication of any motivation on the part of the subject.

1.2. परोपकार is उपकार characterized as पुण्य "meritorious" (holy, sacred) act.

पुण्य करने वाला, यानी एवज में आसमानी शक्ति से कुछ पाने के लिए सौदा करने वाला, कभी भी सही स्पिरिट में परोपकार नहीं कर सकता। (बूंद, 550)

2. All the nouns are + process with the exception of अहसान and उपकार which are ±process. अहसान forms ANP with the postpositions के साथ, के ऊपर and पर; उपकार with के साथ, पर, के प्रति and का; सलूक with के साथ; हित, हितसाधन and भला with का; and भलाई with के साथ and की.

3. के ऊपर, पर अहसान कर--"to oblige someone (by doing him a favor); to do someone a favor"

भारी स्वर में सज्जन ने कहा—आपने मुझ पर बहुत अहसान किया। बेवकूफ साले। (बूंद 205-6)

निस्संदेह इन दोनों नायबों ने कम्पनी के ऊपर बेशुमार अहसान किये थे। अंगरेजों और शुजाउद्दौला के युद्ध के समय शिताबराय ने कदम-कदम पर अंगरेजों का साथ दिया था और उसी से अंगरेजों का अधिकांश काम निकला। (सुन्दर, 232)

When preceded by a conjunctive participle which specifies the thing done, अहसान cannot be pluralized.

मानों वे किसी थर्ड रेट फिल्म का थर्ड रेट गाना थर्ड रेट ढंग से गाकर सुनने वालों पर कोई बड़ा अहसान कर देंगी। (भंवर, 100)

के साथ अहसान कर—"to do someone a favor"

मैं आपकी चिकनी-चुपड़ी बातों में नहीं आ सकता। आपने मेरे साथ कौन-सा अहसान किया है, जिसके बदले में मैं आज आपका कुछ भला करूं। (आदर्श, 67)

4. **के प्रति उपकार कर—"to do someone a favor"**

मुझे कभी इसका भी ध्यान नहीं आता कि मैं किसी के प्रति उपकार कर रहा हूं। तुम लोग मुझे विशेष शक्तिमान बनाकर मेरे अहंकार को न जगाओ। (कथा, 56)

के साथ उपकार कर—"to do a (specific) favor for someone"

सदन ने उनके साथ एक बड़ा उपकार किया था, अफसरों से लिखा-पढ़ी करके उन्हें आये दिन की बेगार से मुक्त करा दिया था। (सेवा, 293)

तुमने मेरे साथ जो उपकार किये हैं, वह मैं कभी न भूलूंगी। (सेवा, ३१८)

पर उपकार कर—"to do someone a favor, to oblige someone"

ज्ञानशंकर ने एक बार उसकी जान बचाई थी, उस पर जबरदस्त उपकार किया था। उस उपकार के बोझ के नीचे दलीप दबा जा रहा था। (धनु, 85)

तुमने मुझ पर बड़े उपकार किये। (लाख, 252)

The-process occurrence of उपकार is illustrated by the following sentence. It is derived from पर उपकार कर-by dropping the पर.

क्योंकि उसका दृष्टिकोण मानवीय नहीं हो पाता। उपकार करने वाले और उपकार किये जाने वाले व्यक्ति के बीच में ईश्वर आड़े आता है। (बूंद, 550)

"Because his view-point (i.e. of the one who is doing someone a favor) does not become humanistic. God stands inbetween the benefactor and the one benefitting".

का उपकार कर—"to contribute to someone's well being, to do someone a favor"

चन्द्र, सूर्य—पर्वत ये सभी मानव का उपकार करते हैं। (शबरी, 41)

...पिछले ग्यारह वर्षों से क्या किया रमला बनर्जी ने? बोर्ड के नाम पर, सरकार के विभिन्न विभागों से पैसे वसूल करके—दुनिया भर की बदचलन बंगालिनों का उपकार किया। (दीर्घ, 17-8)

यह भेष धारण करके अब मुझे ज्ञात हो रहा है कि मैं प्राणियों का बहुत उपकार कर सकता हूं। (सेवा, 163)

ब्राह्मण की प्रार्थना सुनकर सड़क बोली—तुम क्या बच्चों जैसी बातें करते हो। देखते नहीं कि मैं स्वयं लोगों का कितना उपकार करती हूं, उनको इधर-उधर भटकने से बचाती हूं। (कथा, 46)

5. **के साथ सलूक कर—"to do someone a favor, to treat someone favorably"**

बस चलकर एक मकान ठीक कर लूं, भोली क्या मेरे साथ इतना भी सलूक न करेगी? (सेवा, 56)

उमानाथ—मैं अधम पापी सही, पर आपके साथ मैंने जो सलूक किये उन्हें देखते हुए आपके मुंह से ये बातें न निकलनी चाहिएं। (सेवा, 168)

6. **का हित कर—"to do someone a favor, to promote someone's welfare"**

...अथवा तुमने निर्दोष प्राणियों को पीड़ा पहुंचाई होगी, या तुम पाप की कमाई खाते होगे, या तुम सदा निन्दा करते होगे, दो मित्रों के झगड़े में पड़कर उनका हित करने की चेष्टा करते होगे...। (भारत, 40)

बिना प्रयोजन के ही जो प्राणियों का हित करता है वह परमात्मा ही इस संसार में एक वास्तविक मित्र या सखा है। (वैदिक, 22)

7. **का हितसाधन कर—"to promote someone's welfare"**

इससे आशय सर्व हितकारी शासन से है जो बिना व्यक्ति और वर्ग भेद के सम्पूर्ण जनता का हितसाधन करता है। (राजवि, 5)

8. **का भला कर—"to do good to someone"**

मैं आपकी चिकनी-चुपड़ी बातों में नहीं आ सकता। आपने मेरे साथ कौन-सा एहसान किया है, जिसके बदले में मैं आपका कुछ भला करूं! (आदर्श, 67)

When used with one of the various designations of God or some specific deities as the subject, then it represents a formulaic expression meaning "May God bless you."

तुम सुखी हो। भगवान सबका भला करें। (तितली, 09)

भला कर -, when followed by a कि clause is also a formulaic expression meaning "Thank God."

वह तो भगवान ने भला किया कि सम्पादकजी मुझ से सैंकड़ों मील दूर थे, नहीं तो इस घटना ने मेरे दिमाग का संतुलन इस कदर बिगाड़ दिया था कि अगर वह कहीं नजदीक होते तो न जाने क्या हो जाता? (सच, 11)

9. **के साथ भलाई कर—"to do good to someone"**

कहने लगी—राजदान ने मेरे साथ एक ही तो भलाई की (बूंद, 390)

की भलाई कर—"to do someone a good"

ब्रह्मनिष्ठ राग-द्वेष से रहित परमात्मा की ही तरह सब जीवों की भलाई करते हैं। (वैदिक, 22)

28. आशंका, संभावना, अपेक्षा, आशा, उम्मीद

1. आशंका, संभावना, अपेक्षा, आशा and उम्मीद denote one's state of mind in which one entertains the idea or thought of what one anticipates or looks forward to. The nouns also apply to utterances expressing such a state.

आशंका is suspecting (or anticipating with concern) something evil when one apprehends such a possibility or likelihood. संभावना is expecting that which one envisions as likely or regards as possible. अपेक्षा is expecting the coming into effect of something presupposed (i.e. taken for granted) or considered desirable. आशा is expecting (of others) what one intends or believes, or hoping for what one wishes. उम्मीद is expecting what one intends or presumptuously places a reliance on.

2. All the nouns are + process. आशंका and संभावना form ANP with की, and the rest with से or की. Only की permits the occurrence of infinitives.

3. **की आशंका कर—"to be (overly) apprehensive of"**

मल्लिका: तो क्या हुआ ? आप भी मां की तरह व्यर्थ में अनिष्ट की आशंका करने लगे। (आषाढ़, 55)

4. **की संभावना कर—"to be expecting, to expect, to anticipate"**

निकट ही कहीं जापानी हैं यह ज्ञात था और आक्रमण की संभावना भी की जा रही थी। (नदी, 333)

5. **से अपेक्षा कर—"to be desired"**

...इसी कारण उनकी दृष्टि कई स्थलों पर संकुचित रह गई थी और वे अपने समकालीन कई आन्दोलनों को वह सहानुभूति नहीं दे पाये थे जिसकी उनसे अपेक्षा की जाती थी। (मूल्य, 149)

की अपेक्षा कर—"to presuppose"

...अतएव वह (अनुमान) दृष्ट साधर्म्य की अवश्य अपेक्षा करेगा। (भक्तिसुधा, 47)

6. से आशा कर—"to rely upon"

मैं ऐसा अनुभव करता था कि आपत्काल में इन सिद्धों से बहुत अधिक आशा नहीं की जा सकती। (चारु, 11)

से आशा कर—"to take for granted"

स्त्री से मैं शर्म और संकोच की आशा करता था। (राह, 24)

से आशा कर—"to look forward to"

किंतु जब देखता हूं कि वह मुझसे स्नेह और सांत्वना की आशा करने वाली निरीह प्राणी नहीं रह गई है, वह तो अपने लिए एक दृढ़ भूमिका चाहती है, और चाहती है, मेरा पतन, मुझी से विरोध, मेरी प्रतिद्वन्द्विता। (तितली, 109)

की आशा कर—"to rely upon"

अदालत और हाकिमों से तो उन्होंने न्याय की आशा करना ही छोड़ दिया। (सम, 12)

की आशा कर—"to await"

अब आप लोगों से यह नवविवाहित दम्पति आशीर्वाद की आशा करता है। (तितली, 120)

की आशा कर—"to look forward to"

शो समाप्त होने पर विदा लेते हुए सर कृष्ण ने अजित से कहा—आगे फिर मिलने की क्या आपसे आशा कर सकता हूं। (तीन, 42)

की आशा कर—"to expect"

सज्जन स्तब्ध रह गया। उसने कन्या से कभी ऐसा उत्तर पाने की आशा नहीं की थी। (बूंद, 205)

जब तक प्रत्येक परिवार के पास अपना घर न होगा उससे सार्वजनिक स्वास्थ्य के हित में कुछ अधिक आशा नहीं की जा सकती क्योंकि बिना घर के लगाव उत्पन्न हुए स्वच्छता का महत्त्व उन्हें नहीं समझाया जा सकता। (स्वस्थ, 10)

की आशा कर—"to hope, to be hopeful"

आप काम के विषय में चिंतित होंगी, मैं उसके लिए दत्तचित्त हूं। और शीघ्र ही कुछ कर सकने की आशा करता हूं। (नदी, 56)

की आशा न कर—"to have no desire for"

संत कुछ देर तक चुप रहकर फिर बोला—देवताओ ! मैंने तो निष्काम सेवा का व्रत ले रखा है, कर्म के उपरान्त में फल की आशा नहीं करता। (कथा, 56)

की आशा कर—"to hope for"

मैं न्याय विचार के साथ एक गंभीर निराविष्टता, निरपेक्षता की आशा करता था। (जय, 84)

व्यर्थ आशा कर—"to assume"

...कि इस वर्ष के चुनावों में अमरीका एक विभक्त राष्ट्र है हमारे शत्रुओं को भी इस तरह की व्यर्थ आशा करने की जरूरत नहीं है। हमारे खुले चुनाव अमरीका की शक्ति के प्रतीक हैं, दुर्बलता के नहीं। (अमरीका, 57)

की आशा कर—"to expect"

भेड़ पालक गर्मियों में करीब १५ से २० प्रतिशत भेड़ों, शरद् के आरंभ में ५० से ८० प्रतिशत भेड़ों और सर्दियों में थोड़ी सी भेड़ों को सम्भोग के लिए तैयार होने की आशा करता है। (भेड़, 18)

आशा कर—"to look forward to"

मैं आशा करता हूं कि भविष्य में भी आप लोग इसी प्रकार शबरी के प्रति भी आदर दिखाते रहेंगे। मेरा विश्वास है कि आप सब लोग मेरे इस निर्णय से सहमत हैं। (शबरी, 15)

आप तो उनके हितैषी ही होंगे इसलिए मैं आशा करता हूं कि आप रोगी के कल्याण की दृष्टि से मेरे साथ सहयोग करेंगे। (धनु, 151)

आशा कर—"to suspect"

सभी आश्चर्य से मेरी ओर देखने लगे थे, जैसे उन्होंने आशा की थी कि कामिनी के साथ मेरा सम्बन्ध कोई दूसरा ही है। (राह 58)

7. उम्मीद कर—"to look forward to"

. . . मगर दूसरी शाम के लिए मैं उसके साथ की उम्मीद नहीं कर सकता। (राकेश, 60)

की उम्मीद कर—"to expect"

मैं मुख्य मंत्री श्रीमती सुचेता कृपलानी से गोंडा में मुलाकात करने की उम्मीद करता हूं जहां से आजकल वे अपने निर्वाचनक्षेत्र का दौरा कर रही हैं। (आज, 2)

की उम्मीद कर—"to count upon"

बेचारे सिटपिटाकर खड़े के खड़े ही रहे। जिस चेले से वे इतनी उम्मीद करके आए थे, वही दरबार में सबके आगे उनकी इज्जत उतारने लगा। (आदर्श, 67)

"बिना कुछ उम्मीद किये—"without expecting anything in return"

सो जो अपने हों या जिन्हें अपनाने में मजा आता हो उनके सारे नाज उठाने ही होंगे। वक्त पर बिना कुछ उम्मीद किए। (विचित्र, 12)

29. अतिरेक, अतिशयता, ज्यादती

1. अतिरेक, अतिशयता and ज्यादती are applied to an act or a statement described as being excessive. अतिरेक is overdoing or overindulgence implying lack of moderation, अतिशयता is exaggerating, i.e. having the quality of being more than necessary, and ज्यादती is stating in too strong a terms implying a degree of unfairness.

2. All the nouns are +process. Both अतिरेक and अतिशयता form ANP with में, and ज्यादती with से or के साथ. The N post. with these nouns may be optionally dropped. Only में permits the occurrence of infinitives. Only ज्यादती is pluralized.

3. में अतिरेक कर दे—"to overindulge in something"

अतिरेक कर दे—"to overdo"

नारी के अंतरंग सम्पर्क का मौका कभी-कभी तो दो-दो तीन-तीन महीने तक नहीं मिलता, और जब कभी ऐसा अवसर आ जाता है तब वह अतिरेक कर देता है। (बूंद, 86)

4. अतिशयता कर—"to exaggerate"

लिजा, जानती हो क्या? लगता है तुम अपने प्रेम में पड़ी हो। इसी से अतिशयता करती हो। (जय, 415)

5. के साथ ज्यादती कर—"to be unfair, to unfairly overstate someone's case"

सज्जन ने उसे देखा, कहा—तुम अपने और शीला के साथ ज्यादती कर रहे हो। (बूंद, 532)

ज्यादती कर—"to overstate, to exaggerate"

ये तो तुम ज्यादती कर रहे हो महिपाल। (बूंद, 422)

30. सहायता, मदद

1. सहायता and मदद refer to furnishing another person or thing with what is needed, सहायता is aiding or assisting. मदद is a more inclusive term meaning helping, and covers a wide variety of things done

anywhere between giving someone a helping hand and directly participating in or taking over the functions and duties of someone or something. मदद also lacks the formal implications of सहायता.

2. Both nouns a:e +process and form ANP with की and को.

सहायता may be modified by N के लिए or N में, and मदद by N में only. के लिए implies assisting someone so that he can accomplish what is postposed by के लिये. में implies directly participating in the act of assisting or helping. These nouns do not take plural.

3. **की सहायता कर—"to assist"**

अब पहले तुम्हारी मां को स्वस्थ करूंगा फिर गांव की बीमारियों से लड़ूंगा। तुम सब मेरी सहायता करना इस काम में। (खिलौने, 68)

जरा मुझे कुछ कपड़े सिलवाने हैं, क्योंकि कल मेरी वर्षगांठ है। चलो, कपड़े पसंद करने में मेरी थोड़ी-सी सहायता कर दो। (तीन, 24)

...कचनार से स्पष्ट कहना पड़ेगा। मुझको विश्वास है वह समस्या के सुलझाने में सहायता करेगी। (कचनार, 334)

की सहायता कर—"to aid, to assist"

आवाज निकालने में नाक भी हमारी सहायता करती है। (आज, 27)

की सहायता कर—"to render aid"

बच्चे को बचाने के लिए आर्थिक रूप से उसकी सहायता करूं। (बूंद, 503)

के लिये सहायता कर—"to aid, to assist in"

वह धन का उपयोग पिछड़े लोगों के लिये करने में गौरव अनुभव कर रहा है तथा उनके आर्थिक तथा अन्य विकास के लिए सहायता कर रहा है। (अणु, 44)

को सहायता कर—"to render assistance, to come to someone's aid"

...उन्होने शायद यह भी मान लिया है कि साम्यवादी देश दूरी के कारण इन लोगों को सहायता नहीं कर सकेंगे। और कभी ऐसी संभावना हुई तो पश्चिमी देश हमारी सहायता के लिए दौड़ आएंगे। (अणु, 36)

सहायता कर—"to help out"

आप इस समय दस रुपये से सहायता न करेंगे तो सब मर जायेंगे। बिहारी जी आपको...। (तितली 179)

4. की मदद कर--"to help, to participate"

"तो बेटा फिर तुम्हारे दरबार में हमारी सुनवाई नहीं हुई" सास बोली। "जी नहीं। मैं गलत काम में कभी किसी की मदद नहीं किया करता। कन्या जाओ।" "भाभी को मैं अपने पास रखे लेती हूं अम्मा। फिर पहुंचा दूंगी।" (बूंद, 449)

की मदद कर—"to help"

रहमतअली का इकलौता बेटा, शमशेर अली सरकारी काम में बाप की मदद किया करता था। (डगर, 13)

की मदद कर—"to help"

इसी तरह कारीगरों को भी चरखे-करघे के लिए, या जो भी अच्छा हुनर वे जानते हों उसे बढ़ाने के लिए रुपया उधार दे देते थे। गरीबों की शादी-गमी में रुपयों से मदद कर देते थे...। (बूंद, 471)

को मदद कर—"to be helpful"

किन्तु यदि इसमें ऐसी सीधी सादी मशीनों का उपयोग होने लगे जो मनुष्य को कष्टसाध्य कामों में मदद करती हों तो न केवल इससे ईंटों की किस्म ही अच्छी होगी वरन् प्रति व्यक्ति कार्यक्षमता भी काफी बढ़ जायगी। (ईंट, 57)

एक दूसरे को मदद कर—"to help each other out"

संयुक्त निवास से पारस्परिकता की भावना उदय होने से एक दूसरे को दुःख तकलीफ में आपस में मदद करते हैं। (ग्रामीण, 14)

को मदद कर—"to aid"

इनमें से दो चीजें थीं--फास्फोरस और पोटैशियम क्लोरेट। इस दूसरी चीज में आक्सीजन नामक गैस छिपी होती है और यह तो तुम जानते ही हो कि आक्सीजन चीजों को जलने में मदद करती है। (आग, 33)

रुपये की मदद कर—"to assist financially"

दूसरे साहबजादे आई० सी० एस० हैं, वो भी अब इस गली-मुहल्ले और दकियानूस मां-बाप से भला कैसे संबंध रखें? हां, कुछ रुपयों की मदद जरूर करते रहते हैं। (बूंद, 127)

31. विश्राम, आराम

1. विश्राम and आराम both refer to freedom or withdrawal from normal activity for a period of time. विश्राम, when applied to human beings, suggests the absence or suspension of श्रम "labour, fatigue", and therefore is relaxing (in a variety of ways generally not expressed in the

sentence) by not engaging in or withdrawal from anything that fatigues, disturbs or troubles implying the release of physical or mental tension. When applied to things, it refers to their either giving the appearance of inactivity or state of being dormant. आराम is applied to animate beings alone (with कर-), and refers to freedom from any activity by suspending it temporarily. It suggests as an aim the overcoming of physical or mental weariness or the regaining of physical or mental tranquility.

2. विश्राम is +process, and आराम +process. Both nouns do not take plural. Both are generally preceded by determiners like थोड़ा "a little", तनिक "a bit", बहुत "plenty of", and यथेष्ट "enough, necessary, needed" etc., or by phrases indicating specific periods of time. The only exception is the occurrence of सदा के लिये "forever" or the like suggesting complete withdrawal, resignation or termination of one's services. The occurrence of inanimate nouns as subject requires the explicit indication of location.

3. **विश्राम कर पा—"to relax, to take a break"**

"तो क्या मैं तनिक भी विश्राम नहीं कर पाऊंगा?" "मालूम होता है तू चिढ़ गया।" "नहीं, नहीं, चिढ़ूंगा क्यों?" (रूस, 2)

"Can't I relax even a little ?/May I, if you please, take a little break ?"

विश्राम कर चुक—"to finish (taking) one's nap"

निक्षेप: परन्तु यह भी तो कहा था कि आचार्य विश्राम कर चुकें तो तुरन्त आपको सूचना दूं। (आषाढ़, 28)

विश्राम कर—"to take the day off"

रविवार की संध्या को डा० सुमंत और सुमित्रा जी छुट्टी मनाया करते थे। कोई सख्त बीमार हो तो बात अलग है, वरना वे दोनों उस दिन विश्राम किया करते थे। (धनु, 172)

विश्राम कर—"to be lying dormant"

इन दोनों दलों में दोषों के कारण शिथिलता आ गई है। आज दोनों ही सम्प्रदाय, साम्प्रदायिकता की गोद में विश्राम कर रहे हैं। (धर्म, 12)

विश्राम कर—"to be parked" (**implying a temporary parking in a business area or the like**)

मोटरों की कतार दो निकट के चौराहों के बीच विश्राम कर रही थी। (बूंद, 85)

4. **आराम कर—"to take complete rest"**

लाली ने लिखा था कि उसका ब्लडप्रेशर फिर बढ़ गया था। डाक्टर ने उसे आराम करने की सलाह दी है। (जान, 36)

आराम कर—"to rest"

हकीम साहब ने कह रखा है कि खाने के बाद इन्हें कम से कम एक घंटा आराम करना चाहिए। (अंधेरे, 30)

आराम कर—"to recuperate, to rest"

इसीलिए भैया ने कहा कि तुम एक साल आराम करो, अगले साल फाइनल का इम्तहान देना। (राह, 68)

आराम कर ले—"to take a break, to relax, to rest"

खाना खाकर घंटा-आधा घंटा स्वयंसेवकों का भी आराम कर लेने का दस्तूर था। (दुख, 154)

आराम कर ले—"to relax"

वर्षा और आंधी के जोर के खिलाफ बचने और थोड़ा सुस्ताने के लिए वो एक बिल्डिंग के पोर्च के नीचे आकर खड़े हो गए ताकि थोड़ा आराम कर लें, और अगली यात्रा के लिए हिम्मत बटोर लें। (धनु, 14)

आराम कर—"to rest"

यह स्वाभाविक आदत होने से वे चरागाहों में चारा जल्दी-जल्दी खा लेते हैं और बाद में जब वे आराम करते हैं उस समय भोजन को धीरे-धीरे रौंदते हैं। (भेड़, 42)
"...and afterwards when they are resting..."

32. कठोरता, कड़ाई, सख्ती

1. कठोरता, कड़ाई and सख्ती all refer to the severity of one's conduct, behaviour or dealings with others.

कठोरता refers to the callousness or complete lack of sympathy or understanding in one's conduct. कड़ाई stresses the uncompromising inflexibility with which one deals with others. सख्ती refers to the relentless ness of one's behaviour or to the harshness of the measures dealt to others.

2. All the nouns are + process and form ANP with से and के साथ. They are not pluralized.

3. के साथ कठोरता कर—"to be (excessively) severe with"

बाबू जी, मेरा क्या अपराध है। मैं तो आपही लोगों को खोज रही थी ?

अभागिनी। खोज रही थी मुझे या किसी और को—

... दुष्टा। मुझे जल पिला दिया, प्रायश्चित्त करना पड़ेगा।

अब मंगल की समझ में आया कि वह यात्री तारा का पिता है। ... उसने ... तारा से पूछा—क्या यही तुम्हारे पिता हैं? हां, परन्तु मैं अब क्या करूं। ... मेरी मां होती तो इतनी कठोरता न करती। (कंकाल, 33)

4 से कड़ाई कर—"to deal strictly with"

श्री बांके बिहारीजी की रकम दबाने का किसी को साहस न होता था और न अपनी रकम के लिए कोई दूसरा आदमी उनसे कड़ाई कर सकता था। श्री बांके बिहारीजी को रुष्ट करके उस इलाके में रहना कठिन था। (सेवा, 8-9)

5. के साथ सख्ती कर—"to drive/push one relentlessly"

मैं समझता हूं कि तुम भी अपने लड़के के साथ ऐसी सख्ती न करो तो अच्छा होगा। (गांधी, 79)

सख्ती कर—"to deal strictly or severely with"

पुलिस और फौज को सरकशी खत्म करने और अमन कायम करने का फर्ज पूरा करने में जो सख्ती करनी पड़ेगी उसके लिए सरकारी नौकरों, पुलिस या फौज के खिलाफ कोई शिकायत नहीं सुनी जायगी न उसकी कोई जांच पड़ताल होगी। (फूलो, 44)

सख्ती करके—"due to or through (one's) persistence"

माता की बीमारी अब कम हो रही थी। चौधरी और डाक्टर ने सख्ती करके गांव के लोगों को माता के टीके लगवा दिये थे और यह उसी का प्रभाव था। (लाख, 186)

33. अन्तर, फर्क

1. Both अन्तर and फर्क refer to causing something to become different. अन्तर stresses a state of being different in a minor, non-fundamental way, i.e. transforming or changing into something else. फर्क refers to

the state of being different without suggesting the positive implication of अन्तर.

2. Both nouns are +process and form ANP with में. They are not pluralized, and do not permit the occurrence of infinitives before में.

3. में अन्तर कर—"to alter, to make an alteration in"

गर्व तो यह है कि हम कविता का कायापलट कर रहे हैं। कर तो रहे हैं, किन्तु कविता के कायापलट के अर्थ क्या केवल वृत्तों में या थोड़ी-सी उपमाओं में अन्तर कर देने भर के हैं। (अमीर, 25)

4. में फर्क कर—"to modify"

फिर फाजिल वजन वाले को अपना वजन कम करने के लिए अपनी जीवन-पद्धति में कुछ तो फर्क करना ही पड़ेगा। (भूदान, 53)

तुम्हारे कल्चर साहित्य और ऊंची-ऊंची बातों का इतना प्रचार हो जाने पर भी साधारण मनुष्य अपने दृष्टिकोण में कोई फर्क नहीं कर पाया। (बूंद, 423)

34. प्रश्न, सवाल

1. Both प्रश्न and सवाल are applied to interrogative expressions (verbal or gestural), and differ in the kind of motive which prompts one to address a question to another person or to oneself. प्रश्न stresses a question put with the desire to gain familiarity with something through the acquisition of information, whereas सवाल is a more inclusive term implying in addition either something objectionable, inappropriate or a need, an expectation, which prompts one to employ a suitable interrogative expression.

2. Both nouns are +process and form ANP with से. They are freely pluralized unless adjoined by a कि clause. The कि clause, in this case. represents the interrogative expression. Alternatively, the interrogative expressions may be represented in the sentence itself by nominal expressions with one of the postpositions—के सम्बन्ध में "concerning", के विषय में "regarding", के बारे में "with regard to" and के बाबत "about, in connection with". In the latter situation, the specific question or questions asked, may remain unexpressed in the sentence but the interrogative expressions referred to by प्रश्न and सवाल fall into four different categories on the basis of the applicability of the four postpositions. के सम्बन्ध में implies lack of advance knowledge and therefore pertinent questions seeking information, के विषय में implies specific questions about a subject already known, के बारे में implies specific or general questions as may arise in the subject's mind (without any reference to

advance knowledge or the lack of it), and के बाबत is applied to interrogative expressions casually referring to someone or something.

3. **से प्रश्न कर—"to ask someone a question, to inquire about"**

भारतीयों के पास बैठकर वह प्रायः भारत के देहातों, पहाड़ी और प्राकृतिक दृश्यों के सम्बन्ध में इन्द्रदेव से कुतूहलपूर्ण प्रश्न किया करती। (तितली, 22)

"to consider something questionable, to question"

जिस प्रश्न का उत्तर प्रश्नकर्ता को ज्ञात है अथवा जिसके सम्बन्ध में उसकी मान्यता निश्चित है उसके विषय में प्रश्न नहीं करना चाहिए। (भक्तियोग, 6)

के सम्बन्ध में प्रश्न कर—"to question someone, to ask questions"

बादशाह ने उस यात्री-दल के सम्बन्ध में और भी कई प्रश्न किए। अयाज ने सब बातों का उत्तर दे दिया। उसने सौदागरों से उनके बारे में बहुत कुछ पूछ लिया था। (आदर्श, 51-52)

से प्रश्न कर—"to query"

छिः नारी क्या केवल भोग की वस्तु है? उसने अपने से ही प्रश्न किया। (बूंद, 56)

से प्रश्न कर—"to query"

मगर उसमें जिस शक्ति के दर्शन होते हैं वह कहां से आती है? सज्जन ने अबस प्रश्न किया और कहा—मैं—मैं तुमसे एक सवाल करता हूं। तुम बड़ी पढ़ी लिखी, प्रोग्रेसिव और साथ ही ईमानदार महिला हो। (बूंद, 550)

से (अनेक) प्रश्न कर—"to bombard someone with questions, to assail someone with questions"

शास्त्रार्थ आरम्भ हुआ। यामुनाचार्य ने अपने प्रतिद्वन्द्वी महापंडित से इस तरह अनेक प्रश्न किए। (आदर्श, 21)

का प्रश्न कर—"to pose a question"

रुकने से लाभ?—और लीला की आंखों ने अजित की आंखों से एक बहुत बड़ा तथा महत्व का प्रश्न कर डाला। (तीन, 84)

4. **से सवाल कर—"to ask (someone) a question, to indulge in conversation with (someone)"**

यूं मैं किसी लड़की से ज्यादा सवाल नहीं करता क्योंकि वे जरा से परिचय को घनिष्ठता समझने लगती है। (जान, 72)

सवाल कर—"to ask a question"

आशा है, हम जो सवाल करेंगे तुम लोग उसका ठीक-ठीक जवाब दे सकोगे। (बाल, 11, 33)

दूसरा सवाल कर दे—"to fire a question at"

एक क्षण के लिए वह अचकचा गया था। सिगरेट जलाने के बहाने वह उत्तर सोचने लगा था कि उस आदमी ने बड़े स्नेह से दूसरा सवाल कर दिया था, छुट्टी आये हैं? (मांस, 6)

का सवाल कर—"to raise a question of"

भाषा का मैं सवाल नहीं करता, मैं केवल इतना ही पूछ रहा हूं कि जितने उपन्यास आपने पढ़े हैं, उनमें किसका और कौन-सा उपन्यास आपको पसन्द आया है। (तीन, 45)

सवाल कर—"to ask"

यह कहां मुंह उठाये जा रही है? मेरी पत्नी ने फिर सवाल किया। आज के प्रोग्राम के मुख्य प्रबन्धक के साथ जाकर कोई बात करेगी और फिर उसके पास बैठ जायेगी, मैंने अनुमान लगाते हुए कहा (दुग्गल, 138)

के सामने दांत निकाल कर सवाल कर—"to beseech, to importune"

यह कहानी आज से पैंतीस वर्ष पूर्व की है। वह अपनी उधेड़-बुन में था। इसी वक्त एक स्त्री-भिखारिन ने रूखे सिख के सामने आ, दांत निकाल कर सवाल किया। (जुहू, 5)

35. अधिकार, कब्जा

1. अधिकार and कब्जा both refer to the act of taking possession of something, sometimes a person when he is referred to as having taken on some emotive state subconsciously or unwillingly. अधिकार stresses the result, and कब्जा the result and/or the means. Therefore अधिकार may imply a series of acts leading to subjugation, surrender or occupation, and कब्जा a sudden, forcible taking or abrupt seizure, usually by overpowering the opposition.

2. Both nouns are ±process and form ANP with पर and के ऊपर. पर/के ऊपर अधिकार/कब्जा are +process, and their process-counterparts are अधिकार /कब्जे में.

3. **पर अधिकार कर—"to be occupying"**

राजा ने सोचकर मन में देखा तो सचमुच ये वस्तुएं उसके हृदय पर अधिकार

किए थीं। उसने कुटी में आग लगा दी और कमंडलु, दंड आदि नदी में फेंक दिए। (कथा, 74)

पर अधिकार कर ले—"to take possession of"

अंग्रेज अफसर भी ताक में थे ही। उन्होंने धीरे-धीरे भूमि पर अधिकार कर लिया। (ग्रामीण, 34)

पर अधिकार कर ले—"to assume jurisdiction over, to appropriate"

राजभवन के दक्षिण की ओर यशनगर राज्य के सरकारी दफ्तर थे और कचहरी थी जिन पर जमींदारी उन्मूलन के बाद उत्तर प्रदेश सरकार ने अधिकार कर लिया था। (सा सा, 280)

पर अधिकार कर ले—"to capture"

दुश्मन ने अग्नि वर्षा का वेग कई गुना अधिक बढ़ा दिया, मगर यह सब कुछ राने को अपने इस्पाती संकल्प से न डिगा सका, वे अपने कार्य में सफल हुए, रास्ता साफ हुआ और भारतीय सेना ने आगे बढ़कर बाखली पुलिया पर अधिकार कर लिया। (परम, 22)

पर अधिकार कर ले—"to overpower"

लगता है कहीं बेहोश होकर में यहां पर लेट न जाऊं और अनन्त निद्रा मुझ पर अपना अधिकार न कर ले। (सा सा 94)

पर अधिकार कर ले—"to assume ownership of"

उद्योग क्षेत्र में कुछ उद्योगों पर राज्य ने अधिकार कर लिया है जैसे शस्त्रास्त्रों और गोला बारूद का निर्माण, नदी घाटी योजनाएं, अणुशक्ति और रेलें आदि। (भारत, 39)

पर अधिकार कर ले—"to take possession of, to occupy"

उनके सामने सबसे बड़ी समस्या यह थी कि ज्योंही वे एक राज्य या प्रान्त को जीतकर दूसरे पर आक्रमण करते त्योंही शत्रु लोग जीते हुए देश पर पुनः अधिकार कर लेते थे। (आदर्श, 26)

पर अधिकार कर ले—"to manage to gain possession of, to get hold of"

इसके अतिरिक्त जब महंगू के दामाद ने उसकी सभी चल संपत्ति पर अधिकार कर अंत में धोखा दिया तब गोवर्धन ने जातीय पंचायत कर बहुत प्रयत्न किया, किन्तु महंगू के हाथ कुछ नहीं लगा। (व्यास, 13)

को अधिकार में कर—"to predispose someone to one's authority"

सबको अपने अधिकार में करके ईश्वर इसी प्रकार दुनिया में निरन्तर परिवर्तन करता रहता है।

पर अधिकार कर—"to subdue, to curb"

फिर ऐंठने वाले हृदय पर अधिकार किया। वह प्रकृतिस्थ होकर ध्यान से उसकी बातों को सुनने लगा। (तितली, 257)

अधिकार कर—"to occupy"

एक प्रस्तरशिला बीच में पड़ी हुई थी जो कपित्थ के शिशु वृक्षों की अधिक भूमि अधिकार करने की दुरन्त लालसा में बाधक सिद्ध हुई थी। (चारु, 269)

भूमि अधिकार करने की implies ellipsis of में after अधिकार.

4 पर कब्जा कर—"to have one's hold over"

मेरे तन, मन और धन पर उन्होंने इस मजबूती से कब्जा किया है कि उसकी फरियाद किसी भी राष्ट्रसंघ में नहीं हो सकती। (सच, 35)

पर कब्जा कर ले—"to take possession of"

भागते सिपाहियों की पीठ पर धमकाने के लिए निशाना साध रहे छावनी के सिपाहियों ने मराठा गाड़ियों पर कब्जा कर लिया। (बेटी, 22)

पर कब्जा कर ले—"to seize, to captivate"

व्यक्तित्व एक ऐसी वस्तु है जिसकी व्याख्या ही नहीं हो सकती। एक विचित्र शक्ति जो मनुष्यों के हृदयों पर कब्जा कर लेती है—और उनमें यह शक्ति प्रचुर मात्रा में है। (मूल्य, 84)

पर कब्जा कर—"to come to gain possession over"

जिस तरीके से ईस्ट इंडिया कंपनी ने हिन्दोस्तान पर कब्जा किया उससे अधिक बीभत्स और ईसाई सिद्धान्तों के विरुद्ध किसी दूसरे तरीके की कल्पना नहीं की जा सकती। (सुन्दर, 20)

पर कब्जा कर—"to seize, to capture"

भारतीय फौज को राजौरी पहुंचना ही था और राजौरी पहुंचने के पूर्व बाखली की यह पुलिया और नाथपुर पर कब्ज़ा करना परमावश्यक था। (परम, 22)

पर कब्जा करके—"after taking over"

हवेली पर कब्जा करके अचलपुरी ने मानसिंह को कैद कर लिया। (कचनार, 311)

कब्जे में कर ले—"to hold someone down, to overpower, to subjugate"

उसे लगा था कि जिवा को भी, वह इसी तरह हैरान कर देगा और पूरी तरह अपने कब्जे में कर लेगा। (लाख, 233)

कब्जे में कर—"to capture, to have something in one's hold"

गुलाब जैसी छोकरी यहां फिल्म में क्या कमा सकती है और एक बार उसे लेकर बम्बई को कब्जे में किया जा सकता है। (जुहू, 9)

36. ऐश, ऐयाशी, मज़ा, मौज

1. ऐश, ऐयाशी, मज़ा and मौज, though not exactly synonymous terms, have in common the notion of indulging in ease, gratification marked by a lack of restraint. ऐश suggests indulgence in continuous and carefree voluptuousness or just anything which could (relatively speaking) be characterized as luxury, ऐयाशी is one's dispositional predilection for luxury, मज़ा is (commonly understood as "savor", "taste") taking conscious pleasure in sexual relations with women, मौज suggests rollicking (i.e. behaving in a carefree, joyous manner) of a young male adult in the company of a young female adult or refers to (proverbially) merriment.

2. All the nouns are + process. ऐश forms ANP with पर or के साथ. With पर it generally occurs in plural and non-feminine. With के साथ it does not take plural and implies feminine. ऐयाशी forms ANP with की, and both मजा and मौज with के साथ.

3. **पर ऐश कर—"to live wantonly"**

उमर-भर मेरे बेटे पोतों ने मेरी कमाई पर ऐश किये हैं। (बाहों, 12)

से ऐश कर—"to live well or in luxury"

...कि पति के पैसे से ऐश करेंगी मगर आमतौर पर यह नसीब सब को नहीं मिलता। (बूंद, 510)

के साथ ऐश कर—"to enjoy (a woman)"

आप एतबार करें, जितना लुत्फ उस औरत के साथ ऐश करने में नहीं मिला था (उससे) कहीं ज्यादा उनकी बोटी-बोटी उड़ाने में हासिल हुआ। (जुहू, 113)

4. **ऐयाशी कर—"to allow oneself the luxury of, to afford the luxury of"**

सुन्दर सोचता इतनी कम आमदनी पर वह लोग कैसे यह ऐयाशी कर सकते हैं। (दुग्गल, 113)

कोई ऐयाशी कर—"to take to some luxury"

आधी छुट्टी के वक्त आजकल वह कभी कोई चसका लगाते, कभी कोई ऐयाशी करते। (दुग्गल, 119)

5. **के साथ मजा कर—"to have a good time with"**

कैसा मजा किया होगा उस छोकड़ी के साथ। (देश, 65)

6. **के साथ मौज कर—"to rollick, to have fun with"**

रमेश ने आंखें फाड़कर अजित की ओर देखा—"मैं नहीं समझा।" "और मैं समझा भी नहीं सकता हूं, लेकिन इतना कह दूं, तुम प्रभा के साथ खेलो, मौज करो यह समझ करके कि खेलना और मौज करना ही प्रेम है।" (तीन)

वह सिर्फ खाने-पीने और मौज करने के सिद्धान्त को ही अपने आगे रखकर चल रहा है। (बूंद, 472)

He is (seemingly) following the principle of 'eat, drink and be merry."

37. चिन्ता, फिक्र, परवाह

1. चिन्ता, फिक्र and परवाह all refer to one's reflection (generally expressed in form of negative sentences) upon someone else's (sometimes one's own) troubled or oppressed state of mind induced by one's doubts and apprehension, or refer to the modalities of one's mindfulness implying the absence of complacency, indifference or carelessness. चिन्ता is worrying implying somewhat deeper apprehensiveness, फिक्र a mild concern or anxiety stressing a recourse to some means of alleviation, and परवाह the disposition or propensity for care.

When occurring without negation, they refer to one's exercise of one's sense of devotion, attention and care respectively in the execution of what one is doing.

Observe the following contexts :—

लेकिन शर्माजी, यह दिल्ली तो अथाह सागर है, मैं अकेली कैसे वहां रहूंगी ? उत्तर शर्माजी के पास मौजूद था, इसकी आपको चिन्ता नहीं करनी है। दिल्ली में मेरे पास एक अच्छा-सा बंगला है। मैं तो केवल एक कमरे में रहता हूं, आप वहां रहिए आकर...। (सा सा, 172)

रानी मानकुमारी का हृदय तेजी के साथ धड़कने लगा था, मंसूर साहिब, आप यह क्या कह रहे हैं ? सीमा क्या सोचेगी ? लोग मुझे किस तरह इंचार्ज बना देंगे ?

इसकी फिक्र आपको नहीं करनी है, रानी साहिबा! पिछले तजरबों के बाद सीमा आगे से किसी डेलीगेशन में खुद नहीं जाना चाहती और इंचार्ज बनाने की जिम्मेदारी मुझ पर है। (सा सा, 229)

तुमने वृथा के बन्धनों में अपने को जकड़ रखा है। वृथा के वहम अपने इर्द-गिर्द बुन लिये हैं। इन वहमों, इन शंकाओं के जाल तोड़ दो। पाप-पुण्य की बातें छोड़ो। नातेदारों की प्रसन्नता की परवाह न करो।···अपने अन्तर की आवाज का गला न घोंटो, उसकी सुनो और मानो। (धारा, 186)

2. These nouns are + process, and form ANP with की which permits the occurrence of nouns as well as infinitives before it. They are not pluralized. परवाह occurs with negatives more often than without.

3. **की चिन्ता कर—"to devote oneself to"**

बल्कि धामोनी के किले को जल्दी हथियाने की चिन्ता करेगा, जिसमें रक्षा के स्थान में सिर रखने का भरोसा तो मिल जाय। (कचनार, 293)

हरि की हर बात का वह ध्यान रखती। उसकी आवश्यकता की चीजों, उसके कपड़ों, उसके स्वास्थ्य सभी की चिन्ता करती। आती तो हरि की मेज पर बिखरी हुई चीजों को ढंग से सजाने लगती...। मानों उससे पहले हरि का कमरा कभी सजा-संवरा ही न था...। (धारा, 169)

की चिन्ता कर—"to concern oneself with, to devote oneself to"

जो शिष्य गुरु के दोष ढूंढने की चिन्ता करता है, वह कुछ नहीं पाता। (कचनार, 271)

की चिन्ता कर—"to have concern for"

इसलिए अपने देश के भविष्य में रुचि रखने वाले हर अमरीकी नागरिक का कर्तव्य है कि वह अफ्रीका, ऐशिया और लैटिन अमरीका के अपने पुराने मित्रों के भविष्य की भी चिन्ता करे। (अमरीका, 82)

की चिन्ता कर—"to worry (too much) about"

रूप के हाट में इस बात को लेकर हंसी उड़ाई जाती थी, परन्तु पेरियनायकी ने कभी इसकी चिन्ता न की। (सुहाग, 20)

की चिन्ता कर—"to think too much of"

हत्यारे समाज की मैं चिन्ता नहीं करता। (कंकाल, 43)

के लिये चिन्ता कर—"to devote oneself to the care of"

शकुन्तला का विवाह वह शानदार ढंग से करना चाहती है। यह उसके हृदय की विशालता का परिचय देता है। आजकल कौन स्त्री अपनी ननंद की लड़की के लिए इतनी चिन्ता करेगी (बूंद, 434)

के लिये चिन्ता कर—"to devote oneself to, to be overly anxious to"

जिन-जिन सुखों को वह त्यागने के लिए चिन्ता करता है, वे ही उसे धक्का देने का उद्योग करते हैं ...। (कंकाल, 12)

की चिन्ता न कर—"without worrying about or giving any thought to"

आज पहाड़ पर बहुत वर्षा हुई है और नाले में बहुत पानी आ गया था। जो आदमी नूरकलां की डाक लेने आया था वह बाढ़ की चिन्ता न कर नाले में घुस गया, परन्तु पानी उसे बहाकर ले गया ...। (डगर, 14)

को लेकर चिन्ता कर—"to worry over"

सज्जन और कन्या दोनों ही इस विषय को लेकर बड़ी चिन्ता करने लगे। सज्जन ने प्रस्ताव किया कि एकबार वह स्वयं राजा साहब के पास जाकर हवेली को किराए पर लेने की बात उठायेगा। (बूंद, 568)

चिन्ता करके सूख जा—"to fret oneself (about someone)"

तुम आ गये भुवन-गौरा तो चिन्ता करके सूख गई थी। (नदी, 228)

चिन्ता करना छोड़ दे—"to give up on; to give up entertaining (any) apprehension"

इस प्रकार, साख व्यवस्था का परम्परागत आधार हटा लिया गया है किन्तु इससे साख-व्यवस्था पहले की भांति ही सुरक्षित है। लोगों ने यह चिन्ता करना ही छोड़ दिया है कि नोटों के पीछे सोने की आड़ रखी गई है या नहीं। (एमाई, 67)

4. **की फिक्र कर—"to care for"**

तुम भाई हो उसके। पर तुम भी कोई फिक्र नहीं करते उनकी। (लाख, 11)

"You are her brother. But you, too, don't seem to care for them."

की फिक्र कर—"to bother about"

...जीजी की कहानी में भी वह लोग काम की फिक्र नहीं करते, उन्हें भी हमेशा हर

दिन छुट्टी रहती है . ...ओह...फिर तो हम भी तुम्हारी जीजी की कहानी में हैं। जीजी कहती है कि कभी-कभी इस देश के लोग रात के समय बादलों की सवारी पर चढ़ हमारे घरों में भी आते हैं। (परिन्दे, 39-40)

आपको एक बार अपने सामान की फिक्र करनी चाहिए। (नदी, 122)

"You should at least once attend to your baggage (i.e. walk over to the place where your baggage is in order to make sure it is intact)."

की फिक्र कर—"to be concerned about"

कन्या कहने लगी—इस पर्चे के साथ सुबह भल्ले बाबू और दो-तीन साथी एक पर्चे का मसौदा मेरे पास लाये थे। उसमें भी इस अन्याय से ज्यादा पार्टी और भल्ले बाबू की इज्जत बचाने की फिक्र की गई थी। (बूंद, 125)

की फिक्र कर—"to take care of"

उनमें कोई बीमार पड़ता है तो उसके घर जाती है और दवा दारू की फिक्र करती है। (सेवा, 315)

की फिक्र कर—"to attend to"

एक बार जब दिल का दौरा पड़ा, तब भी उनकी किसी ने फिक्र नहीं की थी। (मांस, 65)

की फिक्र कर—"to bother oneself about"

उनकी फिक्र मत करो... उन्होंने घुड़दौड़ में ही बाल पकाये हैं... हां भूल गई, सिर चंदला किया है। उनकी खोपड़ी पर तो एक भी बाल नहीं है। (ढोल, 33)

5. **की परवाह कर—"to care for"**

मेरी तो ऐसी कल्पना है कि अच्छा लेखक हमेशा दूसरों की भावनाओं की परवाह करेगा (राह, 22)

अपने वचन की परवाह न कर—"... ignoring/not caring for what I said"

मुझ पर यह अभियोग न लगे कि मैंने इसे भागने में मदद दी, इसीलिए मैं अपने वचन की परवाह न कर लौटकर गांव में आया हूं। (लाख, 260)

की परवाह कर—"to care for, to give care to"

घोंघो की परवाह भी बहुत करनी पड़ती है। (समुद्र, 128)

मेरे गुस्से की किसे परवाह है? हवा बहती है, आंधी उठती है, बिजलियां चमकती हैं, बर्फ गिरती है—कौन परवाह करता है। (लाख, 225)

"...who cares !"

की परवाह कर—"to care"

मैं घबराकर उससे अलग होने की कोशिश करता पर वह उसकी परवाह नहीं करती थी। बाद में मुझे लगा कि वह जान बूझकर ही स्पर्श करने के मौके ढूंढ़ा करती थी। (धनु, 69-70)

की परवाह कर—"to care for someone"

एक दिन नेता ने विचार किया—इतना बड़ा दल मेरे साथ है कि अन्याय-कारी अमीर, धर्माध्यक्ष और राजा तक मेरी परवाह करते हैं। विरोध करते हुए भी, गालियां देते हुए भी वे मुझसे डरते हैं। जनता मेरे इशारे पर मरने और मारने को तैयार है। (मुक्ता, 40)

अगर तुम मेरी परवाह नहीं करते, तो मेरा धर्म नहीं कि तुम्हारी हर एक आज्ञा का पालन करूं। मिस्टर सेठ ने आंखों में विष भरकर कहा—नतीजा बुरा होगा। (सम, 36)

की कोई खास परवाह कर—"to make no scruples about"

बहिन की लड़की का विवाह भाई के लड़के से नहीं करते—भाई की लड़की भी बहिन के लड़के से नहीं ब्याही जाती। फिर भी मैं चुप था। सोचता था कि मृत्यु शैया पर दादा को वचन दे चुका हूं, इसलिए इन आचार-विचारों की कोई परवाह मैं नहीं करूंगा। (लाख, 133)

की परवाह न कर—"to give a damn about"

आप मेरी इतनी विनय मान जाइएगा। शोहदों के लिए आवाज कसना बिल्कुल मामूली बात है। मैं आवाजों की परवाह नहीं करती। (सम, 75)

उसने अपनी जान की भी परवाह न करके सूर्य से आग चुरा लाने का निश्चय किया। और सचमुच एक दिन वह आग चुरा ही लाया। (आग, 36)

"Without caring about (the danger) to his life..."

अपनी व्यक्तिगत सुरक्षा की परवाह किये बिना राने ने अकेले इस सारी योजना को सफलतापूर्वक क्रियान्वित किया। (परम, 23)

"Without caring for his personal safety..."

38. आहत, घाव, जख्म, घायल, जख्मी

1. आहत, घाव, जख्म, घायल and जख्मी all refer to inflicting a wound

upon someone capable of sustaining an injury. आहत specifically stresses the fact of hurting or causing a hurt by striking (from a distance). घा implies affliction (i.e. the state of pain or distress), and therefore may refer to a significant injury inflicted by an outside agent (through stabbing, piercing, or severe words) or caused internally. जख्म asserts only the infliction of injury, and thus contains no specific reference to its agent or cause. However, unless otherwise expressed, it generally suggests laceration. घायल refers to the state of being afflicted with a घाव and जख्मी to the fact of inflicting upon one a जख्म (suggesting the severity of the act rather than the distress of the one wounded).

2. आहत, घायल and जख्मी are —process, and घाव and जख्म are +process. घाव and जख्म respectively form ANP with में and पर, and both may occur with plural.

3. **को आहत कर—"to hurt"**

मल्लिका—यह आहत हरिणशावक ? . . .यहां ऐसा कौन व्यक्ति है जिसने इसे आहत किया। (आषाढ़, 15)

को आहत कर—"to cause injury to, to hurt, to do damage to"

. . .उस दुखमय विवेक ने मुझे बताया कि क्या चीज है जो अब भी जीवन में आस्था नहीं मिटने देती. . .फिर भी तुमसे दूर क्यों गया—क्यों जाना चाहा ? इसलिए कि सीखा, स्नेह में जब मोह भी होता है तब आघात मिलता है—मिलता ही नहीं, तब व्यक्ति स्वयं उसी को आहत करता है जिसके प्रति स्नेह है। (नदी, 323)

को आहत कर—"to hurt, to distress"

उल्लास-मत्त मंर्नासह की लीलायित गति रुकी नहीं। बोधा को चंचल कटाक्ष से आहत करता हुआ और हल्की-सी स्मित रेखा से बेधता हुआ वह चला ही गया। बोधा अज्ञात आशंका से व्याकुल हो उठे। कुछ बोल नहीं सके। (चारु, 429)

4. **घाव कर जा—"to wound deeply"**

फिर कोवलन की बात उसके कलेजे में घाव कर गई।(सुहाग, 158)
मेरे हृदय में वह देवनंदन का अपमान घाव कर गया। (तितली, 58)

5. **पर जख्म कर—"to make a cut"**

आग पर हाथ रखो तो उसे जलना ही होगा। शरीर पर जख्म करो तो रक्त को बहना ही होता है। (धनु, 131)

6. **को घायल कर दे—"to wound"**

नायक चन्द्रराव ने इस बीच उसे बुरी तरह घायल कर दिया था। (बेटी, 57)

को घायल कर दे—"to hurt deeply"

तेगअली की तलवार ने उन्हें घायल कर दिया। (सेवा, 175)

को घायल कर—"to hurt someone"

पर खुले मैदान में आते ही छावनी के सिपाही उन्हें तक-तक कर तीर और पत्थरों की बौछार से घायल करने लगे। (बेटी, 22)

7. **को जख्मी कर—"to injure, to inflict bodily injuries upon"**

एक दरोगा और चार कांस्टेबिलों को जख्मी किया है। (फूलो, 55)

जख्मी कर—"to hurt (oneself) on"

और कांटों से मुंह जख्मी किये लेते हैं। (थान, 65)

39. स्मरण, याद

1. Both स्मरण and याद refer to calling upon one's faculty of remembering either by having come into the mind again the notion or idea of something previously perceived or just putting it into effect through repetition (in order to fix it in one's mind).

स्मरण implies renewed apprehension (i.e. the act of grasping with intellect) of one's past experience or repeatedly uttering some words. याद is permitting something held in one's memory to occupy one's attention or repeating some words or utterances in order to commit them to memory.

2. Both nouns are ±process, and form ANP with का (की for याद). They do not admit plural.

3. **का स्मरण कर—"to reminisce about, to think of again"**

अम्मा, इस आनंद के समय में आप क्यों दुःख का स्मरण करती हैं ? (शांतला, 30)

का स्मरण कर—"to recall, to reflect upon"

राजमाता कुछ देर तक वहीं बैठी रहीं। अब तक जिन-जिन बातों पर बहस चली थी उनका एक-एक करके उन्होंने स्मरण किया। (शांतला, 56)

का स्मरण कर—"to remember, to mention"

आज स्टीफेनसन को कोई नहीं भुला सकता और उपहास करने वालों का नाम तक कोई स्मरण नहीं करता। (चमत्कार, 37)

का स्मरण कर—"to reflect upon, to think about, to recite mentally"

अथवा पुस्तक में किसी ऐसे वाक्य को पढ़ता है जो इसके हृदय में चुभ जाता है, उसका वह कई बार स्मरण करता है। (चमत्कार, 5)

का स्मरण कर—"to recite mentally"

मैं नीलतारा के नाम का स्मरण कर रहा हूं और रानी और मैना चित्त में उद्भासित हो रही हैं। (चारु, 393)

का स्मरण कर—"to remember, to come to mind again, to bring to recollection"

तुम जानती हो, मैं कितनी नीच प्रकृति का अधम जीव हूं, लेकिन अपनी उन नीचताओं का स्मरण करता हूं तो मेरा हृदय व्याकुल हो जाता है। (सेवा, 343)

का स्मरण करते-करते—"reminiscing"

कृष्णचन्द्र उस भूतकालिक जीवन का स्मरण करते-करते गद्गद हो गये। (सेवा, 223)

का इस तरह का स्मरण किया जाना—"a reflecting/reflection upon, a reference to"

ऐसे बहुत-से प्रेमी संसार में मिलते है, पर निबाहने वाले कम होते हैं। मैंने तेरी मां को ही देखा है।—चाची की आंखों में आंसू भर आये, पर तारा को अपनी माता का इस तरह का स्मरण किया जाना बहुत बुरा लगा। (कंकाल, 47)

का स्मरण करके—"(at the recollection of)"

जिस भयानक अकाल का स्मरण करके आज भी रोंगटे खड़े हो जाते हैं, जिस पिशाच की अग्नि क्रीड़ा में खेलती हुई तुमको मैंने पाया था वही संवत् 55 का अकाल आज के सुकाल से भी सदय था—कोमल था (तितली, 9)

तुम ईश्वर का स्मरण कर प्रतिज्ञा करो कि तुम इस पाप की चर्चा कभी भूलकर भी नहीं करोगी अन्यथा इस पाप के फल से तुम्हारा जीवन कलंकमय और कष्टमय हो जायगा। (फूलो, 96)

3. **की याद कर ले—"to refresh one's memory of, to recall"**

दिन-भर राजकाज करने के बाद वह रोज रात में उसी कोठरी में जाकर अपनी प्रिय

वस्तुओं को देखकर अपने बचपन की याद कर लेता था और अपने मन से कहता था कि ऐश्वर्यशाली पद पाकर अपने असली रूप को भूल मत जाना। (कथा, 18)

की याद कर पा—"to recall"

मैं आज भी उस दिन की घटनाओं की पूरी तरह साफ साफ याद नहीं कर पाता। (परिन्दे, 59)

को याद करता रह—"to remember"

बोला, सुमन तुमने मेरे साथ जो उपकार किया है उसको मैं सदा याद करता रहूंगा। (सेवा, 299)

को याद नहीं कर—"to not wish to recount"

और उससे मुझे बहुत-सी बातें याद आ गयी थीं जिन्हें मैं याद नहीं करती। (नदी, 329)

याद कर ले—"to recollect, to revive one's memory of"

चलो उठो, ठहरो जी। मुझे वो याद कर लेने दो। वो रसखान का कवित्त—कवित्त नहीं, सवैया है। अमां कुछ भी सही। क्या है वो...ऊंह...क्या है कन्या ? है तो कुछ अवश्य, पर क्या है ये याद नहीं। (बूंद, 287)

को बहुत याद कर—"to miss someone"

अब दीवाली पास आ रही है, इसलिए बच्चे मां को बहुत याद करते हैं। मां को गये 6 महीने से ऊपर हो गये हैं, इसलिए सबका दिल मां के लिए उदास है।

याद कर लेने की कोशिश कर—"to try to memorize"

शाहिद पर्चों को दो तीन बार पढ़कर शब्दों को याद कर लेने की कोशिश करता ताकि बिल्कुल सही सही रिपोर्ट दे सके। (फूलो, 52)

याद कर रख—"to memorize, to commit to memory"

—हमने भी कुछ गुर याद कर रखे हैं। (कहा, 33)

की याद कर—

अपनी माता से कहना कि मैंने उनकी याद की है। यह कहते हुए उन्होंने बच्ची के हाथ में एक टोकरी भर फल-फूल भेज दिये। (शांतला, 8-9)

"Remember me to your mother"

के रूप में याद किया जा—"to be remembered as"

मेरा विश्वास है कि तीस वर्ष बाद 1960 के इस दशक को अमरीका के एक महान् मोड़ के रूप में याद किया जायगा। (अमरीका, 47)

40. प्रण, संकल्प, इरादा

1. प्रण, संकल्प, and इरादा all refer to one's entering upon a state of firm determination about or adherence to a course of action. प्रण implies an open avowal of one's decisive choice, संकल्प is (more often a solemn, serious) decision or commitment to devote oneself to a purpose or design, and इरादा is a relatively neutral term referring to one's intent.

2. All the nouns are + process, and form ANP with का which freely permits the occurrence of infinitives before it. These nouns are not pluralized.

3. **का प्रण कर—"to pledge"**

उन्होंने अपने जीवन, अपनी सम्पत्ति और अपने पवित्र सम्मान की कुरबानी देने का प्रण किया...। (अमरीका, 19)

का प्रण कर ले—"to make a resolution"

पुनीता—गाली दूं। तुमको क्या हो गया है, मां? भलाई का बदला बुराई से दूं। मैंने तो प्रण कर लिया है अब गाली नहीं दूंगी। (बांस, 63)

प्रण कर—"to make a resolution or a vow"

आज मैंने भगवान शंकर के सामने प्रण किया है। (कचनार, 366)

का प्रण कर ले—"to have one's mind (already) made up"

हमारा हरकारा स्वयं छत्रपति के शिविर में जाने को तैयार था किन्तु तुम्हारे स्वामी ने स्वयं ही हमें शत्रु मानने का प्रण कर लिया है। (बेटी, 40)

का प्रण कर—"to resolve to"

सज्जन रोज उससे बेलाग रहने का प्रण करता है और वह प्रण कच्चे धागे की तरह बार-बार टूट जाता है। (बूंद, 205)

4. **का संकल्प कर—"to undertake, to enter upon"**

बहुत बड़े काम का संकल्प तुमने किया है बेटा, उसके लिये आवश्यक है कि उस महान संकल्प का आश्रयीभूत चित्त इनके चरणों में चढ़ा दो। (चारु, 184)

इसके पूर्व कभी भी इतने बड़े पैमाने पर भारत ही क्या विश्व के किसी देश में विकास काय करने का संकल्प नहीं किया गया था। (सामुदा, 11)

का संकल्प कर—"to take to"

अभिचार-साधना से ऊबी हुई करुणा ने ही,निर्जन-वास का निश्चय किया हो, तथागत की धर्म-देशना ने ही सरस-प्रेम साधना का संकल्प किया हो। (चारु, 283)

का मन में संकल्प करले—"to take upon oneself (the task of)"

रामनाथ ने पूरे बल से इस लीला का प्रत्याख्यान करने का मन में संकल्प कर लिया। बोले—सुनो राजो, ब्याह तो होगा ही। (तितली, 101)

संकल्प कर ले—"to decide (that)"

उसने भी संकल्प कर लिया कि बालक का अस्पताल में पालन हो जायगा, फिर मैं चली जाऊंगी। (कंकाल, 55)

का संकल्प कर—"to take upon oneself expressly"

राष्ट्रीय स्वच्छता दिवस पर हमने इन स्थानों की स्वच्छता का संकल्प किया और राष्ट्रपति डा० राजेन्द्रप्रसाद ने इसकी उपयोगिता बताते हुए अपने संदेश में लिखा...। (स्वस्थ 24)

का दृढ़ संकल्प कर रख—"to put oneself under the obligation to"

वह वापस नहीं आया क्योंकि उसने कुछ करके दिखाने का दृढ़ संकल्प कर रखा था। (बाल, 11, 49)

5. **का इरादा कर रख—"to intend to, to have the intention of"**

पिछले तीन घंटों का दृश्य उसके मन में फिर उभर आया। उसे ध्यान आया, उसने जब-जब पूछा था कि भाग तो नहीं जाओगे तब-तब भुवन ने बात पलट दी थी, उत्तर नहीं दिया था, तो क्या वह उसे छोड़कर चला जायगा—क्या वैसा इरादा उसने कर रखा है। (नदी, 304)

मैं स्वयं कई दिन से तुम्हारे पास आने का इरादा कर रहा था, लेकिन काम से ही छुट्टी ही नहीं मिलती। (सेवा, 295)

का इरादा कर ले—"to make up one's mind"

इन्होंने भी अपनी मेहनत के रेट बढ़ाने का इरादा कर लिया है। (दुख, 80)

का इरादा कर—"to resolve"

उसने इस काम के लिये अब सीधे इलाहाबाद पहुंचने का इरादा किया। (सुन्दर, 223)

41. कृपणता, कंजूसी, सरफा, किफायत, बचत

1. कृपणता, कंजूसी, सरफा, किफायत and बचत all have in common practice of economy in the use of money or other possessions. Both कृपणता and कंजूसी refer to respectively having the disposition of being niggardly and miserly. सरफा is sparing use (often on necessities) by abstaining and restraining in order to hoard or to let others have the benefit of use, किफायत is frugality suggesting absence of luxury and lavishness, and बचत is trying to save or effect savings by reducing expenditure through use of alternatives (such as buying less expensive items, conserving on use, judicious planning or the like).

2. All nouns are + process and do not admit plural. Both कृपणता and कंजूसी form ANP with की, सरफा with पर or के ऊपर, किफायत with में, and बचत with की or में.

3. **की कृपणता कर–"to scrimp, to be niggardly in providing for"**

प्रोफेसर महाशय का भोजन ऐसे उत्तेजक पदार्थों से सदा शून्य रहता था। मोतीराम अलग से उनका सेवन करता था। ज्ञानवती की रुचि उस ओर देखकर उसने कृपणता नहीं की...। फूलो, (88)

4. **की कंजूसी कर—"to scrimp, to limit too closely"**

वीर—उसने सत्य की ज्यादा कंजूसी नहीं की।

5. **के ऊपर सरफा कर—"to live with frugality"**

कौन इनकी कमाई में से इसने पैसा दे दिया, और फिर अपने ऊपर तो सरफा किया है नहीं। (तुला, 78)

6. **में किफायत कर—"to cut down, to curtail"**

तुम्हें अब अपने रोशनी और पंखे के खर्चे में, पान तम्बाकू के खर्चे में, घोड़े साईस के खर्चे में किफायत करना भारी मालूम होता है, किन्तु भैया मुझे वार्निस वाले जूता पहना कर आप नंगे पांव रहते थे। (सेवा, 74)

7. **पाई-पाई की बचत कर—"to pinch every penny"**

श्यामसुन्दर दिल लगाकर काम करता, जान डालकर काम करता, पाई-पाई की बचत करता, मालिक का पैसा-पैसा बचाता रहता। (दुग्गल, 42)

की बचत कर ले—"to save"

इसकी जगह वह मद का त्याग करके एक शिलिंग रोज की बचत कर ले। (अच्छी, 6)

लाख बचत कर सक—"to economize (in a hundred thousand ways)"

अगर औरत घर में रहे तो लाख बचत कर सकती है। (दुग्गल, 118)

में बचत कर—"to cut down on, to effect a saving in"

अतः तार पंजीकृत करा लेने से तथा इन सरकारी विभागों की जानकारी कर लेने से तार के व्यय में बचत भी की जा सकती है।

42. इकरार, वायदा, प्रतिज्ञा

1. इकरार, वायदा (Sp. Var. वादा) and प्रतिज्ञा all refer to one's holding out to some one an assurance or one's determination to follow a definite course of action (in the future). इकरार implies a binding assurance, usually entered upon by one with another with a mutual understanding. It also carries a strong apprehension that one may falter or back out from one's committed course of action. वायदा is promising to perform, to do or to refrain from something, or resolving to bring about something desired by someone else or pleasing to oneself. प्रतिज्ञा is the expression of one's pledging oneself to an undertaking or simply assenting to do or refrain from doing something.

2. All the nouns are + process and form ANP with से, के साथ and का/की. Only का/की permit occurrence of infinitives. Also both इकरार and वायदा may be pluralized.

3. **से इकरार कर—"to promise, to make a promise"**

निहाल का नम्बरदार की बेटी से बड़ा प्रेम था। उन्होंने तो लाखों इकरार किये हुए थे। (दुग्गल, 127)

से इकरार कर—"to agree, to promise"

छः मास हुए जो कुछ इसने अपनी बेटी के ब्याह के लिए जोड़ा था वह भी ले गया। अचानक उसे कोई जरूरत आन पड़ी थी। और न अब उसने इस फसल की रकम भेजी थी न और कुछ जो उसने इकरार किया था। (दुग्गल, 130)

4. **से वायदा कर—"to promise to"**

कमरे में खामोशी आधे मिनट से भी कुछ अधिक ही रही। सज्जन ने फिर कहा—कल तुमने मुझसे वादा किया था कि मेरे यहां रहोगी। (बूंद, 204)

अरे एक ने भी तो—और वचन मात्र से भी—मुसीबत में उसका साथ देने का वादा नहीं किया। (विचित्र, 11)

से वायदा कर ले—"to be committed to do"

जोखन लाल ने ज्ञानेश्वर राव से वायदा भी कर लिया था कि वह उन्हें उत्तरप्रदेश से राज्यसभा में भी भेज देंगे। (सा सा, 28)

के साथ वायदा कर— "to promise, to agree to"

क्यों ? मेरे साथ तुम चलने का वादा कर चुके हो न ?—मुसकराते हुए अजित ने कहा। तो वादा टूट भी सकता है। प्रभा ने आंखें तिरछी करते हुए कहा। (तीन, 61)

का वायदा कर—"to agree to"

इन्सपेक्टर ने शमशेर अली के आवेदन पत्र पर केवल विचार करने का वादा किया। (डगर, 14)

वर्षों पहले किए अपने वायदे—"the pledge she made years before"

हालां कि दहेज में बड़ा सुन्दर पलंग आया था, पर मां ने वर्षों पहले किये अपने वायदे के अनुसार वही अपने वाला बड़ा, कीमती पलंग सोहाग कक्ष में बिछा दिया था। (कहानी, 45)

5. से प्रतिज्ञा कर—"to promise someone"

यदि मैं जीवित रहा तो ठीक ही है नहीं तो कुकोरी से यह कहकर पताका मेरी स्त्री के पास भेज दी जाय। मैंने रणयात्रा के समय, अपनी स्त्री से शत्रुओं की एक पताका देने की प्रतिज्ञा की है। (काल, 44)

की प्रतिज्ञा कर—"to make a vow"

और इस भारीपन में ही उसे यह भी लग रहा था मानों वह तपोभ्रष्ट हो गया हो। उसने शराब न पीने की प्रतिज्ञा की थी, ब्रह्मचर्यपालन के लिए मां के मन्दिर, और भगवान बुद्ध से लेकर बाबा राम जी तक के उपदेशों की आड़ ली थी। (बूंद, 348)

प्रतिज्ञा कर—"to promise"

रानी : प्रतिज्ञा करते हो। देते हो वचन। मंत्री : हां वचन देता हूं। रानी : (क्रोध से) निकल जाओ यहां से झूठे प्रपंची विश्वासघाती पुरुष (नाटक, 53)

प्रतिज्ञा कर—"to promise"

परन्तु एक प्रतिज्ञा करनी होगी। वह क्या ? मेरा सोना बेच कर कुछ दिनों के लिए मुझे निश्चिन्त बना दो (कंकाल, 67)

की दृढ़ प्रतिज्ञा कर—"to make a pledge"

अपनी सेवा वृत्ति को जागरूक करने की उसने दृढ़ प्रतिज्ञा की। (तितली, 247)

प्रतिज्ञा करते समय—"at the time of making a pledge"

छावनी में तलवार हिलाकर प्रतिज्ञा करते समय तुम्हारी आंखों पर अभिमान का पर्दा पड़ा था, गायकवाड़। (बेटी, 64)

43. अनुवृत्ति, पुनरावृत्ति, आवृत्ति

1. अनुवृत्ति, पुनरावृत्ति and आवृत्ति all refer to saying something verbally (as opposed to writing) again.

अनुवृत्ति is quoting or citing something said by someone else, in part or full. The term is usually applied to something short, often a sentence, a couplet or part of it and the like, and may imply a use of the words of another person in a different context. पुनरावृत्ति is the reiteration of what one has said before. The term applies to saying all over again something long, though not necessarily verbatim. आवृत्ति is saying again or repeatedly something very short.

2. These nouns are +process and form ANP with की. They are not pluralized. With the exception of अनुवृत्ति, they are generally qualified by a suitable determiner indicating the number of times something is repeated, e.g., एक बार "once", बार-बार "again and again", अन्तहीन "endlessly" etc. The words occurring before की आवृत्ति are repeated once.

3. **की अनुवृत्ति कर—"to cite, to quote"**

परन्तु कुमार ने मुझे बचाया। उन्होंने मेरी आर्या के एक अंश की अनुवृत्ति करते हुए परिहासपूर्वक कहा—व्रत की याद से विह्वल होना उचित नहीं, भट्ट। सारी सभा हंस पड़ी। (बाण, 194)

4. **का पुनरावृत्ति कर—"to reiterate"**

लाले की घरवाली फिर एक बार अपनी शिकायत-रामायण की पुनरावृत्ति कर गई। (बूंद, 23)

5. **की आवृत्ति कर—"to say again and again, to repeat"**

...बार-बार एक ही दारुण दृश्य सामने आता है, और मैं सुनता हूं तुम्हारी दर्द-भरी आवाज मुझे पुकारती हुई, प्राण, जाण, जान, अंतहीन आवृत्ति करती हुई एक कराह,

जिसे वर्षा की वह अनवरत टपटपाहट भी नहीं डुबा पाती जो कि उस स्मृति का एक अभिन्न अंग है। (नदी, 261)

44. हस्तक्षेप, दस्तंदाजी

1. हस्तक्षेप and दस्तंदाजी have to do with someone's motivated concern or involvement in the affairs or responsibilities of others, and are applied to any act which, in the judgement of the speaker, indicates or constitutes that concern. हस्तक्षेप stresses a desire to influence the person directly, and दस्तंदाजी implies that the person expressing concern is acting officiously.

2. Both nouns are + process and form ANP with में. They do not occur with plural.

2. में हस्तक्षेप कर—"to interfere in"

गांव के लोग किसी की भी कुटुम्ब व्यवस्था की यद्यपि चर्चा करते तो भी प्रत्यक्ष रूप से उस व्यवस्था में हस्तक्षेप करने के लिए आगे कोई न आता। (लाख, 44)

यों तो मानव जीवन एक अकारण, अनिर्दिष्ट, आकारहीन गतिमयतासा लगता है, पर मेरा ख्याल है, बीच-बीच में विधि मानवों के जीवन में थोड़ा-सा हस्तक्षेप जरूर करती है... एक-एक गोट को उठाकर एक-एक दिशा दे देती है...(नदी, 88)

में हस्तक्षेप कर—"to pry into"

...तब तक मैं इसके सिवा क्या समझ सकती हूं कि उनके जीवन में हस्तक्षेप करने का मेरा कोई अधिकार नहीं है। (नदी, 83)

में हस्तक्षेप कर—"to interfere with, to encroach upon"

इसी प्रकार भारतीय राज्य में किसी भी नागरिक को यह अधिकार नहीं है कि वह दूसरे के अधिकारों और स्वतंत्रता में हस्तक्षेप करे। यहां तक प्रत्येक नागरिक पर राजकीय नियंत्रण है। (भारत, 39)

3. में हस्तक्षेप कर—"to intervene in"

संक्षेप में, राज्य व्यक्ति की उन सब आर्थिक क्रियाओं में हस्तक्षेप कर सकता है जिनमें कुछ अन्य लोगों का शोषण होता हो, उनको धोखा दिया जाता हो उनकी किसी प्रकार से हानि होती हो। (भारत, 34)

4. में दस्तंदाजी कर—"to meddle in, to be inquisitive about"

मैंने उनसे वादा किया था कि उनके लव अफेयर्स में उनकी मर्जी के खिलाफ दस्तंदाजी

नहीं करूंगी। ये बातें जो तुम्हें सन 26 में मालूम हुईं मुझे सन् 25 के ग्यारहवें महीने से ही मालूम हैं । (खत, 34)

में दस्तंदाजी कर--"to meddle with"

अभी तक रूपा की बातें रेणुका सुनती जा रही थी। पर अब उससे नहीं रहा गया । लज्जा, संकोच और शिष्टता को ताक पर रखकर, वह...झल्लाकर उस पर टूटती हुई बोली ...तुम हमारे काम में दस्तंदाजी मत करो। समझे ? (लाख, 90)

45. भेदभाव, पक्षपात, लिहाज, रियायत, तरफदारी

1. भेदभाव, पक्षपात, लिहाज, रियायत and तरफदारी all refer to disregard of non-partisanship or impartiality in what one does. The terms apply to one's attitude or to the effect of such an attitude. भेदभाव is discriminating in favor of or against; पक्षपात is defending or taking a partisan view of someone or something implying one's favorable predisposition; लिहाज is lack of fair and square dealing with someone in order to show deference, consideration or the like; रियायत is withdrawing a stricture already applied or withholding from applying it, and तरफदारी is expressing (through words or acts) one's favorable disposition towards or for someone.

2. All nouns are + process and form ANP as follows—भेदभाव with में, के साथ, के प्रति ; पक्षपात with के प्रति, का; लिहाज with का; रियायत with के साथ; and तरफदारी with की. They do not admit plural.

3. **में भेदभाव कर--"to discriminate in favor of"**

भगवान् कभी अपनी चीजों का विषम बंटवारा नहीं कर सकता। अगर उसने हवा, पानी, प्रकाश और आसमान के वितरण में भेदभाव नहीं किया, तो यह कैसे हो सकता है कि वह जमीन ही सिर्फ मुट्ठीभर लोगों के हाथ में रहने दे। (भूदान, 41)

के साथ भेदभाव कर—"to discriminate against"

वह आग तब सीमित नहीं रहेगी। वह अफ्रीका के उन सब क्षेत्रों में फैलेगी जहां गोरे कालों के साथ भेदभाव करते हैं। (नवभा, 1-4)

के प्रति भेदभाव कर—"to institute discriminative practice"

भारतीय संविधान के अनुसार भारत में धर्म, प्रजाति, जाति, लिंग अथवा जन्मस्थान आदि के आधार पर किसी भी व्यक्ति के प्रति कोई भेदभाव नहीं किया जायेगा। इनमें से किसी भी बात को लेकर किसी भी व्यक्ति को किसी भी सार्वजनिक स्थान पर जाने से नहीं रोका जा सकता । (भारत, 48)

4. का पक्षपात कर—"to favor someone"

...सरकार पर भी प्रत्यक्ष रूप से धनिकों का नियंत्रण रहना, जिससे वह भी धनी-वर्ग का ही पक्षपात करती है। (एमाई, 57)

के प्रति पक्षपात कर—"to take a partisan view of"

वहां मैत्री के प्रति पक्षपात न कर जनता को सचेत करना मेरा परम कर्त्तव्य है। यह मानवता की पुकार है। (बूंद, 554)

5. का लिहाज कर—"to show consideration to"

बूढ़े गंगासिंह को ख्याल आया, मक्खन हलवाई ने अभी तक उसकी रकम नहीं लौटाई थी। तीन बीसी तो सूद हो जाता, यदि इसने कागज लिखवाया होता। और वह सोचता अब वह लिहाज नहीं करेगा। दुग्गल, 121)

का लिहाज करते हुए—"considering"

उसने स्वयं ही चौधरी साहब की सज्जनता और आपसदारी का लिहाज करते हुए पैसे लेने से मना कर दिया था। (सवाल, 117)

6. के साथ रियायत कर—"to excuse"

औरत जात समझ कर हम तेरे साथ रियायत करते हैं तो उसका नाजायज फायदा मत उठा। (धनु, 73)

के साथ रियायत कर—"to condone"

सुमन—इस तरह कह रहे हैं, मानों मेरे साथ बड़ी रियायत कर रहे हैं। (सेवा, 138)

रियायत कर—"to make a concession"

इस संबंध में आचार्य के लिखने या कहने पर समुचित रियायत करने में सरकार को आपत्ति न होगी। (जय, 53)

7. की तरफदारी कर—"to side with"

उल्टा उनका आरोप यह है कि मैं मां, बहनों और भावजों के सामने भीगी बिल्ली बन जाता हूं और जैसा कि मुझे करना चाहिए, उनकी तरफदारी नहीं करता। (सच, 56)

मनुष्य के विचार किस वक्त पलट जायें यह कोई नहीं कह सकता। सच पूछा जाय तो यही आश्चर्य है कि कुछ दिन पहिले तक वह हमारी इतनी तरफदारी क्यों कर रहा था। (लाख, 188)

की तरफदारी कर—"to take sides, to side with"

जो राज्य अधिकारी धन के लोभ से ऐसे मनुष्यों की तरफदारी करके राज्य में विषमता को प्रश्रय देते हैं, वे भी दंडनीय हैं। (वैदिक, 2)

46. अपव्यय, फिजूलखर्ची

1. अपव्यय and फिजूलखर्ची both refer to one's spending money extravagently or thriftlessly. अपव्यय is squandering money by one who is improvident or prodigal, sometimes with no other purpose but to show off. फिजूलखर्ची contains a reference to someone's habit of thriftless spending or to an instance of such an act of spending money beyond one's means.

2. Both nouns are + process. अपव्यय forms ANP with का, and फिजूलखर्ची with पर. They are not pluralized.

3. **का अपव्यय कर—"to squander away, to spend extravagently"**

जिस तरह बहुत दिन तक दारुण दारिद्र्य भोगने के बाद एकाएक कोई अतुल सम्पत्ति का स्वामी हो जाय और अपना संतुलन खोकर धन का अपव्यय करने लगे, कुछ ऐसी ही दशा आज की उच्चशिक्षा प्राप्त अधिकांश आधुनिकाओं की है। (भंवर, 27)

4. **फिजूलखर्ची कर—"to spend wastefully"**

यह जरूर है कि मैं फिजूलखर्ची नहीं करता, फिर भी अपने बच्चों को पूरी तरह खिला-पहना भी नहीं सकता। (बूंद, 104)

उनके किस्से मैंने भी सुने हैं। यह बात दूसरी है कि अपने होश से ही मैंने अपने मायके में फिजूलखर्ची और कंगाली ही बराबर बढ़ती देखी। और अब तो फिजूलखर्ची करने को भी बरसों से कुछ नहीं। (बूंद, 471)

47. आड़, ओट

1. Both आड़ and ओट refer to the act of covering something in order to cut it off from observation or to protect it from observation or attack. आड़ is literally a screen or anything so used (and held) in an upright or horizontal position, and ओट refers to anything that shields or obstructs.

2. Both nouns are ±process, and form ANP with पर. However,

they are used more frequently as —process with or without में. N पर is also freely dropped. They are not pluralized.

3. **आड़ कर ले—"to give someone a cover (on)"**

...सब्जी लेकर लौटी आ रही थी। देखा तो खादी-दीदी की साड़ी पीछे से एक दम भुभुक्का। मैंने तुरंत आड़ कर लिया और हरामियों को गलिया के भगाया। (दीर्घ, 95)

Observe the switch of the gender of आड़ from feminine to non-feminine in the above sentence.

...से आड़ किए—"covering..."

तो देखा कि तितली एक छोटा सा दीप जलाकर अपने आंचल से आड़ किए वहीं आ रही है। (तितली, 127)

आड़ में कर दे—"to place out of sight"

लालटेन आड़ में कर दी गई। (तितली, 194)

4. **ओट कर—"to shield"**

...अधखुली मुट्ठी सिर पर ऐसी लगने लगी मानो चोट से बचने को ओट की गयी हो। (नदी, 57)

को ओट में कर ले—"to shield"

मीरा ने चादर जोड़कर जैसे अपने को ओट में कर लिया। (आकाश, 83)

को नजर-ओट कर—"to obstruct, to cut off from sight"

इसलिए व्यक्ति अपने को नजर-ओट कर हर दूसरे व्यक्ति को गलत बताता है। (बूंद, 583)

नजर-ओट is a compound formation derived from नजर से ओट में.

48. विस्तार, विस्तृत, विकास, विकसित, प्रगति, उन्नति, उन्नत, तरक्की

1. विस्तार, विस्तृत, विकास, विकसित, प्रगति, उन्नति, उन्नत and तरक्की all refer to the acts or processes contemplated or carried out in order to make or become better through someone's or something's moving along a course, or bychanging from one state to another.

विस्तार is literally spreading out, and therefore refers to expanding or extending, implying a giving of greater scope. विकास (lit. unfolding or bursting) is developing through a natural course as well as through the exercise of human energy, ingenuity or the like. प्रगति (lit. going forward) refers to the indication of progress implying a step by step or stage by stage improvement. उन्नति (lit. rising or ascending) refers to an observed state of improvement in someone or something, and तरक्की (lit. growth or growing up) is a relatively colorless term referring to advancement.

2. All the nouns, with the exception of प्रगति and तरक्की are ±process— their – process counterparts being विस्तृत, विकसित and उन्नत respectively. Both विस्तार and विकास form ANP with का, and प्रगति, उन्नति and तरक्की with में and की. These nouns do not take plural.

3. **का विस्तार कर—"to (want to) gain more experience, to increase (one's knowledge, skill etc. by participation in events)"**

निस्सन्देह में अनुभवों का विस्तार करना चाहता था। (राह, 7)

का विस्तार कर—"to expand, to enlarge"

उदयपुर स्थित राजस्थान कृषि कालेज का विस्तार किया जायेगा और जोबनेर के एस० क० एन० कृषि कालेज में अतिरिक्त सुविधाओं की व्यवस्था की जाएगी। (लोक, 11)

का विस्तार कर—"to expand, to increase the scope of"

समाजवादी ढांचे का समाज स्थापित करने के लिए अभी राज्य को अपने कार्यों के क्षेत्र का और भी विस्तार करना पड़ेगा। (भारत, 38)

का विस्तार कर—"to enlarge, to give greater scope to"

मानव को व्यापकता प्राप्त करनी है, स्व की परिधि का विस्तार करना है। (धर्म, 102)

का विस्तार कर—"to expand, to develop"

पिछले साढ़े तीन वर्षों में हमने अपने शांतिकाल में अपनी अर्थव्यवस्था का जैसा विस्तार किया है, वह सर्वथा अभूतपूर्व है। (अमरीका, 100)

4. **को विस्तृत कर—"to extend, to stretch out"**

मानव स्वभाव है, वह अपने सुख को विस्तृत करना चाहता है। (तितली, 46)

विस्तृत कर—to expand, to extend"

...इसलिए कि तुम अपने ही को सब कुछ समझ रहे हो। अपने जीवन की परिधि विस्तृत करो...। उसमें मुझे भी आने दो...दूसरों को आने दो। (सन्यासी, 43)

5. **का विकास कर—"to lead to the development of"**

कुटीर उद्योग धंधे ग्रामीण समुदायों की आर्थिक दशा की उन्नति कर ग्रामीण समुदायों का विकास करते हैं। (ग्रामीण, 30)

का विकास कर—"to develop"

ऐसा आदर्श उपनिषद् कालीन ऋषियों में जीवित था। व्यक्ति और समाज के भीतर छिपी हुई सम्भावनाओं का विकास अधिक सावधानी और विवेक से न किये जाने के कारण पाश्चात्य देशों में भी विकसित न हो सका। (धर्म, 72)

लेकिन हमें उस उत्तमता को भी प्रोत्साहन देना होगा जो किसी प्रतिभाशाली-छात्र को अपनी क्षमता का विकास करने को प्रेरित करती है। (अमरीका, 44)

विकास कर—"to be developed"

हमारे मन ने अभी तक इतना विकास नहीं किया है कि स्वार्थी इच्छाओं को छोड़कर हम संवादपूर्ण विश्व-समाज की रचना में लग जायें। (अणु, 29-30)

का विकास कर ले—"to become mature"

मनुष्य जब अपने व्यक्तित्व का विकास कर लेता है तो उसमें आत्मविश्वास की भावना इतनी दृढ़ हो जाती है कि...। (धर्म, 118)

का विकास कर—"to develop, to evolve"

...मनोविश्लेषण के सिद्धान्त का जो विकास कर रहे हैं...(मूल्य, 118)

6. **विकसित कर—"to develop"**

विश्वविद्यालय में ही मैं कुछ शोर-शरापा और हुल्लड़बाजी करता था...कहना चाहिए कि मैं यह नया गुण अपने में विकसित कर रहा था, परन्तु घर आकर मैं चुपचाप बैठा या सोया रहता था। (राह, 11)

महान समाज वह जगह है जहां बच्चा ज्ञान से अपने मस्तिष्क को समृद्ध बना सके और अपने गुणों को विकसित कर सके। (अमरीका, 39)

विकसित कर—"to unfold (itself), to develop into (predominant trend)"

18वीं और उन्नीसवीं शताब्दी की चिन्तना के फलस्वरूप जिस मर्यादा ने साहित्य में अपने को प्रमुखतम रूप में विकसित किया वह थी सामाजिक प्रगति की मर्यादा। (मूल्य, 105)

विकसित कर—"to evolve"

...युंग ने इस यान्त्रिकता के परिहार के लिए व्यक्तित्व के सृजनात्मक सन्तुलन का सिद्धान्त विकसित किया जिसे वह आत्मा का स्थानापन्न मानता है। (मूल्य, 118)

7. **में प्रगति कर—"to bring about development, to make progress"**

जापान ने मोती-उत्पादन में काफी प्रगति की है। (समुद्र, 129)

की प्रगति कर—"to lead to progress"

व्यष्टिवादी सिद्धान्त का योगदान व्यक्ति के महत्व पर जोर देने में है। इसमें कोई संदेह नहीं है कि समाज और देश की प्रगति व्यक्तियों ने की और आगे भी इनका मार्गदर्शन व्यक्तियों के हाथ में रहेगा...। (भारत, 23)

प्रगति कर—"to progress"

अगर हमें जाति गत संघर्ष को समाप्त करना है तो हमारे सामने एक यही रास्ता है कि हम व्यवस्थित प्रगति करें। (अमरीका, 24)

प्रगति कर—"to move on to perfection"

इस विकास में विज्ञान और समाजशास्त्र ने भी काफी हिस्सा लिया है। दोनों आज बहुत आगे बढ़ गये हैं। इसीलिए आज हमारे नीति-विषयक विचार आगे बढ़े हैं। जैसे समाज आगे बढ़ेगा, नीतिशास्त्र और भी प्रगति करता रहेगा। (भूदान, 82)

8. **में उन्नति कर—"to make progress"**

इसी भावना के फल-स्वरूप मानव ने विज्ञान के क्षेत्र में ऐसी चमत्कारिक उन्नति की है? (बुन, 25)

में उन्नति कर—"to improve"

सामाजिक विधान का उद्देश्य समाज में प्रत्येक के जीवन में इस तरह की उन्नति करना है और उसको ऐसे साधन और अवसर देना है जिनसे कि वह संविधान में निर्धारित नागरिक के अधिकारों को प्राप्त कर सके। (भारत, 46)

उन्नति कर—"to rise higher (in status etc.)"

निक्षेप: मुझे दुख होता है। इन सबके अतिरिक्त उन्हीं व्यवसायियों के मुख से और भी तो कई तरह की बातें सुनी थीं। मल्लिका: कोई व्यक्ति उन्नति करता है तो उसके नाम के साथ कई तरह के अपवाद अनायास जुड़ने लगते हैं। (आषाढ़, 52)

9 **उन्नत कर—"to improve, to elevate"**

उदाहरण के लिए जब तक भारतीय समाज में स्त्रियों की दशा उन्नत न की जाय

तब तक परिवार और विवाह की संस्थाओं में मौलिक परिवर्तन करने की आशा व्यर्थ है। (भारत, 5)

उन्नत कर—"to elevate"

मध्यवर्गीय जन जीवन को सांस्कृतिक दृष्टि से उन्नत करने के लिए यह आयोजन किया गया है। (बूंद, 378)

10. **में तरक्की करके दिखा—"to improve upon"**

अगर वे पढ़-लिख कर भी अपने पुश्तैनी धन्धों को नहीं छोड़ते और उनमें तरक्की करके दिखाते तो आज हिन्दुस्तान की जैसी बुरी हालत हो गई है, न हो पाती। (बुन, 9)

की तरक्की कर—"to make advancement or progress"

पश्चिमी देश विज्ञान की तरक्की करके युद्ध और विनाश फैलाते हैं जबकि हमारे देश के गाँधीवादी लोग विज्ञान की तरक्की के विरुद्ध हैं। (राह, 48)

तरक्की कर—"to advance"

परन्तु यहां स्वार्थ का मतलब है कि हम समूह रूप में तरक्की करेंगे, हम अपनी समस्याओं पर और खास तौर से कमजोरियों पर तटस्थता से विचार करेंगे और अपने को ऐसा बुद्धिमान, व्यावहारिक और कर्मठ नागरिक के रूप में विकास करेंगे, जिसके शरीर और मन की तरक्की से समाज की तरक्की हो...। (राह, 45)

की तरक्की कर दे—"to give someone a raise"

सभी कागजात और हिसाब किताब ठीक था। इसलिए इन्सपेक्टर ने बहुत अच्छा नोट लिखा और दो रुपए उनकी तरक्की कर दी। (डगर, 13-4)

49. व्रत, अनशन, उपवास, उपास, फाका, व्रत-उपवास, भूख-हड़ताल

1.1. व्रत, अनशन, उपवास, उपास and फाका all refer to abstinence from food for a period of time. व्रत which is abstention from self-indulgence, only secondarily refers to fasting on certain occasions as a matter of religious practice among the Hindus (with the implied purpose of atonement). अनशन is voluntarily (or wilfully) abstaining from all nourishment for the attainment of one's objective, generally expressed (sometimes implied). उपवास is fasting voluntarily, or missing meals for a day or a number of days, implying some purpose, or some circumstance which causes such behaviour, and उपास is an informal or dialectal variant of

उपवास usually lacking in the specific implication of the latter. फाका is going hungry in whole or partially.

1.2. भूख-हड़ताल is a compound term meaning "to go on hunger-strike" when occurring with कर-. It is generally used in contexts of अनशन when the purpose other than religious or sacred is to be stressed.

व्रत-उपवास is a binomial compound, and the expression व्रत-उपवास कर means "to practise asceticism, to observe ascetic practices."

मैं व्रत-उपवास खूब करूंगी, मुझको अभ्यास है । (कचनार, 190)

2. All the nouns are + process, and do not take N post., with the exception of व्रत which requires N का. Only फाका admits plural.

3. का व्रत कर—"to observe (Ekādaśī)"

वैष्णवजन एकादशी का व्रत द्वादशी की प्रधानता से ही करते हैं। (भक्ति, 3)

4. अनशन कर —"to abstain from nourishment"

वृन्दावन से प्राप्त नवीनतम समाचारों से ज्ञात हुआ है कि गोवध निषेध के लिए अनशन कर रहे संत प्रभुदत्त ब्रह्मचारी की शारीरिक और मानसिक स्थिति इतनी गंभीर हो गयी है कि आज कई बार वे बेहोश हो गए। (आज, 2)

अनशन कर रख —"to not be eating"

इसके यहां तर माल मिलेगा, कचराकूट का चांस, इसी विचार से मैंने कल शाम से ही अनशन कर रखा है। (विचित्र, 19)

5. का उपवास कर—"to observe a fast, to fast"

इतने से भी सन्तोष न पाकर एक बार, चातुर्मास में उन्होंने हर तीसरे दिन उपवास किया। (गांधी, 4)

उपवास कर—"to go without food"

अब इसी कमजोरी की हालत में तीन दिनों से उपवास भी कर रहा हूं। हम लोगों के पास लकड़ी ईंट, मेज, कुर्सी...को छोड़ ऐसी कोई भी चीज नहीं जिसे ढग णा सकें। (खत, 74)

उपवास करता रह—"to practise abstinence, to be fasting"

एक तरफ पत्नी उपवास करती रही दूसरी ओर भोलानाथ पंजाबिन के साथ शराबी-भजे लेता रहा। (जुहू, 24)

उपवास करके—"without eating"

बेचारा उपवास करके सो रहा। उधर मां चिंता में पड़ी कि सनातन कहां चला गया (बाल, 11, 37)

6. **उपास कर—"to miss a meal"**

देवीदीन ने कहा...सब खायेंगे तो तू उपास न करेगा। (निरु, 83)

7. **फाका कर—"to go hungry"**

अरे बेटा, इन छोटे-मोटे फिकरों से क्या फाका करने लगे? (मित्रो, 9)

फाके कर—"to forbear eating"

हम लोगों को अकेले-अकेले अमृत खाने से स्वजनों के संग फाके करने में भी मजा आता है। (जुहू, 84)

50. लाभ, फायदा, प्रभाव, असर

1. लाभ "profit", फायदा "advantage", प्रभाव "influence" and असर "effect" are the terms employed (in their extended usage) to describe the remedial effects of drugs, medicines or other modes of treatment of diseases, injuries or other such unhealthy conditions of the body; they are thus used only when the subject of a sentence containing any one of these nouns is the name of such a drug, medicine or the like.

Both लाभ and फायदा imply the preventive qualities of the treatment, लाभ stressing the restoration of health or recovery from disease, and फायदा refers to the remedial qualities.

प्रभाव and असर stress the effectiveness of a remedy. प्रभाव implies a quick curative effect, and असर is a term employed when the implications of प्रभाव are to be avoided, or more lasting effectiveness is implied.

2. All the nouns are + process and form ANP with में. They are not pluralized.

3. **में लाभ कर—"to help"**

हैजे का सीजन हो तो बराबर लेने से इस रोग में लाभ करता है। (इलाज, 60)

4. **में फायदा कर "to relieve"**

इलायची का तेल सर्दी, सिर दर्द, वायु वगैरह में लगाने से फायदा करता है। (इलाज, 28)

5. **में प्रभाव कर—"to work a cure"**

रक्त का दबाव भारी हो, सारे शरीर में कटन होती हो, सिर दुखता हो, घुमती आये तब शिलाजीत रसायन को चतुर्मुख रस के साथ देने से तत्काल प्रभाव करती है। (इलाज, 5)

6. **में असर कर—"to reinvigorate, to restore to health"**

वृद्धावस्था से आयी कमजोरी के कारण थकान लगना, सन्धियों का भारी होना, चलने में सांस फूलना, मीठा-मीठा ज्वर बना रहना, इन सब में शिलाजीत रसायन छह मास से एक वर्ष तक लगातार लेने से उत्तम असर करती है। (इलाज, 5)

51. मुकाबिला, मिलान, तुलना

1. मुकाबिला (Sp. var, मुकाबला), मिलान and तुलना all refer to the act of making a comparison between things or persons, or to the assertion of comparability of one object to another in respect to some specific features or characteristics.

मुकाबिला stresses the lack of comparability of the object of comparison to the one it is considered or regarded as comparable to, and the expression, therefore, generally occurs with negation (नहीं) in this meaning. For other uses of मुकाबिल see 52.

मिलाना implies the existence of a similarity which permits or invites comparison. The phrase may or may not be accompanied by the speaker's expression of value-judgement or the like.

तुलना stresses a measuring of one object against or in terms of another, in order to (1) express one's judgement about the likenesses and differences between objects or (2) to explain by analogy (esp. in जा-passive sentences as तुलना की जा सके-).

2. मुकाबिला may take the noun denoting the thing or person being compared (with another) as its subject, and in that case forms ANP with का. In other contexts मुकाबिला resembles मिलान and तुलना in requiring से or के साथ occurring after the noun denoting the measure, and का (की before तुलना) following the object of comparison.

They are all + process, and are not pluralized.

3. **का मुकाबिला कर—"to compare to"**

नारी ने कहा—तुमने सुन्दर रचनायें की हैं नर, परन्तु इनमें से एक भी वस्तु मेरी

सृष्टि का मुकाबला नहीं कर सकती । कह कर उसने अपने बच्चे को गोदी में उठाकर प्यार कर लिया । (बूंद, 139)

का मुकाबिला कर—"to compare to"

सज्जन ने हाल ही में इतनी तेज़ी से ख्याति प्राप्त की है कि महिपाल उसका मुकाबिला नहीं कर सकता । महिपाल को उससे ईर्ष्या होती है परन्तु वह ईर्ष्या निकम्मी है । (बूंद, 537)

के साथ मुकाबिला कर—"to compare with, to liken"

इसलिए कृषि में भेड़ों का अन्य पशुओं के साथ उस समय तक कोई मुकाबिला नहीं किया जा सकता, जब तक उनको बड़ी संख्या में नहीं पाला जाता है । (भेड़, 42)

के साथ मुकाबिला कर—"to compare with"

"रहने दो, उसके साथ इसका मुकाबिला करते हो ?" "वह आई थी तो वह भी ऐसी ही थी... ।" (जान, 156)

4. **से मिलान कर—"to compare with"**

नास्तिक माने जाने वाले जिवा से मिलान करते समय अपनी पत्नी की भावुकता शिवा को बड़ी अभिमानास्पद लगती । (लाख, 44)

का मिलान कर—"to match"

कइयों ने अपनी साड़ी के रंग के साथ सिर के फूलों के रंग का मिलान कर रखा था । (राकेश, 114)

5. **से तुलना कर—"to compare with, to contrast"**

बाबू शिवप्रसाद गुप्त के जीवन और मृत्यु से जब मैं बच्चा महाराज के जीवन और मरण की तुलना करने चलता हूं तो मेरी मति हैरान-परेशान रह जाती है । (खबर, 117)

से तुलना कर—"to compare with"

और घर लौटता भारतभूषण सारी राह बाल्मीकि से अपनी तुलना करता रहा । (विचित्र, 14)

से तुलना कर—"to compare, to contrast"

...यदि भारतीय रुपये की वर्तमान स्थिति की तुलना इसकी युद्धपूर्व स्थिति से करें तो मालूम होगा कि इसका मूल्य (अथवा क्रय शक्ति) बहुत गिर गया है । (एमाई, 52)

से तुलना कर—"to liken"

एडमस्मिथ ने मुद्रा की तुलना एक ऐसी सड़क से की थी जिस पर तनिक भी घास नहीं उगती है। (एमाइ, 29)

के साथ तुलना कर—"to make a comparison"

दोष उसमें भी है, पर सड़ी रूढ़ियों और विषाक्त परम्पराओं के विष से जर्जर समाज के साथ जब उसके द्वारा प्रभावित समाज की तुलना करता हूं तो निराश हो उठता हूं। (चारु, 341)

से तुलना की जा सके—"to be comparable with"

इस समुदाय को मैंने संज्ञा दी है 'वृन्दवार्तिक' की। वार्तिक शब्द लोकनाटकों में आज भी व्यवहृत होता है। 'वृन्दवार्तिक' की तुलना यूनान के कोरस से भी की जा सकती है। (कोणार्क, 9)

52. प्रतिरोध, मुकाबिला, सामना

1. प्रतिरोध, मुकाबिला (Sp. var. मुकाबला) and सामना all refer to meeting or confronting a situation, a condition or a person in an endeavor to offset its effects or to deal with it.

प्रतिरोध stresses an exerting to ward off the hostile or the destructive, मुकाबिला a vigorous striving against the adverse or the hostile, and सामना a facing of the adverse.

2. They all form ANP with का and are not pluralized. They are all + process.

3. **का प्रतिरोध कर—"to resist"**

हाथ मैंने अवश्य तलवार की मूठ पर जमा लिया था और इस प्रकार सावधान था कि किसी भी क्षण किसी आक्रमण का प्रतिरोध कर सकता था। (चारु, 394)

का प्रतिरोध कर—"to resist, to repel, to ward off"

दुनिया को याद है—और हमेशा याद रहना चाहिए—कि जिस आक्रमण का प्रतिरोध नहीं किया जायगा वह बढ़ता ही जायगा। (अमरीका, 54)

का प्रतिरोध करने के लिए अग्रसर हो—"to exert oneself in order to prevent"

राज्य...विशेषतः गायों और बछड़ों तथा अन्य दुधारू और बोझा ढोने वाले पशुओं की नस्ल सुधारने के लिये तथा उनके बध का प्रतिरोध करने के लिये अग्रसर होगा। (भारत, 11)

4. **का मुकाबिला कर—"to combat"**

ज़रा सी उत्तेजना पर हम अंधाधुंध कार्रवाई नहीं करेंगे लेकिन आक्रमण का मुकाबला दृढ़तापूर्वक करते रहेंगे। (अमरीका, 56)

का मुकाबिला कर—"to cope with"

इन सब बातों के जवाब में हम यह दिखलाने का प्रयत्न करेंगे कि अंगरेजों के आने से पहले भारत के ऊपर अन्य विदेशियों के हमले कितने, कब कब और किस ढंग के हुए और भारत ने उनका कहां तक सफलता के साथ मुकाबला किया। (सुन्दर, 11)

का मुकाबला करना पड़ सक—"to encounter (stiff opposition)"

इस बार संसोपा के उम्मीदवार श्री भूमिमंडल के द्वारा कांग्रेस को और अधिक कड़ा मुकाबला करना पड़ सकता है। भूमिमंडल की लोकप्रियता निचले तबके के लोगों में सबसे अधिक है और कहीं पलड़ा पलटने की बारी न आ जाय। (आज, 4)

का मुकाबला कर—"to encounter"

सिराजुद्दौला भी अपने थोड़े से शासनकाल में और ऐसे कठिन समय में जबकि उसे लगातार षड्यन्त्रों और साज़िशों का मुकाबला करना पड़ा, अपने नाना की इस उदार नीति का ठीक ठीक पालन करता रहा। (सुन्दर, 165)

का मुकाबला कर सक—"to cope with, to withstand, to rival"

वही बाजार में पहुंचते ही इतनी चुस्त और चंचल हो जाती हैं कि औसत हिन्दुस्तानी पति उस वक्त उनका मकाबला नहीं कर सकता। (कहा, 18)

का मुकाबला कर "to fight"

जान पड़ता है कि अपने भीतर कुछ लेकर उसका मुकाबला करते हुए ही वह अपने को बिता रहा और बीत रहा है। (सुता, 103)

का मुकाबला कर (सक)—"to cope with, to encounter"

यदि आप विजय और विपत्ति का एक समान मुकाबला कर सकते हैं...। (चमत्कार, 38)

का मुकाबला कर सक—"to cope with"

और आपको पा कर वीणा जी भी दुनिया की किसी भी परिस्थिति का मुकाबला कर सकती हैं...दलीप की समस्या का भी। (धनु, 190)

का मुकाबला कर—"to resist"

कानों के भीतर की हवा बाहर की हवा के दबाव का मुकाबला करती है और उसके कम या अधिक होने से कान को हानि नहीं पहुंचती। (आज, 31)

5. **का सामना कर—"to face"**

पिछली दो पराजयों के बाद दुश्मन फिर दूनी ताकत और निश्चय के साथ भयानक हमला करेगा, नायक जदुनाथ सिंह यह जानता था, फिर भी वह घायल नर शार्दूल अकेला ही आने वाले हमले का सामना करने के लिये तैयार होकर दूने उत्साह और अधीरता से प्रतीक्षा करने लगा। (परम, 11)

का सामना कर—"to encounter, to face"

...कि कोई ऐसा बीच का रास्ता निकल आये जिससे ब्रिटेन को भी कोई विशेष परेशानी का सामना न करना पड़े—। (नवभा, 1-4)

का सामना कर—"to encounter, to run into"

छत्रपति के दिग्विजयी रथ की अप्रतिहत गति को पहली बार भयंकर अवरोध का सामना करना पड़ रहा था। इससे पूर्व अपने प्रबलतम शत्रु को घर्षित करने में भी उन्हें धन-जन की इतनी हानि नहीं उठानी पडी। (बेटी, 59)

का सामना कर—"to face up to, to withstand"

...हम यह भी दिखाना चाहेंगे कि इस तरह के हमले यूरोप के विविध देशों पर भी हुए थे या नहीं और यदि हुए थे तो भारत के मुकाबले में यूरोपियन देशों ने उनका कहां तक सफलता के साथ सामना किया। (सुन्दर, 24)

का सामना कर—"to face"

पर घर लौटने के प्रश्न का कभी न कभी सामना करना तो जरूरी था ही? (धनु, 173)

का सामना करना पड़ सक—"to face, to encounter"

यह अनुमान लगाया जा रहा है कि इस बार राज्य के कई मंत्रियों को पराजय का सामना करना पड़ सकता है। (आज, 4)

का सामना कर—"to combat, to resist"

पर्याप्त फास्फोरस मिलने से फसल के पौधे इतने स्वस्थ हो जाते हैं कि कीट तथा फंजाई के आक्रमणों तथा कुछ निश्चित रोगों का सामना करने की शक्ति उनमें आ जाती है अर्थात् पौधों में इस की जीवन-शक्ति अधिक रहती है। कमी में फसलें शीघ्र रोग ग्रस्त हो जाती है। (खाद, 120)

का सामना कर सक—"to face"

अमरीका दूसरों की किसी भी चुनौती का सामना कर सकता है और करेगा। (अमरीका, 55)

का सामना कर—"to confront, to resist, to face up to"

चलचित्र की तरह उसे वह रात स्पष्ट दिखलाई दे रही थी, जब कि नाना के महल पर डाकुओं का हमला हुआ था। कितनी निर्भीकता और साहस के साथ उसने डाकुओं का सामना किया। (बूंद, 577)

का सामना कर—"to meet"

हमारी निर्बाध उद्यम-पद्धति ने अतीत की गंभीर चुनौतियों का सामना सफलतापूर्वक किया है। (अमरीका, 101)

का सामना करना पड़—"to encounter"

प्रत्येक मनुष्य को किसी न किसी अवस्था में बेकारी का सामना करना पड़ता है। उस समय मनुष्य शिकायत करते हैं कि उनके पास कोई काम नहीं और अपने भाग्य को कोसते हैं। (चमत्कार, 18)

का सामना कर—"to resist, to hold out against"

पठान गुसाइयों का सामना न कर सके। गुसाइयों की तलवारों की बाढ़ के सामने वे टिक न पाये। (कचनार, 242)

का सामना कर सक—"to counteract"

जहां धर्म तर्क का और प्रतिभा अध्ययन का सामना न कर सके, वहां सूझों का दुर्भिक्ष, संकल्पों का मरण और पौरुष को भय के सिवा और हो ही क्या सकता है? (अमीर, 19)

का सामना कर—"to stand up to"

जान पड़ता था, हमारे ऊपर टूट पड़ने के लिये उसका हृदय व्यग्र हो रहा था। पर उसमें इतनी हिम्मत कहां कि हमारी दानवता का सामना करती। (काल, 32)

का सामना करके..."by overcoming"

गंगराज ने मुझे यहां लाकर तुम्हारे पिता के साथ मेरा विवाह कराया। उसके बाद इससे उत्पन्न कठिनाइयों का सामना करके स्वयं गंगराज को मुसीबतों का निवारण करना पड़ा। दूसरे किसी व्यक्ति से यह कार्य नहीं बनता। (शांतला, 33)

का सामना करते हुए—"in the face of"

देश के बड़े बड़े इंजीनियरों के मना करने के बावजूद उन्होंने अनेक संकटों का सामना करते हुए बांध का सफलतापूर्वक निर्माण कर अपने अद्वितीय साहस, कार्यक्षमता एवं निर्माण-कुशलता का परिचय दिया। (बाल, 11, 41)

53. प्रायश्चित, पश्चाताप, रंज, अफसोस

1.1. All these nouns refer to the display of one's distressed state of mind (through words or deeds) in which one feels keenly sorry for something.

प्रायश्चित stresses the public acknowledgement of one's guilt or fault in what one did in order to expiate one's past action.

पश्चाताप stresses one's remorseful concern at the distress of others, or one's repentence for one's past action.

रंज describes one's mental suffering or grief.

अफसोस is merely a display of one's sadness or grief.

1.2. प्रायश्चित कर—is often applied to some of the ritualistic practices among the Hindu orthodox as may be necessitated by the socio-religious sanctions of a community.

2. All the nouns, except रंज (which is ±process), are +process, and are not pluralized. प्रायश्चित forms ANP with का, and the rest with पर or का.

3. **का प्रायश्चित कर—"to expiate, to make amends for"**

मृदुला की आखों से आसुओं की झड़ी लगी हुई थी। बोली—बीमार तो नहीं हूं बहन। विपत्ति से बिंधी हुई हूं। तुम मुझे खूब कोस रही होगी। उन सारी निठुराईयों का प्रायश्चित करने आई हूं। (सम, 10)

का प्रायश्चित कर—"to expiate"

तुम्हारे चरणों तक पर गिरकर अपने पाप का प्रायश्चित कर लेता। (सुहाग, 153)

का प्रायश्चित कर—"to make amends for"

उसी अत्याचार का अब प्रायश्चित कर रहा हूं। (सेवा, 163)

का प्रायश्चित कर—"to make propitiations for, to expiate"

उनका स्वास्थ्य बुरी तरह गिर गया था...पर उन्हे पूर्ण सन्तोष था क्योंकि वे सत्ती की मृत्यु का प्रायश्चित कर रहे थे। (सूरज, 102)

का प्रायश्चित करना पड़—"to ward off by sacred rites, to pay the penalty for"

कल ही कथा होगी, देख लेना। ब्राह्मण खायेंगे बिरादरी जमा होगी। जेल का प्रायश्चित तो करना ही पड़ेगा। तुम हमारे घर दो–चार दिन रहकर तब जाना बहन। (सम, 8)

का प्रायश्चित कर—"to make propitiations for, to propitiate"

पंच फिर विलायत से लौटने वालों की खुशामद करने लगे थे कि भैया प्रायश्चित कर लो। (बूंद, 524)

4. **का पश्चाताप कर—"to regret, to be keenly sorry for, to experience regret for"**

शैला ! तुम्हारा पिता अपने अपराधों का पश्चाताप करता है। वह बहुत सुधर गया है। क्या तुम उसे प्यार न करोगी ? (तितली, 248)

पर पश्चाताप कर—"to regret, to experience regret"

दोनों मित्र अकेले में बैठे बातें करते रहे। महिपाल की मति पर पश्चाताप करते रहे। सज्जन ने एक-दो बार अपना यह भय भी प्रकट किया कि लाज के मारे महिपाल कहीं कुछ कर न बैठे। (बूंद, 578-79)

का पश्चाताप कर—"to do penance for"

सम्राट के प्रतिनिधि ने कहा, "अपराधी ! न्याय की रक्षा के लिये अंतिम बार फिर कह रहा हूं, सम्राट की जय-घोषणा कर पश्चाताप कर ले।" (मुक्ता, 50)

5. **को रंज कर—"to grieve"**

मैं सदके जाऊं तुम्हारी नसीहतों के। तुम तो हिन्दुओं के ढोंगी पंडितों से भी बढ़ गए। मैं बड़े दिन की छुट्टियों में चन्द दिनों के लिए घर लौटी हुई अपनी (जान) को क्यों रंज करती ? (खत, 33)

6. **पर अफसोस कर—"to feel sorry for"**

ये गुमराह औरतें पेशतर नहीं तो शराब का नशा उतरने के बाद जरूर अपनी हालत पर अफसोस करती हैं, लेकिन उस वक्त उनका पछताना बेसूद होता है। (सेवा, 174)

अफसोस कर—"to express grief, to feel sorry for"

लोगों की यही धारणा थी कि रेणुका और मन्दा घर के भीतर ही रह गयी हैं और वे अब वहीं जलकर भस्म हो जाएँगी। दोनों के लिए लोग अफसोस कर रहे थे। पर कर कुछ नहीं सकते थे क्योंकि आग ने समूचे घर को बुरी तरह घेर लिया था। (लाख, 256-57)

54. आमना-सामना, सामना

1. आमना-सामना and सामना refer to occupying a position with the face toward someone or something.

आमना-सामना means "to be face-to-face with" and सामना "to face".

2. Both nouns are +process, and are not pluralized आमना-सामना forms ANP with से and सामना with का.

3. **से आमना-सामना कर—"to be face-to face with"**

कोवलन संयत होकर बैठना चाहता था परन्तु माधवी ने उससे आमना-सामना करने के लिए ऐसा स्थान चुना था जहां उसकी आखें अटक-अटक जाती थीं। (सुहाग, 25)

4. **का सामना कर—"to face"**

बाबू गुलाबचन्द ने उनका सामना करने की गरज से फौरन ही कुरसी उनकी ओर घुमा दी। (बूंद, 41)

55. उद्यम, उद्योग, परिश्रम, तरद्दुद, श्रम, मसक्कत, (मशक्कत) मेहनत

1. All these nouns refer to active expenditure of physical or mental power in producing or attempting to produce a desired result. उद्यम is engaging in a vocation stressing a strong inner impulse towards a course of action, उद्योग is engaging actively in the pursuit of what one undertakes to do, परिश्रम is devoting effort or energy stressing a degree of laboriousness, तरद्दुद is expenditure of effort implying an exertion that is an inconvenience (or that inconveniences the agent), श्रम is labouring implying expenditure of physical effort to the extent that it is fatiguing, difficult or compulsory, मसक्कत (Sp. Var. मशक्कत) contains reference to one's physical distress through the excessive expenditure of physical energy, and मेहनत is effort-making in general marked by one's solicitousness or earnestness.

Both श्रम and मेहनत are also used to denote human activity that produces goods or provides the services in demand in an economy. Though the terms are sometimes used interchangeably, they do carry their original implications.

2. All the nouns are +process, and do not admit plural. उद्यम forms ANP with के लिये, उद्योग with के लिये and का, परिश्रम with के विषय में, के पीछे and के लिये, तरद्दुद and मसक्कत with के लिये, श्रम with पर, and मेहनत with पर and के लिये.

3. **के लिए उद्यम कर—"to engage in a vocation"**

बाप को तो कहता है—तुम गुलाम हो। वह एक अंग्रेजी कंपनी में हैं। बार-बार

इस्तीफा देने का विचार करके रह जाते हैं, लेकिन गुजर-बसर के लिए कोई उद्यम करना ही पड़ेगा। कैसे छोड़ें। (सम, 8)

4. **के लिये उद्योग कर—"to be engaged in the task of"**

आजकल वह कृषकों की सहायता के लिए एक कोष स्थापित करने का उद्योग कर रहे हैं जिससे किसानों को बीज और रुपये नाम मात्र सूद पर उधार दिये जा सकें। (सेवा, 347)

का उद्योग कर—"to make an effort for, to try for"

नहीं ऊब-डूब करते डिब्बों का यूरोप नहीं फिर एक स्वाधीन यूरोप, लेकिन जिसकी स्वाधीनता नये और दृढ़तर पायों पर टिकी हो। मैं तो समझती हूं हम यहां हिंदुस्तान में भी न केवल अपनी वरन् यूरोप की भी स्वाधीनता का उद्योग कर सकते हैं। (नदी, 70)

का उद्योग कर—"(as if) to try to (do something)"

पत्तियाँ भी विरल हो चली थीं; वह रूखी-सूखी लता, किरणें उसमें सहज प्रवेश करके उसे हँसाने का उद्योग कर रही थीं। (तितली, 199)

5. **के लिए परिश्रम कर—"to devote oneself to"**

मैं तो श्रमजीवी हूं शैला। मुझे जो फीस देगा उसी का काम करने के लिए मुझे परिश्रम करना पड़ेगा। (तितली, 204)

के लिये कठोर परिश्रम कर—"to strive hard to, to devote one's efforts to"

तीस वर्षों से...हम मनुष्य की स्वतंत्रता को व्यापक बनाने के लिए कठोर परिश्रम करते आए हैं। (अमरीका, 13)

के पीछे परिश्रम कर—"to be working on, to make a concentrated effort for"

मैं भी इसके पीछे परिश्रम कर रहा हूं। (कचनार, 189)

के विषय में परिश्रम कर—"to strive for"

इसके बाद अरबों का समय आया और जहां तक इस कला को वैज्ञानिक रूप देने और इतिहास की सचाई को कायम रखने का प्रश्न है, शायद किसी भी प्राचीन कौम ने इस विषय में इतना अधिक परिश्रम नहीं किया जितना अरबों ने। (सुन्दर, 1)

परिश्रम कर—"to labour hard, to put out a great deal of labor"

आपके मित्र ने बहुत परिश्रम किया है, मैं उनकी बड़ी कृतज्ञ हूं। (नदी, 68)

6. **के लिये तरद्दुद कर—"to constrain (oneself)"**

"घर जलाने के लिये इतना तरद्दुद करने की क्या जरूरत है, भाटिया ?" मैंने बाल्कनी की ओर बढ़ते हुए कहा। (जानवर, 61)

7. **श्रम कर—"to work, to labour"**

...श्रम कर सकनेवाली एक बिकने योग्य वस्तु। (मूल्य, 123)

श्रम कर—"to work"

जो मनुष्य श्रम नहीं करता...। (बुन, 2)

श्रम कर—"to labour"

कच्ची उम्र में ही कइयों को कठिन श्रम करना पड़ जाता। (कल्याण, 30)

8. **मसक्कत कर—"to trouble, to strain"**

अब लहनार हूं। नहीं तो तुम्हें भला इतनी मसक्कत करनी पड़ती ? (तुला, 82)

9. **के लिए मेहनत कर—"to devote oneself to, to try earnestly"**

वह नंगे पैरों घर भर में दौड़ती थी, और जरा-जरा देर में अपने नये फ्राक मैले कर आती थी। वह उसे रहन-सहन की आदतें सिखाने के लिए रात-दिन मेहनत करता था। (आकाश, 92)

के लिए मेहनत कर—"to work diligently"

तुम्हारे पास मैटर तो बहुत अच्छा है उस्ताद। इसके लिए तुमने मेहनत भी खूब की है। (बूंद, 34)

पर मेहनत कर—"to toil on"

जो लोग जमीन पर मेहनत कर सकते हैं उनके पास आज जमीन नहीं है। (भूदान, 39)

ज्यादा मेहनत कर—"to work hard"

वह ज्यादा मेहनत नहीं करता था, परन्तु अपना पाठ बहुत जल्दी याद कर लिया करता था। (बाल, 1, 25)

लाख मेहनत करके—"...taking great pains"

लाख मेहनत करके वह बाल सेट करती, घर के धंधों में कहीं पका रही, कहीं धो रही,...दो दिन में उसके बाल फिर सीधे हो जाते। उनके घुंघर निकल जाते। (दुग्गल, 80-1)

मेहनत करने वाला—"working man/woman"

वह सिर्फ हिंदुस्तानी और विदेशी मुनाफाखोरों का समझौता है। मेहनत करने वालों का स्वराज्य केवल मेहनत करने वालों की अपनी पार्टी कम्युनिस्ट पार्टी ही कायम कर सकती है। (फूलो, 52)

56. अभिलाषा, आकांक्षा, कामना, इच्छा

1. These nouns refer to states of mind consisting of feeling or desire which is manifested in what one intends to do, or what one sets before one's mind.

अभिलाषा is a longing or desire expressed in one's words or actions suggesting (total) emotional involvement without any reference to attainability or non-attainability.

आकांक्षा is wanting for that which is attainable (but somewhat remote), or aspiring for the unattainable (or difficult to attain).

कामना is making a wish or wishing for something.

इच्छा is expressing a wish for something or having an intention.

2. All the nouns are + process and form ANP with की. They are not pluralized. Infinitives occur freely before की unless इच्छा कर—etc. occur as conjunctive participle, and in that case the infinitive complement before the nouns is dropped. For example वह इच्छा करके भी जा नहीं पाया is in fact to be understood as वह जाने की इच्छा करके भी जा नहीं पाया।

3. **की अभिलाषा कर—"to long for"**

वेदना की अनुभूति को प्रयोगवाद की छटी प्रवृत्ति स्वीकार किया जा सकता है। प्रयोगवादी कवि वेदना से पलायन न करके उसके सान्निध्य की अभिलाषा करते हैं। (निबन्ध, 674)

की अभिलाषा कर—"to express one's desire for"

किन्तु आराध्य का प्रसाद पहले ग्रहण करो, आराधिका का प्रसाद बाद में ग्रहण करने की अभिलाषा करो। (चारु, 182)

अभिलाषा कर—"to hope (for)"

सभी पितृ-हृदय भी यही अभिलाषा करते हैं कि अपनी जोती हुई जमीन, बनाया हुआ घर, पाला हुआ घोड़ा, कमाया हुआ धन इनमें से कोई भी व्यर्थ न हो, बरबाद न हो, सबकी वृद्धि हो, और घर का नाम बना रहे। (शांतला, 32)

4. **की आकांक्षा करने लग—"to want to"**

वही जंगल और पहाड़ जो कभी आपको सुनसान और बीहड़ प्रतीत होते थे, वही नदियां और झील जिनके तट पर से आप आँखें बन्द किये निकल जाते थे, कुछ समय के पीछे एक अत्यन्त मनोरम शान्तिमय रूप धारण करके आपके स्मृतिनेत्रों के सामने आती हैं और फिर आप उन्हीं दृश्यों को देखने की आकांक्षा करने लगते हैं। (सेवा, 223)

की दृढ़ आकांक्षा कर—"to be badly wanting to, to be entertaining an aspiration to, to be aspiring for"

इसलिये डरू इन्दौर सेना की नौकरी छोड़ कर सागर सेना में पहुंच जाने की दृढ़ आकांक्षा करने लगा। (कचनार, 212)

5. **की कामना कर—"to wish"**

उस समान आनंद की कामना तुम्हारे लिए करती हूं, गौरा—तुम्हारे लिए, और भुवन के लिए। (नदी, 330)

कामना करके—"wishing (that)..."

ये कहानियां सभी को खासकर छोटे बच्चों को खुश करें, यह कामना करके भूमिका समाप्त करता हूं। (रूस, 5)

सतत कामना कर—"to long for, to desire"

प्रिय, जबसे तुम बिछड़े मैं नया सृजन नहीं कर पाई। मैं सतत कामना करती हूं, सतत प्रयत्न करती हूं, पर मेरे नये बच्चे नहीं होते। (बूंद, 140)

की कामना कर—"to harbor the feeling of"

इन्द्रिय तृप्ति की चरम सीमा पर जाकर उसके खट्टे-मीठे अनुभवों में से गुजर कर अब वह लौट रहा है, उन पर विजय प्राप्त करने की कामना कर रहा है। (अणु, 44)

6. **की इच्छा कर—"to intend to"**

बाबा राम जी के खिलाफ कुछ भी सोचने की इच्छा वह नहीं करता। (बूंद, 388)

की इच्छा कर—"to express a desire, to wish to"

ताई जो दान पुन्न करने की इच्छा करती उन सबका आयोजन होता। (बूंद, 550)

बहुत इच्छा करके भी—"to have every intention, to try hard"

इस आदर्श को वह बहुत इच्छा करके भी अपने प्रत्यक्ष जीवन में न पा सका। (बूंद, 272)

इच्छा करने से भी—"even though (he) makes every endeavor to..."

सज्जन को इस समय अचानक यह पुराना अनुभव ताजा होकर लगा कि कन्या का प्रेम अति निर्मल, अति निश्छल है। वह इच्छा करने से भी वैसी शुद्धता अपने आप में क्यों नहीं महसूस कर पाता ? (बूंद, 430)

इच्छा कर—"to have a mind to"

"इच्छा मात्र करने की देर है!" "इच्छा मात्र करने की देर है!"—सज्जन को लगा कि मानो क्षणभर में उड़कर उसने सब कुछ सिद्ध कर लिया। इस भावावेश से उसमें स्फूर्ति, आनन्दभरी तन्मयता भर गई। (बूंद, 457-58)

इच्छा कर—"to feel like"

कभी उसकी टांग मेरी टांग से आ सटती, और कभी मेरे कन्धे से उसका कन्धा सट जाता। मैं बुत की तरह स्थिर बैठा था। उसका ऐसा करना मुझे बहुत अच्छा लगता। इच्छा करती कि उसके हाथ को हाथ में लेकर दबाऊं, या झुककर उसका चुम्बन ले लूं। (राह, 93)

की इच्छा कर—"to feel like"

मेरी कोई काम-धाम करने की इच्छा ही नहीं करती। (राह, 83)

की इच्छा कर पा—"to have a desire to, to think of"

आपसे मिलने की इच्छा भी तो नहीं कर पाई मैं, और शायद यह अच्छा ही हुआ। अगर इच्छा करती तो शायद आपसे मिलना न हो पाता। (सा सा, 169)

"It did not even occur to me that I should see you, and perhaps it was good. If I had wished (i.e., had in my mind as an aim), the meeting between you and me would not have taken place."

57. दर्शन, भेंट, मुलाकात

1. These nouns refer to the act of calling upon someone with an objective.

दर्शन is having presence with a superior, and is also used to refer to making a visit to a sacred place.

भेंट is to have audience with a person in authority (with a grievance or complaint) or making a social call upon someone. It may be used in referring to the receiving of visitors by one in authority.

मुलाकात is meeting or seeing someone in order to discuss something.

2. All the nouns are + process. दर्शन forms ANP with का, and भेंट and मुलाकात with से. दर्शन normally occurs in plural form. The other nouns are not pluralized.

3. **के दर्शन कर—"to meet"**

भोगोबान आपका भला करें, गोशाई, आपके दर्शन कर आज तो चित्त प्रसन्न हो गया। आहा! (तुला, 51)

के दर्शन कर—"to see"

एक समय बनारस में प्रेमचन्द जी के दर्शन करने जाकर उनसे रूसी उपन्यास कुपिन-कृत यामा की प्रशंसा सुनकर उसे भी पढ़ चुका था। (कोठे, 29)

के दर्शन कर—"to see"

क्यों जनाब, यह क्या बदतमीजी है कि कोई दस मील पैदल चलकर हजूर के दर्शन करने आये और आगे से जवाब मिलता है फरमाईये।

के अच्छी तरह दर्शन कर—"to take a good look at, to have seen"

अभी तक अधिकांश गली-मुहल्लों की औरतों ने अच्छी तरह से महिला पुलिस के दर्शन भी नहीं किए, इसलिए या तो उनका कोई प्रभाव ही न पड़ेगा...। (बूंद, 396)

का दर्शन कर—"to make a visit to"

मां, इतने कार्यों के होते हुए भी आप समय निकालकर देवी का दर्शन करके आईं, यह कितने आनन्द का विषय है। (शांतला, 28)

4. **से भेंट कर—"to have audience with, to see"**

षड्यन्त्रकारी उच्च पदस्थ राजकर्मचारियों को इस महाभीड़ के कारण इस बात का अवसर ही न मिल सका कि वे कन्नगी को महाराज से भेंट न करने दें। (सुहाग, 263)

से भेंट कर—"to receive (visitors), to see"

छुट्टी के दिन भी वह कोठी में बने हुए दफ्तर में जा बैठता। वहां वह सरकारी काम करता रहता या पढ़ता रहता या मिलने वालों से भेंट करता रहता। (दुग्गल, 30)

से भेंट कर—"to see"

अच्छा अब मैं इधर से जाऊंगी। महीर महतो से एक नौकर के लिए कहा था। उससे भेंट कर लूंगी। नमस्कार। (तितली, 127)

से भेंट कर—"to meet, to like to see"

इंद्र देव ने गहरी सांस लेकर कहा—शैला। क्या इंद्रदेव? मां से भेंट करोगी ; चलूं ? अच्छा, कल सवेरे। (तितली, 29)

से मुलाकात कर—"to see"

आप तुरन्त ही सरपंच से मुलाकात कीजिए और आपस का परिचय लेने देने के बाद उनसे ग्राम-सम्बन्धी सभी आवश्यक बातों का ज्ञान प्राप्त कीजिये...। (बुन, 42)

से मुलाकात कर—"to meet"

मैं मुख्यमंत्री श्रीमती सुचेता कृपलानी से गोंडा में मुलाकात करने की उम्मीद करता हूं। (आज, 2)

से मुलाकात करने के बाद— "after seeing"

"जल्दी क्या है ? थोड़ी ही देर में इस जहाज़ के सबसे बड़े सैनिक अफसर से मुलाकात करने के बाद ही तुम किनारे जाने पाओगे।" गोरी ने भेद-भरे भाव से सुनाया। (जुहू, 83)

58. स्नेह, प्रेम, प्यार, मुहब्बत

1. All these nouns refer to the emotional state of affection in which one feels a strong liking and warmth for someone or something.

स्नेह contains reference to display of affection which is part of one's disposition.

प्रेम (as opposed to घृणा) is applied when emotion is thought of in the abstract, and प्यार (as opposed to नफरत) is generally used in reference to the actual experience of it. Besides this major difference in application, both the nouns differ in their connotations also. प्रेम is cultivated and fervent (feeling of) love, and प्यार is spontaneous and passionate feeling. Also प्रेम implies a sense of attachment (i.e., devotion or loyalty) whereas प्यार stresses a personal fondness.

मुहब्बत is a neutral term referring to the feeling of warmth and tenderness (of sentiment). The noun may, depending upon the object noun, strongly suggest amorousness on the part of the subject noun.

2. Only प्यार is ±process, the rest are +process only. They all form ANP with से, के साथ and को. प्रेम occurs more often with से, and प्यार with को. They are not pluralized.

3. **से स्नेह कर**—**"to have warm feelings for"**

साधारणतः अश्क जी सगे सम्बन्धियों और मित्रों से उसी मात्रा में स्नेह करते हैं जिस मात्रा में इन्हें उनसे स्नेह मिलता है, किन्तु मां, बड़े भाई और सबसे छोटा भाई इसके अपवाद हैं। (धारा, 26)

से स्नेह कर—**"to have affection for"**

उसे जैसे अपने आप से घृणा होने लगी...क्या तितली मुझसे स्नेह करेगी ? मुझ अपराधी से उसका वही सम्बन्ध फिर स्थापित हो सकेगा ? (तितली, 252)

को स्नेह कर—**"to love"**

मैंने अपने हृदय के सम्पूर्ण स्नेह से इनका लालन पालन किया। रानी भी इन्हें इसी प्रकार स्नेह करती थीं। उन्होंने सदा इन्हें अपने पुत्रों के समान माना (चारु, 128)

4. **से प्रेम कर**—**"to love"**

हर : (उसे आलिंगन में भींचते हुए) मैं तुमसे प्रेम करता हूं तीभा ! मैंने कई बार अपने-आपको समझाने की कोशिश की है कि मैं तुम्हें सिर्फ पसंद करता हूं तुमसे मुहब्बत नहीं करता। (भंवर, 110)

से प्रेम कर—**"to love, to feel warmly towards"**

महापुरुष—अच्छा देवदूत, यह तो बताओ कि क्या तुम कभी ऐसे मनुष्यों की सूची भी बनाओगे जो मनुष्य-मात्र से ही प्रेम करते हैं और स्वार्थ को भूलकर सारा समय लोकसेवा में ही लगाते हैं। (कथा, 70)

से प्रेम कर—**"to make love with"**

एक दिन जब राजकुमार राजकुमारी से प्रेम कर रहा था तब अचानक कुतिया ने राजकुमार पर आक्रमण कर उसे काट खाया। (सुहाग, 130)

से प्रेम करने लग—**"to fall in love with"**

लोग कहते थे कि दोनों मेडिकल कालेज में पढ़ते थे तभी एक दूसरे से प्रेम करने लगे थे। आगे चलकर वे विवाह सूत्र में बद्ध हुए और अब तक उनकी प्रीति और पारस्परिक आकर्षण टिका हुआ है। (धनु, 133)

से प्रेम कर—**"to be devoted to"**

भक्त केवल भगवान से प्रेम करता है जिसका स्त्री-पुत्र, गृह-धन तथा देह में प्रेम है वह संसारी है। (भक्तियोग, 2)

से प्रेम कर—**"to have an affair with"**

महिपाल स्वयं भी पत्नी पर अत्याचार करता है वह भी विरहेश की तरह पत्नी

सन्तानों वाला होकर भी अन्य स्त्री से प्रेम करता है। प्रेम वह सचमुच करता है फिर बड़ी और विरहेश के प्रेम को कलुषित क्यों माने। (बूंद, 309)

प्रेम कर—'to adore, to love fervently"

कुंतल : सुनो, सुनो ! हिन्दू स्त्री प्यार नहीं प्रेम करती है। जय : अब संभालो। प्यार और प्रेम में भी अंतर। तुम भी खूब हो कुंतल। (रात, 81)

से प्रेम कर—"to love"

राजा शमशेर बहादुर सिंह से रानी मानकुमारी ने प्रेम किया था उसके मरने के बाद भी रानी साहिबा का अपने पति के प्रति प्रेम मिटा नहीं था। (सा सा, 62)

5. **को प्यार कर—"to be in love with"**

पर विचित्र बात यह है कि वह अब भी रमा चौधरी को पागल की तरह प्यार करता हैं। (ढोल, 37)

को प्यार कर—"to adore"

आशीर्वाद की कृतज्ञता में सिर झुकाकर तितली ने कहा—कितना प्यार करती हो मुझे।

तुमको जो देखेगा, वही प्यार करेगा। (तितली, 94)

को प्यार कर—"to be in love with"

इन्द्रदेव। मैं उस कोठी को बहुत प्यार करती हूं।

कबसे शैला ?—हंसते हुए इन्द्र ने उसका हाथ पकड़ लिया (तितली, 79)

को प्यार कर—"to adore"

अपनी मां को सज्जन बहुत प्यार करता था। वह उसके मन की विचित्रता थी कि जिन खूबियों को वह अपनी पत्नी में देखना पसंद नहीं करता था, उन्हीं के लिए माँ का आदर करता था। चरित्रहीन पिता के विपरीत अपनी मां के चरित्र में उसे सदा शक्ति झलकती दिखाई देती थी। (बूंद, 87)

से प्यार कर—"to be fond of"

इसके अतिरिक्त, पहिले से ही वह मोती से अत्यंत प्यार करती थी। बचपन में ही मोती की मां उसे अनाथ कर गयी थी। तब से उसी ने मोती को अपनी छाया तले बढ़ाया था। (लाख, 19)

से प्यार कर—"to have a love affair with"

तीनों ने अपने यौवनारंभ में किसी ऐसे व्यक्ति से प्यार किया था जिसे वे भिन्न कारणों से अपना जीवन साथी न बना पायी थीं। (भंवर, 43)

से प्यार कर—"to fondle"

उसने बब्बल को उठा तो लिया, लेकिन उससे प्यार न कर सकती थी। (लड़की, 64)

को प्यार कर ले—"to embrace"

युवती के अस्त-व्यस्त घुंघराले बाल, दर्द में एकाग्र बड़ी बड़ी आंखों की पुतलियां, भावावेश से तमतमाया हुआ खूबसूरत गोरा चेहरा, करुण स्निग्ध दृष्टि से देखते-देखते सहसा सज्जन के जी में आया कि उसे प्यार करले। (बूंद, 56)

The expression can be more appropriately rendered in English by the slang term "to neck".

से प्यार कर—"to make love with"

मीरा को लगता कि उससे प्यार करते वक्त भी वह मन-ही-मन चुम्बनों की गिनती करता रहता होगा...तभी तो न उसका आवेश एक चरम पर पहुंचकर एकाएक रुक जाता था। (आकाश, 73)

प्यार कर—"to love"

इन्सान की कमजोरियां भी प्यार करने के काबिल हैं। अब मान भी लीजिए इस बात को। कन्या उसकी तरफ देखकर हंसी। बोली...ये पेट भरे आदमी ही की लॉजिक हो सकती है। (बूंद, 134)

प्यार कर—"to love"

शीला ने सज्जन से कहा...दुर्जन, औरत मर्द के रिश्ते को लेकर मैंने अपनी जिंदगी से एक बात सीखी है...प्रेम थ्योरी नहीं, प्रैक्टिस है, जितना ज्यादा प्यार करोगे रिश्ता उतना ही गहरा बैठता है...(बूंद, 233)

6. **से मुहब्बत कर—"to be given to love making"**

रोमान पसन्द हमेशा अपनी बीवी को छोड़कर दूसरे की बीवी से मुहब्बत करेगा...। (भंवर, 107)

से मुहब्बत कर—"to be attracted towards"

इस एहसास की वजह से मैंने अपने स्कूल के दिनों में उस लड़के को जो मुझ से बेहद मुहब्बत करता था अपने जिस्म के किसी हिस्से को छूने तक नहीं दिया।

59. प्रमाणित, सिद्ध, साबित

1. प्रमाणित, सिद्ध, and साबित are applied to arguments, evidence or

the like adduced by way of proof or disproof of the genuineness, validity or truth of something.

प्रमाणित stresses inducement of factual or authoritative evidence in order to make something acceptable beyond a reasonable doubt, सिद्ध implies contesting an established belief by producing an argument in favour of one's contention, and साबित refers to the adducing of proof (or disproof) of something based on or in the form of demonstrable evidence.

2. All three are adjectives (and therefore—process), and may occur with a sentential complement or a clause connected by का, depending upon the object noun.

3. प्रमाणित कर दे—"to establish"

यह बात विज्ञान ने विशेष करके विद्युत शक्ति, चुम्बक शक्ति और आणविक रचना से प्रमाणित कर दी है। (चमत्कार, 48)

प्रमाणित कर दे—"to establish"

बीरू बाबू ने रिक्शा खरीदने की रसीद दिखाकर रिक्शा पर अपना अधिकार प्रमाणित कर दिया। (तितली, 228)

को प्रमाणित कर दे—"to confirm"

यहां पर इनके दोषों का इलाज किया जाकर इन्हें काम सिखलाये जाते हैं। इस संस्था का मुख्य अधिकारी जब इस बात को प्रमाणित कर देता है कि अब वह अपराध नहीं करेगा तो उसे लाइसेंस दे दिया जाता है। (कल्याण, 40)

को प्रमाणित कर—"to demonstrate the validity of, to substantiate"

बीरबल कहता था कि दृष्टि रखने वाले अल्पसंख्या में हैं। दुनिया में अंधे ही अधिक मिलते हैं। अकबर ने उससे अपने मत को प्रमाणित करने को कहा। (कथा, 67)

को प्रमाणित कर—"to give proof of, to establish"

...विधाता की इच्छा क्या है, क्या नहीं, इसे प्रमाणित करने के लिए आपको शास्त्रों की शरण लेनी पड़ती है, नहीं तो विधाता की इच्छा आपको कैसे मालूम हुई, इसका आप सन्तोषप्रद कोई प्रमाण न दे सकेंगे, उल्टा आप पर असत्य-भाषण का दोष लग जायगा। (प्रतिमा, 3)

को प्रमाणित कर चुक—"to be certified by, to be approved by"

सुधरे औजार जिन्हें खेती का महकमा प्रमाणित कर चुका है ऐसे खेती सुधरे औजार खरीदने के लिए 1000 रु० तक ऋण मिल सकता है। (लोक, 28)

को सही या गलत प्रमाणित कर—"to prove or disprove"

किसी घटना को सही या गलत प्रमाणित करना वास्तविक तथ्यों पर निर्भर करता है। (सामाजिक, 62)

प्रमाणित कर दे—"to have adduced evidence (to prove), to have demonstrated (authoritatively)"

कीन्स ने यह प्रमाणित कर दिया है कि जब श्रमिकों के मौद्रिक पुरस्कार में कमी की जाती है तो वे इसका घोर विरोध करते हैं लेकिन जब कीमतें बढ़ने से उनकी मजदूरी में कमी आती है तो उनका विरोध इतना तगड़ा नहीं होता। (एमाई, 34)

4. **सिद्ध कर—"to convince someone of, to prove oneself to be"**

लगभग दो वर्ष के कठोर संघर्ष के बाद अपने को पूर्ण पागल सिद्ध कर वह लड़की बाहर निकल पाई है। वह लड़की पुरुषमात्र से त्रस्त है पुरुषमात्र से घृणा करती है। (बूंद, 501)

को (adj.) सिद्ध करता रह—"to try to convince someone that..., to demonstrate oneself to be"

सचमुच मेरा कोई विचार नहीं था जब कि मैं कामिनी के सामने अपने को योग्य सिद्ध करता रहा। (राह, 116)

को (adj.) सिद्ध करना चाह—"to be inclined to, to be trying to prove someone to be"

नगर के विलासी राज्याधिकारीगण भी अपनी जान बचाने के लिए नगर के सेठों की क्षणिक लोभवश अंध व्यापारिक नीति को ही महाराज के सम्मुख दोषी सिद्ध करना चाहते थे। (सुहाग, 182)

सिद्ध कर दे—"to demonstrate, to establish (one's own superiority)"

तक्षशिला-नरेश ने उसी समय सिकंदर को लाखों रुपये की सम्पत्ति भेंट करके उसका यथोचित सत्कार किया। उसके बदले में सिकंदर ने तक्षशिला-नरेश को उससे दूनी सम्पत्ति देकर अपना बड़प्पन सिद्ध कर दिया। (आदर्श, 64)

सिद्ध कर दिखा—"to convincingly demonstrate, to have proven, to show"

महिपाल ने जवाब दिया—भारतीय संस्कृति ने बहुत से गणतंत्रों को संभव सिद्ध कर दिखाया है। जायसवाल की 'हिन्दू पालिटी' उठाकर पढ़ जाइए। (बूंद, 345)

5. **गलत साबित कर—"to prove to be wrong, to disprove"**

इतिहास की आदत है कि वह भयावह भविष्य-कथनों को गलत साबित कर देता है। (अमरीका, 44)

"It usually is the case with history that it proves alarming predictions to be wrong."

अपने को...साबित करने के लिये—"in order to prove themselves to be..."

और ये इंजीनियर अपने को मुझ से अधिक योग्य और कुशल साबित करने के लिए यह कहेंगे कि यह झील स्वाभाविक रूप से बन गई है। (सा सा, 255)

निर्मूल साबित करदे—"to disprove the validity of, to refute"

पिताजी, आज आर्य बीज गुप्त ने मुझे ऐसी बातें बतलाईं जिनसे मेरी आँखें खुल गईं। मेरी पुरानी धारणाओं को इन्होंने निर्मूल साबित कर दिया...।" (चित्र, 132)

साबित कर—"to prove"

आगे चलकर उन्होंने अपने को ऐसी विरासत का एक योग्य वारिस साबित किया। (परम, 2)

सचाई को साबित कर दिखा—"to demonstrate the truthfulness of, to establish the truth of"

यह मेरी ईमानदारी पर झूठा कलंक है और मैं अपनी बात की सचाई को साबित कर दिखाऊंगा। (बूंद, 202)

साबित कर—"to be convinced of"

पुलिस अधिकारी श्री इंद्रजीतसिंह ने भी पीपल-ब्रह्म के बारे में कानूनन कुछ करने में तब तक असमर्थता प्रकट की जब तक साफ कोई अपराध होता साबित न किया जाय। (विचित्र, 41)

"The police officer Shri Indrajit Singh expressed his inability to take any legal action about "Pipala-Brahma" until he was convinced that a crime has actually been committed (i.e., he refused to act upon hearsay)."

को (Adj.) साबित कर दे—"to prove someone to be, to convincingly demonstrate that..."

जब मैंने जिरह शुरू की, तो सब बगलें झांकने लगे। मैंने तीनों गवाहों को झूठा साबित कर दिया। उस समय जाने कैसे मुझे चोट सूझती गई। (सम, 5)

साबित करना चाह—"to like to make (it) demonstrably clear that..."

हम यह साबित करना चाहते हैं कि पश्चिमी यूरोप से अच्छे संबन्ध स्थापित करने से पूर्वी यूरोप की प्रगति ही होगी। (अमरीका, 73)

के विश्वास को सच साबित कर—"to prove (oneself to be) up to"

कोई भी सहानुभूतिशील सरकार जनता के विश्वास को सच साबित करने और उसके बच्चों का भविष्य बनाने का ध्यान रखती है। (अमरीका, 46)

60. उपचार, इलाज, चिकित्सा, दवाई, दवादारू, दवा, औषधि, औषधोपचार

1. All the nouns refer to taking preventive and/or corrective measures (medical or otherwise) in order to alleviate any ailment or ailing condition.

उपचार is attending to give medical (or other such remedial) care, often as a first-aid or a temporary preventive measure.

इलाज refers to systematic (prolonged) remedial or corrective treatment.

चिकित्सा (which means the practice of medicine) always refers to the medical treatment given by a medical man.

दवाई (always occurs in pl., see 2 below) is a term meaning "medication" stressing the variety or kind according to the prevailing systems of medicine in India.

दवादारू is a binominal term consisting of दवा "drug, medicine" and दारू "medical or spirituous liquor." It is applied to the use of medications or medicinal things usually available around one's home, and that do not require prescription.

दवा is drug or medicine having a remedical effect, and refers to both receiving or giving medication or medical care.

1.2. The term औषधि which is considered synonymous with दवा primarily refers to herbs and plants having medical effects.

औषधोपचार is a binominal compound consisting of औषधि and उपचार and refers to medications taken internally as well as applied externally.

2. All nouns are +process and form ANP with का (की for चिकित्सा, दवाई, दवादारू and दवा). They all take plural with the exception of चिकित्सा and दवादारू.

3. **का उपचार कर—"to attend to, to treat"**

राजा दलीपसिंह का तुम्हीं ने उपचार किया था? (कचनार, 312)

का उपचार कर—"to treat"

इसके लिए पहला कदम परजीवी कीड़ों का उपचार करना है और जिन भेड़ों को यह रोग भयानक रूप से हो, उनको एक चाय का चम्मच तारपीन का तेल मिला कर दो से चार औंस अरंडी का तेल दिया जा सकता है। (भेड़, 55)

का उपचार कर--"to care for, to be giving care to"

वे लोग संशय करेंगे कि हम अपने बाकी रुपये के लोभ में इसका उपचार कर रहे हैं। (कचनार, 122)

4. **का इलाज कर—"to remedy, to give remedial care to"**

यहां पर इनके दोषों का इलाज किया जाकर इन्हें काम सिखलाये जाते हैं। इस संस्था का मुख्य अधिकारी जब इस बात को प्रमाणित कर देता है कि अब वह अपराध नहीं करेगा तो उसे लाइसेंस दे दिया जाता है। (कल्याण, 40)

का इलाज किया जा-- "to receive medical treatment"

सेना के इस सरकारी अस्पताल में हर एक का मुफ्त इलाज किया जाता। (दुग्गल, 86)

रोगियों का इलाज कर--"to treat the sick"

आजकल सवेरे से दोपहर तक रामेश्वर रोगियों का इलाज करता है और दोपहर बाद लोगों की हजामत कर बाप-दादा का नाम रोशन करता है। सुना है पंजाब विधान सभा और लोक सभा के चुनावों में रामेश्वर की बहुत पूछ रही। (डगर, 43)

का इलाज कर—"to be trying to cure (himself)"

पर वह जानते नहीं हैं कि जो सिगरिट के धुएं से अपना इलाज करने में डटा हुआ है वह दूसरों का इलाज कर पाने का अवकाश नहीं रखता। (खिलौने, 14)

का इलाज किया जा--"to correct, to remedy"

मुसीबत एक हो तो कही जाय, और उसका इलाज भी किया जाय! (कहा, 18)

5. **की चिकित्सा कर—"to give medical care to"**

इस अधिनियम के द्वारा कुष्ठ (कोढ़) के रोगियों को अन्य व्यक्तियों से अलग रखकर उनकी चिकित्सा करने का आयोजन किया गया। (भारत, 56)

6. **लाख दवाइयां कर—"to give every possible (lit. one hundred thousand) medication"**

अंधेरा हो चुका था, जब उसके पिता ने उसे गांव के बाहर जंगल में पड़ा पाया। ज्वर

से जैसे वह फुका जा रहा था। घर लाकर लाख दवाइयां की गईं, डाक्टर आये, हकीम आये, फिर कहीं तेज ने आंख खोली। (दुग्गल, 152)

7. **सब प्रकार की दवादारू कर—"to give all sorts of medications"**

सब प्रकार की दवादारू कर, बहुत ही आग्रह और प्रेम से गरम-गरम थोड़ा दूध पिलाकर मुझे गोद में सटाकर सो गई। (देश, 56)

8. **की दवा कर—"to be under the care of"**

सुधाकर : घर के पास ही एक वैद्य रहते हैं। रमाशंकर—वैद्य की दवा करते हो? अंग्रेजी पढ़कर! तुम यह नहीं जानते कि वैद्य बड़े धूर्त होते हैं। (सन्यासी, 26)

की दवा कर—"to give care to, to treat the sick"

मुरारी बाबू को यह अफसोस भी है कि किशन ने कभी उनका दुख-सुख नहीं पूछा। सिर्फ फर्ज-अदायगी के लिए रुपया भेज देता है...पचासों लोगों की दवा करता है, पर खुद अपने मां-बाप की हारी-बीमारी से उसे कोई मतलब नहीं रहता। (मांस, 60)

की दवा कर—"to soothe, to alleviate"

निरु सुरेश की सचाई की परीक्षा न कर रही थी, उस दृष्टि से हिसाब देखने का उसका उद्देश्य न था, वह केवल अपने मर्ज की दवा कर रही थी उचटते हुए चित्त को एकमुखी करती हुई, पर मरीज सुरेश बाबू उसके प्रश्न से जैसे क्षतस्थान की वेदना का अनुभव करने लगे। (निरु, 75)

9. **औषधोपचार कर—"to give medical treatment to"**

मनमाने जादू-टोने और भ्रमपूर्ण औषधोपचार करके उसके प्राण ले लेंगे। (कचनार, 122)

'They will take his life by indulging in witchcraft and quackery."

61. भरोसा, एतबार, यकीन, विश्वास

61. भरोसा, एतबार, यकीन and विश्वास all refer to one's attitude or response which signifies one's mental acceptance or assent to the truth or accuracy of something or someone, but differ significantly in regard to the character and basis of such an attitude or response.

भरोसा implies an assuredness in another which is complete and absolute. It suggests (often in the absence of any other alternative) a basis for one's choice or decision.

एतबार implies a formulated judgement of trust based on some definite grounds.

यकीन implies satisfaction as to the certainty or truth of some matter suggesting some convincing evidence.

विश्वास is subjective feeling of sureness (often on grounds other than those afforded by senses and reason).

2. All nouns are +process, and form ANP with के ऊपर, पर, में and का with the exception of भरोसा which does not occur with में. None of the expressions takes plural.

3. **पर भरोसा कर—"to trust"**

देवशंकर पर आप भरोसा कर सकते हैं। (सा सा, 86)

पर भरोसा कर—"to rely upon"

इसी कारण प्रोफेसर क्रोबर आदि मानवशास्त्रियों ने इस पद्धति पर पर्याप्त भरोसा किया है। (मानव, 64)

पर भरोसा कर—"to place reliance upon"

जो अदृश्य है उस पर भरोसा कभी भी नहीं किया जा सकता। (सा सा, 250)

पर भरोसा कर—"to place reliance upon"

अमेरिका के खाद्यान्न पर भारत सरकार ने जितना भरोसा किया था अब उसे प्राप्त करने में दिनों-दिन कठिनाई बढ़ती जा रही है। (आज, 4)

पर भरोसा कर—"to depend upon"

गौरी ! रोओ मत ! दिल को मजबूत करो—भगवान पर भरोसा करो। (दीर्घ, 142)

पर भरोसा कर—

वे भगवान् पर भरोसा करती अवश्य हैं पर अपनी समझ पर काम नहीं करतीं। (चारु, 336)

"She places reliance on God but trusts her own judgement nevertheless."

का भरोसा कर—"to reckon on"

"आया तो आ ही गया। नहीं तो—भरोसा यहां किसका कीजिए।" (सुता, 84)

का भरोसा कर—"to count on"

पर मुझे तो आते ही रहना है। यहां से मेरे भूखे जाने का भरोसा तुम न करना। (सुता, 54)

4. **के ऊपर एतबार कर—"to trust, to rely upon"**

दूसरा ख्याल आया कि यह तो अपने ऊपर एतबार करने वालों के साथ दगा होगा। (फूलो, 53)

का एतबार कर—"to trust"

कोतवाल साहब सिपाहियों को यों भी समझाते रहते थे कि मुसलमान हाकिम कौम है। वे हमेशा मुल्क पर हकूमत करते आये हैं।...अंग्रेज हमेशा मुसलमान का एतबार और इज्जत करता है।...खुदा ने अंग्रेजों को ओहदा दिया है और हम लोगों को उसकी मदद करने का हुक्म है। (फूलो, 45)

5. **पर यकीन कर—"to place confidence in"**

"भला बताओ, अब *जोतिस* पर कैसे यकीन न किया जाए?" कर्नल अपनी दृष्टि से शास्त्री जी की महिमा बखान रहा था। (बूंद, 113)

में यकीन कर—"to believe (strongly) in, to entertain a conviction"

फिर बोलो—"दुर्जन, कल तक जिस बात में यकीन करती थी आज वह झूठी साबित हो चुकी है। (बूंद, 233)

का यकीन कर—"to be convinced"

मुनीम ने नीचा सिर किये हुए कहा, "पाँच सेर दूध और पाव भर जलेबी की रसीद। समिति वाले यकीन नहीं करेंगे कि वकील साहब पक्का सवा पांच सेर डाल गये! शक करेंगे कि मुनीम पचा गया।" (दबेपांव, 5)

6. **के ऊपर विश्वास कर—"to put one's faith in"**

हम अपने ऊपर विश्वास करने वालों को कभी निराश नहीं करना चाहते और ऐसे बोझों को उठाने को तैयार हो जाते हैं जिन्हें हम असाध्य समझते थे। (सेवा, 345)

पर विश्वास कर—"to have faith in"

उसकी प्रजा उसके शुभ जन्म पर विश्वास करती है। उसके सैनिक लापरवाह रहते हैं, उनका दृढ़ विश्वास है कि अस्सी वर्ष तक कुछ भी दुर्घटना नहीं घटेगी। (चारु, 13)

पर विश्वास कर ले—"to take something on faith"

मुंह बनाते हुए लीला ने कहा—मिस्टर अजीत! आप भी बड़े भोले आदमी हैं। जिसने जो कुछ कह दिया। उस पर आपने विश्वास कर लिया।" (तीन, 62)

पर विश्वास कर पा—"to have (or acquire) confidence in"

और जनता यद्यपि बड़ी तेजी से उसकी तरफ खिंच रही थी परन्तु सज्जन अब तक जनशक्ति पर हृदय से विश्वास न कर पाया था। (बूंद, 570)

पर विश्वास कर—"to trust, to rely upon"

उन्हें देखते ही डा० ज्ञानशंकर को लगा कि यह कोई पुराना मित्र है जिस पर फौरन विश्वास किया जा सकता है, जो सहायता ही करेगा, कभी नुक्सान नहीं पहुंचाएगा। (धनु, 137)

पर विश्वास कर—"to rely on"

धर्म का निर्मल स्वरूप वास्तविक अर्थों में भारतीय धर्म में है जो तर्कों से अधिक अनुभूतियों पर विश्वास करता है। (धर्म, 93)

पर विश्वास कर—"to give credence to"

जिस बात का शक हुआ उस पर विश्वास करने को मन नहीं करता था। (धनु, 111)

में विश्वास कर—"to give credence to"

मैं जानता था कि मेरे विचारों में कोई दम नहीं, मैं उनमें विश्वास न करता था। (राह, 49)

में विश्वास कर—"to believe in"

विश्व के सभी मानव ईश्वर की सत्ता में विश्वास नहीं करते। (धर्म, 44)

में विश्वास कर—"to have faith in"

हम ऐसी विचार-पद्धतियों में विश्वास नहीं करते जो राज्य की दुहाई देकर व्यक्ति के स्वप्न पर कुठाराघात करती हैं। (अमरीका, 14)

में विश्वास कर—"to believe in"

अजित हंस पड़ा—"नहीं लीला, मैं व्यक्तित्व और ममत्व को बनाए रखने में विश्वास करता हूं—यदि मैंने अपना ममत्व ही खो दिया तो फिर मैं कहां रहा।..." (तीन, 70)

का विश्वास कर—"to trust, to rely on"

कानों का विश्वास करना ठीक नहीं; चलो अपनी आंख से देख लूं तो शायद यह पेचीदा बात मेरी समझ में आ जाए। (कथा, 47)

का विश्वास कर—"to believe, to be taken in by"

आप लोग इनकी चिकनी चुपड़ी बातों का विश्वास न कीजिए। (ढोल, 85)

का विश्वास कर—"to place confidence in, to trust"

लेकिन वह कौन सा ऐसा काम करे जिससे कि लोग उसका विश्वास कर सकें, जनता का विश्वास प्राप्त करने के लिए वह किस प्रकार आत्मोत्सर्ग करे । (बूंद, 571)

62. विचार-विनिमय, विचार-विमर्श, परामर्श, विचार, सलाह-सूत, मशविरा, सलाह

1. All the nouns refer to holding conversation with someone on something problematic.

विचार-विनिमय refers to an exchange of views, and may sometimes mean nothing more than normal communication.

विचार-विमर्श is discussing or holding a group discussion.

परामर्श is conferring with someone in order to seek information or expert opinion (sometimes concurrence prior to decision-making).

विचार (see 63 also) is seeking opinions, views or the like.

सलाह-सूत is to consult another person (mainly to compare views).

मशविरा covers the ground of विचार-विमर्श as well as that of परामर्श but differs from both in the sense that it may imply a preventing or averting of something unpleasant (sometimes even a conspiring against).

सलाह is consulting in order to seek counsel, opinion, advice or the like of someone (not necessarily an expert) or holding (a brief) group discussion in order to come to a concurred opinion.

2. All the nouns are +process, and form ANP with से. If the subject noun is plural, then the N से is replaced by आपस में "amongst themselves". These expressions are not pluralized.

3. से विचार-विनिमय कर—"to exchange views, to communicate"

जिस वातावरण में वह रहता है जिन लोगों से वह विचार-विनिमय करता है वे भारतीय होते हुए भी परम्परागत भारतीय जीवन से करीब-करीब दूर हो चुके हैं। (बूंद, 7)

4. विचार-विमर्श कर—"to discuss"

इसलिये हमें पैगंबर ईसा के इस कथन का पालन करना ही चाहिए, "आओ, अब हम मिल-बैठ कर विचार-विमर्श करें। (अमरीका, 96)

विचार-विमर्श कर—"to be engaged in a discussion"

एक दिन ताई की हवेली में बैठकर बाबा राम जी, [illegible], [illegible] और कन्या। इसी रुपए का उपयोग करने के लिए विचार-विमर्श कर रहे थे। (बूंद, 543)

5. से परामर्श कर—"to confer with"

उन्होंने तुरन्त पुण्डीर को बुलाया और सैनिकों की व्यूह-रचना के विषय में परामर्श किया। (चारु, 251)

से परामर्श कर चुक—"to have consulted someone"

बोधा प्रधान उनसे परामर्श कर चुके हैं। (चारु, 416)

6. से विचार कर—"to seek the opinion of, to discuss with someone"

मैं मिसेज शुक्ला को गाड़ी में बिठा कर आती हूं। कल्याणी, कर्नल की पत्नी से कन्या वाले तुरंत के प्रस्ताव पर विचार कर रही थी। कन्या ने प्रस्तावित किया था कि शकुंतला का विवाह इसी घर से हो। (बूंद 494-95)

7. से सलाह-सूत कर—"to cosult"

उसी दिन शाम को मुहल्ले के एक प्रतिष्ठित रईस-महाजन अपने सजातीय मित्र लाला आनकी सरन से टीके की दावत-महफिल आदि के संबंध में सलाह-सूत करने के तकल्लुफ-भरे बहाने के साथ राजा बहादुर की सवारी आई। (बूंद, 13)

8. मशविरा-कर—"to conspire"

सुबह दस बजे से अब्बा और सूफी साहब एक कोठरी में बंद होकर जाने क्या-क्या मशविरा कर रहे हैं। (खत, 68)

9. से सलाह कर ले—"to consult, to talk to"

मास्टर साहब, मैंने नाटक पढ़ लिये, और भी दो एक लड़कियों से सलाह कर ली। (नदी, 67)

आपस में सलाह कर—"to agree upon among themselves"

देवताओं ने आपस में सलाह करके कहा—एवमस्तु, हम तुम्हें यह वर देते हैं कि तुम्हारे शरीर की छाया जहां भी पीछे और अगल-बगल पड़ेगी, वहां की प्रत्येक वस्तु में नवजीन का संचार हो जायगा। (कथा, 57)

से सलाह कर—"to seek someone's advice"

वह रमेश से सलाह करने आया था कि क्या किया जाय...। (तीन, 50)

सलाह कर ले—"to talk about"

भुवन जोर से हंस दिया। बोला अच्छा, मालविकाग्निमित्र छोड़ जाओ, पढ़ डालूंगा। कल फिर सलाह कर लेंगे। (नदी, 64)

63. मनन, चिन्तन, गौर, ध्यान, विचार, ख्याल, सोच, सोचविचार

1. The nouns मनन, चिन्तन, गौर, ध्यान, विचार, ख्याल, सोच and सोच-विचार all refer to the application of one's mind to any object of thought in the manner of brooding over it for a length of time.

मनन is focusing on or exerting one's mind over something in order to comprehend, understand or grasp its significance or deeper meaning The term is also used in religious contexts to refer to the practice of trying to inculcate the truth of sacred writings in one's mind.

चिन्तन is devoting or directing one's power of observation to something in order to bring it into one's consciousness clearly and vividly or constantly trying to transform the intuitively perceived knowledge of something in one's inner self into a subjective reality for oneself by making it an integral part of one's mode of life or one's disposition. In spiritual or mystic practices, चिन्तन (along with स्मरण, see 39) is prescribed as a necessary form of meditation in order to experience the realization of the ultimate or transcendental reality.

गौर refers to the act of turning one's attention to or the application of one's mind to any object of sense or thought as if one were dwelling on or over it continuously or moodily. By itself the term stresses nothing more than a reference to the subject's appearance in which with his eyes he gives the impression of lingering over something.

ध्यान refers to the state of intellectualization or the exercise of intellect (i.e. the power or faculty of knowing as distinguished from the power to feel and to will), and is therefore esoterically applied to indicate a mental state in which one takes into the mind or dwells upon any object of thought in order to give it an intellectual or rational form or content, or intellectually absorb its significance. In its popular usage it refers to the act of pursuing one's thoughts with complete absorption (often as in a reverie).

विचार is discursive reasoning from premises to conclusion or proceeding from particulars to generalization. The term may refer both to the process of discursive reasoning as well as to its results.

ख्याल is a term referring to intuitive thinking in general or the ideational activity of the mind. The term may therefore be used to refer to any notion or idea one may have about some one or something without the implication that such a notion or idea has any factual relevance or not.

सोच refers to the state of being mentally agitated (in varying degrees) over something. The term implies a temporary state of indecision or hesitation on the part of the subject in a situation where he is expected to respond to a request, demand or the like.

सोच-विचार is a compound term (consisting of सोच and विचार) referring to carefully weighing the pros and cons of a matter at hand before making up one's mind to act upon it or come to a decision about it.

2. मनन, गौर, विचार and ख्याल are ±process, and the rest are +process only. मनन forms ANP with पर, चिन्तन with पर, के ऊपर and का, गौर with पर, ध्यान with का, विचार with पर and का, ख्याल with का, सोच with का and की, and सोच-विचार with पर. None of these nouns is pluralised.

3. **पर गम्भीरता पूर्वक मनन कर—"to delve deeply into"**

इंगलैण्ड में इस स्थिति पर सर ग्रेशम ने गम्भीरता पूर्वक मनन किया। (एमाई, 23)

को मनन कर—"to take to heart"

श्री तुलसीदास जी ने इस मैत्री प्रसंग पर अनेक उपयुक्त बातें लिखी हैं। उन्हें पाठकों को अवश्य मनन करना चाहिए। (वैदिक, 22)

मनन कर—"to contemplate"

इन सभी का आधार उक्त मंत्र है अतः मनन करने के योग्य है। (वैदिक, 34)

मनन कर—"to think, to function"

जिस शक्ति के बिना हमारी आंखें देख नहीं सकतीं, कान सुन नहीं सकते, मन मनन नहीं कर सकता और बुद्धि तर्क नहीं कर सकती...उसी शक्ति को जानना साधक का प्रथम उद्देश्य है। (धर्म, 109)

4. **के ऊपर चिंतन कर—"to ponder over"**

गोकुल—आखरी विषय के ऊपर साधुओं ने काफी विचार और चिंतन किया होगा? (बाँस, 28)

का चिन्तन कर—"to think about"

मानव को उसी वस्तु का चिन्तन करना चाहिए जिसका अभाव उसे कर्म करते हुए भी प्रतीत होता है। (धर्म, 142)

का चिन्तन कर—"to entertain"

साधक जब योग और वेदान्त के निगूढ़ रहस्यमय सिद्धान्तों के परस्पर विरोधी भावों का चिन्तन करता है, तो लगता है, कि ये सब व्यर्थ की बातें हैं। (धर्म, 112)

के हेतु चिन्तन कर—"to turn one's thoughts to, to think of"

आज आवश्यकता इस बात की है कि वह अपने व्यक्तित्व के विकास के साथ-साथ

विश्व के कल्याण के हेतु भी चिन्तन करे, क्योंकि आज का विश्व सिकुड़ कर बहुत छोटा हो गया है। (धर्म, 83)

चिन्तन कर—"to ruminate, to ponder"

मेरा यह मतलब नहीं कि माणिक मुल्ला उसके पास बैठकर यह सब चिन्तन किया करते थे। नहीं, यह सब तो उस परिस्थिति का मेरा अपना विश्लेषण है, वैसे माणिक मुल्ला को तो वह केवल बहुत अच्छी लगती थी और उन दिनों माणिक मुल्ला का मन पढ़ने में भी लगने लगा काम करने में भी, और उनका वज़न भी बढ़ गया और उन्हें भूख भी खुलकर लगने लगी, वे कालज की खेलों में भी हिस्सा लेने लगे। (सूरज, 88-89)

चिन्तन करता रह—"to be engaged in thinking"

यह हमने देख लिया कि मन निरंतर चिन्तन करता रहता है। (चमत्कार, 2)

5. **पर गौर कर—"to muse over"**

मैं अलफ़ाजों खाते-खाते अपने मिजाज की इस उछाल पर गौर करने लगा। (साझे, 14)

पर गौर कर—"to watch"

मैं चुपचाप उसकी भाव-भंगी पर गौर कर रहा था। (तुला, 51)

पर गौर कर—"to be intent upon"

तीसरे सज्जन एक कुर्सी से टिके खड़े थे, और ऐसा मालूम होता था कि वे कलाबाजी खाने की बात पर गौर कर रहे हैं। (तीन, 28)

पर फिर से गौर कर ले—"to reconsider"

पर मकोला इस बातचीत में बुरी तरह उत्तेजित हो चुके थे, "नहीं जोखनलाल आज हम लोगों को फिर से अपनी अपनी स्थिति पर गौर कर लेना होगा।...." (सा सा, 116)

पर गौर कर—"to consider"

...अगर तन्ना घरजमाई बनना पसन्द करे तो इस प्रस्ताव पर गौर किया जा सकता है। (सूरज, 56)

पर गौर कर—"to be absolutely absorbed in thoughts of"

...अपनी सच्ची निष्ठा पर गौर करता हुआ वह अपने चिन्तन मंदिर से जब बाहर आया। (बूंद, 176)

गौर कर—"to notice, for something to dawn upon one"

मैंने अब गौर किया कि मैं सर्दी के मारे झुककर चल रहा हूं। (राह, 60)

गौर करते हुए—"observantly"

किसी अच्छे काम में पहल करने वाले आदमी हमेशा बहुत कम होते हैं। सज्जन बहुत गौर करते हुए बोला—मुझे ऐसा लगता है कि इस समय हमारा देश खुद अपने बारे में बेहद ओछी नज़र से सोचता है। (बूंद, 472)

गौर कर—"to look at"

...मगर जब दूसरे पहलू से गौर करता हूं तब यह एक पति-पत्नीव्रत का सिद्धान्त विकास-नियम का पोषक होकर स्त्री-पुरुष के समाज को कोरी देह-भोग की चेतना से ऊंची सतह पर उठाता है। (बूंद, 95)

गौर कर—"to observe"

मैंने यह गौर किया कि वह शख्स कभी उत्तेजित और क्रोधित नहीं होता और उसकी आवाज़ सदा मीठी होती है। (राह, 59)

बराबर गौर कर—"to observe"

सज्जन एक बार फिर रीझ उठा; उसने बराबर गौर किया है कि कन्या के मनोभाव सीधी रेखाओं और बिन्दुओं की तरह उसके चेहरे और आंखों में आ जाते हैं, उसके तमाम रंग सादे, मगर जानदार हैं। (बूंद, 129)

को गौर कर—"to dwell on, to brood over"

फिर उसके आखिरी कथन के रहस्य को ज्यों-ज्यों गौर करता त्यों-त्यों उलझन में फंसता जाता। (देश, 27-28)

पर गौर कर—"to think of, to dwell on"

हम अपनी ही व्यापकता और चिर विकास पर गौर कहां करते हैं। (बूंद, 546)

6. **का ध्यान कर—"to concentrate on"**

सज्जन मौसम से ज्यादा शास्त्री जी की बातों का ध्यान कर रहा है। शास्त्री जी की बातों से आज उसके मन की अनेक शंकाएं दूर हुई हैं। (बूंद, 112)

का ध्यान कर—"to be thinking of"

मैं अपनी बैठक में बैठा हुआ अपने दो वर्ष के छोटे बच्चे और प्रेममयी स्त्री का ध्यान कर रहा था। (काल, 31)

का ध्यान कर—"to be reflecting on, to think back upon"

इस समय चीनी नक्काशी के बेशकीमत पलंग पर रबड़ के मुलायम गद्दे पर बांह के सहारे सिर उठाए लेटी हुई बड़े घर, अनेक नौकर-चाकरों की स्वामिनी, पिया की प्यारी सुहागिन अपने पिछले जीवन का ध्यान कर मन ही मन छटपटा रही थी। (बूंद, 451)

का ध्यान कर—"to be musing over"

...कदाचित् प्रतापी जयित्र चद्र के अपार धैर्य और साहस का ध्यान कर रही थीं। (चारु, 90)

का ध्यान कर—"to observe, to follow carefully"

इसका परिणाम यह होता है कि वह निवास की अनिश्चितता के कारण स्वास्थ्य सम्बन्धी नियमों का ध्यान नहीं कर पाती। (स्वस्थ, 9)

का ध्यान कर—"to think of"

मनुष्य की एक मुख्य कमजोरी का ध्यान करके उसने कहा—तुम बड़े चतुर हो, इसमें संदेह नहीं, लेकिन एक जगह चूक गए हो, एक त्रुटि न होती तो ये मूर्तियां सजीव लगतीं। (कथा, 35)

का ध्यान कर—"to fix one's mind upon"

जो लोग सांसारिक उद्देश्य को छोड़कर एक मात्र ईश्वर का ध्यान करते हैं, विरक्त बने फिरते हैं, वे भी दोषी हैं क्योंकि अन्य मानवों के हितार्थ वे कुछ नहीं कर पाते। (धर्म, 26)

का ध्यान करके—"musing on"

वहीं दीवार में दुबक कर बैठ रहे। वो चिल्ले की रात फ़क़त मजलिसी-रईसों के कीमती गर्म कपड़ों का ध्यान करके काट दी। (तुला, 37)

का ध्यान करते हुए—"to focus one's mind on"

माणिक मुल्ला चुपचाप गऊ माता का ध्यान करते हुए सो गए। (सूरज, 29)

का ध्यान करते हुए—"to focus one's mind on"

इस समय माचिकब्बे मन-ही-मन जिनेश का ध्यान करते हुए कह रही थीं—अक्क तो शांतला का वीणा-वादन सुन चुकी हैं, ऐसी हालत में फिर से इतने बड़े समारोह का प्रबन्ध उन्होंने क्यों करवाया? (शांतला, 65)

7. पर विचार कर—"to give thought to"

सरकार को उसका स्थायी हल खोजने पर विचार करना चाहिए। (नवभा, 1-4)

पर विचार कर—"to consider"

वेश्याओं की समस्या पर सुधारवादी दृष्टिकोण से ही विचार किया गया है। (नदु, 40)

पर विचार कर—"to consider, to think over"

(मालती चुप रहती है) रमाशंकर मेरी बात पर सहानुभूति के साथ विचार करो। (मालती का हाथ पकड़कर) इधर देखो। (सन्यासी, 78)

पर विचार कर—"to give some consideration to, to consider"

...यदि आपने मेरी बिनती पर विचार नहीं किया तो दो-चार दिन में ही कोई कांड होने वाला है। (देश, 43)

पर विचार कर—"to give thought to"

हिन्दुत्व के नवीन रूप को उपस्थित करते हुए वे समस्त विश्व को यह संदेश देना चाहते थे कि यदि अपनी विविधताओं में सामंजस्य करना चाहते हो तो जरा इन सत्यों पर भी विचार करो जिन्हें भारत सदियों से संजोये हुए है...। (धर्म, 69)

पर विचार कर—"to consider"

हमारे यहां तीन महीने पहले मैटर पर विचार किया जाता है। (बाल, 11-31)

पर विचार करते हुए—"considering, commenting upon, while examining"

इस आन्तरिक और बाह्य क्रमभग्न मनुष्य की समस्या पर विचार करते हुए मैक्स रिकार्ड ने इसके कुछ बहुत महत्वपूर्ण पक्ष उद्घाटित किये हैं। (मूल्य, 31)

पर विचार कर—"to think over"

इन पांच शब्दों में कितना सत्य भरा पड़ा है, उसका पता ज्यों-ज्यों इस पर विचार करो उतना अधिक लगता जाता है। (कल्याण, 28)

पर विचार कर—"to think of, to give some thought to"

क्षण भर के लिए वह झिझक गया। मैनेजर के प्रश्न के साथ ही सभ्यता की जो समस्यायें सहसा उसकी नज़र के आगे कौंव गयीं, उन पर उसने आते हुए विचार नहीं किया था। (नदी, 126)

पर विचार कर—"to think over, to reconsider"

इस आश्रम में ऐसी महिलाओं को लाना अनुचित है। आप लोग इस प्रश्न पर विचार करें। (सम, 55)

पर विचार कर—"to think over, to give thought to"

भारतीय स्त्री ने अभी तक इस समस्या पर निष्पक्ष होकर वैसा विचार नहीं किया जैसा किया जाना चाहिये। (म, 60)

पर विचार कर—"to think about, to think over"

मुझे समय दो कि में परिस्थितियों पर विचार करूं। (चित्र, 52)

पर विचार कर—"to think out"

उसकी बातों से लगेगा कि उसने इन्सान की समस्याओं पर तटस्थता से विचार किया है। (राह, 22)

पर विचार कर—"to reason out"

क्या उन्होंने इस पर भी विचार किया कि क्यों उस युवक का विद्रोह इस चरम सीमा तक पहुंच गया। (सोमा, 77)

पर विचार कर—"to examine"

इस अध्याय में पहले कार्बनिक खादों का वर्णन करेंगे, परन्तु दोनों का अलग अलग अध्ययन करने से पूर्व उन पर तुलनात्मक विचार करना अच्छा है। (खाद, 13)

पर विचार कर ले—"to consider, to think about"

आइए, यहां कुछ जीवधारियों की आत्मरक्षा के साधनों पर विचार कर लें। (बाल, 11-5)

पर विचार करते करते—"reflecting on"

पद्मसिंह ने इस प्रस्ताव को वेश्याओं के प्रति घृणा से प्रेरित होकर हाथ में लिया था, पर अब इस विषय पर विचार करते-करते उनकी घृणा बहुत कुछ दया और क्षमा का रूप धारण कर चुकी थी। (सेवा, 290)

पर विचार करते हुए—"reflecting on"

संस्कृति के विभिन्न पहलुओं पर विचार करते हुए महिपाल ने जाड़े की रात को अपनी ज्ञान चेतना से गर्माने का भरसक प्रयत्न किया। इस पर भी वह इस ख्याल से न उबर सका कि यह कमजोरियों का गुलाम है। (बूंद, 221)

पर विचार कर—"to be reflecting on"

उसके मन में आज बड़ी करुणा थी, वह अपने अपराध पर स्वयं विचार कर रहा था। यदि मेरे मन में मैना के प्रति थोड़ा सा भी स्निग्ध भाव न होता तो क्या घटना की धारा ऐसी चल सकती थी। (तितली, 251)

पर विचार कर—"to ponder over, to reflect on"

शाम को महिपाल के जाने के बाद सज्जन उसकी टूटी हुई मानसिक अवस्था पर विचार करता रहा। इंसान की दुर्बलताएं भी किसी न किसी सत्य के आधार पर फलती-फूलती हैं। (बूंद, 198)

पर विचार कर—"to examine"

अब हम वस्तु विनिमय की कठिनाइयों पर विस्तार से विचार करेंगे। (एमाई, 8)

पर विचार कर—"to discuss"

पाश्चात्य उपन्यास की ह्रासोन्मुखता पर विचार करने के उपरान्त बिना कोई कारण दिये भारतीय उपन्यास की वर्तमान या भावी श्रेष्ठता की उद्घोषणा करने लगते हैं...। (मूल्य, 172)

पर विचार कर—"to think over"

आप न जाइए यू. एन. ओ., न बैठाइए जांच कमीशन, न कीजिए पंच फैसला, खुद ही अपनी-अपनी अक्ल पर थोड़ा जोर डालकर सहानुभूति से इस मसले पर विचार कीजिए, तो मेरी बात को सच पाइएगा। (सच, 57)

पर विचार कर—"to consider, to discuss"

अब हम घर की महत्वपूर्ण समस्या पर विचार करेंगे—वह है चूल्हे की समस्या। (स्वस्थ, 20)

में विचार कर—"to reason with oneself before"

अब तुम ही देख लो...तुम चट से इसका उत्तर न दे सके। प्रश्न यदि सीधा होता तो, इसका उत्तर देने में विचार करने की जरूरत न पड़ती। (लाख, 58)

के सम्बन्ध में विचार कर—"to reason oneself out of"

नर ने अपने सम्बन्ध में विचार करते हुए हठपूर्वक काम की इच्छा और प्रिया की याद को भुलाना शुरू किया। (बूंद, 139)

के सम्बन्ध में विचार करता रह—"to be engrossed with"

सज्जन फिर ब्रह्मचर्य और वनकन्या के सम्बन्ध में विचार करता रहा। (बूंद, 198)

के साथ के सम्बन्ध में विचार कर—"to discuss something with someone"

यहां तक कि एक दिन वह एटकिन्सन के साथ इस सम्बन्ध में विचार करता

रहा कि इतनी अच्छी और मेहनती लड़की को उसके पति ने घर से क्यों निकाल रखा है। (जान, 141)

के सम्बन्ध में विचार कर—"to think about, to think of"

...हरदम रुपए-पैसे, नाते-रिश्ते, लेने-देन आदि के सम्बन्ध ही में विचार करती रहती है फिर भी उसका जीवन जैसा एकनिष्ठ है वैसा उसने कम देखा है। (बूंद, 101)

के लिये विचार कर—"to do the thinking for someone"

बीरबल—दूसरे हमारे लिए विचार करें। दूसरे लोग हमारे लिए काम करें। (बीर, 20)

के लिये विचार कर—"to be considered, to be taken up"

बिलारी मोर्चे की आंच में तपे हर सिपाही को उचित पुरस्कार देने के लिए हम अष्ट प्रधानों की सभा में विचार करेंगे। (बेटी, 95)

का विचार कर—"to consider"

गंगराज—हेमाद्री की सलाह विचार करने लायक है। (शांतला, 53)

का विचार न करते हुए—"irrespective of"

मूल रूप में कल्याण राज्य एक समुदाय है जहां कि राज्य शक्ति को आय के एक अधिक समान वितरण को प्राप्त करने के लिए जान बूझकर प्रयोग किया जाता है और इसी प्रकार प्रत्येक नागरिक के लिये, उसके कार्य और उसकी सम्पत्ति के बाजार भाव का विचार न करते हुए एक बुनियादी न्यूनतम वास्तविक आय निश्चित की जाती है। (भारत, 3)

का विचार कर—"to be thinking of"

तुमको यहां देखना। देखो आज यह कैसी संध्या है। मैं तो लौटने का विचार कर रहा था और मैं कोठी से होती आ रही हूं। भला, आज कितने दिनों पर। (तितली, 124)

का विचार कर—"to deal with (a subject), to give consideration to"

...मीमांसक मत में तत्व ज्ञान का विचार मुख्य रूप में नहीं किया गया है तथापि इस मत में व्यापक नित्य जीव माना गया है, ईश्वर को जीव के कर्म फलों को देने में अस्वीकार किया गया है केवल कर्म ही फल देने में समर्थ है। (वैदिक, 34)

का विचार कर ले—"to decide, to make up one's mind to do something"

एक दिन दृढ़ होकर इसका निपटारा कर लेने का विचार कर लिया। (कंकाल, 158)

का विचार कर—"to think of"

कभी सोचते, भैया को पत्र लिखूं, कभी सोचते चलकर उनसे कहूं, कभी विट्ठलदास को भेजने का विचार करते, लेकिन कुछ निश्चय न कर सकते थे। (सेवा, 265)

का विचार कर—"to decide"

जब्ती की आज्ञा मनसूख होते ही 10,000 प्रतियों का दूसरा संस्करण निकालने का विचार किया गया। (सुन्दर, झ)

का विचार कर—"to mind"

मैं छूत-छात का कुछ विचार नहीं करता। (कंकाल, 94)

का विचार कर—"to mind, to give any thought to"

इस समय उसकी दशा उस रोगी-सी हो रही थी, जो मीठे पदार्थ को सामने देख कर उस पर टूट पड़ता है और पथ्यापथ्य का विचार नहीं करता। (सेवा, 330)

का विचार कर—"to give any thought to"

कहीं का भी लड़का और कहीं की भी लड़की जब एक जगह आ जाते हैं तो विवाह हो जाता है। इनकी जोड़ी ठीक जमी है या नहीं इसका क्या कभी कोई विचार करता है? (लाख, 227)

को बार बार विचार कर—"to cogitate on (the meaning of)"

सभ्यता, संस्कृति, आदर्श, न्याय, सौन्दर्य, सत्य, मानवता आदि बड़े-बड़े शब्दों को बार-बार विचार कर नित नए अर्थों से निखरने वाला कलाकार-साहित्यिक स्वयं अपने ही अपराध से जड़ है। (बूंद, 433)

का विचार कर—"to examine"

उसके सामने ऐसे प्रश्न उपस्थित होते हैं जिनका विचार अब तक दार्शनिक ही करता रहा है और आगे भी उनको दर्शन से पृथक् नहीं किया जा सकेगा। (नक्षत्र, 29)

का विचार करके रह जा—"to think of, to have thoughts of, to reason oneself out"

बाप को तो कहता है—तुम गुलाम हो। वह एक अंग्रेजी कम्पनी में हैं। बार-बार इस्तीफा देने का विचार करके रह जाते हैं, लेकिन गुजर-बसर के लिए कोई उद्यम करना ही पड़ेगा (सम, 8)

का विचार कर—"to be contemplating to"

ऐसा भी हो सकता है कि महाराज ने हमारी भलाई का कोई काम करने का विचार किया हो। (बाल, 11-33)

8. **का ख्याल कर—"to occupy oneself with, to attend to"**

वीणा घर का सारा काम-काज बड़ा चित्त लगाकर करती, पति के आराम और जरूरत का अधिक ख्याल करती पर डा० ज्ञानशंकर मुंह से कुछ नहीं बोलते। (धनु, 115)

का ख्याल कर—"to have some notion of"

जहां तक हो सके हमको रुचि, सामर्थ्य, देश और काल और इनकी अनुकूलता का ख्याल करना होगा, इस तरह किया हुआ काम थकावट को दूर करता है, नवीनता को लाता, प्रतिभा को प्रकाश करके अविश्वास, अरुचि, थकावट आलस्य आदि दोषों का निरसन करता है। (चमत्कार, 45)

का ख्याल कर ले—"to have some regard for"

श्रीमतियां तो अपने पति से व्यवहार करते समय लोक-परलोक का कुछ ख्याल कर भी लेती हैं, लेकिन इन महाशयों को तो न लोक का भय है, न परलोक का। (सच, 19)

ख्याल कर—"to regard"

मेरी दादी अपने छोटे से श्रोता को कहानी सुनाते समय शायद बहुत समझदार ख्याल कर लेती हैं। (तुला, 102)

ख्याल कर—"to consider"

अपने आपको सोशलिस्ट भी ख्याल करते हैं। (बूंद, 48)

ख्याल कर—"to mind"

नहीं-नहीं वह सब कुछ नहीं, आप उन्हें कुछ ख्याल न कीजिएगा हज़रत। (तुला, 68)

बिना ख्याल किये—"without thinking, without entertaining any thought in one's mind"

वह उन बहुत कम लोगों में से थी जो अपने भीतर से अलग होकर सतह पर रह सकते हैं...बर्फ की पतली परत पर—बिना यह ख्याल किये कि वह कभी भी टूट सकती है। (वे दिन, 221)

ख्याल कर—"to mind, to consider"

जहां भाई-भाई और मित्र-मित्र नहा कर एक तौलिये से शरीर पोंछना न केवल बुरा ख्याल न करते थे, बल्कि उन्हें यह मालूम ही न था कि ऐसा करना बुरा है। (धारा, 48)

9. **की सोच कर—"to worry oneself over"**

गुल बेटा, इस बूढ़ी की सोच न कर। (मित्रो, 14)

का सोच कर—"to worry, (here : 'Never mind')"

उसका सोच मत करो। तुम कौन कहानी कह रहे थे। (तितली, 25)

10. **सोच-विचार कर—"to consider, to debate"**

बहुत सोच-विचार करने पर भी उसे कोई उपाय न सूझा। (रूस, 2)

ज्यादा सोच-विचार कर ले—"to think things through, to give something a thorough consideration"

जरनल कौल की किताब ने खलबली मचा दी है। किसी अफसर को नौकरी से हटाने से पहले अब मंत्री लोग ज्यादा सोच-विचार कर लिया करेंगे। (आज, 3)

64. पाप, गुनाह, अपराध, जुर्म, दोष, कसूर

1. पाप, अपराध, दोष and their respective synonymous counterparts गुनाह, जुर्म and कसूर all signify an act of infraction of a law or a moral obligation. The first set of terms has (Hindu) religious overtones significantly absent in the latter.

Thus both पाप (which is an antonym of पुण्य) and गुनाह refer to a breach of an accepted code of conduct involving a penalty, whereas only the former signifies a sin or a sinful act and the latter committing an offense or defaulting.

Both अपराध and जुर्म refer to committing a crime, the former stressing one's marked lack of conscientiousness and the latter having no such significance. Thus अपराध may be used to signify one's display of improbity, lack of conscientiousness or the like to the extent to which one considers oneself blameworthy or responsible or to a crime actually committed, whereas जुर्म refers only to a crime actually committed.

दोष (the antonym of गुण "virtue") "vice" and कसूर "fault" both refer to any act of wrong doing in general unless specified otherwise in the context. However, the former stresses indulgence in acts of moral depravity and the latter a falling short of a standard (or an expected standard) of perfection in disposition or action.

The order in which the above terms appear signifies the fact that पाप, अपराध and दोष carry the general sense that conduct implies an act of breaking or violating, whereas गुनाह, जुर्म and कसूर refer to a breaking or violating.

2. All the nouns are +process, and are freely pluralized unless they are preceded by a conjunctive participle phrase e. g., शादी करके गुनाह or a determiner कोई, यह, ऐसा or the like.

3. **पाप कर—"to do wrong"**

मेरा और शीला का सम्बन्ध आज की लौकिक दृष्टि से अनैतिक भले ही हो पर हम कोई पाप नहीं कर रहे हैं। और जो यह कहा जाय कि मैं एक पत्नीव्रत का पालन न कर सका तब भी कोई पाप नहीं। तीस-चालीस वर्ष पहले तक कितने लोग दो-दो, तीन-तीन पत्नियां रखते थे। (बूंद, 207)

पाप कर—"to engage in any immoral practice"

मैं धर्म का नाम लेकर उसकी आड़ में कभी पाप नहीं करता, क्योंकि मैं मानता हूं कि गुप्त पाप को भी देखने वाला कोई है...। (भारक, 22)

पाप कर—"to do wrong"

उसने मैना का प्राण बचा दिया तो क्या पाप किया। (तितली, 165)

4. **गुनाह कर—"to commit an infraction"**

नास्तिकता से उन्हें चिढ़ थी, यह सच है, पर नास्तिकता कोई गुनाह नहीं। जब तक कोई गुनाह न करे तब तक वह तहसीलदार के चंगुल में कैसे आ सकता था? (लाख, 36)

गुनाह कर—"to do wrong"

लेकिन इसके माने यह भी नहीं कि पति ने शादी करके कोई ऐसा गुनाह कर लिया है कि उससे वह खुद ही नहीं, उसके मां-बाप, बहन-भाई बच्चे-भतीजे सब-के-सब हेय हो गये हों। (सच, 64)

5. **अपराध कर—"to commit a crime"**

गलती किससे नहीं हो जाती—बाबू ने गलती नहीं अपराध किया है। (बूंद, 446)

अपराध कर—"to be guilty of"

मैं यहां बैठी थी, अनिच्छा से ही अकेले बैठे-बैठे तुम्हारी डायरी के कुछ पन्ने पढ़ लेने का अपराध मैंने किया है। (तितली, 114)

अपराध कर—"to be recalcitrant"

शायद मैं स्वामी के साथ विश्वासघात करके एक गुरु अपराध कर देता। (चित्र, 28)

अपराध कर—"to do wrong to someone"

वीणा! वीणा! तुमने यह क्या कर डाला। मैंने तुम्हारा क्या अपराध किया था जो तुमने मेरी स्थिति इतनी विचित्र और दयनीय बना दी है। (धनु, 126)

का अपराध कर—"to blame oneself for, to have made a blunder"

इस तरह के व्यक्तिगत आग्रह को मानने का अपराध एक बार पहले कर चुका हूं, अब दूसरी बार नहीं करना चाहता। (आकाश, भूमिका)

का अपराध कर—"to wrong"

तुमने अपराध किया; पर तुमने जिसके प्रति अपराध किया था, उससे अपना अपराध कह कर अपने अपराध को धो दिया। (चित्र, 28)

अपराध कर—"to treat someone with injustice"

लगता है, उन्होंने नितिन के संग कोई गहरा अपराध किया है...ऐसा अपराध जिसे नितिन खुद नहीं जानता (बहुत पहले चर्चा होती थी नितिन के ब्याह की...अब कोई भूलकर भी इशारा नहीं करता)। (जलती झाड़ी, 59)

6. **जुर्म कर—"to commit crime"**

कोई पादरी यदि बुरे से बुरा जुर्म करता था तो उसे केवल थोड़ा सा जुर्माना देना पड़ता था। (सुन्दर, 13)

7. **दोष कर—"to do wrong"**

पर हमारा अनुभव हमें यही सिखाता है कि बिना कारण के कोई दोष नहीं करता, बिना परिस्थितियों के कोई पाप नहीं करता। (धनु, 141)

दोष कर—"to engage in acts of moral depravity"

एक अच्छे फल के लिए बहुत से दोष करते रहना। (कंकाल, 62)

8. **कसूर कर—"to have failed, to be accused of being derelict in"**

फिर हमारे घर ने ऐसा कौन सा बड़ा कसूर किया है? तुम्हीं इन्साफ करके देखो। (बूंद, 445)

का कसूर कर--"to do wrong (purposely)"

मैं चुपचाप खड़ी रही और सोचती रही कि एक बार तो मैं सचमुच का कसूर करके देखूंगी। (त्यागपत्र, 8)

65. अनादर, निरादर, अपमान, अपमानित, तौहीन, बेअदबी, बेकदरी, जलील, बेइज्जती, बेइज्जत

1. These expressions refer to acting in a manner so as to cause (i. e., to directly bring about or make someone feel) a loss of prestige and honor.

अनादर is absence of respect displayed especially by remaining indifferent to or contemptuously neglecting someone or something.

निरादर is an attempt to show one's lack of esteem or feeling of low estimation for someone.

अपमान and अपमानित are any attempt to offend or affront someone or may refer to one's conduct which is tantamount to an attack on someone's integrity or a violation of his dignity. The terms are also used in reference to someone's conduct not measuring up to standards of moral and social behavior.

तौहीन contains reference to an attempt at vilification in an act of indignity.

बेअदबी is lack of decorum in one's confrontation with someone, tantamount to defiance.

बकदरी is a reference to one's deprecatory disposition manifest in one's lack of proper care, concern or solicitude.

जलील describes the state of someone or something that is affected offensively and depreciatively.

बेइज्जती and बेइज्जत refer to any act or action that does not measure up to standards of decent (moral) behavior or violates the dignity (or dignified character) or integrity of someone or something.

2. All the nouns with the exception of अपमान and बेइज्जती are +process, अपमानित and बेइज्जत being the-process counterparts of अपमान and बेइज्जती respectively. All form ANP with का/की except बेअदबी which takes के साथ. The expressions which are +process do not take plural.

3. **का अनादर कर—"to disregard"**

कुछ दिनों पहले भक्त के रूप में मिलने वाला वर्मा भी इस समय विरहेश का अनादर करने का हौसला दिखला रहा था, विरहेश उसे घूर कर देखने लगा मानों फाड़ खायगा। (बूंद, 230)

का अनादर कर—"to disregard, to disapprove, to show no consideration or regard, to treat with indifference"

मगर मैं तुम्हारी राय का अनादर यों भी न करता। तुम पाठक हो, तुम्हें अपनी राय रखने का हक है। और लेखक के नाते मुझे उस पर गौर करना ही होगा। (बूंद, 35)

4. **का निरादर कर—"to offend"**

हां ! मैंने अपने स्वामी से मना किया, मैंने अपने आराध्य देव का निरादर किया, मैंने अपने कुटिल स्वार्थ के वश होकर उनका अपमान किया। (सेवा, 296)

का निरादर कर—"to affront"

और इसलिए उन सफेद पोशों का निरादर करने की गरज से गांव का चौधरी जो जाति का कुर्मी था, तहसीलदार का बहुत अधिक ढकोसला फैलाता था। (लाख, 33)

5. **का अपमान कर—"to offend"**

उसे लगता था, उसने तुम्हारा अपमान किया और वह खिन्न थी। उसका ख्याल न करना। (जय, 104)

का अपमान कर—"to insult, to disregard"

स्त्री के सौंदर्य का अपमान करने वाला पुरुष, जिसे मैं सब कुछ बिना किसी मूल्य के दे देना चाहती थी, वह उस रस की थाली को ठुकरा दे ? (धनु, 162)

अपमान कर—"to humiliate"

अंधकार में न दीखने वाली लीला के मुख पर क्रोध का भाव उसकी भाषा में उमड़ पड़ा—"कुंवर साहब ! अब लौट चलिए। क्या आप मेरा अपमान करने के लिए यहां लाए हैं ?" लीला का स्वर कांप रहा था। (तीन, 76)

का अपमान कर—"to insult"

...इन साले बड़े आदमियों के लिए हमारी कला का अपमान किया गया है। (बूंद, 385)

का अपमान कर—"to disgrace"

ऐसी शंका करना उसकी राष्ट्रीयता का अपमान करना है। (गोदान, 67)

अपमान कर—"to insult"

फिर एकाएक कठोर होकर बोलीं—जब तक कांग्रेस ने इस काम का भार मुझ पर रखा है, आपको मेरे बीच में बोलने का कोई हक नहीं है। आप मेरा अपमान कर रहे हैं। कांग्रेस कमेटी के सामने आपको इसका जवाब देना होगा। (सम, 80)

6. **को अपमानित कर—"to bring dishonor to"**

क्यों पुरुष अपने आपको और स्त्री को इस तरह अपमानित करता है? इसमें उसे कौन-सा रस मिलता है? होली रस और शृंगार का त्यौहार है। यह गाली क्यों बना? (बूंद, 474)

को अपमानित कर—"to humiliate"

इसी कारण माओ के समर्थक लाल रक्षकों ने उनकी सार्वजनिक भर्त्सना कर उन्हें अपमानित किया है। (आज, 3)

7. **की तौहीन कर—"to insult, to malign"**

यह तुम कैसे कहते हो बदमाश कि मेरे पास पैसे नहीं? त मेरी तौहीन करता है नालायक! निकल जा मेरे मुहल्ले से नहीं तो...। (तुला, 78)

8. **के साथ बेअदबी—"to treat defiantly, to defy"**

एक किसान किसी पुलिस के आदमी के साथ इतनी बेअदबी करे, इसे भला वह कहीं बरदाश्त कर सकता है। सब कांस्टेबलों ने गरीब को इतना मारा कि वह मर गया। (सम, 11)

9. **की बेकदरी कर—"to waste, to dissipate"**

वह जरूर उन लोगों में से होगा जो अपने अमृत-बिन्दुओं की बेकदरी करते हैं और जिन्दगी को ज़लील...जिन्हें इस बात की भी परवाह नहीं कि लड़का हुआ तो जिन्दगी-भर, उनका लहू, अपना गोश्त-पोस्त, अपने दादा का परपोता, अपना बेटा भीख मांगता फिरेगा, औरतों की दलाली करेगा और लड़की होगी, तो अपने पितरों की पत को बेचेगी, पेशा करेगी। (लड़की, 42-43)

10. **को ज़लील कर—"to humiliate"**

शैतान ने मुझे गालियां दी, ज़लील किया। बस, यही रट लगाए हुए था कि देर क्यों की। निर्दयी ने चपरासी से मेरा कान पकड़ने को कहा। (पाच, 19)

11. **की बेइज्जती कर—"to insult"**

मेरी बहन की बेइज्जती क्यों करते हो ?...(होली, 64)

की बेइज्जती कर—"to disgrace"

पर दो सौ की खातिर भैया ने मालिक के बाग की बेइज्जती कर दी। (रात, 99)

12. **बेइज्जती कर—"to assault"**

अब रामरति ने साफ-साफ बतलाया दीदी जी, दोनों को जबर्दस्ती एक कोठरी में बंद करके बेइज्जत किया है—बड़ी मेम के दोस्तों ने। (दीर्घ, 141)

66. आमोद-प्रमोद, आमोद, मनोरंजन, मनबहलाव, तफरीह

1. All the nouns refer to occupying onself or someone else in a pleasant manner. आमोद-प्रमोद is merrymaking or merriment, but when qualified by a time phrase refers to allowing oneself the pleasure of something (in the manner of a playboy). The term has formal or ceremonial implications. आमोद is doing as it pleases one. मनोरंजन is entertaining with a performance (artistic or the like) or taking part in any activity which is entertaining enough to one. मनबहलाव is doing anything that is engaging or amusing enough as a diversion, and तफरीह is any recreational activity.

2. All the nouns are + process and are not pluralized. They form APN with के साथ (for आमोद-प्रमोद and मनबहलाव) or का (for मनोरंजन) except आमोद and तफरीह which do not take N post.

3. **के साथ आमोद-प्रमोद कर—"to divert oneself with"**

काम से छुट्टी पाने पर थकावट मिटाने के लिए बोतल, प्याला और व्यक्ति-विशेष के साथ थोड़े समय तक आमोद-प्रमोद कर लेना ही उसके लिये पर्याप्त था। (कंकाल, 153)

4. **आमोद कर—"to do as it pleases one"**

मिलजुल कर रहना, खाना-पीना और आमोद करना यही उनका काम था। (बूंद, 31)

5. **का मनोरंजन कर—"to entertain"**

तीन दिन तक पहाड़ी नर-नारियां बराबर संगीत और नृत्य द्वारा अपना और अन्य दर्शकों का मनोरंजन करती हैं। (डगर, 31)

का मनोरंजन कर—"to entertain, to amuse"

...इसका प्रयोग करके अपना तथा मित्रों का मनोरंजन करो। (बाल, 1-27)

मनोरंजन कर—"to rejoice"

जीवन-भर ताई को छेड़कर उनकी गालियों से अपना मनोरंजन करने वाले बच्चे बूढ़े-जवान अंतिम बार ताई के साथ चले जा रहे थे। (बूंद, 566)

का मनोरंजन कर—"to entertain"

दिन पर दिन अकबर और बीरबल की घनिष्टता बढ़ती गई। क्यों कि बीरबल अपनी वाक्यपटुता से हमेशा बादशाह का मनोरंजन करते थे। (बाल, 1)

...मनोरंजन करने के लिये—"for fun, for the entertainment of"

मैंने जानबूझ कर मनोरंजन करने के लिए या धोखा देने के लिए किसी को पापी और किसी को पुण्यआत्मा नहीं बनाया है। (सन्यासी, 10)

6. **के साथ मनबहलाव कर—"to divert oneself with"**

आखिर में किसके साथ चंद मिनट मन-बहलाव करूं, यह निश्चय न हो सका। (होली, 1)

7. **तफरीह कर—"to enjoy oneself, to recreate"**

...वे जो वहां आने वालों के लिए तफरीह का सामान प्रस्तुत करते हैं, और वे जो दूसरों को तफरीह करते देखकर लुत्फ ले लेते हैं। (जानवर, 123)

67. आत्मसंकीर्तन, आत्मश्लाघा, गुणगान, बखान, स्तुति, वाह-वाह

1. All these nouns refer to the modalities of expression of praise. आत्मसंकीर्तन is self-glorification through the use of such sentences as involve the occurrence of one's own name repeatedly (with reference to statements of one's own accomplishments. आत्मश्लाघा is applied to an exaggerated reference of one's own or someone else's quality or qualities. गुणगान is talking about the praiseworthy qualities of someone (generally with a motive) or of oneself (as if one were singing a song). बखान is relating repetitiously the pleasing qualities or characteristics of someone. The term may be used as a dignified reference to someone's profuse abuse to another in public. स्तुति is singing religious praises in order to perform worship, and वाह-वाह (which is lit. using the interjectional

particle वाह more than once) is public approbation implying a degree of pleasure and satisfaction. The term usually contains a somewhat slighting reference to the one expressing approbation because it carries a strong implication of being impulsive.

2. All the nouns are +process, and are not pluralized. They all form ANP with की (का for गुणगान and बखान) with the exception that वाह-वाह may also occur with पर. आत्म in आत्मसंकीर्तन and आत्मश्लाघा is equivalent to अपना "one's own" and is idiomatic in these compounds.

3. आत्मसंकीर्तन कर—"to indulge in self-glorification"

यदि वह (कला और जीवन) मिलकर बैठते हैं तो बड़े कलह-प्रिय, बिगड़कर उठते हैं तो बड़े षड्यंत्रकारी, यदि स्पर्द्धा करते तो बड़े छुआछूत-पसंद और आत्मसंकीर्तन करते हैं तो शास्त्रियों और प्रचारकों दोनों को मात देते हैं। (अमीर, 40-41)

4. आत्मश्लाघा कर—"to boast"

मातुल...मातुल का शरीर लोहे का बना है, लोहे का। आत्मश्लाघा नहीं करता। (आषाढ़, 68)

5. का गुणगान कर—"to extol"

वह सबके आगे अपने मुख से अपनी निंदा करके उस जन-नायक का गुणगान करने लगा। (आदर्श, 56)

का गुणगान कर—"to extol, to exaggeratedly speak of"

कन्या कहती रही—हम लोग अपनी महानता का गुणगान करते थकते नहीं और थकना भी नहीं चाहिए (बूंद, 471)

6. का बखान कर—"to praise, to talk repeatedly of"

उसने अपनी पड़ोसिनों से मैके का बखान करना छोड़ दिया। (सेवा, 29)

का बखान कर—"to praise, to relate"

नौकर, जिसे घरवालों से अधिक घर का दर्द था, जिसकी ईमानदारी का बखान उठते-बैठते पति-पत्नी करते रहते थे, जिसकी सचाई के बारे में गली-मुहल्ले, अड़ोस-पड़ोस जान-पहचान वाले सब सौगंध खा सकते थे। (दुग्गल, 45)

का बखान कर—"to abuse (in public as if to extol)"

मुंह में जो भी गालियां आतीं उन्हें देता हुआ रूप। शिया के पुरखों का बखान कर रहा था। (लाख, 246)

7. **की स्तुति कर—"to extol, to worship"**

उस वीर पुरुष की हम सब स्तुति करते हैं जो तीव्र गति वाला है। (वैदिक, 17)

की स्तुति कर—"to worship"

उसकी दृष्टी दाहिने गई तो पोर्ट ट्रस्ट की गुमटी के नीचे कुछ लोग समुद्र-स्नान कर रहे थे। एक पारसी पुरुष और दो स्त्रियां तट पर खड़ी समुद्र की स्तुति कर रही थीं। (जुहू, 7)

की स्तुति कर—"to sing the praises of, to worship"

उसके बाद दोनों ने अपनी-अपनी वीणा हाथ में लेकर, तान आलापकर देवी की स्तुति की। (शांतला, 63)

8. **पर वाह्-वाह् कर—"to applaud, to express one's approval"**

...और उनके प्रशंसक मानवता की इस निर्मम हत्या पर वाह-वाह करते रहे। (कहा, 96)

68. आग्रह, इसरार

1. Both the nouns refer to pressing someone into doing something or pressing a point to someone.

आग्रह stresses an urging usually by a superior, a man of experience or the like, normally (expected to be) taken into consideration more or less seriously.

इसरार is usually pressing a point implying a disregard of opposition, or assertion in the face of opposition. The term lacks the special implications of आग्रह in the sense that in the context where nothing is expressed to the contrary, it (i. e., इसरार) does not imply an intent to comply.

2. Both the nouns are +process, and are not pluralized. They form ANP with पर, का, से or के लिये. Only का and के लिये permit the occurrence of infinitives.

3. **पर आग्रह् कर—"to insist on"**

इसीलिये नाम विशेष पर आग्रह न करके अभिज्ञों ने...। (सुधा, 6)

पर आग्रह् कर—"to urge"

हमारे परिवार के उन्हीं शुभचिन्तक मित्र श्री केवलराम दवे ने, जिन्होंने मुझे इंगलैंड भिजवाया था, इस बात पर आग्रह किया कि मैं बम्बई में जाकर वकालत करूं। (गांधी, 78)

से आग्रह कर—"to plead with"

वे स्वयं उन सिद्धान्तों का प्रयोग करने के लिये व्यग्र थे। इसके लिए उन्होंने अपने समय के कई शासकों से आग्रह किया, परन्तु कोई भी तैयार नहीं हुआ। (आदर्श, 70)

के पास आग्रह कर—"to make an urgent request"

अतः आपका यह कर्त्तव्य है कि पक्की नालियां बनवाने के लिये पंचायत या स्वच्छता कमेटी के पास आप आग्रह कर सकते हैं। (स्वस्थ, 22)

के लिये बार-बार आग्रह कर—"to ask for repeatedly"

कन्नगी लौट पड़ी; शान्त स्वर में बोली, मैं धर्म से विवश हूं, नहीं तो इतनी-सी बात के लिए आपको बार-बार आग्रह न करना पड़ता। (सुहाग, 222)

आग्रह कर—"to insist that..."

मिस खुरशेद ने आग्रह किया—मुआमले को साफ करने के लिए उनका आप लोगों के सामने आना जरूरी है। एकतरफी फैसला आप क्यों करती हैं। (सम, 56)

4. पर इसरार कर—"to insist on"

बंगले में आया-बैरों से 'मेम साहब' और बाहर तमाम लोगों से मिसेज राजदान कहलाने पर वह इसरार करती है। (बूंद, 74-75)

के लिए इसरार कर—"to insist on"

आप बराबर यह जानने के लिए इसरार करते ही रहे कि आखिर मियां घर-बार छोड़कर इस तरह जा कहां रहे हैं। (तुला, 21)

बहुत इसरार करके—"pressing some one into"

सत्ती ने बहुत इसरार करके माणिक को रुपए दिए ताकि उनका काम न रुके और फिर बहुत बिलखकर रोयी। (सूरज, 95)

"Satti pressed Manik into taking the money so that his work was not hampered, and..."

इसरार कर—"to persist in"

माणिक गये और सत्ती जितना इसरार करे जल्दी निकल चलने को कि कहीं महेसर दलाल या चमन ठाकुर न आ पहुंचें उतना माणिक किसी-न-किसी बहाने टालते जायें...। (सूरज, 97)

69. आयोजन, आयोजना, आयोजित, बन्दोबस्त, प्रबन्ध, इन्तजाम, व्यवस्था

1. These terms refer to the act of taking steps in order to bring together (one or more) individuals or parts in a whole as may be called for, or to a given end.

आयोजन refers to any event or activity involving an assemblage of people, and therefore takes as its object nouns denoting meeting, conference, a show, a performance or containing reference to a plot, a scheme or the like that requires elaborate planning and advance preparation (often with a set purpose). Sometimes the noun denoting the event or activity (as the object of आयोजन) may be replaced by an expression referring to the purpose, the noun in that case stresses the skill and contrivancy in the endeavor of the subject noun.

आयोजना (which is the feminine counterpart of आयोजन) may refer to one's faculty of contriving covertly a plan successfully executed or implemented, or it may refer to taking steps towards the accomplishment of one's objective (followed by के लिये) without any overt, formal or ceremonial public display.

आयोजित Is arranging by systematic planning and coordination or may have reference to the mode in which something is constituted.

बन्दोबस्त contains reference to the initial setup of an operation as a step to the implementation or execution of that which is planned or formulated. The term lacks the overt formal and ceremonial implications of आयोजन.

प्रबन्ध, though used interchangeably with इन्तजाम, stresses the subject's skill at devising or effectiveness in carrying out. The term, therefore, may sometimes imply an arranging for in advance (as a verbal agreement or the like), sometimes stressing the supervisory role of the subject noun.

इन्तजाम stresses the fact of doing the needful. It may be used to refer to things actually done by way of an arrangement (as opposed to something (to be) done as a verbal agreement).

व्यवस्था is either putting in a state of order by making a provision for or taking steps to provide for, stressing in both senses a reference to arriving at some conclusion (rather than to an implementation or a carrying out).

2. All the nouns are +process and form ANP with का (आयोजना and व्यवस्था with की), sometimes with के लिये. Both का and के लिये permit the occurrence of infinitives whereas only का occurs with nouns.

The noun आयोजन may be pluralized while referring to more than one sort or kind of event or activity. In that case the sentence usually contains expressions like कई प्रकार/तरह के आयोजित (being an adjective) is -process.

3. **के लिये आयोजन कर—"to endeavor, to strive"**

कन्या सारे हुल्लड़ की, सारे असंतोष को नियंत्रित कर उसे एक रचनात्मक रूप देने के लिए अद्भुत आयोजन कर रही थी । (बूंद, 386)

का आयोजन कर—"to arrange"

वेलफेयर बोर्ड की ओर से हर साल बेबी शो, महिला-शिल्प मेला, फ्लावर-शो के आयोजन किये जाते हैं। (दीर्घ, 13)

का आयोजन किया जा—"to have been planned"

महिपाल के घर आमंत्रित लोगों की भीड़ जुड़ने लगी । सेठ रूपरतन के विशाल लान में प्रीतिभोज का आयोजन किया गया था। (बूंद, 567)

का आयोजन कर—"to devise, to take part in"

बहुधा वह अपने साथियों के साथ उस प्रकार की प्रतियोगिताओं का आयोजन करता था। (परम, 14)

का आयोजन कर—"to be making preparations for, to be plotting"

ताई आज अपने पति पर मूठ चलाने का आयोजन कर रही थीं। प्रारम्भिक विधि हो जाने पर हंड़िया को कास (मन्त्र) से बांधने के लिये नन्दों ने ताई से कहा। (बूंद, 56 162)

का आयोजन कर—"to organize"

ये खबरें उन छोटे-छोटे गुटों की हैं जो गुप्त रहकर हिंसात्मक कार्यवाहियों का आयोजन करते हैं। (अमरीका, 24)

का आयोजन कर—"to plan"

डाक्टर...ने उद्घाटन भाषण दिया था। इस प्रदर्शिनी के लिए भी ऐसे ही उद्घाटन का आयोजन क्यों न किया जाय। (बूंद, 391)

4. **की आयोजना कर—"to be planning for"**

शीघ्र ही तू चन्द्रदीधिति और निपुणिका को लेकर मगध की ओर चला जा। मैं व्यवस्था किये देता हूं। जा चन्द्रदीधिति को मेरी ओर से आशीर्वाद कहना । मैं उसके निरापद

प्रस्थान की आयोजना कर रहा हूं। जब तक कोई व्यवस्था नहीं हो जाती, तब तक उसके देखने की व्याकुलता को मैं दबा रहा हूं। (बाण, 47)

5. **आयोजित कर—"to organize, to arrange to hold (a meeting)"**

अध्यापक को चाहिये कि ... उन गांव वालों की एक सभा आयोजित करे। (बुन, 43)

को आयोजित कर—"to constitute, to organize"

कर-प्रणाली को इस प्रकार आयोजित किया जाय कि इसका भार मुख्यत: धनिक वर्ग पर पड़े। (एमाई, 57)

6. **का बन्दोबस्त कर—"to provide a set up (for the care of)"**

75,000 वर्गमील से भी अधिक वनों का परिअंकन और बन्दोबस्त किया जायेगा। (लोक, 13)

का बन्दोबस्त कर—"after completing the arrangements for"

मगर मेवाड़ में लड़ाई को जारी रखने का बन्दोबस्त करके, फिर देखूंगा। (बीर, 79)

का बन्दोबस्त कर--"to arrange to find"

उधर की एक अच्छी गाय का बन्दोबस्त हमारे लिए कर दो। (दीपावली, 121)

का बन्दोबस्त कर—"to set up"

रानी साहब ! आपके ताल्लुके में नमूने के गांव बसाने का बन्दोबस्त किया जायगा। (तितली, 40)

7. **का प्रबन्ध कर—"to arrange"**

जिस दिन कार्य-क्रम का प्रबन्ध किया गया था उस दिन राजमहल जाने के पहले शांतला तथा लक्ष्मी ने स्नान किया...। (शांतला, 62)

का पूरा प्रबन्ध कर ले--"to make all the arrangements (in advance)"

उसी दिन से वह बेचारी पड़ी है। उधर सुना है कि तहसीलदार ने बेदखली कराने का पूरा प्रबन्ध कर लिया है। (तितली, 68)

का प्रबन्ध कर—"to superintend, to look after the arrangements for"

राज-कर्मचारीगण प्रजा की रक्षा से अधिक दो दिन बाद पधारने वाले महाराज के स्वागत के लिए अन्य दिशा में सजावट का प्रबन्ध कर रहे थे। (सुहाग, 280)

का प्रबन्ध कर—"to procure (the supply of), to be charged with the procurement of"

यह प्रादेशिक फेडरेशन सहकारी भट्टों के ईंधन के लिए कोयले के चूरे का प्रबन्ध करती है। (ईंट, 94)

का प्रबन्ध कर—"to manage (to get), to procure"

कपूर कुछ सूखी लकड़ियां बीन लाया। उर्मिला ने सूखा घास-फूस इकट्ठा किया। कागज़ के टुकड़े भी उसे मिल गए। मोहन ने दियासलाई का प्रबन्ध किया। (आग, 5-6)

का प्रबन्ध कर—"to make arrangements for"

मैं थोड़ी देर में तुम्हारे एकान्तवास का प्रबन्ध करता हूं। (कचनार, 191)

8. **का मुस्तकिल इंतजाम कर—"to make a permanent arrangement for"**

खैर, एक बात बतलाओ, यह तो मैं जानती हूं कि तुम मुझे कैप्टेन राजदान की तरह अपने घर में नहीं रक्खोगे; सेवाय में मेरा मुस्तकिल इन्तज़ाम कर दोगे ? (बूंद, 354)

दूसरा इन्तजाम कर—"to make some other arrangement"

आप अगर मन लगाकर ठीक तरह से पाठ नहीं कर सकते तो कल से मैं दूसरा इन्तजाम कर लूंगा। नहीं धर्मावतार...। (बूंद, 166)

का इंतजाम कर दे—"to provide"

हम लोगों के लिए रोटी, फल और अनाज का इंतजाम कर दीजिए। (रूस, 12)

9. **की व्यवस्था कर—"to arrange for (on one's own), to have (one's own) arrangements for"**

इनके लिये किसान को अधिक धन खर्च करना पड़ता है और बाहर से मंगवाने की व्यवस्था भी करनी पड़ती है। (खाद, 14)

की व्यवस्था कर—"to arrange"

मैं योग्य वर से तुम्हारे विवाह की व्यवस्था करूंगा। (फूलो, 96)

की व्यवस्था कर—"to provide for"

रही लड़की की सुरक्षा की बात सो मैं इतना जानता हूं कि यदि मैं कन्नगी से कह जाऊंगा तो वह निश्चय ही इसे पाल-पोसकर बड़ा करने और इसकी भविष्य की सुखद सात्त्विक व्यवस्था कर लेने तक सती न होगी। (सुहाग, 214)

की व्यवस्था कर—"to provide for the care of"

आधुनिक राज्यवृद्ध, निर्धन, बेकार और अपाहिज नागरिकों की भी व्यवस्था करने लगा है। उनको आर्थिक सहायता दी जाती है। (भारत, 31)

की व्यवस्था कर—"to make a provision for, to provide the N for"

भारत सरकार ने द्वितीय पंचवर्षीय योजना में 2100 मातृत्व कल्याण तथा शिशु स्वास्थ्य केन्द्र खोलने के लिए 3 करोड़ रुपये की व्यवस्था की है। (भारत, 15)

की जीवन-व्यवस्था कर—"to run the life or lives of"

...आज अपनी शादी हो, कल से सारी दुनिया के नर-नारियों की जीवन-व्यवस्था करने में लग जावें, यह स्त्री स्वभाव ही है कि पुरुष के जीवन के लिए वह निरंतर सांचे बनाती चले। (नदी, 320)

70. सम्मान, सम्मानित, मान, आदर, समादर, अदब, कदर, इज्जत, मान-सम्मान, आदर-सम्मान

1. All the terms refer to the pliancy in the disposition or conduct of one who is so disposed to someone or takes such a view of something.

सम्मान stresses the degree of esteem or respect by virtue of one's own dispositional preference or liking or due to some achievement, excellence, status or the like of the object.

सम्मानित is a reference to ceremonial and formal public recognition accorded to one.

मान is the measure of estimation in which one is generally held. The term is applicable to the subject or the object. When applied to the subject it implies an attitude of arrogance.

आदर is feeling or having the feeling of recognition of someone's or something's worth or worthiness.

समादर applies to the act of taking cognizance of someone (by one in authority) as a formal show of courtesy.

अदब is conducting oneself in a decorous manner marked by a show of obeisance.

कदर is recognition of that which commends itself as worthy of appreciation or is worth appreciating.

इज्जत is observance of standards of decency or awareness of someone's dignity.

Both मान-सम्मान and आदर-सम्मान respectively refer to observance of the norms of social etiquette and someone's personal dignity.

2. All nouns are + process, with the exception of सम्मान(सम्मानित being its-process counterpart). They are not pluralized. They form ANP with का (की for कदर and इज्जत). Only मान also occurs with पर (in the sense of being over-bearingly haughty) and with से (in the sense of being arrogant).

3. का सम्मान कर—"to show reverence to"

नहीं, तू भर ले, मैंने यह सोचकर कहा था कि शायद वह मेरे सफेद बालों का सम्मान कर रही है। (जानवर, 71)

का सम्मान कर—"to regard with profound respect"

वह अपने चाचा का बड़ा सम्मान करता था। (सेवा, 63)

का सम्मान कर—"to honor"

इसी अलेगजेंडर ने पेन्सलीन का आविष्कार किया। समस्त विश्व ने उसका सम्मान किया। (बाल, 1-25)

का सम्मान कर—"to treat with due appreciation and regard"

सम्राट् चन्द्रगुप्त द्वितीय स्वयं संस्कृत का विद्वान् और साहित्य का रसिक था तथा विद्वानों का सम्मान करता था। (ज्योति, 19)

का सम्मान कर—"to show deference to"

शायद वह बाहर का कमरा मेरे-जैसे सीधे-साधे विद्यार्थी को ही देती होगी जो बुढ़ियों का सम्मान करता होगा। (राह, 72)

का सम्मान कर—"to venerate, to admire, to be a great admirer of, to value highly"

स्वाधीनता का मैं खूब सम्मान करता हूं और यूरोप से लौटकर मुक्त रहने का महत्त्व और भी समझने लगा हूं। (नदी, 79)

का सम्मान कर—"to venerate, to revere"

आज जो डाकू और हत्यारे भी उनके चरण छूते हैं क्या वे किसी प्रकार का भय खाते हैं ? इस नब्बे पौंड के सूखे शरीर वाले व्यक्ति में ऐसा क्या है कि लोग उसका इतना सम्मान करते हैं। भारत, 77)

का सम्मान कर—"to honor, to pay homage to"

इसलिए आज उज्जयिनी का राज्य ऋतुसंहार के लेखक का सम्मान करना और उन्हें राजकवि का आसन देना चाहता है। (आषाढ़, 20)

का सम्मान कर—"to give due recognition to"

जो अमरीकी दूसरों के अधिकारों का सम्मान करता है उसकी स्वतंत्रता इस कानून से प्रभावित नहीं होती। (अमरीका, 21)

का सम्मान कर—"to value, to esteem, to give due recognition to"

अगर हम वैयक्तिक उद्यम को नहीं जगाते, अगर हम वैयक्तिक उपलब्धि का सम्मान नहीं करते तो हम परिवर्तन के दास ही रहेंगे, स्वामी नहीं बन सकेंगे। (अमरीका, 44)

"If we do not arouse the spirit of personal enterprise, if we do not value the spirit of individual accomplishment. . . ."

4. **को सम्मानित कर—"to honor"**

पति के स्वर्गवास के उपरांत महादेवी अक्क ने गंगराज को महासचिव के पद पर चढ़ाकर सम्मानित किया। (शांतला, 22)

को सम्मानित कर—"to honor"

यह कहकर सिकंदर ने उस चित्रकार को यथेष्ट पुरस्कार देकर सम्मानित किया। (आदर्श, 46)

को सम्मानित कर—"to accord recognition to"

माना कि देरी से किये जाने वाले इस कर्तव्य-पालन में पीढ़ियां उन्हें गौरव के हारों से सम्मानित नहीं करेंगी किंतु यह सन्तोष तो बुढ़ापे में होगा ही कि हमने अपनी भयंकर भूल का परिमार्जन किया। (अमीर, 33-34)

5. **का मान कर—"to hold one in high esteem"**

वह दिन रात इसी सोच-विचार में रहता था कि कोई ऐसी तरकीब करनी चाहिए कि सब पशुपक्षी उसे जंगल का राजा कहने लगें और इस प्रकार सब उसका मान करने लगें। (बाल, 11-21)

का मान कर—"to show appreciation for, to think much of"

अब मुझे मालूम होता है कि मैं ही उसके घर से निकलने का कारण हुआ, मैं उसकी सुन्दरता का मान न कर सका, इसलिए सुमन का भी मुझ से प्रेम नहीं हो सका। (सेवा, 162)

का मान कर—"to have regard for"

बाप का भी वह इतना मान न करता था। (मानसरोवर, 149)

का मान कर—"to be highly regarded"

...इतने वर्षों से ये ऐसी ही बातें कहते और लिखते हैं, छापे और सभाओं की दुनिया इनका मान करती है, फिर भी संसार अपनी सनातन लीकपर ही चला जाता है, (बूंद, 108)

थोड़ा मान करते हुए—"with a touch of arrogance"

हां, हमें मिस्टर लाल से इस बात की सख्त शिकायत है कि पड़ोस में रहते हैं और कभी हमारे यहां झांकते भी नहीं। तारा ने थोड़ा मान करते हुए कहा। (बूंद, 71)

मान कर—"to conduct oneself overbearingly"

उसे बार-बार अपने मान करने पर पछतावा होता था। (सेवा, 296)

"She regretted again and again her overbearing conduct."

से मान कर—"to treat one with insolence"

हा ! मैंने अपने स्वामी से मान किया, मैंने अपने आराध्य देव का निरादर किया, मैंने अपने कुटिल स्वार्थ के वश होकर उनका अपमान किया। (सेवा, 296)

मान किये रह—"to be overbearingly haughty"

धरती धूप की मुस्कराहट के लिए प्रतीक्षा में आकुल हो जाती पर बादल नवोढ़ा माननी की भांति मान किये रहते। (फूलो, 10)

6. **का आदर कर—"to show appreciation, to recognize"**

यदि तुम्हारे मित्र हैं, तो संभवत: वे अपने स्वभाव की नीचता के कारण तुम्हारे गुणों का आदर न करके तुमसे विरक्त रहते हैं। (भारक, 45)

का आदर कर—"to hold one in high regard"

मेरे घर वाले भी तुम्हारा स्वागत करेंगे और तुम्हारे त्याग के लिए न केवल तुम्हारा आदर करेंगे, वरन् मैं और वे इसकी प्रतिपूर्ति करने में कुछ उठा न रखेंगे। (धारा, 187)

का आदर कर—"to show appreciation for, to appreciate"

जो इस रहस्य को ध्यान में रखते हैं वे वर्तमान जीवन के मूल्यों का आदर कर सकते हैं। (धर्म, 139)

का आदर कर—"to respect"

हमें छत्रपति से स्पष्ट कह देना है कि उनके सिपाही यदि अपनी मित्र-रियास्तों की सीमा का आदर न करेंगे तो यह स्वराज्य के लिए अनुचित होगा। (बेटी, 35)

का आदर कर—"to respect, to abide by, to show obeisance to"

राजा सातवाहन देवी के आदेशों का आदर करेंगे।

का आदर कर—"to respect, to abide by"

वह गांव के सदस्यों के आपसी झगड़े निपटाता है और गांववाले उसके फैसले का आदर करते हैं। (भारत, 73)

का आदर कर—"to respect, to acknowledge, to show consideration for"

वहां लोग मनुष्यता नहीं देखते, बल्कि उसकी कुर्सी का आदर करते हैं। (कथा, 16)

का आदर कर—"to recognize"

अपने देश में लोग स्वास्थ्य सम्बन्धी सिद्धान्तों का आदर तो करते हैं परन्तु अज्ञान, भ्रम और आलस्य के कारण उनका उचित रूप से पालन नहीं कर पाते। (स्वस्थ, 1)

का आदर कर—"to respect"

...अष्ट-प्रधान भी शिवा जी की इच्छा का आदर करते किन्तु दुष्ट गायकवाड़ के साथी सरदार नीलो जी और दादा जी प्रभु के कान भरने से सरे नौबत प्रतापराव गूजर ने युद्ध का ही अनुरोध किया। (बेटी, 46)

7. **का समादर कर—"to recognize, to pay homage to"**

नागरिक, वणिक, जैन व्यापारी आदि ऐसे बहुत से लोग थे जिनका समादर करना बाकी रह गया था। (शांतला, 50)

8. **का अदब कर—"to show obeisance, to treat respectfully or with deference"**

इसीलिए बहुएं अपनी सास का अदब करती हैं। (बूंद, 2)

का अदब कर—"to regard with veneration"

मैं बच्चा समझकर ही आप पर और अब अपनी बहूरानी साहबा पर भी हक रखता हूं, मगर चूंकि नमक खाता हूं इसलिए मालिक का अदब करता हूं। (बूंद, 442)

9. **की कद्र कर—"to have a sense of appreciation, to show one's appreciation"**

आप क्या हिन्दी के पाठकों की आदत से परिचित नहीं कि वे किसी भले आदमी की कद्र नहीं करते। (कहा, 68)

की कद्र कर—"to admire"

तुम जिन घरेलू जिम्मेदारियों की वजह से इतना बड़ा त्याग कर रहे हो मैं उनकी कद्र करती हूं। तुम अच्छी तरह जानते हो कि मैं कल्याणी की भी कद्र करती हूं। (बूंद, 492)

की कद्र कर—"to admire, to hold one in high esteem"

वह निराला की बड़ी कद्र करते थे। (अपनी खबर, 16)

की कद्र कर ले—"to show some appreciation"

लेकिन हमारे दोस्तों के आगे तो कभी-कभी हमारी कद्र कर लिया करें, इतना तक उनसे नहीं हो पाता। (सच, 33)

10. **की इज्जत कर—"to praise, to commend"**

दूसरे वालंटियरों ने भी आपको यही यकीन दिलाया कि लाटसाहब ने आपकी बड़ी इज्जत की है। (तुला, 66)

की इज्जत कर—"to treat with respect, to treat one nicely"

देखिये साहब, और बातें बाद में कीजिएगा, पहले इस लड़की को थोड़ी तमीज़ सिखाइये। बड़े भाई की यंह इज्जत करना नहीं जानती,...कह रही थी कि आप काफी में चीनी की जगह नमक पीते हैं। मैंने मना किया तो मुझ पर बिगड़ने लगी। (आकाश, 21)

की इज्जत कर—"to have (some degree) of regard for"

उसने कहा—शीला की मैं इज्जत करता हूं मगर कन्या को उसके मुकाबिले में लाने के लिए हर्गिज तैयार नहीं। (बूंद, 252)

"He said : 'I have a regard for Sheila but I would not go so far as to put her (i. e. Sheila) on a par with Kanya."

11. **का मान-सम्मान कर—"to be mindful of social etiquette"**

मुझ-जैसी सुशिक्षित, समझदार, भले घर की, सबका मान-सम्मान करने वाली सद्-गृहस्थ पत्नी हर एक को मुश्किल से ही नसीब होगी। (कहा, 13)

12. **का आदर-सम्मान कर—"to conduct oneself in a dignified manner"**

मैं अब उस समय की बातों को सोचता हूं तो ऐसा मालूम होता है कि एक बड़े घर की बेटी से ब्याह करने में मैंने बड़ी भूल की और इससे बड़ी भूल यह थी कि ब्याह हो जाने पर उसका उचित आदर-सम्मान नहीं किया। (सेवा, 162)

"...that I did not conduct myself in a manner worthy of her dignity."

71. तिरस्कार, अवहेलना, उपेक्षा, अवमानना, अवज्ञा, नजरअंदाज, अनसुना, अनदेखा

1. All these nouns describe the disposition of one whose conduct is marked by a lack of complaisance, amenability or a marked show of indifference. Secondarily, the terms may suggest the speaker's disapproval of the subject's conduct.

तिरस्कार is taking upon oneself an unmoving disposition or having nothing to do with (anymore) often with a reason.

अवहेलना is remaining unresponsive or not responding in a manner that is called for.

उपेक्षा is applied to that which is not worth viewing, does not merit consideration, or is not worth paying attention to.

अवमानना is applied to that which is esteemed low implying a contempt of some accepted standard.

अवज्ञा stresses a disposition of heedlessness for that which is obvious but not worth taking notice of.

नजरअंदाज is taking on a disposition of not being overtly affected.

Both अनसुना and अनदेखा are not listening to and not seeing implying a disposition or an intent to avoid.

2. All nouns, with the exception of नजरअंदाज, अनसुना and अनदेखा are +process and form ANP with का or की. They are not pluralized.

3. **का तिरस्कार कर—"to disregard"**

...निर्वैयक्तिक हो सकना, निर्वैयक्तिक रूप से घृणा कर सकना, बिना दर्द के सब कुछ का तिरस्कार कर सकना—कितना अच्छा होगा वह । (नदी, 190)

का तिरस्कार कर—"to show indifference to, to ignore"

इसीलिए मैं मधु के साथ इतना घूमा, उसकी आंखों में आंखें डालकर उसकी बातें सुनीं, अपनी बनावटी सज्जनता द्वारा उसको उत्तेजित किया और फिर भी सिनेमा हाल में उसकी प्यार की इच्छा का तिरस्कार किया। (राह, 99)

का तिरस्कार कर—"to discard"

घोर कष्ट सहकर भी सहृदय तोते ने अपने प्रिय वृक्ष का तिरस्कार करके दूसरे का आश्रय लेना उचित नहीं समझा । (भारक, 93)

उपेक्षा से उसका तिरस्कार कर—"to disregard one imprudently"

शैला ने देखा कि एक ठोकर खाया हुआ हृदय अपनी दुरवस्था में उपेक्षा से उसका तिरस्कार कर रहा है । (तितली, 231)

का तिरस्कार कर—"to be devoid of"

उसके कदमों की तेज़ी राजदूतों की शिष्टता और विनम्रता का तिरस्कार कर रही थी। (बेटी, 37)

4. की अवहेलना कर—"to ignore"

राज्य आमतौर से समाज की प्रथाओं, रीति-रिवाजों और परम्पराओं का उल्लंघन नहीं करता।...साधारणतः राज्य इन सामाजिक संगठनों के अधिकारों की अवहेलना नहीं करता। (भारत, 29)

"....ordinarily the state does not ignore the claims of these social entities (or organizations)."

की अवहेलना कर—"to fail to maintain the standard of, to show a contempt for"

इन कविताओं में शैली की एकतानता है। सुरुचि, शिष्टता और सामाजिकता की अवहेलना की गई है। (कहा, 69)

की अवहेलना कर—"to fail to live up to, to treat with contempt"

भाभी भविष्य में कभी मैं तुम्हारे आदेशों की अवहेलना नहीं करूंगा। छोड़कर कभी भागूंगा नहीं, आजीवन साथ निभाऊंगा। (दुःख, 161)

"Dear sister (lit. sister-in-law), in the future (I promise) I'll never fail to live up to your expectations."

की अवहेलना कर—"to neglect, to show disregard for"

शान्ता अब मुंह से कोई ऐसा शब्द न निकालती, जिससे उनके पिता की आत्मा को दुःख हो, उनके जीवनकाल में वह कभी-कभी उसकी अवहेलना किया करती थी, पर अब वह अनुदार विचारों को हृदय में न आने देती थी। (सेवा, 238)

5. की उपेक्षा कर—"to overlook, to fail to appreciate, to omit any reference to"

अधिकांश हिन्दी वालों ने इस उपन्यास की उपेक्षा की थी। (सा सा, 30)

की उपेक्षा कर—"to neglect, to fail to observe or take into account"

किसी भी कला-कृति या प्रवृत्ति का मूल्यांकन करते समय यदि इनमें से एक भी पक्ष की उपेक्षा की गई तो वह समीक्षा एकांगी बन जाती है। (मूल्य, 146)

की उपेक्षा कर—"to slight"

कामिनी ने मेरी जो उपेक्षा की थी, उसके बदले में मैं एक अस्पष्ट प्रतिहिंसा के वशीभूत होकर एक दूसरी लड़की का जीवन बर्बाद करना चाहता था। (राह, 99)

की उपेक्षा कर—"to overlook, to fail to take due notice of, to omit"

उक्त मान्यताओं के कारण प्रतिष्ठित अर्थशास्त्री एक पूंजीवादी अर्थव्यवस्था की वास्तविक कठिनाइयों की उपेक्षा कर दिया करते थे। (एमाई, 30)

की उपेक्षा कर दे—"to ignore, to try to forget"

सेठानी और उसकी लड़की से डांट-फटकार सुनने के पश्चात् जगन्नाथ को लक्ष्मी और दूसरों से प्रशंसा पाकर अतीव प्रसन्नता और सान्त्वना मिलती और अपनी सेठानी को किसी छोटे कुल की समझ कर वह उसकी डांट-फटकार की उपेक्षा कर देता। (धारा, 219)

की उपेक्षा कर जा—"to neglect"

असीम की खोज में लगा चित्त प्रायः सीमा की उपेक्षा कर जाता है। (चारु, 189)

की उपेक्षा कर जा—"to neglect, to overlook"

मिट्टी के ग्राहक हीरे की उपेक्षा करते हैं। (चारु, 278)

की उपेक्षा करते हुए—"ignoring"

उत्तरीय कुछ लटक रहा है और एक हाथ से उसे पकड़ते हुए वेग से अन्दर आते हैं और अभ्यर्थना की उपेक्षा करते हुए बैठ जाते हैं। (कोणार्क, 37)

6. **की अवमानना कर—"to slight"**

फार्मों में बिजली पहुंचा कर, बाढ़ों का नियन्त्रण कर या बैंकों को फेल होने से रोककर क्या सरकार हमारी स्वतन्त्रता की अवमानना करती है। (अमरीका, 46)

7. **की अवज्ञा कर—"to ignore, to neglect to fulfill"**

मुख्य अधिष्ठाता की आज्ञा टल जाय मगर क्या मजाल कि कोई उसके हुक्म की अवज्ञा कर सके। (अच्छी, 2)

की अवज्ञा कर—"to overlook, to do some wrong through an oversight"

फिर गौरा की पीठ को देखते हुए उसे मानों ध्यान आया कि वह उसकी कुछ अवज्ञा कर गया है।—गौरा बात करने आयी थी। (नबी, 288)

की अवज्ञा करते हुए —"ignoring"

दुश्मन ने हमारे जवानों पर आग उगलना शुरु कर दिया, किन्तु मृत्युञ्जयी हवलदार मेजर पीरूसिंह आग की अवज्ञा करते हुए आगे बढ़ते रहे। (परम, 16)

8. **नजर अंदाज कर—"to overlook"**

अगर पैसा होता तो मेरा बड़ा से बड़ा पाप भी दुनियां नजर अंदाज कर जाती...। (बूंद, 218)

को नजर अंदाज कर—"to ignore, to avoid"

अविवेक और असंगति की उपेक्षा कर या यह कहना बेहतर होगा कि उन्हें नजरअंदाज कर एक कल्पित मनोजगत के सौंदर्य में डूबने की प्रवृत्ति...। (मूल्य, 22)

को नजरअंदाज कर—"to avoid"

तारा छोटी बड़ी तीनों अपनी तरफ उठती हुई मर्दानी नज़रों को नजरअंदाज कर और जनाने फैशन पर निगाह दौड़ाती हुई धीरे-धीरे आगे बढ़ रही थीं। (बंद, 72)

को नजरअंदाज करते हुए—"ignoring"

लाला जानकीसरन यह समझते हुए भी कि कर्नल ने बात की आड़ में चोट की है उसे नज़रअंदाज करते हुए बोले...। (बूंद, 335)

9. **अनसुना कर दे—"to pay no attention to"**

मुरारी बाबू ने बात अनसुनी कर दी थी। (मांस, 61)

अनसुनी करते हुए—"to avoid a reference to"

भुवन ने अंतिम बात को अनसुनी करते हुए कहा...। (नदी, 28)

10. **अनदेखी कर जा—"to tend to take no notice of, to miss (through inattention)"**

किन्तु गरज के बावले मनुष्य देखकर भी अनदेखी कर जाते हैं। (सेवा, 196)

को अनदेखा करता रह—"to fail to perceive"

इस प्रत्यक्ष सत्य को समाज न जाने कैसे अनदेखा करता रहा है। (म, 146)

को अनदेखा न कर सक—"to fail to observe"

कोटा के जीवन में यह परिवर्तन इतना उजागर और प्रकट है कि कोई भी यात्री इसके प्रभाव को अनदेखा नहीं कर सकता। (राजवि, 24)

72. संकलन, संकलित, संचय, संचित, संग्रह, एकत्रित, एकत्र, इकट्ठा, जमा

1. All these nouns and adjectives refer to bringing and/or putting together in a variety of ways objects—individuals or things—both mass and count.

Both संकलन and संकलित imply the exercise of care and judgement. The expressions take as their object nouns—generic or abstract—having a representational or informational character about specific or concrete things they stand for. Therefore they imply a selection of that which is relevant, pertinent to the objective, and, if none, then as a matter of personal preference.

Both संचय and संचित imply a laying away of things—valuable, useful, or cherished—usually referred to by their abstract or generic designations or by a reference to their characteristics. The terms strongly suggest increase or growing greater with gradual accumulation.

In technical language, the terms may be applied to refer to storing of chemicals or other similar products (other than raw materials) over a length of time.

संग्रह refers to putting or bringing together things (i. e. both count and mass nouns) in a limited number or quantity, stressing the manner in which they are put or brought together. The noun, when not accompanied by an explicit statement of the manner (or unless the object-noun contains a reference to the manner in which its individual members are related to each other) always implies individuals or entities successively put together in a non-random fashion.

ऐकत्रित stresses a putting or bringing together in a location individuals or entities implying a unity of function or purpose.

एकत्र is putting or bringing together in a location individuals or entities, suggesting a gathering or forming into a mass.

इकट्ठा applies to bringing together individuals or entities from different locations or sources, or the same thing more than once from one and the same source or different sources.

जमा is a reference to togetherness which is subject to stipulation or qualification in terms of a stated mass, quantity or number of individuals or entities, usually implying a purpose.

2. The nouns संकलन, संचय and संग्रह are ±process, the rest being adjectives are −process. The three nouns form ANP with का and are not pluralized.

3. **का संकलन कर—"to cull"**

मंगलदेव कुछ कहता था और विजय बड़ी उत्सुकता से सुनते हुए अपना आदर्श संकलन करता। (कंकाल, 61)

4. **संकलित कर—"to compile"**

उन्हीं के आधार पर आगे की सूचना संकलित की गई है। (ईंट, 86)

संकलित कर—"to put together (with care), to collect"

मनोविज्ञान उनका जीवन भर अध्ययन तथा मनन का विषय रहा है और यह पुस्तक उनके जीवनभर के अध्ययन तथा प्रयोगों का सार है जो उन्होंने अब तक संकलित किए हैं। (चमत्कार, दो शब्द)

5. **का संचय कर—"to rally"**

सामुदायिक विकास आन्दोलन द्वारा प्रत्येक गांव की समूची जनता की शक्ति का संचय किया जाता है और इसकी जनशक्ति तथा अन्य साधनों का प्रभावशाली ढंग से प्रयोग किया जाता है। (सामुदा, 8)

का संचय कर—"to accumulate"

...स्वर्ग में जाकर मनुष्य अपने पूर्व कर्मों का फल ही भोगता है, कोई नया कर्म करके आगे के लिये पुण्य का संचय नहीं कर सकता। (भारक, 39)

का संचय कर—"to amass needlessly"

साधन पथ पर साधक को जीवन-निर्वाह के अतिरिक्त अन्य वस्तुओं का संचय नहीं करना चाहिए। (धर्म, 130)

का संचय कर—"to store"

अत: शुष्क स्थान पर इसका संचय करना चाहिए नहीं तो इसके बड़े-बड़े ढेले बन जाते हैं। इस कारण इसके प्रयोग में कठिनाई होती है। (खाद, 86)

संचय कर—"to save (for future use), to collect"

मघा का जल संचय करना है। (कंकाल, 93)

6. **संचित कर—"to store (over a long period of time)"**

इन दोनों परिवर्तनों में भी कैलसियम सायनामाइड के भार तथा आयतन में वृद्धि होती है। एक वर्ष से अधिक समय तक संचित किये गये कैलसियम सायनामाइड में खराबी होने से डाई सायनों डाइनएमाइड बनता है...। (खाद, 111-12)

संचित कर—"to conserve"

व्यवहारजगत केवल कार्य से सम्बन्ध रखता है, बुद्धि कार्य के स्थूल ज्ञान से लेकर उसे जन्म देनेवाले सूक्ष्म विचार तक जानती है और हृदय तज्जनित सुख-दुःख से लेकर स्वप्न-कल्पना तक की अनुभूतियां संचित करता है । (साहित्यकार, 32)

7. **का संग्रह कर—"to collect, to gather"**

जिन तरीकों से एक विज्ञान इन वास्तविक तथ्यों का संग्रह करता है, उनका वर्गीकरण करता है...। (सामाजिक, 62)

का संग्रह कर—"to gather"

वर्मा की बात काट कर महिपाल बोला—सामाजिक क्रांति लाने वालों को पहले अपनी परम्पराओं का संग्रह तो कर लेना चाहिये, फिर उन्हें समझ कर उनके अच्छे-बुरे को छांटेंगे। (बूंद, 415)

का संग्रह कर—"to gather, to muster together"

आज का शिक्षक अथवा उपदेशक यदि वास्तव में समुन्नत सभ्यता के समीप मानव समुदाय को पहुंचाना चाहता है तो उसे जीवन में जीवैक्य भाव की स्थापना करनी होगी, समस्त सद्विचारों और सद्भावनाओं का संग्रह करना होगा और नवीन संतति को भी दीक्षा देनी होगी । (धर्म, 34)

का संग्रह कर—"to preserve, to store"

सोडियम नाइट्रेट की भांति यह प्रक्लेद्य पदार्थ है। इसलिए वायु-रोधक बोरों में इसका संग्रह करते हैं। (खाद, 96)

का संग्रह कर—"to take down (readings)

वहां पर नाना प्रकार के रेडियो और विद्युत् यंत्रों से घिरे हुए वे तीनों निरंतर प्रयोग करते थे, अनुलेखों का संग्रह करते थे और केन्द्रित रेडियो रश्मियों द्वारा अदृश्य चीजों को पहचानने के नये आविष्कार को सम्पूर्ण सफल और व्यावहारिक बनाने के काम में योग देते थे। (नदी, 333)

संग्रह कर—"to gather"

भारत में अंग्रेजी राज का शुरू का इतिहास ज़ियादातर ईस्ट इन्डिया कम्पनी की रिपोर्टों और कागजों से ही संग्रह करना पड़ता है...। (सुन्दर, 4)

संग्रह कर—"to preserve"

पहले लोग सोना चांदी के रूप में धन संग्रह करते थे लेकिन आजकल शिक्षा के

प्रसार, बेंकिग प्रणाली आदि के कारण बेंक जमाओं के रूप में धन का संचय बढ़ता जा रहा है तथा सोने चांदी के रूप में धन संचय की प्रवृत्ति घटती जा रही है। (एमाई, 77-78)

संग्रह कर--"to muster"

...मगर मामी जी की बड़ी-बड़ी आंखों से बचने का साहस वह अभी संग्रह नहीं कर पाया था। (जुहू, 15)

संग्रह कर—"to collect"

इस कमरे में तो आपने अपने ही धर्म के चार नमूने संग्रह किये हैं। अन्य धर्मों और देशों की प्रेमिकाओं के नमूने संग्रह करना बाकी ही है। (हास्य, 80)

8. **एकत्रित कर—"to assemble"**

बच्चों को फिर एक जगह एकत्रित करके उनको सुदंर गीत सुनाती है और उपदेश देती है। वह सोचती है—आज के बच्चे कल के नागरिक हैं। (शबरी, 29)

एकत्रित कर—"to collect, to assemble"

सामाजिक मानवशास्त्री पहले अपने अध्ययन-क्षेत्र को चुनता है और फिर उस क्षेत्र में जाकर प्रत्यक्ष अवलोकन द्वारा अपने अध्ययन-विषय से सम्बन्धित तथ्यों को एकत्रित करता है और उसी के आधार पर कुछ सामान्य निष्कर्षों को निकालता है। (सामाजिक, 62)

एकत्रित कर—"to amass"

कुछ राज्यों में व्यक्ति के आर्थिक कामों में बिल्कुल रोक टोक नहीं होती और वह चाहे जितना धन एकत्रित कर सकता है। (भारत, 33)

9. **एकत्र कर—"to be crowded together, to be rounded up"**

यहां पशु और मनुष्य में भेद नहीं। सब एक जगह बुरी तरह एकत्र किये गये हैं। कब किसकी बारी आवेगी, कौन कह सकता है। सुना है तुमने महंत का समाचार ? (तितली, 259)

एकत्र कर—"to amass"

प्रायः करों के द्वारा इतनी बड़ी राशि एकत्र करना सहज नहीं होता। अतः देश विदेश से ऋण लेना पड़ता है। (एमाई, 47)

एकत्र कर—"to collect (in a place)"

गजाधर जी आप अस्त्रों को एकत्र करें। (कोणार्क, 60)

एकत्र कर—"to muster"

कुछ भी हो में इसके लिए प्रमाण एकत्र करूंगी। मैं कुछ भी करूंगी इस अन्याय का प्रतिकार करूंगी। (बूंद, 502)

साहस एकत्र करके—"by bringing to bear (a degree of enthusiasm), to call forth"

वह शांत थी। इन्द्रदेव ने साहस एकत्र करके कहा—तब जैसी तुम्हारी इच्छा। (तितली, 113)

"Indradeva responded, trying to overcome his helplessness..."

10. **इकट्ठा कर—"to gather"**

मुझे जाने दो नहीं तो मैं हल्ला मचा कर तमाम मुहल्ले को इकट्ठा कर दूंगी। (मुक्ता, 32)

को इकट्ठा कर—"to attract"

पहले मैंने यह सोचा था कि ये भावुक और मूर्ख लोग हैं, जिन्होंने बहस करने तथा लौंडियों को इकट्ठा करने के लिये यह प्रपंच फैलाया है। (राह, 55)

को इकट्ठा कर—"to round up"

भेड़ों में अपने मालिक के पीछे-पीछे चलने की स्वाभाविक आदत होती है और भेड़पालक खेतों और चरागाहों में उनको इकट्ठा आदि करने में उनकी इस आदत से लाभ उ ाते हैं। (भेड़, 16)

को इकट्ठा कर—"to assemble, to conserve"

हताश होकर उसने अपने सैनिकों को एक जगह इकट्ठा कर लिया और असंख्य मराठा सेना पर प्रहार करने लगा। (बेटी, 57-58)

इकट्ठा कर—"to form in a pile, to press together"

नये गड्ढे खोदने पर जो मिट्टी निकलती है, उसको गड्ढे की लम्बाई के साथ इकट्ठा करते हैं ताकि चौड़ाई पर बैलगाड़ी के आने जाने में कोई बाधा न पड़े। (खाद, 43-44)

इकट्ठा कर—"to gather"

कपूर कुछ सूखी लकड़ियां बीन लाया। उर्मिला ने सूखा घास-फूस इकट्ठा किया। (आग, 5)

चंदा इकट्ठा कर—"to collect donations"

जब बाहर भेजी गई तो बाढ़-पीड़ितों के लिए चंदा इकट्ठा किया और कपड़े की दुकान में कर्ज चुकता किया। (ढोल, 92)

इकट्ठा करके धर दे—"to pile up"

और मैं भी जब तुम्हारे पास आता हूं तो गांव भर का रोना मेरे सामने इकट्ठा करके धर देती हो। और मेरी कोई बात ही नहीं। (तितली, 125)

ताकत इकट्ठी कर कह—"to assert oneself, to bring oneself to saying, to express oneself emphatically"

मैंने अपने जिस्म की तमाम ताकत जबान में इकट्ठी कर उनसे कहा—अब्बा मैं तो अभी पढ़ूंगी। (खत, 61)

11. **जमा कर दे—"to deposit"**

मैं तुम्हारी ओर से यह रुपया जमा कर दूंगा। (सा सा, 244)

जमा कर दे—"to deposit, to pile up"

तो यह वह तरीका था जिससे भारतवर्ष की अनेक देशी रियास्तों का शासन देशी राजाओं से छीन-छीन कर ब्रिटिश सत्ता के चंगुल में जमा कर दिया गया। (सुन्दर, 20)

जमा कर ले—"to pile up"

उसने मैदान के छोर पर ढलान के पास ढंग से पत्थर जमा कर लिये थे। (वे दिन, 117)

(खाते में) जमा कर दे—"to enter (in the account), to deposit"

यदि एक व्यक्ति के खाते में से रुपया निकाला जाता है, तो यह दूसरे व्यक्ति के खाते में जमा कर दिया जाता है। (एमाई, 79)

जमा कर ले—"to accumulate, to save"

उन्होने काशी में नया बंगला बना लिया और कई हजार रुपये भी जमा कर लिए। (नट्टु, 50)

जमा कर—"to save"

उसने कई बार कहा था मक्खन निहाल के लिए जमा करना चाहिए। मक्खन का घी बनाकर लड़के को भिजवाना चाहिए। (दुग्गल, 123)

जमा कर रख--"to be piled up"

कोई काम की चीज़ नहीं सब अल्लम-गल्लम जमा कर रखा है—सब कबाड़ी को दे डालो। मैंने उन्हें प्रभावित करने के लिए ताश के पत्तों का जादू दिखलाया। (परिंदे, 16)

73. समर्थन, अनुमोदन, पुष्टि, पुष्ट, तस्दीक, ताईद

1. All these nouns refer to having or taking upon oneself a disposition or attitude (implying a viewing with favor) that serves, promotes or contributes directly or indirectly to the cause of the other.

समर्थन refers to acts (indicative of or amounting to exercising one's judgement) which directly contribute to a cause promoted by some individual or group, or to such conditions, situations etc. (which in someone's judgement) as are conducive or affirmatory to some trend or something proposed. The term, since it involves a choosing between two or more alternatives, may in some contexts suggest partisanship on the part of the subject noun or his opposition to a contrary view.

अनुमोदन is being in accord with or consenting to something that commends itself or meets with approval.

तस्दीक is that which serves to confirm the truth, validity or genuineness of something stated or presented. The term always implies a comparison or a seeking correspondence between.

पुष्टि (lit. nutrient value) in this context refers to anything that is affirmatory by its vindicatory or sustaining nature.

पुष्ट is serving to have a strengthening or reinforcing-influence.

ताईद is concurring with an opinion, implying affirmation of it or lending support to someone.

2. All the nouns are +process (पुष्ट is-process counterpart of पुष्टि) and form ANP with का (for समर्थन and अनुमोदन and the rest with की). They are not pluralized.

3. **का समर्थन कर**

व्यष्टिवादियों ने निम्नलिखित तीन विभिन्न दृष्टिकोणों से तर्क देकर अपने पक्ष का समर्थन किया है। (भारत, 22)

का समर्थन कर—"to give backing to, to uphold (i.e. by agreeing with)"

सोचा, जिन सामाजिक रीतियों के कारण कुमार जैसे शिक्षित मनुष्य को पीड़ा

पहुंचती है, उनका समर्थन करके वस्तुतः ज्ञान की ओर बढ़ने का उसने विरोध किया है,...। (निरु, 85)

का समर्थन कर दे—"to express one's assent to"

...रेणुका सिर्फ हुंकारी देकर शिवा की बात का समर्थन कर देती। (लाख, 45)

का समर्थन कर—"to endorse unanimously, to give unanimous endorsement to"

सेलेक्शन कमेटी के सदस्यों ने सर्वसम्मति से मिसेस बनर्जी के नाम का समर्थन किया। (दीर्घ, 15)

का समर्थन-सा कर—"to tacitly justify or support the use of, to try to vindicate"

अनुशासनहीनता और हिंसा की बहुत ही दबी जबान से शाब्दिक निन्दा करते हुए भी उन्होंने प्रकारान्तर से बंगाल की हिंसा का समर्थन-सा किया। (दिनमान, 2-23)

का समर्थन कर—"to support"

आपने कहा कि हमारे देश में भी दलों की संख्या में निरंतर वृद्धि होने के कारण महा निर्वाचनों में मतदाताओं के समक्ष उलझन पैदा हो जाती है, इसलिए मतदाता हड़बड़ी में केवल सत्तारूढ़ दल के प्रत्याशियों का समर्थन कर बैठता है। (आज, 3)

का समर्थन कर—"to advocate"

कामिनी ने उस दिन जिन आदर्शों का समर्थन किया था उन्हीं के विपरीत अपने को सिद्ध करने की मैं कोशिश कर रहा था। (राह, 29)

का समर्थन कर—"to back, to quote scriptures in favor of"

...परन्तु इस मार्ग के अपूर्ण और अधकचरे अनुयायी जब किसी व्यसन में लिप्त हो जाते हैं तब वे विज्ञान और तर्क विवाद की सहायता से अपने व्यसनों का शास्त्रोक्त समर्थन करके उस सम्पूर्ण मार्ग को बदनाम कर देते हैं। (कचनार 238)

का समर्थन कर—"to sanction"

गौरा इसे स्पष्ट अन्याय समझती है, पर क्या माता पिता की इच्छा पर अपने को उत्सर्ग कर देना भी एक रास्ता नहीं है ? सारी परंपरा तो इसीका समर्थन करती है कि यही रास्ता है...। (नदी, 75)

का समर्थन कर—"to support, to champion"

19वीं शताब्दी में जान स्टुअर्ट मिल, हर्बर्ट स्पेंसर...तथा माल्थस ने इंगलैंड में व्यष्टि-वाद का जबर्दस्त समर्थन किया। (भारत, 21)

4. **का अनुमोदन कर—"to recommend"**

वास्तव में गृहस्थ न होकर भी मैं वही सब तो करता हूं जो एक संसारी करता है... यद्यपि प्राचीन आर्यों की धर्म नीति में इसीलिये कुटीचर और एकान्तवासियों का ही अनुमोदन किया है; परन्तु संघबद्ध होकर बौद्धधर्म ने जो यह अपना कूड़ा छोड़ दिया है, उसे भारत के सम्प्रदाय अभी भी फेंक नहीं सकते। (कंकाल, 18)

का अनुमोदन कर—"to agree with"

मिस्टर भंडारी सम्भ्रांत अतिथि की हर बात का अनुमोदन कर रहे थे। (जानवर. 103)

अनुमोदन कर—"to approve"

उसी डाक में बंगलौर से पत्र आया कि उसका थीसिस स्वीकृत हुआ है और डाक्टरेट प्रदान करने का अनुमोदन किया गया है। अगले कनवोकेशन में उसे डिगरी मिल जायगी। (नदी, 77)

अनुमोदन कर—"to favor"

पर क्या भुवन दुःख को इष्ट मानता है? क्या रेखा भी वैसा मानती है। विराट् अनुभूति के प्रति खुले रहने का ही क्या वे अनुमोदन नहीं करते विराट् के प्रति समर्पित होने का? (नदी, 44)

का अनुमोदन कर—"to conform to"

इसलिए हम रंगमंच के चाहे जो वर्गीकरण करें और नाट्यसाहित्य के मार्ग निर्धारित करने के लिये चाहे जिन नियमों का प्रतिपादन करें, इन वर्गों और नियमों को सामाजिक परिस्थितियों और जनता की रुचि का अनुमोदन करना ही होगा। (कोणार्क, 108)

5. **की पुष्टि कर—"to speak in favor of"**

...वह कभी भीतर जाते हैं; कभी बाहर आते हैं। आज उनके परिश्रम और उत्साह की सीमा नहीं है। पद्मसिंह ने अपना प्रस्ताव उपस्थित किया और तुले हुए शब्दों में उसकी पुष्टि की। (सेवा, 266)

पुष्टि कर ले—"to verify, to confirm, to validate"

इस समय हमारे सिद्धान्त केवल अनुमानों पर आधारित हैं, लेकिन वैज्ञानिक तब तक चैन से नहीं बैठेंगे, जब तक वे इनकी निरीक्षणों द्वारा पुष्टि नहीं कर लेंगे। (श्रम, 36)

की पुष्टि कर—"to confirm, to corroborate"

ब्रह्मांड में नवजात यौवनपूर्ण एवं प्रौढ़, सब प्रकार के तारों का होना इस बात की पुष्टि करता है। (नक्षत्र, 17)

6. **को पुष्ट कर—"to serve to promote, to reinforce"**

पुराने जमाने में जब वैज्ञानिक और नीतिज्ञ एक ही था, तब विज्ञान नीति को पुष्ट करता था। (नदी, 80)

को पुष्ट कर—"to reinforce"

खून को उन्होंने जीवन का प्रतीक माना। मेरा ख्याल है कि औरत की महावारी में बहने वाले खून ने भी उनकी धारणा को पुष्ट किया होगा। (बूंद, 33)

7. **की तस्दीक कर—"to verify"**

मिसेज़ टंडन दौड़ी हुई आश्रम पहुंची और अन्य महिलाओं को खबर सुनाई। जुगनू उसकी तस्दीक करने के लिए बुलाई गई। (सम, 51)

तस्दीक कर—"to corroborate"

मुद्दई का बयान ही ऐसा था, गवाहों ने उसे तस्दीक किया था...। (देश, 9)

8. **की ताईद कर—"to speak in favor of, to back up"**

मैं आपकी बात की ताईद कर रहा था। (तीन, 10)

की ताईद कर—"to back up"

"हां जाओ!" ठाकुर मितानसिंह ने भी अफसराना लहजे में मैनेजर साहब की ताईद की। (फूलो, 25)

74. आविष्कार, ईजाद

1. आविष्कार is discovering, creating or producing something not previously known. The term does not imply any reference to purposive search and investigation or to the accidental nature of the finding.

ईजाद essentially covers the same ground as does आविष्कार, but in addition may sometimes be used to describe the subject's skill at contriving or concocting something implying some sort of immediacy of purpose or as a matter of expediency.

2. आविष्कार is +process and ईजाद-process. आविष्कार forms ANP with का. These nouns do not take plural.

3. **का आविष्कार कर—"to isolate"**

इसी अलेक्जेंडर ने पेन्सलीन का आविष्कार किया। समस्त विश्व ने उसका सम्मान किया। (बाल, 1-25)

का आविष्कार कर—"to develop, to invent, to evolve"

जीवन के गूढ़ रहस्यों को अंशत: व्यक्त करने के लिए मनुष्य ने जिन भाषा संकेतों का आविष्कार किया है वे प्राय: अपनी रूढ़ परिभाषाओं की सीमा पार कर हृदय और बुद्धि के अनेक स्तरों तक फैल जाते हैं। (साहित्यकार, 25)

का आविष्कार कर—"to devise"

मनुष्य ने किस मोह में पड़कर इस विकट साधना-पद्धति का आविष्कार किया है। (चारु, 143)

का आविष्कार कर—"to discover"

यही होनहार मेरिया विश्व में मैडम मेरी क्यूरी के नाम से प्रसिद्ध हुई जिसने रेडियम धातु का आविष्कार किया। (बाल, 1-25)

का आविष्कार कर—"to make a new discovery"

आज उन्होंने शल्य चिकित्सा में एक अद्‌भुत आविष्कार किया था। (दीपाली, 187)

4. **ईजाद कर—"to invent"**

उसने पशु-पक्षियों के, अपने, नारी के चित्र अपनी गुफा में अंकित किये, प्रिया के नन्हें से खिलौने का ध्यान कर वह खिलौने भी गढ़ने लगा। वह बड़ी दूर का निशाना साधने लगा, उसने धनुष-बाण भी ईजाद कर लिया। (बूंद, 138)

ईजाद कर—"to devise"

जब उस पर तमाम तरकीबें बेकार साबित हुईं तो दारोग़ा साहिब ने अपने तरकश का आखिरी तीर इस्तेमाल किया जो उसकी तरह कमजोर और पढ़े-लिखे राजनीतिक कैदियों के लिये ख़ासतौर से ईजाद किया गया था। (अवध, 94)

ईजाद कर—"to devise"

उस तरीके से बढ़कर दूसरों को यंत्रणा पहुंचाने का तरीका राजनैतिक या धार्मिक, किसी ज़माने में किसी भी ज़ालिम हुकूमत ने कभी पहले ईजाद न किया था। (सुन्दर, 20)

ईजाद कर—"to concoct, to coin"

एक तरफ सरकार का हुनर है और दूसरी तरफ परमात्मा का हुनर है। तुम्हारा

तकरीबन-तकरीबन अभी दफ्तर में ही रहेगा और मेरा तकरीबन-तकरीबन कफ़न में पहुंच जायगा। सालों ने सारी पढ़ाई खर्च करके दो लफ्ज़ ईजाद किये हैं—शायद और तकरीबन ? (जानवर, 88)

75. प्रकाशन, प्रकाशित, प्रगटीकरण, प्रकट, इज़्हार, जाहिर, अभिव्यक्ति, अभिव्यक्त, व्यक्त

1. All these expressions are used to characterize or specify the manner (i. e., verbal, gestural, or any other form) in which a person expresses either his feelings, sentiments, opinions or simply something of informative value. Alternatively they are used to refer to what in the speaker's opinion someone or something reveals, makes manifest or purports to express (such as by his or its appearance, behavior or in some other suitable manner).

प्रकाशन and प्रकाशित both refer to the act or the result of bringing into public view in a variety of ways (such as by displaying a sentiment or feeling in one's writing, by publishing or taking steps in order to make known something which could otherwise escape notice), or that which is set forth in such a manner as if it is luminous or shiny. The expressions usually take as their object nouns suggestive of something in the nature of information or something which is of significant value to someone or in a given context.

प्रगटीकरण and प्रकट both refer to making manifest to the senses (by making it available to sense-experience), or to presenting something which is underlying, concealed or under the surface in a manner that it becomes apparent to someone else. Alternatively, the terms may be used in describing or in referring to either what (for one) is an apparent manifestation of something or what (to one) is apparently manifest in something. These terms, therefore, avoid a direct reference to the intention of the subject (which is the characteristic of अभिव्यक्ति and अभिव्यक्त), or to something which is evident to the speaker in the behaviour or appearance of the subject.

इज़हार and जाहिर simply stress a calling forth or bringing into being of something, or refer to something as being in evidence in what is called forth or brought into being. The terms differ from प्रगटीकरण and प्रकट in emphasizing the sense experience of something evident in what presents itself (but may or may not be intended by the subject).

अभिव्यक्ति and अभिव्यक्त are applied when the subject's intention (i. e., the import of the meaning in his expression) or the significance of something intentional (i. e., having a reference to beyond itself) is being referred to in a composition (i.e., any form of expression—artistic or otherwise) symbolic in nature, or when a reference is desired to the modes of symbolic expression in general, or a symbolic representation of something abstract.

The term अभिव्यक्ति, in modern Hindi literary and critical writings, is used as an equivalent of the English term "expression" in general. When a reference is desired to a specific sense-use of the term "expression" (while referring to expressionism in general or as a particular school of thought), the term अभिव्यंजना "distinct intentional manifestation" is employed.

व्यक्त (as opposed to अव्यक्त "transcendental, i. e., extending or being beyond the limits of ordinary experience") is applied to that which is put forth, represented or expressed within the bounds of ordinary human experience.

2. The nouns प्रकाशन, प्रगटीकरण, इजहार and अभिव्यक्ति are +process, and the adjectives प्रकाशित, प्रकट, जाहिर, अभिव्यक्त and व्यक्त are —process. प्रकाशन, प्रगटीकरण and इजहार form ANP with का, and अभिव्यक्त with की. The nouns in this group are not pluralized.

3. **का प्रकाशन कर—"to bring to light, to exhibit"**

विजयदेव नारायण साही ने जहां एक ओर व्यक्ति या समाज के जीवन को आक्रांत करने वाली अनास्था का स्पष्ट प्रकाशन किया है, वहां दूसरी ओर सम्पूर्ण समाज अथवा व्यक्ति विशेष से अनास्था के तत्त्वों को ग्रहण करने का भी संदेश दिया है। (निबंध, 673)

का प्रकाशन कर—"to publish"

हिन्दी अकादमी डा० सम्पूर्णानन्द के ग्रह-नक्षत्र का प्रकाशन कर गौरव का अनुभव करती है। (नक्षत्र, 6)

4. **प्रकाशित कर—"to reveal"**

सूत्रधार और विष्कंभक को यूनानी कोरस की पद्धति में ढालकर एक नवीन प्रकार के रंगनायक की सृष्टि की जा सकती है जो यवनिका और गर्भों के बिना ही नाटक की पृष्ठभूमि और भिन्न अंकों का एक दूसरे से संबंध प्रकाशित कर सके। (कोणार्क, 106)

प्रकाशित कर—"to disclose"

तुम मेरी आज्ञा के विरुद्ध धर्म के गोपनीय रहस्यों को प्रकाशित कर रहे हो। इसका परिणाम जानते हो? (आदर्श, 24)

प्रकाशित कर दे—"to illuminate"

खेतों में फसल पक जाने के समान जिस शरद ने मेरे काव्य की वृद्धि कर उसे पूर्णता को पहुंचाया, जिसने मेरे अवकाश की कोठी को प्रकाश से प्रकाशित कर दिया, पद और गायन रचते समय जिसने मेरे खुले मन पर आनंद और धैर्य का प्रवाह बढ़ाया...। (संस्मरण, 25)

प्रकाशित कर—"to publicize, to be made known to the public"

कम्पनी के डाइरेक्टरों ने इस तरह की बातों या खबरों को दबा देने में, जिन्हें वे प्रकाशित करना न चाहते थे, शुरू से आखीर तक, बड़ी होशियारी के साथ काम लिया है। (सुन्दर, 4)

प्रकाशित कर—"to publish"

एक बार किसी महाशय ने उर्दू-फारसी का एक साधारण कोश प्रकाशित करके उसका ऐसे विज्ञापन किया कि बहुत से लोग बिना देखे ही उस पुस्तक की प्रशंसा गाने लगे। (आदर्श, 91)

5. **का प्रगटीकरण कर—"to publicize"**

शाम को पड़ोस वाली हवेली का लाउडस्पीकर गली के बाहर हवेली के अन्दर चलने वाली एक मीटिंग का प्रगटीकरण कर रहा था। (बूंद, 397)

6. **प्रकट कर—"to show"**

तितली को अपनी लज्जा प्रकट करने के लिए उठ जाना पड़ा। उसने कहा—क्यों नहीं आऊंगी ? (तितली, 86)

प्रकट कर दे—"to express, to reveal"

मन में उठे विचारों को बाहर प्रकट कर देने से मन का गुबार निकल जाता है...। (लाख, 190)

प्रकट कर दे—"to make known, to reveal"

समुद्र की ओर दृष्टि गड़ाए रखकर ही उसने कन्नगी से कहा तुमसे मैं अपने मन की निर्बलता भी प्रकट कर देना चाहता हूं। (सुहाग, 142)

प्रकट कर—"to give expression to"

इन्सान का गालियों में अपनी कामेच्छा का प्रकट करना भी उसकी उस कुदरती आदत को जाहिर करता है जिसे सभ्यता की ऊंची मीनार पर चढ़ कर हम शरीफ लोग व्यभिचार के नाम से पुकारते हैं। (बूंद, 423)

प्रकट कर—"to divulge"

मंत्री और धनवती वेश्या जो सज्जन को अपना मित्र मानकर उसके सामने अपना असली रूप प्रकट कर चुके थे, वे आज सज्जन का असली रूप देखेंगे। वह सीधी तौर पर धनवती से नज़रें नहीं मिला पा रहा था। (बूंद, 512)

प्रकट कर—"to express"

सोलन ने भी शोक प्रकट करते हुए कहा—सचमुच बड़े दुख की बात है; बेचारे बाप की छाती इसको सुनकर फट जाएगी। (आदर्श, 59)

प्रकट कर—"to express"

निधान मन ही मन असहमत हुआ, परन्तु उसने अपना प्रतिवाद प्रकट नहीं किया। (कचनार, 314)

प्रकट कर—"to express"

भुवन के बारे में भी उसने चिंता प्रकट की—भुवन न जाने कहां है, कैसी स्थिति में और कब लौटेगा या आगे क्या करेगा...। (नदी, 312)

बिना किसी तरह का संदेह प्रकट किए—"without any expression of doubt or suspicion"

सिकंदर ने बिना किसी तरह का संदेह प्रकट किए एक हाथ से प्याले को पिया और दूसरे हाथ से उस पत्र को निकालकर फिलिप के हाथ में दे दिया। (आदर्श, 31)

7. **का इज़हार कर—"to reveal, to express"**

...और अनातोल फ्रांस चूंकि बड़ा ही गहरा बुद्धिवादी था अतः उसने इस कटुता का इजहार जीवन के समस्त आदर्श और गहराइयों का मखौल उड़ाने वाली शैली के रूप में किया हो लेकिन...। (मूल्य, 43)

का इज़हार कर—"to make evident, to reveal"

उसने रोज़ की तरह अपने दिल की गंदगी का इज़हार किया। (विचित्र, 35)

का इज़हार करते हुए—"appearing to be (honest), trying to look (honest)"

मियां, मुझे क्यों जलन होगी? जब तक जमकर काम करता हूं—साधना करता हूं—तब तक मुझे किसी से भी ईर्ष्या नहीं होगी। सज्जन की तरफ से नजर चुराते हुए, कर्नल से नजरें मिलाकर ईमानदारी का इजहार करते हुए महिपाल ने कहा...। (बूंद, 30)

का इजहार करने लग—"to express, to appear to be"

पहले तो वह शक और वसवसे का इज़हार करने लगी, लेकिन जब उसे पता चला कि दरबारी का पूरा नाम दरबारी लाल मेहता है तो उसने झट से इजाजत दे दी, क्योंकि बम्बई में जो लोग मकानों का किराया उगाहते हैं उन्हें मेहता बोलते हैं। (लड़की, 45)

8. **जाहिर कर—"to express"**

कर्नल ने अपनी मजबूरी जाहिर की कि वह दिन में नहीं आ सका। कन्या से उसे पता लगा कि दाग देने के लिए राजा साहब के सुपुत्र ने सज्जन को आदेश देकर पीछे हटा दिया था। (बूंद, 567)

जाहिर कर—"to reveal"

मैं तुमसे झूठ नहीं कहता, इस गीत में भले ही कलात्मकता न हो पर यह उस कविता भरी नई उम्र और नए जोड़े की दिली भावनाएं जाहिर करता है जिसमें बात-बात पर रस बरस पड़ता है। (बूंद, 415)

जाहिर कर—"to express, to give expression to"

बीर—खड़ी हिन्दी तो है जहांपनाह जिसमें कठोर बात आसानी के साथ जाहिर की जा सकती है। मुल्ला—(धीरे से अपने साथी दरबारी से) कितना चालाक है बीरबल, किस तरह से माफ करा लिया इसने। (बीर, 75)

पर जाहिर कर—"to make known to"

दर्शकों में खड़ी नवयुवती गोरी ने भी अपनी राय पुलिस वालों पर जाहिर की। (जुहू, 68)

जाहिर कर—"to show, to try to appear"

आठ दस लोग नोटिस बोर्ड और चिट्ठियों वाले रैक के आसपास खड़े अपने को किसी न किसी तरह व्यस्त जाहिर करने की चेष्टा कर रहे थे। (जानवर, 146)

जाहिर कर—"to bespeak, to reveal"

इन्सान का गालियों में अपनी कामेच्छा का प्रकट करना भी उसकी उस कुदरती आदत को जाहिर करता है...। (बूंद, 423)

9. **की अभिव्यक्ति कर—"to exhibit"**

इस काव्य में मानव के लघु व्यक्तित्व की उस शक्ति पर गौरव तथा अभिमान की अभिव्यक्ति की गई है जो महत्ता की चरम सीमा का स्पर्श करती है। (निबंध, 672)

की अभिव्यक्ति कर—"to manifest"

किस प्रकार भावनाओं की अभिव्यक्ति ऐसे नये प्रतीकों द्वारा करता है जो मूल दमित वासनाओं से सम्बद्ध रूपाकृतियों को व्यंजित भी करते हैं। (मूल्य, 159)

10. **अभिव्यक्त कर—"to exhibit"**

हमारे दैनंदिन जीवन के राग-रंग को प्रस्तुत करने के लिए हमारे संवेदों और स्पन्दनों को अभिव्यक्त करने के लिए जिस रंगमंच की आवश्यकता है वह पाश्चात्य रंगमंच से भिन्न होगा। (आषाढ़, दो शब्द)

अभिव्यक्त कर डाल—"to pour, to give full expression to"

स्वतः प्रेरित कलाकृति उनकी समस्त कल्पना बुद्धि ज्ञान को सहायक उपादान बनाकर अपने को अभिव्यक्त कर डालती है...। (मूल्य, 158)

अभिव्यक्त कर—"to express"

विचारों को अभिव्यक्त करने की योग्यता भी नहीं आती है। (बुन, 4)

अभिव्यक्त करने लग—"to manifest, to be manifest, to become apparent"

बौद्धिक विक्षोभ अपने को अभिव्यक्त करने लगा था। (मूल्य, 56)

11. **व्यक्त कर—"to express"**

मैं उन सबों के प्रति अपनी हार्दिक कृतज्ञता व्यक्त करता हूं। (मूल्य, 12)

व्यक्त कर—"to express"

हिन्दी के प्रसंग में लेखक ने छायावाद और प्रगतिवाद दोनों के प्रति असन्तोष व्यक्त किया है क्योंकि विचार में एकने मूल समस्या का सामना ही नहीं किया और दूसरे ने समस्या को गलत परिप्रेक्ष्य में उठाकर उलझनें बढ़ा दीं। (मूल्य, 11)

व्यक्त कर—"to give expression to"

सच कहूं तो मुझे आप पर थोड़ी ईर्ष्या ही हो रही थी, काफी हाऊस की तो बात खैर छोड़िए वह तो एक प्रतीक बन गया है जिसके सहारे हम जीवन ही के प्रति अपने दृष्टिकोण व्यक्त कर रहे हैं। (नदी, 21)

व्यक्त कर—"to divulge"

उसके विषय में मुझे एक ऋषि द्वारा यह श्राप सौगंध मिला है कि मैं यदि उस बात को किसी के भी सामने व्यक्त कर दूंगा तो उसी क्षण में पत्थर हो जाऊंगा। मुझ से मेरी रानी यही चाह रही है। (नाटक, 33)

व्यक्त कर--"to tell, to disclose"

जल्दी में शर्मा जी बहुतों को निमंत्रण न भेज सके थे। सज्जन ने अपने आने का कारण न व्यक्त करते हुए अपनी मौन मुद्राओं से यह ही प्रकट किया कि जैसे वह कविता सुनने के लिए ही आया है। (बूंद, 351)

व्यक्त कर--"to represent, to express"

नाइट्रो-चाक इसे संक्षिप्त में संकेत द्वारा व्यक्त किया जाता है। (खाद, 95)

व्यक्त कर पा--"to express oneself, to put forth plainly or adequately"

...मैं अपनी बात तुमसे ठीक-ठीक व्यक्त नहीं कर पा रही, पर तुम इसे ठीक-ठीक ही समझना। सज्जन बोला—मैं उसे बिल्कुल ठीक समझ रहा हूं।

व्यक्त कर—"to bring out"

यह इनिशियेटिव, यह पहल हमारे हाथ में है कि हम अपने द्वारा उपलब्ध मूल्य को इसी क्षण आचरण में व्यक्त कर भविष्य का निर्माण करते हैं या नहीं। (मूल्य, 122-23)

व्यक्त कर जा--"to let someone know (one's feelings)".

उसने कामिनी को एक अत्यधिक मामूली और तुच्छ लड़की समझा था और चूंकि वह मेरी सहपाठिनी थी, जिससे मेरा सम्बन्ध विकसित हो सकता है, इसलिए उसको काटने के लिए मधु अपनी घृणा व्यक्त कर गई। (राह, 115)

व्यक्त कर—"to signify, to display, to express"

जिन युगों में एक भू-खण्ड दूसरे से परिचित नहीं था उनमें भी मनुष्य ने वसुधा को कुटुम्ब के रूप में स्वीकार कर अनदेखे सहयात्रियों के प्रति आस्था व्यक्त की है। (साहित्यकार, 28)

में संदेह व्यक्त कर—"to be skeptical, to raise doubt, to express doubt"

हमारी सफलता में संदेह व्यक्त किया जायगा, विलम्ब होगा और निराशा के क्षण भी आएंगे लेकिन हमें लक्ष्य की ओर बढ़ते ही रहना है। (अमरीका, 95)

76. न्याय, इन्साफ

1. Both न्याय and इन्साफ refer to treating someone rightfully, in a just manner, or to acting as a judge in order to dispense justice.

न्याय applies in situations in which the canons or code of conduct (or any such authority) of a society are invoked, and in which evidence is considered or deliberated on in conformity with such laws.

इन्साफ stresses following the dictates of one's own conscience (in the event there is lack of evidence, sometimes even if the evidence indicates to the contrary).

2. Both the nouns are +process and form ANP with के साथ and का. न्याय also occurs with के प्रति. These nouns do not occur with plural.

3. **के प्रति न्याय कर—"to act fairly or justly towards"**

महिपाल सबके प्रति न्याय करता है। (बूंद, 111)

के साथ न्याय कर—"to treat someone in all fairness"

विट्ठलदास से आशा थी कि वह उनके साथ न्याय करेंगे, उनके रूठे हुए मित्रों को मना लावेंगे, लेकिन विट्ठलदास ने उल्टे उन्हीं को अपराधी ठहराया। (सेवा, 271)

का न्याय कर—"to administer justice, to be a (good) judge of"

राजा : जाओ रानी मुझे पूरा विश्वास है कि तुम मंत्री विजयसेन के कुकर्मों का सुदंर न्याय करोगी। (नाटक, 68)

न्याय कर—"to observe impartiality, to rightfully observe the canons of justice"

वह...रिश्वत से सदा दूर भागते थे, और इसी कारण अच्छा न्याय करते थे...। (गांधी, 3)

सोच समझकर न्याय कर—"to administer justice"

इसलिए सोच समझकर न्याय करो। (भारक, 55)

न्याय कर—"to judge"

पर मैं न्याय करने वाला कौन होता हूं...? अपराधी न्यायाधीश नहीं हो सकता। (राजभवन-द्वार की ओर बढ़कर) द्वारपाल...नहीं नहीं कोई नहीं। (नाटक, 19)

4. **के साथ इन्साफ कर—"to display one's sense of impartiality, to do someone justice"**

समस्त अंगरेज़ इतिहास लेखकों में शायद करनल मालेसन एक ऐसा है जिसने सिराजुद्दौला के साथ इन्साफ करने की कोशिश की है। (सुन्दर, 164)

के साथ इन्साफ कर—"to treat one right or rightfully"

मेरे साथ इन्साफ करो, और समाज से कराओ। मेरा घर बसवा दो। (विचित्र, 68)

का इन्साफ कर—"to deal with someone, to give someone his just deserts"

ज़रा आप लोग बगलवाले कमरे में चलें...फिर मैं इनका इन्साफ करूं। मिनटों में इस मस्तान को पस्तान करता हूं। (जुहू, 59)

इन्साफ कर—"to make an impartial decision"

अमां अफसर ने ठीक इन्साफ किया आज के मर्द हिजड़े हो गए हैं। तभी तो ये धांधलीबाजी मच रही है। एक दूसरे जवान बोले। (बूंद, 432)

77. शास्त्रार्थ, वाद-विवाद, तर्क-वितर्क, बहस-मुबाहसा, वाक्-युद्ध, तर्क, बहस, दलील

1. शास्त्रार्थ, वाद-विवाद, तर्क-वितर्क, बहस-मुबाहसा, वाक्-युद्ध, तर्क, बहस and दलील all serve to characterize the variety of ways in which someone engages in a verbal discourse about something with another person or a group of people (or sometimes with oneself).

शास्त्रार्थ refers to the practice of holding verbal duels (usually carried on in the form of questions and answers, and counter-questions and answers) among the Hindu scholars, in which each scholar would demonstrate his mastery of the Hindu scriptures and try to prevail upon the other by expounding and explicating their content and purport.

वाद-विवाद is engaging in a verbal argumentation with another person by putting forth one's own convictions, beliefs, ideas or the like about a subject, a topic or a point, in order to dispute or take exception to the other person's convictions, beliefs or ideas.

तर्क-वितर्क is engaging in a verbal disputation with someone over something by citing arguments, principles or reasons in favor of one's own contention in order to call into question the validity of another person's statement, argument, assertion or the like. The term generally implies a concerted or point-by-point argumentation, and may sometimes be applied to deliberation over something by the subject in his mind (preparatory to making a decision to taking some action).

बहस-मुबाहसा refers to verbal interchange of ideas by a group of two or more people on a subject or a topic (in a manner as if they were thrashing something over).

वाक्-युद्ध (lit. a battle of words) is nothing more than the activity of hurling words back and forth between two people.

तर्क is talking to another person in order to try to persuade, influence or prevail upon him by the use of reason.

बहस is engaging in verbal controversy with someone.

The term दलील is applied to an argument or a reason which is the product of ideational activity or intuitive thinking rather than one based on a systematic understanding of facts and their underlying principles. It is, therefore, used with कर- to indicate the subject's reflecting upon a question or a problem, often referring to his ambivalence in which he hesitates to act (or resists any inducement to act).

2. All these nouns are + process, and form ANP with से or के साथ. When more than one person is being referred to as engaged in the act, both N से and N के साथ are replaced by आपस में or एक दूसरे से/के साथ. Sometimes the sentences with these expressions may contain some specification as to the topic or subject of discourse. This is done by using the appropriate noun with the postposition पर with all the expressions except दलील. Only बहस-मुबाहसा, बहस and दलील are pluralized.

3. **से शास्त्रार्थ कर--"to engage in a verbal duel"**

बन्दी वहां आनेवाले पंडितों से शास्त्रार्थ करता और उन्हें पराजित करने के बाद समुद्र में डुबोने के लिए भेज देता था। (भारक, 8)

4. **आपस में वाद-विवाद कर—" to argue"**

वहां की रानी यामुनाचार्य के व्यक्तित्व से प्रभावित होकर पति से बोली—स्वामी, यह साक्षात् विद्या का अवतार जान पड़ता है। पंडितों के बीच में यह हीरे की भांति चमक रहा है। कोलाहल इसका मान-मर्दन नहीं कर सकता।

राजा ने कहा—क्या कहती हो रानी! यह तो कोलाहल की एक फूंक से उड़ जायगा। बेचारा बकरे की तरह बलिदान के लिए आया है।

इस तरह राजा-रानी आपस में वाद-विवाद करने लगे। (आदर्श, 21)

5. **से तर्क-वितर्क कर--"to plead, to argue"**

उस समय वह अपनी उस कुरूप परन्तु निर्दोष पत्नी का पक्ष लेकर नीरा से तर्क-वितर्क करता रहा था और कई नैतिक, सामाजिक तथा वैयक्तिक सिद्धान्त उसने गिना डाले थे। (धारा, 199)

तर्क-वितर्क कर—"to debate"

यह कानून अत्यन्त सावधानीपूर्वक किये गये तर्क-वितर्क और विचार-विमर्श का परिणाम है। (अमरीका, 20-21)

तर्क-वितर्क कर—"to engage in argumentation"

कुणाल ने इस विषय में अधिक तर्क-वितर्क करना उचित नहीं समझा। (आदर्श, 36)

6. **बहस-मुबाहसा कर—"to discuss, to hold discussion"**

भारतीयता के जोश में ये दोनों अपनी समझ और उम्र से भी ऊंची किताबें एकाग्र होकर पढ़ा करते और उन पर गंभीर बहस-मुबाहसा भी किया करते। (बूंद, 484)

बहस-मुबाहसा कर—"to engage in discussion"

मैंनान के जंगलों में दिन बिताना अलग बात है और जिनीवा में काफी के प्यालों की चुस्की लेते हुये पूंजीवाद की आलोचना और बहस-मुबाहसे करते रहना बिलकुल अलग बात। (दिनमान, 1-6)

7. **से वाक्-युद्ध कर—"to be engaged in a squabble, to squabble"**

भित्तरिया जी से रसमय वाक्-युद्ध करते हुए ताई दालान की ओर चलीं। (बूंद, 152)

8. **से तर्क कर—"to wrangle"**

दुकानदार ने तीनों पुस्तकों के तीन रुपये देने को कहा। तीनों पुस्तकें बिल्कुल नयीं हैं। भाटिया उससे तर्क करने लगा। दुकानदार उसके तर्क का उत्तर न देकर दूसरे ग्राहक से बात करने लगा। (जानवर, 64)

से तर्क कर—"to reason"

परन्तु बीच-बीच में वह अपने हृदय से तर्क भी करती थी—इन्द्रदेव को मैं एक बार ही भूल सकूंगी? (तितली, 148)

तर्क कर—"to argue"

आप यह पूछ सकते हैं कि क्या आप तर्क करते-करते एक गोल चक्कर में नहीं घूम गये। (मूल्य, 160)

तर्क कर—"to reason"

जिस शक्ति के बिना हमारी आंखें देख नहीं सकतीं, कान सुन नहीं सकते, मन मनन नहीं कर सकता और बुद्धि तर्क नहीं कर सकती...उसी शक्ति को जानना साधक का प्रथम उद्देश्य है। (धर्म, 109)

9. **से बहस कर—"to argue"**

जयराम वकील था, उससे बहस करना भिड़ के छत्ते को छेड़ना था। (सम, 68)

के साथ बहस कर—"to argue"

कोई आदमी पहाड़ी को किस तरह रोक सकता है ? और पहाड़ी में अभी तक बाबा नानक का पंजा लगा हुआ है। मुझे ज़रा विश्वास न आया। बाद में किसी ने खोद दिया होगा। मैं अपनी मां के साथ कितनी देर बहस करता रहा। (दुग्गल, 52)

पर बहस कर—"to have a heated discussion on"

प्रकाशक महोदय और मेरे मित्र राजनीति के किसी प्रश्न पर बहस कर रहे थे और जब उनमें से किसी की आवाज़ ज़रा ऊंची हो जाती, तो कोने में बैठा हुआ क्लर्क तीखी क्रुद्ध दृष्टि से उनकी ओर देखने लगता। (परिन्दे, 61)

ज़ोर-ज़ोर से बहस कर—"to wrangle"

शाम को छुट्टी होने पर हम साइकिल पर किसी ऐसे तांगे के पीछे-पीछे जिस पर लड़कियां बैठी होती थीं ज़ोर-ज़ोर से बहसें या बातें करते हुए वापस जाते थे। (राह, 8)

10. **दलीलें कर—"to debate with oneself"**

लड़ाई-झगड़े से सुरखरु हो मंझली अपने कमरे में आयी तो सरदारी लाल का उघड़ा पड़ा बिस्तर देख देर तक दोचिती-सी खड़ी-खड़ी दलीलें करती रही। (मित्रो, 7)

78. जिरह, जिज्ञासा, पूछताछ, दरियाफ़त, पता, मालूम

1. जिरह, जिज्ञासा, पूछताछ, दरियाफत, पता and मालूम all refer to the act of seeking to know by means of asking or questioning.

जिरह is asking a series of questions to establish the truth or the falsehood of a statement made by someone. The term may sometimes be applied in its extended sense to unnecessarily inquisitive argumentation which is irksome or annoying to the addressee.

जिज्ञासा is applied to the posing of specific questions to another person on some subject. The term stresses a strong sense of curiosity on the part of the subject.

पूछताछ is making an inquiry or inquiries in a somewhat casual fashion. The term may sometimes refer to nothing more than the expression of the inquirer's concern for the welfare of another person.

दरियाफ्त applies to an interrogative expression which calls for an informative answer concerning something which the subject has apprehended. The term may sometimes refer to the posing of a question to the addressee in order to draw his attention to something obvious but questionable.

पता refers to the act of ascertaining definitive information about the time of some event or the whereabouts of someone or something.

मालूम is a term of wider application stressing the notion of effort made by the subject to find out what he seeks to know. By itself it says nothing about the use of interrogative expressions or any other means employed in the act of determining something.

The three terms दरियाफ्त, पता and मालूम may take as their object affirmative expressions referring to what one seeks to know or to what one has found out in their respective senses.

2. The nouns जिरह, जिज्ञासा, पूछताछ and पता are +process, and दरियाफ्त and मालूम are — process. जिरह forms ANP with से, जिज्ञासा with के विषय में and से, पूछताछ with से and की, पता with का. None of the +process expressions are pluralized.

3. **से जिरह कर—"to interrogate"**

मैंने उनसे जिरह करनी शुरू की। मैंने भी इतने दिनों घास नहीं खोदी है। थोड़ा-सा कानून जानती हूं। (सम, 5)

4. **के विषय में जिज्ञासा कर—"to be curious about, to express one's curiosity"**

पहले से कुसंस्कार पाये हुए किशोरों ने बोर्डिंग में दो-तीन बार अब्रह्मचर्य के कुचरित्र किये भी। प्रोफेसर महाशय ने अन्य विद्यार्थियों को शिक्षा देने के लिये अपराधियों को बेंत मार कर दंड दिया और बोर्डिंग से निकाल दिया था। दूसरे छात्र कई दिन तक इन अपराधों के विषय में कल्पना और जिज्ञासा करते रहे थे। (फूलो, 85)

5. **के विषय में पूछताछ कर—"to ask about"**

कुछ (विद्यार्थी) कालेज की पढ़ाई की बात कर रहे थे, कुछ नए फिल्म के विषय में पूछताछ कर रहे थे, कुछ फुटबाल मैच की तैयारी कर रहे थे और कुछ रात की म्यूजिक पार्टी का प्रबन्ध कर रहे थे। वे प्रायः जोर से हंस भी देते थे। (तीन, 2)

के सम्बन्ध में पूछताछ कर—"to inquire after"

कल्याणी के घर बराबर आते जाते रहकर आवश्यक वस्तुओं के संबंध में पूछताछ करना, जिस राह से खूबी के साथ दो पैसों की बचत हो वह राह सुझाना कर्नल का ही काम था। (बूंद, 558)

से पूछताछ करने लग—"to ask all sorts of questions"

धर्मशाला वालों ने खून से लथपथ पंडित जी के शरीर को देखा। वे मूर्ख से पूछताछ करने लगे। मूर्ख ने कहा—हमने तो हंसी की थी। हमें क्या मालूम था कि हंसी-हंसी में मित्र की जान चली जाएगी। (कथा, 66)

की पूछताछ कर—"to inquire after"

शांतला ने लक्ष्मी को अपनी छाती से लगाकर इस प्रकार पूछा मानो कोई माता अपने बच्चे की बड़े प्रेम से पूछताछ कर रही हो। (शांतला, 69)

से पूछताछ कर जाया कर—"to call upon someone"

किसी चीज की कमी पड़े तो दलीप से मंगा लेना। मैं उससे कह दूंगा कि वह बीच बीच में तुमसे पूछताछ कर जाया करे। (धनु, 46)

पूछताछ कर—"to ask a question, to question (someone)"

सुमन ने शेष रात मानसिक विकलता की दशा में काटी। चार बजने पर वह गंगा स्नान को चली। वह बहुधा अकेले ही जाया करती थी, इसलिये चौकीदार ने कुछ पूछताछ न की। (सेवा, 255)

पूछताछ कर ले—"to make inquiries"

झील के पास ही डाक-बंगला था, भुवन ने वहां जाकर चौकीदार से कहा कि कुली आवें तो उन्हें कह दे कि वह आगे चला गया है और कुली जल्दी आवें, फिर कुछ और पूछताछ भी कर ली और रेखा के पास लौट आया। (नदी, 128)

6. **से दरियाफत कर—"to pose a question, to inquire"**

जिस समय वे दोनों (हिन्दु मुसलमान) नारकीय नरक की ओर—भयानक दूतों के साथ जा रहे थे, उसी समय स्वर्ग के द्वार की ओर एक जलूस जा रहा था जिसमें देवताओं के बीच में एक तपस्वी नवयुवक दूल्हे की तरह सजा हुआ जा रहा था। दोनों ने दूतों से दरियाफ्त किया, यह किसका जलूस है भाई ?

से दरियाफत कर—"to inquire of"

क्यों जी, सोरावजी ने उससे भी दरियाफ्त किया—क्या अभी थोड़ी देर पहले सेठ मंगलदास के फाटक पर कुछ शोर या हंगामा हो रहा था ?

बिल्कुल नहीं। मुझे तो पता नहीं। सिख ने पुलिस को रूखा जवाब दिया। (जुहू, 50)

7. **का पता कर—"to inquire about"**

रास्ते में गाड़ी का पता भी करते चलेंगे। और टिकट वापस करके नया लेना होगा। (नदी, 121)

8. **मालूम कर—"to learn, to be found out"**

फिर भी, ऐसे कोई विश्वस्त वैज्ञानिक आंकड़े नहीं मिलते हैं जिनसे यह मालूम किया जा सके कि संसार के विभिन्न भागों में आजकल भेड़ की कौनसी नस्लें पाली जाती हैं। (भेड़, 3)

मालूम कर—"to find out"

यदि हमें मालूम हो कि लोहे का टुकड़ा एक सेकेंड में कितने चक्कर लगा रहा है तो हम दो-शाखी सलाख का आवेगनांक मालूम कर सकते हैं। (आज, 38)

मालूम कर चुक—"to know intuitively, to feel"

उसे हृदय में अस्वस्ति मिलती थी, यह वह मालूम कर चुकी है। (निरु, 43)

मालूम कर—"to establish, to ascertain"

मिट्टी के लिये भौतिक विश्लेषण में आमतौर पर मिट्टी की यांत्रिक संरचना सुखाई-व्यवहार, सुखाई-सिकुड़न, सुखाई-बल और अनुकूलतम लोच के लिये नमी मालूम की जाती है। (ईंट, 13-14)

मालूम कर ले—"to know, to have found out"

रमा फिर मुस्कराई, जैसे इस बार मालूम कर लिया हो कि राजन और उसकी पत्नी की आपस में नहीं बनती थी। राजन नये ख्यालातों का नौजवान लगता था। सभ्य, सुशिक्षित और शायद वह पुराने जमाने की गहनों से लदी हुई गांव की लड़की होगी। (ढोल, 15)

मालूम करता रह—"to be able to tell (intuitively)"

अंधेरा होने पर सांस रोक कर वह मालूम करती रही कि हरिप्रसन्न झुंझला रहे हैं। (सुता, 154)

मालूम कर—"to find out"

इंस्पैक्टर साहब का हुक्म था कि ऐसी मीटिंग का समय और स्थान मालूम करके उबेर वक्त रहते उन्हें खबर दे...। (फूलो, 54)

मालूम कर—"to ascertain, to establish"

इस प्रकार प्रत्येक वस्तु का मूल्य अप्रत्यक्ष रूप से अन्य वस्तुओं के रूप में मालूम किया जाने लगा। (एमाई, 15)

मालूम कर—"to find out"

किन्तु इससे आगे चन्द्रसेन को वह क्या जानती है, यह मालूम भी किस प्रकार किया जावे ? (सुता, 149)

79. परिचय, पहचान, जानकारी

1. परिचय, पहचान and जानकारी all refer to the act of getting to know someone or something.

परिचय (used only of people with कर-) refers to becoming socially acquainted with someone for the first time. The term implies the observing of the usual formalities, such as exchange of each other's names, hand-shakes and the like.

पहचान implies the making of another person's acquaintance, generally of someone whom one has not met personally before (but knows otherwise).

जानकारी refers to either becoming familiar with something or having some sort of significant information about something.

2. These nouns are + process. Both परिचय and पहचान form ANP with से and जानकारी with की. These expressions are not pluralized.

3. **से परिचय कर—"to introduce oneself to"**

रमा ने विधवा से परिचय कर लेने के उद्देश्य से पूछा। (ढोल, 13)

से परिचय कर—"to make the acquaintance of, to become acquainted with"

जब भेंट हुई तो सोचा, इस अद्भुत स्त्री से आवश्यक परिचय करना चाहिए। (नदी, 27)

से पहचान कर—"to get acquainted with"

श्रीकान्त इस हरिप्रसन्न के प्रति चिन्तित होता जा रहा है। उसके प्राणों में क्या बेचैनी है कि चुप आराम से बैठना इसके लिए संभव नहीं रह गया था। कहा, "हरि, मुझे मालूम नहीं कि तुम भटके कम हो। जरा दो रोज सुख-चैन से बैठ लो न। सत्या आएगी, उसे पढ़ाना। तुम्हारी भाभी आएंगी उनसे पहचान करना। दुनिया को तुम वीरान क्यों समझते हो?"...(सुता, 113)

5. **की जानकारी कर ले—"to familiarize oneself with"**

अत: तार पंजीकृत करा लेने से तथा इन सरकारी विभागों की जानकारी कर लेने से तार के व्यय में बचत भी की जा सकती है। (आज, 4)

80. व्यय, खर्चा, खर्च

1. व्यय, खर्चा and खर्च refer to expending or consuming some limited resource (e.g., money, time, energy) by putting it to use in a variety of ways.

व्यय is a term used in accounting to refer to an outlay or the creation of a liability for an expense item. It may also be applied to the consumption or depletion of something through use or in referring to the state of an object being used up through mutation.

खर्चा is spending money, incurring an expense for the practice of paying for the services or goods one normally buys. The term implies some sort of opinion of the speaker about the spending habits of the subject.

खर्च is a more general term referring to expenditure or expense (of money, time, energy, skill, etc.) implying using, utilizing or using up one's resources (usually in specified amounts or sums).

2. These nouns are ± process and form ANP with में, पर, and के लिये. Only में permits the occurrence of infinitives before it. These expressions are not pluralized.

3. **व्यय कर—"to undergo the expenses"**

अन्य खादों की ढुलाई तथा फैलाने में जो व्यय करना पड़ता है वह बच जाता है। (खाद, 57)

के लिए व्यय कर—"to spend, to make use of"

उसे ईश्वर की सहायता समझकर दरिद्रों के लिए, अपने दल की आवश्यकता की पूर्ति के लिए, व्यय करने में कोई संकोच नहीं करते। (तितली, 224)

पर व्यय कर—"to make use of, to disburse for"

साथ ही निर्धनों की आय में वृद्धि करने के लिये कर-राशि निम्न कार्यों पर व्यय की जा सकती है...(एमाई, 57)

व्यय कर—"to expend"

एक उपभोक्ता भी मुद्रा की सहायता से अपनी सीमित आय विभिन्न वस्तुओं और सेवाओं पर इस प्रकार व्यय कर सकता है कि उसे अधिकतम संतुष्टि प्राप्त हो। (एमाई, 51)

व्यय कर—"to consume"

अमोनियम सल्फेट...मिट्टी के चूने को व्यय करता है...(खाद, 04)

4. **खर्चा कर—"to incur an expenditure"**

दूसरी समितियों को इन कामों में खर्चा भी अधिक करना पड़ेगा और फिर भी ये उनका उतना अच्छा प्रबन्ध नहीं कर सकेंगी जितना कि राज्य कर सकता है। (भारत, 30)

5. **खर्च कर—"to spend"**

जयराम ने झंडे को ज़मीन पर खड़ा करके कहा—भाइयो, महात्मा गांधी का हुक्म है कि आप लोग ताड़ी, शराब न पियें। जो रुपये आप यहां उड़ा देते हैं, वह अगर अपने बाल-बच्चों को खिलाने-पिलाने में खर्च करें, तो कितनी अच्छी बात हो। (सम, 68)

खर्च कर—"to spend"

पहली पंचवर्षीय योजना में पिछड़े वर्गों पर व्यय किया धन और द्वितीय पंचवर्षीय योजना में अनुमानित व्यय तथा अब तक खर्च किये हुये धन का अनुमान निम्नलिखित तालिका से लग जायेगा...(भारत, 16)

खर्च कर—"to squander"

महिपाल सोचने लगा कि ऐसे चुनाव से क्या लाभ ? करोड़ों रुपये खर्च करके भी जनता का सही मत न जाना जा सका। सच तो यह है कि जनता का किसी राजनैतिक पार्टी में विश्वास नहीं, क्योंकि समय ऐसा है कि जिनमें सहानुभूति और सद्भावना का प्रायः लोप हो गया है। (बूंद, 435)

खर्च कर—"to spend"

भगौती : पन्द्रह तो क्या काका, मैं पांच सौ रुपये खर्च करने के लिए तैयार हूं। चुप हो जाता है। वह भूत हांकना नहीं जानता काका। (अंधा, 146)

खर्च कर—"to spend"

आप यहां कितना रुपया महीना खर्च करते हैं ? (तीन, 18)

खर्च कर—"to use up"

जय : पिताजी मेरे नाम बैंक में पचहत्तर हज़ार रुपये जमा कर गए। मैं उन्हें नहीं खर्च करना चाहता। मैं सोचता हूं जिसके पास बैंक-बैलेंस में जितना ही अधिक धन होगा। उसमें उतनी ही अधिक शक्ति होगी। (रात, 127)

खर्च कर—"to squander"

हां, बारातियों के स्वागत-सत्कार में कन्यापक्ष वालों ने काफी कुछ खर्च कर डाला है। (दुख, 91)

खर्च कर—"to spend on"

दारोगा जी मन-ही-मन हिसाब लगाने लगे कि कितने रुपये दहेज में दूंगा और कितने खाने-पीने में खर्च करूंगा। (सेवा, 12)

खर्च कर—"to use up"

यह क्या है कि वह अपनी तमाम फूलों की मेहनत मेरे ही कमरे में खर्च कर देता है। (बूंद, 166)

खर्च कर—"to use, to expend"

सालों ने सारी पढ़ाई खर्च करके दो लफ्ज़ ईजाद किये हैं शायद और तकरीबन। (जानवर, 88)

खर्च कर—"to use, to use up"

मैं जैसे यही कह रहा था कि उस दिन तुमने लेखकों, कवियों और असभ्यों की आलोचना में अपनी विद्वता खर्च की थी। (राह, 42)

खर्च कर—"to spend"

चतुर भेड़पालक जो अधिक पैसा नहीं खर्च करना चाहता...(भेड़, 30)

खर्च कर—"at the expense of"

आये दिन इकन्नी-इकन्नी के पीछे तो हत्यायें होती हैं, अरबों रुपये और बेशकीमत दिमाग खर्च कर दुनिया को भिस्मार करने के लिए बम बनाये जाते हैं। (बूंद, 242)

खर्च कर—"to spend"

ईश्वर है या नहीं इस समस्या पर उसने गंभीरता से एक क्षण भी खर्च नहीं किया। (बूंद, 165)

81. विनिमय, आदान-प्रदान, लेन-देन

1. These expressions refer to the act of giving something to someone in return for receiving something (else) from him.

विनिमय implies conversion (i.e. exchanging one thing for a specified equivalent).

आदान-प्रदान is reciprocal giving and receiving lacking in the specific implication of विनिमय.

लेन-देन (dialectal variant : लैन-दैन) refers to the practice of giving and taking in general with no reference to reciprocity. The term is often used in referring to the practice of money-lenders, or to someone's act, which in the opinion of the speaker, constitutes an unfair exchange.

2. विनिमय is ± process, and both आदान-प्रदान and लेन-देन are + process. They all form ANP with का and are not pluralized.

3. का विनिमय कर—"to exchange"

जब तक वस्तुओं का मूल्यांकन नहीं होता तब तक उनका विनिमय नहीं किया जा सकता क्योंकि प्रत्येक पक्ष अपनी वस्तु के लिए अधिक से अधिक प्रतिफल पाने का हठ करेगा। (एमाई, 77)

विनिमय कर—"to barter, to trade"

चूंकि एक गाय बराबर दस बकरियां और पचास आम बराबर एक बकरी के, तो एक गाय पांच सौ आमों से विनिमय की जा सकती है। (एमाई, 16)

4. का आदान-प्रदान कर—"to exchange"

विरहेश और बड़ी ने तीन बार इस थैली के सहारे पत्रों का आदान-प्रदान किया है। (बूंद, 229)

का आदान-प्रदान कर—"to exchange"

अन्यान्य वस्तुओं के समान ही विचारों का भी आदान-प्रदान किया जा सकता है। (सुधा, 30)

से का आदान-प्रदान कर—"to interchange, to exchange"

जैवन्स के शब्दों में "तुलनात्मक कम आवश्यकवस्तु से तुलनात्मक अधिक आवश्यक-वस्तु के आदान-प्रदान करने को वस्तुविनिमय कहते हैं।" (एमाई, 6)

आदान-प्रदान कर—"to interchange"

दोनों की आंखें एक क्षण के लिए मिलीं—स्नेहपूर्ण आदान-प्रदान करने के लिए। मधुबन उठ खड़ा हुआ, तितली बाहर चली आई। (तितली, 34)

5. लेन-देन कर—"to engage in money-lending"

रामटहल—नहीं डाक्टर साहब, अभी बीस बाईस साल से यहां आये हैं। लैन-दैन किया। गरीबों के मकान मोल ले लिये और यह इतनी बड़ी जायदाद खड़ी कर ली। (खिलौने, 20)

82. दरगुजर, गवारा, सहन, बर्दाश्त

1. दरगुजर, गवारा, सहन, and बर्दाश्त all characterize the state of one who undergoes, suffers, experiences or puts up with a person, thing, situation or the like which in various ways is harmful, unpleasant or disagreeable to him.

दरगुजर stresses the disposition of one who is given to (the habit of) being proof against or not being readily or easily affected by some situation or condition which confronts him. The term implies the speaker's mild disapproval of the subject's act of intentionally disregarding (such as when he tries to lightly pass over) or sometimes failing to take due notice of something said by the speaker or someone else.

गवारा is almost exclusively applied by the speaker in making an assertion about something (such as another person's or the speaker's request, expectation or the like) which does not agree or meet with the subject's habit, disposition or temperament, or is inappropriate in some ways (in the opinion of the subject). In situations where the speaker addresses the subject directly, the term implies that the speaker is fully aware of the subject's habit but somehow still expects that the subject will comply with the speaker's or the other person's request.

सहन stresses the limits of the subject's (persons s well as things) forbearance (i.e. exercise of patience or restraint) or ability to remain unaffected in the face of or when being subjected to adversity, impropriety or evil. When used with negation the term refers to the subject's (i. e. some individual's) inability to put up with something any longer implying that the limit of his patience has been reached.

बर्दाश्त refers to the subject's capacity to withstand or endure affliction, or afflictive or counteractive circumstances.

2. दरगुजर, गवारा and बर्दाश्त are all —process, and सहन is ±process, However, the + process occurrence of सहन is very rare. सहन forms ANP with का and is not pluralized.

3. **को दरगुजर कर—"to pass over, to disregard"**

कुछ हास्यरस का लेखक समझ कर मेरे इस मार्मिक निबंध को भी हंसी में दरगुजर करना चाहें...(सच, 57)

को दरगुजर कर जा—"to take something lightly, to disregard, to hold back from"

वे दरारें कैसी थीं, कैसे हमारी भावना और चिन्तन के क्षेत्रों में वे एक विघटन

उत्पन्न करती रहीं, और क्यों उस समय हमें उन्हें दरगुजर कर जाना पड़ा और आज अकस्मात् वे कैसे अनावृत होकर अपने समस्त भयंकर परिणामों को साथ लेकर हमारे सामने खड़ी हो गई हैं ...(मूल्य, 81)

4. **को गवारा न कर—"to be incompatible"**

फिर मुंशी जी की इन्सानियत और शराफ़त इस बात को कतई गवारा नहीं कर सकती कि आपके निमंत्रण को नामंजूर कर आपके दिल को दुख पहुंचाए। (तुला, 125)

गवारा कर—"to care to"

मेरे मित्र बहुत थोड़े हैं, और भुवन मास्टर साहब तो शायद पत्र लिखना ही गवारा न करें। (नदी, 69)

गवारा कर—"to stand"

कितनी ही ढीठ क्यों न बने, पर नारी की निर्लज्जता की एक सीमा होती है—प्रेमी के पत्र, अपनी आंखों के सामने, पति द्वारा पढ़े जाना, वह गवारा न कर सकी। (सोमा, 295)

5. **का सहन कर—"to experience"**

परन्तु दुख का सहन करना कई बार असह्य ही नहीं असंभव प्रतीत होता है...। (चमत्कार, 35)

को सहन कर—"to tolerate"

जितनी शरण वे दे सके थे, दी थी। उससे ज्यादा दूर तक वे मुझे सहन नहीं कर पाये थे। (मांस, 116)

को सहन कर पा—"to withstand"

विद्यावती घटनाओं के इस भीषण संघात को सहन न कर पाई। (नदी, 54)

को सहन न कर सक—"to pull through, to bear with"

पट्टाभिषेक के चौथे साल ही हमारे बड़े पुत्र बल्लाल राजा बुरे ग्रह के शिकार होकर स्वर्ग सिधार गए। उस समय आप ही लोगों की सहायता तथा सहानुभूति के बल पर मैं अपने दुख को सहन कर सकी। (शांतला, 23)

को सहन कर—"to endure"

यही आशा और यही विश्वास ऐसे दुर्दिन को सहन करना संभव बनाते हैं। (चमत्कार, 33)

को (स्वेच्छा से...) सहन कर—"to go through"

दुख को स्वेच्छा से और ज्ञानपूर्वक इस बुद्धि से सहन करना उसको बहुत कुछ कम करने में सहायता देता है। (चमत्कार, 34)

को सहन करने वाला हो—"to be able to sustain"

इस नस्ल की भेड़ें छोटे कद की और विपरीत परिस्थितियों को सहन करने वाली होती हैं और कम चराई की परिस्थितियों का उन पर कोई प्रभाव नहीं पड़ता है। (भेड़, 12)

को सहन कर—"to bear"

ऐसा न करें तो कल लोग क्या कहेंगे ? यही न कि वे अपनी पत्नी को काबू में नहीं रख सके, वे दब्बू थे, अपनी नौजवान पत्नी के गुलाम थे नपुंसक थे—छिः। ऐसे आरोपों को उनका पुरुषत्व कैसे सहन करेगा। (धनु, 123)

को सहन कर—"to put up with"

भोली जनता चुपचाप उनके अत्याचारों को ईश्वरीय क्रीड़ाओं के रूप में दैवी आदेश समझते हुए सहन करती रहती है। क्योंकि उन्हें समझाया जाता है कि इनके सब उपदेश इनके नहीं होते, वरन् ये जो कुछ भी कहते हैं उसका आधार दैवी आदेश होता है। (धर्म, 19)

को सहन कर सक—"to tolerate"

मोम में विशेष प्रकार की गंध होती है जिसे कीड़े सहन नहीं कर सकते इसलिए हमारा कान उनसे बचा रहता है। (आज, 29)

को (बड़ा कष्ट) सहन करना पड़—"to be overly subjected to"

भारतवर्ष में अनेक स्थानों पर संयुक्त परिवार का रिवाज है। इनमें स्त्रियों को बड़ा कष्ट सहन करना पड़ता है और उनका समुचित विकास नहीं हो पाता। (भारत, 44-45)

को (भारी नुकसान) सहन करना पड़—"to be subjected to (heavy losses)"

मुद्रा रहित अवस्था में जब लगान और मजदूरी का भुगतान वस्तुओं के रूप में दिया जाता था तब किसानों और श्रमिकों को भारी नुकसान सहन करना पड़ता था। (एमाई, 39)

को सहन कर—"to resist"

अम्लता को बहुत सी फसलें सहन नहीं कर सकतीं और भयंकर अम्लता होते ही पौधों की बढ़वार पूर्ण रूप से रुक जाती है। (खाद, 105)

सहन कर—"to put up with"

अपने मद में चूर होकर तुम मुझे बार बार अपमानित करती हो। मैं अब यह कदापि सहन न करूंगा तुम्हारी दृष्टि में तुच्छ और नगण्य बन कर अब मैं अपने को पीड़ित होने दूंगा। (बूंद, 140)

सहन कर—"to tolerate"

गरीबों का प्रेम भी ये पूंजीपति लोग सहन नहीं कर सकते। आप तो दरवाज़े बन्द कर अपनी प्रियतमा से हासविलास करते...। (बूंद, 230)

सहन कर सक—"to forbear with"

यही तो मेरा एक अपराध है। तो क्या इतना-सा विचलन भी मानवता का ढोंग करने वाला निर्मम संसार या क्रूर नियति नहीं सहन कर सकती ? वह उपेक्षा करने के योग्य साधारण-सी बात नहीं थी क्या ? (तितली, 251-52)

सहन कर सक—"to bear"

नारी के विरह में नर निर्माता बन गया। तरह तरह की रचनाओं में अपना मन उलझाये रखकर भी वह एक क्षण के लिए अपना अकेलापन सहन न कर सका। हरदम उसे अपनी प्रिया की याद सताती थी; परन्तु डर के मारे वह उसके पास जाने का साहस नहीं करता था। (बूंद, 130)

6. **को बर्दाश्त कर पा—"to put up with, to tolerate"**

जो भी हो, दोनों तरह से लोगों को यह अच्छा नहीं लगा था, क्योंकि किसी को बुरा देखकर लोग बर्दाश्त नहीं कर पाते और अच्छा बनते देखना उनसे सहा नहीं जाता। (मांस, 124)

को बर्दाश्त कर सक—"to give in"

मालिक अब बर्दाश्त न कर सका। चल तुझे दो हजार रूबल दूंगा। मेरे सामने से दूर हट जा। (रूस, 5)

को बर्दाश्त कर सक—"to stand, to withstand"

एक किसान किसी पुलिस के आदमी के साथ इतनी बेअदबी करे, इसे भला वह कहीं बर्दाश्त कर सकती है। (सम, 11)

बर्दाश्त कर—"to bear"

मैं रोज खा रही हूं ये कोड़े। और मां चुपचाप बर्दाश्त कर रही है। (लाख, 31)

को बर्दाश्त कर पा—"to be able to bear with"

ईसाई सभ्यता की साढ़े उन्नीस सदियों और भारतीय सभ्यता की उससे भी तीन चार हजार वर्ष पुरानी उच्चनैतिकता का गुमान करने वाले आज के सभ्यजन, विचारक, समाज सेवक क्यों कर इस बेहूदगी को बर्दाश्त कर पाते हैं। (बंद, 433)

को बर्दाश्त कर —"to tolerate"

मुल्ला साहब, घूरे के भी दिन फिरते हैं। अच्छे से अच्छे शाही जमाने में हिन्दुओं के धर्म को बर्दाश्तभर ही तो किया गया है, अब जमाना आया है कि उसको इज्जत भी मिल रही है। (बीर, 99)

बर्दाश्त कर सक—"to contain (anger)"

चार दिन के लिये क्यों जमाने भर से बिगाड़ करें। साहब अब क्रोध को न बर्दाश्त कर सके। (पांच, 17)

को चूड़ियां पहन कर बर्दाश्त कर—"to put up with something without doing anything about it, to let go unchallenged"

क्या वे अपने पुरुषत्व की इस चुनौती को चूड़ियां पहनकर बर्दाश्त कर लेंगे। (धनु, 122)

को बर्दाश्त कर—"to put up with"

जितने-जितने हम अपनी कल्पना में कठिनाइयों और असफलताओं के आगे नहीं झुकते और उनको बर्दाश्त करके आगे बढ़ने का संकल्प करते है उतनी-उतनी हमारी प्रच्छन्न शक्तियां उमड़ती हैं और हममें आगे बढ़ने की क्षमता आती है। (चमत्कार, 34)

बर्दाश्त किये जा—"to be able to sustain"

सुख के दिन उसने देखे थे। उन सुख के दिनों में उसने जो आराम पाया था, उसकी बदौलत ही आज वह भूख बर्दाश्त किये जा रही थी। (लाख, 49)

बर्दाश्त कर—"to tolerate"

अगर यहाँ की पुलिस उनको बचा न देती तो मैं दिखा देता कि यह दूसरा शहर है, यहां की कल्चर दूसरी जरूर है, लेकिन गुण्डाशाही बर्दाश्त नहीं की जाती यहां...। (राह, 38)

बर्दाश्त कर—"to tolerate"

सज्जन उसकी अपनी इच्छा का ही पुरुष रूप है। जिस स्त्री ने अब तक किसी पुरुष का रंगीन नजरों से अपनी ओर देखना बर्दाश्त नहीं किया, जिसने इससे पहले अपने तीन प्रेम याचकों को दुत्कार दिया था वह सज्जन के आगे सब तरह से परास्त है। (बूंद, 288)

बर्दाश्त कर—"to tolerate"

पुरुष अपने पौरुष का अपमान एवं लांछन नहीं सह सकता, बाकी सब कुछ बर्दाश्त कर सकता है। (धनु, 37)

बर्दाश्त कर--"to put up with"

साहब मैं सच कहता हूं—मैं सब कुछ सह सकता हूं, लेकिन हुजूर मैं गालियां बर्दाश्त नहीं कर सकता...। (बाहों, 133)

के साथ बर्दाश्त कर रह—"to put up with"

कहती जाओ, कहती जाओ ! तुम्हारे इस मजाक के नश्तर को मैं बड़े धीरज के साथ बर्दाश्त कर रहा हूं। (बूंद, 451)

बर्दाश्त कर—"to suffer"

सज्जन बोला—पुराने लोगों को अपने पैसे की रक्षा करने के लिए कितनी घुटन बर्दाश्त करनी पड़ती थी। (बूंद, 51)

बर्दाश्त कर—"to put up with"

परन्तु वह हरगिज बर्दाश्त नहीं कर पाती—वे हैं महिपाल की बातें। अपने 24 वर्ष के वैवाहिक जीवन में अपने पति के जीवन—ढर्रे और विचारों को कभी सच्चे मन से ग्रहण नहीं कर पाई ! उसके मन में वर्षों से एक छिपी हुई शंका है। (बूंद, 107-8)

बर्दाश्त कर—"to withstand (danger)"

कोई भी खतरा बरदाश्त करने को तैयार रहें...। (मूल्य, 90)

फजीहत...बर्दाश्त कर जा—"to swallow (insults)"

काफी फजीहत हुई रामसागर की, मगर मुंह लटकाए सब कुछ बर्दाश्त कर गया। (दुख, 59)

बर्दाश्त कर ले—"to be capable of holding"

नमक मिला हुआ पानी कुछ अंश और सर्दी बर्दाश्त कर लेता है। (समुद्र, 89)

बर्दाश्त कर--"to survive, to withstand"

तारा देवी बोली—देखती नहीं है, रोज शाम को एक घंटा-डेढ़ घंटा गायब रहती है।...अंडा-मछली की गर्मी उतारे बिना बांकीपुर की गर्मी कैसे बर्दाश्त कर सकती है। (दीर्घ, 68)

बर्दाश्त कर—"to forbear, to bear"

नहीं तो, मैंने ये कभी नहीं कहा कि गर्वों से लड़ना चाहिए। हम दोनों एक दूसरे के साथी हैं, अपनी अपनी अच्छाइयों बुराइयों के साथ हैं। अगर हमारा साथ सच्चा है तो हमें एक दूसरे के लिए बर्दाश्त भी करना होगा। (बूंद, 418)

83. गुफ्तगू, वार्तालाप, वार्ता, बातचीत, गपशप, बात, खुसर-पुसर, खुस-पुस

1. These expressions refer to the act of engaging in conversation with another person in a variety of ways, on a variety of topics.

गुफ्तगू applies to the act of holding a conversation or a brief discussion with someone on something important, problematic or the like.

वार्तालाप is orally exchanging opinions, ideas, observations, sentiments and the like with another person about a variety of matters or topics.

वार्ता applies strictly to that which is the subject matter of a conversation or an oral discourse (such as a parable, a story, an incident, sometimes a serious continued negotiation) carried on or conducted by two or more persons participating as narrator and listeners or as negotiators.

बातचीत is talking to someone or entering into conversation with someone informally or in a round-about way, usually with some specific objective or aim in mind. If no objective or aim is implied or expressed in the context, the term may refer to the act of socializing with someone through conversation.

गपशप applies to the act of talking to another person in a light and familiar manner or conversing without ceremony with a friend or an acquaintance.

बात is used as a general term referring to the act of talking with someone, or to make a reference to what a third person intends to do or has done. In the latter sense the term implies a comment by the speaker on the subject's intention to act in a particular way or to the act itself. When a specific reference is made to something done by the subject (such as by using a suitable adjectival expression before बात) then the noun refers to some incident (i.e., something said or done by the subject) in which the subject's involvement is characterized by the speaker as an act of wisdom, stupidity or the like (अक्लमन्दी की बात, बेवकूफी की बात).

The sentences with बात कर—, when the expression is not intended as a comment upon the subject's act, usually contain some expression referring to the mode or manner of talking or speaking.

खुसर-पुसर and खुस-पुस are used when two or more persons are carrying on some conversation or talking to each other in a low voice with or without the intention of concealing the contents of their conversation from other persons. खुसर-पुसर is used to express the idea of words whispered back and forth over a period of time whereas खुस-पुस applies to passing the word from one person to another in a whispered tone.

2. All the nouns are +process, and form ANP with के साथ or से. In addition वार्ता and बात may also occur with की. Only बात can be pluralized.

3. **के साथ गुफ्तगू कर—"to confer with, to consult"**

वह कप्तान के साथ एक बहुत अहम मामले पर गुफ्तगू करने आए थे।

4. **से वार्तालाप कर—"to chat with someone"**

अभी-अभी भोजन समाप्त करके प्रभु अपने शयन-गृह के सामने वाले बरामदे में बैठे विष्णु से वार्तालाप कर रहे थे। (शांतला, 85)

वार्तालाप कर—"to be engaged in conversation about"

सब लोग एक साथ बैठे हुए काशी नगर के सुन्दर दृश्यों पर वार्तालाप कर रहे थे (चित्र, 149)

वार्तालाप करते—"talking to (each other)"

दोनों वार्तालाप करते थोड़ी दूर आगे बढ़े ही थे कि उन्होंने देखा कि दो आदमी परस्पर झगड़ रहे हैं। (शबरी, 40)

5. **की वार्ता कर—"to be talking about"**

अनेक लोग आपस में हंसी-मजाक करते हुए प्राकृतिक और अप्राकृतिक मैथुन की वार्ता कर गोमती की धार के विपरीत एक रसधार बहाते हुए बड़े ही रस-मग्न हैं। (बंद, 406)

6. **से बात-चीत कर—"to talk to"**

अपने अन्तःपुर की रानियों के साथ वह संस्कृत में ही बातचीत किया करता था। (ज्योति, 19)

से बातचीत कर—"to talk with"

आज वे लोग चाची से बातचीत करने घर आयेंगे, और कदाचित इसी बहाने लड़की को भी देख लेंगे। (परिन्दे, 23)

से बातचीत कर—"to get in touch with"

इसी बीच में उसने शहर में जाकर मिशनरी सोसाइटी से भी बातचीत की थी। (तितली, 75)

से बातचीत कर—"to talk with, to enter into conversation with"

शैला बड़ी असुविधा में पड़ी। वह अपरिचित से क्या बातचीत करे। उसने पूछा—आप क्या चाहती हैं? (तितली, 27)

से बातचीत कर—"to talk to"

अनवरी ने धीरे से प्रसंग छेड़ दिया—मिस शैला। आपको इन देहाती लोगों से बातचीत करने में बड़ा सुख मिलता है। (तितली, 35)

बातचीत कर—"to talk about"

बातचीत का यह इंटरमिटेंट तरीका कुछ बुरा नहीं है, ये बीच-बीच के ब्रेक अपने-आप में तटस्थता दे देने वाले हैं, फिर बातचीत कोई कैसी ही करे। (नदी, 34)

मीठी बातचीत कर—"to talk to someone nicely, to say something nice"

कुछ मीठी बातचीत भी की या गाल फुलाए बैठी ही रही ? (निरू, 65)

हंस-खुलकर बातचीत कर—"to open up with someone, to speak to"

वह बाबू के रोज़मर्रा आने वाले मित्रों में नहीं हैं; बाबू के मित्र हैं, यह कहना भी कठिन है शायद इसलिए कि उम्र में वह बाबू से आधे हैं और कोशिश करने पर भी बाबू उनसे हंस-खुलकर बातचीत नहीं कर पाते। (जलती झाड़ी, 26)

के साथ बातचीत कर—"to speak to"

सिकंदर ने पौरव से अधीनता स्वीकार कराने के लिये उसके पास दूत भेजे। पौरव ने दूतों को उत्तर दिया कि मैं अपनी सेना सहित युद्ध के मैदान में सिकंदर और उसकी सेना के साथ बातचीत करूंगा। (सुंदर, 26)

बातचीत करते—"talking to"

शायद उन्होंने यह सोचकर मुझे क्षमा कर दिया हो कि मैं गांव से आया हूं ; इसलिए किसी भी स्त्री-पुरुष को बातचीत करते देखकर सिर्फ एक ही दृष्टिकोण से सोचने का अभ्यस्त हूं। (राह, 20)

से बातचीत करते समय—"while talking to"

...अब्रहम लिंकन दूसरों से बातचीत करते समय प्रायः छोटी-छोटी कथाएं बहुत कहता था। (कथा, 3)

7. के साथ गपशप कर—"to talk to (...I would like to have a friendly conversation with...before going to bed)"

हरि—नहीं मालूम ? खैर, मैं सोचता था कि तसवीर छोड़ू या खुद उससे छूटूं और आज श्रीकान्त के साथ गपशप करता हुआ सोऊं। (सुता, 166)

के यहां कुछ गपशप कर—"to spend some time (gossiping, chatting, etc.) at someone's place"

तो चलो प्रभा के यहां ही कुछ गपशप की जाय। (तीन, 58)

8. **से बात कर—"to speak to"**

आप उनसे बात करें। यदि उन्होंने नांही कर दी तो मेरी नांही अभी ले लीजिए। (बांस, 41)

से गुप्त बातें कर—"to speak to someone in private or confidentially"

मैं एक प्रसिद्ध रसायनी हूं; लोहे से सोना बनाने की विद्या जानता हूं परम गुणाग्राही धर्ममूर्ति मंत्री जी से इस विषय में कुछ गुप्त बातें करना चाहता हूं। आदर्श, 86)

के साथ बात कर—"to talk to"

...कि आदमी अपने परिचितों के साथ उस सहजता और खुलेपन के साथ बात नहीं करता जिससे अपरिचित लोगों के साथ करता है। (राकेश, 26)

की बातें कर—"to talk about"

वह धर्म परिवर्तन की भी बातें करती है। उसे हिन्दू आचार-विचार अच्छे लगते हैं। रहन-सहन, पहिनावा और खाना-पीना ठीक ठीक। जैसे मेरे कुटम्ब की स्त्रियां भी उसे अपने में मिला लेने में हिचकेंगी नहीं। (तितली, 111)

बात कर—"to speak to"

स्वरूपा मैं चिल्लाती हूं या तू चिल्लाता है? कह दिया कि मेरे सामने अकड़ कर बात मत किया कर। (खिलौने, 41)

से बढ़ बढ़ कर बातें कर—"to speak to someone boastfully (implying exceeding one's authority, limitations or the like)"

मेरा खेत भी जोतता है, और मुझी से बढ़ बढ़ कर बातें करता है। (तितली, 39)

शक्ति से बाहर की बात कर—"to speak boastfully (here, 'don't say what you can't do')"

...अपनी शक्ति से बाहर की बात न करो युवक। विशु: (जो अब तक मौन हो इस वार्तालाप को सुनता रहा है) नहीं सौम्य उसे अपनी बात पूरी कहने दो। (कोणार्क, 36)

9. **खुसर-पुसर कर—"to whisper back and forth, to speculate in whispered tones"**

परन्तु सभी घबराए हुए थे और आपस में खुसर-पुसर कर रहे थे। (बाल, 11-33)

खुसर-फुसुर—"to gossip about"

औरतें घंटों अकेली बैठी खुसुर-फुसुर करती रहतीं। मर्द अपने गांव की बातें करते... (दुग्गल, 115)

10. **खुसपुस कर—"to talk gibberish"**

अकबर––(उन दोनों से) तुम दोनों क्या खुसपुस कर रहे हो ? पियो और जोर से बोलो। ताड़ी पियो, जबान का ताला खुल जायगा। (बीर, 75)

खुस-फुस कर—"to whisper, to say"

कन्चनपुरी तुमको भी उस दिन लक्ष्यबेध के उत्सव के बीच में बुलाकर उससे खुसफुस नहीं करनी चाहिये थी। (कचनार, 236)

84. प्रयोग, परीक्षण, परीक्षा, तजुर्बा, आजमाइश, निरीक्षण, मुआइना, परख, जांच, निरीक्षण-परीक्षण, जांच-परख, पहचान, पड़ताल, जांच-पड़ताल

1. These expressions describe the manner in which one exercises one's faculty of perception or power of vision upon someone or something in order to ascertain whether something is the case, or to find out or learn with certainty something about the worth, quality, significance or condition of the object.

प्रयोग (lit. extending the use of something) is applied to any tentative provisional or experimental use or application of something (such as the adoption of an expression, a style of composition or the like) in order to (or sometimes expecting or hoping to) produce or bring about a desired result, or create a new effect. It is also used to refer to the act or the action of making any sort of laboratory experimentation with some product or a raw material involving trial and error in order to find new uses or applications for that product or material. The term makes a strong reference to the mental attitude of the subject in the process of testing to see if something works.

परीक्षण (lit. subjecting something to a critical and overall examination) stresses an act or an operation carried out under conditions or in a manner determined by the experimenter in order to verify, establish or illustrate some suggested or known truth or to discover something unknown. The term may therefore refer to the application of any of the recognized methods of testing (such as the use of chemical reagents or other such methods employed for testing purposes in a laboratory) or the use of any suitably devised diagnostic procedure or a series of procedures (such as planned experiments, trials or the like) which would, as the case may be, satisfy the requirements of a critical and overall examination.

परीक्षा refers to the act of testing something, i.e., anything done to put an object to a decisive test by means of experiment, use, experience, or comparison with a (given) standard. In ordinary language, the term simply makes a reference to the act of seeing or trying something for oneself.

तजुर्बा stresses the notion of experience or insight gained by the subject in the form of practical wisdom or direct knowledge resulting from what one has encountered, undergone, or lived through. The term may, therefore, be used to describe the subject's participation in an event or his direct observation of it as if he were experimenting with something or making an experiment.

आजमाइश stresses the state of one who is being subjected to some sort of trying condition (usually indicated by using the appropriate noun as the subject of the sentence) or is being put to a test. The term is also used of a thing when it is being tried out in a manner usually expressed in a sentence, or is being tested for its strength, endurance, worth, accuracy, truth or utility.

निरीक्षण applies to the act of viewing or looking steadily and intently or with studious and prolonged attention at someone or something, implying an effort made to see through or penetrate below the surface, or grasp the observable facts or the details of an event.

मुआइना applies to the act of looking at something, usually with a sustained attention, (or by shifting one's eyes back and forth or from one part of the object to another) as one would normally do when one is busy repeatedly looking over or going over the details of something as if trying to mentally recapitulate.

परख refers to one's ability to perceive something visually or to test something not directly observable so that its properties can be observed or comprehended

जांच describes the activity of one who is engaged in examining (such as by feeling, touching, holding in one's hand or by using some instrument), looking over or going over something in order to sense or come to know or recognize it mentally (esp. something hidden or obscure) or in order to judge the relative state of something in terms of some requirements or criteria set forth in advance.

निरीक्षण-परीक्षण describes the activity of one who mentally observes something (such as by forming an idea about the object) and then repeatedly puts his observation to a test, thus subjecting something to careful scrutiny, generally to establish the characteristic tendencies or trends.

जांच-परख describes the subjects engaging in the act of closely or minutely observing or his ability to observe the minute details of something in order to arrive at the object's relative worth.

पहचान refers to the subject's ability to discern or recognize something (i.e., to make out or perceive the correct identity of an object) on the basis of one's previous experience or with the assistance of some sort of information given to one in advance.

पड़ताल describes the act of one who is mentally trying to picture something (such as the cause of an event, or something about some object) by obtaining some clues from what is available or is directly observable, stressing a reliance on one's intuition rather than the application of the methods of testing.

जांच-पड़ताल describes the activity of one who is cautiously and carefully examining the details of something (usually by touching, feeling or going over the evidence and at the same time exercising his intuition) in order to figure out or mentally picture to himself something unknown about a phenomenon, or in order to make sure that something is in fact the way it is described or appears to be.

2. All the nouns, with the exception of निरीक्षण are + process. निरीक्षण is ± process, though its — process occurrence is relatively rare. They all form ANP with का (परीक्षा, आज़माइश, परख, जांच, जांच-परख, पहचान, पड़ताल and जांच-पड़ताल with की). Only तजुर्बा and परख are pluralized.

3. **पर प्रयोग कर—"to perform an experiment"**

सर्वप्रथम उन्होंने बेला की मधुर ध्वनि पर बत्तख को आत्म विभोर होते देखकर कुछ अन्य पशुओं पर भी वाद्य के प्रयोग किए। (बाल, 11-42)

पर प्रयोग कर—"to try as an experiment"

इसे खाद के रूप में प्रयुक्त करने के अनेक प्रयोग विभिन्न फस्लों पर डा० धर ने

किये हैं। शीरे में साधारण रूप से लगभग 3% नाइट्रोजन, 3 से 5% पोटाश...चूना तथा कार्बानिक पदार्थ काफी मात्रा में रहता है। (खाद, 73)

का प्रयोग कर—"to experiment"

कहा जाता है कि मूंगफली से सर्वप्रथम दूध बनाने का प्रयोग एक नीग्रो वैज्ञानिक डा० कार्बर ने किया था। (योजना, 5-20)

पर प्रयोग कर—"to conduct an experiment"

...इन सभी महत्वपूर्ण पहलुओं पर सिनेमा की इस नई शैली ने प्रचुर प्रयोग किये हैं, नागरिक रंगमंच जिससे यथेष्ट लाभ उठायेगा। (कोणार्क, 101)

4. **के साथ परीक्षण कर—"to experiment with"**

क्या अब भी वह जीवन के साथ परीक्षण करने में वैसा ही उदात्त है? (सुता, 11)

का परीक्षण कर—"to test, to detect"

अमोनियम सल्फेट के जलीय घोल में फैरिक क्लोराइड घोल की कुछ बूंदें मिलाने से इस पदार्थ का परीक्षण कर सकते हैं। यदि अमोनियम सल्फेट में सल्फो सायनेट मिला हुआ है, तो घोल रक्त के समान लाल बन जाता है। (खाद, 100)

का परीक्षण कर—"to put to a test"

निरन्तर अन्याय से जूझो, निरन्तर जड़ता से संघर्ष करते जाओ, निरन्तर सड़ी गली मृत्युग्रस्त रूढ़ियों का परीक्षण करते रहो। (चारू, 410)

पर...का परीक्षण कर—"to experiment with (sounds)"

...कुछ वैज्ञानिकों ने जीव जंतुओं पर संगीत के कुछ मधुर परीक्षण करके यह अनुभव किया है कि मनुष्य की भांति जीव-जन्तुओं पर भी संगीत का प्रभाव पड़ता है। (बाल, 11-42)

परीक्षण कर—"to conduct experiments"

अनुसंधान केन्द्रों में किये गये भेड़ के परीक्षणसम्बन्धी प्रजननों और ग्रामीण क्षेत्रों में उत्तम किस्म की भेड़ें पालने के लिये किये गए परीक्षणों से पता चला है कि अधिक चुनाव द्वारा ऊन की किस्म में काफी सुधार किया जा सकता है। (भेड़, 57)

5. **की परीक्षा कर—"to ascertain, to determine"**

जो ईंटें पानी में डालने से मुलायम हो जाती हैं, उन्हें तोड़ कर फिर पानी में डाल देते हैं फिर उनकी कोमलता की परीक्षा करते हैं। (ईंट, 12)

की परीक्षा कर—"to determine"

आर्किमीदीज को क्या प्राप्ति हुई थी कि वह स्नान करते समय जल से एकाएक निकलकर खुशी से उछल उठा था और पागल के समान चिल्लाया था "मैंने पा लिया, मैंने पा लिया", केवल एक नया विचार कि सोने में कितनी मिलावट है इसकी सुगमता से परीक्षा कैसे की जा सकती है। (चमत्कार, 42)

की परीक्षा कर ले—"to see for oneself"

किग ने उसे और चिमटाकर कहा—आज तुम्हें भी पिलाऊंगा प्रिये ! तुमको पीना होगा। फिर हम दोनों लिपटकर सोयेंगे। नशे में प्रेम कितना सजीव हो जाता है, इसकी परीक्षा कर लो। (सम, 53)

की सचाई की परीक्षा कर—"to put someone to a test, to test someone"

निरू सुरेश की सचाई की परीक्षा न कर रही थी, उस दृष्टि से हिसाब देखने का उसका उद्देश्य न था, वह केवल अपने मर्ज की दवा कर रही थी उचटते हुए चित्त को एकमुखी करती हुई, पर मरीज सुरेश बाबू उसके प्रश्न से जैसे क्षतस्थान की वेदना का अनुभव करने लगे। (निरू, 75)

परीक्षा कर—"to test"

खाना मैं बहुत बढ़िया बना सकता हूं परीक्षा कर इत्मीनान कर लें। (जुहू, 21)

की परीक्षा कर—"to judge, to try to ascertain, to give an expert opinion on"

उसने नम्रतापूर्वक सिकंदर से कहा—श्रीमान, मेरी प्रार्थना है कि आप अपने घोड़े को इसके (चित्र के) सामने खड़ा करके तब इसके गुण-दोष की परीक्षा करें। (आदर्श, 45)

की परीक्षा कर—"to put to the test"

हां, पहले मैं तुम्हारे त्याग की ही परीक्षा करूंगी, फिर दूसरों के किवाड़ खट खटाऊंगी। (तितली, 203)

परीक्षा कर—"to see for oneself"

"सत्य अपने अंतर की पीड़ा से जाना जाता है।" वही मानते हो, तो ठीक है, वही क्यों न परीक्षा करके देखो। (नदी, 27)

की परीक्षा कर—"to ascertain"

किन्तु उसकी वही दशा थी, जैसे कोई मनुष्य भय से आंखें मूंद लेता है। वह नहीं

चाहता था कि अपने संदेह की परीक्षा करके कठोर सत्य का नग्न रूप देखे। (तितली, 153)

6. **का तजुर्बा कर—"to try something out"**

हर बात को वह मुंह में डालकर एक नया तजुर्बा करना चाहता था। (लड़की, 59)

तजुर्बा कर—"to experience"

इस चक्कर में कौन पड़े ? एक बार तजुर्बा करके देख लिया, और भुगत लिया। (वनु, 79)

7. **की आजमाइश कर—"to test"**

आपस का सहयोग और सहानुभूति नष्ट होकर सभी भूखे जानवरों की तरह एक दूसरे पर अपने दांतों की तेजी की आजमाइश कर सकें। (मूल्य, 42)

की आज़माइश कर—"to put something to a test"

मुझे समझ में नहीं आया कि यह कामिनी कब से मेरे मन में चुपके से प्रवेश कर मेरी शक्ति की आजमाइश कर रही है! (राह, 42)

8. **का निरीक्षण कर—"to inspect"**

उन्होंने रहमत अली के साथ जाकर डाकखाने का निरीक्षण किया। (डगर, 13)

का निरीक्षण कर—"to inspect"

महन्त ने किले का निरीक्षण किया। टूटी फूटी दीवारों की मुरम्मत के लिये कारीगर और मजदूर लगा दिये। (कचनार, 317)

का निरीक्षण कर—"to inspect"

प्रधान मंत्री श्रीमती इंदिरा गांधी ने बिहार और उत्तर प्रदेश के बाढ़ पीड़ित क्षेत्रों का हवाई जहाज से निरीक्षण किया है। हो सकता है कि वे इन क्षेत्रों की सहायता के लिये कुछ बड़े कदम उठायें (नवभा, 1-4)

का निरीक्षण कर—"to gaze at"

शैला बड़े कुतूहल से भारतीय वातावरण में नीले आकाश जलती धूप और सहज ग्रामीण शांति का निरीक्षण कर रही थी। वह बातें भी करती जाती थी। (तितली, 23)

का निरीक्षण करते रह—"to watch"

मछुए अक्सर उनका निरीक्षण करते रहते हैं और किसी जगह उन्हें पानी पर झुके देख जान जाते हैं कि मछलियां वहां हैं। (समुद्र, 117)

का निरीक्षण कर—"to examine"

बच्चा होने के बाद डाक्टर ने फिर उसका निरीक्षण किया। फिर वार्ड में दूध-सी सफेद चादर वाले एक पलंग पर उसे लिटा दिया गया। (दुग्गल, 87)

का निरीक्षण कर—"to look at, to survey"

प्रोफैसर के प्रवेश करते ही क्लास-रूम में निस्तब्धता छा गई। कुर्सी पर बैठकर प्रोफैसर साहब ने क्लास का आदि से अन्त तक निरीक्षण किया। (तीन, 7)

का निरीक्षण करता हुआ—"to be intently gazing at, while examining"

मुंशी नोट का निरीक्षण करता हुआ जम्हाई लेकर उठ खड़ा हुआ और बोला, "तो अगले हफ्ते आऊं?" (जानवर, 54)

का निरीक्षण कर—"to examine, to take a good look at (oneself in the mirror)"

कपड़े बदल कर वह आदमकद शीशे के सामने जा खड़ा हुआ। उसने नख से शिख तक अपना निरीक्षण किया और सन्तुष्ट होकर मुस्कराया। (धारा, 202)

का निरीक्षण कर—"to oversee"

उपदेश देते हुए जब अन्त में कहा कि ईश्वर सबका निरीक्षण करता है, उसके पास एक-एक दाने का हिसाब रहता है तब झल्लाते हुए ननी ने कहा...(तितली, 225)

का निरीक्षण कर—"to observe"

आइए, गर्मी की ऋतु में दिन के समय हम न्यू इंगलेंड के समुद्रतट पर इस साम्राज्य का निरीक्षण करें! बाहरी बालू या चट्टानों के पार लहरें खेल रही हैं। (समुद्र, 69)

निरीक्षण करके—"by observing"

इस प्रकार के अनुशीलन के आधार पर हम स्वयं कुछ दिन निरीक्षण करके अपने पथ प्रदर्शन के लिए ऐसे नियम बना सकते हैं जो कि हमारे कामों को अधिक पुष्ट और सफल बना सकें। (चमत्कार, 52)

को निरीक्षण कर लो—"to take a look at, to examine"

महन्त ने कहा, 'जो हो, इनको तुम भी पास से निरीक्षण कर लो, वैद्यराज।' (कचनार, 315)

9. **का मुआइना कर—"to take a look at"**

कोई पन्द्रह मिनट में अनेक डिब्बों का मुआइना करके आंखों आंखों से प्रत्येक में मिल सकने वाली जगह के घन इंच और वर्ग इंच का हिसाब लगाने के बाद जब भुवन ने

एक डिब्बे में खिड़की के रास्ते अपना छोटा सा बक्स और संक्षिप्त बिस्तर अंदर ढेल दिया। (नदी, 12)

का मुआइना कर—"to inspect"

जेलर ने कई बार फांसी-सेल का मआइना किया। (देश, 100)

10. **की परख कर—"to observe"**

मौत का डर छुटाने के लिए मैंने मरते हुए मनुष्यों की बारीकी के साथ परख की है। (कचनार, 273)

की परख कर—"to appreciate, to discern"

किन्तु इस कारीगरी की ठीक-ठीक परख आप ही कर सकती हैं। (रूस, 14)

की परख कर—"to test, to ascertain"

पानी में डाल कर भी ईंटों की मजबूती की परख की जाती है। इसके लिए ईंटें पानी में 24 घंटे तक डुबोयी जाती हैं। (ईंट, 12)

की परख कर—"to make a test"

ईंटों के गुण धर्मों को जानने के लिए जो परखें की जाती हैं इनको दो वर्गों में रखा जा सकता है। (ईंट, 54)

की परख कर—"to test"

यहां पर जिन मिट्टी के नमूनों की परख की गयी है उनके सिकुड़ने और लोच धर्म सारणी 14 में दिये गये हैं। (ईंट, 84)

की परख कर—"to discern"

हम मुसलमानों को तो मालिक की मर्जी पर अपने को छोड़ देना पड़ता है, फिर सुख दुख की अलग अलग परख करने की किसको पड़ी है। (तितली, 36)

परख कर—"to make a test"

(1) ऐसी परखें जो बिना उपकरण से की जाती हैं और (2) ऐसी परखें जिनमें प्रयोगशाला के उपकरणों की आवश्यकता पड़ती है। (ईंट, 54)

11. **की जांच कर—"to search"**

आखिर जब उसने उस व्यापारी की जांच की तो पता चला कि उसने बहुत-सी अमूल्य चीजें पेट पर बांधी नहीं थीं बल्कि उसकी तोंद ही कुछ विचित्र प्रकार से बनी हुई थी। (शबरी, 19-20)

की जांच कर—"to determine, to investigate"

हम इस बात की भी पूरी जांच करना चाहेंगे कि...भारत के अन्दर इस्लाम मत का प्रचार वास्तव में किस ढंग से और किन उपायों से किया गया, हिन्दुओं के साथ भारत के मुसलमान शासकों का व्यवहार आद्योपांत किस ढंग का रहा...(सुन्दर, 12)

की जांच कर—"to examine"

सामान्य ज्ञान के किसी प्रश्न के उत्तर की जांच करते समय भाषा का ज्ञान दिया जा सकता है। (बुन, 23)

की जांच कर—"to subject something (in this context a computer) to a thorough check-up"

इसके एक दिन काम न करने पर बहुत बड़ा नुक्सान होता है, इसलिए इसकी माह दो माह पर डाक्टरी जांच की जाती है। (बाल, 1-57)

की जांच कर—"to take a look at, to examine"

शाम को जब भी भेड़ें घर को लौटें, तब भेड़पालक को चाहिए कि वह उन भेड़ों की जांच करे जो अपने शरीर को किसी खंभे आदि से रगड़ने की कोशिश करती हैं...(भेड़, 52)

की जांच कर—"to review"

जब गंगराज व्यवस्था की जांच कर ही रहे थे कि विजय-सिंहासन सभा-भवन के मंगल-वाद्य-यंत्रों ने यह घोषित किया कि अब अरुणोदय हो गया है। (शांतला, 36)

की जांच कर—"to go over"

आईये हम सफ़ाई के नियमों की जांच करें। (स्वस्थ, 1)

की जांच कर—"to search through"

तीन दिन वह कामनरूम में हर एक के सामने रोती और झुंझलाती रही। चौथे दिन रात को उसने दो व्यक्तियों की उपस्थिति में ताला खोला और सामान की जांच की। (जानवर, 22)

की जांच कर—"to investigate"

आज सुबह एक स्थानीय दैनिक पत्र ने अपनी सम्पादकीय टिप्पणी में कन्या के लेख की तारीफ करते हुए सरकार से इस मामले की जांच करने की मांग की थी। उसने चुनाव लड़ने वाली तमाम पोलिटिकल पार्टियों से यह अपील की थी कि वे अपनी हार जीत के लिए मानवता का गला न घोंटे। (बूंद, 165)

की जांच कर—"to determine"

ईंटों की चपटी सतह के आपस में टकराने से उत्पन्न हुई ध्वनि से ईंटों की उत्तमता की जांच की जाती है। (ईंट, 12)

की जांच कर—"to investigate, to ascertain"

इसमें नमूने की बनी ईंटों को पका कर उनकी सिकुड़ने तथा आकार में हुए परिवर्तनों की जांच करते हैं। (ईंट, 10)

की जांच कर—"to verify, to determine"

आदिम समाजों में जाकर वास्तविक अवलोकन द्वारा अपने इन निष्कर्षों की यथार्थता की जांच करने की आवश्यकता इन विकासवादी लेखकों ने अनुभव नहीं की। (सामाजिक, 63)

की जांच कर—"to test"

इस जांच से यह पता लगाया जाता है कि जांच की जाने वाली मिट्टी के मिश्रण में किस अनुपात से बालू और पानी की मात्रा डाली जाय। (ईंट, 10)

की जांच कर—"to examine"

डा० सुमित्रा देवी ने वीणा की डाक्टरी जाँच की और बतलाया कि शारीरिक स्थिति कमजोर है, मानसिक स्थिति भी अशांत मालूम होती है इसलिए जरा सावधानी लेनी चाहिए। (धनु, 134)

की जांच कर—"to look for"

जहां आप केवल रूप देखते हैं वहां आपके पिता बराबर का कुल, लड़की के गुण तथा अन्य कई बातों की जांच करते हैं, जिनकी आप रूप की तृष्णा के आगे परवाह नहीं करते, पर जो जीवन को सुखी बनाने के लिए नितांत आवश्यक हैं। (तीन, 56)

12. **का निरीक्षण-परीक्षण कर—"to scrutinize"**

मानव-वृत्तियों की विकसनशील अनन्तता साहित्य में निरन्तर नूतन उत्थानों को जन्म देती रही है। साहित्य का नियन्ता किंवा आलोचक इन उत्थानों की गतिविधियों का निरीक्षण-परीक्षण कर उनके स्वरूप का निर्धारण करता है। (निबन्ध, III)

13. **की जांच-परख कर ले—"to judge the worth of"**

हां भाभी, आपके मैके वाले पत्थरों से लेकर मटर की फलियों तक की जांच-परख अच्छी कर लेते होंगे। (बूंद, 393)

की जांच-परख कर—"to examine closely"

भौजाई उनके बालों को हाथ से इस तरह सहला रही थी मानो दुकान में मोल-तोल करने से पहले किसी कपड़े की जांच-परख कर रही हों। (परिन्दे, 15)

14. **की पहिचान कर—"to tell"**

...किसी वस्तु के मुद्रा होने या मुद्रा न होने की पहिचान इसके कार्यों से की जानी चाहिए। (एमाई, 69)

की पहिचान कर—"to recognize, to tell"

अनुभूति के आधार पर ही "सत्यं शिवं सुन्दरम्" की पहचान की जा सकती है। (धर्म, 97)

की पहिचान कर—"to tell the identity of"

एक बार एक जौहरी के यहां मोतियों का एक ढेर देखकर उसने उत्तम मोती छांटकर एक ओर रखना आरम्भ किया और फिर सहसा वह उनकी पहचान करना भूल गई, थककर दृष्टि हटा ली और उसकी आंखें फिर खोएपन के अथाह सागर में डूब गईं। (सुहाग, 266)

15. **की पड़ताल कर—"to investigate"**

ऐसे आदमियों की पड़ताल करनी होगी जो रिआया को भूखी और नंगी रखते हैं। (फूलो, 52)

की पड़ताल कर—"to investigate, to search into (a matter)"

भोजन करते करते रेखा देवी औंधे मुंह सूपप्लेट पर गिर गयीं हत्या के कारण का कोई अनुमान नहीं हो सका। लखनऊ के स्टार पत्रकार चन्द्रमाधव पड़ताल कर रहे हैं। (नदी, 25)

की पड़ताल करके देख ले—"to take a searching look at"

पर आत्म-बलिदान आत्म-प्रवंचना नहीं है, यह खूब अच्छी तरह पड़ताल करके देख लेना चाहिए। (नदी, 76)

16. **की जांच-पड़ताल कर—"to review"**

विकास अधिकारी हर कर्ज लेने वाले का पृथक पृथक खाता रखेगा और इस आवेदन की जांच-पड़ताल करेगा। (लोक, 29)

की जांच-पड़ताल कर—"to investigate"

...हमारी सरकार का पहला काम होगा मंत्रिमंडल के भूतपूर्व सदस्यों की सम्पत्तियों आदि की जांच-पड़ताल करने के लिए एक आयोग नियुक्त करना। (आज, 4)

85. अचम्भा, आश्चर्य, अचरज

1. अचम्भा, आश्चर्य, अचरज all refer to one's state of surprise mixed with wonder in which one reacts to (or expresses oneself on) something and is at the same time puzzled, curious or in doubt about it.

अचम्भा refers to something inexplicable, strange, puzzling or the like, आश्चर्य to something extraordinary, unusual or something not very likely but not altogether irrational or impossible, and अचरज to something hard to believe or beyond one's expectation.

2. These nouns are + process and form ANP with पर. The N पर occurring with all three may be replaced by an expression with a conjunctive participle. The nouns often occur with a कि clause as their object. They are not pluralized.

3. अचम्भा कर—"to be puzzled"

पंडित मूलराज की प्रतिभा का सिक्का सारे गांव पर जमा हुआ था। लोग प्रायः अचम्भा करते थे कि इतने योग्य होते हुए भी वे शहजादपुर रहने पर ही संतोष क्यों किये हुए हैं और अम्बाला के गवर्नमेंट हाई स्कूल के हैडमास्टर क्यों नहीं बन जाते? (डगर, 40)

4. आश्चर्य कर—"to wonder about"

मुझे इससे प्रसन्नता ही हुई थी; परन्तु मैं आश्चर्य यह कर रहा था कि जब मैं नहीं था, तो वह अपना सामान किससे मंगाती थी। (राह, 72)

आश्चर्य कर—"to be surprised"

अगर हो सका तो धूप निकल आने पर वह इन्दु को उन छतनार पेड़ों के नीचे ले जाएगा जिनमें मधुमक्खियों के छत्ते हैं, और वहीं बैठकर, उसे अपने बहुत पास महसूस करते हुए वह घटना सुनाएगा कि कैसे एक भालू शहद पीने के लिए पेड़ पर चढ़ गया था...इन्दु आश्चर्य करेगी और एकदम पूछेगी 'तुमने कैसे देखा?' (कमल, 56)

आश्चर्य कर—"to wonder, to find unusual"

मैं कभी-कभी आश्चर्य करता कि वह विधवा होकर शृंगार-पटार कैसे करती थी। (राह, 66)

आश्चर्य कर—"to wonder, to find surprising"

आकाश के देवता लोग भी उस महापुरुष को दूर से देखकर आश्चर्य करते थे कि मृत्युलोक में इस शरीरधारी ने देवत्व कैसे प्राप्त कर लिया। (कथा, 54)

5. **पर अचरज कर—"to express surprise"**

चारों ओर ताई के इस छठी भोज को लेकर चर्चा चल रही थी। चारों ओर इस बात पर अचरज किया जा रहा था। (बूंद, 417)

अचरज कर—"to be astonished, to express wonderment"

और, अगर एक बार, मनुष्य प्रकृति सौंदर्य में विचरण करने या प्रकृति को देखकर अचरज करने योग्य नहीं रहा तो उसका आध्यात्मिक ह्रास शुरू हो जायगा...। (अमरीका, 42)

86. उद्यत, प्रस्तुत, तैयार, सहमत, राजी

1. These adjectives describe the mental attitude of someone who feels steady sincerity and intentness of purpose towards some goal, and is in a frame of mind in which he is prepared to enter upon a course of action.

उद्यत describes the promptitude of one who is aroused to act in a particular manner or is entering into a course of action by an inspiration of the divine will or in answer to one's own inner conscience.

प्रस्तुत describes the mental state of one who sets himself off on a definite course (such as by making himself available or by offering oneself) by overcoming his ambivalence (i.e., the state of mind in which one oscillates between "Should I" or "Shouldn't I").

तैयार stresses readiness for or commitment to some course of action. The term is generally accompanied by an expression referring to the means employed, especially expense of energy, used in order to overcome indifference, hesitation or opposition in oneself or in another person.

सहमत (lit. having the same or a similar disposition or a frame of mind) is used when someone is brought around or persuaded to commit himself to a course (generally proposed by another) through the use of arguments, evidence or any other similar means of influencing or prevailing upon the decisions of another person.

राजी refers to someone's disposition of willingness or to the state of one who is agreeable to do something, generally implying a reference to the state of mind in which a person expresses himself by saying "O.K. I'll do it" or "It's all right with me" or by using other such expressions. The term implies some sort of persistence on the part of the person who is doing the persuading, and who is finally able to extract the promise from or to prevail upon the other.

Both **सहमत** and **राजी** may take as their object sentences with negation when a reference is made to someone's effort to persuade (or convince) another person to refrain from a course of action.

2. All these expressions being adjectives are —process. They are generally accompanied by some noun phrase with the postposition **पर** or **के लिए**. **पर** occurs with expressions denoting the condition on which the object noun is prepared to enter upon a course, and **के लिए** the proposed course of action.

3. को उद्यत कर दे—"to prompt someone"

इसने शंकराचार्य को माता से सन्यासी होने की अनुमति प्राप्त करने के लिए प्राणों से हाथ धो बैठने के लिए उद्यत कर दिया। (चमत्कार, 26)

4. को प्रस्तुत कर—"to set off (on a course), to commit oneself to"

अब भी वह किसी ऐसे पुरुष को क्षमा नहीं कर सकती। परन्तु सज्जन की बात निराली है, सज्जन उसका पुरुष है यह बात उसके मन में स्पष्ट होकर उसे हर प्रकार से समर्पण के लिए प्रस्तुत कर चुकी है। (बूंद, 368)

5. मार-मार कर तैयार कर—"to coerce someone into, to force someone to submit to"

मेरे और उसके बीच कुछ भी आड़े नहीं आया सिवाय शरीरों के। आदमी का शरीर बहुत डरपोक होता है, शर्मीला भी। बात-बात में संकुचित हो जाता है, झिझकता है। बिना प्राकृतिक ज़रूरत के उसे हर बात के लिए मार-मार कर तैयार करना पड़ता है। (मांस, 113)

तैयार कर—"to be preparing oneself for"

सवेरे तड़के ही वह मार्निंग वाक् के लिए चला जाएगा, दिन भर बाहर बिताएगा। इसी तरह की बातें सोचते हुए वह कल्याणी का सामना करने के लिए मन तैयार करता चला। (बूंद, 216)

तैयार कर—"to prepare mentally, to condition oneself"

लाख कोशिश करने पर भी मैं उन्हें यह न समझा पाई कि इस हैवानियत के खिलाफ जनमत तैयार करने में आबरू नहीं जायगी। (बंद, 143)

तैयार कर—"to prepare/create a (favorable) atmosphere (in order that something be well)"

अहिंसा की योजना में कानून नहीं आ सकता, ऐसी बात नहीं। लेकिन पहले लोकमत का प्रदर्शन होना चाहिए। उसके पहले हवा तैयार करनी पड़ती है......और फिर वे कानून बनाते हैं तो उस कानून में भी कत्ल का रंग चढ़ जाता है। (भूदान, 75)

6. **को सहमत कर—"to convince, to persuade"**

...तो वह उसे पुराने ढंग का बिना बाँह का ब्लाउज़ सिलवाने के लिए बहका देती है। और सहमत करने के लिए बड़े रोचक तर्क उपस्थित करती है कि स्लीव्ज़ नारी की दासता का चिन्ह है, जब उसे सात पर्दों के अन्दर रखा जाता था। अब जिंदगी आजादी चाहती है। (भंवर, 17)

7. **राजी कर ले—"to persuade"**

निरंजन:...मैंने उनसे पूरे विस्तार में बातें कीं। अन्त में मैंने उन्हें महज़ इस बात पर राज़ी कर लिया कि यदि तुम आज उनके सामने जाकर उन्हें धीरज बंधा दो, तो वे स्ट्राइक खत्म कर देंगे। (रात, 123)

पर राजी कर ले—"to prevail upon someone."

उसे किसी तरह अपने साथ शादी करने पर राजी कर लो। (बूंद, 81)

राजी कर—"to persuade"

मैं अपने निजी प्रभाव से उन्हें पांच-पांच रुपये स्वीकार कर लेने के लिए राजी कर लूंगा और इस तरह तुम सस्ते में निपट जाओगे। (लाख, 143)

राजी कर ले—"to induce someone to, to prevail upon someone"

उन्होंने हर तरह से ज्वालासिंह को उल्टा-सीधा समझा कर मना लिया और गांव की पिछली घटना के सम्बन्ध में (बेगारवाली घटना) तहकीकात करने के लिए उन्हें राजी कर लिया। (नंदु, 47)

87. अनुशीलन, अभ्यास, मुताल्या, अध्ययन, पढ़ाई

1. अनुशीलन, अभ्यास, मुताल्या, अध्ययन and पढ़ाई all refer to the application of the mental faculties to a specific matter or to the acquisition of knowledge or skill in a particular field.

अनुशीलन is following up on the disposition or character of something by repeatedly or constantly applying oneself to it or to the study or examination of it.

अभ्यास is practicing in order to train oneself in a subject, to perfect one's skill or ability to perform with a tool or an instrument, or to learn some subject, a skill or a particular field of study or of interest to one as by taking lessons from someone over a period of time.

मुताल्या refers to the act of going over something as if subjecting it to scrutiny or scanning.

अध्ययन is a term of wider application referring to the act of going through (i.e., subjecting to a thorough examination, consideration or study) a subject, the content of a book, a problem or some phenomenon. The term usually suggests strong scholarly overtones.

पढ़ाई is a general term referring to the act of doing some special reading on some subject or reading about something for a specific purpose. The term may also be applied to occupying oneself with the formal study of a subject, a course or working towards a degree in an academic institution.

2. Among these nouns only अनुशीलन is ± process. The rest are + process. All form ANP with का (पढ़ाई with की), and अध्ययन can occur with पर too. They are not pluralized.

3. का अनुशीलन कर—"to study"

साधू हम चाहते हैं कि संतमार्ग का थोड़ा सा अनुशीलन करो। (बांस, 27)

अनुशीलन कर—"to follow"

प्रत्येक मनुष्य यदि वह अपने मन का अनुशीलन करे तो देखेगा कि एक दिन में ही ऐसा समय भी आता है जब ऐसा प्रतीत होता है कि उसके मन की समग्र शक्तियां प्रफुल्लित हो उठी हैं और ऐसा भी जब कि उसकी शक्ति अतीव क्षीण होती है। (चमत्कार, 48-49)

अनुशीलन कर—"to reflect upon"

सद्धर्म में कुतर्क का प्राबल्य बढ़ रहा है, आयुष्मन्! संयत बनकर आचार्यों के वाक्य का तात्पर्य अनुशीलन कर। (बाण, 45)

4. का अभ्यास कर—"to study something constantly"

ऐसे कार्यों के लिए हर देश में शांति आंदोलनों की आवश्यकता है जिससे शांति के लिए जनमत-संग्रह हो सके तथा ये शांतिसंस्थाएं लगातार अंतर्राष्ट्रीय परिस्थिति का अभ्यास करती रहें और सतर्क तथा सक्रिय रहें। (अणु, 26)

अभ्यास कर—"to repeat the words"

जो पुरूष केवल वेद के शब्दों का ही अभ्यास करता रहता है और अर्थज्ञान से शून्य रहता है वह शब्दों का भार ढोने वाला वास्तविकता से बहुत दूर है। (वैदिक, 38)

का अभ्यास कर—"to acquire mastery (through long practice)"

गन्धर्व-कन्याओं की भांति सुन्दर लगनेवाली इन समवयस्क दोनों बालाओं ने अनेक वर्षों तक साथ-साथ रह कर बड़े ही परिश्रम के साथ इस कठिन संगीत-विद्या का अभ्यास किया था। (शांतला, 65-66)

अभ्यास कर—"to learn"

पुरानी खाट पर बैठकर वह बड़े मजे में उनसे बातें करती, साड़ी पहनने का उसने अभ्यास कर लिया था—और उसे फबती भी अच्छी। (तितली, 22)

का अभ्यास कर—"to practice"

चिड़ियां डालों से कूदने और फिर ऊपर को उड़ने का अभ्यास कर रही थीं और कौए पोर्च के सिरे पर चहलकदमी कर रहे थे। (जान, 83-84)

अभ्यास करना पड़—"to learn by practice"

प्रत्येक वस्तु को समुचित आकार प्रकार में देखने के लिए बच्चों को अभ्यास करना पड़ता है। (बाल, 1-58)

5. **का मुताल्या कर—"to go over"**

पुलिस का आदमी इस अर्से में हादसे की तमाम कैफियत का मुताल्या कर चुका था।

का मुताल्या कर—"to scan, to go over, to flip pages"

जब मैं गैलरी में वापिस आया तो वह खातून मेरी रेसों की किताब का मुताल्या कर रही थी और उसके पास चाय की ट्रे पड़ी थी।

6. **पर अध्ययन कर—"(for some study) to be underway"**

......इस तथ्य को दृष्टि में रखकर यहां पर मिट्टियों के गुणों, उनमें उपस्थित लवण, बनी ईंटों के पकाने सम्बन्धी जानकारी ईंटों का रंग आदि पर अध्ययन किया जा रहा है। (ईंट, 85)

का अध्ययन कर चुका—"to make a study of, to observe"

केशव, मैं बहुत से स्वभावों का अध्ययन कर चुका हूं, मुझे किसी के चरित्र का अध्ययन करने में बड़ा आनंद मिलता है...(व्यास, 20)

का अध्ययन कर--"to observe"

नीहारिकाओं का अध्ययन करने से ऐसा लगता है कि यह निरंतर एक दूसरे से दूर हटती जा रही हैं। (नक्षत्र, 23)

का अध्ययन कर—"to examine"

इस अध्याय में पहले कार्बनिक खादों का वर्णन करेंगे, परन्तु दोनों का अलग अलग अध्ययन करने से पूर्व उन पर तुलनात्मक विचार करना अच्छा है। (खाद, 13)

का अध्ययन कर--"to study"

बेणी माधव के बूढ़े ताऊ...ने, बारह साल काशी में रह कर महामहोपाध्याय शिवकुमार मिश्र से व्याकरण शास्त्र का अध्ययन किया था। (दुख, 101)

का अध्ययन कर—"to examine closely"

अश्क ने समाचार-पत्र के एक साधारण रिपोर्टर के रूप में जीवन आरंभ करके ...निम्न मध्यवर्ग और उच्च मध्यवर्ग के जीवन को बड़े निकट से देखा है और उसका जागरूक तथा सूक्ष्म अध्ययन किया है। (भवंर, 10)

का अध्ययन कर--"to investigate"

लोकप्रिय कलाकार भिखारी ठाकुर के विषय में बहुत कुछ सुनकर और उनके 'बिदेशिया' के नाम पर जुट पड़ने वाली जनता की मनोवृत्ति का अध्ययन कर मैं इस निष्कर्ष पर पहुंचा हूं कि......(कोणार्क, 97)

का अध्ययन कर—"to be observing something closely, to be engaged in the study of"

अनवरी इस कुटुम्ब की मानसिक हलचल में दत्तचित होकर उसका अध्ययन कर रही थी। न जाने क्यों, तीनों चुप होकर मन ही मन सोच रही थीं। (तितली, 41)

का अध्ययन कर—"to look at something closely, to view something with sustained attention"

दृष्टि का भाव ऐसे हो जाता है जैसे किसी बहुत सूक्ष्म पदार्थ का अध्ययन कर रहा हो। (आषाढ़, 110)

का अध्ययन कर--"to observe closely"

यमुना भयभीत होकर विजय के आतुर मुख का अध्ययन करने लगी। कुछ न बोली। (कंकाल, 88)

का अध्ययन कर—"to study"

कुशल नाविक समुद्र की सतह पर उसकी लहरों, ज्वार-भाटों और धाराओं का अध्ययन करता है। (समुद्र, 134)

अध्ययन कर—"to study"

मैं इधर मनोयोग पूर्वक पढ़ रही हूं। जितना ही मैं अध्ययन करती हूं उतना ही यह विश्वास दृढ़ होता जा रहा है कि जो कुछ सुन्दर और कल्याणमय है...(तितली, 247)

7. **पढ़ाई कर—"to study hard"**

...मैं तो बड़ी कसकर पढ़ाई करूंगा......उतनी मेहनत करोगी। (नदी, 62)

पढ़ाई कर—"to continue one's studies"

मैं आगे पढ़ाई नहीं कर रही। संगीत के लिए आयी हूं। एक वर्ष यहां और एक वर्ष मैसूर में रहूंगी इतनी दूर स्पष्ट दीखता है और इसमें इतना काम है कि आगे देखना अभी जरूरी नहीं जान पड़ता। (नदी, 77)

पढ़ाई कर—"to study"

तुम देखो खेती का काम, और मैं पढ़ाई करूंगी। हम लोगों को इस भीषण संसार से तब तक लड़ना होगा जब तक वह लौट नहीं आते। (तितली, 214)

88. अन्वेषण, गवेषणा, आत्मान्वेषण, अनुसन्धान, छानबीन, तहकीकात, तलाश, तलाशी, खोज, ढूंढखोज

1. These expressions represent in a variety of ways someone's search for information, knowledge about something or the ultimate truth about something, a search which takes place over a period of time.

अन्वेषण refers to the act of seeking to know or pursuing the unknown subjectively and informally. The term may sometimes be applied to the results of an inquiry where the reference to any systematic methodological research is not intended.

गवेषणा applies to a diligent search or probing of the unknown, or to anything done in the course of such a search or probe (such as sustained, minute examination of phenomena).

आत्मान्वेषण is a compound term consisting of आत्मा and अन्वेषण referring to the attainment of self-knowledge.

अनुसन्धान is striving to attain by searching (literally as well as figuratively) or following or proceeding through systematically or step by step to one's end or objective. The term usually applies to scholarly or scientific pursuits (the noun denoting such pursuits are juxtaposed before अनुसन्धान with the postposition पर). It may also refer to the act of reasoning with oneself when trying to apprehend the underlying causes of a surface phenomenon.

छानबीन refers to the activity of sifting through (lit. छान "sifting" and बीन "picking the relevant") in a manner as may be called for in a given situation in order to determine the facts of the case.

तहकीकात describes the state of one who is in the process of making an inquiry or is trying to get to the bottom of something, aiming to unearth the facts behind an event, or conditions to support or refute suspicions, charges or allegations made by one party against another. The term is usually used in reference to judicial inquiries or probes.

तलाश is trying to seek out and discover someone or something at some (implied) location.

तलाशी is searching a place or a person with a view to uncovering something concealed.

खोज refers to any pursuit with a view to finding someone or something, or to that which one comes upon accidently or by design.

ढूंढखोज refers to the act of going in search of or looking for (as if one were scouting for) someone or something.

2. All the nouns, with the exception of तलाश (which is ± process), are + process. अनुसन्धान forms ANP with पर and का. All the rest form ANP with की only, अन्वेषण with का. Only अन्वेषण, अनुसन्धान and खोज can be pluralized.

3. **का अन्वेषण कर—"to explore"**

वैज्ञानिकों को समुद्र के इन घास के मैदानों का अन्वेषण करने में बड़ा मजा आता है। (समुद्र, 60)

के बारे में अन्वेषण कर—"to make an attempt to explore"

प्राचीन भारत में इस बारे में कि मानसिक भाव, मानव चरित्र और धनप्राप्ति में कोई सम्बन्ध है या नहीं, अन्वेषण किए गए हैं और वर्तमान काल में, मनोवैज्ञानिक दृष्टि से इस सम्बन्ध पर पर्याप्त प्रकाश डाला गया है। (चमत्कार, 19-20)

का अन्वेषण कर—"to come upon"

संस्कृति वास्तव में वह जीवन पद्धति है जिसकी स्थापना मानव व्यक्ति तथा समूह के रूप में करता है। यह उन आविष्कारों का संग्रह है जिनका अन्वेषण मानव ने अपने जीवन को सफल बनाने के लिए किया। (धर्म, 29)

अन्वेषण कर—"to engage in the exploration of, to explore"

पदार्थ अपनी सूक्ष्मतम अवस्था में शक्ति ही है। वैज्ञानिक जब इस स्थूल तथ्य से आगे अन्वेषण करता है, तो एक नये क्षितिज के दर्शन करता है। (अणु, 3)

का अन्वेषण कर—"to conceptualize"

...शिल्प और सौन्दर्य बोध का अन्वेषण करते रहे। (मूल्य, 147)

का अन्वेषण कर—"to probe"

प्रयोग सभी कालों के कवियों ने किये हैं। किन्तु कवि क्रमशः अनुभव करता आया है कि जिन क्षेत्रों में प्रयोग हुए हैं, आगे बढ़कर अब उन क्षेत्रों का अन्वेषण करना चाहिए जिन्हें अभी छुआ नहीं गया था जिनको अभेद्य मान लिया गया है। (निबन्ध, 668)

4. **के सम्बन्ध में गवेषणा कर चुक—"to try to probe into"**

हां, परिच्छिन्न रूप के सम्बन्ध में वैज्ञानिक यथेष्ट गवेषणा कर चुके हैं...। (धर्म, 48)

5. **आत्मान्वेषण कर—"to realize one's real or ideal self, to achieve self-realization"**

...औपन्यासिक पात्र अगर आत्मान्वेषण कर पाता है या उस ओर उन्मुख होता है। (मूल्य, 164)

आत्मान्वेषण कर—"to discover one's own self"

...अपने जीवन की विभिन्न घड़ियों में विभिन्न स्तरों पर आत्मान्वेषण करता है... (मूल्य, 165)

6. **पर अनुसंधान कर—"to make new researches"**

फिर इस विषय पर हिन्दुस्तान के 33 करोड़ देवी-देवता घर-घर में नित्य नये अनुसन्धान कर रहे हैं, इसलिए अभी से इस शास्त्र को लिपिबद्ध करना ठीक नहीं। (कहा,)

पर अनुसंधान कर—"to conduct researches"

ऐसी मनोदशा में मैं विद्यार्थियों को क्या पढाऊंगा, दर्शन-शास्त्र पर मुझे आगे जो अनुसंधान करने हैं वे क्या करूंगा और उन पर जो गंभीर पुस्तकें लिखना चाहता हूं वह क्या लिखूंगा। (धनु, 126)

का अनुसंधान कर—"to find out, to try to make out (for oneself)"

सुमन बहुत देर तक वहां बैठी कार्य से कारण का अनुसन्धान करती रही। (सेवा, 44)

का अनुसंधान कर—"to look upon, to examine"

जब तक बुद्धि कुतर्की बनी रहती है तब तक वह सद्विचारों का सम्पादन करने में असमर्थ बनी रहती है और वह प्रत्येक वस्तु का अनुसन्धान अपने ही कुतर्कों के बल पर करती हुई अपने तर्कों को श्रेष्ठ समझने की अभ्यस्त बनी रहती है। (धर्म, 127-28)

अनुसन्धान कर—"to conduct a systematic study"

स्वच्छ शौचालयों का प्रचलन और प्रयोग बढ़ाने के लिए वैज्ञानिक अनुसन्धान भी कर रहे हैं जिससे कि यह पता लग सके कि किस प्रकार की टट्टियां कहां के लिए उपयोगी हैं। (स्वस्थ, 19)

अनुसन्धान कर—"to follow up, to pursue"

यह विषय मनोवैज्ञानिक दृष्टि से मंथन और अनुसन्धान करने योग्य है। (चमत्कार, 8)

अनुसंधान कर—"to search for (someone)"

जब आप उस दिन कुछ व्याकुल से दिखे और आपने कहा कि उसका मेरा सादृश्य है तब मैंने गांव में अनुसंधान किया। ढूंढ़ने में समय लगा। अन्त में खोज ठिकाने लग गई। (कचनार, 343)

7. **की छानबीन कर—"to conduct an inquiry"**

यदि कोई निष्पक्ष ट्रिब्यूनल इस भयानक रक्तपात की छानबीन करे तो संसार को पता चल जाय कि शान्ति के पुजारी महात्मा ईसा के इन अनुयायिओं ने अपने साम्राज्य की आवश्यकताओं के लिए किस हृदयहीन कूटनीति से लाखों की हत्या कर डाली है। (धारा, 138)

की छानबीन कर—"to sift"

यह क्रांति धर्म के इन पक्षों के कारण हुई जिनको आज का समाज जागृत करना चाहता तो है, किंतु उनकी छानबीन करके ही विश्वास करना चाहता है। (धर्म, 68)

की छानबीन कर—"to conduct an investigation"

और यह आखरी प्रश्न पूछते ही उनका सौम्य चेहरा इतना प्रखर हो गया जैसे पुलिस का अफसर छानबीन कर रहा है। (मनु, 140)

की छानबीन कर—"to sift through, to ransack"

मैं अभी लिये आता हूं। आश्चर्य है मैंने सारे ठौर ठिकानों की छानबीन की, परन्तु कपड़ों के सन्दूक को नहीं ढूंढा। (खिलौने, 46)

अपने स्वभाव-चरित्र की छानबीन कर—"to undergo the process of self-evaluation"

ईसा के आगे सबने शुद्ध हृदय से स्वयं अपने-अपने—स्वभाव चरित्र की छानबीन की। उस समय हर एक को इस तरह का अनुभव हुआ: बुरा जो देखन मैं चला, बुरा न दीखा कोय। जो दिल खोजा आपना, मुझसा बुरा न कोय। (आदर्श, 8)

की छानबीन कर—"to investigate"

स्वतंत्रता के बाद भारत में स्वास्थ्य की स्थिति के बारे में छानबीन करने के लिए जो कमेटी बनाई गई थी उसने भी अपना मत व्यक्त करते हुए लिखा था... (स्वस्थ, 5)

8. **की तहकीकात कर—"to investigate"**

क्या आप वह पत्र मुझे दिखा सकेंगे? आप उसे देखकर क्या करेंगे? ख्वाम-ख्वाह आपका मन खराब होगा। और वह पत्र मेरे पास है भी नहीं। मैंने पुलिस के हवाले कर दिया है। पुलिस उसकी तहकीकात कर रही है। (धनु, 190)

तहकीकात कर—"to inquire about"

उन्होंने गुप्त रीति से तहकीकात की। संदेह जाता रहा। सारा रहस्य खुल गया। (सेवा, 14)

पर तहकीकात कर—"to order an inquiry or investigation"

मैजिस्ट्रेट ने उस पर तहकीकात करने का आश्वासन दिया। (बूंद, 236)

के बारे में तहकीकात कर—"to inquire about, to investigate"

मेरे चरित्र के बारे में आप तहकीकात कर सकते हैं। (धनु, 142)

तहकीकात कर—"to make an inquiry, to inquire"

उसके बाएं हाथ में तीन अक्षर गोदे हुए थे जिनसे मालूम होता है कि उसका नाम दलीप था। पुलिस क्षेत्रों में तहकीकात करने से मालूम पड़ा कि वह एक बेकार नौजवान था जिसकी नौकरी हाल ही में छूट गई थी। (धनु, 195)

9. **की तलाश कर—"to look for"**

इसके बाद तुम आंखें मूंद कर मेरी किसी कविता को उठा लो और उसमें जगह-जगह छन्द भंग, पुनरावृत्ति, ग्राम्यप्रयोग और अश्लीलता की बारीकी से तलाश करो। (कहा, 69)

को तलाश कर दे—"to help one find, to find"

आप यदि मेरी मां को तलाश कर दें तो कितनी बड़ी बात होगी। (बांस 49)

की तलाश करनी पड़—"to have to search through"

बीर—जाने समझे की छानबीन क्या ? तलाश तो पर्दे की तहों की करनी पड़ती है। (बीर, 72)

की तलाश करता रहा—"to look for"

दो साल वह बेकार रहा। एक साल काम की तलाश करता रहा। आज कल विश्राम कर रहा है। (जानवर, 52)

की तलाश कर—"to discover"

तभी उसने जीवन के विभिन्न स्तरों पर वहन करनेवाले, उससे सम्पृक्त केन्द्रीय पात्रों की तलाश की थी—यथार्थ की तलाश की थी, जिसकी साक्षी हैं वे कहानियां, जो इस दौर में लिखी गयीं। (मांस, 7)

की तलाश कर—"to be in search of, to be on the lookout for"

उनकी व्याकुल आंखें केवल एक ही वस्तु की तलाश कर रही थीं—बत्तीस लक्षणों से सम्पन्न किशोरी, जिसके हाथ की रेखाएं उसे रानी से भी कुछ बड़ी बनाने का इंगित करती हैं। (चारु, 71)

की तलाश कर—"to get oneself (a wife)"

ऐसी पत्नी की तलाश करो कि जिसके प्रति स्वयं आत्म-समर्पण किया जा सके। (सच, 53)

तलाश कर—"to find"

तू भी क्या कहेगी कि लड़का न ढूंढा, ऐसा वर तलाश किया है कि सारा गांव देखने को उमड़ेगा। (डगर, 49)

तलाश कर—"to look for"

मकान तलाश करने के लिए मुझको लिखा है जैसे मैं इस कमरे के बाहर कभी कदम भी रखता होऊं। (खिलौने, 13)

10. **की तलाश कर—"to search"**

लड़की के कायुनिस्ट होने के शक को लेकर घर की तलाशी भी लगे हाथ पुलिस ने कर डाली थी। (बूंद, 52)

11. **की खोज कर—"to seek for or after"**

वहां शक्ति का वैषम्य रहेगा ही। परन्तु इतने वैषम्य के भीतर भी एक साम्या-

वस्था है। आज तक संसार के बड़े-बड़े मनुष्यों ने उसी की खोज की है। जीवन की अमरता और बचने का रास्ता वहीं से निकलता है। (प्रतिमा, 52)

की खोज कर—"to conduct researches for"

...वह उत्तरोत्तर युद्ध के शक्तिशाली आयुधों की खोज कर रहा है...(अणु, 12)

की खोज कर—"to discover"

डाक्टर मिश्र ने अखबार के पृष्ठों को जल्दी-जल्दी उलटते हुए कहा—डाक्टर चाको भी अजीब हैं। उन्होंने मुझसे कल मजाक में हंसते हुए कहा कि गनपत सिंघ लेन सेंटर की लेडी हेल्थविज़िटर और वर्किंग विमेन्स हास्टल की सुपरिन्टेंडेंट ने एक नई बीमारी की खोज की है। (दीर्घ, 132)

की खोज कर—"to seek"

कुंवर नारायण जी मानते हैं कि वासना के माध्यम से व्यक्ति अलौकिक तथ्यों की खोज कर सकता है—(निबंध, 676)

की खोज कर—"to explore, to search through"

फिर वह इन खंडहरों की खोज करने लगा। (आज, 11)

की खोज कर—"to try to find out"

हमारे यहां से हटते ही घामोनी वाले इस बात की खोज करेंगे कि हम कहां जा रहे हैं। (कचनार, 121)

की खोज कर—"to be searching for"

नौकरी की खोज करते-करते निराश हो जाते हैं। (बुन, 39)

की खोज कर—"to seek"

जहां तक वस्तु का प्रश्न है अश्क जी अपनी रचनाओं के लिए वस्तु की खोज जीवन से ही करते हैं। (भंवर, 47)

की खोज कर—"to track down"

दो खास काम थे—एक तो पाकिस्तानी एजेंटों का पता लगाना और दूसरा मज़दूरों में बदअमनी फैलाने वाले कम्युनिस्टों की खोज करना। (फूलो, 49)

की खोज कर—"to discover, to make a discovery, to establish something as a fact"

आधुनिक आहार विज्ञान ने इस बात की खोज की है कि भोजन को उस समय तक

उचित रूप में काम में नहीं लाया जा सकता था। शरीर उस समय तक ठीक तरह से काम नहीं कर सकता, जब तक उसमें विभिन्न किस्म के विटामिन नहीं हैं। (भेड़, 45)

की खोज कर—"to seek to discover"

पाश्चात्य देशवासियों ने वस्तु जगत के रहस्यों की खोज करने की दिशा में ही प्रयत्न किया। (धर्म, 74)

की खोज कर—"to scour"

पिछले कुछ वर्षों में अनेक देशों के जहाजों ने इस श्रेणी की ओर खोज की है, जिससे इसके बारे में जानकारी और बढ़ गई है। (समुद्र, 22)

खोज कर—"to search, to make a search"

गोमती के किनारे-किनारे कुरिया घाट से लेकर बंधे तक खोज की गई कि शायद कहीं महिपाल के कपड़े रखे हुए मिल जांय पर श्रम बेकार गया। (बूंद, 580)

12. **की ढूंढ-खोज कर—"to search, to look for"**

मैं उस स्त्री के अनुसन्धान के लिये आया था जो मेरी है। मेरा मन कहता है कि वह यहीं कहीं है शायद आपको न मालूम हो। मैं जाता हूं। उसकी ढूंढ-खोज करूंगा। (कचनार, 197)

89. अनुवर्तन, अनुगमन, अनुकरण, अंधानुकरण, अनुसरण, नकल, पीछा

अनुवर्तन, अनुगमन, अनुकरण, अंधानुकरण, अनुसरण, नकल, and पीछा are used when someone or something is referred to or described as coming behind another or coming after in the path or a pattern set by another.

अनुवर्तन is used when something is described as conducting or behaving in compliance with or in obeisance to the wishes or the expectation of another.

अनुगमन is used when someone is referred to as following the steps of another or going after another literally as well as figuratively, usually on his own choosing.

अनुकरण is following the directions or the lead given or set by another (sometimes with the added implication that one neither knew any better, nor exercised one's originality, or that one simply followed suit because that was just the thing to do.)

अंधानुकरण is applied when someone is described as following another, or some principles, a practice, a code or the like without any regard to the exercise of rational discrimination or restriction.

अनुसरण is used when someone or something is described as literally following the other (such as in a time sequence) or when a person's conduct is described as having been modelled after another It may also be used to refer to someone who in some respects has taken after another.

नकल is applied to any act or action which amounts to making (sometimes referring to the act of making) a duplication of an original.

पीछा is a relatively neutral term referring to the act of going after or in the direction of someone (implying an effort on the part of the subject to catch up with the object).

2. These nouns are + process, and form ANP with का (नकल with की). They are not pluralized.

3. का अनुवर्तन कर—"to comply with, to abide by"

परन्तु क्या मन मन्ता की रुचि का अनुवर्तन करता है...(सुधा, 5)

4. का अनुगमन कर—"to trail along after someone"

बुद्धिमान सिर का विनाश क्यों हुआ ? क्योंकि दुष्परिणाम को जानते हुए भी उसने मूर्ख का अनुगमन किया था। (कथा, 61)

अनुगमन कर—"to trail behind, to follow"

कन्या बाबा जी को भोजन कराने ले गई। सज्जन ने केवल चुपचाप अनुगमन किया। (बूंद, 460)

5. का अनुकरण कर—"to imitate"

प्रतिभा के आचरण को सूक्ष्मता से देखें तो पता चल जाता है कि उसने प्रोफ़ैसर नीलाम की व्यक्तिगत विशेषताओं का अनुकरण भर किया है, उन्हें वह आत्मसात् नहीं कर पायी है। (भंवर, 16)

का अनुकरण कर—"to follow"

"देखो उधर देखो"—पहले एकदम मेरी निगाहें बिट्टो के इशारे का अनुकरण नहीं कर सकीं...और फिर अकस्मात् वहीं जमकर टंगी रह गयीं...(परिन्दे, 22)

का अनुकरण कर—"to follow someone's lead"

महाराजा अशोक चल्ल ने बड़ी श्रद्धा से उन्हें प्रणाम किया और बोधा प्रधान ने भी उन्हीं का अनुकरण किया। (चारू, 367)

का अनुकरण कर—"to follow"

धार्मिक गुरुओं के अन्दर निहित स्वार्थ और अहंकार की भावनाएं उन्हें व्यापक दृष्टि

न प्रदान कर सकीं, अन्यथा आज के विद्वानों को धर्म के पथ से हटकर वे अंधविश्वासों के अनुकरण करने का उपदेश न देते। इतना ही नहीं, वे परिस्थिति के अनुकूल नये नियमों की खोज करना भी पाप समझते हैं। (धर्म, 18)

का (अंशतः) अनुकरण कर—"to strive to copy, to follow the example or pattern of"

उन्होंने उन प्रणालियों अथवा पद्धतियों का अंशत: अनुकरण तो किया लेकिन चालू प्रणालियों से सीधा सम्बन्ध नहीं जोड़ा। (कोणार्क, 96)

6. **का अंधानुकरण कर—"to follow blindly"**

धर्म इसलिए सुरक्षित नहीं रहता कि उसका अनुयायी अंधानुकरण करता है। (धर्म, 23)

7. **का अनुसरण कर—"to follow"**

अपने आपके प्रति सच्चे रहो तो जिस प्रकार रात्रि दिन का अनुसरण करती है आप किसी भी मनुष्य के प्रति झूठे नहीं होंगे। (चमत्कार 28)

के पदचिन्हों का अनुसरण कर—"to follow in someone's footsteps."

तुलाराम शास्त्री भी बिना अनुभवी हुए आचार्य कहलाना हिमाकत समझते हैं, ऐसा जान पड़ता है। इस सिलसिले में वे मेरे पदचिन्हों का अनुसरण करते हुए ताजे अनुभवों का मजा लूट रहे हैं। (तुला, 11)

का अनुसरण कर—"to follow, to model (one's conduct, life) after, to abide by"

इसी पद्धति द्वारा हमारी सभ्यता में सत्संस्कृति प्रविष्ट होगी। इस लक्ष्य की पूर्ति का साधन है अपने अतीत के विस्मृत सिद्धान्तों का अनुसरण करना। (धर्म, 34-35)

का अनुसरण कर—"to comply with"

अपढ़ पंचानंद को यह कैसे ज्ञात हो सकता था कि अंग्रेजों ने जो कानून बनाया था उसमें कागजात गवाह और शिनाख्त के बिना कोई कार्य नहीं हो सकता और अब उनकी कुर्सी पर बैठने वाले उसी कानून का अनुसरण कर रहे हैं। (व्यास, 6)

का अनुसरण कर—"to conform to"

वह एक बार जान्हवी की इच्छा से परिचित होकर जीवन भर उसका अनुसरण करती है। (नदु, 80)

का अनुसरण कर—"to ensue"

भावनाओं और विचारों को पहिले शुद्ध हो जाने की आवश्यकता है, क्रियायें तो उनका अनुसरण करती ही रहती हैं। (धर्म, 150-51)

का अनुसरण कर—"to try to conform to"

वह केवल गुरुजनों, समाज के अदब-कायदों, वरासत में मिली वहां की संस्कृति का अनुसरण करती जा रही थी। (निरु, 35)

का अनुसरण कर—"to take after"

परन्तु राजा राम मोहन राय को भारत में एक नवीन युग का अग्रदूत कहे जाने का मुख्य कारण यह था कि उनके कार्यों से समाज के विभिन्न पहलुओं में समाज सुधार की एक लहर सी आ गई। लोगों ने उनका अनुसरण करके देश के विभिन्न क्षेत्रों में समाज सुधार का झंडा उठाया। (भारत, 62)

का अनुसरण कर—"to trail along after"

अन्य पशुओं की भांति भेड़ों में रोग के लक्षण इतनी आसानी से पता नहीं चल पाते। भेड़ों का स्वास्थ्य बुरी तरह खराब होने पर भी वे अपने नेता का अनुसरण करती हैं। (भेड़, 51)

का अनुसरण कर—"to trail"

शब्द का अनुसरण करते हुए हम दोनों पहुंचे तो देखा कि मैना रक्त से भीगी हुई एक अपूर्व तेजस्विनी महिला की गोद में गिर पड़ी है। (चारु, 436)

8. की नकल कर—"to take after"

अंगरेजों के बाप-दादा अभी डेढ़ दो सौ साल पहले लुटेरे थे। हमारे-तुम्हारे बाप-दादा ऋषि-मुनि थे। लुटेरों की संतान पिये, तो पीने दो। उनके पास न कोई धर्म है न नीति, लेकिन ऋषियों की सन्तान उनकी नकल क्यों करे ? (सम, 69)

की नकल कर—"to copy"

उसके मुंह में कड़वाहट सी आ जाती, खास तौर पर जब उसे इम्तियाज़ के सामने सलूट देनी पड़ती। वह भूल न सकता था कि स्कूल में इम्तियाज़ उसकी कापियों की नकल किया करता था...(फूलो, 43)

की नकल कर—"to reproduce"

अपने इस सब कथन के समर्थन में हम केवल थोड़े से यूरोपीय विद्वानों की सम्मति नकल करते हैं। (सुन्दर, 3)

की नकल कर—"to imitate"

वह कई बार अपने गांव गया, वहां वह सबसे सरल प्रेम से मिला। ग्रामबंधुओं को उचित सहायता देकर सबसे उसने यही कहा कि भाइयो, सरल जीवन न त्यागना, हमारी नकल न करना। (कथा, 16)

की बोली की नकल कर—"to mimic"

मालिक ने अपनी स्त्री को जंगल में ले जाकर एक पेड़ में छिपा दिया और उसने कहा कि यहां से कोयल की बोली की नकल करो। (रूस, 4)

की नकल कर—"to mimic"

गौरा ने एक बार नकली झल्लाहट की अर्थभरी दृष्टि से उसकी ओर देखा, और मुस्कराकर बोली, शिशु, शिशु, शिशु। भुवन ने भी मुस्कराकर उसकी नकल करते हुए कहा, जुगुनु, जुगनू और क्षणभर की अवधि देकर खिलकर, हिडिम्बा। (नदी, 305)

इम्तिहान में नकल करता हुआ—"stealing (an answer) in the examination"

यदुनाथ ऐसे सिटपिटाकर बोला, मानो इम्तिहान में बालक नकल करता पकड़ लिया गया। (विचित्र, 82)

9. **का पीछा कर—"to chase"**

शायद इसी से मैं लड़कियों का पीछा करने लगा था, क्लास से भागने लगा था... (राह, 42)

का पीछा कर—"to stalk, to chase"

जिस तरह बिल्ली चूहे का पीछा करती है, उसी तरह वे उनका पीछा करती हैं। (समुद्र, 102)

का पीछा कर—"to follow"

मुझे दो एक बार शक भी हुआ कि कोई मोटर हमारा पीछा कर रही है पर नयन कुमारी ने बात टाल दी। (धनु, 73)

का पीछा कर—"to hover over, to trail"

मेरा रास्ता अकेला था—मुझे अकेले ही जाना था। पर निराशा के घने अंधकार में डूबे हुए मन को कहीं दूर एक चिनगारी अब भी धुंधला उजाला दे रही थी। उस भयानक रात की नीरव शांतता में एक झूठी परछाई मेरा पीछा कर रही थी। (मांस, 45)

का पीछा कर—"to run after"

वह भेड़ों का पीछा करती हुई घुटनों तक कीचड़ में लथपथ हो जाती थी, तो मा उसे डांट देती थी। वह मां की डांट की तरफ कभी ध्यान नहीं देती थी। (आकाश, 97)

का पीछा कर—"to run after"

यूनिवर्सिटी की लड़कियों का मैंने पीछा किया था, उन पर व्यंग्यबाण छोड़े थे, लेकिन

उनकी सभ्यता और शिष्टता का मैं इस तरह अभ्यस्त था कि वे बहस करें और दूसरों की आलोचना, यह मुझे बहुत ही छिछली बात लगी। (राह, 24)

का पीछा कर—"to follow up"

और क्योंकि जिन्दगी में, और कुछ बन सकने की सम्भावना अपने में न पाकर, मैं कवि बनना तय कर चुका था, इसलिए मैंने प्रेरणा का जोरों से पीछा करना आरम्भ कर दिया। (सच, 1)

का पीछा कर—"to go after (in order to overtake)"

कन्या तुरन्त अपने ड्राइवर को सज्जन का पीछा करने भेज, वैद्य जी को लेती हुई ताई के घर पहुंची तो... (बूंद, 565)

90. उल्लेख, जिक्र, चर्चा

1. उल्लेख, जिक्र and चर्चा are used to describe the act of someone, who by putting forward in his own words (through speech or in writing) brings up some topic (such as in the course of a conversation with another person), makes a reference to something said or done by another in some suitable context in order to call it to the attention of his addressee, or refers to the source of his information about something for the benefit of his addressee.

उल्लेख is used when a specific or explicit reference to someone or something is desired in a context in order to point out to the addressee something characteristic of, peculiar to or noteworthy about that person or thing. The term is also employed to make reference to something explicitly stated in a document (a book or the like) or something specifically said by someone in some context (such as by citing, quoting or naming the source). When used with negation, उल्लेख strongly implies an intentional or deliberate omission of something (such as a person's name, a piece of information or the like) in a context where it belongs or should be specified).

जिक्र refers to something brought up casually or incidentally, or to the act of making a reference to someone or something incidentally, in passing or in an oblique manner. The term often implies an intentional conjecture or approval (or of disapproval as the case may be) by one who, in a given context, is referred to as doing the talking.

चर्चा applies to almost anything about which one talks about or speaks (usually in a light or familiar manner, unless qualified by an expression to the contrary) generally with the intention to inform. The term strongly suggests that the speaker is merely ascribing an act or an expression to the subject, regardless of whether or not it has been done or said by him.

This noun may also be applied to anything (such as an expression, a word, or the like) which the speaker wants to bring to the attention of the addressee in situations where he does not specifically care to make a reference to the exact context of the occurrence of such an expression.

2. These nouns are +process. उल्लेख forms ANP with का. Both जिक्र and चर्चा with से and का. का occurs with expressions denoting the topic of conversation and से with the nouns denoting the addressee. Sometimes का may be substituted by के सम्बन्ध में and के बारे में.

चर्चा occurs in both masculine and feminine genders. It is pluralized only in the masculine. उल्लेख and जिक्र are not pluralized.

3. **का उल्लेख कर—"to mention"**

...अतः इस क्रम-भग्नता का उल्लेख बार-बार यदि पश्चिमी लेखक संसार के अन्त को प्रतीक बनाकर करता है तो यह स्वाभाविक ही है। (मूल्य, 31)

का कई बार उल्लेख कर—"to mention ostentatiously, to brag about"

वह कई बार उन दावतों का उल्लेख कर चुकी थी, जो उसके यहां जन्म-दिवसों पर हुई थीं और जिनमें बड़े-बड़े अफसर, जिलाधीश तथा मुख्य मन्त्री तक आए थे। (राह, 78)

का कोई उल्लेख नहीं किया था—"said nothing about"

लेकिन चन्द्रमाधव ने भुवन को पत्र लिखने में लगभग एक महीने की देर कर दी थी। और जब लिखा था तब रेखा का कोई उल्लेख नहीं किया था। (नदी, 52)

का उल्लेख कर—"to cite"

इस सम्बन्ध में उस घटना का उल्लेख किया जा सकता है, जब उसकी सहेली नीलिमा पूरी बाहों वाला नये फैशन का ब्लाऊज सिलाने की चर्चा करती है तो वह उसे पुराने ढंग का बिना बांह का ब्लाऊज सिलवाने के लिए बहका देती है...(गबर, 17)

का उल्लेख कर—"to recount, to describe, to speak of"

व्यक्तिगत इच्छा को महत्व देते हुए कविवर अपने बाल्य-जीवन की एक घटना का उल्लेख करते हैं। (प्रतिमा, 8)

का उल्लेख करते हुए—"referring to"

फार्स्टर अविवाहित था, उसका उल्लेख करते हुए लारेन्स ने लिखा...(मूल्य, 47)

का उल्लेख कर—"to mention"

रामायण में भी इस नदी का आदर के साथ उल्लेख किया गया है। (शबरी, 11)

का उल्लेख कर—"to quote"

इनकी जड़ तो समाज में धर्म-गुरुओं के सम्प्रदाय-स्वार्थ और उनकी लोलुपता से फैली है, यद्यपि वे धर्मग्रन्थों का ही उल्लेख करते हुए दृष्टांत भी दे दिया करते हैं। यदि वे वास्तव में अपने पूर्वजों के ज्ञानादर्श पर चलते तो भारत का कल्याण होता। (धर्म, 16)

का उल्लेख कर—"to specify"

जबकि वस्तु के गुणों अथवा कार्यों की चर्चा की जाती है तो यह उसका वर्णन होता है और जब वर्ग और विशेषक का उल्लेख किया जाता है तो यह उस वस्तु की परिभाषा होती है। (एमाई, 60)

का उल्लेख कर—"to refer to"

अब तक के विवेचन में 'कल्याणकारी राज्य' का बारम्बार उल्लेख किया गया है। (भारत, 7)

का उल्लेख कर—"to describe, to make a specific reference to"

भारतीय संविधान के अनुच्छेद 41 में बेकारी, बीमारी, वृद्धावस्था आदि की दशा में राज्य की सहायता तथा सामाजिक सुरक्षा का उल्लेख किया गया है। (भारत, 10)

का उल्लेख कर—"to speak of someone"

हर ऐक्सीलेंसी ने कला की महिमा बखानते हुए अपने पास खड़े अंतर्राष्ट्रीय ख्याति-प्राप्त लखनऊ निवासी देशपूज्य वयोवृद्ध कलाकारों का बड़े आदर के साथ अपने भाषण में उल्लेख किया। (बूंद, 383)

4. का जिक्र कर—"to mention someone by name"

उन्होंने अपने भाषण में सज्जन का जिक्र न किया बल्कि सब कलाकारों को देश की राष्ट्रीय संस्था के साथ सहयोग करने के लिए धन्यवाद दिया। (बूंद, 383)

के सामने का जिक्र कर—"to bring up a subject before someone"

जब कभी हम दूसरी कौमों के सामने अंगरेज़ कौम की सचाई और ईमानदारी का जिक्र करते हैं तो वे भारत की ओर इशारा करके बड़ी हिकारत के साथ हमारा मज़ाक उड़ा सकते हैं। (सुन्दर, 20)

से का जिक्र कर—"to speak to someone about something"

प्रभु से एक बार इसका जिक्र करके निश्चय कर दीजिएगा। मारसिंगमय्या तथा माचिकब्बे दोनों खुशी से अपनी स्वीकृति देंगे। (शांतला, 51)

का जिक्र कर—"to be mentioned, to mention"

अंतिओकस के बाद भारत पर कुछ इस तरह के हमलों का जिक्र किया जाता है जिन्हें सचमुच सफल हमले कहा जा सकता है। (सुंदर, 27)

का जिक्र कर—"to talk about"

परिचय हो जाने पर मिस कान्ति ने दोनों आदमियों से हाथ मिलाया और हंसती हुई बोली, बाबा आप लोगों का जिक्र कर रहे थे। (सेवा, 203)

से का जिक्र कर—"to casually mention, to casually bring something to someone's attention"

म्युजियम के नौजवान अधिकारी से मैंने उस चित्र की ओर संकेत करके इस बात का जिक्र किया। (दुग्गल, 73)

का जिक्र कर—"to tell of, to describe, to relate"

बहुतों के बेटों को विशू के बेटे ने कारखाने में भरती करवा दिया और लोग उसके एहसान का जिक्र करते न थकते। (दुग्गल, 166)

का जिक्र करते हुए—"referring to"

कुणाल ने पिछले पत्र का जिक्र करते हुए सब कुछ कह सुनाया। उसे सुनकर अशोक को बड़ा ही आश्चर्य हुआ, क्योंकि उसने इस तरह की बात कभी लिखी क्या सोची भी नहीं थी। (आदर्श, 39)

से के बारे में जिक्र कर—"to tell someone about something"

लेकिन जिस रोजगार के बारे में मैं अभी आपसे जिक्र करूंगा, उसमें पंजी की बिल्कुल ही आवश्यकता नहीं। (कहा, 45)

5. **की चर्चा कर—"to talk about"**

पर आज कोई बेसुरा तर्क भी मैं छेड़ने नहीं जा रहा हूं। मैंने निश्चय किया है कि अब अपनी बात नहीं किया करूंगा, हर किसी से उसके प्रिय विषय की चर्चा किया करूंगा। (नदी, 94)

की चर्चा कर—"to speak of"

उन्होंने बहुत बार तुम्हारी और इस घर की चर्चा की है। जिन दिनों मेघदूत लिख रहे थे, उन दिनों प्राय: यहां का स्मरण किया करते थे। (आषाढ़, 69)

की चर्चा कर—"to discuss"

भारतीय रंगमंच और नाटक के पारस्परिक सम्बन्ध और विकास की चर्चा करते हुए मैंने पहले भी यह मत प्रकट किया था कि सिनेमा के प्रचंड वैभव के बावजूद हमारे रंगमंच का पुनरुत्थान अवश्यम्भावी है। (कोणार्क, 91)

की चर्चा कर—"to bring up, to speak of"

तुम ईश्वर का स्मरण कर प्रतिज्ञा करो कि तुम इस पाप की चर्चा कभी भूलकर भी नहीं करोगी अन्यथा इस पाप के फल से तुम्हारा जीवन कलंकमय और कष्टमय हो जायेगा। (फूलो, 96)

की चर्चा कर—"to recount"

माधवी ने अपने एक-पुरुष-व्रत की, सात्विक मर्यादाओं की, बार-बार कुछ इस प्रकार चर्चा की कि सुनने वाला यदि चाहे तो माधवी के इस गुण को कहीं अपने लिए भी प्रयुक्त और समर्पित होते देख सकता था। (सुहाग, 208)

से के सम्बन्ध में चर्चा कर—"to talk to someone about"

किसी न किसी प्रकार इस रहस्य का उद्घाटन करने की उसकी इच्छा होने लगी। कर्नल से भी उसने इस सम्बन्ध में चर्चा की। उसने मंडल के संबन्ध में अक्सर अफवाहें सुनी थीं। (बूंद, 508)

से चर्चा कर—"to speak to"

मैंने आपको इसीलिए कष्ट दिया प्रोफेसर साहब, कि मैं आपकी पत्नी की हालत के बारे में आपसे चर्चा करना चाहता था। (धनु, 139)

की चर्चा कर दे—"to obliquely refer to"

बातचीत के सिलसिले में चन्द्र ने एक उच्च अधिकारी से अमुक रियासत की राजकुमारियों की गवनस की कुछ चर्चा कर दी थी। फिर पूछे जाने पर उसकी नेकी सच्चरित्रता और लगन की बड़ी प्रशंसा की थी। (नदी, 53)

की चर्चा कर—"to bring up (a subject), to mention"

पहले दो तीन साल तक तो पद्मसिंह को सन्तान का ध्यान ही नहीं हुआ। यदि भामा इसकी चर्चा करती तो वह टाल जाते। (सेवा, 243)

से चर्चा कर—"to mention to someone"

शर्मा—इसकी चर्चा तो लाला भगत राम ने एक बार मुझसे की, लेकिन खेद यह है कि तुमने अब तक मुझसे इसे छिपाया, नहीं तो मैं भी कुछ सहायता करता। (सेवा, 306)

की चर्चा कर—"to discuss"

अत: हम क्रमशः शारीरिक सफाई, घर की स्वच्छता और गांव की सफाई की चर्चा करेंगे। (स्वस्थ, 1)

की चर्चा कर—"to speak of"

जबकि वस्तु के गुणों अथवा कार्यों की चर्चा की जाती है तो यह उसका वर्णन होता है और जब वर्ग और विशेषक का उल्लेख किया जाता है तो यह उस वस्तु की परिभाषा होती है। (एमाई, 60)

चर्चे कर—"to gossip about"

जनता चार दिन तक शौक से चर्चे करेगी फिर यही सब अत्याचार होते रहेंगे। (बूंद, 148)

पर चर्चा कर—"to discuss"

...इस विषय पर अगले व्याख्यान में हम चर्चा करेंगे। (नक्षत्र, 6)

की चर्चा करते हुए—"referring to"

गांधी जी के आन्दोलन की चर्चा करते हुए वाइसराय ने कहा—गांधी जी के कार्यक्रम की सफलता में एक इंच भर कसर रह गई थी, मैं हैरान और परेशान खड़ा था। (सुन्दर, क)

की चर्चा करते—"to talk about"

किन्तु उन्हें अपनी बीमारी की चर्चा करते अच्छा लगता था। (परिन्दे, 47)

91. समाधान, इत्मीनान, तसल्ली

1. समाधान, इत्मीनान and तसल्ली all refer to the state of someone who is assured in mind about the truth or rightness of his judgment of or about something, or to someone's state of inner quietude (in which one is no longer disturbed, bothered, or annoyed by something, or does not find something disturbing, bothering or annoying to oneself any longer, or regards something or the continued presence of something as no longer meddling or interfering with what one is engaged in).

समाधान stresses the effort made in the resolution of something which is involved, complex or problematic by performing what is needed or through an act of putting together (creating as a unified whole) before oneself or another person the parts or segments of the source or the cause of disquietude so that everything can be seen in its right perspective. The term may be used of a thing which is inherently capable of providing or effecting the resolution of some problem, as may be called for in some situation.

इत्मीनान applies to anything that a person does (or is asked to do by another) to make himself sure of the validity or genuineness of something in order to avoid a possible or a probable source of annoyance or anxiety.

तसल्ली stresses the notion of one's need (or the awareness of such a need) to return to a state of inner quietude, and is therefore applied to anything that the person himself does or seeks to do in order to satisfy such a need. The term may be used to describe the state of mind of one who, being helpless for some reason, merely seeks release from disquietude rather than doing something in some way to allay it.

2. These nouns are + process and are not pluralized. They form ANP with का (की for तसल्ली). These expressions (with the exception of समाधान) usually require a sentential complement which is attached to the main sentence with कि. The कि clause is elided in some contexts as in the example...शोभा उसे खींचकर तसल्ली कर लेती। (दुग्गल, 111)

3. **का समाधान कर दे—"to resolve"**

जहां कोई पात्र किसी समस्या के समाधान के लिए चिंतित और व्यग्र होता है, गजाधर अपने साधुवेश में वहीं हाज़िर हैं, और समस्या का समाधान कर देते हैं। (नदु, 35)

का समाधान कर दे—"to solve"

समय बड़ा बलवान होता है। वही अपने आप ही कई समस्याओं का समाधान कर देता है ऐसा विचार उनके मन में आये बगैर नहीं रहा।

का समाधान कर—"to satisfy, to appease"

किंतु हिन्दूधर्म मानव की सभी जिज्ञासाओं का समाधान करता है। उसे कुछ निरे तर्कयुक्त बुद्धि-आश्रित तार्किक दोषी भी ठहराते हैं, क्योंकि वह अति अनुभवगम्य और रहस्यमय है। वह परलोक को सामने रखकर चलता है। (धर्म, 21)

का समाधान कर ले—"to relieve"

बहुत देर तक इसी तरह अनाप-शनाप बककर, मन का समाधान कर लेने के बाद रूपा चल दिया। (लाख, 246)

का समाधान कर--"to answer, to allay"

वे सब सभासदों से मिल चुके थे और इस विषय में उनकी शंकाओं का समाधान कर चुके थे, लेकिन मेम्बरों में कुछ ऐसे सज्जन भी थे जिनकी ओर से घोर विरोध होने का भय था। (सेवा, 171)

का समाधान कर---"to convince"

उसका कहना है कि जब अन्य देश शस्त्रसज्ज हैं, तब जर्मनी ही क्यों अपने हथियार छोड़ दे। उसके पूर्व के कुछ साम्यवादी देश भी हथियार छोड़ देंगे, यह बात उसका समाधान नहीं करती। (अणु, 38)

4. **इत्मीनान कर ले—"to satisfy"**

खाना मैं बहुत बढ़िया बना सकता हूं। परीक्षा कर इत्मीनान आप कर लें। (जुहू, 21)

5. **की तसल्ली कर—"to calm"**

वह सिर्फ होटल की बड़ी तख्ती पढ़ते-पढ़ते ही खड़ा हो गया, और उसके भीतर चाय पीने वाले लोगों की तरफ देखकर ही मन की तसल्ली करने लगा। (बनु, 159)

तसल्ली कर ले—"to make sure"

घर को ताला यदि शोभा लगाती तो सुन्दर देख लेता कि ठीक लगा है कि नहीं और यदि सुन्दर लगाता तो शोभा उसे खींच कर तसल्ली कर लेती। (दुग्गल, 111)

तसल्ली कर ले—"to console oneself"

परन्तु अन्त में उसने यह सोचकर मन ही मन तसल्ली कर ली कि परमात्मा का लिखा हुआ सारा ज्ञान उसके पेट में मौजूद है। (बाल, 1)

तसल्ली कर ले—"to make sure"

पहले उसने चाहा, किवाड़ खोलकर भीतर जाये या कम-से-कम झांककर तसल्ली कर ले, फिर न जाने क्यों उसे विश्वास हो गया कि रेखा कमरे में है और सोयी है या कम-से-कम बिस्तर में तो है और वह वैसे ही दबे-पांव लौट गया। (नदी, 221)

92. उद्भासित, प्रज्वलित, प्रदीप्त, उद्दीप्त, ज्योतित, आलोकित

1. These adjectives are all applied in describing something which is bright and glowing, or in order to make a reference to the effect upon oneself of something (which appears to one as) bright and glowing. These terms are used more often in their figurative rather than literal application.

उद्भासित applies to something which comes forth or appears in a bright manner (i.e., appears brighter than its surroundings), or becomes strikingly visible to the eye in the midst of dark surroundings.

प्रज्वलित describes the effect of the coming to light or life again of an object which was very dim, previously emitted practically no light or, although not completely dead, had lost its fieriness.

प्रदीप्त refers to the state of being fully lighted or ignited. In its figurative application it describes the state of someone who is awakened to a full awareness of some feeling or sentiment in his mind.

उद्दीप्त stresses the heightened effect upon one or the intensity of something inflamed or lighted.

ज्योतित describes something which is brought into prominence by focusing or directing some light-source upon it (such as by the use of a spotlight).

आलोकित describes something which is illuminated enough to be visible or perceptible, or makes a reference to its source of light.

2. All the expressions being adjectives are –process.

3. **को उद्भासित कर रख--"to illuminate"**

ऐसा लगता था कि किसी ने अंधेरी रात में राजमार्ग पर दिया जलाकर उसे उद्भासित कर रखा है। (चारु, 17)

उद्भासित कर दे—"to beam"

सरस्वती या कोई भी अन्य बुद्धि या कला का देवता मनुष्यों के हृदय में अपनी एक किरण प्रेरणा के रूप से उद्भासित कर देता है। (मूल्य, 157)

को उद्भासित कर—"to adorn"

दूसरी ओर इस द्वाररक्षिणी के कान में के दन्तपत्र उसके चिक्कन कपोल मण्डल को उद्भासित कर रहे थे। (बाण, 22)

4. **प्रज्वलित कर—"to ignite"**

इस युवक की प्रतिभा ने मुझे मुग्ध कर लिया है। राजीव, तुम नहीं जानते। मुझे प्रधान के पद से कोई मोह नहीं। मोह है तो यही कि कोणार्क पूरा हो जाये।...आज इस युवक ने ठण्डी होती हुई राख को फूंक मार कर प्रज्वलित कर दिया है। (कोणार्क, 42)

प्रज्वलित कर—"to rekindle"

क्या यह अंगारे की चिंगारी फिर नहीं प्रज्वलित की जा सकती ? क्या इस राख के आवरण को सर्वथा दूर नहीं किया जा सकता ? क्या उन दोनों के बीच प्रीति का मंगल-दीप फिर से नहीं जलाया जा सकता ? (धनु, 169)

प्रज्वलित कर—"to light"

उनका दृढ़ विश्वास था कि विश्व के अन्धकार में आर्यों ने अपनी ज्ञान-ज्वाला प्रज्वलित की थी। (तितली, 96)

5. **प्रदीप्त कर ले—"to kindle"**

ऐसी धारणा जब तक एक व्यक्ति अन्य व्यक्तियों के प्रति नहीं बना लेता, अपने हृदय में प्रेम-ज्योति प्रदीप्त नहीं कर लेता, तब तक वह मानवता के नित्य स्वरूप से अनभिज्ञ रहता है। (धर्म, 87)

6. **उद्दीप्त कर—"to kindle"**

ऐसी धारणा से जब तक एक व्यक्ति अन्य व्यक्तियों को न अपना ले, सर्वात्मा के लिए अपने हृदय में प्रेम-ज्योति उद्दीप्त न कर ले, तब तक वह मानवता के स्वरूप से तथा निज आत्मा के स्वरूप से अनभिज्ञ रहता है। (धर्म, 117-18)

उद्दीप्त कर दे—"to ignite, to kindle"

जिस बात ने मेरे चित्त में आसक्ति की आंधी बहा दी है उसी बात ने रानी के चित्त में विवेक का प्रदीप उद्दीप्त कर दिया है। (चारु, 93)

7. **ज्योतित कर दे—"to illuminate"**

हठात् संगीत रुक जाता है। क्षण भर के लिए पूर्ण मौन और निबिड़ अंधकार ! फिर अंधकार को चीरती हुई प्रकाश की मंद रेखा तीन आकृतियों को ज्योतित कर देती है—मंच के एक सिरे पर अग्रभाग में खड़े हुए सूत्रधार और दो वाचिकाएं। (कोणार्क, 19)

8. **आलोकित कर—"to flash"**

...काम के दबाव में उसका मन नौकुछिया अधिक नहीं भागा था—यों भी उसकी प्रवृत्ति पीछे देखने की नहीं थी, हठात् कभी अतीत की किरण मानव को आलोकित कर जाए वह दूसरी बात है—पर श्रीनगर की झील और नौकुछिया का अन्तर स्वयं मन पर चोट करता था। (नदी, 143)

आलोकित कर—"to light the path (of)"

उनका यह आदर्श इस देश की अनेक पीढ़ियों का पथ आलोकित करता रहेगा। (परम 23)

आलोकित कर दे—"to illuminate"

बड़ी-बड़ी लाइटें उन चित्रों को आलोकित कर देती हैं। (बूंद, 388)

आलोकित कर—"to brighten up"

सोचा था उसके सहारे खुद को, सारी दुनिया को बदल डालेगा...मगर ज्यों-ज्यों उस सत्य का प्रकाश बढ़ता गया, त्यों-त्यों वह प्रकाश उसके हर कर्म को, हर विचार को आलोकित करने के लिए प्रखर होता गया। (बूंद, 197)

आलोकित कर—"to lead the way"

बिजली अंधेरी रात में प्रिय के समागम के लिए आतुर अभिसारिकाओं के पथ को आलोकित करती हुई दिखाई देती है। (ज्योति, 25)

93. मगजमारी, मगजपच्ची, माथापच्ची

1. These expressions describe the state of someone who is wastefully expending his mental energy in some way (as when one is persistently trying to think through by fixing one's mind on something not worthwhile, groping unsuccessfully for words, or engaged in the act of figuring out or trying to figure out something without much success or under physically exacting circumstances).

मगजमारी refers to the state of one who persists in a mentally trying experience (by overtaxing one's strength).

मगजपच्ची is applied to the state of one who is overstraining himself (as if by groping for or after words or expressions in trying to express himself in a suitable manner).

माथापच्ची is applied to the state of one who is laboriously thinking or cogitating over words or expressions (as if one were struggling with them) by repeating those words or expressions in an effort to represent one's ideas as perfectly as possible. The term may sometimes be used with negation as a figurative reference to one's lack of intellectual interest in a subject or to one's concern with something trivial.

2. These nouns are +process, and are not pluralized. Both मगजमारी and माथापच्ची form ANP with में ; and मगजपच्ची with के लिये. Only में occurs with infinitives.

3. **में मगजमारी कर—"to toil over"**

अब इस वक्त अखबारों में मगजमारी करोगे ? (दुख, 19)

4. **के लिए मगजपच्ची कर—"to strain for, to grope in vain for"**

बड़ी-बड़ी शाश्वत भावनायें, रस, छन्द और अलंकार—जिनके लिए महाकवि लोग मगजपच्ची करते-करते मर गए। (कहा, 60)

5. **में माथापच्ची कर—"to strain oneself over"**

मुझे एक-एक श्लोक लिखने में घटियों तक माथापच्ची करनी होती है। (बाण, 110)

माथापच्ची कर—"to wrestle with"

प्रस्तुत पंक्तियों का बड़ी माथापच्ची करने पर ही यह अर्थ निकाला जा सकता है कि कवि किसी कार्य में व्यस्त है कि उसका लड़का ई से ईश्वर उ से उल्लू रटता हुआ उसके पास आता है और सहसा कवि से अपनी मां जी के विषय में प्रश्न करता है। (निबन्ध, 678)

माथापच्ची कर—"to concern oneself with"

वह उस समय के विद्यालयों में, ज्ञान के लोभ में, अधिक काल तक माथापच्ची नहीं करता रहा। (मुक्ता, 111)

लेकर माथापच्ची कर—"to make a fuss about, to concern oneself with"

प्रचलित धारणा है कि बुद्धिजीवी स्त्री के आवेग शिथिल होते हैं। अगर किसी को चट से फ्रिजिड वूमन का बिल्ला दे दिया जा सकता हो तो उसे लेकर माथापच्ची कौन करे। (नदी, 16)

94. धारणा, भावना, भावन, अनुगत, अवगत, लक्ष्य, लक्षित, उपलक्षित, प्रत्यक्ष, साक्षात्कार, बोध, ज्ञान, दर्शन, अनुभव, अनुभूति, तजुर्बा, महसूस, अहसास

1. Strictly speaking the expressions in this group are not synonyms of each other, but they are discussed together because they all serve to characterise in a variety of ways the product of the cognitional processes.

धारणा applies to any idea, belief or view held by someone about another person or about the state of things to come, which in the speaker's opinion is more or less colored by the subject's feelings, sentiments or biases, is vague and half-formed, or is not founded in facts or experience (i.e., the speaker's own experience). Therefore the term may at times suggest a reference to the subject's mental apprehension about the state of things in advance of their realization.

भावना refers to the state of harboring a particular feeling for the expected or desired outcome of an event, or to the induced state of mind in which one experiences the special or typical effect of what one seeks or wishes for (in anticipation of its realization).

भावना refers to the state of subjectively experiencing or having the mental conception of the form or the symbolic representation of something (abstractly, in contrast to what is perceived by the senses), usually colored by one's own orientation, beliefs, feelings or sentiments but considered nonetheless true or real by the individual who has such an experience or mental conception.

अनुगत is applied when one acts suddenly or responds in a particular manner on becoming belatedly aware of some situation or one's predicament.

अवगत is used when the thought of something (usually in the immediate environment not noticed or perceived by one) suddenly dawns upon one or when one suddenly comes to realize something purely by accident or in a situation where one could have easily missed it.

लक्ष्य is applied to anything that is the object of one's attention or refers to someone's state of being or becoming cognizant of another person or thing in the immediate environment.

लक्षित is used to describe or stipulate the manner in which the subject exhibits his awareness of something or responds to the object of his attention.

उपलक्षित is applied to the state of becoming aware of something while one is at the same time focusing one's attention on something else, implying that the former is in some way dependent upon the latter.

प्रत्यक्ष is strictly applied to that which is directly present before the eyes or the vision, and is therefore perceptible or can be perceived or felt. In its extended meaning, it is therefore used to refer to any act of inducement of knowledge or the experience of anything as if it is directly present before one's own (used with कर—) or another person's (used with करा—) eyes.

साक्षात्कार (lit. meeting with the eye) describes the act or the result of coming across or grasping (such as by directly experiencing, perceiving intuitively, or coming to the realization of something as a result of deep reflection) the significance, truth or reality of something. The term because of its literal meaning is also applied in making a reference to someone's encountering another unknown person or thing, sometimes under unexpected circumstances.

बोध refers to an integrated mental picture or to the act of mentally grasping the complete picture or knowledge of the true or real substance through the exercise of one's faculty of intellect. The term usually implies a reference to one's ability to penetrate appearances and abstract from the observable phenomena.

ज्ञान describes the act or the result of getting to know, arriving at an understanding of or the state of having knowledge of, information about or insight into something through intuition or indirection.

दर्शन describes or stipulates the result (i.e., coming to a state of mind in which one realizes or exhibits an understanding of the facts, existence or the significance of something) of someone's act of viewing or looking at something often from a specific or particular standpoint or in a specific or peculiar way.

अनुभव describes the content or the particular effect of one's act of perceiving or apprehending something in the environment or applies to the knowledge, skill, or practice derived from direct observation of or participation in events.

अनुभूति applies to the state of being conscious of the impression or having a sensation of an external object or condition arrived at through or as if through an interpretation of sensory stimuli.

तजुर्बा applies to the effect (usually in the form of practical wisdom or knowledge) gained by one's confrontation (such as by actively participating in or passively undergoing) with a situation, event or person.

महसूस describes someone's awareness or feeling of a particular nature resulting from a particular stimuli, or applies to the result of (i.e., the subjective state of) perceiving by tactile, muscular, integumental or other sensation excited by some physical stimulus.

अहसास applies to the state of mind of someone who has come to realize, recognize or perceive the fact or the existence of something, usually implying a direct confrontation with situations or conditions attendant upon the object or content of one's realization, etc.

2. The nouns धारणा, भावना, भावन, साक्षात्कार, बोध, ज्ञान, दर्शन, अनुभूति, तजुर्बा and अहसास are + process, लक्ष्य and अनुभव are ±process, and the adjectives अनुगत, अवगत, लक्षित, उपलक्षित, प्रत्यक्ष and महसूस are − process. Of the ones which are+process, साक्षात्कार forms ANP with के साथ, से and का, लक्ष्य with पर, धारणा, भावना and अनुभूति with की, and the rest with का. Only धारणा, दर्शन and अनुभूति can be pluralized.

3. की धारणा कर—"to envision, to conceive"

...कितने कवियों और लेखकों ने इस संसार का अन्त होने की जो धारणाएं कीं उसका ऐतिहासिक सन्दर्भ में एक विशेष अर्थ था। (मूल्य, 30)

4. की भावना कर—"to imagine, to conceive of"

सभी कर्मचारी अपने मकानों, मोटरों पर वी लिख रहे थे, इसका मतलब यही कि यदि अधिक लोग हमारे विजय की भावना करेंगे तो हमारी विजय होगी। (सुधा, 34)

की भावना कर—"to suppose"

जब आप किसी लकड़ी के बने हाथी में हाथी की भावना करते हैं, तब आपकी चेतना से लकड़ी का लोप हो जाता है, परन्तु लकड़ी का अस्तित्व तो बराबर बना ही रहता है। (भारतीय दर्शनसार, 330)

की भावना कर—"to conceive of"

जब आप उसमें लकड़ी की भावना करते हैं, तब हाथी गायब हो जाता है, परन्तु लकड़ी वहां बराबर मोजूद रहती, सदा रही है और सदा रहेगी। (भारतीय दर्शनसार, 330)

5. का भावना कर—"to contemplate"

इसीलिए भावुकों ने कहा है...अर्थात् भगवान् ! भक्त अपनी बुद्धि से आपके जैसे जैसे रूप का भावन करता है, आप वैसे-वैसे ही स्वरूप को धारण करते हैं। (सुधा, 21)

6. अनुगत कर—"to realize"

सेंतूचन्द—(सनकी कहकर मन के पछतावे के कारण जरा बल खा जाता है, फिर अपने को उसके मण्डल में कुछ पहुंचा हुआ अनुगत करके) पर बहुत गहरे हैं ! बहुत गहरे !! (खिलौने, 97)

7. **अवगत कर—"to take notice of"**

जसवन्त—(गोमती के स्वर में मरवा डालने की दृढ़ता और प्रखरता को अवगत न करके) मैं स्त्री नही हूं—पेट भरने के लिए निकल पड़ी हूं। (वीर, 34)

को अवगत कर दे—"to let someone know"

...और यह कहा है कि यदि पत्र पढ़ने के बाद आप कुछ बतावें तो फौरन लौटकर उससे हमें अवगत कर देना। (शांतला, 6)

अवगत कर—"to dawn on"

महन्त ने अवगत किया, कचनार का दलीपसिंह के पास अधिक ठहरना ठीक नहीं। (कचनार, 327)

अवगत कर—"to perceive, to become conscious of"

केवल (सलिल से) और चाचा जी आप में परिवर्तन कैसे हुआ। सलिल—खिलौने की खोज से (केवल का चेहरा खिलौने से अपना सम्बन्ध अवगत करने के कारण तमक जाता है)। (खिलौने, 67)

8. **पर लक्ष्य कर—"to mark, to pay special attention to"**

तुमने शायद इन शब्दों पर लक्ष्य नहीं किया, मुझे तो कहीं तनिक भी आपत्ति की बात नहीं दीखी, बल्कि मेरे प्रति अतिरिक्त ध्यान के लिये मुझे और कृतज्ञ होने का कारण ही जान पड़ा। (जय, 53)

लक्ष्य कर—"to observe"

वहां आपके विषय में बातें होती रहीं, मैंने लक्ष्य किया कि उनकी बातों में बार-बार एक छिपी ईर्ष्या व्यक्त हो उठती है जिसका कारण न समझ सकी। (नदी, 96)

लक्ष्य कर—"to notice"

उसने बिल्कुल सफेद धोती पहन रखी थी—बहुत छोटी-छोटी सफेद बूटी वाली चिकन की, गहने वह यों भी नहीं पहनती थी और आज चन्द्र ने लक्ष्य किया उसके हाथों पर साधारण एक-एक चूड़ी और एक अंगूठी भी नहीं, स्फटिक से घिरी हुई निष्कंप लौ की तरह वह अपने में सिमटी बैठी थी। (नदी, 174)

लक्ष्य कर—"to note"

परिचय के समय उसने लक्ष्य किया था कि रेखा के पास रूप भी है और बुद्धि भी है किन्तु बुद्धि मानो तीव्र संवेदना के साथ गुंथी हुई है और एक रूप अदृश्य अस्पृश्य कवच-सा पहने हुए है, पर इस आरंभिक धारणा को उसने तूल नहीं दिया था। (नदी, 16)

लक्ष्य कर—"to look at"

गोपूमल मुझे लक्ष्य करके बोला "इस शख्स का मेजा खराब है!" "मेरी तकदीर खराब है!" भाटिया ने संशोधन किया। (जानवर, 62)

लक्ष्य कर—"to aim at"

श्रीराम एवं सुग्रीव की मित्रता को लक्ष्य करके किष्किंधा कांड में श्री तुलसीदास जी ने इस मैत्री प्रसंग पर अनेक उपयुक्त बातें लिखी हैं। (वैदिक, 22)

को लक्ष्य करके—"turning to (Shantala), (lit. fixing her gaze on Shantala)"

लड़कियां बहुत जल्दी बढ जाती हैं। (शांतला को लक्ष्य करके) शांतला क्या तुम भी भूल गई। (शांतला, 47)

लक्ष्य कर—"to perceive"

...उसकी वाणी के अतिरिक्त अग्नेश को लक्ष्य कर भुवन ने उसकी ओर देखा, दोनों की आंखें मिलीं। (नदी, 147)

9. **लक्षित करना—"to notice"**

गिरजे में उस दिन और उससे अगले दिन पाल की सीट खाली रही। इस बात को लक्षित हर एक ने किया मगर किसी ने इस बारे में दूसरे से बात नहीं की। पाल ईसाई नहीं था मगर फादर फिशर के आदेशानुसार स्टाफ के हर सदस्य का गिरजे में उपस्थित होना अनिवार्य था। (जानवर, 145)

लक्षित कर—"perceiving, noticing"

यह लक्षित करके कि उसकी आवाज की तरफ किसी का ध्यान नहीं गया, वह बाहें फैलाकर तना-तना सा चलने लगा। (जानवर, 125)

लक्षित करके कह—"to direct one's remarks to"

तीन-चार व्यक्तियों के पकड़ने पर वह व्यक्ति मारने से हटा। उसकी पत्नी लोगों को लक्षित करके कहने लगी। (जानवर, 131)

10. **उपलक्षित कर— "to observe, to notice"**

एक ओर मानव अपनी अल्पज्ञता व क्षुद्रता का अनुभव करता है और दूसरी ओर संसार की अकिंचनता को भी वह उपलक्षित करता रहता है। (धर्म, 44)

11. **प्रत्यक्ष कर—"to realize"**

फिर हम समर्थित सत्य को प्रत्यक्ष करते हैं। साध्य तत्त्व को सम्पूर्ण रूप से योग द्वारा ही प्रत्यक्ष किया जा सकता है। (धर्म, 55)

प्रत्यक्ष कर—"to express"

विश्व: मेरा हृदय...

मालती—कुछ नहीं। उसे वश में करो।...

मालती—विश्व-विभव, अन्तर्विभूति, उत्सर्ग मिलन को मेरे।
कब तक चलते और रहेंगे, जग के सपने घेरे ?

यह तुम्हीं ने लिखा है न ? अपनी इस अनुभूति को प्रत्यक्ष न कर सकोगे ? विश्व-कान्त—मैंने जो कुछ लिखा है...कदाचित् सब मिथ्या है। मालती—वही तो सच है। उसका सम्बन्ध तुम्हारी आत्मा से है।

आत्मा के सुख के लिये शरीर का सुख छोड़ दो। (सन्यासी, 70-71)

को प्रत्यक्ष करा—"to transform something into reality"

किन्तु जिन्होंने प्रत्यक्ष ज्ञान की प्राप्ति की है, इतना ही नहीं जो प्रत्यक्ष ज्ञान को प्रत्यक्ष करा देने की क्षमता भी रखते हैं, उनकी दी हुई उक्ति भी सबको समझाने और विश्वास कराने में युक्तिगुक्त नहीं होती। (धर्म, 47)

12. **से साक्षात्कार कर—"to confront, to come face to face with"**

सत्य से साक्षात्कार करने में उसे भी डर लगा। (धनु, 32)

के साथ साक्षात्कार कर—"to come across, to meet with"

परमात्मा की प्रेरणा से लाखों करोड़ों योनियों में होता हुआ जीव उन योनियों के गुण-दोष लेकर मनुष्य योनि में आया। इस योनि में बुद्धि ने ज्ञान के साथ साक्षात्कार किया। बुद्धि और ज्ञान ने मनोबल को प्रबल किया। (कचनार, 219)

का साक्षात्कार कर—"to perceive"

इतना याद रख कि पुरुष वस्तु-विच्छिन्न भावरूप सत्य में आनन्द का साक्षात्कार करता है, स्त्री वस्तु-परिगृहीत रूप में रस पाती है। (बाण, 84)

का साक्षात्कार कर—"to perceive"

हिन्दू धर्म...उन द्रष्टाओं की देन है जिन्होंने धार्मिक सत्यों को केवल सोचा और समझा ही नहीं, वरन् अपने दिव्य चक्षुओं से उसका साक्षात्कार भी किया। (धर्म, 16-17)

का साक्षात्कार कर—"to perceive"

हम अपनी अंतरात्मा से निर्देशित होकर अपने विवेकपूर्ण आचरण के द्वारा जिस अंश तक उस नियति का साक्षात्कार करते हैं उसी अंश तक मानव नियति वास्तविक होती है। (मूल्य, 36)

का साक्षात्कार कर—"to discover"

उन्होंने अपनी पैनी दृष्टि से जिन सत्यों का साक्षात्कार किया, उनका खुलकर प्रयोग एवं प्रचार भी किया। (श्रमण)

का साक्षात्कार कर—"to experience"

भारतीय ऋषियों ने धार्मिक सिद्धांतों को केवल जाना ही नहीं, वरन् उसका साक्षात्कार भी किया। अपनी परोक्षानुभूति के द्वारा ही वे हमारे धर्म के मूल प्रवर्तक माने जाते हैं। (धर्म, 17)

का साक्षात्कार कर—"to encounter"

अपने जीवन संघर्ष में महाकवि ने जो पारिवारिक जीवन से सम्बन्ध रखने वाली सुख-दुख...की अनुभूतियों का साक्षात्कार किया, उनका कलापूर्ण सरस चित्रण उनकी अमर रचनाओं में हुआ है। (ज्योति, 35)

का साक्षात्कार कर—"to experience, to see"

मां, आज के वे क्षण मैं कभी नहीं भूल सकती। सौंदर्य का ऐसा साक्षात्कार मैंने कभी नहीं किया। जैसे वह सौंदर्य अस्पृश्य होते हुए भी मांसल हो। मैं उसे छू सकती थी, देख सकती थी, पी सकती थी। (आषाढ़, 8)

का साक्षात्कार कर—"to envision"

एक दिन सूर्यास्त के समय उद्यान-गृह की छत पर अकेला खड़ा कोवलन अस्ताचलगामी सूर्य की रंग-बिरंगी छटा से निखरे हुए बादलों को देखते-देखते अपनी डूबती हुई तेजोमयी चेतना का साक्षात्कार करने लगा। (सुहाग, 149)

का साक्षात्कार कर—"to discern"

निदिध्यासन और सम्यक्‌दर्शन के द्वारा ही मनुष्य मूल सत्य का साक्षात्कार करता है। (धर्म, 91)

13. **का बोध कर—"to perceive"**

वह वस्तुओं को उसके खंडित रूप में न देखकर उसकी सम्पूर्णता का बोध कर लेता है। (धर्म, 96)

का बोध कर दे—"to help someone grasp"

...भिन्न-भिन्न देवताओं ने आकर ब्रह्म की षोडश कलाओं का उपदेश देकर ब्रह्म के स्वरूप का बोध कर दिया... (वैदिक, 41)

धारणा, भावना, भावन, अनुगत, अवगत, लक्ष्य, लक्षित, उपलक्षित, प्रत्यक्ष, साक्षात्कार, बोध, ज्ञान, दर्शन, अनुभव, अनुभूति, तजुर्बा, महसूस, अहसास

14. **का ज्ञान कर—"to acquire the knowledge of"**

यह स्पष्ट है कि अनेक जन्म के साधनों से प्राणी की उपासना में उन्नति होती है। जन्म-जन्म में मार्ग परिवर्तन करने से यथेष्ट लाभ सम्भव नहीं है। अतः पूर्व की उपासना के संस्कार का ज्ञान करके उसी उपासना में प्रवृत्त होना चाहिये। (सुधा, 13)

का ज्ञान कर ले—"to find out"

सूर्य को देखकर हमने दिशा का ज्ञान तो कर लिया, परन्तु उतने से आगे कुछ नहीं। (चारु, 258)

15. **का दर्शन कर—"to try to see"**

विविधता में समता का दर्शन करो। (धर्म, 68)

का दर्शन कर—"to perceive"

उनकी कल्पना थी कि संसार में जो कुछ है, सब सुन्दर है, अतएव वनराजि, वृक्ष-पंक्ति, लता-कुंज तथा पत्र-पुष्प और पराग में अनुपम सौंदर्य का दर्शन कर प्रकृति के गूढ़ रहस्यों को उद्घाटित करने में वे सफल हुए। (ज्योति, 17-18)

का दर्शन कर—"to meet with, to encounter"

वैज्ञानिक जब इस स्थूल तथ्य से आगे अन्वेषण करता है, तो एक नये क्षितिज के दर्शन करता है और अपने आपको किसी आधिभौतिक, गुह्य क्षेत्र में खोया पाता है। (अण, 3)

चेतना का दर्शन कर—"to come to realize"

अपनी जिम्मेदारी को सदियों तक अदा करने के बाद ही इंसान ने इस चेतना का दर्शन किया कि उसके समाज का एक छोटा अंश जबर्दस्ती उसका भाग्यविधायक बना हुआ है। (बूंद, 427)

का दर्शन कर—"to discover"

संयुक्त होकर दोनों ने नये सत्य का दर्शन किया। (बूंद, 141)

का दर्शन कर ले—"to see through"

प्राचीनकाल के ऋषियों को द्रष्टा की उपाधि इसलिए दी जाती थी कि वे अपनी सहज वृत्तियों तथा अनुभूतियों का प्रत्यक्ष अनुभव करने वाले होते थे, वे सत्य के वास्तविक स्वरूप का दर्शन कर लेते थे। (धर्म, 95-96)

अंतः सत्य के दर्शन कर—"to have an insight, to come across or perceive the inner truth"

—जब कोई मनुष्य आदर्शों को कर्म से अधिक बातों के सहारे बढ़ाता हुआ दीख पड़े

तो समझ लेना कि यह झूठा है। महीपाल भी झूठा है दोस्त ! उसने बहुत बरसों पहले एक बार अंतः सत्य के दर्शन किये थे। (बूंद, 197)

16. का अनुभव कर—"to suffer from"

कामिनी की पहले दिन की बात सुनने के बाद मैं अपने में एक अजीब हीनता का अनुभव करने लगा था। (राह, 41)

का अनुभव कर—"to feel (attracted to), to experience"

इसीलिए मैंने उसके शरीर की ओर आकर्षण का अनुभव किया था। (राह, 99)

का अनुभव कर—"to feel"

पति के इस प्रेम-प्रदर्शन के कारण वीणा जरा-सी मुस्कराई। भीतर ही भीतर उसने थोड़ी सी उष्णता का अनुभव किया...(धनु, 36)

का अनुभव कर—"to have no experience of"

यह भी सोचो कि तुम्हारे न रहने से उस अबला शान्ता की क्या गति होगी, जिसने अभी संसार के ऊंच-नीच का कुछ अनुभव नहीं किया है, तुम्हारे सिवा उसका संसार में कौन है ? (सेवा, 257)

का अनुभव कर चुक—"to have undergone"

उसको ऐसा लगा कि मानो वनकन्या भी उसकी नीचता को पहचान गई है, जिसके कारण सज्जन खुद बड़ी ग्लानि का अनुभव कर चुका है। (बूंद, 164)

का अनुभव कर—"to come across"

शांतला ने इसके पहले कभी ऐसी उदय रवि-चंद्रिका का अनुभव नहीं किया था। बाल रवि की शीतल किरणों ने अभी-अभी खिलने वाले कमलों को सुनहले रंग से रंग दिया था। (शांतला, 45)

का अनुभव कर—"to gain insight into, to have direct experience of"

पद्मसिंह को अब दालमंडी जाने का बहुत अवसर मिलता था और वह वेश्याओं के जीवन का जितना ही अनुभव करते थे उतना ही उन्हें दुःख होता था। (सेवा, 320)

का अनुभव करता था—"to have come across"

मनुष्य समाज बहुत प्राचीन काल से इस तथ्य का परोक्ष और प्रत्यक्ष रूप में अनुभव करता आया है...(चमत्कार, 27)

अनुभव कर—"to sense"

धीरे-धीरे बिना रमेश के जाने हुए अजितकुमार उसके जीवन में पूरी तौर से आ गया। रमेश एक तूफान का अनुभव करता था; पर देख न पाता था। (तीन, 34)

अनुभव कर—"to have empathy with, to regard with empathy, to empathize"

व्यक्ति के जीवन में और समाज के जीवन में बहुत अंतर नहीं है। जिस तरह कविता में सारे संसार के दुख-सुख का अनुभव करते हो...उसी तरह कर्तव्य में करो। विश्वकान्त—मुझसे क्या हो सकेगा...मैं तो अपने से ही ऊब रहा हूं। (सन्यासी, 42-43)

का अनुभव कर—"to feel"

इंद्रदेव मित्रों के निमंत्रण से लौटकर सड़क के किनारे, मुंह पर अत्यंत शीतल पवन का तीखा अनुभव करते हुए बिजली के प्रकाश में धीरे-धीरे अपने मेस की ओर लौट रहे थे। (तितली, 19)

शक्ति का अनुभव कर—"to be excited, to be worked up"

निहत्थे थे, अशक्त थे; पर हरेक अपने अंदर अपार शक्ति का अनुभव कर रहा था। पुलिस पर धावा कर दिया। सिपाहियों ने इस बाढ़ को आते देखा तो होश जाते रहे। (सम, 14)

का अनुभव कर—"to partake of"

बच्चा आग को छूकर ही आग के खतरे से अवगत होता है, इसी तरह कलाकार भी जीवन की हर सांस का अनुभव करना चाहता है।(राह, 21)

(सुख) का अनुभव कर—"to enjoy"

मनुष्य अपने सुख का अनुभव आप ही करता है और दुख को लोगों में बांटता फिरता है। (शबरी, 9)

के प्रति प्रतिष्ठा का अनुभव कर—"to take pride in"

इसलिये जरूरत इस बात की है कि मानव की समस्याएं हल करने के लिये कोई मानवीय तरीका खोजा जाय। अगर ऐसा कोई तरीका निकलता है, तो सारी दुनिया उसकी ओर देखती है। इसलिए आपको अपने देश के इस अहिंसक तरीके के प्रति प्रतिष्ठा का अनुभव करना चाहिये। (भूदान, 83)

गौरव का अनुभव कर—"be elated over, to take pride in"

हिन्दुस्तानी एकेडेमी डा० सम्पूर्णानन्द के 'ग्रह-नक्षत्र' का प्रकाशन कर गौरव का अनुभव करती है। (नक्षत्र, 6)

अनुभव कर—"to gain experience of, to perceive"

सो वह उपन्यासों की काल्पनिक दुनिया में ही जीवन का सत्य और स्पन्दन अनुभव करने का प्रयत्न करती। बम्बई के जीवन में यह स्पन्दन कुछ अधिक सजीव हो उठा ऐसा उसने अनुभव किया। (धनु, 26)

को अनुभव करते हुए—"feeling the sense of"

'तुम्हारे लिए बैठ रहा हूं,' यह कह देकर और भाभी का उत्तर अपने भीतर लेकर, जिस स्थल पर उस भाभी के दोनों हाथों ने उसकी बांह को पकड़ कर बैठा लिया था वहां मानो उस स्पर्श को अब भी अनुभव करते हुए हरिप्रसन्न कुर्सी में बैठा अपने में डूबता गया। (सुता, 81)

अनुभव कर—"to feel the sense of (satisfaction)"

उसने अपने आप में वही सन्तोष अनुभव किया जो प्यासे को पानी से मिलता है। (बूंद, 280)

अनुभव कर—"to experience"

हम प्रेम को समझ सकते हैं, उसको अनुभव कर सकते हैं, पर उसकी परिभाषा करना हमारी शक्ति के बाहर है। (तीन, 51)

अनुभव कर—"to become cognizant of the fact that..."

इतने वर्षों में पहली बार आज अपने सतीत्व की हत्या हो जाने पर हर ऊहापोह से मुक्त हो अपने-आपको वह वेश्या अनुभव कर रही थी। (सुहाग, 254)

अनुभव कर—"to imagine oneself as"

वह अपने आपको चिर संस्कारी हिन्दू वैष्णव अनुभव करने का प्रयत्न कर रहा था। वह अपने अंदर उस भक्ति प्रपात के दर्शन करना चाहता था जिसने इस देश के जनसाधारण में से न जाने कितनों को असाधारण बना दिया है। सूर मीरा आदि के जी की लगन जिस लाल से लगी वह कौन है क्या है ? (बूंद, 256)

के प्रतिबद्ध अनुभव कर—"to feel committed to"

इसका उद्देश्य यह है कि लोग स्वतंत्रता के प्रति और अधिक प्रतिबद्ध अनुभव करें लोग अधिक न्यायप्रिय बनें...(अमरीका, 21)

अनुभव कर—"to realize"

सदा की तरह इस समय भी अपनी विवशता अनुभव कर उसे अपने ऊपर खीज आ रही थी। (बंद, 109)

अनुभव कर—"to feel (such as by touch)"

मनुष्य एक साथ देख सकता है, अनुभव कर सकता है और सुन सकता है। (श्रम, 37)

अनुभव कर—"to have any direct experience of, to perceive, to notice"

यूनीवर्सिटी में रमेश प्रभा को देखता था और नमस्कार कर लेता था। प्रभा सुन्दरी थी। उसकी सुन्दरता पर रमेश ने पहले कभी ध्यान न दिया था। प्रभा में प्रतिभा थी; पर उस प्रतिभा को रमेश ने पहले कभी अनुभव न किया था। (तीन, 43)

अनुभव कर—"to feel, to know"

हम वही कह सकते हैं जो हम अनुभव करें और वे जब तक, उन्हें कुछ कहना नहीं होता और कहने में जल्दी कर बैठते हैं, कुछ कह नहीं पाते। (सन्यासी, 6)

अनुभव किया जा—"to be felt"

चारों ओर यह अनुभव किया गया था कि प्रगति की कसौटी ही बदली जानी चाहिए। (मूल्य, 110)

अनुभव कर—"to feel, to understand"

आदिम समाजों में जाकर वास्तविक अवलोकन द्वारा अपने इन निष्कर्षों की यथार्थता की जांच करने की आवश्यकता इन विकासवादी लेखकों ने अनुभव नहीं की। (सामाजिक, 63)

अनुभव कर—"to feel"

संसार के कीचड़ में रहकर भी कमल की तरह निर्लिप्त बनकर ऊपर उठो। तुम देखोगे कि ईश्वर सूर्य की तरह अपने प्रकाश से तुम्हारी आत्मा के एक-एक दल को खोल देंगे। उस समय तुम अनुभव करोगे कि उसका प्रकाश तुम्हारे भीतर व्याप्त होकर तुम्हें आनन्दित कर रहा है। (कथा, 78)

अनुभव कर—"to feel"

इन स्त्रियों की बातें सुनती हूं, और अनुभव करती हूं कि मैं गृहस्थिन तो पहले ही नहीं थी, अब शायद स्त्री भी नहीं रही। कितनी दूर, कितनी दूर हैं मुझसे ये बातें। (नदी, 123)

...वह अनुभव कर रहा था..."he felt"

किसी वीर सैनिक की भांति वह अनुभव कर रहा था। मानो वह किसी भारी मोर्चे को सर करने जा रहा है । (धारा, 200)

अनुभव करती हुई—"feeling"

उठकर जल्दी से बढ़कर लड़के को पकड़कर एक अननुभूत स्पर्शसुख अनुभव करती हुई, खींचकर बोली—अभी तो आप आये, बातचीत जम भी न पायी कि चलने लगे। (निरु, 56)

अनुभव करने लग—"to feel, to come to realize (that)"

जब हम यह अनुभव करने लगेंगे कि प्रत्येक व्यक्ति स्वच्छता के प्रति अपना उत्तर-दायित्व निभाने में लगा है तो अपना स्वतंत्र देश एक स्वच्छ देश बन जाएगा। (स्वस्थ, 26)

17. **की अनुभूति कर—"to gain an experience of"**

...उसी की परिस्थितियों में अपने को रखकर उसी की अनुभूतियां करके उसी के आत्मान्वेषण के दर्द में...(मूल्य, 169)

की अनुभूति कर—"to feel vividly"

अभी सवेरा था, शरीर में उस कोमल धूप की तीव्र अनुभूति करती हुई तितली, अपने गोभी के छोटे से खेत के पास, सिरिस के नीचे बैठी थी। (तितली, 93)

18. **का तजुर्बा कर—"to suffer, to experience"**

सीता एक ऐसे डर से कांपे जा रही थी जो अपनी इस छोटी-सी जिन्दगी में उसने कभी न देखा था, जिसका तजुर्बा उसने अपने पिता की मौत पर भी न किया था। (लड़की, 50)

19. **महसूस कर—"to feel"**

मैंने उसके कंधों को धीरे से छुआ। उसने मेरी अंगुलियों का स्पर्श महसूस किया होगा तभी तो उसने गर्दन को तनिक हिलाया, कंधों को सिकोड़ा...(परिन्दे, 35)

महसूस कर—"to sense"

बच्चे बार-बार मां बाप की घबराहट को देखते इसी अपरिचित शोर को सुनते, इस नये तूफान को महसूस करते और फिर अधिक तेज़ी से टीनों को बजाने लगते। (दुग्गल, 93)

महसूस कर—"to feel"

अगर हो सका तो धूप निकल आने पर वह इन्दु को इन छतनार पेड़ों के नीचे ले जाएगा जिनमें मधुमक्खियों के छत्ते हैं, और वहीं बैठकर उसे अपने बहुत पास महसूस करते हुए वह घटना सुनाएगा कि कैसे एक भालू शहद पीने के लिए पेड़ पर चढ़ गया था...इन्दु आश्चर्य करेगी और एकदम पूछेगी, तुमने कैसे देखा ? (कमल, 56)

महसूस कर—"to feel, to be aware of"

विकेन्द्रीकरण की विशेषता इसी में है कि जनसाधारण को पल-पल पर उसकी अनुभूति हो सके और वह अपनी जिम्मेदारियों को महसूस करती रह सके। (राजवि, 5)

महसूस कर—"to have become aware of"

अपने पूव अनुभवों के साथ मंडल के ये दृश्य जोड़ते हुए उसने उन कारणों को भी महसूस किया जिनसे स्त्रियां इस रास्ते पर आती हैं (बूंद, 510)

महसूस कर—"to feel"

पानी से भीजे हाथ से बच्चों के बदन में सिरहन हुई ताई के हाथ ने उसे तीन बार महसूस किया। (बूंद, 21)

महसूस कर—"to feel, to sense"

डाक्टर शीला के चेहरे को देखकर कन्या महसूस कर रही थी कि बात कुछ बिगड़ गई है। (बूंद, 496)

दिल से महसूस कर—"to sincerely feel, to feel in one's heart"

कन्या बोली—खैर जाने दो, मैं एक बात जानना चाहती हूं क्या तुम दिल से यह महसूस करते हो कि मैंने अपने पिता को गिरफ्तार करवाकर कोई अनुचित कार्य किया है, और क्या इसमें तुम्हारी सहमति नहीं थी सज्जन ? (बूंद, 372)

महसूस कर—"to feel"

सज्जन ने महसूस किया कि वह युवती भावावेश में है फिर और किसी न किसी रूप में उमड़ना चाहती है। (बूंद, 56)

महसूस कर—"to feel"

कन्या ने महसूस किया कि वह जीवन में पहली बार किसी पुरुष के आकर्षणपाश में पूरी तौर पर बंध गई है। और इसके साथ ही साथ आत्म-प्रशंसा का फाटक लगाकर नैतिकता के गढ़ में सुरक्षित रहने वाली अहंकारिणी नारी को...(बूंद, 261)

महसूस कर रहा—"to feel"

सज्जन यों भी अपने आपको ठगा हुआ ही महसूस कर रहा था। (बूंद, 315)

महसूस कर —"to feel"

...और वह अपने को सदा से गहरे शून्य एकांत में पड़ी हुई महसूस करती। (जानवर, 33)

को दूर महसूस कर—"to feel"

रवि जब ऐसी बात कह देता था, तो वह अपने को उससे बहुत दूर महसूस करती थी। (आकाश, 74)

अपराधिनी सी महसूस कर—"to feel"

फादर फिशर ने उसे पाल वाला क्वार्टर दे दिया था, इसलिए वह अपने को अपराधिनी सी महसूस करती थी। (जानवर, 147)

सर्दी महसूस कर—"to feel"

मोहन और कपूर भी सर्दी महसूस कर रहे थे। (आग, 9)

महसूस कर—"to feel (somewhat stranger)"

सज्जन इन रिश्तेदारों के साथ अजब-अजब सा महसूस कर रहा था। (बूंद, 443)

जिम्मेदारी महसूस कर—"to feel"

अकस्मात उसने अजीब तरह की जिम्मेदारी महसूस की और उनके कमरे में जाकर उसने सब सामान करीने से लगाना शुरू कर दिया था। (मांस, 11)

पास महसूस कर—"to feel"

...और वहीं बैठकर उसे अपने बहुत पास महसूस करते वह घटना सुनाएगी कि कैसे एक भालू शहद पीने के लिए पेड़ पर चढ़ गया था...(कमल, 56)

महसूस कर—"to feel"

पता नहीं तब इन्दु कैसा महसूस करेगी, और क्या कहेगी। (कमल, 52)

महसूस कर—"to feel, to become aware of"

सज्जन सुनकर स्तंभित रह गया। कर्नल ने जो निश्चित कदम उठाया था उससे मन में कहीं ठंडक महसूस करते हुए भी वह स्तंभित रह गया, फिर फौरन झटके से खड़ा हुआ। (बूंद, 380)

महसूस करते हुए—"realizing"

कर्नल ने एक नजर महीपाल के चेहरे पर डालकर परिस्थिति के गांभीर्य को महसूस करते हुए कहा—अच्छा, शाम को तुम्हारा कहीं एपाइंटमेंट तो नहीं है? आज सनीमा चलेंगे—जरा काफी-हाऊस का चक्कर भी लगाया जाएगा बहुत दिन हो गये। (बूंद, 37)

गलती महसूस करना जान—**"(to be bold enough) to avow (one's wrong doing), to acknowledge one's mistake"**

वह बेवकूफी करता है पर अपनी गलती महसूस करना भी जानता है। गल्तियों से ऊपर उठना भी जानता है। तुम मेरी बात मानो। (बंद, 367)

2. **का अहसास कर—"to perceive, to realize"**

अगर हम इस सचाई का अहसास नहीं करेंगे कि दुनिया के सब देश एक दूसरे पर निर्भर हैं तो हम इनमें से एक परिवर्तन लाने में भी सफल नहीं हो सकेंगे। (अमरीका, 52)

95. अनिवार्य, आवश्यक

1. Both अनिवार्य and आवश्यक refer to the act of laying down some-requirement (in the form of a rule, direction or the like) to be met with by someone under some specified conditions.

अनिवार्य (which lit. means that from which there is no turning away) is generally used to refer to a requirement (minimum or basic) the fulfilment of which is insured under a law or is designated by some appropriate authority.

आवश्यक applies to that which is either a necessity by reason of the nature of a thing or an obligation, an imperative set forth in order to achieve a desired objective.

2. Both the expressions, being adjectives, are — process.

3. **को अनिवार्य कर दे—"to institute (something) as a compulsory requirement, to make something compulsory"**

उनके अनुसार राज्य को कृषि और ग्रामोद्योगों का विकास करना चाहिए, नशाखोरी बन्द करना चाहिए, बेसिक शिक्षा को अनिवार्य कर देना चाहिए...(भारत, 26)

4. **आवश्यक कर देना—"to institute (a craft) as an obligatory requirement or as a required subject**

इस प्रकार बालकों को कोई-न-कोई उद्योग करना आवश्यक कर दिया था। (बुन, 13)

96. आनन्दित, निहाल, तुष्टि प्रसन्न, खुश

1. These expressions are applied in describing or making a reference to the state of someone (i.e., the object) who is pleased with a person or a thing for a variety of reasons.

आनन्दित is a reference to the sensation or the feeling of pleasure in the abstract or to the actual state of mind induced by a pleasurable experience.

निहाल describes the state of one who is overwhelmed with happiness caused by or brought about through an overabundance of riches, wealth, material comforts or the like.

तुष्टि makes reference to the induced state of mind in which one feels satisfied or contented because of the fulfilment of some need or desire.

प्रसन्न refers to the state of being somewhat overly pleased at something, particularly as a result of an effort made by someone. When used of human subjects, the word implies a thwarting of adverse consequences, an attempt to curry favour or the like.

खुश describes the state of possessing a happy or pleasant feeling, or anything done to bring about or induce happiness or a pleasant response. It is generally understood as a normal state of mind and, therefore, in contexts where there is a mention of some deliberate or overt effort made by the subject to make someone happy, it strongly implies an attempt to cheer up someone who is angry, displeased, unhappy, indifferent or needs some light-hearted entertainment. प्रसन्न, which is often confused with खुश, never occurs in such contexts, even as a term of abstract reference.

2. These expressions, (with the exception of तुष्टि which is + process) being adjectives, are − process. तुष्टि forms ANP with की. They are usually accompanied by expressions denoting the means with which one person pleases another. This is done by using the appropriate noun with से or a conjunctive participle expression. In some cases the noun denoting the means is also used as the subject in a sentence.

3. को आनन्दित कर—"to satisfy, to soothe"

मुझे अपने स्पर्श सुख से आनन्दित करो, जिससे मैं प्रसन्न होकर नई सृष्टि रचूं। (बंद, 140)

को आनन्दित कर—"to bring joy to someone"

संसार के कीचड़ में रहकर भी कमल की तरह निर्लिप्त बनकर ऊपर उठो। तुम देखोगे कि ईश्वर सूर्य की तरह अपने प्रकाश से तुम्हारी आत्मा के एक-एक दल को खोल देंगे। उस समय तुम अनुभव करोगे कि उसका प्रकाश तुम्हारे भीतर व्याप्त होकर तुम्हें आनन्दित कर रहा है। (कथा, 78)

4. **को निहाल कर दे—"to make someone abundantly happy"**

बुढ़िया—डाक्टर साहब मैं उसको बिल्कुल अच्छा कर लूंगी। मुझको उसके पास भिजवा दीजिए। भगवान आपको सुखी रखें, निहाल कर दें। (बांस, 59)

5. **की तुष्टि कर—"to satisfy, to gratify"**

इस आन्तरिक और बाह्य संकटों के द्विविध पाटों में पिसा हुआ मनुष्य कभी टूटे साधनों से गौरव की तुष्टि करने की प्रवंचना में भटकने लगता है। (मूल्य, 30)

6. **को प्रसन्न कर—"to entertain"**

मैं कहता हूं—ये सभी मेरे मेहमान हैं, इन्हें दोतल्ले पर ले चलो। इनको चायपान से प्रसन्न करो। (जुहू, 56)

को प्रसन्न कर—"to please"

सज्जन पहले भी अक्सर कुछ लोगों को प्रसन्न करने के लिए अनुचित काम करता था, विषयभोग में उसकी रुचि पूरी तौर पर रहती थी—पर इसके कारण उसका मन कभी नहीं उखड़ा। (बूंद, 387)

को प्रसन्न कर—to appease"

श्यामदुलारी ने माधुरी को भी प्रसन्न करने का उपाय निकाल ही लिया। (तितली, 44)

को प्रसन्न कर ले—"to win someone's favour, to pacify"

तहसीलदार की मेहमानदारी यथोचित रीति से करके उसने उन्हें प्रसन्न कर लिया था। (लाख, 35)

को प्रसन्न कर—"to please, to appease"

ऊपर दिये गए इस एक ही प्रसंग से प्रो० ज्ञान के व्यक्तित्व का असली रूप प्रकट हो जाता है। वास्तव में प्रतिभा को प्रसन्न करने के लिए वे सब कुछ करने के लिए तैयार हैं और इनकी बौद्धिकता भी इस प्रयास का अंग है। (भंवर, 36)

को प्रसन्न कर—"to please"

क्या अब से वह केवल कुछ लोगों को प्रसन्न करने और अपने विषय-भोग की चिंता में लगे रहने के सिवा और कोई ढंग का काम नहीं करेगा ? (बूंद, 387)

प्रसन्न कर—"to stimulate"

दिमाग़ की कमज़ोरी दूर करता है। चित्त प्रसन्न कर शरीर में शक्ति लाता है। (इलाज, 74)

7. **को खुश कर दे—"to bring delight to, to entertain"**

कैसे गर्दन के गिर्द अपनी बाहें लपेट लेती थी और छोटी-छोटी बातों से खुश कर देती थी। (दुग्गल, 136)

की तबीयत खुश कर दे—"to immensely please someone"

बिन्नो, तुमने मेरी तबीयत खुश कर दी। बस, अब तुम...। (बंद, 366)

को खुश कर दे—"to conciliate"

पत्नी पति की शिकायत लेकर आयी उसने पत्नी को खुश कर दिया। (दुग्गल, 70)

को खुश कर--"to cheer someone up"

सज्जन उसे खुश करने की गरज से बोला--नहीं भाई, कुछ कह लो, जादू-टोने में शक्ति तो जरूर होती है। (बंद, 17)

को खुश कर—"to please"

मैं, अब तक उसे और तुझे धोखा देने और दुनिया को खुश करने की कोशिश कर रहा था। मगर इस वक्त कव्वाली के बहाने अल्लाह ने मेरे मुंह पर थप्पड़ मारे हैं। (खत, 66)

खुश कर—"to satisfy"

अबे मुनाफा इसमें नहीं, गाहक की तबीयत खुश करने में होता है। तुम लोग साले क्या खाके गाहकी फैलाओगे ? (बूंद, 39)

को खुश कर—"to bring some entertainment to someone, to entertain"

ये कहानियां सभी को, खासकर छोटे बच्चों को खुश करें, यह कामना करके भूमिका समाप्त करता हूं। (रूस, भूमिका)

(अपना) दिल खुश कर—"to amuse oneself"

सलीके और फैशन की तो यह हालत है कि जब कभी दिल खुश करने के लिए ऊंची एड़ी का जूता पहनकर घर में छाता तानकर खड़ी हो जाती है तो बड़ी-बड़ी लेडियां उसके आगे पानी भरें। (तुला, 39)

97. मनस्थ, आत्मसात्, हृदयंगम

1. मनस्थ, आत्मसात् and हृदयंगम all refer to the process of absorbing and retaining something in one's mind.

मनस्थ describes the process of concentrating on something which is gradually absorbed or assimilated.

आत्मसात् is the integration of new facts or situations with what one already knows; the process of interpreting facts and responding to them.

हृदयंगम describes the process of concentrating intensively on something in order to understand it deeply and thoroughly, and thus master it.

2. All these expressions being adjectives are —process.

3. **को मनस्थ कर—"to fix something in one's mind"**

राजकीय तक्षक विशाख और कलाकार अमेघ की पुत्री प्रति प्रातःकाल स्नान के पश्चात् देवता की मूर्ति के सम्मुख उपस्थित होते और एक घड़ी तक एक दूसरे को निहारते। मनोयोगपूर्वक इस दर्शन का प्रयोजन तक्षण के लिये एक दूसरे की आकृति को मनस्थ करना होता था। (फूलो, 38)

4. **को आत्मसात् कर—"to assimilate"**

प्रतिभा के आचरण को सूक्ष्मता से देखें तो स्पष्ट पता चल जाता है कि उसने प्रोफ़ेसर नीलाभ की व्यक्तिगत विशेषताओं का अनुकरण-भर किया है, उन्हें वह आत्मसात् नहीं कर पायी है। (भंवर,16)

को आत्मसात् कर—"to adapt"

प्रयोगवाद कविता की एक नूतन शैली विशेष है जो कवि द्वारा अनुभूत 'सत्य' को पाठक तक पहुंचाने के लिए विभिन्न प्रयोगों को आत्मसात् करती है। (निबंध, 668)

को आत्मसात् कर—"to absorb"

नाजी बिना यथार्थवाला मनुष्य होता है। वह किसी यथार्थ, किसी देश या किसी

व्यक्ति को पदाक्रान्त कर सकता है, उसे दबोच सकता है पर विघटित और क्रमहीन होने के कारण उसे आत्मसात् नहीं कर सकता अत: उसे नष्ट कर देने की कोशिश करता है। (मूल्य, 33)

5. **को हृदयंगम कर—"to take to heart"**

अब एक प्रार्थना अभिनय करने वालों से है। वे इस नाटक को कई बार पढ़ें तब खेलें जीवन की समस्याओं पर इसमें जो कुछ कहलवाया गया है उसको हृदयंगम करें तो अभिनय खरा उतरेगा। (वीर, 5)

को (भली-भांति) हृदयंगम कर ले—"to comprehend"

इस प्रयास में उपन्यासकार को यह तत्व भी भलीभांति हृदयंगम कर लेना चाहिए कि वैज्ञानिक, मनोविश्लेषक, पत्रकार या राजनीतिक कमिस्सार इन सब का मार्ग उपन्यासकार का मार्ग नहीं है। (मूल्य, 173)

को हृदयंगम कर पा—"to imbibe"

इसके पहिले कि हम इस गहन उत्तरदायित्व को भलीभांति हृदयंगम कर पाते, हमारे सामने एक दूसरी ऐतिहासिक चुनौती प्रस्तुत हो गई। (मूल्य, 64)

98. अमान्य, निषेध, वर्जन, वर्जित, अस्वीकार, अस्वीकृत, नामन्जूर, नापसन्द इन्कार, मनाही, मना, ना, नाहीं

1. अमान्य, निषेध, वर्जन, वर्जित, अस्वीकार, अस्वीकृत, नामन्जूर, नापसन्द, इन्कार, मनाही, मना, ना, नाहीं are used to refer to something which is inconsistent with or contrary to some accepted standard or one's own ideas, and is therefore prohibited, excluded or to be avoided in a given situation or under some negative imperative conditions.

अमान्य refers to setting aside or overriding (through one's own act, action or decision not to go along with) a practice customarily followed, a decision or a suggestion made by someone on the grounds that such a practice, decision, suggestion or the like is at variance with one's own ideas or beliefs.

निषेध is applied to any practice (sometimes an act) which on the basis of some principles or premises is excluded from a code of conduct or formal procedures based on those principles or premises. The term may also be used to describe a practice (based on or regarded to be based on false values or beliefs) which contravenes or stands in the way of what is believed to be right morally and ethically.

When used of human subjects निषेध refers to an assertion to the contrary of what has been said or affirmed by another person, usually in the form of a reference to some imperative conditions or to one's own past experience.

वर्जन applies to that which one seeks to avoid (usually by acquiring a disposition of detachment or indifference towards something) on the grounds of expediency, untoward consequences or impropriety.

वर्जित the non—process counterpart of वर्जन, is used when one person asks another to avoid what the latter is tempted to do.

अस्वीकार is to show, express or indicate in a variety of ways a positive unwillingness to accept something (i.e., regard it as proper, suitable or normal; acknowledge or recognize it as appropriate, permissible or inevitable) or to go along with (or comply with) another person's request, suggestion, wishes or the like.

अस्वीकृत is a term of limited application referring to an instance of refusal to have anything to do with something. It may take a non-human subject referring to some dogma, philosophical view or the like.

नामन्जूर refers to the act of refusing to grant someone's petition, or request, or turning down a request made by someone.

नापसन्द refers to the act of giving an indication of one's positive dislike for something (sometimes, someone) presented to someone, or set forth or described before someone in order to be accepted or taken as may be called for in a given situation. The term may be used to refer to something which does not agree with or conform to someone's (i.e., the subject's) personal bias, predilection or disposition.

इन्कार refers to the act of denying or to an instance of denial by someone implying a refusal, usually outspoken, to accept as true, to grant or concede, or to acknowledge the existence or the claims of someone or something.

मनाही (मनाई) refers to an instance of banning something, i.e., prohibiting by legal means, social pressure, or authority the activities or performance of someone or the dissemination or the use of something.

मना refers to responding or answering to another person's request, offer to help or requesting someone to desist from doing something by using anyone of the negative expressions (such as in English "No, thank you," "Please don't do that," "No !").

ना refers to answering another person's request (usually put in the form of an interrogative expression) or any Hindi interrogative expression beginning with क्या with the word नहीं "no". The term may apply to the use of appropriate gestures or such means other than the use of language employed to indicate both a question and its answer.

नाहीं refers to refusing to accede to another person's request or giving another person an indication of one's unwillingness to go along with his suggestion (usually put forth in affirmative sentences) by using negative participles न or नहीं in sentences with verbal expressions चाह—अच्छा लग—, जरूरत हो—or the like.

2. All these expressions with the exception of निषेध, वर्जन and इन्कार, are —process. वर्जन is +process, and both निषेध and इंकार are ±process. वर्जन and निषेध form ANP with का, and इन्कार with से. All three nouns—निषेध, वर्जन and इन्कार—do not take plural.

3. को अमान्य कर—"to dismiss"

कल्याणी और कन्या के बीच होने वाले निश्चय को अमान्य कर शकुन्तला का विवाह सज्जन की शाहनजफ वाली कोठी से करने के बजाय रूपरतन की कोठी से करने की व्यवस्था की। (बूंद, 554)

को अमान्य कर—"to do away with, to cast off"

इनसान...वर्ग मुक्त हो, पीड़ा मुक्त हो, इस डिकेडेंट, रुग्ण, ह्रासशील समाज से और स्वयं अपने-आपसे बाहर होकर इसके सब मानों-प्रमाणों को तोड़ गिराये, इसकी मान्यताओं को अमान्य कर दे...(नदी, 191)

को अमान्य कर—"to reject"

इतना ही नहीं मैं यह भी समझता हूं कि तुम्हारे हिताहित के विषय में तुम्हारी धारणा को वे अमान्य नहीं करेंगे उससे क्लेश होगा तब भी नहीं। (नदी)

को अमान्य कर—"to repudiate, to go against"

संतान को पढ़ा-लिखा कर फिर अपनी इच्छा पर चलाना चाहने का मतलब है स्वयं अपनी दी हुई शिक्षा-दीक्षा को अमान्य करना। (नदी, 73)

4. **का निषेध कर—"to prohibit"**

भारतीय संविधान सब प्रकार की अस्पृश्यता, भिखमंगी, मनुष्यों के व्यापार और बलात् श्रम का निषेध करता है। (भारत, 48)

का निषेध कर—"to contravene, to deny"

...जो आज ध्वस्त मानवीय अंतरात्मा को पुन: स्थापित करना चाहता है उसके लिए यह आवश्यक हो जाता है कि वह इस अवर्तमान महामानव की प्रतिमा को तोड़ने का प्रयास करे क्योंकि वह झूठे मूल्यों की जननी है क्योंकि वह सामान्य मानवीय यथार्थ और मानवीय गौरव का निषेध करती है और अंतरात्मा के ध्वंसावशेषों पर अपनी महत्त्वाकांक्षा का प्रासाद खड़ा करना चाहती है। (मूल्य, 26)

को निषेध कर—"to warn"

उसने हाथ जोड़ कर महन्त को बहुत धीमे स्वर में निषेध किया। "महाराज, कोई औषधि कुछ उल्टी न बैठे कहीं। वैसे ही आराम मिल रहा है।" (कचनार, 321)

का निषेध कर—"to condemn"

किंतु कुछ हो इसमें संदेह नहीं हो सकता कि भारतवर्ष के साथ हमारे शुरू के सम्बन्ध में बहुत सी ऐसी बातें हुई हैं जिनको याद करके कोई भी सदाचारप्रेमी मनुष्य कांप उठेगा और जिनका कोई भी सच्चा ईसाई घृणा के साथ निषेध किए बिना नहीं रह सकता। (सुन्दर, 19)

5. **का वर्जन कर—"to shun, to avoid"**

कर्मत्याग से अभिप्राय है श्रेष्ठ कर्म करते हुए कर्मफलों और उनके अभिमानों तथा आसक्ति का वर्जन करना। (धर्म, 140)

6. **वर्जित कर—"to bar"**

गुसाइयों की इच्छा धामोनी की लूट करने की थी, परन्तु अचलपुरी ने वर्जित किया। (कचनार, 311)

वर्जित कर—"to restrain"

द्वार पर ठिठकी महारानी ने आंख के इशारे से उसे वर्जित किया। (बेटी, 43)

7. **अस्वीकार कर—"to deny"**

वासनाओं की आंधी शरीर-जन्य है। उनके अस्तित्व को अस्वीकार करने से काम नहीं चलता। (धनु, 183)

अस्वीकार कर—"to avoid, to refuse to accept"

मैं भीतर ही भीतर कामिनी को प्यार करता था, परन्तु ऊपर से उसको अस्वीकार करता था। (राह, 41)

अस्वीकार कर दे—"to reject"

हमने इस मान्यता को अस्वीकार कर दिया है कि सरकार का काम बल-प्रयोग या नियंत्रण है। (अमरीका, 99)

अस्वीकार कर दे—"to refuse to accept"

क्या यह मेरे लिए गौरव की वस्तु नहीं है ? मैंने उनका त्यागपत्र अस्वीकार कर दिया। (तितली, 207)

...अस्वीकार करके..."by declining"

अजित ने गंभीरतापूर्वक कहा—और याद रखना तुम मेरे उपहार को अस्वीकार करके मेरा अपमान करोगे। (तीन, 32)

अस्वीकार कर दे—"to turn down"

कर्नल ने उससे महीपाल पर मुकदमा न चलाने के लिए आग्रह किया और कर्नल की आशा के प्रतिकूल सज्जन ने उसके आग्रह को अस्वीकार कर दिया। (बूंद, 563)

को अस्वीकार कर दे—"to decline"

उन्होंने बड़े प्रेम और आग्रह के साथ अनुरोध किया कि महाराजाधिराज द्वारा आयोजित उत्सव में वे सम्मिलित हों, पर भट्टिनी ने दृढ़-शान्त कण्ठ से अस्वीकार कर दिया। (बाण, 264)

8. **को अस्वीकृत कर—"to reject"**

कम्युनिज्म व्यक्ति को पूर्णतया अस्वीकृत कर केवल एक अमूर्त निराकार समूह को प्रतिष्ठित करता है। फिर उस समूह के दायित्व को निर्धारित करने का काम राज के हाथ में होता है। (मूल्य, 50)

9. **नामन्जूर कर दे—"to refuse"**

उनके पूछने पर भी दंड में हाथ बंटाने से परिवारियों ने नामन्जूर कर दिया था। (विचित्र, 14)

नामन्जूर कर—"to turn down"

फिर मुंशी जी की 'इन्सानियत और शराफत' इस बात को कतई गवारा नहीं कर सकती कि आपके निमंत्रण को नामन्जूर कर आपके दिल को दुख पहुंचाए। (तुला, 125)

अमान्य, निषेध, वर्जन, वर्जित, अस्वीकार, अस्वीकृत, नामंजूर, नापसन्द, इन्कार, मनाही, मना, ना, नाहीं

नामन्जूर कर—"to refuse"

यह मेरी तरफ से इनकी नजर है। उम्मीद है आप नामंजूर न करेंगे। (जुहू, 69)

10. **नापसन्द कर—"to dislike"**

आप लखनऊ आवें यह सुझाने की धृष्टता तो नहीं कर सकता, मेरी अपात्रता के अलावा लखनऊ की घटनाओं का भी स्मरण कराया जाना आप नापसन्द करेंगी। (नदी, 256)

नापसन्द कर—"to dislike"

इसी कारण मैंने मन ही मन कामिनी का व्यवहार नापसन्द किया था। (राह, 41)

नापसन्द कर—"to reject, to express one's dislike for"

यदि तुम्हारी बहन को कोई देख कर नापसन्द कर दे तो ? (धारा, 197)

11. **से इन्कार कर—"to deny"**

देश के विकास में नारियों के योगदान का मूल्यांकन करने का गंभीर प्रयास नहीं किया गया है। फिर भी इससे शायद ही कोई इन्कार कर सके कि भारतीय नारी ने इस दिशा में बहुत लम्बे कदम रखे हैं। (श्रम, 31)

से इन्कार कर—"to refuse"

मुखिया के भाषण में बड़ा जोश चढ़ रहा था। तभी एक मनुष्य दौड़ता हुआ आया और पंचों का अभिवादन कर बोला—हुजूर जिवा लुहार यहां आने से इन्कार करता है। (लाख, 108)

से इन्कार कर—"to contradict"

किसी भी जमींदार ने आज तक मेरे विचार से इन्कार नहीं किया। (भूदान, 90)

से इन्कार कर—"to deny"

अकबर की जन्मजात प्रतिभा से कोई इन्कार नहीं कर सकता। (पीर, 3)

से इन्कार कर दे—"to flatly refuse (to do something)"

न जाने वह दिन कब आयेगा, जब हमारे भाई बन्द ऐसे हुक्मों की तामील करने से साफ इन्कार कर देंगे, जिनकी मंशा महज कौम को गुलामी की जंजीरों में जकड़े रखना है। (सम, 85)

से इन्कार कर—"to decline"

रामशरण जैसे चिलम पीने से इन्कार न कर सका था वैसे ही सोंठ फांककर दूध का कटोरा भी उसने पी लिया। (फूलो, 18)

को इन्कार कर दे—"to turn someone down"

पहली बार जीवन में उसको महसूस हो रहा था कि उसकी हार हो रही है। पहली बार जीवन में उसने कोई चीज मांगी थी और ईश्वर ने जैसे उसे इन्कार कर दिया हो। पहली बार जीवन में उसने कहीं हाथ डाला था और उसकी मुट्ठी खाली लौट आई थी। (दुग्गल, 121)

से इन्कार कर—"to deny"

हम इससे इन्कार नहीं कर सकते कि मनुष्य अपने स्वार्थों की पूर्ति के लिये प्रयत्नशील है। (स्वस्थ, 1)

को इन्कार कर—"to avoid"

रिवाल्वर को हाथ में लेकर रगों में स्फूर्ति आती है, श्रीकान्त! नीति कुछ कहे, और नीति तो सदा ही विवादास्पद है, किन्तु प्राणों की स्फूर्ति को तो एकदम कैसे इन्कार किया जा सकता है? (सुता, 102)

12. **की मनाही कर दे—"to bar, to forbid"**

सार्वजनिक सभा तथा जुलूस निकालने की मनाही कर दी गई है। (आज, 3)

की मनाही कर दे—"to forbid"

कुएं पर बर्तन साफ करने, कपड़े धोने और नहाने की मनाही कर देनी चाहिए। (स्वस्थ, 15)

13. **मना कर दे—"to decline"**

मणि नानावती को वह अपनी चायदानी में से चाय देने लगी तो उसने हल्का सा धन्यवाद देकर मना कर दिया। पीटर ने अपना चेहरा ऐसा गंभीर बनाए रखा जैसे उसकी बात करने की आदत ही न हो। (जानवर, 137)

मना कर—"to refuse"

जो व्यक्ति इसे भुगतान के रूप में लेना मना करता है उसे राज्यदंड का भागी होना पड़ता है। (एमाई, 86)

मना कर—"to refuse"

मैंने तो कभी मना नहीं किया। ठीक है पर मेरी दुनियां बदल गई है। अच्छा, मैं जाता हूं। (बूंद, 492)

मना कर—"to desist"

ज्ञानवती ने देखा मोतीराम नहीं मानेगा और वह मना भी नहीं कर पा रही थी। सिर चकरा जाने से उसका विरोध शिथिल हो गया था। (फूलो, 92)

मना कर—"to urge someone not to"

कितना मना किया है कि इतना काम न किया करो, पर तुम मानती ही नहीं। घर में वह नौकरानी है माली है वह! (रात, 83)

मना कर—"to forbid"

सूका: उस तरह था तब भी मुझे रोज भूज रहा था, आज इस तरह है तब भी मुझे जिंदा मछली की तरह भूज रहा है......वैद ने मुझे मना किया है कि उसे भीतर आड़े में ही रखना, पुरवा हवा न लगने पाये। (अंधा, 134)

14. ना कर दे—

सेक्रेटरी ने मोटर मंगाने की आज्ञा चाही तो महाराजकुमार ने इशारे से ना कर दिया। (मुक्ता, 94)

ना कर—

उदास क्यों हो? भाभी से महाभारत हो गया? महीपाल ने गर्दन हिलाकर ना की। सज्जन ने फिर पूछा—तुम्हें कोई न कोई चिंता जरूर है। सुबह कर्नल ने बतलाया कि कल तुम्हारे साले की शादी थी यहां। "शादी परसों थी कल बड़ाहार था।" (बूंद, 180-81)

ना ना करते हुए—

इन दो वस्तुओं को छोड़कर कन्नगी के पास अब और कुछ नहीं रहा और इसीलिए भोले मन की ना ना करते हुए भी कन्नगी देवन्ती को रोक न सकी। (सुहाग, 197)

15. नाहीं कर—

शीला ने अपना शाल जबरदस्ती दे दिया, सर्दी तेज होने की वजह से महीपाल ने भी नाहीं न की। सड़क पर आकर वह सोचने लगा—अब कहां जाऊं। (बूंद, 215)

से नाहीं कर—

अब परसोतम बेचारे से नाहीं करते न बन पड़ा। चुपचाप पांच रुपये निकाल कर दे दिये। (तुला, 96)

नाहीं कर दे—

उसने पूछा—चचा, तुमने ब्याह क्यों नहीं किया? बुआ तो कहती थी, लड़की बड़ी अच्छी है। तुम्हीं ने नाहीं कर दी। (तितली, 262)

99. आतिथ्य, अतिथि-सत्कार, मेहमानदारी, आदर-सत्कार, सत्कार, आवभगत, स्वागत, सुस्वागत, इस्तकबाल, खातिर, खातिर-तवाजा, खातिरदारी

1. आतिथ्य is treating someone (who is a guest) to one's hospitality with a marked show of formality, exuberance and care for details. The term implies a graciousness on the part of the guest who, by accepting the hospitality, enhances the status of the host.

अतिथि-सत्कार is according someone (who is not a guest) the treatment of a guest.

मेहमानदारी is entertaining someone (as a guest). The term lacks the ritualistic overtones of आतिथ्य and अतिथि-सत्कार. It does imply a sense of earnestness or an exertion on the part of the host, and may thus lend itself to a variety of interpretations about the motives of the host.

आदर-सत्कार is receiving someone in a worthy and decorous manner implying an observance of some sort of protocol.

सत्कार stresses a dignified, hospitable treatment accorded to someone. The term often requires some sort of expression in the sentence of the means used.

आवभगत implies the feeling of warmth or cordiality in the manner in which one treats or receives a visitor, a friend or a guest.

स्वागत (स्वागत) refers to the act of welcoming someone, or is applied to anything that is welcome to one, stressing in both cases the subject's attitude of pleasure towards someone or something. This attitude sometimes implies an assertion of the subject's ability to confront and cope with unpleasantness or hostility without being overwhelmed by it.

सुस्वागत is a somewhat pedantic term (coined by prefixing सु twice before आगत), stressing something done to make (unduly) welcome the arrival of someone.

इस्तकबाल is a relatively neutral term stressing the courtesy or cordiality with which one greets a visitor.

खातिर stresses the subject's disposition of the care, in varying degrees, with which he treats someone, anticipates his needs or favours him.

खातिर-तवाजा contains a reference to the disposition of care and concern in an act of hospitality.

खातिरदारी contains a reference to one's sense of obligation to a visitor, a guest or the like.

2. These expressions are ±process and form ANP with का (मेहमानदारी, आवभगत, खातिर, खातिर-तवाजा and खातिरदारी occurs with की). Only खातिर can occur with plural.

3. का आतिथ्य कर—"to welcome"

तहसीलदार ने श्यामलाल बाबू का आतिथ्य करने के लिये, उनसे जो कुछ हो सका था, आमोद प्रमोद का सामान इकट्ठा किया था। (तितली, 138)

4. का अतिथि-सत्कार कर—"to treat someone to one's hospitality, to accord welcome as a guest"

राजा : मैं उसके लिए प्रस्तुत हूं, पर उसके पूर्व...मैं तुम्हारा अतिथि-सत्कार करना चाहता हूं। प्रेतात्मा : अपने राजमहल का ठंडा पानी पिलाकर ? (नाटक, 23)

5. की मेहमानदारी कर—"to entertain, to show hospitality"

तहसीलदार की मेहमानदारी यथोचित रीति से करके उसने उन्हें प्रसन्न कर लिया था...(लाख, 35)

की मेहमानदारी कर—"to entertain"

सुना है उसके यहां एक कोई लड़की है जो जादू जानती है। वह मालदार बकरों की ऐसी मेहमानदारी करती है कि वे अपनी कलेजी तक काढ़ और भून कर उनके भोग के लिये रख देते हैं। (जुहू, 45)

6. का आदर-सत्कार—"to greet, to receive"

...नगर के समस्त नागरिकों तथा अधिकारियों को उत्सव के लिए निमंत्रण दिया गया है। सब लोग आयेंगे ही। सबका, उनके स्थानमान के अनुसार, आदर-सत्कार करना पड़ेगा। अमात्यों को इस सम्बन्ध में आदेश दिया जा चुका है। (शान्तला, 30)

7. का सत्कार कर—"to entertain, to receive"

लेकिन मैं ही जानता हूं कि अपने घर में अपनी सहेलियों का सत्कार करने में 'वे' कितनी स्वतन्त्र हैं और अपने ही घर में अपने मित्रों की आवभगत करने में मैं कितना परतन्त्र हूं ? (कहा, 13)

का से सत्कार—"to be treated to"

शकुन्तला को बुलाकर आदेश दिया कि छिद्दू का पकवानों से सत्कार किया जाय,

उसके कपड़े बेहद गीले हो गए हैं लिहाजा उसे महीपाल की एक पुरानी कमीज़ और धोती भी दी जाय। (बूंद, 474)

का सत्कार कर—"to respect"

अशोक ने फिर कहा—कुणाल ! मेरा मन कैसे मानेगा, मेरी इच्छा का सत्कार करके कुछ मांगो। (आदर्श, 40)

8. **की आवभगत कर—"to receive"**

लेकिन मैं ही जानता हूं कि अपने घर में अपनी सहेलियों का सत्कार करने में वे कितनी स्वतन्त्र हैं और अपने ही घर में अपने मित्रों की आवभगत करने में मैं कितना परतन्त्र हूं। (कहा, 13)

की आवभगत कर—"to receive, to welcome"

गांववालों ने पंडित जी की खूब आवभगत की। (बाल, 1)

9. **मुस्कान से स्वागत कर दे—"to greet someone with a smile"**

दोनों ही कुछ बोल नहीं सके, रेखा ने एक दुर्बल मुस्कान से उसका स्वागत कर दिया और पड़ी रही। (नदी, 240)

का स्वागत कर—"to welcome, to accept"

इस संघर्ष में एक ओर वे लोग हैं जो भविष्य का स्वागत करते हैं और दूसरी ओर वे लोग हैं जो उससे कतराते हैं। (अमरीका, 13)

का स्वागत कर—"to hold a meeting to welcome"

मुझे याद है कि युद्ध से लौटे सैनिकों का हमने अपने छोटे से स्कूल की इमारत में स्वागत किया था। (अमरीका, 61)

का स्वागत कर—"to welcome"

...और कह देना कि इन शब्दों की पूरी जिम्मेदारी मैं ले रहा हूं और इसके हर परिणाम का मैं स्वागत करूंगा। (जय, 84)

का स्वागत कर—"to be welcome to one"

मैजिस्ट्रेट जो कठोर-से-कठोर दंड प्रदान करे, उसका स्वागत करूंगी। अब मैं पुलिस के किसी आक्षेप या असत्य आरोपण का प्रतिवाद न करूंगी; क्योंकि मैं जानती हूं, मैं जेल के बाहर रहकर जो कुछ कर सकती हूं, जेल के अन्दर रहकर उससे कहीं ज्यादा कर सकती हूं। (सम, 17)

का स्वागत कर—"to be welcome, to be received hospitably"

यदि संयोग से कोई पढ़ा-लिखा आदमी फिर से गांव में जा पहुंचे और वहां रहने लगे तो वह चाहे कितना ही सुखी हो, देहात का वातावरण उसका स्वागत नहीं करता। (डगर, 37)

का विशेष स्वागत किया जा—"to be especially welcome"

प्राण हथेली पर रख कर, इन्सान मुसीबत से कैसे जूझा—ऐसी कहानियों का विशेष स्वागत किया जाएगा। (बाल, 11-23)

10. **का सुस्वागत किया जा—"to be accorded a cordial welcome"**

...और पलक-पांवड़े बिछाते अतिथि महोदय का सुस्वागत किया जाता। (कहा, 31)

11. **का इस्तकबाल कर—"to greet, to receive"**

और मुस्करा कर मेरा इस्तकबाल करते हुए फरमाया, कहो, भाई बख्तावर, यह सब क्या माजरा है? (तुला, 64)

12. **की खातिर कर—"to treat with care, to have regard for"**

वह पहले से ही उसकी खातिर करते थे, अब कुछ आदर भी करने लगे और सुभद्रा तो उसे लड़के के समान मानने लगी। (सेवा, 294)

की खातिर कर—"to treat someone with respect"

उनकी सादगी, उनका उत्साह, उनकी विनय, उनकी मृदुवाणी कांग्रेस पर उनका सिक्का जमाये देती थी। हर आदमी उनकी खातिर सम्मान की सीमा तक करता था, पर उनकी स्वाभाविक नम्रता उन्हें अपने दैवी साधनों से पूरा-पूरा फायदा न उठाने देती थी। (सम, 64)

की खातिर कर—"to treat someone with care"

बाहर से किसी प्रकार का मानसिक आघात पाकर मनिया फिर अपनी पत्नी की खातिर करने लगा। छोटे भाई को अपनी पत्नी का लाड़ करते देख उसके मन में भी हौंस हुई। (बूंद, 66)

की खातिरें कर करके—"with solicitude"

अपने बेटे निहाल में जैसे बूढ़े गंगासिंह की जान हो। किस तरह उसने पाला था। उसकी खातिरें कर करके, उसे लाड कर करके। (दुग्गल, 125)

13. **की खातिर-तवाज़ा कर—"to entertain"**

"...हमें उल्लू बनाने के लिए यह खातिर-तवाज़ा कर रहा है...ओह!" मस्तान नशे में चिल्लाने लगा...। (जुह, 59)

14. **की खातिरदारी कर—"to wait on"**

पनवाड़ी के यहां से दो डिबियां चार मीनार की ले लीं। फिर इस तरह आगे चला जैसे घर पर मेहमान आये हों, जाकर उनकी खातिरदारी करनी हो। (आकाश, 63)

100. मीमांसा, समीक्षा, विवेचन, विवेचना, आलोचना, टीका-टिप्पणी, टीका, टिप्पणी, अर्थ, मूल्यांकन, विश्लेषण

1. These expressions are applied to characterize the intellectual activity of someone who expresses himself or discourses about a given subject, topic or matter with a particular viewpoint or in order to express any kind of value judgment about it.

मीमांसा is applied to any discourse in which someone engages in deep reflection, which constitutes contemplative consideration involving recall and re-examination of the particulars of a case (i.e., the individual specific separate phenomena or the instances of a phenomenon). The goal of such an examination is ultimately to relate those particulars to some given generalizations, or to evolve from those particulars a system of generalizations so as to bring into relief what seems to be conflicting and contradictory in them.

समीक्षा is applied to the act or the result of going over or examining something critically and with a view to judging or appreciating the properties of any formulation, statement, expression, work of art, or literature. The term may be applied to any discourse involving such a judgment or appreciation, and is commonly used of one who is (professionally or otherwise) engaged in so doing, such as in the acts of analysis, artistic evaluation, or appreciation of works of arts.

विवेचन is any verbal statement or presentation of some subject-matter or a point of view in which one displays one's knowledge and the exercise of one's faculty of discriminating (truth from falsehood, reality from semblance) and classifying things according to their real properties. The term may be used in discoursing on any subject in the manner indicated above.

विवेचना refers to an act or an instance of विवेचन involving a setting forth of the meaning or the purpose of a formulation or concept, usually in order to make such a formulation or concept comprehensible to others.

आलोचना refers to any discourse, statement or remark involving a measured judgment or evaluation of a person's conduct or his work, usually with a view to pointing out its weak points, demerits and failings.

The term is used along with मीमांसा and समीक्षा (आलोचना more so than the other two) to refer to the practices and the works of professional literary critics.

टीका-टिप्पणी applies to the critical observation or opinionated remarks, usually of someone who habitually criticizes or delights in it. These remarks express an opinion (usually not well-founded in reason and knowledge) concerning either what one has seen or heard or some subject at hand.

टीका is applied to any interpretative note or observation (or a series of notes or observations) which serves to illustrate and explain the meaning of the text of a writing. It may also be applied to an observation or evaluative judgement made by someone (as, for instance, a newspaper reporter) in regard to the context of a situation. The term is used in the former sense to refer to the traditional scholarly practice of writing commentaries on the Hindu scriptures and to other authoritative scholarly and scientific works or texts.

टिप्पणी is any casual public expression of one's opinion or judgment (usually unfavorable or sarcastic) concerning a person's conduct, made with the intention of humiliating or bringing vengeance upon him.

अर्थ applies to the restatement or to the particular interpretation of a passage, an expression, a word, or the like giving its meaning in another form (i.e., by using equivalent words or expressions in the same language or by providing its translation equivalent in another language) usually in clear, simple and understandable terms, or in a manner as suits the purpose or is called for in a given context.

मूल्यांकन applies to any act or result of evaluating something (such as by literally or figuratively putting a price tag on something, or by expressing one's judgment concerning the relative worth, quality, significance, amount, degree or condition of something) in some specific given terms or on the basis of any given criteria or principles.

विश्लेषण refers to any presentation in which one engages in the act of or reports the results of one's analysis of any structured whole, any complex situation or problem, any substance, an observed phenomenon, or anything which could be viewed as an abstract whole consisting of constituents or component parts, in order to understand its nature, determine its essential features, or to arrive at an answer or a solution of some sort. The term is usually accompanied by an expression referring to the purpose or to some specific method or mode of analysing (such as the use of some special laboratory techniques or other methods of analysis used in a particular field or area) unless it is implied or assumed in the context.

2. All the expressions are +process. मीमांसा, समीक्षा and आलोचना form ANP with की, विवेचना with पर and की, विवेचन, मूल्यांकन and विश्लेषण with का, and टीका-टिप्पणी, टीका and टिप्पणी with पर. Only टीका-टिप्पणी and टिप्पणी are pluralized.

3. **की मीमांसा कर—"to recapitulate, to review"**

उन्होंने सारगर्भित वक्तृता देते हुए इस प्रस्ताव की मीमांसा की। (सेवा, 181)

4. **की समीक्षा कर—"to review something critically"**

उपरोक्त परिभाषाओं की समीक्षा करने से यह स्पष्ट हो जाता है कि सामुदायिक विकास ग्रामीण जनता के रूढ़िवादी विचारों में परिवर्तन लाकर प्रगतिशील मार्ग पर उन्हें लाने का प्रयत्न करता है। (सामुदा, 4)

5. **का विवेचन कर—"to discuss"**

उत्पादन की क्रिया में मुद्रा किस प्रकार सहायता करती है इसका हम सविस्तार विवेचन पहले कर चुके हैं। (एमाई, 51)

का विवेचन कर—"to expound something critically"

...इस सिद्धान्त की असंगति का तर्कपूर्ण विवेचन किया है। (मूल्य, 160)

का विवेचन कर—"to examine critically"

...चतुर्वेदी ने प्रयोगवाद में आस्थामूलक वृत्तियों का विवेचन करते हुए लिखा है... (निबन्ध, 674)

का विवेचन कर—"to examine"

अभी तक हमने मुद्रा के महत्व का विवेचन किया है वह एक पूंजीवादी अर्थ-व्यवस्था के बारे में ही विशेष रूप से था। (एमाई, 46)

का विवेचन कर—"to discuss"

सामान्य सिद्धान्तों के बाद अब सामाजिक विघटन के विभिन्न पहलुओं का विवेचन किया जा सकता है। (भारत, 67)

का विवेचन कर—"**to comment upon**"

और इतना ही नहीं, बेबी और छोटी मुन्नी की माताएं भी सुना है एक दूसरे के गले में बाहें डालकर हंस-हंसकर प्रेम से अपने पतिदेवों की बुराइयों का विवेचन करती हैं। (तुला, 107)

6. **विवेचना कर**—"**to give (render) an interpretation**"

अभी कुछ दिन पहले, मैंने वासुदेवशरण जी का एक निबन्ध पढ़ा था, कल्पवृक्ष, उसमें उन्होंने शिव संकल्प की सुन्दर विवेचना की है।

की विवेचना कर—"**to explain, to explicate**"

अमेघ मुस्कराकर बाल-बुद्धि के योग्य उत्तर देने की चेष्टा करता और फिर यह भूल कर कि श्रोता केवल अबोध बालिका है, वृद्ध कलाकार कला के षडंग तत्वों की विवेचना करने लगता। (फूलो, 33)

पर विवेचना कर—"**to present an exposition**"

ईसा की 11वीं सदी में प्रसिद्ध मुसलमान इतिहास लेखक, अलबेरूनी ने इतिहास कला पर बड़ी सुन्दर वैज्ञानिक विवेचना की है। (सुन्दर, 1)

विवेचना कर—"**to discuss**"

बात रुक गई। दोनों ही विचार, विवेचना करते-करते एक जगह प्रायः छके से अनुभव करने लगे। (बूंद, 552)

7. **की आलोचना कर**—"**to disapprove, to censure**"

सुधी समालोचक यदि मेरी इस हरकत पर अचम्भित हों तथा इसकी आलोचना करें तो मैं बुरा न मानूंगा। (कोणार्क, 7)

की तीव्रतम आलोचना कर—"**to denounce, to criticize vehemently**"

...कार्नफोर्थ के नेतृत्व में नये ब्रिटिश मार्क्सवादी विचारकों ने काडवेल की तीव्रतम आलोचना की है। (मूल्य 159)

की आलोचना कर—"**to examine critically**"

व्यष्टिवाद की अनेक विद्वानों ने आलोचना की है और उसके वास्तविक गुणों की ओर भी संकेत किया है। (भारत, 22)

की आलोचना कर—"**to criticize**"

आपका उनसे जरा भी मतभेद हुआ और वह आपके जानी दुश्मन हो गये, आपसे

बोलना तो दूर रहा आपकी सूरत तक न देखेंगे, बल्कि अवसर पायेंगे तो अधिकारियों से आपकी शिकायत करेंगे, अपने मित्रों की मंडली में आपके आचार-विचार, रीति-व्यवहार की आलोचना करेंगे, आप ब्राह्मण हैं तो आपको भिक्षुक कहेंगे, क्षत्रिय हैं तो आपको उजड्ड गंवार कहेंगे। (सेवा, 249)

की आलोचना कर—"to pass judgement upon"

वह चाहता है, स्त्रियां सुन्दर हों, अपने को सजा कर निकलें और हम लोग देखकर उनकी आलोचना करें। (तितली, 153)

की आलोचना कर—"to criticize"

सलिल—(व्यंग के साथ) मेरा एक अपराध और है—सरकार की आलोचना करता हूं और सरकारी कर्मचारियों के निकम्मेपन की भी। (खिलौने, 94)

की घोर आलोचना कर—"to criticize"

मिशनरियों ने जनता का ध्यान हिन्दू समाज के अनेक दोषों की ओर खींचा। उन्होंने विशेषत: बाल-विवाह, कन्या-वध, बहु-विवाह...विधवा पुनर्विवाह के निषेध की घोर आलोचना की। (भारत, 61)

की आलोचना कर—"to condemn"

कप्तान ईस्टविक, जिसे ठीक उन्हीं दिनों कई साल सिंध में रहने और सिंध के देशी शासकों और वहां की प्रजा दोनों से मिलने-जुलने का अवसर मिला...इस लज्जाजनक झूठ की आलोचना करते हुए दूसरे यूरोपीयन विद्वान ग्रैस का नीचे लिखा वाक्य नकल करता है। (सुन्दर, 6)

3. **पर टीका-टिप्पणी कर—"to pass judgement upon, to comment on"**

मगर यह बलिप्रथा गलत थी या सही, इस पर अपनी आज की विकसित बुद्धि से टीका-टिप्पणी करना, या अपने आदिम पुरखों की निंदा-प्रशंसा के चक्कर में पड़ना गलत है। (बूंद, 33)

के सम्बन्ध में टीका-टिप्पणी कर—" comment on"

लाला जानकीसरन के यहां नये-पुराने जमाने, कांग्रेसी हुकूमत, माया-मोह, ज्ञान, वैराग्य से लेकर टीके की दावत तक के सम्बन्ध में टीका-टिप्पणी और विचार-विनिमय करते हुए राजाबहादुर ने तरह-तरह की खातिरदारियों से भरे दो घंटे गुजार दिए। (बूंद, 14)

पर टीका-टिप्पणी कर—"to carp about"

लेकिन मेरे सिद्ध-प्रसिद्ध 'कविराज'—पोयेट-लॉरियट—होने के कारण हर एक को

मेरे ही सामने मेरी इन बुरी आदतों पर टीका-टिप्पणियां करने का साहस जरा कम होता है। (तुला, 50)

9. **पर टीका कर—"to comment upon"**

चीन की वर्तमान आंतरिक स्थिति पर टीका करते हुए न्यूयार्क टाइम्स ने अपने अग्रलेख में कहा है। (आज, 3)

10. **पर टिप्पणी कर—"to comment upon"**

अब सारी बदनामी उन्हीं पर आवेगी, विरोधी दल उनकी हंसी उड़ावेगा, उनकी उद्दण्डता पर टिप्पणियां करेगा और यह सारी निन्दा उन्हें अकेले सहनी पड़ेगी, कोई उनका मित्र नहीं, कोई उन्हें तसल्ली देने वाला नहीं। (सेवा, 271)

11. **का अर्थ कर—"to express the meaning"**

इस मंत्र का कुछ लोग ऐसा भी अर्थ करते हैं। (वैदिक, 39)

का अर्थ कर—"to paraphrase"

मेधा का अर्थ यास्क मुनि ने इस प्रकार किया है... (वैदिक, 16)

का अर्थ कर—"to think"

माता के टीके लगवा लेने के कारण ब्राह्मणों में यह बीमारी नहीं आई, यह सच था। परन्तु दीगर लोग इसका अर्थ यह करते कि शीतला माता स्वयं ब्राह्मण होने के कारण वह अपने जाति वालों पर कुपित नहीं हुई। (लाख, 158)

का अर्थ कर—"to interpret"

प्रश्न अर्जुन कर रहा है। महाभारत के टीकाकार ने अर्जुन का अर्थ किया है सरल चित्त। (भक्तियोग, 6)

12. **का मूल्यांकन कर—"to set a value"**

जैसे, एक व्यापारी वर्ष के अन्त में अपना चिट्ठा तैयार करते समय विभिन्न व्यावसायिक सम्पत्तियों का मूल्यांकन तो करता है लेकिन उन्हें बेचने का इरादा नहीं रखता। ऐसी दशा में वह कहेंगे कि मुद्रा मूल्यांकन का कार्य तो करती है लेकिन विनिमय माध्यम का नहीं। (एमाई, 78)

का मूल्यांकन कर—"to judge"

किसी भी व्यक्ति के व्यक्तित्व और विकास का मूल्यांकन हम सरलता से कर सकते हैं। व्यक्ति के चरित्र से ही उसके जीवन और विकास का मूल्यांकन हो सकता है।

का मूल्यांकन कर—"to assess the worth of"

विश्व की प्रत्येक वस्तु का अपना विशिष्ट इतिहास होता है। सृष्टि की हर वस्तु अपने स्थान पर विशिष्टता रखती है। उसकी महत्ता का मूल्यांकन लोग अपने-अपने दृष्टिकोण से करते हैं। वास्तव में वस्तु का बड़ापन उसके गुण और उसकी पवित्रता से प्रकट होता है। (शबरी, 12)

का मूल्यांकन कर—"to estimate"

देश के विकास में नारियों के योगदान का मूल्यांकन करने का गंभीर प्रयास नहीं किया गया है फिर भी इससे शायद ही कोई इंकार कर सके कि भारतीय नारी ने इस दिशा में बहुत लम्बे कदम रखे हैं। (श्रम, 31)

का मूल्यांकन कर—"to estimate"

समीक्षक को किसी भी कृति की सामाजिक उपादेयता का मूल्यांकन करते समय इन जटिल सूक्ष्मताओं का पूरा ध्यान रखना चाहिए। (मूल्य, 154)

13. **का विश्लेषण कर—"to expound"**

कम्युनिस्ट चीन में हाल ही की महान् सांस्कृतिक क्रान्ति के सिद्धान्त का विश्लेषण करते हुए चायना रिपोर्ट ने माओत्सेतुंग की मन:स्थिति और उनके जीवन-दर्शन का विश्लेषण किया है। (दिनमान, 1-6)

का विश्लेषण कर—"to explicate"

...मनोविज्ञान आदि अन्य कितनी ही वैज्ञानिक पद्धतियों का आश्रय ग्रहण करके इन जटिलताओं का विश्लेषण करने का प्रयास किया है। (मूल्य, 154)

का विश्लेषण कर—"to analyze"

इस दृष्टि से यहां पर देश के अलग-अलग भागों की ईंटों की मिट्टियों का विश्लेषण किया गया। (ईंट, 71)

का विश्लेषण कर—"to subject something to analysis"

सिंचाई और शक्तिविभाग की प्रयोगशाला में ऐसी मिट्टियों का यांत्रिक विश्लेषण किया गया जो स्पर्श करने और देखने में ईंटों के बनाने के योग्य मिट्टी लगती थी और इनकी तुलना नासिक के प्रसिद्ध भट्टों की ईंटों मिट्टियों से की गई। (ईंट, 84)

का विश्लेषण कर—"to explain"

अंत में माणिक मुल्ला ने एक कहानी सुनायी जिसमें उनके कथनानुसार उन्होंने इसका विश्लेषण किया था कि प्रेम नामक भावना कोई रहस्यमय आध्यात्मिक या सर्वथा वैयक्तिक

भावना न होकर वास्तव में एक सर्वथा मानवीय भावना है, अतः समाज से अनुशासित होती है और उसकी नींव आर्थिक-संगठन और वर्ग-सम्बन्ध पर स्थापित है। (सूरज, 25)

101. स्वाध्याय, पारायण, पाठ

1. स्वाध्याय refers to the practice of regularly reciting or perusing a sacred text.

पारायण applies to the act of reading or reciting a sacred text in the manner of going over it from one end to the other.

पाठ refers to the act of reciting (i.e., repeating from memory or reading aloud, esp. before an audience) any short or long sacred verse or any other verse in the manner of sacred verse.

2. स्वाध्याय and पारायण are +process and पाठ is ±process. They all form ANP with का and do not take plural.

3. **स्वाध्याय कर—"to be continually reading sacred texts"**

किंतु ऐसी निर्मल बुद्धि उसी व्यक्ति की हो सकती है, जो आत्मशुद्धि के मार्ग में अनवरत स्वाध्याय करता हो एतदर्थ अपनी साधना के प्रति ईमानदारी रखता हो।

4. **का पारायण कर—"to go over, to recite"**

दोनों जने बातचीत करते-करते बाग के अन्दर दाखिल हुए तो पंडित जी ब्रह्मवैवर्त पुराण का पारायण कर रहे थे। (दुख, 168)

5. **का पाठ करते जा—"to repeat"**

प्रोफ़ेसर अपनी आत्मा की सद्गति के लिए, मृत्यु के समय मन को शांत और पवित्र रखने के लिये 'ओ३म्' शब्द और गायत्री मंत्र का पाठ करते जा रहे थे। (फूलो, 95)

पाठ कर—"to recite"

वे हिन्दी-कवियों के परम्परागत स्वर में नहीं, बल्कि हाल की एक फिल्म के लोकप्रिय तर्ज पर पाठ कर रहे थे। (राह, 14)

का पाठ कर—"to recite, to read aloud"

मंदिर के पास एक बड़ी-बड़ी खिचड़ी मूंछों और कसरती देह वाले ब्राह्मण पालथी मारे रामचरित मानस का पाठ कर रहे थे। (बूंद, 517)

पाठ कर ले—"to recite"

...मैंने गर्भाधान का मंत्र पाठ कर लिया था। (फूलो, 95)

102. विवरण, वर्णन, चित्रण, चित्रित, बयान

1. विवरण, वर्णन, चित्रण, चित्रित and बयान are used to characterize the manner in which another person (i.e., the subject) represents in his own words or represents himself verbally on a given subject, topic, matter or the like for the knowledge or understanding of others.

विवरण applies to any descriptive statement or account (long or short) which is grounded in facts and serves to represent or stands for the object as its verbal representation.

वर्णन is used of any objective verbal description or an act of describing in order to make a reference to the subject's intention to communicate a particular effect, or to his use of some specific mode, style or technique of verbal representation. When no such referencse is expressed or implied in the context, the term means describing something in a manner (such as in a language or in terms) that suits the purpose.

चित्रण is applied to any verbal representation, often colored by one's imagination, of a phenomenon (i.e., an event or fact observed or experienced by the subject) in a manner as if one were presenting its image or lifelike imitation. The term may, therefore, be extended to any picturesque verbal description in which the subject (i.e., the author) employs an appropriate style of exposition in order to create a particular artistic effect on the mind of his reader or addressee.

चित्रित is applied to the result of the act represented by चित्रण or a specific instance of it. The term is, therefore, always accompanied by an expression referring to the effect a verbal representation has on its reader or to some attribute or viewpoint (supposedly or actually) present in it.

बयान applies to any account given, statement made or description set forth by someone of an event, an incident, one's own experience (such as through one's involvement in an event or with another person) or just any noteworthy occurrence or happening. The term usually implies a rendering in more or less straightforward terms, with emphasis on the substance of what is said or stated by another rather than how it is said.

2. The nouns विवरण and चित्रण are +process, वर्णन and बयान are ±process. The adjective चित्रित is −process. All +process expressions form ANP with का. None of the nouns in this group is pluralized.

3. का विवरण कर—"to state"

और अनेक कार्यों के लिए भी ऋण और अनुदान दिये जाते हैं जैसे शिक्षा का विकास, पिछड़े वर्गों की स्थिति सुधारने और मजदूरों को राहत पहुंचाने के लिए उनका अन्य अन्यत्र विवरण किया जाएगा। (लोक, 29-30)

का विवरण कर—"to describe"

मैकियावेली ने जब यह बातें कही थीं तो मनुष्य जाति के कल्याण का दावा नहीं पेश कर रहा था, वह केवल शासक कैसे सत्ता हस्तगत करता है, कैसे अपनी व्यक्तिगत महत्वाकांक्षा पूरी करता है, और सत्ता की तृष्णा के क्षण में कैसे उसके लिए अंतरात्मा निरर्थक सिद्ध हो जाती है इसका विवरण मात्र कर रहा था, बिना एक पैगम्बर का लबादा ओढ़े हुए। (मूल्य, 25)

4. का वर्णन कर—"to describe, to discuss"

इस पुस्तक में आगे स्थान-स्थान पर समाज कल्याण के इन विभिन्न पहलुओं का विस्तारपूर्वक वर्णन किया जायेगा। (भारत, 17)

का वर्णन कर—"to describe"

यहां हम केवल सुविधाओं का वर्णन कर रहे हैं जिनका लाभ सामान्य बुद्धि के स्वस्थ व्यक्ति और सब प्रकार के प्रगतिशील समूह उठा सकते हैं। (लोक, 30)

का वर्णन कर—"to depict"

बुराई का केवल बुराई को दर्शाने के लिये वर्णन करना, गन्दगी का केवल गन्दगी को उछालने के लिये प्रस्तुत करना, मेरी राय में किसी अमरकला का विषय नहीं हो सकता। (दुग्गल, 9)

का वर्णन कर—"to describe"

पिछले अध्यायों में हम कार्बनिक खादों के बारे में वर्णन कर चुके हैं। इन खादों में पौधों के लगभग सभी पोषक तत्व रहते हैं पर सूक्ष्म मात्रा में। (खाद, 79)

का भावभरा गर्वभरा वर्णन कर—"to eloquently describe"

चार वर्ष पहले आंतों में कोलाइटिस रोग हो जाने से कल्याणी बहुत बीमार थीं। कर्नल के साथ डा० शीला सिंग इलाज करने के लिए उसके घर आई थीं। महीपाल से बातें

करने पर उन्हें उसके प्रति बौद्धिक आकर्षण हुआ। कर्नल ने भी अपने मित्र की प्रसिद्धि और महानता का भाव भरा, गर्वभरा वर्णन किया। (बूंद, 209)

का बेपर्दा रूप वर्णन कर—"to depict"

वाल्मीकि जैसे ऋषि भी रावण के मुख से सीता का जैसा बेपर्दा रूप वर्णन करते हैं, या सीता के विरह में रामचन्द्र अपने छोटे भाई के सामने जैसी खुली-खुली बातें करते हैं। (बूंद, 422)

का वर्णन कर—"to recount"

पहले कुछ सभ्य समाज की विलासिता का उल्लेख करूंगा, तब पुलिस के हथकड़ों की कलई खोलूंगा, इसके पश्चात् वैवाहिक अत्याचारों का वर्णन करूंगा। (सेवा, 222)

का वर्णन कर—"to portray"

अयोध्याकाण्ड के आरम्भ में, रामचन्द्र के युवराजतिलकोत्सव की तैयारी के सिलसिले में भी, महाकवि ने अयोध्या की महत्ता का वर्णन गौरवशाली किया है। (अपनी खबर, 42)

का वर्णन कर—"to state"

दूसरे शब्दों में, इन परिभाषाओं में यह बताने के स्थान पर कि मुद्रा क्या है मुद्रा की विशेषताओं का वर्णन किया जाता है। (एमाई, 59)

का वर्णन किए जा—"to recount, to describe"

ममानी साहिबा नज्जो के गुणों का वर्णन किए जा रही हैं। (थान, 177)

का वर्णन कर—"to put into words, to express"

बहुत दिनों के बिछुड़े हुए पिता-पुत्र अकस्मात् एक दूसरे से मिलकर इतने प्रसन्न हुए कि उसका वर्णन नहीं किया जा सकता। (आदर्श, 39)

का वर्णन कर—"to relate"

वह जिस प्रसंग का वर्णन कर रही है उसके नायकों में उसका भी श्रेय है। यह सज्जन के निकम्मे मन में सन्तोष भरने लगा। कन्या दूरी के नाते का एक और पर्दा उठाकर निकट आ गई। (बूंद, 399)

वर्णन कर—"to relate"

जगदीश मुझसे इतना हिल गया था कि अपने जीवन की छोटी-से-छोटी घटना तक मेरे सम्मुख सरल शब्दों में वर्णन करते उसे संकोच न होता। (होली, 108)

5. का चित्रण कर—"to represent in words, to portray"

नारी के इस दुखद इतिहास का वे जिस प्रभावशाली ढंग से चित्रण कर पाई हैं उतना शायद इतिहासकार नहीं कर पाता।...लेकिन ये कहानियां विवशता का चित्रण ही नहीं करतीं, विवशता से लोहा लेने की प्रेरणा भी देती हैं।

का चित्रण कर—"to represent"

अंत में मैंने फिर पूछा कि सूरज के सात घोड़ों से उनका क्या तात्पर्य था और सपने सूरज के सातवें घोड़े से कैसे सम्बद्ध हैं तो वे बड़ी गम्भीरता से बोले कि "देखो ये कहानियां वास्तव में प्रेम नहीं वरन् उस जिन्दगी का चित्रण करती हैं जिसे आज का निम्नमध्य वर्ग जी रहा है।" (सूरज, 113)

का चित्रण कर—"to depict"

जमींदार-किसान-संघर्ष का चित्रण करते हुए उन्होंने अदालत की कार्रवाइयों, वकीलों, डाक्टरों, पुलिस अफसरों आदि का भी खाका खींच दिया है। (नदु, 43)

का चित्रण कर—"to portray"

उनके नाटकों के अध्ययन से पता चलता है कि नारी के किसी भी रूप का चित्रण करते समय अश्क पूर्ण तन्मयता का परिचय देते हैं। (भंवर, 10)

का चित्रण कर—"to portray"

यह अवश्य है कि एक ओर जहां आधुनिक नारी का चित्रण करते समय उन्होंने उसकी सामाजिक प्रगति के प्रति हमदर्दी दिखायी है वहीं दूसरी ओर उसके अभिजातवर्गीय बुर्जुआ संस्कारों वाली उच्छृंखलता की खिल्ली भी उड़ाई है...(भंवर, 11)

6. चित्रित कर—"to depict"

जिन अमीरों (शासकों) ने कभी जीवनभर किसी मादक द्रव्य को अपने पास नहीं आने दिया, जो तम्बाकू के धुएं तक से बचते थे और जो स्त्री जाति के सतीत्व की रक्षा का गैर मामूली ध्यान रखते थे उनको नेपियर ने शराबी और कुचरित्र चित्रित किया है। (सुन्दर, 7)

चित्रित कर दे—"to portray"

पुराने जमाने में विद्वान अपनी-अपनी कौमों के विस्तृत और पूरे-पूरे इतिहास लिखने के बजाय कल्पित या अर्धऐतिहासिक कथाओं के जरिये अपने समय के उच्च से उच्च नैतिक, सामाजिक और धार्मिक आदर्शों को चित्रित कर देना ज्यादा अच्छा समझते थे।(सुन्दर, 2)

चित्रित कर—"to represent"

इन सब बातों में कन्या-सज्जन का किस्सा हवाई जहाज की पर्चेबाजी की चर्चा भी एकबारगी जोर पकड़ गई। धनवानों के खिलाफ जनता की सहज घृणा ने सज्जन को जिस तरह चित्रित किया उससे वहाँ उसके विरुद्ध बड़ी दूषित हवा फैल गई। (बूंद, 301)

चित्रित कर—"to represent"

ऋतुराज वसन्त को कवि ने प्रेमियों के सच्चे संदेशवाहक के रूप में चित्रित किया है। (ज्योति 26)

चित्रित कर—"to picture"

...मनुष्य के आत्मान्वेषण की वृत्ति को सीमित, सतही, कुण्ठित या लक्ष्य-भ्रष्ट चित्रित किया गया है। (मूल्य, 171)

चित्रित कर—"to picture"

उसके आत्मान्वेषण को पूर्णप्रसार और उसकी आत्मोपलब्धि को पूरी गहराई तक उतरकर चित्रित नहीं करते...(मूल्य, 173)

चित्रित कर—"to depict"

उपन्यास में चित्रित मानव निरपेक्ष स्थिति में चित्रित नहीं किया जाता...(मूल्य, 164)

7. **का बयान कर—"to relate"**

चलने से पहले उसने अम्मा से कुछ रुपये मांगे थे, तो वह अपना रोना रोने लगी थी और तंगहाली का बयान करने लगी थी। (मांस, 28)

का बयान—"to describe"

इन सब बातों का हम आगे चलकर और अधिक विस्तार के साथ बयान करेंगे। (सुन्दर, 18)

का बयान कर—"to describe, to talk about someone (openly)"

लेकिन क्या बताएं, उनमें से कुछ महाशय तो इस कदर हमदर्द होते हैं कि उनकी भलमनसाहत का खुले शब्दों में बयान नहीं किया जा सकता। (कहा, 19)

का बयान कर—"to describe"

हम दोनों के बीच जो कुछ भी कमजोरियां तुमने देखी हैं उनको ज्यों का त्यों बयान करना। (बूंद, 560)

बयान कर—"to describe someone as..."

और जिसके व्यक्तिगत चरित्र में कोई ऐसा दोष न था, जो उस समय के 99 प्रतिशत नरेशों या अंग्रेज शासकों में न पाया जाता हो उसे अंग्रेजी पुस्तकों में पहले दरजे का दुराचारी बयान किया जाता है। (सुन्दर, 7-8)

बयान कर—"to describe"

तो मेरे वकील सर तेजबहादुर सप्रू ने अदालत में यह कहा था कि पुस्तक के अन्दर एक भी घटना ऐसी बयान नहीं की गई है, जिसकी सचाई के बारे में किसी तरह का कोई प्रश्न उठ सके। (सुन्दर, ञ)

बयान कर बैठ—"to divulge"

बड़ी दर्द की मारी भोलेपन के साथ अपना विरहेश-प्रेम बयान कर बैठी। नन्दो को एक थाह मिली। (बूंद, 162)

बयान कर—"to describe"

यहां तक कि बड़े से बड़े या अच्छे से अच्छे मुगल बादशाहों को हिन्दुओं और हिन्दोस्तान ने लिए अधिक से अधिक मीठी छुरी कह कर बयान किया जाता है। (सुन्दर, 10)

बयान कर—"to recount, to relate"

...ब्रिटिश भारतीय इतिहास की जो पुस्तकें आजकल हमें मिलती हैं उनमें से अधिकांश में...ऐतिहासिक घटनाओं के सिलसिले के सिलसिले गलत बयान किए जाते हैं और अनेक व्यक्तियों के चरित्र को सफेद की जगह काला और काले की जगह सफेद रंगकर हमारे सामने पेश किया जाता है, अनेक सच्ची घटनाओं का पता तक नहीं चलता और अनेक कल्पित घटनायें सच्ची कहकर बयान की जाती हैं। (सुन्दर, 3)

बयान कर—"to describe"

मगर मैं भी उस घटना को जानता हूं और दिलचस्पी से बयान कर सकता हूं। उस भाटिया जौहरी की तबीयत की सेठानी की कहानी सुन उसने एक खूबसूरत पंजाबी नौजवान को उसे तकाया...(जुहू, 46)

बयान कर—"to describe"

जीवन का अनुभव ही मनुष्य का इतिहास है—वह मनुष्य चाहे कलाकार हो या कोई भी हो। लेकिन अनुभव तो गूंगे की बात के समान होता है। खुद अपने ही मन के अनुभव को इंसान स्पष्ट रूप से बयान नहीं कर पाता। (बूंद, 285)

बयान कर—"to relate, to tell"

जैसे किसी नाली में रुकी हुई वस्तु भीतर से पानी का बहाव पाकर बाहर निकल पड़े, उन्होंने जान्हवी से सारी कथा बयान कर दी। (सेवा, 183)

बयान कर—"to describe"

अब हम उन सब हमलों को एक-एक कर बयान कर चुके हैं जो मुसलमानों के हमले से पहले भारत पर हुए थे। (सुन्दर, 30)

नमक मिर्च लगाकर बयान कर—"to speak gloatingly of, to exaggerate"

उसने सुमन का सारा चरित्र खूब नमक मिर्च लगाकर सुभागी से बयान किया। (सेवा, 185)

बढ़ा-बढ़ाकर बयान कर—"to relate in exaggerated terms"

रास्ते में विट्ठलदास ने आज के सारे समाचार बढ़ा-बढ़ाकर बयान किये और अपनी चतुराई को खूब दर्शाया। (सेवा, 202)

103. निरावरण, अनावृत, उजागर, उद्घाटन, उद्घाटित, रोशन, पर्दाफाश, जगजाहिर, भंडाफोड़

1. These expressions are used to describe (by stipulating as if one has uncovered or laid something bare) the manner in which someone makes public or reveals the characteristic disposition or trait of a person or thing about which very little was known before.

निरावरण stresses the subject's persistence in trying to get at something which is undercover or refers to the effort made by him in uncovering something (as if by removing or stripping off its cover).

अनावृत denotes the effect of someone's act of (literally as well as figuratively) making an opening into something (such as by removing its cover or clearing away an obstruction) so that it is open to view or accessible (in the sense of becoming or being receptive or responsive) to influence from without.

उजागर describes the state of something which stands out from its setting or environment, or is highlighted or brought into prominence (such as by setting off by contrast with or against something else).

उद्घाटन applies to the act of unfolding or unveiling something for the first time or presenting it in such a form that the basis behind the mysterious, baffling or uncouth in it is revealed or becomes available for a full public viewing.

उद्घाटित describes or delineates for the addressee or the reader something which has been brought out or prominently displayed by someone or forms the characteristic feature of someone's work. The term may be used in situations when a person gives out or reveals some information about someone or something (such as a secret or the like.)

Both उद्घाटन and उद्घाटित are also applied when someone makes public something which is little known or known only to a few or divulges a piece of information about another person. When used in this sense the terms make no reference to the subject's intention.

रौशन (lit. that which is luminous i.e., bathed in or exposed to steady light) describes the acts or deeds of someone who is exposing another person or bringing him into prominence (such as when one is much talked about in public for some reason and thus earns a good or bad name).

पर्दाफाश (lit. tearing apart the cover or covering of something) is applied to the act of bringing into light the true identity of something as by clearing away the shroud of mystery enveloping or surrounding an object. The term is also applied to an act of impromptu revealing of some fact about another person.

जगजाहिर refers to any act or action of revealing the true identity of someone or making something (such as a closely guarded secret or the like) public by the use of any means of mass communication (such as a newspaper report, posters or the like), usually by providing sufficient evidence or furnishing proof in support of what is made public.

भंडाफोड़ (lit. smashing or breaking a pitcher) is applied to describe someone's act or his intention to act in a manner that is tantamount to betraying a secret or disclosing a secret, usually with a motive.

2. All the expressions, with the exception of उद्घाटन and पर्दाफाश are —process. Both उद्घाटन and पर्दाफाश are + process, and form ANP with का. They are not pluralized.

3. **निरावरण कर—"to lay bare"**

मानो आडंबर टिक न सकेगा, चीर-फाड़कर यह आदमी वास्तव को एकदम निरावरण कर रहेगा। मैंने कहा "फिर भी आप ऋषि शब्द को महत्व देते हैं।" (जय, 115)

4. **अनावृत कर—"to open, to uncover"**

यही उत्तम विचारों के आने के लिए द्वार को अनावृत करना है। (सुधा, 30)

5. **उजागर कर—"to bring out, to highlight"**

बाहरी दुनियां में संघर्ष की कठोरता में अधिक लिप्त रहने से जीव की यह कोमलता, यह सुन्दरता छिप जाती है। ऐसा क्यों होता है? इसे उजागर करने के लिए दुनिया भर में तीज-त्योहार, मेले, उत्सव, संस्कार-समारोह हुआ करते हैं फिर भी यह कठोरता, क्रूरता का दृश्य ही प्रमुख रूप से क्यों हमारे मनों में छाया रहता है? (बूंद, 546)

उजागर कर—"to bring out, to emphasize"

बुराई का स्थान कला में अवश्य है, यदि वह बुराई अपने पास पड़ी हुई अच्छाई को उजागर कर दे, अच्छाई और अच्छी लगने लग जाय, प्यारी लगने लग जाय। (दुग्गल, 9)

उजागर कर—"to illuminate"

कुप्पी का प्रकाश उसके आधे चेहरे को उजागर किए था। और आधा चेहरा गहन कालिमा में डूबा अदृश्य था। (कमल, 43)

6. **का उद्घाटन कर—"to unveil, to present"**

प्रस्तुत पुस्तक में डा. सम्पूर्णानन्द ने ब्रह्माण्ड की रहस्यलीला का सरल रूप में उद्घाटन किया है। (नक्षत्र, 5)

का उद्घाटन कर—"to uncover"

परन्तु सज्जन के मन में एक आग जाग चुकी थी। वह इस रहस्य का उद्घाटन करने पर तुला हुआ था। उसने अपनी इच्छा दूसरों से गुप्त रखी। (बूंद, 508)

का उद्घाटन कर—"to expose"

प्रेमचन्द ने अंग्रेजी साम्राज्यवाद की नकली आदर्शोन्मुखता का ही उद्घाटन नहीं किया...(नदु, 87)

का उद्घाटन कर—"to bring into public view"

यह बात उसे इस समय भी बिल्कुल सही जंचती है मगर इसके साथ ही साथ

महीपाल यह भी जानता है कि सज्जन केवल गंदगी का उद्‌घाटन करने की दृष्टि से ही काम नहीं कर रहा। (बूंद, 537)

का उद्‌घाटन कर—"to reveal"

वे उसके मन में प्रवेश कर ऐसी गहरी बातों का उद्‌घाटन कर जाते हैं जिससे वह चौंक उठता है। (बूंद, 388)

का उद्‌घाटन कर—"to perform the inauguration ceremony, to inaugurate"

सबसे पहले मुख्य मन्त्री ने कार्यक्रम का उद्‌घाटन किया। फिर कलाकार रंगमंच पर आये, उनका परिचय दिया गया। (दुग्गल, 137)

7. उद्‌घाटित कर—"to uncover"

पर रेखा के व्यक्तित्व की चुनौती को उसने इस प्रकार नहीं टाला, टालने की बात ही उसके मन में नहीं आयी; रहस्यमयता की चुनौती स्वीकार करना तो और भी अधिक टांग अड़ाना है, क्योंकि किसी का रहस्य उद्‌घाटित करना चाहने वाला कोई कौन होता है? यह भी उसने नहीं सोचा। (नदी, 17)

उद्‌घाटित कर—"to reveal"

उनकी कल्पना थी कि संसार में जो कुछ है सब सुन्दर है, अतएव वनराजि, वृक्ष-पंक्ति, लता-कुंज तथा पत्र-पुष्प और पराग में अनुपम सौन्दर्य का दर्शन कर, प्रकृति के गूढ़ रहस्यों को उद्‌घाटित करने में वे सफल हुए। (ज्योति, 17-18)

उद्‌घाटित कर—"to reveal"

इस आन्तरिक और बाह्य क्रम-भग्न मनुष्य की समस्या पर विचार करते हुए मैक्स पिकार्ड ने इसके कुछ बहुत महत्त्वपूर्ण पक्ष उद्‌घाटित किये हैं। (मूल्य, 31)

8. रोशन कर—"to illuminate, to expose, to bring clearly to view"

मगर दूसरों की गलतियों को सूरज की तरह रोशन करने में तुम सब एक आवाज से शामिल होते हो। (बूंद, 469)

का नाम रोशन कर—"to glorify (the name of), to recount the good deeds of"

आजकल सवेरे से दोपहर तक रामेश्वर रोगियों का इलाज करता है और दोपहर बाद लोगों की हजामत कर बाप-दादा का नाम रोशन करता है। (डगर, 43)

9. **का पर्दाफाश कर—"to reveal"**

मोपासां ने भी बड़ी निर्भयता से उच्चवर्गीय नैतिकता का पर्दाफाश किया। (मूल्य, 42)

का पर्दाफाश कर—"to reveal"

शायद ही संसार का कोई कवि, लेखक या उपन्यासकार ऐसा बचा हो, जिसके गुण-दोषों का हमने उस दिन पर्दाफाश न कर डाला हो। (सच, 28)

का पर्दाफाश कर—"to expose"

उनकी चालाकी का पर्दाफाश करने का जिवा लुहार हमेशा प्रयत्न करता। (लाख, 102)

10. **जगजाहिर कर—"to expose"**

इस आबरूदार वेश्या को क्यों न जगजाहिर किया जाए ? (बूंद, 511)

जगजाहिर कर—"to make public"

महीपाल बोला—इस कम्बख्त मुहल्ले वालों ने तुम्हारे खिलाफ अखबारों में शिकायत छपवाकर और तो जो कुछ बुरा किया सो किया इस सीक्रेट अड्डे का पता जगजाहिर कर दिया यह बहुत ही बुरा किया। बड़ी मुश्किलों से गए हैं कवि जी यहां से। (बूंद, 16)

11. **का भंडाफोड़ कर दे—"to betray"**

कहो तो तुम्हारे ही मुहल्ले के अच्छे-अच्छे घरों की इज्जत का भंडाफोड़ कर दूं। बाकी नहीं, हम तो यह सोचते हैं कि जैसी अपनी इज्जत वैसी सबकी। अपनी धोती तले सभी नंगे हैं, किसकी कहने जाऊं ? (बूंद, 519)

का भंडाफोड़ कर—"to disclose"

उसने अंदाज कर लिया कि यही ज्ञानशंकर वीणा का प्रेमी है। उसी को हाथ में लेकर वीणा की केस का भंडाफोड़ करके अप्रत्यक्ष रीति से डाक्टर सुमन्त पर भी छींटे उछाले जा सकते हैं। (धनु, 163)

का भंडाफोड़ कर दे—"to reveal, to betray"

मैं उनके गोप्य का भंडाफोड़ कर दूंगा। मैं सारे यूनिवर्सिटी क्षेत्रों में उसकी बदनामी करा दूंगा। (धनु, 164)

का भंडाफोड़ कर—"to unmask"

आइए आइए आजकल तो आपने खूब नाम पैदा किया है, बाबू साहब। हः-हः-हः ऐसा

अच्छा भंडाफोड़ किया है महिला मंडल का, कि तबियत खुश हो गई। बैठिए-बैठिए। (बूंद, 518)

का भंडाफोड़ कर—"to make public"

एक घृणित षड्यंत्र का भंडाफोड़ करने के लिए स्वयं षड्यंत्रकारी बना प्रेमी का ढोंग किए, एककुलीन गुप्त व्यभिचारिणी सुन्दरी के साथ घनवती के जाने के बाद अकेले में बैठा हुआ सज्जन... (बूंद, 515)

का भंडाफोड़ कर—"to betray"

हम अपनी काम-वासना को अस्वाभाविक रूप से दबाए रहते हैं, फलतः वह जहां-कहीं भी थोड़ी-सी सुराख पाती है, निकल भागकर हमारा भंडाफोड़ कर देती है। (देश, 60)

का भंडाफोड़ कर—"to make public"

वह आपको ब्लैकमेल करना चाहता है, आपका भंडाफोड़ करने के बहाने आपसे रुपया ऐंठना चाहता है, या आपको उसकी बरखास्तगी की नोटिस वापिस लेने को मजबूर करना चाहता है। (घनु, 190)

104. उत्सर्ग, बलिदान, निछावर, विसर्जन, विर्साजित, परित्याग, त्याग, बलि, कुर्बानी, कुर्बान

1. The expressions in this group are applied to describe the act of someone who foregoes something available to him for the sake of another person or for a cause, or gives up something of value to himself.

उत्सर्ग (lit. a spontaneous pouring forth or pouring out) describes the gift of oneself or of something of value, to a cause. It emphasizes the spontaneity of the gift, which is given willingly and without hesitation.

बलिदान is an objective description (i.e., of the speaker who is not directly involved in the act) to an offering or a sacrifice, both literally as well as figuratively. It implies the speaker's commendation or condemnation (as the case may be) of the subject's act in which he dedicates or devotes himself or misapplies his energies to a cause, his beliefs or ideals.

निछावर (न्यौछावर) is making a propitiatory offering or a sacrifice, or devoting one's energy and resources to a cause in the manner of making a propitiatory offering or sacrifice, selflessly and unrelentingly. The term may sometimes imply the taking of a calculated risk by the subject (at least in the opinion of the speaker) or a setting aside of one's own likes, dislikes or preferences for the sake of another person.

विसर्जन is letting something go (in the manner of giving up, giving forth or giving out) in an impassioned state of mind, or in a state of mind in which one is overcome by an emotion or feeling. The term implies the speaker's approval of the subject's act.

विसर्जित is applied to describe the consequence or result of the act of letting go (which is indicated by विसर्जन) rather than the act itself. The term by its very nature does not make reference to the subject's exercise of his will, or to the speaker's approval or disapproval of the subject's act, and is, therefore, open for a variety of implications, depending upon how the speaker construes the subject's act. It is usually accompanied by some expression to indicate this fact unless it is clear in a given context.

परित्याग is giving up or doing away with something completely, and once and for all.

त्याग refers to the act of giving up, withdrawing from or severing one's connection with something or someone voluntarily, of one's own choosing (in response to a cause) or in submission to one's own conscience or to any kind of pressure.

बलि is making a sacrifice (in the form of an oblation before a deity or an act of immolation) as a ritualistic offering.

कुर्बानी is making a sacrifice of something, offering to make a sacrifice, or acknowledging a sacrifice made by someone.

कुर्बान is offering or declaring one's intention to make a sacrifice literally or figuratively. The term is often used as an interjectional expression to give vent to one's feeling when one is struck by some extraordinary quality of another person (say his witticism, the beauty of a woman or the like).

2. All the expressions, with the exception of विसर्जित and कुर्बान (which are − process only), are ±process. They form ANP with का (की for बलि and कुर्बानी). Only कुर्बानी can be pluralized.

3. **का उत्सर्ग कर दे—"to lay down one's (life)"**

...हमें आज्ञा मिली है कि सैंकड़ों लाठियां खाने पर भी हम हिंसा के कार्य न करें—हंसते-हंसते अपने प्राणों का उत्सर्ग कर दें।

उत्सर्ग कर—"to renounce, to give over"

मैंने भले ही बुरा किया हो प्रिये, पर एक नारी के प्रेम में अपना सब कुछ उत्सर्ग करके अपनी पतनशीलता में भी ऐसा अनोखा उदाहरण रखा है कि कोई उसकी मार्मिकता के प्रभाव से बच नहीं सकता। (सुहाग, 213)

उत्सर्ग कर—"to give oneself over"

गौरा इसे स्पष्ट अन्याय समझती है, पर क्या माता पिता की इच्छा पर अपने को उत्सर्ग कर देना भी एक रास्ता नहीं हैं ? (नदी, 75)

उत्सर्ग कर—"to give up"

सहसा रेखा के प्रति एक गहरे कृतज्ञ भाव ने उसे द्रवित कर दिया, कैसे यह स्त्री सब-कुछ इस तरह उत्सर्ग कर दे सकती है, बिना कुछ प्रतिदान मांगे, बिना कोई सुरक्षा चाहे—बल्कि सुरक्षाओं की सब संभावनाओं को लात मार कर क्यों ? क्योंकि वह भुवन को प्यार करती है ? (नदी, 137)

उत्सर्ग कर—"to dedicate oneself totally to, to give oneself over to"

मैं सोच रही थी...किसी तरह कुछ भी करके, अपने को उत्सर्ग करके आपके ये घाव भर सकती...तो अपने जीवन को सफल मानती...(नदी, 299)

4. का बलिदान कर—"to sacrifice"

छत्रपति की काली आंखों में तेज का सूर्य चमक रहा था, "इसके लिए अगर हमें कुछ होनहार सैनिकों का बलिदान करना पड़े तो कोई चिंता नहीं।..." (बेटी, 105)

का बलिदान कर—"to make a sacrifice of, to deprive one of"

...यदि व्यापक मानवीय गौरव की स्थापना हो सकती है तो उसी स्थिति में कि समाज के प्रत्येक छोटे से छोटे व्यक्ति के गौरव को वही महत्व दिया जाय जो बड़े से बड़े व्यक्ति को मिलता है। जब महामानव और लघुमानव का भेद कर एक के गौरव का बलिदान कर दूसरे के गौरव की वृद्धि न की जाय। (मूल्य, 27)

का बलिदान कर—"to renounce"

हम अपने क्षुद्र स्वार्थों पर बड़े-बड़े आदर्शों का बलिदान करते समय गर्व का अनुभव करते हैं। (बेटी, 74)

बलिदान कर—"to renounce, to" sacrifice

उसने एक साधारण नर्तकी पर गृहस्थी के सुख को बलिदान कर दिया। (चित्र, 166)

बलिदान कर—"to consecrate oneself to"

जिन्होंने जीवन को परमार्थ की वेदी पर बलिदान कर दिया है,...उन्हीं का एकमात्र जीवन सफल है...(धर्म, 156)

बलिदान कर—"to sacrifice"

हा भारत! यह विपत्ति तेरे सर से कब टलेगी। संसार में ऐसे-ऐसे पाषाण-हृदय मनुष्य पड़े हुए हैं, जिन्हें इन दुखियारियों पर ज़रा भी दया नहीं आती। ऐसे अंधे, ऐसे पाषाण, ऐसे पाखण्डी समाज को जो स्त्री को अपनी वासनाओं की वेदी पर बलिदान करता है, कानून के सिवा और किस विधि से सचेत किया जाय। (सम, 26)

बलिदान कर दे—"to immolate"

उसे क्या पता कि सनातन ने अपनी मां के लिए बलिदान कर दिया। (बाल,11-51)

5. **का न्योछावर कर दे—"to immolate oneself (for the sake of)"**

इस शिक्षा ने भिक्षुओं में अगम्य-स्थानों में धर्म प्रचार करने की, अगनित क्लेशों को सहने की, अपने धर्म की प्रचार-वेदी पर प्राणों का न्योछावर कर देने की वह स्फूर्ति और प्रेरणा भर दी कि आज भी इस धर्म की दुन्दुभि संसार के कोने-कोने में बज रही है। (भारतीय दर्शनसार, 175)

न्योछावर कर दे—"to give up something for the sake of someone"

उसका मतलब यही था कि उसने अपना हृदय मेरे ऊपर न्योछावर कर दिया है, परन्तु मैं जान-बूझकर उसको मान्यता नहीं देता। (राह, 117)

निछावर कर—"to stake"

दूसरों को आराम पहुंचाने के लिए वह तन तोड़कर मेहनत कर सकती है, अपनी जान तक निछावर कर सकती है। यह विशेषता महीपाल को दूसरी स्त्रियों में प्रायः कम या नहीं के बराबर ही दिखलाई पड़ी है। (बूंद, 101)

निछावर कर दे—"to forsake, to give away"

बाबा जी ने सज्जन और कन्या को बहुजनहिताय, बहुजनसुखाय अपना-अपना सर्वस्व निछावर कर देने के लिए कहा है। (बूंद, 499)

निछावर कर—"to perish, to pine for"

एक दूसरे के लिए उन्होंने हर क्षण हर पल दीवानगी के साथ अपने को निछावर किया। (बूंद, 205)

न्योछावर कर—"to sacrifice"

पतंगें और क्षुद्र जीव अग्नि पर प्राण न्योछावर कर देते हैं। (चमत्कार, 56)

6. **का विसर्जन कर—"to purge oneself of"**

कुमार बाहुबली ने कितना घोर कार्योत्सर्ग झेला, कैसा दुर्द्धर्ष तपश्चरण किया, आरम्भ से ही उन्होंने सब सुखों का विसर्जन किया किन्तु उनको कैवल्य प्राप्त नहीं हुआ। (नीलम, 21)

का विसर्जन कर ले—"to rid oneself of"

अहंकार के समूल विनष्ट हुए बिना भले ही मनुष्य सद्‌गुणी और सत्यभाषी बना रहे, किन्तु जब तक उसका विसर्जन नहीं कर लेता वह आत्मतत्त्व से बहुत दूर रहता है। (धर्म, 150)

प्राण विसर्जन कर—"to commit suicide"

कृष्णचन्द्र ने बहती धार में जाकर प्राण विसर्जन कर दिए। (नदु, 28)

(गीतों के रूप में) विसर्जन कर ले—"to break into"

बाध्य होकर अपने आप में ही बातों को पचा लेने की आदत-सी डाल लेने के बाद भी, गीतों के रूप में विसर्जन कर लेने के उपरान्त भी, मन की वे बातें इतनी बच जाती थीं कि वह कभी-कभी रात में ऊंचे चौबारे वाली छत पर चुपचाप चढ़ चन्द्र-ताराओं को साक्षी बनाकर प्रिय के प्रति अपनी बातों को वायुमंडल में लय कर देती थी। (सुहाग, 133-134)

7. **विसर्जित कर दे—"to unburden oneself of"**

मंगल क्या है ?—देवता है ? उसी समय उसे अपने तिरस्कृत हृदय-पिंड का ध्यान आ गया। उसने मन में सोचा—पुरुष को उसकी क्या चिन्ता हो सकती है, वह तो अपना सुख विसर्जित कर देता है, जिसे अपने रक्त से सींचना पड़ता है, वही तो उसकी व्यथा जानेगा। (कंकाल, 99)

8. **का परित्याग कर—"to dismiss"**

जगत् के दुःख-कातर प्राणियों के उपकार के लिए तुम अपने समस्त संकल्प-विकल्पों का परित्याग करो। (चारु, 116)

का परित्याग कर—"to forsake"

क्या हम अपनी समृद्धि और शांति का परित्याग कर अपने पूर्व ग्रहों के हाथों दीवालिया बनने के लिए तैयार हैं। (अमरीका, 25)

का परित्याग कर दे—"to abandon"

अप्रस्तुत-योजना में प्रयोगवादी कवियों ने पुराने उपमानों का इस प्रकार परित्याग कर दिया है जैसे दूध में पड़ी हुई मक्खी को निकाल कर फेंक देते हैं। (निबन्ध, 677)

का परित्याग कर दे—"to give up, to abandon"

परिणामत: सन् 1921 की नवीन आर्थिक नीति के अन्तर्गत अनेक संकीर्ण साम्यवादी धारणाओं का परित्याग कर दिया गया। (एमाई, 48)

9. **का त्याग कर—"to renounce"**

भाई की उन्नति के लिए अपनी पत्नी के गहने तक बेच डालने में उसे कभी मोह नहीं हुआ। वही महीपाल आज आर्थिक वैभव के लिए कौन-कौन महत् सिद्धान्तों का त्याग नहीं कर रहा? वह कितना पतित हो गया है? (बूंद, 537)

का त्याग कर—"to abandon, to forsake"

व्यर्थ यों भी है कि जय उसका त्याग न करेगा। (जय, 87)

प्राणों का त्याग कर—"to give one's life"

धन्य वे वीर हैं जो धर्म और राष्ट्र के लिए अपने प्राणों का त्याग करके वीरगति को प्राप्त करते हैं। (वैदिक, 21)

का त्याग कर—"to except"

जब उनमें किसी एक विशेषता को अधिक बढ़ाया जाता है, तब कुछ हद तक अन्य दो विशेषताओं का त्याग करना ही पड़ता है। (भेड़, 38)

कामना का त्याग कर—"to practise self-abnegation"

चलो, मैं तुम्हें घर पहुंचा दूंगी। वहां तुम सबसे पहले अपने स्त्री-बच्चों के लिए अपनी कामना का त्याग करो। उन्हें सुखी बनाओ, ईश्वर की तरह उनके हृदय में समा जाओ। इस तरह सबको अपना लो। (कथा, 79)

का त्याग कर—"to do away with, to give up"

गत 150 वर्षों में हमारी सभ्यता में स्वार्थ का ही बोलबाला रहा है। इसी बात का प्रयत्न रहा है कि हमारा भौतिक वैभव किस तरह बढ़ता चले। लेकिन हमने नैतिक तथा आध्यात्मिक मूल्यों की ओर दुर्लक्ष किया और अपने जीवन से उनका त्याग कर दिया। (अणु, 27)

का त्याग कर—"to shun"

कर्म करो, करते ही रहो जब तक जीवित रहो, किन्तु फलासक्ति और अभिमान का त्याग करते हुए। (धर्म, 140)

का त्याग कर—"to abandon"

सन् 1949 में जब हम इस संधि में सम्मिलित हुए थे तब इतिहास में पहली बार अमरीका ने अपने एकाकीपन का त्याग किया था। (अमरीका, 71)

का त्याग कर—"to forsake"

बहस में भी महीपाल यह अस्वीकार न कर सका कि शीला के प्रति उसे प्रेम है। परन्तु उस प्रेम का वह त्याग कर रहा है—एक बड़े सिद्धान्त के लिए। कुटुम्ब व्यक्तिगत प्रेम से बड़ी वस्तु है। (बंद, 496)

का त्याग कर—"to abandon"

ऐसे भी समाचार हैं कि रूस में परदे के पीछे शासक वर्ग पर यह दबाव डाला जा रहा है कि वे युद्ध से पीछे हटें, बलात् साम्यवाद फैलाने के विचार का त्याग करें...(अणु, 22)

का त्याग कर—"to depart from, to leave"

कुशीनगर में जब भगवान् का वैशाखी पूर्णिमा को परिनिर्वाण हुआ तो जम्बूद्वीप के सभी भिक्षुओं ने समझा कि भगवान् ने पृथ्वी का त्याग किया। परन्तु उनकी लीला अपरम्पार है। तुषित-लोक से वे फिर इस लोक में लौट आये और यहां उन्होंने चीनाचार की साधना का प्रवर्तन किया। (चारु, 67)

का त्याग कर—"to quit, to leave"

तब उसे क्या करना चाहिए? आज की रात महीपाल के लिए निश्चय की रात थी। क्या वह सदा के लिए घर का त्याग कर रहा है? अब वह कभी घर लौट कर न जायगा। महीपाल के भाव भरे पीड़ित मन ने उत्तर में कहा—हां। (बूंद, 216-17)

त्याग कर—"to give up"

पुरुषों की इस प्रवृत्ति से पढ़ी लिखी लड़कियों की बिडम्बना दुगुनी हो उठती है कि वे उन्हें प्राप्त तो करना चाहते हैं लेकिन कुछ त्याग करना नहीं चाहते। (भंवर, 28)

त्याग कर—"to make (any) sacrifice"

आर्य बीजगुप्त के लिए वह सबसे बड़ा त्याग कर सकती है। (चित्र, 119)

त्याग कर—"to make a great sacrifice, to forego"

तुम जिन घरेलू जिम्मेदारियों की वजह से इतना बड़ा त्याग कर रहे हो मैं उनकी कद्र करती हूं। तुम अच्छी तरह जानते हो कि मैं कल्याणी की भी कद्र करती हूं। (बूंद, 492)

त्याग कर—"to relinquish"

शैला घबरा गई। वह अभी तो इन्द्रदेव के सर्वस्व त्याग करने का दृश्य देखकर आई है। (तितली, 208)

शस्त्र त्याग कर—"to lay down arms"

जब तक सारी आर्यभूमि विदेशियों के अपवित्र पद-संचार से मुक्त नहीं हो जाती, तब तक वे शस्त्र त्याग नहीं करेंगे। (चारु, 428)

त्याग कर—"to give away"

बौद्धिक रूप से कन्या इस त्याग का विरोध नहीं कर सकती फिर भी त्याग करते हुए उसका मन उदास है, रह रह कर कचोट रहा है। (बूंद, 462)

त्याग कर—"to give up"

महीपाल और कर्नल के साथ के कारण सज्जन को भी सुबह के वक्त विशुद्ध अहिंसात्मक नाश्ता करने की आदत पड़ गई है किन्तु अंडा-टोस्ट या आमलेट का मोह त्याग करने पर भी सुबह दूध बादाम का अधसेरा चढ़ाने वाले कसरत प्रिय महीपाल से प्रभावित होकर भी सज्जन चाय पीना नहीं छोड़ सका। (बूंद, 28)

त्याग कर—"to discharge"

घाट के किनारे मल-मूत्र त्याग करना अथवा कूड़ा-कचरा फेंकना गंदी आदतें हैं। (स्वस्थ, 23)

10. **की बलि कर—"to make an offering, to sacrifice"**

परलोक में मृत व्यक्ति की सुख सुविधा के लिए पशुओं, स्त्रियों की बलि भी की जाती थी। (बूंद, 33)

11. **की कुर्बानी कर—"to sacrifice"**

अलीअहमद ने ललकार कर कहा बाजा बन्द करो, नहीं तो हम लोग गाय की कुर्बानी करेंगे। (होली, 79)

12. **कुर्बान कर—**

दिल ने चाहा कि उस अदा पर वहीं अपने को सौ बार कुर्बान कर दूं। (तुला, 109)

105. सन्तोष, सब्र, चैन

1. सन्तोष, सब्र, and चैन are all applied to indicate the subject's attitude of or disposition toward taking recourse to a state of mental repose for a variety of reasons.

सन्तोष is applied to a state of mind in which one feels as if he is satisfied or contented either through the fulfillment of his needs or wants or the attainment of a desired end. Alternatively, the term may be applied in situations where a reference is made to someone's exercise of forbearance and restraint (usually construed as an indication of the fact that the subject has no other recourse in a given situation).

सब्र stresses either the notion of exercising one's patience or acting or feeling as if one were pleased or gratified in a situation or under circumstances when one can either do no better or have anything more suitable.

चैन applies to the state of mental and physical tranquility as well as ease in which one is no longer disturbed or disquieted. Alternatively, the term may be used to refer to a state of mental as well as physical relief induced or caused by the removal or abatement of any situation which constantly agitates or nags at one.

2. All the expressions are + process and are not pluralized. सन्तोष forms ANP with से or पर, सब्र with से or का and चैन with में or की. The N post. with all three expressions may be dropped, and a conjunctive participial expression used in its place.

3. **से संतोष कर—"to be satisfied with"**

हम लोगों का सिद्धान्त है कि या तो हम केस नहीं लेते हैं और यदि लेते हैं तो हम रोग को जड़ से दूर करने की कोशिश करते हैं। केवल दवाइयां या इंजेक्शन देने से ही सन्तोष नहीं करते। (धनु, 139)

पर सन्तोष कर—"to be satisfied with"

यदि मुद्रा न हो तो उन्हें उत्पादकों पर निर्भर रहना पड़ेगा अर्थात् जो भी और जितनी वस्तु उन्हें दे दी जायगी उस पर ही उसको सन्तोष करना पड़ेगा। (एमाई, 35)

पर सन्तोष कर—"to be contented with"

पंडित मूलराज की प्रतिभा का सिक्का सारे गांव पर जमा हुआ था। लोग प्राय: अचम्भा करते थे कि इतने योग्य होते हुए भी वे शहजादपुर रहने पर ही सन्तोष क्यों किये

हुए हैं, और अम्बाला के गवर्नमेंट हाई स्कूल के हैडमास्टर क्यों नहीं बन जाते ?। (डगर, 40)

सन्तोष कर—"to be satisfied with"

नवल ने उंगली चटखाई और कहा—आदमी होते तो एक आध नज़र देखकर ही सन्तोष कर लेते। (दुख, 54)

सन्तोष कर—"to take pleasure in, to take comfort in"

वह मूर्ति समाप्त कर चुकी थी कुछ काल से वह उसे केवल सब ओर से देखकर अपना सन्तोष कर रही थी। (फूलो, 39)

सन्तोष कर—"to remain contented"

सन्तोष करने को मैं ही एक रह गई हूं ? सारी दुनिया मौज करे और मैं सन्तोष करके बैठी रहूं ? और वह रोती रही।

सन्तोष कर—"to console oneself with"

यदि उनके परिवार का कोई व्यक्ति बीमार पड़ता है तो वे अपना दुर्भाग्य समझकर सन्तोष कर लेते हैं। (स्वस्थ, 9)

सन्तोष कर—"to take consolation or comfort (in the fact that)"

तब बुद्ध बोले—गौतमी ! अब तुम यह मानकर सन्तोष करो कि केवल तुम्हारे ही ऊपर ऐसी विपत्ति नहीं पड़ी है, सारे संसार में ऐसा होता है और लोग ऐसे दुख को धैर्यपूर्वक सहते हैं। (आदर्श, 6)

सन्तोष कर—"to be satisfied"

गंगा मैया की तरफ मुंह करके कहो तो सन्तोष कर लूंगी। (दुख, 65)

सन्तोष कर—"to be satisfied, to be pleased"

गांव के लोग उनका गाना सुनकर जो कुछ दे देते, उसी को खा-पीकर दोनों सन्तोष कर लेते और वहीं पेड़ के तले रात काट लेते थे। (आदर्श, 37)

4. **सब्र कर ले—"to be patient"**

मैं दूध दूंगी। पर कुछ देर और तुम सब्र कर लो। (दुग्गल, 110)

सबर कर—"to be patient"

बाबा ने कहा भाई मरदाने सबर करो। अगले गांव पहुंचकर जितना तुम्हारा जी चाहे पानी पी लेना। (दुग्गल, 50)

सब्र कर—"to manage to restrain oneself"

सुमन का यहां एक-एक दिन एक-एक साल की तरह कटता था, लेकिन सब्र किये पड़ी हुई थी। (सेवा, 319)

सबर कर ले—"to console oneself with"

...अपने-अपने हिस्से के ढाई लाख लेकर उन्होंने सबर कर लिया और मां बाप को उनके हाल पर छोड़ दिया। (साझे, 12)

सबर कर—"to keep on putting up with something"

दुःखी दुनियां सब्र नहीं कर सकती। वह सब्र तो रखती है, लेकिन आदमी के सब्र की भी एक हद होती है। (भूदान, 86)

सब्र कर ले—"to console oneself with"

श्यामसुन्दर ने कभी इस तरह मिन्नत-मनौअल नहीं की थी। उसे बहुत बुरा लगा। फिर उसने सोचा कि मालिक के पास रुपये नहीं थे तो वह कहां से पैदा कर देता और श्यामसुन्दर ने सब्र कर लिया। (दुग्गल, 43)

सब्र कर ले—"to be consoled (by the fact...)"

और चन्दा ने मन में सब्र कर लिया था, यही सोचकर कि कुल-देवता का अंश तो उसे जीवन-भर पूजने को मिल गया था। (कमल, 23)

5. **में चैन कर—"to find relief in, to find comfort in"**

मैंने भी सोचा कि अपनी कमाई में तो चैन कर चुका, इस अवसर पर क्यों चूकूं, सभी शौक पूरे कर लिए। (सेवा, 143)

चैन कर—"to take pleasure in doing something"

उनके गले सस्ता माल मढ़ कर यूरोप वाले चैन करते हैं। (सेवा, 158)

106 प्रस्तुत, पेश, उपस्थित, हाज़िर

1. प्रस्तुत, पेश, उपस्थित and हाज़िर all refer to the subject's bringing something into view, of something of which he has some knowledge or insight into. They differ considerably as to the manner in which the speaker considers this conception or knowledge is manifested to others.

प्रस्तुत is applied when the subject is trying to draw attention to something, usually because of its noteworthiness, importance or relevance, which has not previously been apparent, by creating a description or other representation of it. The term emphasizes the creative capacity of the subject in communicating his insight or displaying his talent in performing.

In its extended meaning प्रस्तुत may be applied to something made available for public viewing for the first time.

पेश is a somewhat neutral term applied to anything that is brought or put forward before someone for action, consideration or acceptance.

उपस्थित (lit. that which is standing or situated horizontally across from one) refers to the appearance or emergence of something which has come about by the efforts of the subject of उपस्थित कर. The term usually carries the implication that the object is the result of considerable effort deliberately made by the subject.

हाजिर is a relatively colorless term referring to anyone or anything which is before someone, is in the view of someone or is at hand. It does not have the special implications of उपस्थित.

2. These expressions are – process.

3. **प्रस्तुत कर—"to depict"**

बरसाने की होली उस काल के सामाजिक जीवन की झांकी किसी हद तक आज भी प्रस्तुत कर देती है। (बूंद, 478)

प्रस्तुत कर—"to manifest, to represent"

...आत्मोपलब्धि के इसी तत्त्व को उसके विविध रूपों में प्रस्तुत किया है। (मूल्य, 165)

प्रस्तुत कर—"to produce"

जब तक कलाकार में अंतःप्रेरणा नहीं जागती तब तक वह सजीव कलाकृति नहीं प्रस्तुत कर पाता। (मूल्य, 156)

प्रस्तुत कर—"to make available, to present"

उसने सिर्फ नये रूपककारों को प्रकाश में ला बैठाया, बल्कि पुरानी कृतियों के लिए भी एक नवीन क्षेत्र प्रस्तुत कर दिया। उसने एक नई मांग पेश की जिसके जवाब में हिन्दी लेखक को अपनी कलम साहित्य के इस विस्मृत क्षेत्र में चलानी पड़ रही है।(कोणार्क, 101)

प्रस्तुत कर—"to depict, to represent"

दोनों-आमने-सामने कुर्सियों पर बैठ गए । गोल मेहराबों और खंभों वाला चौकोर कमरा अंधेरे और अकेलेपन का वातावरण प्रस्तुत कर रहा था। दीवाल पर बने दो छोटे रोशनदानों के सिवा यह कमरा बाहरी दुनिया से एकदम कटा हुआ था। (बंद, 492)

प्रस्तुत कर—"to depict"

मानव अस्तित्व को उसकी पूर्णतम जटिलता, गहनता, रस-मयता, अपराजेयता और श्रेष्ठता के साथ अभी तक हिन्दी उपन्यास में प्रस्तुत नहीं किया जा सका। (मूल्य, 173)

प्रस्तुत कर—"to represent, to express"

इसकी व्याख्या को ऐतिहासिक पद्धति अपना कर ही अधिक सरलता से प्रस्तुत किया जा सकता है? (मानव, 65)

प्रस्तुत कर—"to manifest, to represent"

हमारे दैनंदिन जीवन के राग रंग को प्रस्तुत करने के लिए हमारे संवेदों और स्पन्दनों को अभिव्यक्त करने के लिए जिस रंगमंच की आवश्यकता है वह पाश्चात्य रंगमंच से कहीं भिन्न होगा। (आषाढ़, 3)

प्रस्तुत कर—"to make available"

ऐसी स्थिति में इस बात की बहुत बड़ी आवश्यकता थी कि कोई ऐसी पुस्तक प्रस्तुत की जाय, जिसमें इन व्यापक समस्याओं का बौद्धिक स्तर पर समाधान मिल जाय। (निबन्ध, III)

प्रस्तुत कर—"to introduce, to bring forward"

आर्थिक क्रांति के लिए उन्होंने खादी और कुटीर उद्योग का प्रचार किया। उन्होंने शिक्षा के क्षेत्र में भी क्रांतिकारी विचार प्रस्तुत किये। (भारत, 64)

प्रस्तुत कर—"to perform one's program, to give a performance"

एक बार फ्रेंच गायिका किसी द्वीप में अपना संगीत कार्यक्रम प्रस्तुत करने के लिए गई। (एमाई, 10)

प्रस्तुत कर—"to present"

रातों रात महीपाल ने एक लिखित आयोजना बना डाली जिसमें वह तमाम आदर्श प्रस्तुत किए गये थे जो कि राजा साहब और सेठ रूपरतन के श्रीमुखों के द्वारा उच्चरित हुए थे। (बूंद, 558)

प्रस्तुत कर—"to illustrate, to depict"

विशेषतया डास्टावस्की की कथा कृतियों में मानवीय अंतरात्मा का जो विराट मानचित्र प्रस्तुत किया गया था वह एक विशाल पैमाने पर घटित होते हुए विघटन का सूचक था। (मूल्य, 20)

प्रस्तुत कर—"to depict, to represent"

बुराई का केवल बुराई को दर्शाने के लिये वर्णन करना, गन्दगी का केवल गन्दगी को उछालने के लिये प्रस्तुत करना, मेरी राय में किसी अमर-कला का विषय नहीं हो सकता। (दुग्गल, 9)

प्रस्तुत कर—"to present"

वस्तुतः हिन्दी में नाटक छप पहले जाते हैं—उन्हें रंगमंच पर बाद में प्रस्तुत किया जाता है। (कोणार्क, 7)

प्रस्तुत कर—"to present"

अन्त में उन्होंने कुछ ऐसे सवैये सुनाकर सबका मन मोह लिया जिनमें भारत की आर्थिक दुरवस्था के चित्र प्रस्तुत किये गए थे। (राह, 15)

प्रस्तुत कर—"to obtain, to produce"

बीच में गोवर्धन के ऊपर बहुत सुन्दर मंडप बनाकर उसमें श्रीकृष्ण भगवान प्रतिष्ठित किए गए थे। सज्जन से इस विवाह के लिए आचार्य श्रीधर महापात्र ने राधा और कृष्ण की स्वर्ण प्रतिमायें प्रस्तुत की थीं। (बूंद, 540)

प्रस्तुत कर—"to produce, to compose"

प्रणय की अठखेलियों और भाग्य के थपेड़ों के आधार पर कोणार्क के खंडहरों का सहारा ले एक रोचक कथापट प्रस्तुत कर देने से मुझे संतोष नहीं हुआ। (कोणार्क, 13)

प्रस्तुत कर—"to portray"

और इस आदर्श नारीरूप की प्रतिष्ठा करने के लिये अश्क ने अपनी कृतियों में नारी के अन्य सभी रूपों के बड़े तीखे व्यंग्यचित्र अंकित किए हैं—और भंवर की नायिका 'प्रतिभा' का चरित्र इन व्यंग्य-चित्रों में सबसे अधिक चटख रंग-रेखाओं में प्रस्तुत किया गया है। (भंवर, 12)

के लिए प्रस्तुत कर—"to introduce one to"

कन्या को इस प्रसंग में अभी कोई जानकारी न थी। आज धनवती देवी वैद्यशास्त्रिणी प्रभाकर महान् कलाकार के लिए एक ऐसी प्रेरणा सामग्री प्रस्तुत करने का वचन दे चुकी थी जो साधारणतया सबको सुलभ नहीं होती। (बूंद, 512)

का प्रतीक प्रस्तुत कर—"to portray symbolically, to give symbolic representation to"

अश्क ने जगन के रूप में ऐसे युवकों का प्रतीक प्रस्तुत किया है जिनका प्रेम बिल्कुल सतही होता है। (भंवर, 38)

4. **पेश कर दे—"to introduce"**

कानूनी—तो लो अबकी यह कानून भी असेंबली खुलते ही पेश कर दूंगा। (सम, 25)

पेश कर—"to put forward, to introduce"

उसने न सिर्फ नये रूपककारों को प्रकाश में ला बैठाया, बल्कि पुरानी कृतियों के लिए भी एक नवीन क्षेत्र प्रस्तुत कर दिया। उसने एक नई मांग पेश की जिसके जवाब में हिन्दी लेखक को अपनी कलम साहित्य के विस्मृत-क्षेत्र में चलानी पड़ रही है। (कोणार्क, 101)

पेश कर—"to introduce"

पंडित जी प्रसन्न हो गए। बोले तब हमारी शंका निर्मूल नहीं थी। अच्छा सवा हाथ की होती है न? भाई साहब ने अपनी हंसी दबाते हुए उसमें तरमीम पेश की और कहा कि सवा हाथ की तो नहीं सवा बालिश्त की होती है। (बूंद, 523)

पेश कर—"to present, to introduce"

यदि इस विषय पर अधिक बहस कीजिएगा तो मैं प्रमाण में पुराणों को पेश करूंगा जिनमें ऐसी अनेक कथाएं हैं जिनसे यह साबित होता है कि...। (खत, 81)

(की सेवा में) पेश कर—"to bring into the presence of, to introduce into"

बिलारी युद्ध में प्राप्त कोष को श्रीमंत की सेवा में पेश करो पेशवा मोरोपंत ने साकू जी को आज्ञा दी। (बेटी, 95)

पेश कर—"to present or introduce someone to another person"

भूरे को दामाद बना लेने के बाद ठाकुर मितानसिंह ने उसे मोरियल मिल की दरबानी में भरती करा लिया और दामाद को बड़े साहब के सामने पेश कर कहा—यह हजूर के गुलाम का लड़का है। मैं बूढ़ा हो गया हूं...(पूणो, 23)

पेश कर—"to present, to represent"

इन गालियों में नारी पुरुष द्वारा एक अत्यंत अपमानजनक तरीके से पेश की जाती है। नर-नारी के बीच का काम-व्यवहार पृथ्वी पर सुलभ सर्वोच्च आनन्द है। मनुष्य अन्य

अनेक प्राणियों के साथ आदिकाल से अब तक इस सत्य का पीढ़ी दर पीढ़ी अनुभव करता आया है। साहित्य कलाओं आदि पर काम संबंध ने सबसे अधिक प्रभाव डाला। (बूंद, 479)

पेश कर—"to introduce (something as evidence)"

अपनी स्वर्गीया भाभी का पत्र पेश कर दिया। मजिस्ट्रेट ने उस पर तहकीकात करने का आश्वासन दिया। (बूंद, 236)

(के सामने) पेश कर—"to personally present (in front of someone)"

महाराजा रणजीतसिंह के पास लौटने पर सिपाहियों ने उन लड़कों को उनके सामने सजा देने के लिए पेश किया। (आदर्श, 89)

पेश कर—"to present"

प्रेम के विषय में बात करते समय वे कभी-कभी कहावतों को अजब रूप में पेश किया करते थे। (सूरज, 18)

पेश कर—"to introduce into evidence"

असल में हम दोनों ईश्वर के शव की खोज में निकले थे। उसने कहा ईश्वर मर तो गया है पर उसका शव जब तक अदालत में पेश नहीं किया जाता, मृत्यु की घोषणा नहीं हो सकती। (मांस, 113)

5. **उपस्थित कर—"to advance, to propound"**

...अब तक तुम कम्युनिस्ट लोग समाज में कौन सा आदर्श उपस्थित कर चुके हो? कन्या बोली—पहली बात तो यह कि मैं कम्युनिस्ट पार्टी की मेम्बर नहीं हूं। हां, ये कह सकते हो कि कम्युनिज्म से बहुत काफी प्रभावित जरूर हुई हूं। (बूंद, 469)

उपस्थित कर—"to set forth"

समय-समय पर प्रकट होकर यह आदर्श ऐसे मनुष्यों ने जगत के सामने उपस्थित किया है। (वैदिक, 36)

उपस्थित कर—"to set forth, to propound"

स्वामी विवेकानन्द ने भारतीय संस्कृति का एक अत्यंत प्रगतिशील और तेजस्वी रूप उपस्थित किया। (भारत, 63)

उपस्थित कर—"to present (a show), to put on (a show)"

बंदर दांत दिखाने, गुर्राने, नाराज होने का दृश्य अच्छी तरह उपस्थित करता है। (बाल, 11-6)

उपस्थित कर रख—"to create"

रंगमंच और दर्शक के बीच में चलचित्र ने जो व्यवधान उपस्थित कर रखा है, उसको उसने भर देना चाहा है। (मादा, 9)

उपस्थित कर—"to bring about"

वह अपने स्वार्थ की सिद्धि के लिए तो इस कृपा से लाभ उठाता ही था, पर साथ ही बदला लेने की गरज से गांव में झगड़े उपस्थित करके वह गांव के सब दर्जे के लोगों को जितना संभव हो सकता, उतना अकारण तंग भी करता था। (लाख, 35)

उपस्थित कर—"to call up, to bring (back) to mind"

इतना ही पाजी तो मधुबन भी था लड़कपन में, यह भी अपने बाप का बेटा है न। राजो के मन में मधुबन के बाल्यकाल का स्नेहपूर्ण चित्र उपस्थित करते हुए मोहन उसको सांत्वना दिया करता। (तितली, 262)

उपस्थित कर—"to create"

विश्व प्रेम से प्रेरित होकर सत्य को ही सर्वदा व्यवहार में लाने का प्रयत्न करना चाहिए। समाज में जो लोग अव्यवस्था उपस्थित करते हैं उन्हें उपऋत के द्वारा शांत करना चाहिए। (वैदिक, 9)

उपस्थित कर—"to present, to display"

"मैं बिलारी में प्राप्त कोष उपस्थित करके दरबार का रंग नहीं बिगाड़ना चाहता श्रीमंत!" (बेटी, 95)

उपस्थित कर—"to propose, to advance"

पिछले पृष्ठों में रंगमंच की जो त्रिमुखी योजना मैंने उपस्थित की है वह एक संकेत है इसी मार्ग की ओर। मैं यह कहने की धृष्टता नहीं करूंगा कि हिन्दी भाषी समाज इस संकेत को आंख मूंदकर मान ले। (कोणार्क, 102)

उपस्थित कर—"to propound"

यूं तो विभिन्न राजनीतिज्ञों और विचारकों ने राज्य के कार्यों के विषय में अपने-अपने सिद्धांत उपस्थित किये हैं परन्तु मोटे तौर से आधुनिक काल में निम्नलिखित सिद्धांत गणिका प्रचलित हैं...(भारत, 20)

6. **हाज़िर कर दे—"to bring before"**

तो उसमें क्या है। जिस वक्त इच्छा हो आपके प्रिय लेखक को कान पकड़कर हाजिर कर दूं। चलिये अभी ही चलें उसके यहां। वे दोनों घर ही गये होंगे। (बूंद, 124)

हाज़िर कर—"to make someone appear before"

रानी—तो मेरी इच्छा है कि मंत्री विजयसेन को कारागार से मुक्त किया जाय।
राजा—स्वीकार। और आज्ञा करो रानी।
रानी—और उसे मेरे सामने हाजिर किया जाय। (नाटक, 68)

पर हाज़िर कर—"to have something ready or at someone's disposal"

आप सुबह जरा और जल्दी दो ढाई बजे निकल चलें। गंगा पार पक्की सड़क है, बारह मील घुमाकर ठीक टाइम पर हाजिर कर दिया करूंगा। तीन दिन की तो बात है। (सूरज, 42-43)

107. अभियान, प्रयाण, प्रस्थान

1. अभियान, प्रयाण and प्रस्थान are all applied in making a ceremonial or formal reference to someone who sets out in any direction, moves from or leaves a place or undertakes any similar activity.

अभियान stresses either the idea of setting out (lit. as well as fig.) in the direction of one's goal, or the attainment of one's objective. The term may be applied to any expeditionary undertaking in which more than one person takes part and which involves hazards and risks (usually known to or anticipated by its initiators).

प्रयाण usually implies the notion of accretion in the act of gradually moving from one state or condition to another, either emphasizing a gradually accelerated pace or the effect upon someone of something which he is undergoing. It may be applied to a situation in which one sets out or sets forward from a place to his destination or where he is destined to go. The term may only in the latter sense be figuratively used to describe the death of some religious or other leader.

प्रस्थान is used in reference to the departure of a group of people or an individual alongwith his retinue for an expressed destination. The term may thus be applied as a formal reference to someone's act of leaving a place (such as when an actor leaves the stage depicting a particular scene or some dignitary departs from the scene of an incident).

2. These expressions are +process, and are not pluralized. अभियान forms ANP with के विरुद्ध, के हेतु and के लिए, प्रयाण with की ओर and प्रस्थान with की ओर, के लिए or को.

3. **के विरुद्ध अभियान कर—"to undertake an expedition"**

मैंने इस बार ग्रह-नक्षत्रों के विरुद्ध अभियान किया था। (चारु, 131)

के विरुद्ध अभियान कर—"to wage a war against"

जाओ बेटा, अधर्म के विरुद्ध अभियान करो। (चारु, 289)

के हेतु अभियान कर—"to leave for"

युद्ध के हेतु अभियान करने वाले मनुष्य के जीवन का मूल्य क्या? महत्त्व क्या? (यादव, 191)

4. **की दिशा में प्रयाण कर—"to depart for"**

इससे ग्रामीण समुदाय का आधार टूट गया और विघटन की दिशा में ग्रामीण समुदायों ने प्रयाण किया। (ग्रामीण, 35)

5. **की ओर प्रस्थान कर—"to move in the direction of, to set forth for"**

तुम यहीं रहकर आचार्य शिष्य की सहायता करोगे और मुझे तुरन्त ही आयुष्मान् सिंह की सहायतार्थ गंगा तट की ओर प्रस्थान करना होगा।

को प्रस्थान कर—"to leave (on)"

चन्द्रवार की रात को ही आर्य बीजगुप्त देश पर्यटन को प्रस्थान करेंगे। (चित्र, 184)

के लिए प्रस्थान कर—"to set out for, to leave for"

श्रीचन्द्र ने हरद्वार के लिए प्रस्थान किया। (कंकाल, 14)

की ओर प्रस्थान कर—"to set out"

...और कनक कसौटी रेखा की भांति अपनी छटा दिखाता हुआ अलकापुरी की ओर मंद गति से प्रस्थान करता है। (ज्योति, 26)

की ओर प्रस्थान कर—"to head towards"

अतः नौकरी के द्वारा धन कमाने की लालसा से उन्होंने मैदान में स्थित एक बड़े नगर की ओर प्रस्थान किया। (एमाई, 10)

के लिए प्रस्थान कर—"to have already departed, to have already set out"

...कि पृथ्वीराज की कोई बहुत बड़ी सेना महोबे पर आक्रमण करने के लिए प्रस्थान कर चुकी है। (चारु, 81)

को ओर प्रस्थान कर—"to leave for"

दृढ़काय कहारों ने पालकियों को लेकर राजमहल के सभा-भवन की ओर प्रस्थान किया। (शांतला, 47)

प्रस्थान कर—"to be leaving for, to be setting out for"

तुम्हारे प्रथम पुष्पों को देखकर जो आनन्द से नाच उठती थी, वही शकुन्तला आज अपने पति के घर प्रस्थान कर रही है। (ज्योति, 27)

प्रस्थान कर—"to withdraw, to leave"

पुकारते ही दस लाठियां निकल सकती थीं। तहसीलदार ने समझ-बूझकर धीरे से प्रस्थान किया।

प्रस्थान कर—"to deposit, to leave"

निश्चित समय पर जुलूस ने प्रस्थान किया। उसी वक्त पुलिस ने मेरी गिरफ्तारी का वारंट दिखाया। वारंट देखते ही तुम्हारी याद आई। (सम, 17)

प्रस्थान कर—"to depart from, to leave"

वेश बदलकर रात-रात भर घूमा करता...दोनों नृत्यवत् गतियों से प्रस्थान करते हैं। (नाटक, 14)

प्रस्थान कर—"to set out, to depart from"

परन्तु आचार्य शिष्य के वहां से प्रस्थान करते ही जैसे उसके संकोच का यह आवरण विलग हो उठता। (दत्तक पुत्री, 50)

108. विज्ञापन, परिचित, आगाह, हिदायत, सूचित, खबर

1. विज्ञापन, परिचित, आगाह, हिदायत, सूचित and खबर all refer to the act of communicating a piece of information in a variety of ways or are used in referring to something (usually by using the noun denoting that concept as the subject of the sentence) in a way which informs someone in an indirect way of the existence of something, and conveys some notion of its condition or state to him.

विज्ञापन (lit. making widely known) applies to any act or effort made by someone to solicit public attention and interest in something one has to offer. The term may be used as a subjective or conjectural reference to someone who appears to be trying to gain publicity, and has done something worthy of public attention.

परिचित applies to any effort made by someone (such as through discussion, explanation, etc.) which is intended to convey to another the significance or importance of something, or its characteristics or nature. The term may take as its subject any noun (denoting a mental or psychic process) which serves as a means to reveal the characteristics or significance of something to someone.

The adjective परिचित occurs more often with करा— than with कर—.

आगाह refers to letting someone know of an impending event or makes reference to anything which serves to remind one of the consequences or the outcome of what one proposes to do in the immediate future.

हिदायत applies to anything (told to someone) that serves as a guide for him or directs him to act in a particular way in a given situation, or informs him of what he is expected to do.

सूचित refers to any kind of communication, verbal or written, which informs someone either directly or indirectly of the details of an event or happening.

खबर (lit. that which serves to bring about in one's mind the awareness of someone or something) is applied to any information or news about someone or something which is communicated, conveyed or transmitted by one person to another.

2. विज्ञापन, हिदायत and खबर are + process and the rest are − process. विज्ञापन forms ANP with का and हिदायत and खबर with को. These three nouns are not pluralized.

3. **का विज्ञापन कर—"to advertise"**

एक बार किसी महाशय ने उर्दू-फारसी का एक साधारण कोश प्रकाशित करके उसका ऐसे विज्ञापन किया कि बहुत-से लोग बिना देखे ही उस पुस्तक की प्रशंसा गाने लगे। (आदर्श, 91)

का विज्ञापन कर—"to publicize"

वे प्रथम श्रेणी के लेखकों को अपने शिविर में ले आयेंगे और उनकी बैसाखी लगाकर दो हाथ ऊंचे खड़े होने का विज्ञापन करते रहेंगे। (मूल्य, 59)

का विज्ञापन कर—"to advertise, to make a public announcement"

गत शिवरात्रि को शहर के एक सिनेमा वाले ने सारी रात का प्रोग्राम रखकर तीन-तीन तस्वीरें दिखाने का विज्ञापन किया। (विचित्र, 79)

विज्ञापन कर—"to tell everybody, to publicize"

फूलचन्द—(मुस्कराकर) तो क्या मैं कोई विज्ञापन कर रहा हूं ? मैंने तुम्हारे सिवाय और किसी से नहीं कहा।

मन्दाकिनी—इसलिए कहती हूं कि ब्याह की बातचीत माता-पिता या अभिभावक द्वारा होनी चाहिए। (बांस, 44)

4. को से परिचित कर—"to help one know oneself, to reveal"

जप हमको अपने आप से परिचित कराता है, उसकी गहराइयों का ज्ञान प्राप्त कराता है, उसकी उलझनों को हमारे सम्मुख लाता है और कुछ दार्शनिक सिद्धांतों का प्रत्यक्ष दर्शन कराता है। (चमत्कार, 3-4)

को से परिचित करा—"to impart to someone the knowledge of"

ग्रामीण जनों को विज्ञान और टेक्नालोजी की प्रविधियों और प्रक्रियाओं से परिचित कराया जाय, जिससे वे उनका लाभ उठा सकें। (सामुदा, 8)

को से परिचित करा—"to familiarize someone with"

कृषकों को उनकी समस्याओं से परिचित कराता है और यह एक प्रकार का क्रियात्मक अभ्यास है। (सामुदा, 4)

को से परिचित करा—"to acquaint someone with"

उन समस्याओं के हल से कृषकों को परिचित कराता है। (सामुदा, 12)

को से परिचित करा—"to acquaint someone with"

सज्जन ने तो हमें यह बतलाया था कि मुहल्ले के लोगों को कला की विशेषताओं से परिचित कराने के लिए यह प्रदर्शनी की जा रही है...(बूंद, 385)

को से परिचित करा—"to help someone learn, to make someone know"

सामुदायिक विकास कार्यक्रम लोगों को विधियों तथा दर्शन से परिचित कराता है। (सामुदा, 12)

5. **को से आगाह कर—"to caution, to forewarn"**

मैंने जानबूझकर तुम्हें इन बातों से आगाह नहीं किया। मैं अपनी नर्गिस को तुमसे ज्यादा चाहती हूं। (खत, 34)

को आगाह कर—"to forewarn"

तुझे आगाह करने आया हूं बताने आया हूं, मैं कल उसे अपने कब्जे में करूंगा जिसे तू अपनी बीबी समझना चाहता है। (खत, 78)

आगाह कर—"to serve to caution someone against, to arouse in someone's mind the awareness of"

पर पत्नीत्व के संस्कार भी उभर-उभर कर सामने आ जाते हैं, आगाह करते हैं...। (धनु, 82)

6. **को हिदायत कर—"to instruct"**

इनको हिदायत करते-करते देर हो गई। (ढोल, 31)

7. **सूचित कर—"to inform, to tell someone of"**

कर्नल को सूचना हुई। डा० जयपाल को भी बुलाकर सूचित किया गया। पुलिस को भी सूचना दी गई। (बूंद, 580)

सूचित कर—"to indicate"

पर ये तथा ऐसे अन्य दृष्टिकोण ऐतिहासिक परिप्रेक्ष्य से नितान्त अपरिचय ही सूचित करते हैं। (मूल्य, 91)

सूचित कर—"to give an indication of"

मेरे पत्र की किसी बात का उत्तर तुमने नहीं दिया; और परीक्षाफल तक नहीं सूचित किया—क्या मैंने कभी कल्पना की थी कि तुम्हारा परीक्षाफल रजिस्ट्रार को तार देकर मंगाना पड़ेगा। (नदी, 73)

सूचित कर—"to let someone know"

दिल्ली पहुंचें तो मुझे सूचित कीजिएगा। मैं कुछ दिन के लिए वहां जाने की सोच रहा हूं। (नदी, 95)

सूचित कर—"to inform, to let someone know, to intimate"

उन्होंने मेरे लिए भी आशा प्रकट की है कि मैं पुराने घावों को ही न सहलाती रह कर भविष्य का निर्माण करूंगी। उन्हें मेरे भविष्य में विश्वास है, और उनका अनुरोध है कि जब भी कुछ महत्त्वपूर्ण मेरे जीवन में घटे तो उन्हें सूचित करूं। (नदी, 271)

सूचित कर—"to indicate, to serve to denote, to express the notion of"

मुद्रा शब्द का प्रयोग विनिमय के माध्यम तथा मूल्य-मान दोनों को ही सूचित करने के लिए किया गया है। (एमाई, 64)

सूचित कर—"to reveal, to indicate, to bespeak"

उसकी यह भंगिमा ही सूचित कर देती है कि वह अपने वातावरण से किस कदर बेज़ार है। और दूसरे ही क्षण उसकी यह बेज़ारी मुखर हो उठती है, जब वह अंगड़ाई लेकर कहती है...(भंवर, 15)

8. **को खबर कर—"to inform"**

फिर अस्पताल में रुकने तक कोई नहीं बोला। उतरते ही डाक्टर ने कहा नर्स टामस आपरेशन-रूम तैयार कराओ। डाक्टर रेबर्न को खबर करो। इम्मीजिएट आपरेशन। (नदी, 234)

को खबर कर दे—"to advise, to inform"

अगर यह सम्भव नहीं होता तो वह जहाज को इस ऊंचाई पर ले जाता है कि वह पैराशूट लेकर कूद सके और ऐसा करने से पहले वह कंट्रोल रूम को खबर कर देता है। (बाल, 11-46)

को खबर कर दे—"to notify"

पुलिस को भी खबर कर दी गई थी, वह भी आ गई। (डगर, 61)

को खबर करने आ—"to inform"

स्वर चिढ़ से कर्कश होकर फट गया, झटके से दाहिना हाथ बढ़ाकर उन्होंने कहा—जब उनकी अर्थी निकले तब खबर करने आना। (बूंद, 10)

को खबर कर—"to let someone know"

भाभी शीला पेटीकोट ही में भागी आती, दादी को आखिरी सांसों में देखकर आंखें फैलाती, चिल्लाती, हाय ! कोई उनको खबर करो...(लड़की, 6)

109. टालमटोल, आनाकानी, आगापीछा, तकल्लुफ, संकोच, लज्जा, शर्म, बहाना

1. The expressions in this group are all applied to make a reference to someone's state of mind in which he holds back from any act or action for some reason or in a variety of ways.

टालमटोल is applied to situations in which one tries to put off an impending act or something inevitable by using any sort of delaying tactics.

आनाकानी is applied to a positive show of one's reluctance or to a display of one's disinclination or reluctance to go through with something or act in a manner proposed by another.

आगापीछा stresses the state of indecision, uncertainty or doubt in one who is acting in a manner such that he is trying to hold back or hold off doing something for some reason or is vacillating in making up his mind.

तकल्लुफ is strictly applied to a state of hesitancy in accepting a gift, a favor etc. as a mark of one's appreciation of its value or to any act in which one conforms to any formal or conventional modes of conduct (usually construed by the speaker as some sort of hesitation on the part of the subject).

संकोच (lit. contracting, narrowing etc.) is applied to describe a variety of situations in which one shrinks from doing something or avoids a direct encounter with a situation or a person usually with a motive or intention. If no specific reference to the subject's motive or intention is expressed in the sentence or contained in the context, then the term strongly implies that the subject's avoiding a situation or a person is characterized by his sense of propriety, is a positive display of his modesty or his regard for the feeling of others.

लज्जा refers to the state of mind in which one is overcome or affected by a natural impulse to withdraw or retract oneself from attention, notice, publicity, notoriety; or to avoid pushiness, overbearing behavior, arrogance etc. The term, therefore, strongly suggests the notion of conducting oneself with modesty, and thus exercising considerable restraint at the outset in an encounter with a person or a situation.

शर्म describes with approval the state of one who is bashful or shy, or may be applied disapprovingly to the act of the person who does not conduct himself properly or in a worthy manner (because he lacks a sense of shame).

बहाना is applied to the act of making an excuse for not doing or wanting to do something, or to the act of doing something under some pretext, pretense or cover.

2. All the nouns in this group are +process, and with the exception

of बहाना, they are not pluralized. बहाना forms ANP with का, लज्जा with से, शर्म with की or से, and the rest with से.

3. टालमटोल कर—"to put things off, to avoid the issue"

जल्दी सुनाइये और फिर मेरी बात का उत्तर दीजिये। मैं टालमटोल नहीं करने दूंगी। (बांस, 51)

टालमटोल कर—"to hesitate over"

अब तो टालमटोल करने या समझाने-बुझाने की बात ठीक नहीं है। इसका ध्यान रखना होगा कि तुम्हारी विवाह की उम्र बीत न जाय। (शांतला, 233)

4. में आनाकानी कर—"to hesitate, to be hesitant"

उसके गुसाईं हो जाने के कारण सागर राजा को उसे जागीर प्रदान करने में बाधा नहीं होगी, और भोंसले का कृपापात्र होने के कारण भोंसले उसको स्वीकार करने में आनाकानी नहीं करेगा। (कचनार, 33)

में आनाकानी कर—"to be disinclined"

मन के अभाव को भरने के लिए मान से फूल-फूलकर वह कोवलन के निमित्त मानी गई मणिमेखला देवी की मानता इतनी धूमधाम से करना चाहती थी कि प्रिय के कानों तक बातें पहुंचें, पर पेरियनायकी इसके लिए स्वीकृति देने में आनाकानी करती थी। (सुहाग, 136)

में आनाकानी कर—"to hesitate"

इसलिए तितली की सहायता करने में तुम आनाकानी कर रहे हो न? (तितली, 204)

में आनाकानी कर—"to be reluctant to, to be afraid to"

अब गांव की बहन-बेटियां घर के बाहर निकलने में आनाकानी करती हैं। (होली, 67)

में आनाकानी कर—"to be reluctant to"

वे किराया देने में आनाकानी करते हैं और मांगने पर गाली-गलौज पर उतर आते हैं...। (राह, 67)

आनाकानी कर—"to show no interest"

विट्ठल—हां, किया तो था लेकिन जिस प्रकार आप एक बार मौखिक सहानुभूति

प्रकट करके मौन साध गये, उसी प्रकार अन्य सहायकों ने भी आनाकानी की, तो भाई अकेला चना तो भाड़ नहीं फोड़ सकता ? (सेवा, 126)

आनाकानी कर—"to give no particular response to the contrary"

वीणा, जो अपने आपको नगण्य मानती थी कुछ कीमत पा गई, अस्तित्व पा गई। जिस पुरुष के कारण उसे यह अस्तित्व मिला उसके प्रति उसको कृतज्ञता लगी। और इसी में से जब विवाह का प्रस्ताव उत्स्फूर्त हुआ तब वीणा ने विशेष आनाकानी नहीं की। (धनु, 22)

आनाकानी—"to respond negatively"

माणिक ने जब आनाकानी की तो जमुना बोली, देखो माणिक तुमने नमक खाया है और नमक खाकर जो अदा नहीं करता उसे पाप पड़ता है। (सूरज, 31-32)

5. **में आगापीछा कर—"to waver, to show reluctance"**

पर चीन में अफीम खाने की कुप्रथा मिटाने के लिये सरकार ने इतनी भीषण हानि उठाने में जरा भी आगा-पीछा नहीं किया। (सेवा, 179)

में आगापीछा कर—"to make excuses"

शोक ! आप आंखों से देख रहे हैं कि हिन्दू जाति की स्त्री कुएं में गिरी हुई है, और आप उसी जाति के एक विचारवान् पुरुष होकर उसे निकालने में इतना आगापीछा कर रहे हैं। (सेवा, 98)

में आगापीछा कर—"to be unable to or to take too long to make up one's mind"

आप विचित्र जीव हैं, सीधी-सी बात में भी इतना आगापीछा करने लगते हैं। (सेवा, 261)

आगापीछा कर—"to try to stall"

उन्होंने बताया था कि अशोक चल्ल के सेनापति और मंत्री कुछ आगापीछा कर रहे हैं। (चारु, 414)

आगापीछा कर—"to waven, to vacillate"

पंडित जी उसके व्याख्यान से चिढ़कर बोले—तू इस तरह आगापीछा करता रहेगा तो एक पग भी आगे नहीं बढ़ेगा। व्यर्थ की बातों में दिमाग क्यों उलझाता है ! (कथा, 63)

6. **तकल्लुफ कर—"to beat around the bush"**

देखो सज्जन मैं तकल्लुफ करूंगा नहीं। (बूंद, 343)

7. में संकोच कर—"to not be above (doing something)"

तो आप भी पैसे के लिए अपने घर के पुरुषों को होम करने में संकोच न करेंगी। (गोदान, 73)

में संकोच कर—"to hesitate"

जो पड़ोसी पहले दियासलाई की डिबिया देकर भूल जाते थे, वे अब तीलियों तक का हिसाब रखने में संकोच न करते थे। (धारा, 86)

में संकोच कर—"to have no restraint on"

उसे ईश्वर की सहायता समझ कर दरिद्रों के लिए अपने दल की आवश्यकता पूर्ति के लिए व्यय करने में कोई संकोच नहीं करते। (तितली, 224)

में संकोच कर—"to be reluctant in"

और जो कहीं उसने घृणावश मुझसे गले मिलने में संकोच किया तब तो उसी क्षण विष खा लूंगी। (सेवा, 258)

में संकोच कर—"to refrain from, to restrain oneself from"

हां, निर्णय हो जाने पर उसे अपने अनुभव को बताने में कदापि संकोच न करना चाहिए और कठोर शब्दों को मधुर शब्दों से ढकने का प्रयत्न करना चाहिए। (धर्म, 121)

में संकोच कर—"to avoid, to shrink from"

चरित्र की दुर्बलता के कारण मित्र से भी मिलने में संकोच करता है। (कंकाल, 106)

8. से लज्जा कर—"to act with demureness towards"

फूलो पांच बरस की बच्ची थी तो क्या, वह जानती थी, दूल्हे से लज्जा करनी चाहिए। (फूलो, 7)

9. शर्म कर—"to be embarrassed"

दीनानाथ—भीतर जाओ।
किरणमयी—भीतर क्यों? मैं शर्म नहीं करती। (सन्यासी, 94)

शर्म कर—"to be ashamed"

हाय, शरम करो, कैसी बात करते हो? अच्छा, मैं बताऊं? पहले तेरे एक लड़की होगी, फिर दो लड़के होंगे, फिर एक लड़की होगी...। (जानवर, 118)

10. बहाना कर—"to make the pretense or excuse of"

विट्ठलदास को सन्देह हुआ कि सुमन 30 रु० मासिक स्वीकार नहीं करना चाहती, इसलिये उसने कल उत्तर देने का बहाना करके मुझे टाला है। (सेवा, 122)

बहाना कर—"to make the excuse of"

...पर उनकी उदारता मेरे दिल-दिमाग में बस गयी थी। शाम को मित्र एकत्र हुए तो मैंने सिरदर्द का बहाना कर उन्हें धता बताई। (हास्य, 91)

का बहाना कर—"under the pretense of"

ब्याह का बहाना करके कल मेरे साथ बलात्कार करने का उसने संकल्प कर लिया। (कचनार, 179)

का बहाना कर—"to pretend to be (serious)"

परन्तु मुझे देखकर वे ठिठक गईं और गम्भीर होने का बहाना करने लगीं। (राह, 19)

का बहाना कर—"to pretend to be"

किन्तु नायक सरलता का बहाना कर रहा था। (बेटी, 20)

का बहाना कर—"to pretend"

लड़की डरने का बहाना करती एक हल्की सी चीख हंसी के ठहाकों के बीच डूब जाती... फिर कोई एकोर्डियन बजाने लगता। (वे दिन, 77)

का बहाना कर—"to pretend to be (asleep)"

अब मुझे पता चला कि अलहना ने सोने का बहाना भर किया था। (चारु, 260)

का बहाना कर—"to make a pretense of"

और इसमें भी मैं ऐसी कोई खास जूठन नहीं मानता। अजी हमारे यहां तो पहले ये आमकायदा था। रईस लोग नाममात्र की जूठन का बहाना कर अपने नौकरों-चाकरों को अक्सर अच्छी से अच्छी चीजें खिला-पिला देते थे। (बूंद, 470)

का बहाना कर—"to make an excuse, to make something an excuse for"

मां डायन है। दादी को पानी नहीं देती। जान-बूझकर धुआं करती है। गीली लकड़ियों का बहाना करती है। हर एक से लड़ती-झगड़ती रहती है। (बचपन, 0)

बहाना कर—"to make some excuse or other, to pretend something or other"

गजानन्द ने कितनी ही बार चाहा कि उन्हें लावें, पर वह कोई न कोई बहाना कर दिया करते थे। (सेवा, 348)

का बहाना कर—"to pretend to be (sick)"

आठ दिन बीत गए, लेकिन वे किसी बात का अकाट्य उत्तर नहीं सोच पाए। नवें दिन वे बीमारी का बहाना करके पड़ गए। और क्या करते ! दरबार में जाकर नाक कटाने में क्या लाभ था ! (कथा, 26)

का बहाना करके—"under the pretext of"

देशी नरेशों को धोखा दे-देकर एक दूसरे से लड़ाया गया; पहले उसमें से किसी एक को उसके विपक्षी के विरुद्ध मदद देकर गद्दी पर बैठाया गया और फिर किसी न किसी दुर्व्यवहार का बहाना लेकर उसे भी तख्त से उतार दिया गया। (सुंदर, 21)

बहाना कर—"to pretend"

वह संदिग्ध दृष्टि से मेरे डफलकोट की ओर देख रही थी। मैंने बहाना किया कि मैं चेक नही समझता हूं। (वे दिन, 14)

का बहाना कर—"pretending to be"

...भारी-सी आवाज़ में उत्तर देकर महीपाल ने टेबिल-लैंप जलाया और अपनी मेज के कागजात इस तरह उलटने लगा जैसे कोई जरूरी कागज ढूंढ रहा हो। व्यस्त होने का बहाना करते हुए उसकी पीठ अपनी पत्नी की तरफ थी, वैसे ही बोला...(बूंद, 99)

बहाना न कर—"to pretend"

मैं उनसे डरती नहीं...अगर उन्होंने सचमुच शराब पी रखी हो और बहाना न कर रहे हों। (वे दिन, 107)

110. परिचर्या, खिदमत, टहल, सेवा, सेवा-इलाज, सेवा-शुश्रूषा, सेवा-पूजा, सेवा-टहल, सेवा-कार्य

1. These expressions are used to characterize or specify the nature of the activity of someone who looks after another person, provides any service that benefits or helps another or devotes himself to any self-assigned task.

परिचर्या (lit. moving or walking around someone) is applied when someone attends to the needs of or gives care to a sick person.

खिदमत refers to a variety of services performed by one (usually by one who is given to a sense of duty or in the line of duty) for the sake of a cause or another person.

टहल denotes the activity of one who performs duties or chores for someone or in the house of someone. The term usually implies either that sort of work which requires no knowledge of any special skill or an occupation appropriate to a menial. It may, therefore, be used (unless otherwise specified in a sentence) to express the subject's dislike for what he is made to do.

सेवा is a term of broader application referring to the duties, work or business performed or discharged by one in any capacity or as a matter of regular practice, usually in a way specified in the sentence.

सेवा-इलाज, सेवा-शुश्रूषा, सेवा-पूजा and सेवा-टहल are coordinate compound terms formed by juxtaposing इलाज "treatment, treating", शुश्रूषा "obsequiousness", पूजा "worship, worshipping", and टहल "duty, chore" with सेवा.

सेवा-कार्य refers to the practice of engaging in any sort of volunteer work of one's own free will for which one receives no compensation.

2. All these nouns are +process and form ANP with की and are not pluralized.

3. की परिचर्या कर—"to care for, to attend to the need of"

तीन रात कचनार ने परिचर्या की। (कचनार, 103)

की परिचर्या कर—"to attend to, to watch over, to look after"

आप बतला सकते हैं राजा दलीपसिंह की परिचर्या कौन करता था। (कचनार, 315)

4. खिदमत कर—"to do something for someone"

इस कदर खिदमत चन्द्रकान्त करता था वह बड़े फख्र से अपने दोस्तों में बयान करता था।

की खिदमत कर—"to work for"

मैं क्या नौकर हूं कि इसके दोस्तों की खिदमत करती फिरूं।

खिदमत कर—"to do something for someone"

मैनेजर—साहब ने मुझे यह पूछने के लिए भेजा है कि हम आपकी क्या खिदमत कर सकते हैं।

5. टहल कर—"to work for someone"

मुझे तन ढकने के लिए बस्तर चाहिए, क्योंकि मैं चौबीस घंटे तुम्हारे घर में टहल करती हूं। (अंधा, 95)

6. **सेवा कर—"to serve someone wholeheartedly"**

वह उसके सुख सम्मान का पूरा ध्यान रखता था। युवक भी उसके सद्व्यवहार से प्रभावित होकर तन-मन से उसकी सेवा करने लगा। (आदर्श, 55)

सेवा कर—"to serve"

मिसेज़ सक्सेना ने निराश होकर कहा—महाशय जयराम, आपने मेरे साथ बड़ा अन्याय किया है और मैं इसे क्षमा न करूंगी। आप लोगों ने इस बात का आज नया परिचय दे दिया कि पुरुषों के अधीन स्त्रियां अपने देश की सेवा भी नहीं कर सकतीं। (सम, 67)

ग्राम सेवा कर—"to perform services for, to work for"

"ग्राम सेवक, शिक्षक, ग्रामोद्योग कुशल, स्वास्थ्य रक्षक और गाँव की पूरी सफाई रखने में समर्थ होगा, तो वह समग्र ग्राम-सेवा कर सकेगा।" (स्वस्थ, 22)

सेवा कर—"to serve (others), to perform services for (others)"

इस कथा का तात्पर्य यह है कि सच्चा लोक-सेवक वह है जो दूसरों की सेव करके उनका उद्धार करे और कभी उसका श्रेय न ले। (कथा, 58)

की सेवा कर—"to serve"

चूंकि हमारी सरकार उन सब लोगों के कुल योग से बनी है जिनकी सेवा वह करती है इसलिए इस देश के वास्तविक स्वरूप का निर्धारण ये बातें ही करेंगी कि हमारी निजी पसन्द क्या है ? हम व्यक्तिगत रूप से किन प्रतियोगिताओं में सम्मिलित होते हैं। (अमरीका, 47)

की बड़ी सेवा कर—"to do a great service to, to serve a cause"

यदि तुम समझकर विरोध करते हो तो निस्संदेह तुम समाज और साहित्य की बड़ी सेवा कर रहे हो, किन्तु समझकर, यह याद रहे। (सन्यासी, 7)

समाज सेवा करने वाला—"worker, volunteer"

पहले समाज सेवा करने वाले सब निःशुल्क कार्य ही किया करते थे और जो समाज सेवा करने के लिए वेतन लेता था उसे सेवक नहीं समझा जाता था। (कल्याण, 15)

सेवा कर—"to do (something), to work on (something)"

धृष्टता क्षमा हो तो मैं कुछ सेवा करने का अवसर चाहता हूं। (चारु, 20)

की सेवा कर—"to serve"

एक भंगी स्वच्छता करके, कृषक अन्न का उत्पादन करके, बुनकर वस्त्र बुनकर, शिक्षक

पढ़ाकर प्रशासन की सेवा करते हैं। इसी प्रकार जो कोई भी परमात्मा की सेवा करना चाहते हैं उन्हें भगवान के चरणों में अपनी सेवा समर्पित करने का अधिकार है। (भक्ति, 13)

सेवा कर—"to stake one's life in the service of"

मुझे हत्याओं से घृणा है, पर स्वदेश से प्रेम है। इसलिए स्वत: प्राण देकर उसकी सेवा करूंगा, स्वयं किसी पर तलवार न उठाऊंगा। (काल, 96)

की सेवा कर—"to serve"

नायक का कर्तव्य प्रजा की सेवा करना, उसके सुख दुखों का ख्याल रखना और उसकी रक्षा करना मानती है। केवल मानना ही नहीं बल्कि इस जिम्मेदारी का अक्षरश: पालन भी करती है। (शबरी, 30)

की सेवा कर—"to serve, to entertain"

हम पुरुष लोग मल्लविद्या और व्यायाम-कौशल से लोगों का मनोरंजन करते हैं और हमारी स्त्रियां नाच-गाकर बड़े लोगों की सेवा करती हैं। (चारु, 319)

की सेवा कर—"to serve"

इनका काम नाच-गान के द्वारा देवता की सेवा करना था। (चारु, 279)

सेवा कर—"to greatly serve, to serve the cause of"

रूस में देश की बड़ी सेवा करती रही। (बुन, 15)

7. **सेवा-इलाज कर—"to treat someone, to take care of someone"**

उसने कहा—यहां एक छोटा सा पागलखाना है। एक साधु उनकी सेवा-इलाज वगैरा करते हैं। (बूंद, 241)

8. **सेवा-शुश्रूषा कर—"to attend to"**

इस जीव को देखते हो। पहचान सकते हो! यह मल्लिका है जो धीरे धीरे बड़ी हो रही है और मां के स्थान पर अब मैं इसकी सेवा-शुश्रूषा करती हूं। (आषाढ़, 97)

की सेवा-शुश्रूषा कर—"to attend to the needs of"

कहीं बस्ती में कोई बीमार पड़ा हो तो पता लगते ही तुरन्त उस झोपड़ी के पास पहुंच जाती है उसकी सेवा-शुश्रूषा भी करती है और चिकित्सा का प्रबन्ध भी। (शबरी, 101)

9. **सेवा-पूजा कर—"to worship"**

उसने अपनी दादी को, मां को यहां घंटों बैठकर सेवा-पूजा करते हुए या कथा पुराण सुनते हुए देखा है। (बूंद, 166)

10. सेवा-टहल कर—"to perform the duties or chores of"

उसका काम था, महिला-आश्रम में महिलाओं की सेवा-टहल करना; पर महिलायें उसकी सूरत से कांपती थीं। (सम, 44)

11. सेवा-कार्य कर—"to do volunteer work"

हमारे मंडल में चरित्र पर बड़ा ध्यान रखा जाता है। बाईस वर्ष हो गए मुझको यह सेवा-कार्य करते हुए मैं आपसे कहता हूं चन्द्रमा में कलंक है परन्तु हमारी चन्द्रमुखियां निष्कलंक हैं। (बूंद, 505)

सेवा-कार्य कर—"to do volunteer work"

नील कोठी का काम तुम्हारे योग्य नहीं है। मिस्टर स्मिथ यहां पर अपने पिछले थोड़े-से दिन शांति से सेवा-कार्य करते हुए बिता लेंगे, और तुम से दूर भी न रहेंगे। (तितली, 249)

111. व्याख्या, स्पष्टीकरण, स्पष्ट, खुलासा, साफ

1. व्याख्या (lit. an instance of speaking or discoursing on something in a manner that is understandable or comprehensible) applies to any statement (set forth in intelligible or familiar language or terms) which embodies an exposition, interpretation or characterization of the meaning or purport of something not immediately plain or explicit (such as a term, a concept, an utterance of some principle or dogma). The term may also be applied to the rendition of the meaning of a concept in the light (or on the basis) of a chosen dogma, principle or one's own belief.

स्पष्टीकरण specifically applies to the act of someone who is trying to explain or is offering an explanation (such as by giving reasons or causes) for his own or someone else's conduct in order to clarify or make it (i.e., something said or done by the person himself or by someone else) acceptable to another.

स्पष्ट (lit. that which is clear, plain or evident) applies to anything said or done (such as by restating one's position on a particular issue, offering an explanation for one's conduct or the like) by someone in order to enhance or affirm the understanding of something in the mind of another. The term may also be used in referring to something which serves to explicate (or enhance the effect of) the meaning or the sense of some utterance.

खुलासा describes the words used by someone or applies to anything that serves as a clue in order to simplify for another something difficult or complex for him to comprehend or understand.

साफ (lit. clear or clean) is a general term referring to anything done or said by someone in order to clarify or clear up another person's confusion or misunderstanding about something (implying an effort to remove that which obstructs one's judgement or unnecessarily entangles the matter at hand).

2. व्याख्या, स्पष्टीकरण and खुलासा are +process, and the rest are – process. व्याख्या forms ANP with की, and both स्पष्टीकरण and खुलासा with का. Of these three nouns only व्याख्या takes plural.

3. की व्याख्या कर—"to render an exposition of"

व्यवहार के प्रसंग में बुद्धि, भौतिक सत्य की एक प्रकार से बाह्य और सीमित व्याख्या कर सकती है, किन्तु सार्वभौम सत्य से अपरिचित होने के कारण वह पथप्रदर्शन कराने में लंगड़ी हो जाती है। (धर्म, 78)

की व्याख्या कर—"to formulate a definition of"

लेकिन उसे इस विषय में सावधान रहना चाहिए कि लोकतंत्र की व्याख्या करते समय उसे आज की आवश्यकताओं को ध्यान में रखना है। (अमरीका, 5)

की व्याख्या कर—"to expound upon, to speak on the subject of"

...भौतिकवाद की व्याख्या करते हुए यह स्पष्ट कहा था कि वस्तुसत्य को धारणा द्वारा नहीं वरन् सक्रियता द्वारा हृदयगम करना चाहिए। (मूल्य, 116)

की व्याख्या कर—"to interpret"

इनकी व्याख्या वे यों करते थे कहानी का आदि वह है जिसके पहले कुछ न हो बाद में मध्य हो, मध्य वह है जिसके पहले आदि हो बाद में अंत हो, अंत उसे कहते हैं जिसके पहले मध्य हो बाद में रद्दी की टोकरी हो। (सूरज, 19)

की व्याख्या कर—"to explain the profundities of"

बृहदारण्यकोपनिषद के मैत्रेयी ब्राह्मण में महर्षि याज्ञवल्क्य ने अपनी पत्नी मैत्रेयी को प्रेमतत्त्व की व्याख्या करके समझाया है। यह सारा ब्राह्मण इसी [illegible] का निरूपण है। (नैतिक, 27)

की व्याख्या कर—"to explain the meaning of"

धीर शर्मा ने श्लोक की व्याख्या करते-करते एक छोटा-सा व्याख्यान ही दे डाला। (चारु, 97)

की व्याख्या कर—"to explain the nature of"

पूर्व इसके कि प्रचलित धारणानुसार समाज कल्याण की व्याख्या की जाए, यह जान लेना आवश्यक है कि इस शब्द तथा इस विषय का विकास कैसे हुआ। (कल्याण, 14)

की व्याख्या कर—"to explain the intent of"

ज्ञानवती गुरुकुल में बारह वर्ष की शिक्षा पूर्ण कर चुकी थी। उसने संस्कृत और वैदिक साहित्य का यथेष्ट ज्ञान प्राप्त किया था। वह महाभाष्य और निरुक्त की व्याख्या कर सकती थी। शरीर उसका गुरुकुल के कठिन जीवन से दुबला और रूखा जान पड़ता था। परन्तु वह स्वस्थ थी। (फूलो, 87)

की व्याख्या कर—"to render a distorted exposition of, to give a distorted account of"

नये सृजन में सहायक न होकर उसे कुण्ठित कर डालता है, पुरानी परम्पराओं को नये रूप में विकसित न करके उनके प्रति गलत दृष्टिकोण बना लेता है, इतिहास की विकृत व्याख्यायें करने लगता है...(मूल्य, 144)

की संकीर्ण व्याख्या कर—"to give a narrow definition of, to define narrowly"

हां, संस्कृति की संकीर्ण व्याख्या करने वाले कुछ विद्वानों ने रूढ़ संस्कारों के कारण ही उसे संकुचित सीमा में आबद्ध करने का प्रयास किया है।

4. **का स्पष्टीकरण कर—"to explain"**

क्या गर्धभिल्ल इतना अशक्त और स्वाभिमान से हीन है कि उस अहंकारी आचार्य के समक्ष अपने शील और चरित्र का स्पष्टीकरण कर गया। (यादव, 205)

का स्पष्टीकरण कर—"to explain the significance of"

इसका नाम सूरज का सातवां घोड़ा क्यों रखा गया इसका स्पष्टीकरण भी अंत में मैंने कर दिया है। (सूरज, 21)

5. **स्पष्ट कर—"to elucidate"**

स्वरों में वार्तालाप की-सी विविधता हो। वाणी के साथ-साथ हाथों से संकेत और चेहरे पर भावाभिनय द्वारा वार्ता और पद्य के अर्थ को और भी स्पष्ट किया जाय। मतलब यह कि सूत्रधार और वाचिकाएं अनुभवी और सिद्धहस्त अभिनेता अभिनेत्री ही होने चाहिएं। (कोणार्क, 86)

स्पष्ट कर—"to state clearly"

भारतीय संस्कृति की व्यापकता और विशालता के परिचायक औपनिषदिक यह स्पष्ट करते हैं कि भारतीय संस्कृति केवल भारतीयों के लिए ही नहीं...(धर्म, 32)

स्पष्ट कर—"to define"

यदि हम इस जिज्ञासा की उपेक्षा न करें, निरर्थक उलझनों से मुक्त करके इसको स्पष्ट करें। (चमत्कार, 56)

स्पष्ट कर—"to make clear, to disclose"

इतना ही नहीं। मैं अब इसलिए चिंतित हूं कि अपना और तुम्हारा संबन्ध स्पष्ट कर दूं। (तितली, 77)

स्पष्ट कर दे—"to dispel, to put an end to"

और मेरी स्वतंत्र स्थिति इन प्रवादों को स्वयं ही स्पष्ट कर देगी। (तितली, 78)

स्पष्ट कर दे—"to make (something) clear"

अंत में यह भी स्पष्ट कर देना चाहता हूं कि इस लघु उपन्यास की विषय-वस्तु में जो कुछ भी भलाई-बुराई हो उसका जिम्मा मुझ पर नहीं माणिक मुल्ला पर ही है। मैंने सिर्फ अपने ढंग से वह कथा आपके सामने प्रस्तुत कर दी है। अब आप माणिक मुल्ला और उनकी कथाकृति के बारे में अपनी राय बनाने के लिए स्वतन्त्र हैं। (सूरज, 114)

स्पष्ट कर दे—"to clarify, to explicate"

तृतीय अंक का अंतिम दृश्य, जिसमें मूर्ति धराशायी होती है रंगमंच की दृष्टि से अधिक स्पष्ट कर दिया गया है। (कोणार्क, 8)

स्पष्ट कर—"to clarify (a situation), to explain (one's predicament)"

अपनी परिस्थिति को स्पष्ट करते हुए उसने अखबारों में अपना वक्तव्य दिया, साथ ही मुहल्ले वालों का विश्वास प्राप्त करने के उपाय सोचने लगा। (बंद, 9)

6. **का खुलासा कर—"to clarify, to elucidate"**

साइंस एक दिन जरूर इसका खुलासा करेगी। या तो इस धारणा को मजबूत बनायेगी—या फिर सदा के लिए खत्म कर देगी। (बूंद, 231)

7. **साफ कर—"to clear up"**

मिस सुरतोब ने आग्रह किया।—मुआमले को साफ करने के लिए उनका आप लोगों के सामने आना जरूरी है। (सम, 56)

साफ कर—"to clarify, to clear (someone's mind of)"

सज्जन ने विचारमग्न होते हुए कहा—तुम्हारी बात ने मेरा मन बेहद साफ किया है,

मैं तुम्हारा बड़ा शुक्रगुजार हूं दोस्त। मगर—मगर क्या तुम यह नहीं मानते कि हर व्यक्ति को लेकर कुछ ऐसी भी बातें हैं जो अलग-अलग लोगों के जीवन में अलग-अलग किस्म के एक्सिडेंट्स बनकर आती हैं। (बूंद, 427-28)

112. निर्णय, निश्चय, निश्चित, सुनिश्चित, निस्तारा, निपटारा, फैसला, तय

1. निर्णय, निश्चय, निश्चित, सुनिश्चित, निस्तारा, निपटारा, फैसला and तय all refer to the mental or intellectual processes involving the exercise of one's judgement in order to come to a conclusion, arrive at a choice or solution about something, or to make up one's mind about some future course of action. The terms equally apply to the results of such mental or intellectual processes.

निर्णय involves a reference to any determinative criteria or basis (such as a consideration of the facts or the pros and cons of the matter, contrast and comparison with other similar or different objects, appeal to authority or one's knowledge and experience or the like) which leads one to form a conclusive judgement. Alternatively the term may be used to make a reference to any method of determination which enables one to come to a conclusion or which forms the basis of one's conclusion. It specifically excludes any reference to one's personal preference or choice.

This term, therefore, refers to the act of deciding something definitely and firmly as well as to the result of such an act. In the former sense it is either applied to the subject's act itself or in making a reference to anything (by using the appropriate noun as the subject in the sentence) which in the speaker's opinion acts or serves to determine the attributes or the character of the object of निर्णय कर. In the latter sense it is solely used to refer to some sort of pronouncement about a matter by the speaker.

निश्चय describes the act of decision making as well as a decision made by someone (such as by making up one's mind to do something or about something) including the exercise or one's personal preference or choice (sometimes even one's whims). The term may also be used to make a reference to the attributes or qualities of a thing which, in the opinion of the speaker, serve to make up or give to it a particular character.

निश्चित applies to anything about which one makes sure or certain with another person or in one's own mind. The term also makes a reference to someone's formulation (such as a description or an account of something given by someone) which serves to fix the character or the scope of something. In the latter sense the term is usually accompanied by expressions referring to the subject's choice of a particular or specific way of rendering such a formulation.

सुनिश्चित is taking steps (such as by defining, delimiting or formulating) to set or fix the limit, scope or the character of something in a manner that is appropriate, proper or called for.

निस्तारा describes the act of settling or resolving some matter finally by resorting to any means which could enable one to discriminate facts from fiction or truth from falsehood or to ascertain the truth or falsehood of something.

निपटारा (निबटारा) applies strictly to the act of disposing of any matter (i.e., treating or handling something with the result of finishing or finishing with) such as by settling a dispute, taking care of some business or the like.

फैसला is applied to any judgement, conclusion or decision made by someone, or to anything done by the subject that serves to settle some matter finally. By itself the term contains no reference to any basis or method of determination used by the subject or to the subject's personal preference or choice.

तय is applied to anything that one decides, intends or sets out to do as if it were a limit or a goal set by one for oneself, fixed for one by another, or fixed by one with another (usually for oneself and the other person as well).

2. The nouns निश्चय, निस्तारा, निपटारा and फैसला are +process, निर्णय is ±process, and the rest of the expressions are −process. Both निश्चय and फैसला form ANP with का and पर, and the rest with का only. Only निर्णय, निश्चय and फैसला can be pluralized.

3. **का निर्णय कर—"to determine"**

उसके बाद भेड़ की लगभग आयु और उसकी उपयोगिता का निर्णय करने के लिए यह बात देखी जाती है कि उसके पहले दो दांत और बाद के पक्के दांत कितने घिसे हैं। दांतों की बनावट में परिवर्तन से भेड़ की आयु का अन्दाजा हो जाता है। (भेड़, 21)

का निर्णय कर—"to pass a judgement on"

अकेला खेतों में घूमता क्यारी-क्यारी फिरता, बूढ़ा गंगासिंह सोचता अब वह बाजार

में खड़े होकर झूठ सच का निर्णय नहीं किया करेगा, झूठे को झूठा नहीं कहा करेगा, सच्चे को सच्चा नहीं जतलायेगा। (दुग्गल, 121)

का निर्णय कर—"to settle (such as a question)"

जब एक सर्वसम्मत परिभाषा बन जाएगी, तब इस बात का निर्णय कि कौन कार्य समाज कल्याण में पड़ते हैं, परिभाषा से किया जाएगा। (कल्याण, 19)

का निर्णय कर—"to decide"

अब वह वक्त आ गया है कि हम खुद को और दुनिया को यह बता दें कि इस राष्ट्र के भविष्य का निर्णय सड़क के बदमाश और रात के लुटेरे नहीं करेंगे। (अमरीका, 25)

का निर्णय कर—"to take a decision on"

महीपाल पर मान-हानि का मुकदमा चलाने अथवा न चलाने का अंतिम निर्णय भी वह वहां से लौटने पर ही करेगा। (बूंद, 565)

का निर्णय कर—"to judge"

दंतुल : तो राजपुरुष के अपराध का निर्णय ग्रामवासी करेंगे ! ग्रामीण युवक, अपराध और न्याय का शब्दार्थ भी जानते हो ? कालिदास : शब्द और अर्थ राजपुरुषों की सम्पत्ति हैं, यह जानकर आश्चर्य हुआ। (आषाढ़, 18)

का निर्णय कर—"to determine, to decide on"

उन्हें छिपा रखने से साबित हो गया कि वह सत्यासत्य का निर्णय नहीं करना चाहता, केवल जनता को प्रसन्न करने के लिए नित्य गालियां बकता जाता है। (सेवा, 276)

निर्णय कर—"to make a decision, to rightly exercise one's judgement"

बुद्धि के समक्ष जब तक संशय न रखा जाय उसे निर्णय करने का अवसर ही नहीं मिलता। (धर्म, 121)

निर्णय कर—"to determine"

वह भी नहीं मानी, तो "टास" से निर्णय करने का फैसला हुआ। टास किया और वह हार गयीं। (परिन्दे, 29)

निर्णय कर—"to come to a decision"

नहीं, नहीं दलीप सिंह अवश्य मर गया। सुमन्तपुरी अवश्य कोई दूसरा आदमी है। निर्णय कर लेने पर भी मानसिंह निश्चय नहीं कर पा रहा था, और निश्चय कर लेने पर वह दृढ़ नहीं हो पा रहा था, और न स्मृतिपटल पर से घटनायें टल रही थीं। (कचनार, 199)

निर्णय कर—"to deliberate on, to engage in argumentation as to..."

इनमें से कौन सत्य है कौन मिथ्या यह निर्णय करना हमारा उद्देश्य नहीं, यहाँ पर केवल यह संकेत किया जा रहा है कि...(मूल्य, 109-10)

निर्णय कर—"to act as determinant of, to predetermine"

हमारी शिक्षा, पठन क्षेत्र, प्रकृति जीवन के प्रति हमारा दृष्टिकोण आदि निर्णय करते हैं कि हमारा मन किस ओर झुकेगा। परन्तु विचार से अच्छी पुस्तकों के अध्ययन से हम इस झुकाव को यदि वह बुरा है बदल सकते हैं। (चमत्कार, 35)

4. **का निश्चय कर—"to serve to determine, to make up"**

कुरूप या बेपढ़ी-लिखी बड़े आदमी की बेटी का छोटे परिवार में विवाह हो जाने से लड़की की सामाजिक स्थिति गिर जाती है। परन्तु सामाजिक स्थिति का निश्चय करने वाले कारण देशकाल के अंतर से बदलते रहते हैं। (भारत, 74)

का निश्चय कर—"to persist in one's decision to"

...शायद ही कोई एक अंगरेज ऐसा होगा, जिसने बहुत थोड़े समय के अन्दर अपनी विशाल पूंजी सहित इंगलिस्तान लौट जाने का निश्चय न कर रखा हो।(सुन्दर, 225)

पर निश्चय कर—"to make a decision about, to conclude, to come to a conclusion about"

इसलिए परीक्षा करके तब किसी विषय पर निश्चय करना चाहिए। (भारक, 55-56)

निश्चय कर—"to ascertain, to determine with certainty, to find out for a certainty"

प्रभु से एक बार इसका जिक्र करके निश्चय कर दीजिएगा। (शांतला, 51)

निश्चय कर—"to decide"

एक दिन देवताओं ने आपस में सभा करके निश्चय किया कि ऐसे महात्मा को वरदान देकर पुरस्कृत करना चाहिए। (कथा, 54)

निश्चय कर—"to follow one's convictions"

मनुष्य अपनी कामना के अनुसार विचार करता है और विचार के अनुकूल ही निश्चय करता है। (धर्म, 57)

निश्चय कर—"to be satisfied, to be convinced"

वाट्सन भी चुपचाप होकर सोच रहे थे। उन्होंने कहा—मैंने कागज पत्र देखकर निश्चय कर लिया है कि शेरकोट पर तुम्हारा स्वत्व है। (तितली, 237)

निश्चय कर ले—"to decide"

और उसी क्षण मैंने अचानक निश्चय कर लिया ... उस रात जब मैं सोने लगा, तो लग रहा था मानो एक भारी बोझ दिल से हट गया है। (परिन्दे, 53)

निश्चय कर—"to come to a decision"

तुम्हारा पत्र मिला है। सोचती हूं कि चलो, हो ही आऊं कुछ दिन पहाड़ पर, मगर कुछ निश्चय नहीं कर पाती हूं। यों अभी सोचने और निश्चय करने के लिए काफी समय भी तो है। (नदी, 87)

निश्चय कर ले—"to make a decision"

मैंने एक साथ कई निश्चय कर लिये। वह बात समाप्त हो गयी। माँ बहुत रोयीं-धोयीं पर मान लेंगी ऐसा विश्वास है। (नदी, 76)

निश्चय कर—"to make sure, to find out for certain"

उस समय मैंने सुना कि वह मुझे पुकार रहे हैं पर जब तक में यह निश्चय कर सकं कि वह कहाँ है उन्हें निर्दयी लहरों ने ग्रस लिया। (सेवा, 256)

5. **निश्चित कर—"to determine"**

लोचमान मिट्टी के संयोगशीलता के गुण को निश्चित करता है। (ईंट, 16)

निश्चित कर—"to fix"

मूल रूप में कल्याण राज्य एक समुदाय है जहाँ कि राज्यशक्ति को आय के एक अधिक समान वितरण को प्राप्त करने के लिए जान-बूझ कर प्रयोग किया जाता है और इसी प्रकार प्रत्येक नागरिक के लिए, उसके कार्य और उसकी सम्पत्ति के बाजार भाव का विचार न करते हुए एक बुनियादी न्यूनतम वास्तविक आय निश्चित की जाती है। (भारत, 3)

निश्चित कर—"to establish"

...अच्छी किस्म की ईंटे तैयार करने वाली मिट्टियों के प्रतिमान निश्चित किये गये हैं। इन परखों से अब यह संभव हो गया है कि मिट्टियों में उपस्थित अवगुणों का पता लग सके। (ईंट, 14)

से निश्चित कर—"to fix, to establish"

मुद्रा के रूप में विभिन्न व्यक्तियों का पारिश्रमिक सरलता से निश्चित कर दिया जाता है तथा इसका अग्रिम भुगतान भी संभव होता है। (एमाई, 46)

निश्चित करना पड़—"to be determined"

उत्पादन अनेक व्यक्तियों द्वारा संयुक्त रूप से किया जाता है। प्रत्येक के लिए अलग-अलग विधि से पारिश्रमिक निश्चित करना पड़ता है। (एमाई, 46)

निश्चित कर—"to decide on"

वनकन्या ने चार-पाँच चीजें निश्चित कीं जिसे उपस्थित स्त्रियों को सुनाया। (बूंद, 396)

निश्चित कर—"to arrange with someone to do something"

सज्जन सुबह जब इस मंदिर में आया था तभी लंच के लिए यह जगह कन्या से निश्चित कर गया था। (बूंद, 316)

निश्चित कर दे—"to determine"

1948 में देश की नई उद्योग नीति में सरकार ने राष्ट्रीय हित की दृष्टि से उद्योगों के योजनाबद्ध विकास और नियंत्रण की पूरी जिम्मेदारी राज्य की मान ली है। निजी उद्योगों का एक विशेष क्षेत्र निश्चित कर दिया गया है। (भारत, 36)

निश्चित कर—"to determine"

फिर भी यह एक आविष्कार था, जो किसी विलक्षण बुद्धि वाले व्यक्ति ने, जिसे हर समय वस्तुओं के पारस्परिक विनिमय-अनुपात निश्चित करने की असुविधा उठानी पड़ती थी सम्पन्न किया। (एमाई, 14)

निश्चित कर दे—"to establish"

किसी विलक्षण बुद्धि वाले व्यक्ति की समझ में यह आया कि कोई एक प्रधान वस्तु निश्चित कर दें और फिर अन्य वस्तुओं व सेवाओं के मूल्य इसके आधार पर नियत कर दिए जाएं तो वस्तु विनिमय की अनेक कठिनाइयां समाप्त हो जाएं। (एमाई, 13)

निश्चित कर—"to decide"

बरसाना में उन्होंने लंच करना निश्चित किया था। ऊंची पहाड़ी पर स्थित श्रीराधा जी के विशाल और सुंदर मंदिर में पहली मंजिल पर छज्जे के पास बनी हुई चबूतरी पर दोनों अपना टिफिन कैरियर खोलकर बैठे थे। (बूंद, 316)

निश्चित कर—"to establish"

अतः राजनीतिक दृष्टिकोण से राष्ट्रीय रंगमंच की रूपरेखा निश्चित नहीं की जा सकती, नहीं की जानी चाहिए। (कोणार्क, 93)

निश्चित कर—"to determine"

राष्ट्र और समाज, संस्कृतिक्षेत्र के नेता और शासन, सभी को परम्परा, परिस्थिति और उपकरणों को ध्यान में रखते हुए नये रंगमंच की रूपरेखा निश्चित करनी है, और जहां तक सम्भव हो उस निश्चित योजना के अनुसार साधन एकत्र कर रंगमंच के आन्दोलन को चलाना है। (कोणार्क, 102)

निश्चित कर—"to determine"

हां, मुद्रा के संदर्भ में वस्तुओं के मूल्य अवश्य निश्चित किये जाते हैं। (एमाई, 79)

निश्चित कर—"to decide on"

विवाह का समस्त प्रबन्ध निश्चित किया गया। महीपाल की जल्दी के कारण सज्जन भी उठा। कन्या हवेली की ओर चली गई। उसकी पाठशाला अभी चल ही रही थी। (बूंद, 529)

निश्चित कर—"to establish, to determine"

दूसरी ओर साम्यवादी देशों में व्यक्ति के आर्थिक कार्यों पर अधिक से अधिक रोक-टोक होती है अर्थात् अधिकांश सम्पत्ति पर राष्ट्र का अधिकार होता है और राज्य व्यक्ति की आर्थिक क्रियाओं का प्रतिमान निश्चित करता है तथा धन का स्वयं वितरण करता है।

निश्चित कर—"to be determined"

पूंजीवादी अर्थ-व्यवस्था में समस्त वस्तुओं व सेवाओं के मूल्य मुद्रा में बताये जाते हैं और इन मौद्रिक मूल्यों के आधार पर यह निश्चित किया जाता है कि कौन-कौन सी वस्तु उत्पन्न की जायें...(एमाई, 46)

6. सुनिश्चित कर—"to determine"

राज्य काम की न्यायोचित तथा मानवोचित दशाओं को सुनिश्चित करने के लिए प्रसूति की सहायता के लिए व्यवस्था करेगा। (भारत, 10)

7. का निस्तारा कर—"to get to the truth of the matter"

बनवारी लाल ने फिर झूठ-सच का निस्तारा करने को भाई से पूछा—सरदारी लाल, यह तेरी ब्याही परणायी है, तू ही जी पर हाथ रख कह दे कि यह सब झूठ है। (मित्रो, 8)

8. का निबटारा कर—"to settle (a quarrel)"

इसका कारण यह है कि अगर लोग शिकायत और विवाद का निबटारा अपने आप ही करने लगेंगे तो सभी की स्वतन्त्रता खतरे में पड़ जायेगी। (अमरीका, 93)

का निपटारा कर—"to settle, to decide on, to take care of (a problem)"

वेणी माधव के हाथ में कापी थी। दुखमोचन लेने लगे तो रोक कर उसने कहा—नहीं दुखन, पहले इस बात का निपटारा कर दो! वह काम तो खैर होगा ही...(दुख, 47)

का निपटारा कर—"to dispose of, to take care of"

अपने सारे कार्यों का निपटारा करके उन्होंने मुंह में दो पान दबाए और बड़े सन्तोष से चबाने लगे। (घनु, 53-54)

का निपटारा कर—"to settle a dispute"

...राजकृष्ण ने मेरे आंकड़ों के आधार पर ही झगड़े का निपटारा किया है...(आकाश, 83)

पर निपटारा कर—" to punish, to take care of"

ठहरो, इन आदमियों से उस सवाल पर मैं खुद निपटारा किये लेता हूं। (नीलम, 31)

निपटारा कर—"to settle"

अच्छा न आवें, इस काम से छुट्टी मिली तो एक बार मैं स्वयं जाऊंगा और सदा के लिए निपटारा कर जाऊंगा। (सेवा, 333)

9. **का फैसला कर—"to settle a duel, to test each other's strength"**

यदि दो पहलवान अपनी शक्ति का फैसला करना चाहें तो उन्हें एक ही अखाड़े में लड़ना होगा। दोनों अगर अलग-अलग अखाड़े में ताल ठोंकते रहे तो उससे बल परीक्षा हो नहीं सकती। (प्रतिमा, 8)

का फैसला कर—"to settle (a dispute)"

कहीं पारस्परिक झगड़ा होता हो तो उस झगड़े का फैसला करती है और दोनों पक्ष वालों को समझाती है। (शबरी, 30)

का फैसला कर—"to come to a decision about"

इसमें तनिक भी सन्देह नहीं कि अगर मेरे पूज्य पिताजी ने मेरी शादी न करने का फैसला, बिना मुझसे पूछे ही कर लिया होता...(कहा, 8)

पर फैसला कर—"to base one's judgement on, to rule on"

क्षमा देवी कुछ कानून जानती थीं। बोलीं—मैजिस्ट्रेट पुलिस के बयान पर फैसला करेगा। मैं ऐसे कितने ही मुकदमे देख चुकी। (सम, 5)

पर फैसला कर—"to judge someone (on the basis of)"

जयराम ने उसी नम्र आग्रह के साथ कहा—आप मेरे पिछले रेकार्ड पर फैसला कर

रही हैं। आप भूलती जाती हैं कि आदमी की अवस्था के साथ उसकी उद्दण्डता घटती जाती है। (सम, 66)

फैसला कर—"to not be able to decide"

तेज़ आ रही मोटर ने जग्गू को बचाने की कोशिश की, किन्तु जिस ओर मोटर हुई जग्गू उसी ओर हो गया। ऐसे जैसे गड़बड़ा कर आदमी फैसला नहीं कर पाता। (दुग्गल, 60)

फैसला कर ले—"to make one's mind up, to make a decision"

—कोई भूला-भटका सा क्षण आता है, जब मन फैसला कर लेता है। (परिन्दे, 63)

एकतरफी फैसला कर—"to settle unilaterally, to decide arbitrarily"

मिस खुरशेद ने आग्रह किया—मुआमले को साफ करने के लिए उनका आप लोगों के सामने आना जरूरी है। एकतरफी फैसला आप क्यों करती हैं। (सम, 56)

दो टूक फैसला कर—"to settle once and for all"

क्यों न वह सदैव के लिए इस मानसिक यन्त्रणा की समाप्ति कर दे—नरेन्द्र की भांति दो-टूक फैसला करे! (धारा, 200)

10. तय कर—"to decide, to resolve, to be sure about"

वह अनिश्चित सा उसकी ओर देखने लगा मानो तय न कर पा रहा हो कि वह किस बात से ज्यादा प्रसन्न होगी। उसके जाने से या न जाने से। (वे दिन, 41)

तय कर—"to decide, to fix"

18 नवम्बर, 1962 का वह दिन, चीनियों ने तय किया था कि वे शाम की चाय चुशूल में बैठकर पियेंगे। (परम, 31)

तय कर—"to come to a decision"

मुझे जरूर एक न एक हुनर सीख लेना चाहिए, जैसे कि ज्यादा लोग सीखते हैं। अब जार ने मंत्रियों से सलाह कर यह तय किया कि जार के लड़के के लिए किमखाब का काम सीखना सबसे अच्छा होगा। (रूस, 9)

तय कर—"to make up one's mind"

सब कुछ सोच-समझकर सतीश ने तय किया कि वह किसी बीमा कम्पनी की ऐजन्सी ले लेगा। (तुला, 91)

तय कर—"to come to a conclusion"

अन्त में उसने तय किया, 'कलावती के सामने कायदे का ही बर्ताव किया होता तो अच्छा होता। वह ललिता सरीखी सुलभ नहीं है।' (कचनार, 210)

तय कर—"to decide"

हमने तय किया कि महात्मा जी जब गोष्ठी वाले कमरे के बाहर निकलें तब अचानक लपक कर पावन चरण-स्पर्श किया जाये। (अपनी खबर, 120)

तय कर—"to arrange"

वह अपनी मां से साफ-साफ यह नहीं कह सकता था कि उनके द्वारा तय किये गये किसी रिश्ते को वह पसन्द नहीं कर सकता। तीन बरस बाद मुंह पर रेखें फूट आने पर वह सोचने लगा कि मां द्वारा पसन्द की गई सुंदर से सुंदर लड़की भी...(बूंद, 87)

तय कर—"to decide to"

उन्हें रुपयों की जरूरत हुई तो यह तय किया कि छोटा भाई घर पर रहेगा और बड़ा भाई जावेगा शहर और कुछ रोजगार धंधा करके घर रुपये भेजेगा। (रूस, 1)

तय कर—"to decide (mutually), to agree (among themselves)"

बहरहाल बड़े मियां, जुम्मन और बरीदी ने मिलकर यह तय किया कि कादिर को, चाहे कुछ भी हो, घर लौटाकर ले जाया जायगा। (तुला, 25)

तय कर—"to come to a decision"

मन में यह तय करके वह भाग रहे व्यक्ति के पीछे दौड़ पड़ा। (लाख, 254)

तय कर—"to decide to"

इसलिए तथा नेपथ्य के स्वरों की अव्यवहारिकता के कारण, मैंने यह तय किया कि सूत्रधार उसके साथ दो वाचिकाओं को उपक्रम और उपसंहार के पात्रों का रूप दिया जाए। (कोणार्क, 9)

तय कर—"to decide, to settle, to take care of"

पांचवीं गुप्त मीटिंग हड़ताल के लिए आखिरी बातें तय करने के लिये की जानी थी। मिल से छुट्टी होते ही शाहिद को कहा गया कि ग्वालटोली के चार साथियों...को खबर दे आये। (फूलों, 51)

तय कर—"to make a decision, to decide on"

कन्या को यह महसूस हुआ कि स्त्रियों की गतिविधि पर सहसा पुलिस बन्धन का

प्रभाव बड़ा बुरा पड़ा। महिला पुलिस को बुलाने की बात आखिरी वक्त पर तै की गई थी। (बूंद, 395)

तय कर—"to decide to"

इस समय सज्जन को 'अपनी', पर महीपाल को 'अपनी' की धुन फिर चढ़ आई। उसके बार-बार इसरार करने पर भी महीपाल ने अकेले ही रिक्शे पर जाना तै किया। (बूंद, 536)

तय कर—"to fix, to determine, to settle"

समस्त साधनों के पुरस्कार मुद्रा में ही तय किये और चुकाये जाते हैं। (एमाई, 51)

तय कर—"to arrive at a decision, to think of a course of action"

शीघ्र ही वह कुछ तय कर लेगी, और बिलकुल नहीं ही कर सकी तो फिर भुवन दा को बुला भेजेगी। (नदी, 75)

तय कर—"to resolve"

उसके बारे में मैं कभी तय नहीं कर पाता कि वह मुझे अच्छी लगती है या बुरी लगती है, वह बू नहीं है, महज एक हल्का सा रंग है जो बाबा के कमरे की हवा में तिरता रहता है। (परिन्दे, 80)

तय कर—"to decide, to resolve"

जब मुसाफिर नहीं होती तब मेहमान होती हूं—और दोनों में कौन अधिक उखड़ा है यह कभी तय नहीं कर पायी। (नदी, 32)

तय कर ले—"to make one's mind up"

और अब तो मैंने तय कर लिया है कि कभी तो मैं अपने बच्चों की ससुराल इस पागलखाने को बनने दूं। (थान, 45)

तय कर ले—"to decide, to determine"

...और तय कर लिया कि किवाड़ के आगे लगे सामान के ढेर के कारण इधर-उधर न जा सकने पर भी खिड़की के रास्ते घुस सकेगा,... (नदी, 12)

तय कर ले—"to decide"

हमने तय कर लिया था कि विवाह के बाद कुछ दिनों तक मैं और नीरजा एक मित्र के घर रहेंगे। नीरजा अपने पिता को एक पत्र में सब कुछ विस्तारपूर्वक लिख देगी। (परिन्दे, 56)

तय कर ले—"to come to a decision"

एकाएक कल्याणी के सामने खड़े होकर महीपाल बोला—बस, मैंने तय कर लिया है—शिवचरण दुबे के लड़के से बात पक्की किये लेता हूं। उनके विचार और कर्म दोनों अच्छे हैं, उनका लड़का भी बड़ा सुशील है, एन्जीनीयरिंग पास करेगा इस साल। क्या समझीं। (बूंद, 106)

तय कर ले—"to make up one's mind"

क्योंकि पिछली रात उसने मार्क्सवाद के सवाल पर मुझे नीचा दिखाया था और सच्चे संकीर्ण मार्क्सवादियों की तरह मैं झल्ला उठा था और मैंने तय कर लिया था कि वह सही बात भी कहेगा तो मैं उसका विरोध करूंगा। (सूरज, 52)

तय कर ले—"to come to a decision"

वह घर पर पद्मसिंह के साथ भोजन करने बैठता तो निश्चय कर लेता था कि आज इस विषय को छेड़कर तै कर लूंगा, पर उसका इरादा कभी पूरा न होता, उसके मुंह से बात ही न निकलती। (सेवा, 294)

तय कर ले—"to come to a conclusion"

और इन दो दिनों तक मेरे दिल पर क्या-क्या बीती है, इसका अंदाज तुम्हें भी नहीं है। पर मैंने यह तय कर लिया है, कर्नल, कल्याणी से मेरा समझौता नहीं हो सकता। देखो—। देखो-वेखो कुछ नहीं। (बूंद, 274)

तय कर ले—"to make up one's mind"

मेरा भी खुदा है। मैंने तो यह तय कर लिया है, भीख मांगूंगी तो उन्हीं के साथ और तख्त पर बैठूंगी तो उन्हीं के साथ। (खत, 38)

तय कर ले—"to make up one's mind"

उससे वह काफी हद तक शांत, गंभीर और संतुलित हो गई थी। कन्या ने एक तरह से मन-ही-मन यह तय सा कर लिया था कि उसे कभी अपने ही समान संस्कारी, सिद्धांत-वादी पुरुष मिल गया तो वह विवाह कर लेगी। (बूंद, 201)

तय कर ले—"to settle"

हम लोग मिल-जुलकर सारे मामले को तय कर लें तो दोनों ही लाभ में रहेंगे। (आदर्श, 63)

तय कर ले—"to make up one's mind"

माफ करना अब्बा मैंने कहा इसीलिए मैं यहां से घर नहीं जाना चाहती, नहीं जाऊंगी। मैंने तय कर लिया है। (खत, 62)

से तय कर—"to fix, to arrange"

शकुंतला का ब्याह शिवचरण दूबे के लड़के से तय करूंगी। (बूंद, 107)

से तय कर—"to arrange"

कुंतल: पहले मेरी शादी पिताजी ने कहीं एक दूसरे लड़के से तय की थी। सुन्दरम्—तो—कुंतल: विवाह की तारीख भी निश्चित हो गयी फिर... (रात, 40)

से तय कर दे—"to arrange"

नि—वह पुरुष कोई भी हो सकता था? कु—हां, वह पुरुष कोई भी हो सकता था—कोई भी, जिससे लड़की के मां-बाप शादी तय कर दें। (रात, 73)

तय कर दे—"to fix"

राष्ट्रीय अभियान की सीमाएं तय कर दी थीं। (मूल्य, 84)

113. निर्वाह, वहन, गुजारा, गुजर

1. निर्वाह, वहन, गुजारा and गुजर all apply to situations in which one persists in a course of action or way of life, in spite of adverse or unsatisfactory circumstances.

निर्वाह refers particularly to the perseverance of someone who persists in the face of adverse circumstance or who endures hardship without complaint.

वहन is used when someone bears with difficult circumstances, when such endurance arises out of necessity (rather than by choice of the person involved) or is an inevitable outcome of a situation which the subject accepts.

Both गुजारा and गुजर make reference to the continuation of someone's action or state which he carries on in, or of some state of affairs. गुजारा generally refers to circumstances persisting over a long period of time (such as a chosen way of life or a permanent disposition). गुजर applies to any single condition or circumstance through which one goes or to one's act of resorting to any temporary measure or means of subsisting, usually under unforseen circumstances or conditions, which are not going to last very long.

2. All the nouns are +process, and do not admit plural. **निर्वाह** forms ANP with के साथ, पर and का, **वहन** with **का,** गुजारा with में and गुजर with पर.

3. **के साथ निर्वाह कर—"to live with"**

परसराम एक अशिक्षित और फूहड़ लड़की के साथ निर्वाह करने की कल्पना से पागल-सा हो गया... (भंवर, 28)

पर निर्वाह कर—"to subsist on"

भेड़ें खेतों और चरागाहों पर निर्वाह करती हैं और वहां से वे आंतरिक परजीवियों को ले लेती हैं। सबसे कष्टदायक कीड़े वे होते हैं, जो भेड़ के पेट के चौथे भाग में अपना घर बनाते हैं। (भेड़, 53)

पर निर्वाह कर—"to maintain oneself"

बस, यही उसका खेत है जिस पर वह सब्जियां पैदा कर अपना निर्वाह कर लेता है। (राजवि, 23)

का निर्वाह कर—"to have to fulfill (a duty)"

मुझे पुत्र धर्म का निर्वाह करना है। मातृ भक्ति, जो मुझमें सच्ची थी कृत्रिम होती जा रही है। क्यों ? इसी खींचा-तानी से। अच्छा तो मैं क्यों इतना पतित होता जा रहा हूं। (तितली, 110)

का निर्वाह कर—"to fulfill all expectations"

मलिका : यह क्या आवश्यक है कि तुम उन सब अपेक्षाओं का निर्वाह करो ? (आषाढ़, 47)

का निर्वाह कर—"to abide by"

वस्तुतः मानवीय गरिमा के प्रति संवेदनाजन्य अंतरात्मा की पुनः प्रतिष्ठा का एक वेदनापूर्ण दायित्व है जिसका निर्वाह हमें प्रतिक्षण करना पड़ता है। वे ही अर्थवान क्षण हैं, आत्मोपलब्धि के क्षण हैं, आत्मोपलब्धि के—क्योंकि उन्हीं में हम अपने को पाते हैं—अर्थात् अर्थहीन शून्यता अयथार्थमूलक अनस्तित्व से मुक्त कर अपने को सार्थक पाते हैं। (मूल्य, 35)

का निर्वाह कर जा—"to endure, to carry on"

वह नई परिस्थिति होगी और मुझे विश्वास है कि मैं भली प्रकार उसका निर्वाह कर जाऊंगी। (सुहाग, 138)

का निर्वाह कर—"to carry through, to fill"

लोकनायक श्री जवाहरलाल नेहरू के निधन के बाद राष्ट्र में जो स्थान रिक्त हुआ उसका आपने जिस असाधारण योग्यता तथा अपूर्व क्षमता के साथ निर्वाह किया वह सदैव स्मरणीय रहेगा। (आज, 1)

का निर्वाह कर—"to maintain properly"

सारे जिले और तहसीलें सड़कों से जोड़ दी गई हैं।...सड़कें पक्की और उत्तम हैं और इनका अच्छा निर्वाह किया जा रहा है। (लोक, 3)

का निर्वाह कर—"to hold out, to endure"

मैं आपसे कोई सहायता नहीं चाहती, केवल एक सुरक्षित स्थान चाहती हूं, चक्की पीसूंगी, कपड़े सीऊंगी, और किसी तरह अपना निर्वाह कर लूंगी। (सेवा, 129)

निर्वाह कर—"to make a living"

...भूरे खां एक मामूली देहाती, जो सब्जी और आम बेचकर निर्वाह करता है। (डगर, 44)

निर्वाह कर—"to hold out"

वाट्सन हतबुद्धि होकर चुप हो गये। शैला ने तितली को ईर्ष्या से देखा। यह गंवार लड़की ! अपनी वास्तविक स्थिति में कितनी सरलता से निर्वाह कर रही है। (तितली, 236)

जीवन-निर्वाह कर—"to support oneself, to maintain"

अभी मेरी बैरिस्टरी अच्छी तरह नहीं चलती, तो भी कई महीनों में सादगी से जीवन-निर्वाह करने के लिए मैं रुपये जुटा लेता हूं। (तितली, 193)

4. का वहन कर—"to carry on"

उसका कृश शरीर पीला मुख और मन्दगति देखकर अनुमान होता है कि उसका स्वास्थ्य बिगड़ा हुआ है, और इस भार का वहन करना उसे कष्टप्रद है। (सम, 25)

वहन कर—"to bear"

अपने यथार्थ को वहन करते हुए, निरन्तर बदलते परिवेश को देखते हुए, लिखने का प्रयास ही मेरा प्रयास है। (मांस, 9)

वहन कर—"to bear"

यदि मैं चित्रकार होता तो कल्पना का सारा भार तूलिका को वहन करना पड़ता। (डगर, 38)

वहन कर—"to bear under a load"

चूंकि पानी उसका भार वहन करता चला गया, इसलिए उनका आकार बढ़ता ही चला गया। (समुद्र, 108)

वहन कर—"to bear with"

बेचारे बड़े परेशान थे। कहते थे कि मेरे पैरों में तो जैसे भौरी पड़ गई है। नाहक बेचारों को बड़े-बड़े भत्तों का बिल बनाने की तकलीफ उठानी पड़ती और उनके पैसों का बोझ वहन करना पड़ता। (वनु, 52)

वहन कर—"to be engaged in the conduct of life"

तभी उसने जीवन को विभिन्न स्तरों पर वहन करने वाले, उससे सम्पृक्त केन्द्रीय पात्रों की तलाश की थी—यथार्थ की तलाश की थी, जिसकी साक्षी हैं वे कहानियां, जो इस दौर में लिखी गयीं। (मांस, 7)

5. **में गुजारा कर—"to live within (one's means)"**

उसे आयलमैन की मजदूरी में ही गुजारा करना पड़ता था। (फूलो, 51)

गुजारा कर—"to live on"

कबूतर—मैं तो, कन-कन बीन कर गुजारा करता हूं। तो भी लोग मेरी घात में लगे रहते हैं। (बाल, 11-12)

गुजारा कर—"to maintain, to live (in poverty)"

इतिहास में उसने कई खलीफाओं और बादशाहों का जिक्र पढ़ा था जो स्वयं गरीबी में गुजारा करके इन्साफ करते थे। (फूलो, 48)

6. **पर गुजर कर—"to live off (the land)"**

गांव में थोड़ी-सी जमीन थी, उसी पर गुजर करते थे। (बाल, 11-36)

गुजर कर—"to do without"

यह भी मुश्किल है, वह भी मुश्किल है। सर झुकाएं गुजर करें क्योंकर। (खत, 52)

गुजर कर—"to maintain oneself on"

रात भर तुम अपने दोनों कम्बल उसे उढ़ाते हो और आप सिगड़ी के सहारे गुजर

करते हो। उसके बदले आप पहरा देते हो, अपने सूखे लकड़ी के तख्तों पर उसे सुलाते हो, आप कीचड़ में पड़े रहते हो। (दीपाली, 79-80)

गुजर कर—"to make a living from"

उफ़! कितनी शक्ति का अपव्यय हो रहा है। (रिपोर्ट निकालकर) ओह। 50 लाख आदमी केवल भिक्षा मांगकर गुजर करते हैं। (सम, 19)

गुजर कर—"to live"

इस कारण उनका बड़ा परिवार बढ़ई सरदार जी के बड़े परिवार की बनिस्बत ज्यादा जगह में आराम से गुजर करता था। (बूंद, 8)

114. अर्पण, आत्मार्पण, अर्पित, समर्पण, आत्मसमर्पण, समर्पित, प्रदान, दान, भेंट, नजर, अदायगी, अदा

1. The expressions in this group are used to describe the manner in which someone gives away or gives up something, or relinquishes his hold over it for a variety of reasons. The terms are applied both figuratively as well as literally.

अर्पण describes the act of consigning (such as by making over, by uttering appropriate words or by performing a ritual) the desert (usually earned by performing a sacred rite, reading or reciting a sacred text or the like) by one person to another (whether living or deceased) in order to bring emancipation to the latter.

The term also stresses the solemnity with which one commits one self (such as by engaging in constantly and continuously with full awareness) to the attainment of a sacred goal or objective.

आत्मार्पण stresses the spirited disposition or devotion in one who gives oneself over (such as by abandoning or surrendering) absolutely to another or to a cause.

अर्पित makes reference to the object (usually something tangible) which passes from one person to another, or describes the solemnity with which someone accepts the consequence of his dedication or devotion to a sacred cause.

समर्पण stresses the completeness and thoroughness in the act of one who gives himself up or unflinchingly gives away something for a cause or to another person.

आत्मसमर्पण makes reference to the notion of acquiescence or resignation in one's act of giving oneself up (as may be called for in a given situation) voluntarily or when under pressure.

समर्पित makes reference to the result of one's act of giving oneself up or giving away something by specifying the manner of giving or naming something given.

प्रदान either makes reference to a cause (i.e., something which produces an effect), by using the appropriate noun in the subject spot in the sentence, in order to describe the effects it brings about (by using the appropriate expressions in the object spot), or may refer to the act of a superior who gives something (such as a gift, a title, a degree or the like) in a wide variety of ways to someone.

दान (lit. the act of giving or the thing given to another) is a term reserved for referring to any act of gratuitous giving (such as in charity, or for a religious or humanitarian cause).

भेंट refers to the act of presenting or handing over something concrete to a superior in his esteem or as a token or mark of one's respect for him. In contexts where no such reference is intended or implied, the term may refer to the giving away of something to anyone with the intention of gaining his favor.

नजर applies to the act of bringing something (usually of appreciable value) in the presence or before someone usually with the intention of presenting it (sometimes giving it away without anything in return) to him.

अदायगी makes reference to the payment of dues in order to meet an obligation or to fulfill a promise or commitment made to someone.

अदा refers to the act of paying back in money, services or the like in order to discharge an obligation incurred by one or in order to compensate someone else for his services.

2. आत्मार्पण, प्रदान, दान, भेंट and अदायगी are ±process, and rest of the expressions are -- process only. आत्मार्पण forms ANP with पर, प्रदान with का, दान with का, and both भेंट and अदायगी with की. All the +process expressions do not take plural.

3. अर्पण कर दे—"to dedicate"

समाप्ति के बाद उसका फल दादी के निमित्त अर्पण कर देतीं, ताकि दादी की जान आसानी से निकल जाए। (लड़की, 6)

अर्पण कर—"to dedicate, to consign"

...मानव जीवन की अंतिम विजय (अहंकार का हनन) तो तभी सम्भव है जब मनुष्य पूर्णरूप से अपने सम्पूर्ण जीवन को अभ्यास के हेतु अर्पण कर दे। (धर्म, 125)

अर्पण कर—"to consign"

दीया किया और उसके कान के पास मुंह करके बड़ी श्रद्धा के साथ न सिर्फ गीता का सत्तरहवां अध्याय बल्कि महात्तम भी पढ़ा और उसका पुरा फल दादी के निमित्त अर्पण किया। (लड़की, 36)

4. पर आत्मार्पण कर—"to dedicate oneself, to give oneself over to"

जो सच्चे हृदय से परमात्मा पर आत्मार्पण करते हैं उनके कुशल-मंगल की जिम्मेदारी परमात्मा स्वयं अपने ऊपर लेते हैं। (शांतला, 104)

5. अर्पित कर—"to offer, to present"

उन गुंडों को ऐसा कुचल दिया जावे कि वे फिर सिर न उठा सकें। गांव वालों को उनकी गायें लौटा दी जायें और उन गुंडों से एक सौ मुहरें जुर्माना वसूल करके प्रभु को अर्पित कर दी जायं। (शांतला, 5)

अर्पित कर—"to commit oneself to, to dedicate oneself"

उस दायित्व को ग्रहण करने की चेतना, उसके प्रति अपने को अर्पित करने की आस्था लगभग उन सभी कवियों में है...(मूल्य, 178)

श्रद्धाञ्जलि अर्पित कर—"to eulogize"

इस अवसर पर देश के उच्चतम अधिकारियों और नेताओं ने उन्हें श्रद्धाञ्जलि अर्पित की। (परम, 34)

अर्पित कर—"to commit (power) to someone, to entrust someone with"

विष्णु : किन्तु मैंने आज अपना पद इस युवक को अर्पित कर दिया है। (कोणार्क, 49)

अर्पित कर—"to make an offering of"

नर ने गर्व के साथ अपनी रची हुई सृष्टि नारी को अर्पित कर दी। (बूंद, 139)

अर्पण, आत्मार्पण, अर्पित, समर्पण, आत्मसमर्पण, समर्पित, प्रदान, दान, भेंट, नजर, अदायगी, अदा

अर्पित कर—"to make an offering"

वीर्य के प्रतीक के रूप में दही चढ़ाया गया, फूलहार आदि अर्पित किए गए। एक ब्राह्मण ने भाषा के मंत्र पढ़ने आरंभ किए। (बूंद, 479)

6. **समर्पण कर—"to sacrifice oneself, to give up one's life"**

यदि उसे कोई चिन्ता हो तो मैं उस चिन्ता को दूर करने के लिए अपने प्राण तक समर्पण कर दूंगा। (सेवा, 213)

समर्पण कर—"to give oneself over"

वे दोनों एक दूसरे के निकट आए, निकट आते रहे, आते रहे, और उनका द्वैत नष्ट होकर वे एक दूसरे में समा गए—जैसे लता वृक्ष से लिपट जाती है—जैसे सरिता सागर में अपना समर्पण कर देती है। और चाँदनी खिलती रही,...और समुद्र गर्जन करता रहा। (धनु, 156)

समर्पण कर—"to sacrifice everything for"

ऐसे पति के लिए तो वह पत्नी सब समय अपने सर्वस्व का समर्पण करने के लिए तैयार रहती है। (धनु, 181)

समर्पण कर—"to surrender, to yield"

किसी भी अधिनायकवादी आतंक के सम्मुख समर्पण कर दे। (मूल्य, 177)

7. **आत्मसमर्पण कर—"to consecrate oneself to"**

भगवान् को परिपूर्ण रूप से आत्मसमर्पण किए बिना यह बुद्धि नहीं आती। (चारु, 226)

8. **समर्पित कर—"to hand over, to pass on"**

जिस प्रकार ईश्वर की दी हुई वस्तु जब समाज रूपी नारायण को समर्पित कर दी जाती है उसका यथाधिकार बंटवारा कर दिया जाता है तब सभी लोग सुखी रहते हैं। (वैदिक, 3)

समर्पित कर—"to give oneself over"

पति की मृत्यु के बाद उसने अपने को पूर्णरूपेण समर्पित कर दिया—समाज-सेवा के लिए। (दीर्घ, 16)

समर्पित कर—"to present"

सबने उनकी रचना की सराहना भी की। इससे उत्साहित होकर वे उसे गांधी जी के कर-कमलों में समर्पित करने उनके पास पहुंचे। (आदर्श, 99-100)

समर्पित कर—"to surrender oneself to, to yield to"

सज्जन ने उसकी बातों से यह अनुमान भी किया, अपने पति के प्रति तीव्र घृणा होने के कारण ही वह अनजाने पुरुषों को देह समर्पित कर मानो पति से गुप्त बदला लेती है। (बूंद, 516)

9. **का प्रदान कर—"to give"**

जैसे कोई परम कारुणिक चिकित्सक किसी कुपथ्यप्रिय, अदीर्घदर्शी अबोध शिशु को उसके अभीष्ट कुपथ्य रूप में दिव्य महौषध प्रदान करता है। (सुधा, 5)

प्रदान कर—"to give to, to bring about"

वही बात जो कि एक व्यक्ति को प्रसन्नता प्रदान करती है दूसरे को असह्य वेदना का कारण हो जाती है। संकट को स्वेच्छा से बर्दाश्त करने का अभ्यास डालना जहां संकट को कठोर नहीं रहने देता, वहां चरित्र को भी उच्च करता है। (चमत्कार, 34)

प्रदान कर—"to grant"

हे जिनेश, ये दोनों तुम्हारी पुत्रियां हैं! मां शारदा, इन बच्चों को धैर्य तथा कंठ-श्री प्रदान करके उबारो! (शांतला, 65)

प्रदान कर—"to bestow upon"

सृजन का क्षण वस्तुतः इस रिक्तता, विघटन और विच्छिन्नता के क्षण से बिल्कुल पृथक् होता है। उसमें हम क्षण को एक संगति, एक अर्थ, एक क्रम प्रदान करते हैं। (मूल्य, 35)

प्रदान कर—"to confer upon"

उसके गुसाईं हो जाने के कारण सागर राज्य को उसे जागीर प्रदान करने में बाधा नहीं होगी और भोंसले का कृपा पात्र होने के कारण भोंसले उसको स्वीकार करने में आनाकानी नहीं करेगा। (कचनार, 233)

प्रदान कर—"to bring about, to give"

मुद्रा धन अथवा पूंजी के विभिन्न रूपों को एक सामान्य रूप और तरलता प्रदान करती है। (एमाई, 75)

प्रदान कर—"to give"

मैजिस्ट्रेट जो कठोर-से-कठोर दंड प्रदान करे, उसका स्वागत करूंगी। अब मैं पुलिस के किसी आक्षेप या असत्य आरोपण का प्रतिवाद न करूंगी; क्योंकि मैं जानती हूं, मैं जेल के बाहर रहकर जो कुछ कर सकती हूं, जेल के अन्दर रहकर उससे कहीं ज्यादा कर सकती हूं। (सम, 17)

प्रदान कर—"to bestow upon"

नररत्न, हम तुम्हारे कर्मों पर मुग्ध होकर तुम्हें कोई वरदान देना चाहते हैं; बोलो क्या चाहते हो ? मांगो तो हम तुम्हें ऐसी शक्ति प्रदान करना चाहते हैं कि तुम्हारे स्पर्शमात्र से बड़े-बड़े रोगी चंगे हो जाएं। (कथा, 54)

प्रदान कर—"to accord"

...और कभी (युरोपीय चिन्तन ने) मनुष्य को मूलत: बर्बर असंस्कृत पशु मानकर उसकी पाशविक अचेतन वृत्तियों को ही सर्वोपरि मान्यता प्रदान की। (मूल्य, 29)

प्रदान कर—"to supply"

जब पौधे भूमि में दबा दिये जाते हैं, तो सड़कर सम्पूर्ण पोषक तत्त्वों को घुलनशील तथा उपलब्ध दशा में भूमि को प्रदान कर देते हैं। (खाद, 57)

प्रदान कर—"to give"

उन्होंने इस समस्या को हल करने के लिए तीन सुझाव दिये हैं। पहला यह कि विकासोन्मुख देश खाद्यान्न उत्पादन को सर्वोच्च प्राथमिकता प्रदान करें। जिन देशों में खाद्यान्नों का अभाव है वे परिवार नियोजन कार्यक्रमों पर विशेष ध्यान दें। (आज, 3)

प्रदान कर—"to grant"

उसी डाक में बंगलौर से पत्र आया कि उसका थीसिस स्वीकृत हुआ है और डाक्टरेट प्रदान करने का अनुमोदन किया गया है, अगले कनवोकेशन में उसे डिगरी मिल जायेगी। (नदी, 77)

प्रदान कर—"to grant"

अल्प आय वर्ग गृह निर्माण योजना के अंतर्गत 3480 गृहों के निर्माण के लिए ऋण प्रदान किये जायेंगे। (लोक, 17)

प्रदान कर—"to accord"

महाराज ने उसे रथ का आदर भी प्रदान किया। (फूलो, 32)

प्रदान कर—"to make something available, to provide"

संक्षेप में, श्रम विभाजन को बढ़ावा देकर, पूंजी का संचय संभव बनाकर, इसकी गतिशीलता में वृद्धि करके,...मूल्य-समंत्र के द्वारा भावी मांग का अनुमान प्रदान करके, मुद्रा ने उत्पादन में आश्चर्यजनक वृद्धि ला दी है। (एमाई, 51)

प्रदान कर—"to impart"

संघर्ष के इन लम्बे वर्षों ने इस पुरानी मान्यता को नयी अर्थवत्ता प्रदान की है कि

कोई भी मनुष्य या समुदाय या राष्ट्र किसी द्वीप की भांति कट कर अलग-अलग नहीं रह सकता। (अमरीका, 78)

प्रदान कर—"to afford"

संयुक्त स्वरूप आवश्यकता की समस्त वस्तुओं व सुविधाओं का अवसर प्रदान करता है। (ग्रामीण, 41)

10. **दान कर—"to give away (one's daughter in marriage)"**

कन्या का दान करे वह पिता कहां है ? उनकी अनुमति कहां है। (जय, 112)

दान कर—"to offer"

...कि उसे कार्त्तिक-भर सुबह गंगा नहाकर चंडी देवी को पीले फूल और ब्राह्मणों को चना जौ और सोने का दान करना चाहिए। (सूरज, 41)

दान कर—"to make a sacrifice of"

वह ईश्वर राक्षस है, वह खुदा शैतान है, जिसके नाम पर हिंसा की अग्नि में स्नेह का दान किया जाय। (होली, 39)

दान करते समय—"in giving"

कला में अमीर और गरीब का भेद नहीं है, पूजा-भावना में द्वेष नहीं है, जीवन के स्नेह को दान करते समय भेद-बुद्धि नहीं है। (अमीर, 57)

दान कर—"to give away"

स्वाभाविक अभिभावक को...नाबालिग की जायदाद के किसी भाग को गिरवी रखने, बेचने, खर्च करने या दान कर देने का अधिकार नहीं होगा। (भारत, 51)

11. **भेंट कर—"to hand over, to present"**

किसी की कोई चीज़ किसी रजवाड़े के मन भा जाती, उसे वह उनकी भेंट करनी होती थी। (दुग्गल, 13)

को भेंट कर दे—"to offer (to give), to dedicate, to surrender to"

बोल, देवी का कोप दूर करना चाहता है तो अभी प्रतिज्ञा कर कि लोभ और मोह छोड़कर सब कुछ अतुल पराक्रम महाराज सात वाहन को भेंट कर देगा। (चारू, 368)

की भेंट कर—"to present to"

यूनानियों की किताबों से यह भी पता चलता है कि चन्द्रगुप्त ने सेल्यूकस की लड़की के साथ शादी कर ली। इस सबके बदले में चन्द्रगुप्त ने पाँच सौ हाथी सेल्यूकस को भेंट

किए और सेल्यूकस ने अफगानिस्तान की सरहद को पार कर अपने देश का रास्ता लिया। (सुन्दर, 27)

को भेंट कर—"to make an offering"

तक्षशिला-नरेश ने उसी समय सिकंदर को लाखों रुपये की सम्पत्ति भेंट करके उसका यथोचित सत्कार किया। उसके बदले में सिकंदर ने तक्षशिला-नरेश को उससे दूनी सम्पत्ति देकर अपना बड़प्पन सिद्ध कर दिया। (आदर्श, 64)

भेंट कर—"to present"

एक बार किसी धनी भक्त ने स्वामी रामकृष्ण परमहंस को एक बहुत बढ़िया ऊनी दुशाला भेंट किया। स्वामी जी ऐसी चीज़ों के शौकीन तो थे नहीं, फिर भी प्रेमी भक्त के आग्रह से उसको लेकर लापरवाही से ओढ़ने-बिछाने लगे। (आदर्श, 94)

12. **की नजर कर—"to give"**

उसने सोचा, क्यों न यह कंगन सुमन बाई की नजर करूं। (सेवा, 104)

नज़र कर—"to give"

सच कहूं तो अपने उस विवाहोत्सव में महाराजाधिराज ने मुझे इतनी चीज़ें नज़र की थीं...(मुक्ता, 122)

नज़र कर दे—"to present"

बेहतर यह है कि मैं इसे जार को नज़र कर दूं। (रूस, 17)

13. **की अदायगी कर—"to pay dues"**

सभी राष्ट्रों को संयुक्त राष्ट्र संघ को अपने-अपने हिस्से के रुपये-पैसे की अदायगी करनी होगी। (अमरीका, 95)

14. **अदा कर—"to play an important part in something"**

किसी मिट्टी की रासायनिक और खनिज संरचना उससे बनी ईंटों के सूखने और पकाने सम्बन्धी गुण धर्मों पर काफी असर डालती है और पकी ईंटों के भौतिक और रासायनिक गुणों को निश्चित करने में महत्त्वपूर्ण भाग अदा करती है। (ईंट, 13)

अदा कर—"to thank, to be grateful"

मैं जनाब की इस हमदर्दी के लिये शुक्रिया अदा करने की इजाजत चाहता हूं। (तुला, 111)

अदा कर—"to play the role of"

उनसे पिटने का मुझे इतना डर था कि भरत तो भरत वह धमकाता तो मैं कमसिनी भूल दशरथ का पार्ट भी अदा करके रख देता रावण का भी ! (अपनी खबर, 30)

अदा कर—"to carry out"

अपनी जिम्मेदारी को सदियों तक अदा करने के बाद ही इंसान ने इस चेतना का दर्शन किया कि उसके समाज का एक छोटा अंश जबर्दस्ती उसका भाग्य विधायक बना हुआ है। (बूंद, 427)

अदा कर—"to pay back"

आप दोनों का प्रेम और विश्वास फिर लौट आवे और आपका वैवाहिक जीवन पूर्ण सुखी और आनंदमय हो जाए यही हमारे ऋण को अदा करने का एकमात्र उपाय है। (धनु, 189)

अदा कर—"to repay"

मैंने उसे जो दूध पिलाया था, उसे वह खून से अदा कर रहा था। (सम, 14)

115. सतर्क, सजग, सचेष्ट, सचेत, सावधान, होशियार

1. The expressions in this group refer to an induced state of mind in which someone (i.e., the object of the verb कर-) exercises care and caution, or is not remiss about the task at hand, something impending in the situation or the like. The terms are, therefore, used with कर- in situations when someone (by his act) or something serves to remind, inform or warn another person in a wide variety of ways to act with care and caution.

सतर्क stresses a disposition of caution and care usually exercised by one who having once suffered some mishap wants to avoid having a similar experience again.

सजग refers to an induced state of mind in which one displays one's keen sense of awareness (i.e., a state of heightened perception and ready comprehension and appreciation) of one's obligations or duties.

सचेष्ट implies a passage from the state of inaction or inactivity to one of active apprehension or continued watchfulness usually about the activities of another person.

सचेत stresses the regaining of consciousness or awareness by someone who has been prodded by another to abandon his ignorance, forgetfulness or inattention.

सावधान stresses the disposition of watchfulness in one who has been alerted or put on guard by someone else against another person's clandestine activity. The term may also be used to refer to something (such as an incident, event or the like) which serves to arouse this disposition of watchfulness in one.

होशियार stresses the notion of one's exercise of care and caution or state of steady watchfulness resulting from another person's having alerted one or having given one special information regarding a situation or problem in advance of one's confrontation with it. The term is also used to describe one's skill or dexterity in coping with a situation or a predicament, usually because of one's unusual ability to sense things which are not immediately obvious.

2. All the expressions in this group are—process.

3. **सतर्क कर दे—"to make someone cautious"**

सोई हुई आत्मा को जगाने के लिए हमारी भूलें एक प्रकार की दैविक यन्त्रणायें हैं, जो हमको सदा के लिए सतर्क कर देती हैं। (सेवा, 233)

4. **सजग कर—"to arouse one's sense of duty"**

व्यर्थ की भावुकता से चंचल हृदय को कर्त्तव्य के कोड़े से सजग करती महारानी हाथ की छांव देकर... (बेटी, 47)

5. **सचेष्ट कर—"to make someone aware, to arouse someone to awareness of"**

अत: वह कुमार कोणिक को सचेष्ट कर उठा और सावधान कर उठा उसे पितृवर की एक नई आस्था की ओर से। (दत्तक पुत्री, 130)

6. **सचेत कर—"to caution someone, to draw someone's attention to"**

एक बार उसने नर्गिस से गम व्यवहार न करने के लिये इशारे-इशारे मुझे सचेत भी किया था। (खत, 77)

को सचेत कर—"to warn someone"

शबरी ने उस अत्याचार को देख लुटेरा दल को सचेत किया कि वह खून खराबे को हरगिज सहन नहीं कर सकती है। शबरों ने सार्थवाहों का माल छीन लिया। (शबरी, 19)

सचेत कर—"to awaken someone"

पद्मसिंह इस मायाजाल को तोड़ना चाहते थे, वह उन भूली हुई आत्माओं को सचेत किया चाहते थे, वह उनको इस अज्ञानावस्था से मुक्त किया चाहते थे...(सेवा, 320)

को सचेत कर—"to awaken (someone's sense of responsibility)"

...उसकी दायित्व-भावना को सचेत करता है—संक्षेप में यदि वह उसे जीवन-प्रक्रिया के प्रति उद्‌बुद्‌ध करता है...(मूल्य, 152)

सचेत कर—"to draw someone's attention to"

सर कृष्ण ने अजित को हाथ से सचेत करते हुए कहा—"कुंवर साहब आप क्या सोच रहे हैं? लीजिए सिगरेट पीजिए।"—यह कहकर उन्होंने अपना सिगरेट केस अजित के सामने बढ़ा दिया। (तीन, 88)

7. सावधान कर दे—"to alert"

रूपा लुहार से घनिष्टता करके समय-समय पर उसके द्वारा रचे जा रहे षड्‌यंत्रों का पता उसने जिवा को देकर सावधान कर दिया था। (लाख, 241)

को सावधान कर—"to caution"

ईसा की 11वीं सदी में प्रसिद्ध मुसलमान इतिहास लेखक अलबेरूनी ने इतिहास कला पर बड़ी सुन्दर वैज्ञानिक विवेचना की है और इतिहास के विद्यार्थियों को सावधान किया है कि हर इतिहास लेखक की अपनी-अपनी स्वाभाविक प्रवृत्तियों से कितनी तरह की भ्रांतियां पैदा हो सकती हैं जिनसे बच सकना लेखक के लिए अत्यंत कठिन है। (सुन्दर, 1)

से सावधान कर—"to alert"

पत्र-लेखक ने उसको फिलिप से सावधान करते हुए लिखा था कि फारस के बादशाह ने आपको दवा के साथ विष देकर मारने का गुप्त षड्‌यंत्र किया है...(आदर्श, 31)

के प्रति सावधान कर—"to make someone mindful of"

दुख भी मनुष्य को उसके ध्येयों के प्रति सावधान करता रहता है। (धर्म, 131)

8. को होशियार कर दे—"to caution someone"

हालांकि गेटकीपर ने नंदो को होशियार कर दिया था कि बाबू की माली हालत घर को देखते हुए बहुत अच्छी नहीं मालूम देती, फिर भी नंदो को विश्वास न आया। (बूंद, 295)

होशियार कर दे—"to warn, to caution"

सज्जन अपने मन-दर-मन में बार-बार कन्या की देह को पाने के लिए उतावला हो

जाता है, और कन्या का व्यक्तित्व उसे सौ हाथ पहले ही से बा-अदब-बा मुलाहिज़ा होशियार कर देता है। (बूंद, 175)

होशियार कर—"to caution, to warn"

उसका होश जाग उठा था। उसका होश उसे होशियार कर रहा था कि तर्क से परे अपनी बहक में अब न डोले। (बूंद, 387)

116. निरूपण, निरूपित, निर्धारण, निर्धार, निर्धारित, प्रतिपादन, प्रतिपादित

1. निरूपण specifies the act of setting forth in words or applies to the use of some specific words or expressions in a manner such that the basic, essential or real form, character or outline of something abstract (such as a concept, principle, method or the like) is clearly set off against some background or in some context.

निरूपित applies to any particular form or character peremptorily imposed upon or assigned to something in some specific way, usually indicated or expressed in the sentence (such as by a legal decree or the like), in order to define, determine or delineate its scope, function or application.

निर्धारण applies to the act of laying down or setting up (such as by establishing authoritatively, prescribing, defining or the like) a principle, code or dogma, or the form, scope or outline of something by specifying, particularizing or enumerating the characteristics or the features of that thing. The term is also used to point out something (i.e., the subject of the sentence) which serves as a determinant of the specifics or particulars of something else (i.e., the object).

निर्धार applies to the act of making an advance determination of or fixing in one's mind the specific details of something, usually implying the subject's intention to control or regulate the course of events to come.

निर्धारित refers to any course of action, to an objective or to a mode of conduct which is laid down or determined peremptorily or stated in a manner such that the limits or scope of it precludes any contradiction or uncertainty.

प्रतिपादन is applied to anything (such as a statement or exposition of some principle, doctrine or a dogma) set forth or stated effectively and authoritatively by one who is seemingly or in fact the originator (and therefore viewed as the exponent or the proponent) of such a principle, doctrine or dogma. The term may be used in its extended meaning either to refer to any didactic discourse or doctrinal statement, or in order to make a reference to the erudite disposition of someone (i.e., the subject).

प्रतिपादित is used to make reference to someone who champions, advocates or sometimes gives the appearance of advocating a view. The term may also be applied to any discourse which, in the opinion of the speaker, purports to advocate or express some view (with distinct implication that the subject may not have intended to or in fact does not advocate such a thing).

2. The terms निरूपण, निर्धारण, निर्धार and प्रतिपादन are +process and form ANP with का. They are not pluralized. The rest of the expressions in this group are—process.

3. का निरूपण कर—"to characterize"

अर्थात् जैसे उपनिषदों में यह ब्रह्म नहीं है, नेति-नेति कहकर ब्रह्म के स्वरूप का निरूपण किया गया है उसी तरह उन कहानियों में यह प्रेम नहीं था यह भी प्रेम नहीं था, यह भी प्रेम नहीं था कहकर प्रेम की व्याख्या और सामाजिक जीवन में उसके स्थान का निरूपण किया गया था। (सूरज, 112)

निरूपण कर—"to formulate, to delineate (the form of)"

वे महानुभाव यदि तर्क के स्वरूप को ठीक-ठीक निरूपण कर सकें, तो उन्हें यह पता लग सकेगा कि धर्म तथा देवता पर तर्क कुछ काम कर सकता है या नहीं। (भक्ति सुधा, 41)

निरूपण कर—"to expound on, to describe"

आधुनिक संकट प्रकृति का निरूपण करते हुए यह स्पष्ट किया जा चुका है कि यह केवल आर्थिक राजनीतिक या सामाजिक संकट नहीं वरन् मानव जीवन के मौलिक प्रतिमानों का संकट है। (मूल्य, 101)

का निरूपण कर—"to set forth"

इस प्रकार भक्तिशास्त्र में जो द्वादश संख्या का महत्त्व है, उसी की परम्परा में गीता के बारहवें अध्याय को ही 'भक्तियोग' का निरूपण करने के लिए उपयुक्त चुना गया है। (भक्तियोग, 3)

4. **निरूपित कर—"to fix, to assign"**

...इसमें विनिमय के माध्यम का कार्य करने की शक्ति कानूनी रूप में निरूपित की गई होती है। (एमाई, 80)

5. **का निर्धारण कर—"to act as a determinant of, to determine"**

यह उपयोग सुविधा ही कार्यक्षमता, संतोष तथा रहन-सहन के स्तर का निर्धारण करती है। (ग्रामीण, 51)

का निर्धारण कर—"to state, to specify"

उक्त विवेचना के पश्चात् ग्रामीण समुदाय की अब हम नीचे लिखी विशेषताओं का निर्धारण कर सकते हैं जिनसे ग्रामीण समुदाय का अर्थ और भी स्पष्ट हो जायगा। (ग्रामीण, 25)

का निर्धारण कर—"to set up"

आज वे हमारे दाय की अंग हैं। राष्ट्रपति को चाहिए कि इस दाय में से अपने युग के अनुकूल लक्ष्यों का निर्धारण करे और मार्ग प्रदर्शन में इसकी सहायता ले। (अमरीका, 5)

निर्धारण कर—"to fix, to establish"

मानव-वृत्तियों की विकसनशील अनन्तता साहित्य में निरन्तर नूतन उत्थानों को जन्म देती रही है। साहित्य का नियंता किंवा आलोचक इन उत्थानों की गतिविधियों का निरीक्षण-परीक्षण कर उनके स्वरूप का निर्धारण करता है। (निबन्ध, 111)

का निर्धारण कर—"to determine"

चूंकि हमारी सरकार उन सब लोगों के कुल योग से बनी है जिनकी सेवा वह करती है इसलिए इस देश के वास्तविक स्वरूप का निर्धारण ये बातें ही करेंगी कि हमारी निजी पसन्द क्या है? (अमरीका, 47)

6. **का निर्धार कर—"to exercise one's faculty of forethought, to think about beforehand"**

वह सेनानायक ही क्या जो बहुत पहले से सब बातों का निर्धार न कर ले। (कचनार, 291)

7. **निर्धारित कर—"to lay down, to assert"**

अनुभूति के पश्चात् जिन पदार्थों को हम जीवन में मूल्यवान समझते हैं उनको आसानी से दूसरों के हित के लिए भी निर्धारित कर सकते हैं। (धर्म, 97)

निर्धारित कर ले—"to decide on"

मैं अब तक तो केवल वह दृश्य देख रहा था। किन्तु क्षण-भर में मैंने अपना कर्त्तव्य निर्धारित कर लिया। मैंने कहा—काले खां, भूलना मत, मेरा नाम है रामनाथ... (तितली, 58)

निर्धारित कर—"to fix"

तत्पश्चात् एक ऐसा संनियम बनाया जाय, जो कि मजदूरी की निम्नतम दरें निर्धारित कर दे और इससे कम पर कोई काम न करा सके। (एमाई, 57)

निर्धारित कर—"to lay down"

वह स्वयं ही खेल की नीति निर्धारित करता था और अन्य खिलाड़ी उसकी चापलूसी करते थे। (राह, 35)

निर्धारित कर—"to set up"

विश्व के विभिन्न समाज-शास्त्रियों ने ग्रामीण समुदाय को नगरीय समुदाय से अलग करने के कुछ मापदंड निर्धारित किये हैं।

निर्धारित कर—"to determine"

इसके विकास का ऐसा लक्ष्य निर्धारित किया गया था कि अक्टूबर सन् 1953 तक यह कार्यक्रम देश के समस्त ग्रामीण क्षेत्र में फैल जाय। (सामुदा, 16)

निर्धारित कर—"to fix, to determine"

भले ही उत्पादन के लक्ष्य कोई तानाशाह ही क्यों न निर्धारित करे देश के विभिन्न साधनों को तो इन उद्देश्यों की पूर्ति में उपयुक्त रीति से लगाना केवल एक मूल-तंत्र के आधार पर ही सम्भव हो सकता है... (एमाई, 49)

निर्धारित कर—"to determine"

क्यों न हमारा विवेक ही प्रगति की मर्यादा निर्धारित करे? (मूल्य, 108)

8. **का प्रतिपादन कर—"to set forth"**

जीवन की समस्त शक्ति लगाकर पहले क्षण एक सत्य का प्रतिपादन करता है परन्तु दूसरे ही क्षण पता चलता है कि वह जिस भूमि पर खड़ा था बिल्कुल कच्ची थी। वह केवल सन के छूछे गोले छोड़ रहा था। (दीपाली, 184)

का प्रतिपादन कर—"to preach"

एक चेतारामी संप्रदाय निकला उसने अजब मत का प्रतिपादन किया कि चतुर्मुखी

ब्रह्मा से इस्तीफा दिलवाकर उसके स्थान पर एकमुखी अल्ला और त्रिमुखी दत्तात्रेय दोनों को बिठलाया। (बूंद, 46)

का प्रतिपादन कर—"to harp on"

बुद्धि को पहले सत्य जिज्ञासा की प्रेरणा से शुद्ध कर लेने की भी आवश्यकता होती है, अन्यथा वह अपने ही मत का प्रतिपादन करती रहेगी और यदि कुछ ऐसे तर्कों और युक्तियों से प्रमाण भी प्रस्तुत करने में समर्थ हो, जो विपक्षी के मतों का खंडन करने में समर्थ हों तो भी उसके अन्दर शंका बनी ही रहती है। (धर्म, 86)

का प्रतिपादन कर—"to propound, to set forth"

वे कहते हैं कि स्वयं अनुग्रह करके अर्जुन को सम्पूर्ण रूप से आश्वस्त करने के लिए भगवान के जिस द्विभुज मानुषरूप का प्राकट्य हुआ बारहवें अध्याय में उसकी उपासना का प्रतिपादन किया गया है। (भक्तियोग, 4)

का प्रतिपादन कर—"to expound"

आप (ब्रह्म सत्य जगन्मिथ्या) के तत्व का प्रतिपादन करते हैं, संसार को मायावत् मानकर असार समझते हैं पर उसी संसार के एक श्रेष्ठ तत्व मानव के प्रति घोर उदासीन हैं। (धनु, 183)

प्रतिपादन कर—"to establish (by proof)"

विज्ञान के जितने भी भेद हैं, वह बस अंततोगत्वा किसी प्रकार की शक्ति का प्रतिपादन करते हैं...(नक्षत्र, 31)

9. प्रतिपादित कर—"to advocate"

नीत्शे ने ही पहली बार बड़े बल से यह प्रतिपादित किया कि वह मनुष्य जो आज है, जो वर्तमान है वह निरर्थक है। (मूल्य, 24)

प्रतिपादित कर—"to expound"

मार्क्स ने इसी तत्व को पहचाना था और उसने जो दर्शन प्रतिपादित किया उसने उसमें स्पष्ट रूप से यह कहा कि यह सारा दोष वस्तुतः इस व्यवस्था का है जिसमें वर्ग वैषम्य के कारण प्रत्येक मूल्य मिथ्या सिद्ध हो रहा है। (मूल्य, 28)

को प्रतिपादित कर—"to advocate"

स्पष्ट है कि नीत्शे का यह अवर्तमान् को प्रतिपादित करने वाला दर्शन सामान्य मानवीय गौरव का विरोधी था। (मूल्य, 25)

117. प्रमाद, ढील, गफलत, लापरवाही, कोताही

1. प्रमाद, ढील, गफलत, लापरवाही and कोताही all refer to the disposition of the subject to be careless or remiss in his actions, and implies some sort of criticism or reprobation on the part of the speaker of the sentence towards this negligence.

प्रमाद refers to a state of mind in which someone acts under an impulse, conducts himself without restraint, check or limitation, or is simply overly self-indulgent (as if he were drunken or intoxicated) without any regard or concern for the feelings of others, his own obligation or duties or the like. The term is, therefore, applied to any situation in which one overlooks something or is inadvertently unsolicitous, and it may, depending upon the gravity or seriousness of the situation, imply a degree of censure of the subject's act for his wantonness or his being unduly remissive.

ढील makes reference to the languid disposition of the subject or to the undue laxity or slackness of his conduct in dealing with a particular situation (implying more or less giving free reins to someone else).

गफलत is applied to situations in which one is remiss or negligent in the performance of one's work or duty, or misses responding to something or acts casually or lightheartedly as if one were not (mentally or otherwise) quite up to the situation.

लापरवाही is applied to any act characteristic of the subject's disposition of carelessness or negligence (usually implying that the subject should have exercised or should exercise a little more prudence, judgement or caution).

कोताही is applied to any act or situation in which a reference is desired to the fact that the subject did not put in enough effort or exercise enough care or caution in doing something (usually in order to produce a desired or expected result). The term may also be used in referring to any situation in which, according to the speaker's opinion, the subject exhibits a lack of care, concern or interest in applying himself to his task.

2. All the nouns are +process, and form ANP with में with the exception of कोताही which occurs with से or में. They are not pluralized. Only में permits the occurrence of infinitives before it.

3. में प्रमाद कर—"to be callous, careless"

रेखा ने गंभीर होकर माफी मांगी। सहसा उसे ध्यान हुआ भुवन को यों खींच लाने में भावुकता का कितना बड़ा प्रमाद उसने किया है। (नदी, 127)

में प्रमाद कर—"to be negligent"

स्वाध्याय, चिंतन एवं निदिध्यासन में कभी भी प्रमाद न करना चाहिए (धर्म, 131)

4. में ढील कर—"to be lax in, to be slack in"

अतः प्रकट है शिशु-कल्याण का वह कार्य प्रशासनिक तथा सामाजिक सहायता से सम्पन्न किया जाना आवश्यक हो जाता है, जिसके करने में या तो माता-पिता असमर्थ होते हैं अथवा ढील करते हैं। (कल्याण, 29)

5. में गफलत कर—"to be negligent"

क्योंकि सूझ का क्षण तो लड़ाकू लड़कियों की तरह होता है। वह निर्माण में गफलत करने पर गुस्सा होकर चला जाता है और फिर लौटकर नहीं आता। (अमीर, 29)

में गफलत कर—"to be remiss"

सच कहता हूं, अपना स्तर क्रमशः ऊंचा उठाने में मैं कभी गफलत न करता, अगर इस बार इन्होंने ही आगे बढ़कर मुझे न छेड़ा होता। (हास्य, 78)

6. में लापरवाही कर—"to be careless in, to be slovenly"

स्वतंत्रता के बाद भारत में स्वास्थ्य की स्थिति के बारे में छानबीन करने के लिए जो कमेटी बनाई गई थी उसने भी अपना मत व्यक्त करते हुए लिखा था कि इस पर विचार करने पर कि स्वच्छता के साधारण नियमों के अज्ञान या उनके व्यवहार में लापरवाही करने के कारण कितने अधिक रोग उत्पन्न होते हैं, यह पता चलेगा कि अकेले स्वास्थ्य शिक्षा पर व्यय की गयी धनराशि किसी भी कार्य पर किए गए व्यय से अधिक लाभदायक सिद्ध होगी। (स्वस्थ, V)

में लापरवाही कर—"to neglect to"

...इन दिनों तुम्हें खाने-पीने में लापरवाही नहीं करनी चाहिये—उसने कहा। (जलती झाड़ी, 150)

लापरवाही कर—"to be neglectful of (her health)"

तरह-तरह से उसने जुगनू को समझाया था कि वह अपनी सेहत की खातिर कहीं और चली जाय। जरूरत के लिए सौ पचास रुपये भी ले जाय, पर इस तरह लापरवाही न करे...... (मांस, 27)

लापरवाही कर जा—"to be careless (in handling)"

तस्वीरें उतारे जाते समय अनभिज्ञ दास कुछ लापरवाही कर गया। सज्जन ने फौरन ही बोझ को संभाला और दूसरे मजदूरों के बोझ को वह स्वयं ही उतारने लगा। (बूंद, 378)

7. में कोताही कर—"to shirk (work, an obligation)"

कभी-कभी इसमें स्वयं उसे काफी परिश्रम करना पड़ता, पर वह मानता था कि अध्यापन का श्रेष्ठ सम्बन्ध वही होता है जिसमें अध्यापक भी सीखता है और इस परिश्रम में कोताही नहीं करता था। (नदी, 62)

से कोताही कर—"to shirk from"

इस बात के नतीजे से वह खुद घबरा रहा था लेकिन खुदा के रूबरू वह अपने फर्ज से कोताही कैसे करता? (फूलो, 54)

118. अंगीकार, अंगीकृत, तस्लीम, कबूल, मंजूर, धारण, ग्रहण, अख्तियार, स्वीकार

1. These expressions make reference to the subject's disposition or attitude of acquiescence to a person, object, situation or value. Alternatively they may be used to describe the way in which someone or something takes on, assumes, acquires or develops a particular appearance, form, shape, characteristic or the like (usually implying that the subject is either predisposed to some kind of influence from without or is acting in acquiescence to it in a given situation).

अंगीकार refers to the act of taking something by free choice (such as by adopting an attitude or acceptance towards a person or a belief, or by acquiring a disposition of regarding someone or something as appropriate for oneself). The term also makes a reference to the subject's behavioral disposition in which he takes to doing something as if he were obligated by circumstances or committed to take such a course.

अंगीकृत emphasizes the result or the consequence upon the subject of his act (which is indicated by अंगीकार) of taking over or upon himself the duty, job or responsibility of another person.

तस्लीम applies to the act of giving another person an indication (verbal or otherwise) that one concurs with him in the truth of an allegation or that one consents to go along with a situation or something proposed by another.

कबूल applies to the act of verbally acknowledging the truth of an assertion or accepting an offer made by another person.

मंजूर applies to the act of assenting to something proposed by another or expressing one's willingness to go along with someone's request, demand or the like.

धारण describes a disposition of holding, maintaining or holding on to something, or refers to the act of taking on a specific appearance or form in a wide variety of ways. The term is equally applied to persons as well as things.

ग्रहण stresses the notion of positive acceptance of something (i.e., that which presents itself before one) in the subject or emphasizes reference to the subject's accustomed attitudes and moods in being receptive to the effects of environments around him. The term may be equally applied to things in making reference to their being inherently disposed to some characteristic traits which they exhibit or as a result of their being in harmony with such effects.

अख्तियार (इख्तियार) makes a reference to characteristics, properties or functions which someone or something is inherently given to, or describes something as being inherently capable of developing or culminating into a given state or the like. The term always implies that the speaker assumes something to be the case or makes such a conjecture on the basis of his knowledge of the latent qualities or the potential characteristics of something or someone (i.e., the subject) to which the term is being applied in a given context.

स्वीकार is the most neutral term in this group. It broadly describes the subject's acceptance of something proposed, given or offered by another person, or is used in referring to a situation in which someone agrees, consents or accepts to do something at the request of another person or in response to a given situation as if he were condescending to do so.

2. Only धारण is ±process. The rest of the expressions in this group are −process. धारण forms ANP with कर. It is not pluralized.

3. अंगीकार कर—"to accept"

उसकी निज की आत्मा की रक्षा की चिन्ता और सिद्धांत प्रीति से अधिक निजी भी वहाँ कुछ है, यह इला की उदात्त वृत्ति अंगीकार करना नहीं चाहती। (जय, 110)

अंगीकार कर ले--"to take on, to acquire"

हमारा पहला सम्पर्क संवेगात्मक होता है, लेकिन वह इतना सबल हो जाता है कि आचरण की अनुरूपता, चेतन या अचेतन अनुकरण द्वारा अनिवार्य हो जाती है और उसके गुणों और दोषों को हम पूरी तरह अंगीकार कर लेते हैं। (भंवर, 16)

अंगीकार कर पा—"to accept"

......लेकिन नीलाभ के प्रति उसकी जो स्वप्नदर्शिता है उसी के कारण यह हरदत्त को अंगीकार नहीं कर पाती। (भंवर, 39)

अंगीकार कर—"to take to"

अहं की प्रेरणा से उसने साधूपन अंगीकार किया। (खिलौने, 87)

अंगीकार कर—"to accept, to recognize as appropriate or inevitable"

अतएव हमें अपने को सुरक्षित रखने के लिए अपनी संस्कृति को अंगीकार करना होगा। (धर्म, 41)

अंगीकार कर—"to accept"

इसलिये धामोनी की जनता उसको अंगीकार करेगी। (कचनार, 235)

अंगीकार कर—"to take to (a course of death), to commit suicide"

सो, एक तरफ तो उनकी दर्शनसंबंधी पुस्तकें होंगी, लोग उनकी सराहना करेंगे, हालांकि उनकी संख्या बहुत थोड़ी होगी और दूसरी तरफ हज़ारों-लाखों लोग तो यही कहेंगे कि पत्नी के व्यभिचार से दुःखी होकर प्रोफेसर ज्ञानशंकर जी ने आत्महत्या कर ली, एक कायर की तरह मृत्यु अंगीकार की, जीवन से मुंह मोड़ लिया। (धनु, 126)

4. अंगीकृत कर—"to take upon oneself, to take over"

देवरानी के प्रेम से अंगीकृत किया हुआ गृहकार्य अंत में रेणुका के भाग्य के साथ सदा के लिए ही बंध गया। (लाख, 43)

5. तस्लीम कर—"to accept"

और बारह बरस की ऐसी उम्र नहीं जिसमें कि किसी को आसानी से गोद में उठाकर खिलाया जा सके। बहरहाल, बहुत-सी ऐसी बातें हैं जिनको कि बगैर सिर उठाये ही तस्लीम करना होता है। (तुला, 62)

तस्लीम कर—"to admit"

बिल्कुल ठीक कहा था। तस्लीम करती हूं, मानती हूं। (खत, 15)

तस्लीम कर ले—"to concede"

"छुट्टी ? हां, हमारी भी छुट्टी है—वैसे भी हर रोज छुट्टी ही रहती है।" पहली बार मैंने अपनी बेकारी को बिना हयाशर्म के तस्लीम कर लिया। (परिन्दे, 38)

6. **कबूल कर—"to confess"**

देखो मेरी बात को गलत न समझना। मैं सच्ची कहती हूं, मेरा भगवान साक्षी है। मैं अपने उनको बहुत लौ करती हूं दिलोजान से करती हूं। वो भी मुझसे बहुत लौ करते हैं। पर एक जगह पर अपना कपट कबूल करती हूं। (बूंद, 61)

कबूल कर—"to acknowledge"

माणिक मुल्ला : इसी बात को ध्यान में रखते हुए माणिक-कथाचक्र की इस प्रथम शृंखला का नाम 'सूरज का सातवां घोड़ा' रखा था। सम्भव है यह नाम आपको पसन्द न आवे इसलिए मैंने यह कबूल कर लिया कि यह मेरा दिया हुआ नहीं है। (सूरज, 114)

कबूल कर—"to admit"

जी हां। संदेह नहीं, सच बात है। उसने खुद कबूल किया है। (धनु, 141)

कबूल कर—"to admit"

हसीना—मुझको और कुछ न चाहिए। सब कुछ पा गई। बड़े आदमियों के लिए सबसे ज्यादा मुश्किल काम है अपनी गलती का कबूल करना। गलती कबूल कर लें तो उनकी यही सजा है। (बीर, 105)

कबूल कर—"to accept"

सालारजंग बोले—मैं आपके यहाँ की कोई चीज कबूल नहीं कर सकता। (बूंद, 444)

7. **मंजूर कर—"to admit"**

जी नहीं, आंखों से तो कुछ नहीं देखा। उसके प्रेमी का रूमाल मिला था, सो उसने मंजूर कर लिया। (धनु, 141)

मंजूर कर—"to agree to"

मेरे साथ मंदा का विवाह करना मंजूर करो। आज ही सगाई कर दो। (लाख, 206)

मंजूर कर—"to accept"

तुम हमको चुनौती देना चाहते हो, सज्जन, तो हम चुनौती भी मंजूर करते हैं। मर-भुखों के आगे कितने जूठे टुकड़े डालोगे ? मरभुखे लाखों हैं सज्जन। (बूंद, 569)

मंज़ूर कर—"to submit"

हमारी जगह पर अगर सौ मुसलमान, अंग्रेज या सिख होते तो कभी भी ऐसी ज़िल्लत में रहना मंजूर न करते। (खत, 74)

मंज़ूर कर—"to agree to"

यही सोच-विचार कर मजदूर ने शर्त मंजूर कर ली। (रूस, 1)

मंज़ूर कर—"to make a pledge"

सेनापति की आँखों में लोभ झलकने लगा। उसने कहा—अच्छी बात है। लेकिन तू कसम खाकर मंजूर कर कि जार तुझे जो कुछ दें उसमें से आधा मुझे देगा। (रूस, 17)

मंज़ूर कर—"to approve"

...उसका साठ हज़ार का क्लेम मंजूर हुआ है जिसमें से आधा उसे नकद मिलेगा और आधा जायदाद के रूप में। पीछे बैठी हुई स्त्री रो रही थी कि बेड़ा गर्क हो क्लेम मंजूर करने वालों का जो उन्होंने उसका केवल अट्ठारह हजार का ही क्लेम मंजूर किया है...। (जानवर, 113)

मंज़ूर कर—"to accept"

एक गिद्ध रोज़ आता था और उसके जिगर के एक हिस्से को खा लेता था, लेकिन साहसी प्रोमेथ्यूस ने अपने साथियों के लिए खुशी-खुशी अपनी जान देना मंजूर कर लिया। (आग, 36)

8. **धारण कर—"to assume a positive state of mind, disposition or determination"**

महीपाल भावावेश में हाथ उठाकर बोल उठा...अर्थात् संकल्प का धारण करो। फिर कर्म का स्मरण करो। कितना सोचा था, कितना कर पाया।...वाह-वाह, कैसा अनूठा सत्य हमारे पुरखे बोल गए हैं।

धारण कर—"to accept"

पुत्र की भविष्य-आशा में गांव वालों के भी असह्य लांछन नत-मस्तक होकर धारण किये थे। (निरु, 74)

धारण कर—"to wear"

मोतियों को कोई समुद्र में नहीं डालता। जो डालता है, वह उन्हें खो देता है। आदमी का काम है सागर-तल में से मोती निकाल कर उसको गले में धारण करना। (कथा, 99)

धारण कर—"to turn into"

पद्मसिंह ने इस प्रस्ताव को वेश्याओं के प्रति घृणा से प्रेरित होकर हाथ में लिया था, पर अब इस विषय पर विचार करते-करते उनकी घृणा बहुत कुछ दया और क्षमा का रूप धारण कर चुकी थी। (सेवा, 290)

धारण कर—"to appear to be"

बाबा जी बोले—अपनी विजय के दिन बड़ा मौन धारण किया है राम जी ? बाबा जी, सुनो, ताई बाबा जी को इशारे से बुलाकर अलग ले गईं और धीरे से पूछा, जंतर-मंतर भी सिद्ध हैं बाबा जी ? (बूंद, 363)

धारण कर—"to take on"

वह जल जो मनुष्य को जीवन प्रदान करता है, जो पृथ्वी के कणों को एक-में-एक जोड़ता है वह मृत्यु की संज्ञा धारण कर लेता है। (सा सा, 315)

धारण किये—"holding"

श्रीकृष्ण छंगुलिया पर गिरिवर को धारण किये खड़े हैं, उनके साथ ही और दूसरे गोप-बाल लकड़ियां लिए पहाड़ के बोझ को साध रहे हैं।...यह गोवर्द्धन सात-पांच की लाकड़ी एक जने का बोझ बन कर कृष्ण की छंगुलिया पर उठ गया। (बूंद, 421)

धारण कर—"to wear, to put on"

सोम जब फौजी वर्दी देखता तो उसका मन उन दिनों की कल्पना में खो जाता जब वह भी ऐसी पोशाक धारण करेगा। (परम, 3)

धारण कर—"to adopt"

मुद्रा के रूप में चाँदी के कार्य का विश्लेषण करते हुए जेनाफेन ने एक विचित्र रुख धारण किया। (एमाई, 22)

धारण कर—"to don"

नत मस्तक हो उसे उठाया, अपने शीर्ष पर धारण किया, और फिर सावेग संथागार सत्र के लिये चल पड़े। (दत्तक पुत्री, 2)

धारण कर—"to be feigning himself (to be worried or concerned)"

चिंतामग्न मुद्रा धारण कर कर्नल ने कहा—"यार, वो बड़ी जादूगरनी है। तुमने अच्छा नहीं किया।" (बूंद, 17)

धारण कर—"to be disguised"

सज्जन की यह योजना उस पूतना के समान है जो अपने स्तनों में विष लगाकर वात्सल्य का ढोंग करती हुई सुन्दर रूप धारण कर श्रीकृष्ण को दूध पिलाने आई थी। (बूंद, 554)

धारण कर—"to assume"

जिस प्रकार किसी द्रव को जिस बर्तन में रखते हैं वह उसी बर्तन के समान रूप धारण कर लेता है, इसी तरह मुद्रा के रूप में रखी गई सम्पत्ति अपने स्वामी की इच्छानुसार किसी भी वस्तु के रूप में बदली जा सकती है अर्थात् उससे कोई भी वस्तु खरीद सकते हैं। (एमाई, 75)

धारण किये हुए—"having donned, wearing"

बटु मंगलकारी पीत वस्त्र धारण किये हुए होइसलेश्वर के पीछे-पीछे चल रहा था। उसके शरीर की कांति में गुराई के साथ ललाई मिली हुई थी। (शांतला, 37)

धारण कर—"to be dressed"

सहसा एक सुन्दर सजीला युवक रेशमी सूट धारण किये, जूते चरमर करता हुआ अंदर आया। (सम, 50)

9. **ग्रहण कर—"to turn into"**

उस तेजोराशि को एक भव्य पुरुष का आकार ग्रहण करते हुए शांतला ने देखा। (शांतला, 46)

ग्रहण कर—"to take"

जो जाति वितरण करना ही जानती है और ग्रहण करना नहीं जानती उस जाति की संस्कृति एक न एक दिन अवश्य समाप्त हो जायगी। (धर्म, 36)

ग्रहण कर—"to adopt, to take over"

जगत को मिथ्या मानने वाले लोग अपने प्रति भले ही अत्याचार न करते हों, किंतु समाज के प्रति यह भावना बना कर सामाजिक ध्येयों से परे होकर वे एक भयंकर अत्याचार करते हैं। उनके आचरण को कई व्यक्ति बिना विचारे हुए ग्रहण कर लेते हैं। (धर्म, 13)

ग्रहण कर—"to absorb"

सोडियम नाइट्रेट के नाइट्रेट आयन्स को पौधे शीघ्र ग्रहण करते हैं और सोडियम आयन्स मृदा में ही रह जाते हैं। (खाद, 89)

ग्रहण कर—"to take (the place of)"

जो भी वस्तु उपयुक्त जंची, वही विनिमय का माध्यम बनाई गयी, और जब दूसरी वस्तु प्रथम वस्तु की तुलना में अधिक अच्छी प्रतीत हुई तब उसने पुराने माध्यम का स्थान ग्रहण कर लिया। (एमाई, 15)

ग्रहण कर—"to accept"

परन्तु जो वह हरगिज बरदाश्त नहीं कर पाती...वे हैं महीपाल की बातें। अपने चौबीस वर्ष के वैवाहिक जीवन में अपने पति के जीवन-ढर्रे और विचारों को कभी सच्चे मन से ग्रहण नहीं कर पाई। उसके मन में वर्षों से एक छिपी हुई शंका है। (बूंद, 107-8)

ग्रहण कर—"to accept"

सच बात तो यह है कि कविश्री की टीका में कविश्री ने कवि-सुलभ स्वच्छन्दता का उपयोग किया है और इसलिए जो कोई उसके सीधे अर्थ को ग्रहण करेगा वह अपने को बड़ी ही बेढब स्थिति में पावेगा। (प्रतिमा, 1)

ग्रहण कर—"to embrace"

इस प्रकार संक्षेप में, समाज सुधार समाज के मूल्यों अथवा ढांचे में ऐसा परिवर्तन है जिससे कि सम्पूर्ण समुदाय का जीवन उन नवीन प्रतिमानों को ग्रहण करता है जो कि समाज की प्रगति के लिए आवश्यक हैं। (भारत, 61)

ग्रहण कर—"to adopt, to accept"

धात्विक मुद्रा का मूल्य उत्पादन लागत से निर्धारित होता है, इस विचार को मिल ने ग्रहण किया। (एमाई, 26)

ग्रहण कर—"to acquire"

मल्लिका : मां, आज तक का जीवन जिस किसी तरह बीता ही है आगे भी बीत जायेगा। आज जब उनका जीवन एक नई दिशा ग्रहण कर रहा है, मैं उनके सामने अपने स्वार्थ का उद्घोष नहीं करना चाहती। (आषाढ़, 25)

ग्रहण कर—"to adopt"

आधुनिकता की एकरूपता को भारतीय जाग्रत महिलाओं ने अनेक रूपों में ग्रहण किया है, जो स्वाभाविक ही था।

ग्रहण कर—"to take (someone's advice)"

ब्राह्मण ने उसके उपदेश को ग्रहण किया...(कथा, 52)

ग्रहण कर—"to take (one's seat)"

मल्लिका : मैं समझ नहीं पा रही किस रूप में मुझे आपका आतिथ्य करना चाहिए आप आसन ग्रहण कर लें तो मैं आपके लिये...(आषाढ़, 70)

ग्रहण कर—"to adopt (a point of view)"

...कुछ अर्थशास्त्रियों ने मुद्रा के प्रति उदार दृष्टिकोण अपनाया है जबकि अन्य अर्थशास्त्रियों ने संकुचित दृष्टिकोण ग्रहण किया है। इसके विपरीत अर्थशास्त्रियों का एक ऐसा वर्ग भी है जिसने उक्त दोनों के मध्य का दृष्टिकोण अपनाया है। (एमाई, 64)

ग्रहण कर—"to accept, to receive"

राजमाता ने उसे (उस फूल को) दोनों हाथों से ग्रहण करके आंखों पर रख लिया और मन ही मन कहा—ऐ माता, तुम्हारी करुणा अपार है...(शांतला, 28)

ग्रहण कर—"to absorb"

शैशवकाल में ही शिशु अपनी माता से शिक्षा को अधिक सुगमता से ग्रहण कर लेता है। (धर्म, 11)

ग्रहण कर—"to succeed"

...यह हमारी जाति की रीति है कि नायक के कार्यभार से निवृत्त होने के बाद उसका ज्येष्ठ पुत्र या पुत्री ही उस पद को ग्रहण कर सकती है। (शबरी, 16)

ग्रहण कर—"to have taken over"

लेकिन अंत में देखने में यही आता है छोटी इकाई बड़ी इकाई का उत्तरदायित्व ग्रहण किये हुए होती है। (ग्रामीण, 31)

ग्रहण कर—"to acquire (as a modification of existing behavior), to learn a lesson"

सबसे बड़ी शिक्षा जो हमें विफलता से ग्रहण करनी चाहिए और सबसे बड़ा सदुपयोग जो हम उसका कर सकते हैं वह है जीवन में एक नए और अच्छे मोड़ की झांकी प्राप्त करना जिससे कि जीवन अधिक समृद्ध और अधिक सार्थक हो सके। (चमत्कार, 36)

ग्रहण कर—"to accept"

दालान में ऊंचे तकिये के सहारे महंत जी प्रायः बैठकर भक्तों की भेंट और किसानों का सूद दोनों ही समभाव से ग्रहण करते। (तितली, 176)

ग्रहण कर—"to accept"

तुम भी मुझे भगवान के प्रसाद की तरह मिली हो कन्या। मैं तुम्हें ग्रहण करने में देर नहीं करना चाहता। सज्जन की आंखों में अतृप्ति की उत्तेजना चमक उठी। (बूंद, 228)

ग्रहण कर—"to receive in one's mind"

शैला ने अपने मन का समस्त बल एकत्र करके उससे आदर्श ग्रहण करने का प्रयत्न किया। वह एक क्षण में सुन्दर स्वप्न देखने लगी, जिसमें आशा की हरियाली थी। (तितली, 247)

ग्रहण कर—"to accept"

इसी व्यक्ति ने राजकोष के लिए मानाइहन का दान ग्रहण किया था और राजाज्ञा से माधवी द्वारा अपहरण किये गए कोवलन के महाकोष का पुनरपहरण भी। (सुहाग, 233)

ग्रहण कर—"to aequire"

किन्तु यहां पर यह संकेत कर देना आवश्यक है मानवीय मूल्य मर्यादाओं को अपनी सहज प्रकृति से ग्रहण करने वाले साहित्य ने मनोविश्लेषण की यान्त्रिकता को कभी भी यथावत् नहीं स्वीकार किया था। (मूल्य, 118)

ग्रहण कर—"to take to (arms)"

आपके चरणों की शपथ लेकर मैं प्रतिज्ञा करता हूं कि मैं मनुष्य जाति के कल्याण के लिये शस्त्र ग्रहण करूंगा, किसी भी क्षुद्र स्वार्थ या सुखलिप्सा को इस पवित्र संकल्प में कलुष-लेप करने का अवसर नहीं दूंगा। (चारू, 78)

10. **अख्तियार कर—"to become, to develop into"**

उनका विश्वास तो यहां तक था कि मैगनीशियम भविष्य की धातु का दर्जा अख्तियार कर लेगी। (समुद्र, 131)

अख्तियार कर—"to adopt a course"

उन्होंने कहा कि कर्मचारियों के आंदोलन को कुचलने के लिए प्रदेश सरकार ने जो रास्ता अख्तियार किया है वह अमानवीय है। (आज, 4)

अख्तियार कर—"to adopt (such a method), to take (such a course)"

अगर हम ऐसा तरीका अख्तियार करते हैं, तो सारा-का सारा समाज ऊंचा उठता है। (भूदान, 135)

अख्तियार कर—"to adopt (the intellectual outlook or disposition of children)"

लोग जब बूढ़े होते हैं तो ऐसे ही अनजाने फिसलकर बच्चों की मानसिक प्रवत्तियां अख्तियार कर लेते हैं...। (नदी, 249)

इख्तियार कर—"to become"

—जिसने प्रोग्रेस करके शादी की सूरत इख्तियार कर ली। (बूंद, 127)

इख्तियार कर—"to take to"

इतने बड़े विद्वान का निस्संकोच भाव से यह कार्य इख्तियार करना महत्त्व रखता है। (निरु, 27)

11. स्वीकार कर—"to choose to be"

मनुष्य के समक्ष दो ही विकल्प हैं, या तो वह इन्द्रियों की दासता को स्वीकार कर ले अथवा जिधर-किधर इन्द्रिय-सुखों का आकर्षण उसे खींचे, उधर ही उसकी जीवनधारा प्रवाहित हो और फिर इन्द्रिय निग्रह का वह अपने जीवन के गुप्त अव्यक्त भावों को प्रकट कर उसका अधिकाधिक विकास करे। (धर्म, 123)

स्वीकार कर—"to submit"

यों वह हर तरह की खुशामद किया करते थे, लेकिन यह अपमान स्वीकार न कर सके। (सम, 42)

स्वीकार कर—"to recognize"

इसके विपरीत इस पद्धति के अन्तर्गत सिद्धान्तों के महत्त्व को पूर्णतया स्वीकार किया जाता है। (सामाजिक, 63)

स्वीकार कर—"to have accepted the supremacy of"

काबुल से लेकर इराक, शाम, टरकी, बैबिलोन, मिस्र और कुछ भाग यूनान का भी इस ईरानी विजेता की अधीनता स्वीकार कर चुका था। (सुन्दर, 25-26)

स्वीकार कर—"to make a confession to"

वह किस मुंह से इन्द्रदेव से उसकी सहायता के लिए कहे। यदि नहीं कहती है तो अपनी सब दुर्बलताएं तितली से स्वीकार करनी होंगी। (तितली, 200)

स्वीकार कर—"to concede"

उधर सर्वदलीय पहाड़ी नेताओं के प्रतिनिधिमंडल ने अपनी स्थिति बताते हुए यह मांग रखी कि पृथक् पहाड़ी राज्य की मांग स्वीकार की जानी चाहिए। (आज, 4)

स्वीकार कर—"to admit"

मन्दा चुप रही। अपनी भूल स्वीकार करने के सिवाय मुझे कोई चारा न था। (लाख, 99)

स्वीकार कर—"to confess"

मनुष्य के सामने हम कब अपना अपराध स्वीकार करते हैं ? यदि अपराध साबित भी हो जाता है तो भी हम उसे स्वीकार नहीं करते—और बिना किसी हिचक के कह देते हैं कि हम पर झूठी तोहमत लगायी जा रही है। (लाख, 112)

स्वीकार कर—"to recognize"

सेल्यूकस ने चन्द्रगुप्त को सिंधु नदी से पूरब के समस्त देश का अधिराज स्वीकार किया, और इसके इलावा काबुल, कंधार, हिरात और बलूचिस्तान भी उसी के हवाले कर दिये। (सुन्दर, 27)

स्वीकार कर—"to admit"

...इस ग्रन्थ का विद्वान रचयिता, सय्यद गुलाम हुसेन अपने ग्रन्थ में स्वीकार करता है कि सम्राट शाहआलम और अंग्रेजों के संग्रामों के दिनों में उसे (सय्यद गुलाम हुसेन को) लोभ देकर अंग्रेजों ने अपनी ओर मिला लिया था। (सुन्दर, 8)

स्वीकार कर—"to confess"

भारी कदम रखते हुए शिवा घर की ओर जा रहा था। भगवान के सामने उसने अपना अपराध स्वीकार कर लिया था पर उसका मन अभी भी उसे लगातार काट रहा था। (लाख, 111)

स्वीकार कर—"to subscribe"

समाज के सदस्यों में अपनी स्थिति और कार्यों को स्वीकार करने की तत्परता तभी होगी जबकि उन पर समाज का नियन्त्रण रहे। (भारत, 71)

स्वीकार कर—"to undertake"

पारिभाषिक रूप से कल्याण राज्य का निर्णायक तत्व राज्य के द्वारा लोगों के लिए शिक्षा, सफाई, जीविकोपार्जन के साधन आदि के विषयों में कुछ मौलिक जिम्मेदारियों को स्वीकार करना और...(भारत, 8)

स्वीकार कर—"to admit"

अपने स्वप्नदर्शी स्वभाव से वह स्वयं अवगत है और अपनी इस कमजोरी को स्वीकार भी करती है कि उसकी प्रकृति शादी के अनुकूल नहीं है क्योंकि उसके दिमाग के किसी कोने में आजाद और कलचहं जिंदगी का कुछ ऐसा सुन्दर, सजीव और पवित्र चित्र अंकित है कि विवाह से उस चित्र का भ्रष्ट हो जाना अनिवार्य है। (भंवर, 14)

स्वीकार कर—"to accept (the challenge)"

हमारे लिए दो रास्ते हैं—हम इस चुनौती को स्वीकार करें या अपनी पीठ दिखायें, इस पर काबिज हों या इसे अपने पर काबू पा लेने दें। (अमरीका, 25)

स्वीकार कर—"to tolerate, to accept, to condone, to reconcile oneself to"

आप ही बताइये महाराज, अगर कदम्बवास के हत्यारे को नाटी माता स्वीकार कर लेतीं तो कितनी बड़ी कृतघ्नता होती। (चारु, 320)

स्वीकार कर—"to accept"

कवि महोदय सोचते थे कि वे एक-एक पंक्ति में अपना गुणगान देखकर गद्गद हो जाएंगे और बड़े हर्ष से उस भेंट को स्वीकार कर लेंगे। (आदर्श, 100)

स्वीकार कर—"to accept"

इसलिए उसे जब ताश कम्पनी की नौकरी मिली तो उसने बगैर हील-हुज्जत के स्वीकार कर ली। (राकेश, 55)

स्वीकार कर—"to hold by"

हम देखते हैं कि विवेक-हीन पशु इन्द्रियपरक जीवन व्यतीत करते-करते वासना की दासता को स्वीकार किये रहता है, जबकि एक विवेक-युक्त पुरुष ऐसी दासता से सर्वथा मुक्त रहता है। (धर्म, 127)

गर्दन हिलाकर स्वीकार कर—"to nod 'yes'"

शादी की बात हुई है ? हूं। कब, अभी हाल में ही ? कन्या ने गर्दन हिलाकर स्वीकार किया। (बूंद, 366)

119. अपदस्थ, बेदखल

1. Both **अपदस्थ** and **बेदखल** refer to an act or action of someone who dispossesses another person of something or takes away something vested in him.

अपदस्थ (lit. the one who has been dispossessed of rank, status or the like) describes the act of taking away of possession, position or whatever is vested in one as a distinction or mark of special privilege. The term, therefore, always requires a human object and an explicit mention of something that is taken away from the object noun.

बेदखल is a term of wider application referring to the act of dispossessing someone of something which rightfully (or otherwise) belongs to him. It equally applies to persons (i.e., who have been dispossessed of something) as well as to things (i.e., what someone has been dispossessed of). बेदखल (more so than अपदस्थ) carries the implication of the speaker's judgement involving condemnation of the subject's act.

2. Both the terms are adjectives, and therefore —process.

3. **अपदस्थ कर—"to divest one of one's authority or privilege"**

उनसे सब अधिकार लेकर मैं उनको अपदस्थ करके नहीं रखना चाहती। (तितली, 207)

4. **बेदखल कर—"to confiscate"**

कुमार के बेदखल किये बाग के एक आम के वृक्ष के नीचे सुरेश कुर्सी पर बैठे थे। (निरु, 60)

120. अन्धकार, अन्धेरा

1. Both अन्धकार and अन्धेरा are applied in making a reference to the state of being dark (i.e., absence or lack of light or illumination).

अन्धकार refers to the absence of light such as that caused by sunset, at nightfall or during the night. The term may be used to describe situations when there is not enough light (as one would normally expect such as just before sunset) due to some external cause.

अन्धेरा is a term of wider application and denotes absence of light or a lack of illumination in any degree (relative to what one would normally like to have in a given situation or environment). It may be used figuratively to describe the state of someone who is ignorant of the facts, nature or characteristics of something, or in order to make a reference to some inherently misleading cause or agent which, through one's preoccupation with or overindulgence in something does not permit him to see things in a different light.

2. Both the terms are +process and form ANP with में. They are not pluralized.

3. असमय अन्धकार कर—"to cause an untimely twilight"

घिरे हुए मेघों ने आज असमय अन्धकार कर दिया है। (आषाढ़, 35)

4. अंधेरा कर— "to obscure (the light)"

अर्थात् किताबी विद्वान कुरान आदि पुस्तकों से घिरे रहते हैं, वे आत्मा की स्वप्रकाश ज्योति को ढांपते हैं और उजियाले में अन्धेरा करते हैं। (चमत्कार, 30)

APPENDIX I

List of the Sources of the Data

(All the works are listed below in the alphabetic order of their coded references).

1. अंधा — लक्ष्मीनारायण लाल, *अंधा कुआं*, भारती भंडार (प्रयाग, 1957), प्रथम संस्करण ।
2. अंधेरे — मोहन राकेश, *अंधेरे बन्द कमरे*, राजकमल प्रकाशन प्रा० लि० (दिल्ली, 1961), प्रथम संस्करण ।
3. अचल — वृन्दावन लाल वर्मा, *अचल मेरा कोई*, मयूर प्रकाशन (झांसी, 1959), सप्तम संस्करण ।
4. अच्छी — शचीरानी गुर्टू (सम्पादिका), *अच्छी कहानियां*, साहित्य सदन (देहरादून, no date) ।
5. अजात — जयशंकर प्रसाद, *अजातशत्रु* भारती भंडार (प्रयाग, 1966), बीसवां संस्करण ।
6. अणु — दिलीप, *अणुयुग और हम*, अखिल भारतीय सर्व-सेवा-संघ-प्रकाशन (वाराणसी, 1962), प्रथम संस्करण ।
7. अतीत — महादेवी वर्मा, *अतीत के चलचित्र*, भारती भंडार (प्रयाग, 1962), आठवां संस्करण ।
8. अद (अपराध) — कौशलकुमार राय, *अपराध और दंडशास्त्र*, चौखम्बा विद्याभवन (वाराणसी, 1965), प्रथम संस्करण ।
9. अधूरा — प्रकाश पंडित, *अधूरा स्वप्न*, राजपाल एण्ड सन्ज (दिल्ली, no date) ।
10. अनदेखे — राजेन्द्र यादव, *अनदेखे अनजान पुल*, राजपाल एण्ड सन्ज (दिल्ली, 1963), प्रथम संस्करण ।
11. अनबूझे — उमाशंकर, *अनबूझे सपने*, भारतीय ग्रंथ निकेतन (दिल्ली, 1967) ।
12. अनुभूति — डा० नगेन्द्र, *विचार और अनुभूति*, नेशनल पब्लिशिग हाउस (दिल्ली, no date), तृतीय संस्करण ।
13. अनुसंधान — डा० नगेन्द्र, *अनुसंधान और आलोचना*, नेशनल पब्लिशिंग हाउस (दिल्ली, 1961), प्रथम संस्करण ।
14. अप (आत्महत्या) — परिपूर्णानन्द वर्म्मा, *आत्महत्या तथा कामवासना के अपराध*, साहित्य निकेतन (कानपुर, 1966), प्रथम संस्करण ।

15.	अपने खिलौने	भगवतीचरण वर्मा, *अपने खिलौने*, भारती भंडार (प्रयाग, 1957) ।
16.	अपराध (अद)	see (8) above .
17.	अमरीका (अम)	लिण्डन बी० जानसन, *मेरे सपनों का अमरीका*, रवीन्द्र प्रकाशन (नई दिल्ली, 1964) ।
18.	अमर	आनन्दकुमार, *अमर कथाएं*, राजपाल एण्ड सन्ज (दिल्ली, no date) ।
19.	अमीर	माखनलाल चतुर्वेदी, *अमीर इरादे गरीब इरादे*, भारतीय ज्ञान-पीठ (वाराणसी, 1964), तृतीय संस्करण ।
20.	अमृत	अमृतलाल नागर, *अमृत और विष*, लोक भारतीय प्रकाशन (इलाहाबाद, 1966), प्रथम संस्करण ।
21.	अवध	ख्वाजा अहमद अब्बास, *अवध की शाम*, नीलाभ प्रकाशन (इलाहाबाद, 1956), द्वितीय संस्करण ।
22.	आकाश	मोहन राकेश, *फौलाद का आकाश*, अक्षर प्रकाशन प्रा० लि० (दिल्ली, 1966), प्रथम संस्करण ।
23.	आग	रमेशचन्द्र वर्मा, *आग हमारी मित्र व शत्रु*, राजपाल एण्ड सन्ज (दिल्ली, 1966), तीसरा संस्करण ।
24.	आज	केशवसागर, *आवाज*, राजपाल एण्ड सन्ज (दिल्ली, 1960), प्रथम संस्करण ।
25.	आत्मदाह	आचार्य चतुरसेन शास्त्री, *आत्मदाह*, हिन्दी साहित्य मंडल (दिल्ली तथा जयपुर, 1953), तीसरा संस्करण ।
26.	आदर्श	आनन्द कुमार, *आदर्श कथाएं*, राजपाल एण्ड सन्ज (दिल्ली, 1966), पांचवां संस्करण ।
27.	आदि	उपेन्द्रनाथ अश्क, *आदिमार्ग*, नीलाभ प्रकाशन (इलाहाबाद, 1961), तृतीय संस्करण ।
28.	आध	कृशन चन्दर, *आधे घंटे का खुदा*, राजपाल एण्ड सन्ज (दिल्ली, no date) ।
29.	आधु	महाराष्ट्र राष्ट्रभाषा सभा (प्रकाशक), *आधुनिक हिन्दी कहानियां* (पूना, 1962), प्रथम संस्करण ।
30.	आनंद	मुल्कराज आनंद, *हिन्दुस्तान की कहानी*, राजकमल प्रकाशन (दिल्ली, 1956), द्वितीय आवृत्ति ।
31.	आलो	केशनी प्रसाद चौरसिया, *आलोचना के प्रतिमान*, युनाइटेड बुक डिपो (इलाहाबाद, 1966), प्रथम संस्करण ।
32.	आवाज	रांगेय राघव, *आखिरी आवाज*, राजपाल एण्ड सन्ज (दिल्ली, 1962), प्रथम संस्करण ।
33.	आविष्कार	विनोदकुमार, *आविष्कारों की कहानियां*, राजपाल एण्ड सन्ज (दिल्ली, 1966), चौथा संस्करण ।

34.	आषाढ़	मोहन राकेश, *आषाढ़ का एक दिन*, राजपाल एण्ड सन्ज (दिल्ली, 1958)।
35.	इलाज	चंद्रशेखर गोपाल ठक्कुर, *घरेलु इलाज*, भारतीय ज्ञानपीठ प्रकाशन (बनारस, 1965), प्रथम संस्करण।
36	ईंट	ओम्प्रकाश शर्मा, *ईंट निर्माण में विज्ञान*, कौंसिल आफ साइंटिफिक एण्ड इण्डस्ट्रियल रिसर्च (नई दिल्ली, 1964), प्रथम संस्करण।
37.	ईमान	जगदीश शर्मा, *धर्म और ईमान* देहाती पुस्तक भंडार (दिल्ली 1962), प्रथम संस्करण।
38.	उखड़	राजेन्द्र यादव, *उखड़े हुए लोग*, साहित्य सदन (देहरादून, 1964), द्वितीय संस्करण।
39.	उत्तमी	यशपाल, *उत्तमी की मां*, विप्लव कार्यालय (लखनऊ, 1959), दूसरा संस्करण।
40.	उत्तरी	आवन रसेल, *उत्तरी तथा दक्षिणी ध्रुवों की कहानियां*, हंसराज रहबर (अनुवादक), राजपाल एण्ड सन्ज (दिल्ली, 1966), चौथा संस्करण।
41.	उद्भव	सुरेश सिन्हा, *हिन्दी कहानी, उद्भव और विकास*, अशोक प्रकाशन (दिल्ली, 1966), प्रथम संस्करण।
42.	उलझन	जार्ज बर्नर्ड शा, *डाक्टर की उलझन*, शिवदान सिंह चौहान तथा श्रीमती विजय चौहान (अनुवादक), राजपाल एण्ड सन्ज (दिल्ली, 1960), प्रथम संस्करण।
43.	उषा	राजानन्द, *उषा और आदित्य*, विक्रेता प्रकाशन संघ (दिल्ली, 1962), प्रथम संस्करण।
44.	ऊंचे	रमेश वर्मा, *ऊंचे पर्वत*, हिन्दी पाकेट बुक्स प्रा० लि० (दिल्ली, no date)।
45.	एक	मोहन राकेश, *एक और जिन्दगी*, राजपाल एण्ड सन्ज (दिल्ली, (1961), प्रथम संस्करण।
46.	एक बूंद	सच्चिदानन्द वात्स्यायन, *एक बूंद सहसा उछली*, भारतीय ज्ञानपीठ (काशी, 1960), प्रथम संस्करण।
47.	एटम	इरा एम० फ्रीमैन, *एटम की कहानी*, विराज एम० ए० (अनुवादक), राजपाल एण्ड सन्ज (दिल्ली, 1966)।
48.	एडीसन	जी ग्लैबुड क्लार्क, *महान् आविष्कारक एडीसन*, विराज एम० ए० (अनुवादक), राजपाल एण्ड सन्ज (दिल्ली, 1960)।
49.	एमाई	एस० सी० मित्तल, *एडवांस्ड मानीटरी एकानामिक्स*, कैलाश पुस्तक सदन (ग्वालियर, 1965), प्रथम संस्करण।
50.	ऐतिहासिक	गोपीनाथ तिवारी, *ऐतिहासिक उपन्यास और उपन्यासकार*, साहित्य रत्न भंडार (आगरा, 1958), प्रथम संस्करण।

51.	औरत	मोपासां, *एक औरत की जिन्दगी*, शिवदान सिंह चौहान तथा श्रीमती विजय चौहान (अनुवादक), हिन्द पाकेट बुक्स प्रा० लि० (दिल्ली, no date)।
52.	कंकाल	जयशंकर प्रसाद, *कंकाल*, भारती भंडार (इलाहाबाद, 1967), ग्यारहवां संस्करण।
53.	कचनार	वृन्दावनलाल वर्मा, *कचनार*, मयूर प्रकाशन (झाँसी, 1959), पंचमावृत्ति।
54.	कच्चा	दुर्गाप्रसाद खत्री (सम्पादक) *कच्चा रंग*, लहरी बुक डिपो (वाराणसी, 1964), प्रथम संस्करण।
55.	कटाई	शकुन्तला वर्मा, *भारतीय कटाई-सिलाई विज्ञान*, किताब महल प्रा० लि० (इलाहाबाद, no date)।
56.	कथा	आनन्द कुमार, *मनोरंजक कथाएं*, राजपाल एण्ड सन्ज (दिल्ली, 1966), नवां संस्करण।
57.	कमल	राजेन्द्र यादव (सम्पादक), *कमलेश्वर, श्रेष्ठ कहानियाँ*, राजपाल एण्ड सन्ज (दिल्ली, 1966), प्रथम संस्करण।
58.	कभू	प्रेमचन्द, *कर्मभूमि*, हंस प्रकाशन (इलाहाबाद, 1960), आठवां संस्करण।
59.	करामात	श्रीकांत व्यास, *कैदी की करामात*, शिक्षा भारती (दिल्ली, 1966), चौथा संस्करण।
60.	कर्ब	प्रेमचन्द, *कर्बला*, गंगा ग्रंथागार (लखनऊ, 1959), षष्ठावृत्ति।
61.	कर्मयोग	जयदयाल गोयन्दका, *कर्मयोग का तत्त्व*, गीता प्रेस (गोरखपुर, 1965), प्रथम संस्करण।
62.	कलंक	नैथेनियल हाथार्न, *कलंक*, आशुतोष (अनुवादक), राजपाल एण्ड सन्ज (दिल्ली, 1958)।
63.	कला	पांडेय बेचन शर्मा उग्र, *कला का पुरस्कार*, आत्माराम एण्ड सन्ज (दिल्ली, 1955)
64.	कल्याण	विद्यासागर शर्मा, *समाज कल्याण*, आत्माराम एण्ड सन्ज (दिल्ली, 1962), प्रथम संस्करण।
65.	कल्याणी	जैनेन्द्र कुमार, *कल्याणी*, पूर्वोदय प्रकाशन (दिल्ली, 1961), द्वितीय संस्करण।
66.	कश	कृश्न चन्दर, *कश्मीर की कहानियां*, राजपाल एण्ड सन्ज (दिल्ली, 1966), तृतीय संस्करण।
67.	कहा	गोपाल प्रसाद व्यास, *मैंने कहा*, आत्माराम एण्ड सन्ज (दिल्ली, no date)
68.	कहानी	इन्द्रनाथ मदान (सम्पादक), *कहानी और कहानी*, रामचंद एण्ड कम्पनी (दिल्ली, 1966), प्रथम संस्करण।

69. काया — पांडेय बेचन शर्मा उग्र, *यह कंचन सी काया*, आत्माराम एण्ड सन्ज (दिल्ली, 1964)।

70. काल — पांडेय बेचन शर्मा उग्र, *काल कोठरी*, आत्माराम एण्ड सन्ज (दिल्ली, 1964)।

71. काला — श्रीकांत व्यास, *काला फूल*, शिक्षा भारती (दिल्ली, 1964)।

72. किनारे — नीरज, *नदी किनारे*, आत्माराम एण्ड सन्ज (दिल्ली, 1964), तीसरा संस्करण।

73. कुछ — सम्पूर्णानन्द, *कुछ स्मृतियाँ और कुछ स्फुट विचार*, ज्ञानमंडल प्रा० लि० (बनारस, 1962), प्रथम संस्करण।

74. कुण — आचार्य श्यामसुन्दर सुमन, *कुणाल*, भाग्योदय प्रकाशन (मथुरा, 1962), प्रथम संस्करण।

75. कुतिया — शौकत थानवी, *कुतिया*, नारायणदत्त सहगल एण्ड सन्ज (दिल्ली, 1961), द्वितीय संस्करण।

76. कुबड़ा — विक्टर ह्यूगो, *पेरिस का कुबड़ा*, श्रीमती विजय चौहान तथा शिवदान सिंह चौहान (रूपान्तरकार), हिन्द पाकेट बुक्स प्रा० लि० (दिल्ली, no date)।

77. कैद — राजेन्द्र यादव, *जहां लक्ष्मी कैद है*, राजकमल प्रकाशन प्रा० लि० (दिल्ली, 1960), द्वितीय संस्करण।

78. कैदी — कृश्न चन्दर, *सपनों का कैदी*, हिन्दी पाकेट बुक्स प्रा० लि० (दिल्ली, no date)।

79. कोठे — अमृतलाल नागर, *ये कोठेवालियां*, राजकमल प्रकाशन प्रा० लि० (दिल्ली, 1961), प्रथम संस्करण।

80. कोणार्क — जगदीश चन्द्र माथुर, *कोणार्क*, भारती भण्डार (इलाहाबाद, 1966), नवां संस्करण।

81. कोलम्बस — आर्मस्ट्रांग स्पेरी, *कोलम्बस*, महावीर अधिकारी (अनुवादक), राजपाल एण्ड सन्ज (दिल्ली, 1966)।

82. कोश — रामचन्द्र वर्म्मा, *शब्दार्थक ज्ञानकोश*, शब्दलोक प्रकाशन (वाराणसी, 1959), प्रथम संस्करण।

83. क्यों — यशपाल, *तुमने क्यों कहा था मैं सुन्दर हूँ*, विप्लव कार्यालय (लखनऊ, 1965), तीसरा संस्करण।

84. क्षणदा — महादेवी वर्मा, *क्षणदा*, भारती भंडार (इलाहाबाद, 1958), प्रथम संस्करण।

85. खत — स्टीफेन ज्विग, *एक अनजान औरत का खत*, शरद देवड़ा (अनुवादक), हिन्द पाकेट बुक्स प्रा० लि० (दिल्ली, no date)।

86. खतूत — पांडेय बेचन शर्मा उग्र, *चंद हसीनों के खतूत*, हिन्द पाकेट बुक्स (दिल्ली, no date)।

87.	खबर	पांडेय बेचन शर्मा उग्र, *अपनी खबर*, राजकमल प्रकाशन प्रा० लि० (दिल्ली, 1960), प्रथम संस्करण।
88.	खरा	अरिगपूडि, *खरे खोटे*, भारती साहित्य सदन (दिल्ली, 1957), प्रथम संस्करण।
89.	खाद	रणवीर सिंह शर्मा तथा दयाराम, *खाद एवं उर्वरक*, एशियन पब्लिशर्ज (मुजफ्फरनगर, 1964), प्रथम संस्करण।
90.	खाली	महेन्द्र मीत, *खाली समुद्र*, भारत बुक स्टाल (कानपुर, 1962), प्रथम संस्करण।
91.	खिलौने	वृन्दावनलाल वर्मा, *खिलौने की खोज*, मयूर प्रकाशन (झांसी, 1965), पंचमावृत्ति।
92.	गध	कृश्न चन्दर, *एक गधे की आत्मकथा*, हिन्द पाकेट बुक्स प्रा० लि० (दिल्ली, no date)
93.	गधे	कृश्न चन्दर, *एक गधे की वापसी*, हिन्द पाकेट बुक्स प्रा० लि० (दिल्ली, no date)।
94.	गरजन	कृष्ण चन्द्र, *गरजन की एक शाम*, राजपाल एण्ड सन्ज (दिल्ली, no date)।
95.	गरा	उपेन्द्रनाथ अश्क, *गर्म राख*, नीलाभ प्रकाशन (इलाहाबाद, 1956)।
96.	गरिमा	नवलकिशोर, *निबन्ध गरिमा*, पब्लिशिंग हाउस (जयपुर, no date)।
97.	गांधी	हरिभाऊ उपाध्याय (संपादक), *संक्षिप्त आत्मकथा*, सस्ता साहित्य मंडल (दिल्ली, 1939)।
98.	गिरी	हिमांशु श्रीवास्तव, *रथ से गिरी बांसुरी*, भारतीय ग्रंथ निकेतन (दिल्ली, 1967), प्रथम संस्करण।
99.	गुज	के० एम० मुन्शी *गुजरात के गौरव*, भाग 1, रजनी साहित्य सदन (दिल्ली, no date)।
100.	गुरु	कामता प्रसाद गुरु, *हिन्दी व्याकरण*, नागरी प्राचारिणी सभा (काशी, 1962)।
101.	गुलाब	उषा प्रियंवदा, *जिन्दगी और गुलाब के फूल*, भारतीय ज्ञानपीठ (काशी, 1961), प्रथम संस्करण।
102.	गोदान	प्रेमचंद, *गोदान*, सरस्वती प्रेस (इलाहाबाद, 1960)।
103.	गोवि	सेठ गोविन्ददास, *गोविन्ददास ग्रन्थावली*, तीसरा खण्ड, भारतीय विश्व प्रकाशन (दिल्ली, 1958)।
104.	गोविंद	सेठ गोविन्ददास, *गोविन्ददास ग्रन्थावली*, दूसरा खण्ड, भारतीय विश्व प्रकाशन (दिल्ली, 1957)।
105.	गौरव	के० एम० मुन्शी, *गुजरात के गौरव*, भाग 2, नवयुग प्रकाशन (दिल्ली, no date)।

106. ग्रामीण — पी० एन० खरे, *ग्रामीण समाजशास्त्र*, गया प्रसाद एण्ड सन्ज (आगरा, 1962)।

107. ग्रास — गंगा मिश्र महेश, *ग्रामीण समाजशास्त्र*, नंद किशोर एण्ड सन्ज (वाराणसी, 1965), प्रथम संस्करण।

108. घड़ी — रमेश कुमार माहेश्वरी, *घड़ी की कहानी*, राजपाल एण्ड सन्ज (दिल्ली, no date), दूसरा संस्करण।

109. घर में — शिवरानी प्रेमचन्द, *प्रेमचन्द घर में*, आत्माराम एण्ड सन्ज (दिल्ली, 1956)।

110. घोंसला — किशोर साहू, *घोंसला*, हिन्द पाकेट बुक्स प्रा० लि० (दिल्ली, no date)।

111. चन्द्र — जयशंकर प्रसाद, *चन्द्रगुप्त*, भारती भंडार (इलाहाबाद, 1966), चतुर्दश संस्करण।

112. चट्टान — कर्तार सिंह दुग्गल, *चील और चट्टान*, साहनी प्रकाशन (दिल्ली, no date)।

113. चमत्कार — जयवंतराम, *मन के चमत्कार*, आत्माराम एण्ड सन्ज (दिल्ली, 1962), प्रथम संस्करण।

114. चांद — कृश्न चन्दर, *पूरे चांद की रात*, राजपाल एण्ड सन्ज (दिल्ली, 1966), चौथा संस्करण।

115. चांदनी — गिरधर गोपाल, *चांदनी के खंडहर*, साहित्य भवन प्रा० लि० (इलाहाबाद, 1962), नवीन संस्करण।

116. चार — सुदर्शन, *चार कहानियां*, हिन्दी ग्रन्थ रत्नाकर प्रा० लि० (बम्बई, 1957), तीसरा संस्करण।

117. चारु — हजारी प्रसाद द्विवेदी, *चारुचंद्रलेख*, राजकमल प्रकाशन प्रा० लि० (दिल्ली, 1963)।

118. चित्र — भगवती शरण उपाध्याय, *भारतीय चित्रकला की कहानी*, राजपाल एण्ड सन्ज (दिल्ली, 1966), पांचवां संस्करण।

119. चित्रलेखा — भगवती चरण वर्मा, *चित्रलेखा*, भारती भंडार (प्रयाग, 1961), सोलहवां संस्करण।

120. चीड़ — निर्मल वर्मा, *चीड़ों पर चांदनी*, भारतीय ज्ञानपीठ (वाराणसी, 1964), प्रथम संस्करण।

121. चौराहे — फणीश्वर नाथ रेणु, *कितने चौराहे*, राधाकृष्ण प्रकाशन (दिल्ली, 1966), प्रथम संस्करण।

122. जग — ब्र० जगदीश विद्यार्थी, *वैदिक प्रश्नोत्तरी*, आर्य साहित्य भवन (दिल्ली, 1965)।

123. जगत — देवेन्द्रकुमार, *विज्ञान जगत*, राजपाल एण्ड सन्ज (दिल्ली, 1965) पांचवां संस्करण।

124. जय — जैनेन्द्र कुमार, *जयवर्धन*, पूर्वोदय प्रकाशन (दिल्ली, 1965), द्वितीय संस्करण।

125. जलती झाड़ी — निर्मल बर्मा, *जलती झाड़ी*, राजकमल प्रकाशन प्रा० लि० (दिल्ली, 1964)।

126. जहां — प्रकाश पंडित, *जहां फूल खिलते हैं*, राजपाल एण्ड सन्ज (दिल्ली, 1962)।

127. जहाज — इलाचन्द्र जोशी, *जहाज का पंछी*, राजकमल प्रकाशन प्रा० लि० (दिल्ली, 1956), द्वितीय संस्करण।

128. जातक — चन्द्रिका प्रसाद मिश्र, *जातक कथाएं*, साहित्य प्रकाशन मंदिर (ग्वालियर, no date)।

129. जादू — लेविस कैरोल, *जादू नगरी*, श्रीकांत व्यास (अनुवादक), राजपाल एण्ड सन्ज (दिल्ली, 1966), पांचवां संस्करण।

130. जानवर — मोहन राकेश, *जानवर और जानवर*, राजकमल प्रकाशन प्रा० लि० (दिल्ली, 1958), प्रथम संस्करण।

131. जिन्दगी — रामनाथ सुमन, *नई जिन्दगी*, राजपाल एण्ड सन्ज (दिल्ली, 1961), प्रथम संस्करण।

132. जिराह — बालशौरी रेड्डी, *जिंदगी की राह*, राजपाल एण्ड सन्ज (दिल्ली, no date)।

133. जी — पांडेय बेचन शर्मा उग्र, *जी-जी-जी*, आत्माराम एण्ड सन्ज (दिल्ली, 1955)।

134. जीते — काशीराम चावला, *मन जीते जग जीत*, मलिक बुक शाप (लुधियाना, 1964)।

135. जीव — गंगाप्रसाद उपाध्याय, *जीवात्मा*, कला प्रेस (प्रयाग, 1964)।

136. जुहू — पांडेय बेचन शर्मा उग्र, *जुहू*, हिन्द पाकेट बुक्स प्रा० लि० (दिल्ली, no date)।

137. जैनेन्द्र 1 — जैनेन्द्र कुमार, *जैनेन्द्र की कहानियां*, भाग एक, पूर्वोदय प्रकाशन (दिल्ली, 1962), तृतीय संस्करण।

138. जैनेन्द्र 2 — जैनेन्द्र कुमार, *जैनेन्द्र की कहानियां*, भाग दो, पूर्वोदय प्रकाशन (दिल्ली, 1962), तृतीय संस्करण।

139. जैनेन्द्र 4 — जैनेन्द्र कुमार, *जैनेन्द्र की कहानियां*, भाग चार, पूर्वोदय प्रकाशन (दिल्ली, 1963), तृतीय संस्करण।

140. जैनेन्द्र 5 — जैनेन्द्र कुमार, *जैनेन्द्र की कहानियां*, भाग पांच, पूर्वोदय प्रकाशन (दिल्ली, 1961), तृतीय संस्करण।

141. जैनेन्द्र 6 — जैनेन्द्र कुमार, *जैनेन्द्र की कहानियां*, भाग छः, पूर्वोदय प्रकाशन (दिल्ली, 1963), तृतीय संस्करण।

142. जैनेन्द्र 7 — जैनेन्द्र कुमार, *जैनेन्द्र की कहानियां*, भाग सात, पूर्वोदय प्रकाशन (दिल्ली, 1963), तृतीय संस्करण।

143. जैनेन्द्र 8 — जैनेन्द्र कुमार, *जैनेन्द्र की कहानियां*, भाग आठ, पूर्वोदय प्रकाशन (दिल्ली, 1964), तृतीय संस्करण ।

144. जैनेन्द्र 9 — जैनेन्द्र कुमार, *जैनेन्द्र की कहानियां*, भाग नौ, पूर्वोदय प्रकाशन (दिल्ली, 1964), तृतीय संस्करण ।

145. ज्योति — जगदीश चन्द्र जैन, *विश्व साहित्य के ज्योति पुंज*, हिन्दी ग्रन्थ रत्नाकर प्रा० लि० (बम्बई, 1962) ।

146. झलक — श्रीमती रामेश्वरी नेहरू, *मानव विकास की एक झलक*, साहित्य केन्द्र (वाराणसी, 1962) ।

147. झांसी — वृन्दावन लाल वर्मा, *झांसी की रानी*, मयूर प्रकाशन (झांसी, 1965), आठवां संस्करण ।

148. टाम — मार्क ट्वेन, *बहादुर टाम*, श्रीप्रकाश (अनुवादक), राजपाल एण्ड सन्ज (दिल्ली, no date) ।

149. टी सेट — भगवती प्रसाद वाजपेयी, *टूटा टी सेट*, भारतीय ग्रंथ निकेतन (दिल्ली, 1962) ।

150. टीला — रांगेय राघव, *मुर्दों का टीला*, किताब महल प्रकाशन (इलाहाबाद, 1963), तृतीय संस्करण ।

151. टेढ़े — भगवतीचरण वर्मा, *टेढ़े-मेढ़े रास्ते*, भारती भंडार (प्रयाग, 1965), पंचम संस्करण ।

152. ठेले — धर्मवीर भारती, *ठेले पर हिमालय*, भारती प्रेस प्रकाशन (इलाहाबाद, 1958), प्रथम संस्करण ।

153. डगर — राजेन्द्रलाल हांडा, *गांव की डगर पर*, मौलिक साहित्य प्रकाशन (दिल्ली, 1966) ।

154. डायरी — डा० सत्य प्रकाश संगर, *मिनिस्टर की डायरी*, राजकमल प्रकाशन प्रा० लि० (दिल्ली, 1966) ।

155. ढोल — अरिगपुडि, *दूर के ढोल*, राजकमल प्रकाशन प्रा० लि० (दिल्ली, 1957) ।

156. तितली — जयशंकर प्रसाद, *तितली*, भारती भंडार (इलाहाबाद, 1966), बारहवां संस्करण ।

157. तीन — भगवतीचरण वर्मा, *तीन वर्ष*, भारती भंडार (इलाहाबाद, 1965), सातवां संस्करण ।

158. तीर्थ — प्रेमचन्द, *प्रेमतीर्थ*, सरस्वती प्रेस (बनारस, 1958), आठवां संस्करण ।

159. तीस — श्रीकांत व्यास, *तीस मार खां*, राजपाल एण्ड सन्ज (दिल्ली, no date) ।

160. तुला — अमृतलाल नागर, *तुलाराम शास्त्री*, भारती भंडार (इलाहाबाद, 1948), द्वितीय संस्करण ।

161. तूफानी — उपेन्द्रनाथ अश्क, *तूफानी लहरों में हंसता मांझी*, नीलाभ प्रकाशन (इलाहाबाद, 1966), प्रथम संस्करण।

162. तेल — प्रभाकर माचवे, *तेल की पकौड़ियां*, भारतीय ज्ञानपीठ (बनारस, 1965), द्वितीय संस्करण।

163. त्याग — जैनेन्द्र कुमार, *त्याग पत्र*, पूर्वोदय प्रकाशन (दिल्ली, 1963), इक्कीसवां संस्करण।

164. थान — शौकत थानवी, *सांच को आंच* (दिल्ली, 1954)।

165. दत्तक पुत्री — शिवकुमार कौशिक, *वैशाली की दत्तक पुत्री*, आत्माराम एण्ड सन्ज (दिल्ली, 1961)।

166. दबे पांव — वृन्दावन लाल वर्मा, *दबे पांव*, मयूर प्रकाशन (झांसी, 1959), द्वितीय आवृत्ति।

167. दर्शन सार — बलदेव उपाध्याय, *भारतीय दर्शन सार*, सस्ता साहित्य मंडल (दिल्ली, 1962)।

168. दश — लक्ष्मीनारायण लाल मिश्र, *दशाश्वमेध*, हिन्दी भवन (जालन्धर, 1964), दसवां संस्करण।

169. दहक — विष्णु प्रभाकर, *हंसते निर्झर दहकती भट्टी*, नेशनल पब्लिशिंग हाउस (दिल्ली, 1966)।

170. दाय — विष्णु प्रभाकर, *ये रेखायें ये दायरे*, हिन्दी ग्रन्थ रत्नाकर प्रा० लि० (बम्बई, 1963)।

171. दावानल — नानक सिंह, *दावानल*, वोरा एण्ड कम्पनी (इलाहाबाद, 1966)।

172. दाह — उदयशंकर भट्ट, *दाहर अथवा सिंध पतन*, आत्माराम एण्ड सन्ज (दिल्ली, 1962)।

173. दिनमान — *साप्ताहिक दिनमान*, बैनेट कोलमैन एण्ड कम्पनी, दिल्ली।

174. दिल — कृश्न चन्दर, *दिल दौलत और दुनिया*, राजपाल एण्ड सन्ज (दिल्ली, no date)।

175. दीदी — उपेन्द्र नाथ अश्क, *अंजो दीदी*, नीलाभ प्रकाशन (इलाहाबाद, no date)।

176. दीपाली — सुदर्शन, *दीपाली*, वोरा एण्ड कम्पनी पब्लिशर्स प्रा० लि० (इलाहाबाद, 1965), तृतीय संस्करण।

177. दीपिका — महावीर प्रसाद पाण्डेय, *चिकित्सा तत्त्व दीपिका*, शान्ति प्रकाशन (दिल्ली, 1965)।

178. दीर्घ — फणीश्वर नाथ रेणु, *दीर्घतपा*, ग्रन्थ कुटीर (पटना, 1963)।

179. दीवारों — मन्नु भण्डारी, *बिना दीवारों के घर*, अक्षर प्रकाशन प्रा० लि० (दिल्ली, 1965)।

180. दुख — नागार्जुन, *दुखमोचन*, राजकमल प्रकाशन प्रा० लि० (दिल्ली, 1958), द्वितीय संस्करण।

181. दुग्गल — कर्तारसिंह दुग्गल, *मोतियोंवाले*, भारतीय ज्ञानपीठ (काशी, 1958)।

182. दुनिया — देवराज दिनेश, *दुनिया रंगबिरंगी*, हिन्द पाकेट बुक्स प्रा० लि० (दिल्ली, no date)।

183. दूत — उदयशंकर भट्ट, *मुक्तिदूत*, आत्माराम एण्ड सन्ज (दिल्ली, 1960)।

184. दूसरा — शैलेश मटियानी, *दूसरों के लिए*, प्रतिभा प्रकाशन (इलाहाबाद, 1967)।

185. देरीना — सत्यप्रकाश संगर, *हमदमे देरीना का मिलना*, राजकमल प्रकाशन प्रा० लि० (दिल्ली, 1963)।

186. देवता — धर्मवीर भारती, *गुनाहों का देवता*, भारतीय ज्ञानपीठ (काशी, 1962), सातवां संस्करण।

187. देश — रामवृक्ष बेनीपुरी, *पतितों के देश में*, बेनीपुरी प्रकाशन (मुजफ्फरपुर, 1964)।

188. दो फूल — राबर्ट लुई स्टीवेन्सन, *गुलाब के दो फूल* (हिन्दी अनुवाद), राजपाल एण्ड सन्ज (दिल्ली, 1957)।

189. धर (धरती) — लक्ष्मी नारायण मिश्र, *धरती का हृदय*, किताब महल (इलाहाबाद, no date)।

190. धर्म — स्वामी राम, *युग धर्म क्या ? एक आधुनिक दृष्टि*, साहित्य भवन प्रा० लि० (इलाहाबाद, 1966)।

191. धारा — उपेन्द्रनाथ अश्क तथा कौशल्या अश्क, *दो धारा*, नीलाभ प्रकाशन (इलाहाबाद, 1965), तृतीय संस्करण।

192. नक्षत्र — सम्पूर्णानन्द, *ग्रह-नक्षत्र*, हिन्दुस्तानी एकेडमी (इलाहाबाद, 1965)।

193. नगर — भगवतशरण उपाध्याय, *भारतीय नगरों की कहानी*, राजपाल एण्ड सन्ज (दिल्ली, no date)।

194. नदी — स० ही० वात्स्यायन, *नदी के द्वीप*, सरस्वती प्रेस (वाराणसी, 1966)।

195. नद्द — नन्ददुलारे वाजपेयी, *आधुनिक साहित्य*, भारतीय भण्डार (इलाहाबाद, 1958), द्वितीय संस्करण।

196. नवरंग — सत्येन्द्र शरत्, *नवरंग*, साहित्य सदन (देहरादून, 1965), दूसरा संस्करण।

197. नवनीत 1 — *नवनीत मासिक*, नवनीत प्रकाशन लि०, जुलाई, 1962।

198. नवनीत 2 — *नवनीत मासिक*, नवनीत प्रकाशन लि०, मई, 1962।

199. नाटक — लक्ष्मीनारायण लाल, *नाटक तोता मैना*, लोक भारती प्रकाशन (इलाहाबाद, 1962)।

200. नाना — रामकुमार वर्मा, *नाना फडनवीस*, रामनारायण बेनी प्रसाद (इलाहाबाद, 1964)।

201. निबन्ध — रामसागर त्रिपाठी तथा शांतिस्वरूप गुप्ता, *बृहत् साहित्यिक निबन्ध*, अशोक प्रकाशन (दिल्ली, 1966)।

202. निरु — सूर्यकांत त्रिपाठी निराला, *निरुपमा*, भारती भंडार (प्रयाग, 1962), नवां संस्करण।

203. निर्वासित — इलाचन्द्र जोशी, *निर्वासित*, भारती भंडार (प्रयाग, 1959), छठा संस्करण।

204. निष्कर्ष — वासुदेव, *विचार और निष्कर्ष*, भारतीय साहित्य मन्दिर (दिल्ली, 1956)।

205. नीति — आनन्द कुमार, *नीति कथाएं*, राजपाल एण्ड सन्ज (दिल्ली, 1966), नवां संस्करण।

206. नील — शौकत थानवी, *नीलोफर*, एन० डी० सहगल एण्ड सन्ज (दिल्ली, 1966)।

207. नेह — विश्वम्भरनाथ शुक्ल, *नेह की नदी*, जवाहर पुस्तकालय (मथुरा, 1965)।

208. नेहरू — जवाहर लाल नेहरू, *स्वाधीनता और उसके बाद*, पब्लिकेशन्स डिवीजन, सूचना तथा प्रसारण मंत्रालय, भारत सरकार (दिल्ली, 1954)।

209. नोट — शरद देवड़ा, *एक आलोचक की नोटबुक*, अपरा प्रकाशन (कलकत्ता, 1964)।

210. पथ — महादेवी वर्मा, *पथ के साथी*, भारती भंडार (इलाहाबाद, 1958), प्रथम संस्करण।

211. पनघट — सुदर्शन, *पनघट*, बोरा एण्ड कम्पनी (बम्बई, 1954) चौथा संस्करण।

212. पपी (पीयूष) — प्रेमचन्द, *प्रेम पीयूष*, सरस्वती प्रेस (बनारस, 1958), दूसरा संस्करण।

213. पपू — प्रेमचंद *प्रेमपूर्णिमा*, सरस्वती प्रेस (बनारस, 1959), द्वितीय संस्करण।

214. परख — जैनेन्द्र कुमार, *परख*, हिन्दी ग्रन्थ रत्नाकर कार्यालय प्रा० लि० (बम्बई, 1941), द्वितीय संस्करण।

215. परम — उमाकांत मालवीय, *परमवीर*, राजरंजना प्रकाशन (इलाहाबाद, 1965)।

216. परि — निर्मल वर्मा, *परिन्दे*, पीपुल्स पब्लिशिंग हाऊस प्रा० लि० (नई दिल्ली, 1960)।

217. पश्चिम — सावित्री देवी वर्मा, *पश्चिम भारत की लोक कथाएँ*, पब्लिकेशन्स डिवीजन (दिल्ली, 1962)।

218.	पांच	प्रेमचन्द, *पांच फूल*, हंस प्रकाशन (इलाहाबाद, 1959), नवां संस्करण।
219.	पांचल	मोहन राकेश, *पांच लम्बी कहानियां*, राजकमल प्रकाशन प्रा० लि० (दिल्ली, 1960)।
220.	पांव	रामकृष्ण कौशल, *चढ़ती पगडंडियां, अनथके पांव*, हिन्दी प्रचारक पुस्तकालय (वाराणसी, 1965)।
221.	पाठ 1	*स्वास्थ्य शिक्षा पाठमाला* भाग 1, विकास अन्वेषणालय, नियोजन विभाग, उत्तर प्रदेश सरकार (लखनऊ, 1962)।
222.	पाठ 2	*स्वास्थ्य शिक्षा पाठमाला*, भाग, 2, विकास अन्वेषणालय, नियोजन विभाग, उत्तर प्रदेश सरकार (लखनऊ, 1962)।
223.	पाप	कमल शुक्ल, *पाप और पुण्य*, सन्मार्ग प्रकाशन (दिल्ली, 1966)।
224.	पारस	सुदर्शन, *सुदर्शन की कहानियां*, राजपाल एण्ड सन्ज (दिल्ली, no date)।
225.	पाश्चात्य	अवधविहारी लाल कपूर, *पाश्चात्य दर्शन-दर्पण*, रत्न प्रकाशन मन्दिर (आगरा, 1961)।
226.	पीपल	अमृतलाल नागर, *पीपल की परी*, संध्या प्रकाशन (दिल्ली, 1963)।
227.	पीयूष (पपी)	See (212) above.
228.	पीला	ख्वाजा अहमद अब्बास, *लाल और पीला*, नीलाभ प्रकाशन (इलाहाबाद, 1957)।
229.	पुकारुं	रांगेय राघव, *कब तक पुकारुं*, राजपाल एण्ड सन्ज (दिल्ली, no date)।
230.	पुरस	किरण कुमारी गुप्ता, *पुरस्कार*, विनोद पुस्तक मन्दिर (आगरा, 1955)।
231.	पुरुष	आनन्द कुमार, *महापुरुषों की कथाएँ*, राजपाल एण्ड सन्ज (दिल्ली, 1966), नवां संस्करण।
232.	पूर्व	वृन्दावन लाल वर्मा, *पूर्व की ओर*, मयूर प्रकाशन (झांसी, 1962), दसवां संस्करण।
233.	पेरिस	ख्वाजा अहमद अब्बास, *पेरिस की एक शाम*, नीलाभ प्रकाशन (इलाहाबाद, 1961)।
234.	पैंतरे	उपेन्द्रनाथ अश्क *पैंतरे*, नीलाभ प्रकाशन (प्रयाग, no date)।
235.	पैदा	रांगेय राघव, *इन्सान कब पैदा हुआ*, किताब महल प्रा० लि० (इलाहाबाद, no date)।
236.	पोली	पांडेय बेचन शर्मा उग्र, *पोली इमारत*, आत्माराम एण्ड सन्ज (दिल्ली, 1964)।
237.	प्रकाश	त्रिलोक चन्द गोयल, *प्रकाश की कहानी*, राजपाल एण्ड सन्ज (दिल्ली, 1956), दूसरा संस्करण।

238. प्रताप — गणेशचन्द्र जोशी, *महाराणा प्रताप*, दी स्टूडेंट्स बुक कम्पनी (जयपुर, 1964)।

239. प्रति — जयशंकर प्रसाद, *प्रतिध्वनि*, भारती भंडार (इलाहाबाद, 1961), छठा संस्करण।

240. प्रतिमा — सूर्यकान्त त्रिपाठी निराला, *प्रबन्ध प्रतिमा*, भारती भण्डार (इलाहाबाद, 1963), द्वितीय संस्करण।

241. प्रयोग — रामचन्द्र वर्म्मा, *हिन्दी प्रयोग*, साहित्य रत्नमाला कार्यालय (वाराणसी, 1964), नौवां संस्करण।

242. प्रश्न — जैनेन्द्र कुमार, *प्रश्न और प्रश्न*, पूर्वोदय प्रकाशन (दिल्ली, 1966)।

243. प्रेमचन्द — नार्मन जाईड तथा अन्य, *ए प्रेमचन्द हिन्दी रीडर*, ईस्ट वेस्ट सेन्टर प्रेस (होनोलुलु, 1962)।

244. प्रेमा — प्रेमचन्द, *प्रेमाश्रम*, हंस प्रकाशन (इलाहाबाद, (no date)।

245. प्रेमिका — कंथरविला, *प्रेमिका*, श्यामू सन्यासी (अनुवादक), राजपाल एण्ड सन्ज (दिल्ली, 1954)।

246. प्यार — लिगोटाल्सटाय, *प्यार की जिंदगी*, हिन्द पाकेट बुक्स प्रा॰ लि॰ (दिल्ली, 1959)।

247. प्यास — कृश्न चन्दर, *प्यास*, हिन्द पाकेट बुक्स प्रा॰ लि॰ (दिल्ली, no date), चौथा संस्करण।

248. प्यास एक — ल॰ दा॰ नवरे, *प्यास*, विश्वभारती प्रकाशन (नागपुर, 1965)।

249. फर — राजेन्द्र यादव (सम्पादक), *फणीश्वरनाथ रेणु, श्रेष्ठ कहानियां*, राजपाल एण्ड सन्ज (दिल्ली, no date)।

250. फाग — पांडेय बेचन शर्मा उग्र, *फागुन के दिन चार*, रणजीत प्रिंटर्स एण्ड पब्लिशर्स (दिल्ली, 1960)।

251. फूल — सुदर्शन, *फूलों का गुच्छा*, राजपाल एण्ड सन्ज (दिल्ली, no date)।

252. फूलों — यशपाल, *फूलों का कुर्त्ता*, विप्लव कार्यालय (लखनऊ, 1969), चौथा संस्करण।

253. बअ — महेश नारायण, *बड़ों से मिलने के विचित्र अनुभव*, कल्याणदास एण्ड ब्रदर्स (बनारस, 1962)।

254. बक — प्रकाश पंडित, *बक रहा हूं जुनून में*, भारतीय ज्ञानपीठ प्रकाशन (वाराणसी, 1965)।

255. बकवास — शौकत थानवी, *बकवास*, वनयुग प्रकाशन (दिल्ली, no date)।

256. बचपन — कृष्ण बलदेव वैद, *उसका बचपन*, सरस्वती प्रेस (बनारस, 1957)।

257. बटन — श्रीकांत व्यास (रूपान्तरकार), *चांदी का बटन*, राजपाल एण्ड सन्ज (दिल्ली, 1966)।

258. बल — नागार्जुन, *बलचनमा*, किताब महल प्रा० लि० (इलाहाबाद, 1965), तृतीय संस्करण ।

259. बांके — भगवतीचरण वर्मा, *दो बांके*, भारती भंडार (इलाहाबाद, 1955),

260. बांस — वृन्दावन लाल वर्मा, *बांस की फांस*, मयूर प्रकाशन (झांसी, 1963), पांचवां संस्करण ।

261. बाण — हजारी प्रसाद द्विवेदी, *बाण भट्ट की आत्मकथा*, हिन्दी ग्रन्थ रत्नाकर प्रा० लि० (बम्बई, 1958) ।

262. बाल 1 — *बाल-भारती*, पब्लिकेशन्स डिवीजन, भारत सरकार दिल्ली, जून, 1966 ।

263. बाल 10 — *बाल-भारती*, पब्लिकेशन्स डिवीजन, भारत सरकार दिल्ली, मार्च, 1966 ।

264. बाल 11 — *बाल-भारती*, पब्लिकेशन्स डिवीजन, भारत सरकार दिल्ली, अप्रैल, 1966 ।

265. बिजली — अजयकुमार (अनुवादक), *बिजली की कहानी*, राजपाल एण्ड सन्ज (दिल्ली, 1960) ।

266. बीर — वृन्दावन लाल वर्मा, *बीरबल*, मयूर प्रकाशन (झांसी, 1965), छठा संस्करण ।

267. बुन — जे० पी० पाण्डेय, *बुनियादी शिक्षा व्यवहार में*, भदौरिया पब्लिशिंग हाउस (जयपुर, no date) ।

268. बूंद — अमृतलाल नागर, *बूंद और समुद्र*, किताब महल प्रा० लि० (इलाहाबाद, 1964), दूसरा संस्करण ।

269. बेटी — नरेश मिश्रा, *सह्याद्रि की बेटी*, तरंगिणी प्रकाशन (इलाहाबाद, 1965) ।

270. बैसाखियों — रमेश बख्शी, *बैसाखियों वाली इमारत*, अक्षर प्रकाशन प्रा० लि० (दिल्ली, 1966) ।

271. भंवर — उपेन्द्रनाथ अश्क, *भंवर*, नीलाभ प्रकाशन (इलाहाबाद, 1961) ।

272. भक्ति — स्वामी अखंडानन्द सरस्वती, *भक्तियोग*, भक्तियोग ट्रस्ट (बम्बई, no date) ।

273. भटका — भीष्म साहनी, *भटकती राख*, राजकमल प्रकाशन प्रा० लि० (दिल्ली, 1966) ।

274. भवन — भगवतशरण उपाध्याय, *भारतीय भवनों की कहानी*, राजपाल एण्ड सन्ज (दिल्ली, 1966), चौथा संस्करण ।

275. भाद — हरेन्द्र प्रसाद सिन्हा, *भारतीय दर्शन की रूपरेखा*, बुकलैंड (कलकत्ता, 1965), द्वितीय संस्करण ।

276. भार — तनसुखराम गुप्त, *भारतीय महापुरुष*, भाग 1, सूर्य प्रकाशन (दिल्ली, 1962) ।

277.	भारक	आनन्द कुमार, *भारतीय कथाएं*, राजपाल एण्ड सन्ज (दिल्ली, 1965), छठा संस्करण ।
278.	भारत	रामनाथ शर्मा, *भारत में समाज-कल्याण और सुरक्षा*, केदार नाथ रामलाल (मेरठ, 1964), द्वितीय संस्करण ।
279.	भालू	विलियम फाकनर, *भालू*, सूर्यकुमार जोशी (अनुवादक), राजपाल एण्ड सन्ज (दिल्ली, 1959) ।
280.	भिन्न	रोशन लाल सुरीरवाला, *लंगड़ी भिन्न* भारत प्रकाशन मन्दिर (अलीगढ़, 1964) ।
281.	भूले	भगवतीचरण वर्मा, *भूले बिसरे चित्र*, राजकमल प्रकाशन प्रा० लि० (दिल्ली, 1961), दूसरी आवृत्ति ।
282.	भेड़	एस० एस० खोत, *भेड़ और ऊन*, कृषि सूचना सेवा विस्तार निदेशालय, खाद्य और कृषि मंत्रालय, भारत सरकार (नई दिल्ली, 1962) ।
283.	भोजन	ज्योतिलाल भार्गव, *स्वास्थ्य के लिए भोजन*, राष्ट्रीय साहित्य सदन (लखनऊ, 1963) ।
284.	भौगोलिक	कृपाशंकर गौड़ *भारत की भौगोलिक समीक्षा*, हिन्दी प्रचारक पुस्तकालय (वाराणसी, 1965), चतुर्थ संस्करण ।
285.	म (महादेवी)	महादेवी वर्मा, *शृंखला की कड़ियां*, भारती भंडार (इलाहाबाद, 1958) ।
286.	मण्टो	उपेन्द्रनाथ अश्क, *मण्टो : मेरा दुश्मन*, नीलाभ प्रकाशन (इलाहाबाद, 1956)
287.	मक	मोहन राकेश, *मृच्छकटिक*, राजकमल प्रकाशन प्रा० लि० (दिल्ली, 1962) ।
288.	मछली	राजकमल चौधरी, *मछली मरी हुई*, राजकमल प्रकाशन (दिल्ली, 1966) ।
289.	मछुआ	राजेन्द्र यादव (अनुवादक), *एक मछुआ एक मोती*, हिन्द पाकेट बुक्स प्रा० लि० (दिल्ली, no date) ।
290.	मणि	एन० चन्द्रशेखरन नायर (सम्पादक), *निबन्ध-मणि*, प्रगति प्रकाशन (आगरा, 1967) ।
291.	मनो	एस० एस० माथुर, *समाज मनोविज्ञान*, विनोद पुस्तक मन्दिर (आगरा, 1964) ।
292.	ममता	हरिकृष्ण प्रेमी, *ममता*, राजपाल एण्ड सन्ज (दिल्ली, no date) ।
293.	मरकत	बच्चन (अनुवादक), *मरकत द्वीप का स्वर*, राजपाल एण्ड सन्ज (दिल्ली, 1965) ।
294.	मशीन	जगतराम साहनी, *मशीनों की दुनिया*, हिन्द पाकेट बुक्स प्रा० लि० (दिल्ली, 1959) ।

295.	महादेवी (म)	see (285) above.
296.	महिला	कांतिमोहन (अनुवादक), *आज की वैज्ञानिक महिलाएं*, राजपाल एण्ड सन्ज (दिल्ली, 1966), द्वितीय संस्करण ।
297.	मांस	कमलेश्वर, *मांस का दरिया*, अक्षर प्रकाशन प्रा० लि० (दिल्ली, no date) ।
298.	मादा	लक्ष्मीनारायण लाल, *मादा कैक्टस*, राजकमल प्रकाशन प्रा० लि० (दिल्ली, 1959) ।
299.	मान 1	प्रेमचन्द, *मानसरोवर*, भाग 1 , सरस्वती प्रेस (बनारस, 1960), नवां संस्करण ।
300.	मान 2	प्रेमचन्द, *मानसरोवर*, भाग 2, सरस्वती प्रेस (बनारस, 1957), सातवां संस्करण ।
301.	मान 4	प्रेमचन्द, *मानसरोवर*, भाग 4, सरस्वती प्रेस (बनारस, 1958), आठवां संस्करण ।
302.	मान 5	प्रेमचन्द, *मानसरोवर*, भाग 5 , सरस्वती प्रेस (बनारस, 1958), पांचवां संस्करण ।
303.	मान 6	प्रेगनन्द, *मानसरोवर*, भाग 6, सरस्वती प्रेस (बनारस, 1959) ।
304.	मान 7	प्रेमचन्द, *मानसरोवर*, भाग 7, सरस्वती प्रेस (बनारस, 1960) ।
305.	मान 8	प्रेमचन्द, *मानसरोवर*, भाग 8, सरस्वती प्रेस (बनारस, 1960), बारहवां संस्करण ।
306.	मानव (सामाजिक)	रवीन्द्रनाथ मुकर्जी, *सामाजिक मानवशास्त्र की रूपरेखा*, सरस्वती सदन (मसूरी, 1962) ।
307.	मुक्ता	पाण्डेय बेचन शर्मा उग्र, *मुक्ता*, आत्माराम एण्ड सन्ज (दिल्ली, 1964) ।
308.	मित्रो	भैरव प्रसाद गुप्त, *मित्रो और अन्य कहानियां*, धारा प्रकाशन (इलाहाबाद, 1963) ।
309.	मिला 1	पद्मसिंह शर्मा कमलेश, *मैं इनसे मिला*, पहली किश्त, आत्माराम एण्ड सन्ज (दिल्ली, 1952) ।
310.	मिला 2	पद्मसिंह शर्मा कमलेश, *मैं इनसे मिला*, दूसरी किश्त, आत्माराम एण्ड सन्ज (दिल्ली, 1952) ।
311.	मुद्रा	आरिगपुडि, *मुद्राहीन*, भारती साहित्य सदन (दिल्ली, 1960) ।
312.	मूंगे	श्रीकांत व्यास (रूपान्तरकार), *मूंगे का द्वीप*, राजकमल एण्ड सन्ज (दिल्ली, no date) ।
313.	मूल्य	धर्मवीर भारती, *मानव मूल्य और साहित्य*, भारतीय ज्ञानपीठ (काशी, 1960) ।
314.	मैला	फणीश्वरनाथ रेणु, *मैला आंचल*, राजकमल प्रकाशन प्रा० लि० (दिल्ली, 1963), तृतीय संस्करण ।

315. मोति — गंगाधर मधुकर, *मोतियों वाले हाथ*, राजकमल प्रकाशन प्रा० लि० (दिल्ली, 1963)।

316. मोरा — राजेन्द्र यादव (सम्पादक), *मोहन राकेश, श्रेष्ठ कहानियां*, राजपाल एण्ड सन्ज (दिल्ली, 1966)।

317. मौसम — हरिश्चन्द्र विद्यालंकार, *मौसम की कहानी*, राजपाल एण्ड सन्ज (दिल्ली, no date), चौथा संस्करण।

318. म्यान — नानकसिंह, *एक म्यान दो तलवारें*, राजपाल एण्ड सन्ज (दिल्ली, no date)।

319. यह — प्रकाश पंडित, *यह सच है*, हिन्द पाकेट बुक्स प्रा० लि० (दिल्ली, no date)।

320. यांत्रिकी — आर्नल्ड सोमरफेल्ड, *यांत्रिकी*, जगदबिहारी (अनुवादक), सूचना विभाग, उत्तर प्रदेश सरकार (लखनऊ, 1962)।

321. याद — कांतिमोहन (अनुवादक), *याद*, हिन्द पाकेट बुक्स प्रा० लि० (दिल्ली, no date)।

322. यायावर — स० ही० वात्स्यायन, *अरे यायावर याद रहेगा*, सरस्वती प्रेस (बनारस, 1953)।

323. यूक्रेन — शुभा वर्मा, *यूक्रेन की लोक कथाएं*, दूसरा भाग, हिन्द भवन (जालन्धर तथा इलाहाबाद, 1962,)।

324. ये वे — जैनेन्द्र कुमार, *ये और वे*, पूर्वोदय प्रकाशन (दिल्ली, 1954)।

325. योग — आचार्य हेमचन्द्र, *योगशास्त्र*, श्री ऋषभचन्द जौहरी (दिल्ली, 1963)।

326. रंग — प्रेमचंद, *रंगभूमि*, भारतीय प्रकाशनालय, (इलाहाबाद, no date)।

327. रक्त — लक्ष्मीनारायण लाल, *रक्तकमल*, राजकमल प्रकाशन प्रा० लि० (दिल्ली, 1963), द्वितीय संस्करण।

328. रजत — रामकुमार वर्मा, *रजत रश्मि*, भारतीय ज्ञानपीठ (काशी, 1963), द्वितीय संस्करण।

329. रथ — मामा वरेरकर, *एक रथ दो पहिये*, विद्या प्रकाशन मन्दिर (दिल्ली, 1963)।

330. रसायन — रमेशचन्द्र वर्मा, *रसायन की कहानी*, राजपाल एण्ड सन्ज (दिल्ली, 1966), तृतीय संस्करण।

331. रसीली — विश्वनाथ, *रसीली कहानियां*, राजपाल एण्ड सन्ज (दिल्ली, no date)।

332. रहस्यमयी — रामनाथ सुमन (अनुवादक), *रहस्यमयी*, राजपाल एण्ड सन्ज (दिल्ली, 1958)।

333. राकेट — रांगेय राघव (अनुवादक), *राकेट की कहानी*, राजपाल एण्ड सन्ज (दिल्ली, 1966), द्वितीय संस्करण।

334. राकेश — मोहन राकेश, *आखिरी चट्टान तक*, राजकमल प्रकाशन प्रा० लि० (दिल्ली, 1961)।

335. राक्षस — लक्ष्मीनारायण मिश्र, *राक्षस का मन्दिर*, हिन्दी प्रचारक पुस्तकालय (बनारस, 1958), तृतीय संस्करण।

336. राखी — वृन्दावन लाल वर्मा, *राखी की लाज*, मयूर प्रकाशन (झांसी, 1962), बारहवां संस्करण।

337. राज — मागीलाल महेचा, *राजस्थान के राजपूत* (जोधपुर, 1965)।

338. राजनय — बी० के० उपाध्याय, *भारतीय राजनय तथा विदेश नीति*, विश्वभारती प्रकाशन (आगरा, 1967)।

339. राजवि — *राजस्थान विकास*, पंचायत एवं विकास विभाग, राजस्थान सरकार, (जयपुर, अक्तूबर, 1966)।

340. राजहंस — मोहन राकेश, *लहरों के राजहंस*, राजपाल एण्ड सन्ज (दिल्ली, 1964), द्वितीय संस्करण।

341. रात — लक्ष्मीनारायण लाल, *रातरानी*, नेशनल पब्लिशिंग हाऊस (दिल्ली, 1966)।

342. राब — श्रीकान्त व्यास (अनुवादक), *राबिन्सन क्रूसो*, राजपाल एण्ड सन्ज (दिल्ली, no date), सातवां संस्करण।

343. राह — अमरकांत, *कटीली राह के फूल*, राजकमल प्रकाशन प्रा० लि० (दिल्ली, 1963)।

344. रूप — राजेन्द्रपाल सिंह, *अनुसंधान की रूपरेखा*, गया प्रसाद एण्ड सन्ज (आगरा, 1966)।

345. रूस — अरुण घोष, *रूस की कहानियां*, इंडियन प्रेस प्रा० लि० (इलाहाबाद, 1962)।

346. रेखा — बनारसीदास चतुर्वेदी, *रेखाचित्र* भारतीय ज्ञानपीठ (काशी, 1963), द्वितीय संस्करण।

347. रोक — प्रियकुमार चौबे, *सामान्य रोगों की रोकथाम*, चौखम्बा विद्याभवन (बनारस, 1962)।

348. लड़की — राजेन्द्रसिंह बेदी, *लम्बी लड़की*, हिन्द पाकेट बुक्स प्रा० लि० (दिल्ली, no date)।

349. लज्जा — इलाचन्द्र जोशी, *लज्जा*, भारती भंडार, (इलाहाबाद, 1964), पांचवां संस्करण।

350. लता — गुलाबदास ब्रोकर, *लता*, हिन्द पाकेट बुक्स प्रा० लि० (दिल्ली, no date)।

351. लहर — यादवचन्द्र जैन (अनुवादक), *लहरों के बीच*, राजपाल एण्ड सन्ज (दिल्ली, no date)।

352. लाख — मामा वरेरकर, *सात लाख में एक*, रामचन्द्र रघुनाथ सर्वटे (अनुवादक), लोक चेतना प्रकाशन (जबलपुर, 1961)।

353. लोक — *लोक युग का राजस्थान*, सार्वजनिक सम्पर्क विभाग, राजस्थान सरकार (जयपुर, 1961)।

354. लोक कथा — आनन्द कुमार, *लोक कथाएं*, राजपाल एण्ड सन्ज (दिल्ली, no date)।

355. वरा — लक्ष्मीनारायण मिश्र, *वत्सराज*, हिन्द भवन (जालन्धर और इलाहाबाद, 1959)।

356. वायु — धर्मपाल शास्त्री (अनुवादक), *वायुयान की कहानी*, राजपाल एण्ड सन्ज (दिल्ली, no date), चौथा संस्करण।

357. वासना — दास्तायवस्की, *वासना*, राजपाल एण्ड सन्ज (दिल्ली, 1959)।

358. विकास — अ० अ० अनन्त, *बच्चों का विकास और उनकी शिक्षा*, मगध राजधानी प्रकाशन (पटना, no date)।

359. विचार — कुमारी ज्ञानवती, *साहित्य—कुछ विचार*, ज्ञानलोक प्रकाशन (लखनऊ, 1965)।

360. विचित्र — पांडेय बेचन शर्मा उग्र, *चित्र-विचित्र*, आत्माराम एण्ड सन्ज (दिल्ली, 1964)।

361. विज्ञान — कृष्ण कुमार अग्रवाल, *आधुनिक उधान विज्ञान*, भारत पब्लिशिंग हाउस (कानपुर, 1964)।

362. विमर्श — दशरथ राज, *सूर साहित्य विमर्श*, प्रभात प्रकाशन (दिल्ली, 1964)।

363. विवर्त — जैनेन्द्र कुमार *विवर्त*, पूर्वोदय प्रकाशन (दिल्ली, 1957), दूसरा संस्करण।

364. वितस्ता — लक्ष्मीनारायण मिश्र, *वितस्ता की लहरें*, आत्माराम एण्ड सन्ज (दिल्ली, 1962), चतुर्थ संस्करण।

365. विवेचन — डा० नगेन्द्र, *विचार और विवेचन*, नेशनल पब्लिशिंग हाउस (दिल्ली, 1964), द्वितीय संस्करण।

366. विश्लेषण — डा० नगेन्द्र, *विचार और विश्लेषण*, नेशनल पब्लिशिंग हाउस (दिल्ली, 1961), द्वितीय संस्करण।

367. वृन्दा — लक्ष्मीनारायण लाल, *मन वृन्दावन*, नेशनल पब्लिशिंग हाउस (दिल्ली, 1966)।

368. वे दिन — निर्मल वर्मा, *वे दिन*, राजकमल प्रकाशन प्रा० लि० (दिल्ली, 1964)।

369. वैदिक — श्री स्वामी जी महाराज, *वैदिक उपदेश*, भाग 1, पीताम्बर पीठ, संस्कृत परिषद् (वनखण्डेश्वर, दतिया, 1965)।

370. वैदिक 1 — श्री स्वामी जी महाराज, *वैदिक उपदेश*, भाग, 2, पीताम्बर पीठ, संस्कृत परिषद् (वनखण्डेश्वर, दतिया, 1966)।

371. वैभव — रामेश्वर तांतिया, *विदेशों का वैभव*, इंडियन प्रेस (इलाहाबाद, 1965)।

372.	वोल्गा	राहुल सांकृत्यायन, *वोल्गा से गंगा*, किताब महल प्रा० लि० (इलाहाबाद, 1960), द्वितीय संस्करण ।
373.	व्यतीत	जैनेन्द्र कुमार, *व्यतीत*, पूर्वोदय प्रकाशन (दिल्ली, 1962), तृतीय संस्करण ।
374.	व्यास	विनोदशंकर व्यास, *अस्सी कहानियां*, नागरी प्रचारिणी सभा (काशी, 1962) ।
375.	शक	उदयशंकर भट्ट, *शक-विजय*, मसिजीवी प्रकाशन (नई दिल्ली, 1955), तृतीय संस्करण ।
376.	शबरी	बालशौरि रेडी, *शबरी*, शिक्षा भारती (दिल्ली, 1961) ।
377.	शरा	पांडेय बेचन शर्मा उग्र, *शराबी*, आत्माराम एण्ड सन्ज (दिल्ली, 1961) ।
378.	शरीफा	मन्मथनाथ गुप्त, *शरीफों का कटड़ा*, राजपाल एण्ड सन्ज (दिल्ली, 1966) ।
379.	शहर	उपेन्द्रनाथ अश्क, *शहर में घूमता आईना*, नीलाभ प्रकाशन (इलाहाबाद, 1963) ।
380.	शांतला	के० वी० अय्यर, *शांतला*, साहित्य अकादमी, (दिल्ली, 1960) ।
381.	शिकार	श्यामरी भटनागर, *शिकार*, हिन्द पाकेट बुक्स प्रा० लि० (दिल्ली, no date) ।
382.	शिशु	ओम कृष्ण चोपड़ा, *शिशु जन्म*, हेमकुंड प्रेस (नई दिल्ली, 1963) ।
383.	शेखर	स० ही० वात्स्यायन अज्ञेय, *शेखर, एक जीवनी*, पहला भाग, सरस्वती प्रेस (बनारस, 1958) ।
384.	शौर्य	रमणलाल वसन्तलाल देसाई, *शौर्य-तर्पण*, श्यामू सन्यासी (अनुवादक), वोरा एण्ड कम्पनी प्रा० लि० (बम्बई, 1960) ।
385.	श्रम	*श्रम जीवी*, श्रम विभाग, उत्तर प्रदेश सरकार, (लखनऊ, मार्च, 1967)।
386.	संगीत	भगवतशरण उपाध्याय, *भारतीय संगीत की कहानी*, राजपाल एण्ड सन्ज (दिल्ली, 1967), चौथा संस्करण ।
387.	संग्राम	प्रेमचन्द, *संग्राम*, सरस्वती प्रेस (इलाहाबाद, 1962) ।
388.	संघर्ष	शिवदान सिंह चौहान तथा विजय चौहान (अनुवादक), *संघर्ष* हिन्द पाकेट बुक्स प्रा० लि० (दिल्ली, no date) ।
389.	सन्तुलन	प्रभाकर माचवे, *सन्तुलन*, आत्माराम एण्ड सन्स (दिल्ली, 1954) ।
390	संत	रामलाल, *संतों के संस्मरण*, शिवलाल अग्रवाल एण्ड कम्पनी (आगरा, 1965) ।
391.	सक	के० डी० ठक्कर तथा रामनारायण तिवारी, *सच्ची कहानियां*, राजपाल एण्ड सन्ज (दिल्ली, no date) ।

392. सगर — उदयशंकर भट्ट, *सगर विजय*, मसिजीवी प्रकाशन (दिल्ली, 1956), छठा संस्करण।

393. सच — गोपाल प्रसाद व्यास, *कुछ सच कुछ झूठ*, आत्माराम एण्ड सन्ज (दिल्ली, 1958)।

394. सज्जन — सज्जन सिंह, *लद्दाख की डायरी* सत्साहित्य प्रकाशन (दिल्ली, 1955)।

395. सत — रामकुमार वर्मा, *सत्य का स्वप्न*, किताब महल प्रा० लि० (इलाहाबाद, 1953)।

396. सदा — आनन्दकुमार, *सदाचार की कथाएं*, राजपाल एण्ड सन्ज (दिल्ली, 1966), आठवां संस्करण।

397. सदानीरा — डा० रामगोपाल शर्मा दिनेश *सदानीरा*, पीतम प्रकाशन मन्दिर (आगरा, 1965)।

398. सन — लक्ष्मीनारायण मिश्र, *सन्यासी*, हिन्दी प्रचारक पुस्तकालय (वाराणसी, 1961), तृतीय संस्करण।

399. सपना — भगवती प्रसाद वाजपेयी, *सपना बिक गया*, प्रभात प्रकाशन (दिल्ली, 1965)।

400. सफर — बलराज साहनी, *पाकिस्तान का सफर*, हिन्द पाकेट बुक्स प्रा० लि० (दिल्ली, no date)।

401. सब्ज — कन्हैयालाल कपूर, *सब्ज बाग*, हिन्द पाकेट बुक्स प्रा० लि० (दिल्ली, no date)।

402. सभ्यता — डा० रामविलास शर्मा, *मानव सभ्यता का विकास*, विनोद पुस्तक मन्दिर (आगरा, 1956)।

403. सम (समर) — प्रेमचन्द, *समर यात्रा*, सरस्वती प्रेस (बनारस, 1958), छठवां संस्करण।

404. समर (सम) — see (403) above.

405. समा — महावीर प्रसाद मुरारका, *समाजवाद—एक अध्ययन*, भारती प्रकाशन (बम्बई, 1962)।

406. समुद्र — रमेशचन्द्र वर्मा (अनुवादक), *समुद्र की कहानी*, राजपाल एण्ड सन्ज (दिल्ली, 1966), तीसरा संस्करण।

407. सवाल — दुष्यंत कुमार, *छोटे छोटे सवाल*, राजकमल प्रकाशन प्रा० लि० (दिल्ली, 1964)।

408. सागर — कुमार (अनुवादक), *सागर तल की खोज*, राजपाल एण्ड सन्ज (दिल्ली, 1966), द्वितीय संस्करण।

409. सात — मुल्कराज आनंद, *सात समुन्दर पार*, राजपाल एण्ड सन्ज (दिल्ली, no date)।

410. सात नाटक — रमेश मेहता, *सात नाटक*, चौ० बलवन्तराय (दिल्ली, 1957)।

411. सानि — शांति स्वरूप गुप्त, *साहित्यिक निबन्ध*, अशोक प्रकाशन (दिल्ली, 1966), चतुर्थ संस्करण ।

412. सामाजिक (मानव) — see (306) above.

413. सामुदा — दूधनाथ सिंह, *सामुदायिक विकास एवं कृषि प्रसार*, नन्दकिशोर एण्ड ब्रदर्स (वाराणसी, 1965) ।

414. सा सा — भगवती चरण वर्मा, *सामर्थ्य और सीमा*, राजकमल प्रा० लि० (दिल्ली, 1965), द्वितीयावृत्ति ।

415. साह — लक्ष्मीनारायण सुधांशु, *साहित्यिक निबन्ध*, राजकमल प्रकाशन प्रा० लि० (दिल्ली, 1964) ।

416. साहित्य — डा० इन्द्रनाथ मदान, *आलोचना और साहित्य*, नीलाभ प्रकाशन (इलाहाबाद, 1964) ।

417. साहित्यकार — महादेवी वर्मा, *साहित्यकार की आस्था तथा अन्य निबन्ध*, लोक भारती प्रकाशन (इलाहाबाद, 1962) ।

418. सितार — केशव सागर (अनुवादक), *सितारों की कहानी*, राजपाल एण्ड सन्ज (दिल्ली, 1966), चौथा संस्करण ।

419. सिद्धान्त — गुलाबराय, *सिद्धान्त और अध्ययन*, आत्माराम एण्ड सन्ज (दिल्ली, 1965), छठा संस्करण ।

420. सिपाही — श्रीकांत व्यास (रूपान्तरकार), *वीर सिपाही*, शिक्षा भारती (दिल्ली, no date) ।

421. सिहो — लक्ष्मीनारायण मिश्र, *सिन्दूर की होली*, भारती भंडार (इलाहाबाद, 1965), दसवां संस्करण ।

422. सीपी — ज्ञानेन्द्र कुमार भटनागर, *सीपी मेरे प्राण*, अपोलो प्रकाशन (जयपुर, 1965) ।

423. सीमा — विमला शर्मा, *सीमा*, अमृत बुक कम्पनी (नई दिल्ली, 1966) ।

424. सुखदा — जैनेन्द्र कुमार, *सुखदा*, पूर्वोदय प्रकाशन (नई दिल्ली, 1965), द्वितीय संस्करण ।

425. सुता — जैनेन्द्र कुमार, *सुनीता*, पूर्वोदय प्रकाशन (दिल्ली, 1964) ।

426. सुधा 1 — हरिहरानन्द सरस्वती, *भक्तिसुधा*, भाग 1 (कलकत्ता 1967) ।

427. सुधा 2 — हरिहरानन्द सरस्वती, *शक्ति सुधा*, भाग 2 (कलकत्ता, 1967) ।

428. सुधा 3 — हरिहरानन्द सरस्वती, *भक्ति सुधा*, भाग 3 (कलकत्ता, 1967)

429. सुन्दर — सुन्दरलाल, *भारत में अंगरेजी राज*, सूचना और प्रसारण मंत्रालय, भारत सरकार (दिल्ली, 1960) ।

430. सुम — प्रेमचन्द, *सप्त सुमन*, हंस प्रकाशन (इलाहाबाद, no date) ।

431. सुमन — अम्बालाल जोशी, *अभिनव एकांकी सुमन*, कृष्ण ब्रदर्स (अजमेर, 1966) ।

432. सुल — नरेन्द्र शर्मा, *सुलगते हृदय*, पैरामाउन्ट पब्लिकेशन्ज (दिल्ली, 1962)।

433. सुहाग — अमृतलाल नागर, *सुहाग के नूपुर*, राजकमल प्रकाशन प्रा० लि० (दिल्ली, 1963), द्वितीय संस्करण।

434. सूनी — सर्वेश्वरदयाल सक्सेना, *एक सूनी नाव*, अक्षर प्रकाशन प्रा० लि० (दिल्ली, 1966)।

435. सूरज — धर्मवीर भारती *सूरज का सातवां घोड़ा*, भारतीय ज्ञानपीठ (काशी, 1963), तृतीय संस्करण।

436. सेठ — अमृतलाल नागर, *सेठ बांके लाल*, किताब महल प्रा० लि० (इलाहाबाद, 1960)।

437. सेवा — प्रेमचन्द, *सेवासदन*, हंस प्रकाशन (इलाहाबाद, no date)।

438. सोमा — सोमावीरा, *धरती की बेटी*, (दिल्ली, 1962)।

439. स्कन्द — जयशंकर प्रसाद, *स्कन्दगुप्त विक्रमादित्य*, भारती भंडार (इलाहाबाद, 1966), पन्द्रहवीं आवृत्ति।

440. स्वत — रामानन्द तिवारी, *स्वतन्त्रता का अर्थ*, भारती मंदिर [भरतपुर, (राजस्थान), 1963]।

441. स्वर्ण — कमल शुक्ल, *स्वर्ण-कमल* साहित्य केन्द्र प्रकाशन (दिल्ली, 1966)।

442. स्वस्थ — *स्वस्थ भारत*, स्वास्थ्य मंत्रालय, भारत सरकार, केन्द्रीय स्वास्थ्य शिक्षा ब्यूरो (नई दिल्ली, 1962)।

443. हार — हरी जुत्शी, *मैं हार गया*, नवयुग ग्रन्थागार (लखनऊ, 1962)।

444. हास्य — हरिश्चन्द्र व्यास, *हास्य कथाएं*, आलोक प्रकाशन (बीकानेर, no date)।

445. होली — पांडेय बेचन शर्मा उग्र, *ऐसी होली खेलो लाल*, आत्माराम एण्ड सन्ज (दिल्ली, 1964)।

Index of nouns and adjectives described in Studies in the Semantic Structure of Hindi, volume I

अ